ARAB PATRIOTISM

ARAB PATRIOTISM

THE IDEOLOGY AND CULTURE OF POWER IN LATE OTTOMAN EGYPT

Adam Mestyan

PRINCETON UNIVERSITY PRESS
PRINCETON AND OXFORD

Published by Princeton University Press, 41 William Street, Princeton, New Jersey 08540
In the United Kingdom: Princeton University Press, 6 Oxford Street, Woodstock, Oxfordshire OX20 1TR
press.princeton.edu
Cover image: Postcard of the Azbakiya Garden Theater. Courtesy of the Rare Books and Special Collections Library, The American University in Cairo

First paperback printing, 2020
Paperback ISBN 978-0-691-20901-2
Cloth ISBN 978-0-691-17264-4
British Library Cataloging-in-Publication Data is available
This book has been composed in Charis SIL

Contents

List of Illustrations vii

List of Tables ix

Notes on Transliteration, Names, Titles, and Currency xi

Introduction 1

PART I: THE MAKING OF THE KHEDIVATE 17

1. The Ottoman Origins of Arab Patriotism 21

2. The Ottoman Legitimation of Power: The Khedivate 50

3. The European Aesthetics of Khedivial Power 84

PART II: "A GARDEN WITH MELLOW FRUITS OF REFINEMENT" 121

4. A Gentle Revolution 125

5. Constitutionalism and Revolution: The Arab Opera 164

PART III: THE REINVENTION OF THE KHEDIVATE 199

6. Hārūn al-Rashīd under Occupation 203

7. Behind the Scenes: A Committee and the Law, 1880s–1900s 238

8. Distinction: Muṣṭafā Kāmil and the Making of an Arab Prince 268

Conclusion: The Ottoman Origin of Arab Nationalisms 303

Illustrations

Figure I.1. The Ottoman Empire, early 1860s xii

Figure I.2. The Rulers of Egypt xiii

Figure 2.1. Ismail in 1845 52

Figure 2.2. Ismail after 1867 53

Figure 3.1. The Comédie of Cairo, 1869 91

Figure 3.2. The Khedivial Opera House and the Circus, between 1869 and 1872 95

Figure 3.3. A poster of Eldorado du Caire, 1869 98

Figure 3.4. *Allegory of the Joining of the Two Seas*, 1869 113

Figure 3.5. A painting of Ibrahim Pasha in the hall of the Khedivial Opera House 114

Figure 4.1. Title page of *Wādī al-Nīl* journal, 22 October 1869 143

Figure 5.1. Sheikh Salāma Ḥijāzī, possibly in 1913 188

Figure 6.1. The troupe of Sulaymān Qardāḥī in Paris, 1889 233

Figure 8.1. Muṣṭafā Kāmil in 1893 296

Tables

Table 3.1. Theaters and Playhouses in Khedivial Cairo, 1868–1879 99

Table 3.2. Personnel du service de l'entretien du matérial, 1878 109

Table 4.1. Publications of *Wādī al-Nīl* Printing Press, 1866–1878 134

Table 5.1. Political Events and the Performances of the Arab Opera, April 1882 193

Table 6.1. Comparison between the French Proposal, the Advertised Arabic program, and the Staged Plays of *al-Jawq al-Waṭanī* in the Khedivial Opera House, March–April 1886 221

Table 7.1. État nominatif du personnel de l'Opéra pour le mois de janvier 1904 249

Table 8.1. List of 230 Subscribers to the Seasons of Santi Boni and Soschino in the Khedivial Opera House, 1885–1886 284

Notes on Transliteration, Names, Titles, and Currency

Arabic words are transliterated following the system of the *International Journal of Middle East Studies* (IJMES) without the initial *hamza*. Colloquial Egyptian Arabic expressions are transcribed according to their pronunciation in today's Cairo. Ottoman Turkish is transliterated according to the modern Turkish alphabet and pronunciation. Arabic or Turkish words found in the *Oxford Dictionary of English* are used accordingly (Koran, not *Qurʾān*; sheikh, not *shaykh*). Muslim months and days are transliterated according to Arabic vocalization, following the IJMES standard (*Rajab* and not Turkish *Receb* or *Raceb*; *jumʿa*, not *cuma*).

Where a person gave his or her name in Latin script consistently, I have respected that practice (e.g., Fahmy); however, I have made some exceptions (Khayyāṭ, not Kaïat; Qardāḥī, not Cardahi) to maintain consistency with the earlier literature. In the case of elite Ottomans in Egypt, I transcribe their names according to the Ottoman Turkish conventions (Khedive Ismail, not Ismāʿīl; Said, not Saʿīd). The names of those, like Ismāʿīl Ṣiddīq, who are remembered as Egyptians are transcribed according to the Arabic. Where a military or administrative title has an English equivalent I have used it (Pasha and not Pacha, Paşa, or *Bāshā*; Bey, not *Bīk*). "Efendi," after Ryzova, is written without the double f.

In this period, 1 Egyptian pound (*ghinī*, LE = livre égyptienne) was 100 piasters (*qirsh/ghirsh*, *qurush/ghurūsh*), and 1 piaster was equivalent to 40 *paras*. Currency exchange rates vary. In 1875, 1 British pound ("sovereign") was equivalent to 195 piasters (1.95 LE); 1 French franc was 7 piasters 20 paras. (Murray, *A Handbook*, 8–9.) In 1878, 1 French franc was 3.8 piasters (table 3.2). In 1885, 1 LE was 26 francs (*Baedeker's Lower Egypt* [1885], 5).

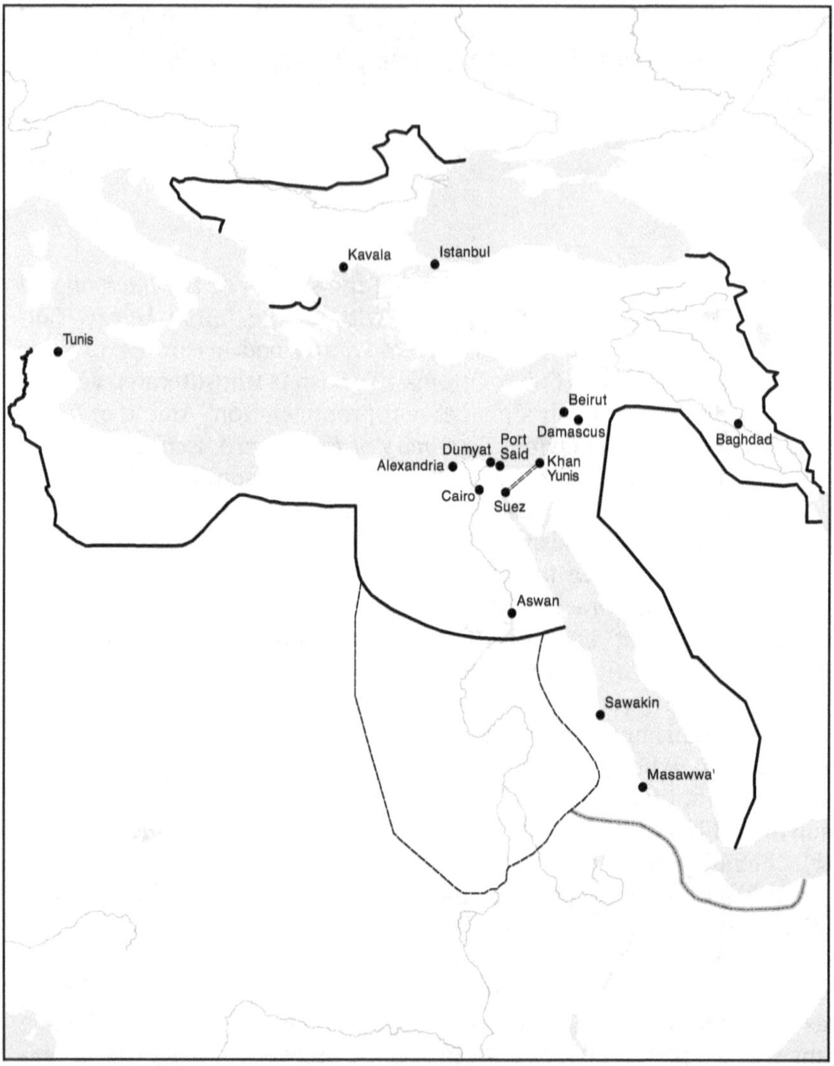

FIGURE I.1. The Ottoman Empire, 1860s

THE solid black line indicates the approximate boundaries of the Ottoman Empire in the early 1860s. The dashed line indicates the approximate boundaries of the Ottoman-Egyptian sphere of the Sudan after the conquests of Mehmed Ali and his descendants. The double-dashed line indicates the boundary of the Egyptian province in the Sinai according to the 1841 firman. The shaded-dotted line indicates the approximate additions in Africa to Ottoman-Egyptian sphere of interest in the mid-1860s.

Source: Map prepared prepared by Fei Carnes, Harvard Center for Geographical Analysis. Copyright © Fei Carnes.

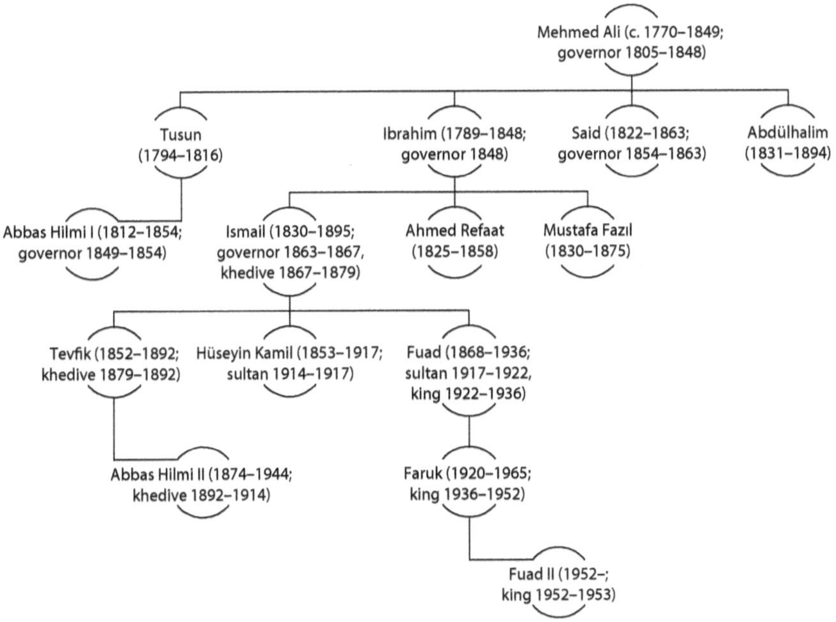

FIGURE I.2. The Rulers of Egypt

ARAB PATRIOTISM

INTRODUCTION

This book is a study of patriotism in the Egyptian province of the Ottoman Empire. What can we learn by re-examining Egypt's nineteenth-century history, not as the tale of progress towards a sovereign nation-state but as the saga of an Ottoman province? What are the consequences of reframing a national narrative in an imperial context?

I argue that the imperial context requires a new theory of national development. The imperial origins of patriotic ideas in provinces complicate standard accounts of how present-day nation-states came to be. Empires provide a fundamentally different structure of political power from that of national settings. The case of the Ottoman Empire is even more complex since the sultans were caliphs of Sunni Islam. Within the imperial system, the ideas and practices specific to provinces reveal the hidden architecture of the empire's networks. By retelling Egypt's nineteenth-century history as an Ottoman province, we follow the ways in which ideas, practices, and power struggles were enacted and constituted through these networks and imperial hierarchies.

In order to understand this complex story, we have to put aside the standard views of nationalism and religion. In the nineteenth-century Ottoman Empire, including the Egyptian province, two historical trajectories of political thought converged: Muslim concepts of just rule commingled with European notions of homeland framed by a centralizing imperial system. This discursive matrix manifested itself as *patriotism*. This book offers a new definition of this concept, based on the Ottoman Egyptian example.

Patriotism in Arabic (*waṭaniyya*) became manifest in two aspects. Firstly, it was an empire-wide ideology of power that provided a tactical vocabulary for Arabic-speaking elites to negotiate co-operation among themselves and with the Ottoman system. In the Egyptian province, it served the goal of achieving a tacit *compromise* with the semi-independent governor. Secondly, patriotism was a communal emotion, a physical experience of togetherness, constituted in and through public occasions. Such experiences allowed elite and ordinary individuals to imagine themselves as part of a community. Importantly, these were not just any experiences, but experiences that were made possible by new, *public* practices, institutions, and technologies.

This book, therefore, focuses on performance culture as a key aspect of patriotism. Stages and theater buildings were new public spaces, and going to the theater was a new public ritual in the nineteenth-century Ottoman Arab world. Arabic journalism and theater were intertwined enterprises and together built up a fragile public sphere. Arabic musical theater was connected to patriotism in Arabic journals. Prewritten musical plays performed on stages, involving women, in front of a seated audience, were innovations that creatively absorbed earlier practices like Arabic poetry, singing, and popular mimetic performances. Language was made compatible with the new spaces. The study of performance culture is crucial to understand what *being public*, hence *being a patriot*, meant in the changing Ottoman urban world.

Moreover, plays provide access to plural, often opposing, definitions about what exactly the community of the homeland is. Plays were written by learned and talented individuals; and their ideas often served political and business interests. Plays could also function as petitions. In general, during a performance, ideas are translated into experience and, *vice versa*, experience influences ideas. Plays, their performances, and reception can convey the change in the realm of subversive ideas before such change manifests itself in political action, but plays can also represent and serve official doctrine. Importantly, entertainment and journalism are commercial enterprises, and so the practices of patriotism also illuminate the history of Arab capitalism. Not only local or global but also imperial factors influenced the content, staging, and reception of plays. The Ottoman Egyptian elites, as we shall see, instrumentalized Western European opera for their own representation. *Arab Patriotism* therefore demonstrates the impure construction of nation-ness in the black box of culture.

For analytical clarity, I maintain a clear distinction between patriotism and nationalism. Modern nationalism is typically defined as an ideology of solidarity, organized around the idea of "the nation" (based on birth, *natio*) in a sovereign political unit.[1] I understand patriotism, by contrast, as an ideology of solidarity associated with the political use of the "homeland" (living territory, *patria*) without the explicit demand for a sovereign polity. Both can be mass phenomena for which intellectuals and political elites articulate the core ideas; their practices are similar. Whereas patriotism has generally been considered positive, nationalism has a darker reputation. As the historian Johan Huizinga once declared, "[nationalism] flourishes in the sphere of competition and opposition."[2]

[1] Dawisha, *Arab Nationalism*, 13; Smith, "Biblical Beliefs," 414; Osterhammel, *The Transformation of the World*, 404–405.

[2] Huizinga, "Patriotism and Nationalism," 154.

A patriot would die for the homeland; a nationalist would purify the nation. This is admittedly oversimplified (many patriots would perhaps gladly purify the nation), and there have been calls to forget patriotism altogether,[3] but this distinction allows us to discuss the patriotic idea at a particular historical juncture.

Patriotism is the expression of nation-ness that can emerge in various contexts, mostly imperial ones. Nation-ness is a narrative quality of identification connected to the use of the "homeland" as a political argument.[4] This type of narration appears as political temporality in the form of history or *historicization*.[5] Patriotism can precede nationalism, but it can also instantiate a muted nationalism within an imperial framework that makes allowance for a type of federal state. Nationalism begins when the patriotic ideas and experiences of a particular group are articulated in conjunction with arguments for an independent polity. When such a polity is attained, the ideology transforms into a state "theory of political legitimacy."[6] There is nothing romantic about patriotism. It also legitimizes power. Between its first murmurs in empires and the realization of a fully sovereign state, there are various ways in which the patriotic idea can serve governments. This book traces one of those ways in the context of the Ottoman Empire.

Modern Egypt as an Ottoman Province: The Khedivate

What does the framing of Egypt as an Ottoman province tell us precisely? Egypt became an Ottoman province in 1517 when the sultan's army conquered Cairo. The province was never fully integrated: the seventeenth and eighteenth centuries saw rebellious localized Turkic-Egyptian military alliances. After the brief French occupation (1798–1801), they were gradually crushed. Even within the province there were power struggles between peasants of Upper Egypt and the military leaders in Cairo, the seat of local power.

Administratively, Egypt was an *eyalet* (province) until 1867 when its designation changed to *hidiviyet* (khedivate). An *eyalet* was the largest administrative unit in the Ottoman imperial system in which the governor (*vali*), who was sent from the empire's center, was responsible for tax collection and redistribution. The governor, assisted by the chief judge

[3] Cohen and Nussbaum, *For Love of Country*.

[4] Anderson coined "nation-ness" (*Imagined Communities*, 4) but never defined it.

[5] Ricoeur, "Narrative Time," 182–184; 189.

[6] Gellner, *Nations and Nationalism*, 1–7.

(*kadı*), also appointed from the imperial center, represented "the executive power of the sultan on all matters."[7] This is why, behind the words *eyalat* and *hidiviyet*, the Ottoman administrative language understood *vilayet*, "governorship," as the main designation of an imperial unit that owed tribute and soldiers to the center.

Throughout the nineteenth century, the governorship of the Egyptian province was in the hands of one Turkish-speaking family. They were neither local Egyptians nor sent from the imperial elite. This position explains their quest to belong to both the province and the empire in order to maximalize their security. While Istanbul attempted to reassert stricter control over its provinces in the nineteenth century (excepting those of Algiers and Tunis, which were lost to the French), the province of Egypt continued to experience a degree of autonomy. The governors of Egypt represented the sultan without being fully subject to him.

This was the achievement of Mehmed Ali (r. 1805–1848), a Turkish-speaking mercenary in the Ottoman army and founder of the dynasty. His political maneuvering made possible the special path taken by late Ottoman Egypt. After leading his new army to occupy the Syrian provinces in the 1830s, international pressure obliged him to retreat—but only on the condition that he receive the right to hereditary governorship in 1841. Thereafter his family stood between the distant sultan and the peoples in the Nile valley, making Cairo a rival center to Istanbul in the late Ottoman world.[8] The nineteenth-century history of Egypt as an Ottoman province is thus a history of the struggle of Mehmed Ali's descendants with both the center and each other over the resources of the Nile Valley.[9] From 1867 they used the title "khedive" exclusively. Their family intrigues, played out through the sultanic administration, greatly influenced the lives of ordinary Egyptians. Nineteenth-century Egyptian history is also a history of localized imperial legal codes, Turkish administrative orders, Egyptian participation in imperial wars, tribute to the central treasury, imperial censorship, and Egypt's subjection to a Sunni caliphate that belonged to the House of Osman. It is a history of networks: close commercial ties with the Hijaz and the Greater Syrian and the Balkan provinces; the intellectual networks of the Arabic-speaking Ottoman urban centers. It is a history of African conquests (Sudan and Ethiopia) in the name of the sultan and of gaining the right to contract foreign loans. In sum, it is the history of making the khedivate.

This book argues that it is not a coincidence that the idea of the homeland develops forcefully as a political argument in Arabic in the new

[7] EI2, "Eyalet" (Halil İnalcik).
[8] Fahmy, *Mehmed Ali*, 74.
[9] Toledano, *State and Society*, 3.

regime from the 1860s. The khedivate and political patriotism in Egypt were connected.

Patriotism as a Historiographical Problem

Positing Arab patriotism as both an imperial phenomenon and the particular ideology of the Egyptian khedivate requires critical engagement with two historical traditions. The first is the history of the Egyptian nation-state. The writing of this history began in the nineteenth century with the khedivial government itself, which sought to present itself as a sovereign nation-state well before this was a political reality. The second historical tradition concerns the development of Arab nationalism or "Arabism."

Writing about the khedivate is a delicate exercise. Until 1952, the prevailing narrative was a glorified royalist history in which the rulers of the khedivate were "daring modernizers" responsible for ushering in an age of reform and "independence."[10] The pendulum has since swung fiercely in the opposite direction. After the 1952 military coup d'état, the agenda of the historian ʿAbd al-Raḥmān al-Rāfiʿī became the official state doctrine. Al-Rāfiʿī divided history into a "political history" (the khedives, the Ottomans, and the British) and a "national history" (the nation).[11] Following him, Egyptian and non-Egyptian historians have generally preserved the divide between politics and nation.[12] To the best of my knowledge, no attempt has been made to understand the khedivate as a theoretical problem in historical scholarship.[13]

The history of the period of the British occupation has typically been written from the standpoint of imperial and colonial history, as if Egypt was suddenly out of the Ottoman reach.[14] Only James Jankowski made an analytical distinction between religious (Ottomanism), territorial, and

[10] Di Capua, *Gatekeepers*, 38–43; 91–140.

[11] Al-Rāfiʿī, *Muṣṭafā Kāmil*, 320.

[12] Mohammed Sabry (French thesis 1924; Arabic translation 2006), ʿAbd al-Raḥmān al-Rāfiʿī's interwar Arabic works, Jamal Mohamed Ahmed (1960 in English), Nadav Safran (1961 in English), Luwīs ʿAwaḍ (1969 in Arabic), Anouar Abdel Malek (1969 in French, 1983 in Arabic), Charles Wendell (1972 in English), Israel Gershoni-James Jankowski (1987 in English), Gershoni (1992 in English); Ziad Fahmy (2011 in English). There is a branch of Marxist history substituting the "nation" with the "people": Sālim, *Al-Quwa al-Ijtimāʿiyya*; Cole, *Colonialism and Revolution*; and a Foucauldian history starting with Mitchell, *Colonising Egypt*; Fahmy, *All the Pasha's Men*.

[13] Recent publications about the history of the offence against the ruler are promising. ʿAshmāwī, *Al-ʿAyb fī al-Dhāt al-Malikiyya*; Rizq, *Al-ʿAyb fī Dhāt Afandīnā*.

[14] The two canonical works are Berque, *Egypt*; Tignor, *Modernization*.

ethnic/linguistic nationalisms in this period.[15] Recent authors have investigated the nature of British rule and the way the occupation influenced political, social, and gender identities and practices, including nationalism.[16] Few study the continued Ottoman networks of occupied Egypt.[17]

In contrast, building upon the work of historians Ehud Toledano and Khaled Fahmy, this book situates the history of nineteenth-century Egypt within the Ottoman world until the 1890s.[18] The British occupation does not represent a break in this regard; as we shall see, the Ottoman context continued to inform patriotism in Egypt during the occupation.[19]

The other historiographical axis, associated primarily with the theorist Sāṭiʿ al-Ḥuṣrī (1880–1967), articulates a distinction between territorial nationalism (*waṭaniyya*) and pan-Arab nationalism (*qawmiyya*).[20] This distinction becomes manifest in the twentieth century in the contrast between the state nationalisms of new countries such as Egypt, Lebanon, and Syria on the one hand, and the vision of all Arabs united in a giant state on the other. The distinction continues to resonate in Arabic scholarship, although we are in a post-*qawmiyya* age today.[21]

Numerous valuable attempts have been made to connect nineteenth-century discourses to the twentieth-century pan-Arab idea (*qawmiyya*).[22] The scholarly consensus now is that the idea of an independent, united Arab polity became popular among intellectuals and army officers, especially Greater Syrians and Iraqis, only after 1908 during the Second Constitutional Period in the Ottoman Empire.[23]

However, we lack the conceptual tools to interpret the dominant ideas in Arabic *before* 1908. These ideas are typically understood as only the "origins," "prehistory," and "early stirrings" of either nation-state nationalism or pan-Arabism. Rashid Khalidi argues that this early Arabism is not identical with the pan-Arab idea (the giant Arab state) but does not explain its nature.[24] Youssef M. Choueiri uses the term "cultural Arabism" to describe nineteenth-century ideas but does not provide a clear explanation of their

[15] Jankowski, "Ottomanism and Arabism."

[16] Russell, *Creating the New Egyptian Woman*; Baron, *Egypt as a Woman*; Jacob, *Working Out Egypt*; Barak, *On Time*.

[17] Fahmī, *Al-ʿAlāqāt al-Miṣriyya*.

[18] Toledano, *State and Society*; Fahmy, *All the Pasha's Men*. A useful publication is Ihsanoğlu, *The Turks in Egypt*, without theoretical claims.

[19] Toledano, "Forgetting Egypt's Ottoman Past."

[20] Choueiri, *Arab Nationalism*, 112–116; Dawisha, *Arab Nationalism*, 85.

[21] Ḥijāzī, *Al-Waṭaniyya al-Miṣriyya*, 11–12.

[22] Hourani, *Arabic Thought*, ch. 4; Duri, *The Historical Formation*.

[23] Dawn, *From Ottomanism to Arabism*; Tauber, *The Emergence*; Khalidi et al., eds., *The Origins*; Kayalı, *Arabs and Young Turks*; Dawisha, *Arab Nationalism*, 14–27.

[24] Khalidi, "Arab Nationalism," 1365.

function and their relationship to what he terms "political Arabism" in the twentieth century.[25] He calls for the restoration of the "Ottoman option" in historiography, by which he means the understanding of Ottomanism among Arabs "as a response to European penetration."[26] Aziz Al-Azmeh suggests there is no contradiction in theorizing a "civic Ottoman patriotism, combined with an Arab linguistic and local patriotism," although he provides clues to such a theorization only in passing.[27]

Bringing the empire and culture back into the study of national development significantly alters our understanding of the Arab historical trajectory in two regards. First, it shows the local structure of political power and the relationship between local Arabic-speaking and imperial elites within the Ottoman system. Second, unlike the dominant theory of tracing Arabism to modernist Muslim thought (the usual chain is Muḥammad ʿAbduh, ʿAbd al-Raḥmān al-Kawākibī, Rashīd Riḍā) and to some Christian intellectuals, I argue that Arabness had an earlier, noncolonial Ottoman mode. In this mode, revivalism and invented traditions were deployed to negotiate compromises within the various Ottoman subsystems. I use the term "Arab patriotism" to describe this complex mode of politics in the Egyptian province.

Patriotism as Theoretical Problem

The theoretical problem of Arab patriotism in the Ottoman Empire lies in recognizing the emergence of imagined national communities in an empire that was, simultaneously, a mosaic of religious collectivities and a Sunni caliphate. Put another way, the problem is how to account, theoretically, for local patriotic ideas that were not premised on a fundamental rejection of empire.

Local Patriotisms and Imperial Networks

One has to leave behind the received definitions of nationalism to understand how imperial networks can contribute to local patriotic ideas and how a provincial governing family could insert itself among these ideas.

Ehud Toledano suggests two simultaneous strategies of the "power elite" in the Ottoman Empire after the seventeenth century: localization and Ottomanization. Turkic military-administrative elites became culturally "local" in provinces, while at the same time local notable families

[25] Choueiri, *Arab Nationalism*, 65–70.
[26] Choueiri, *Modern Arab Historiography*, 205.
[27] Al-Azmeh, "Nationalism and the Arabs," 73.

started to learn Ottoman Turkish and participate in imperial governance. The elaborate balance of these two processes slowed down the disintegration of the empire and, according to Toledano, explains that separatism was not welcomed in the Arab provinces.[28]

Recently, Alexei Miller and Stefan Berger have argued that "nations emerged in empires" partly as the consequence of "the nation-building project which was conceived and implemented in the imperial core" but which never aimed at a complete homogenization of citizens.[29] In the Ottoman Empire, indeed, there was a central Ottoman ideology manufactured largely in the imperial core. This model accounts for the centralized production of imperial nations and accommodates the existence of plural patriotisms while giving more analytical attention to the former than to the latter.

My suggestion is that the various patriotisms in the Arab provinces were the nineteenth-century forms of the Ottomanization/localization strategy. There was an interaction between centrally produced imperial and local patriotisms. The "local-Ottoman," typically Muslim, elite did embrace patriotism and developed their own local versions. These provincial patriotisms did not aim at the external sovereignty of a people but at the acknowledgement of the localized representation of (Ottoman) power as a form of internal sovereignty. The various provincial elites designed various degrees of this acknowledgment.

These local discursive patriotisms were based on imperial networks. I use "network" here to refer to commercial, religious, and linguistic connections, as well as shared intraimperial political interests. I identify at least four urban hubs: Cairo, Beirut, Tunis, and Damascus, each of which came to stand for different aims and political agendas.[30] Beyond the Arab provinces, Istanbul was the main center of translating Ottoman imperial patriotism into Arabic. Imperial framing means the translation of ideas from the central language and the experience of this language in everyday life, such as in the army and in school. It also works in the other direction—that is, the central language reacts to and absorbs provincial and global discourses. The Ottoman case is interesting since it used Arabic words (*waṭan* as pronounced in Turkish *vatan*) with Turkish and Persian grammar, thus "translation" to Arabic did not occur between languages but between mental maps which shared the same words. The Ottoman Arab urban network was also part of a larger Mediterranean and global networks, and transmitted other ideologies later.[31]

28 Toledano, "The Emergence of Ottoman-Local Elites," 155–156.
29 Berger and Miller, eds., *Nationalizing Empires*, 4.
30 Hourani was close to such a formulation in *Arabic Thought*, ch. 4.
31 Khuri-Makdisi, *The Eastern Mediterranean*, 94–134.

Mediating the empire is the work of patriotism. Mediation occurs in order to preserve the precarious position of elite individuals between the center and the province and to avoid violence. As we shall see, patriotism within Egypt entailed a special pact between elites and the governor. The khedives also supported the Ottoman Arabic networks as part of their larger imperial game. Thus not only the imperial core but elite provincial interests—and the factual power of these local elites—contributed to the development of empire-compatible patriotic ideas in Arabic.

Nation-ness and Islam: Non-Colonial Time?

Since the Ottomans increasingly represented the empire as the Sunni caliphate in the nineteenth century, one has to account for the co-existence of patriotic ideas and Muslim loyalty.[32] Why was there no major clash between these collective principles—nation-ness and revelation—until the twentieth century? This question can be illuminated by the problem of time.

Benedict Anderson explains the origins of nationalism through the loss of a religion-based politics and the loss of the dynastic realm in eighteenth-century Europe. Emptied, measurable, clock-time became filled with the idea of the nation, "a cultural artifact," as Anderson describes it, and this singular form of the imagined community was used in other territories as well.[33] On Barak brings an original counter-argument. He shows that anticolonial nationalism in British-occupied Egypt was "predicated on rejecting and subverting" the supposedly universal empty, homogenous time by employing "counter-tempos."[34] Thus he points out that Anderson's model worked exactly the opposite way in colonial Egypt: nationalism resisted empty time.

While these applications of Walter Benjamin's theory about time on nationalism are important, I argue that there was patriotism before (anticolonial) nationalism in the Ottoman Empire and specifically in its Egyptian province. This patriotism relied on a particularly complex structure of revelation-based and nation-based practices.

Cracks in the supernatural architecture of the temporal world could occur without major eruptions because the worldly power was still a Muslim one. Avner Wishnitzer argues that Ottoman temporal culture became a domain of competing social roles and that "ruptures" occurred in the Muslim time-divine order continuum in the nineteenth century.[35]

[32] Deringil, *The Well-Protected Domains*, 17.
[33] Anderson, *Imagined Communities*, 26.
[34] Barak, *On Time*, 83.
[35] Wishnitzer, *Reading Clocks, Alla Turca*, 8.

Nation-ness and revelation-based practices co-existed because Muslim governments approved the patriotic ideas and older social practices could transmute into new ones. There was an indigenous, modernizing power structure in which nation-ness co-mingled with revelation-based practices in the context of informal European imperialism and gunboat diplomacy. The assumption of this book is that this situation is different from direct European colonialism. Egypt is not India.

Patriotism in Arabic

There is also a conceptual problem of translation from Arabic sources. *Waṭaniyya* in the nineteenth century has rarely been translated as "patriotism."[36] Bernard Lewis has repeatedly suggested that patriotism, understood in English as the "calm loyalty of free men to the country of their birth," had less appeal to Arabs than nationalism.[37] Since the interwar years *waṭaniyya* and *qawmiyya* have often been interchangeable words in spoken Arabic; Adeed Dawisha prefers to translate *waṭaniyya* in twentieth-century Egypt as "state nationalism."[38] Eliezer Tauber warns that the distinction between nationalism and patriotism is entirely European and cannot be applied to Arabic thought before the First World War; yet he neither defines these concepts nor proposes a solution.[39] The distinction, in casual historical parlance, is indeed based on (western) European examples (and has a specific resonance in English).

The classical Arabic use of the "homeland" (*waṭan*) was a subjective literary topos of loss, grief, and desire whose "affective structure," as Yaseen Noorani shows, was transformed in the nineteenth century into a political summons to solidarity.[40] In this book, we shall follow some of the main features of this transformation. A number of neologisms and phrases appeared to accompany this change such as "patriot" (*waṭanī*), "the sons of the homeland" (*abnāʾ al-waṭan*), or "patriotic service" (*khidma waṭaniyya*). The very same Arabic words were often used in Ottoman Turkish, too. Like the German concept of *Heimat*,[41] the exact territorial meaning of homeland remained fluid in late Ottoman Arabic texts. Its reference point was clearest in Egypt where the Nile Valley was a well-defined unit and where the governors attempted to attach themselves to the homeland. "Border" was not yet a concept connected to the

[36] One of the rare examples: Duri, *The Historical Formation*, 155–161, in Lawrence Conrad's translation.

[37] Lewis, "Patriotism and Nationalism," 71–98.

[38] Dawisha, *Arab Nationalism*, 98, 101.

[39] Tauber, *The Emergence*, 245.

[40] Noorani, "Estrangement," 25.

[41] Applegate, *A Nation of Provincials*; Blickle, *Heimat*.

identification between individual and territory. Earlier than the idea of freedom, the idea of homeland in Arabic became politicized by the mid-nineteenth century.[42]

As we shall see, Arabness was an idea only belatedly connected to the mental category of *waṭan* in khedivial Egypt. The idea of Arabness as a moral principle and linguistic quality served as a common ground between elites. The pages that follow will reveal that intellectuals and powerful figures in late Ottoman Egypt attempted to use patriotism, as in Europe and the United States, for various political ends.

Patriotism as a Methodological Problem

How can one access an ideology of this sort, which traveled between sites and mediated competing scales of belonging and rule? And how can we access its experience? For, patriotism was a communal experience as well as an ideology. In tracing the life of ideas, one cannot limit oneself to searching libraries for printed materials. Ernest C. Dawn suggests that the ideological origins of pan-Arabism are to be found in a limited number of texts; others challenge this view.[43] This book dissects the very making of such texts in a historical anthropology and social history based on the extensive use of archival and nonarchival sources.

Memory: The Making of Modern Muslim Aesthetics

The use of aesthetics as a technique of power was characteristic of Europe from Louis XIV to Nazi Germany. But its use was not limited to Europe. The makers of patriotism in Egypt were highly educated Muslim intellectuals who made an effort to translate the power of the khedives. They were keenly aware of the difficulty of using the patriotic idea in a caliphate. They turned to Muslim memory (and, by this gesture, invented it in a novel form) to experiment with new textual and visual aesthetic forms and to explore potential resources for patriotic identification. The textual domain contained the genres of Arab-Islamic-Ottoman poetry and history-writing. Medieval Muslim political discourse used poetry, history, tales, proverbs, and theological treatises in order to address matters of justice and the relationship between ruler and ruled.[44] The petition, as

42 Abu-'Uksa, *Freedom in the Arab World*, 13.

43 Al-Azmeh, "Nationalism and the Arabs"; Dawn, "From Ottomanism to Arabism," 397; Khalidi, "Ottomanism and Arabism," in his *Origins of Arab Nationalism*; Watenpaugh, *Being Modern*, 7.

44 Al-Azmeh, *Muslim Kingship*, 43, 73, 79.

a specific political-aesthetic genre characterized by flowery praise of the ruler, was a legitimate means of political communication in the Ottoman domains. Praise could manipulate official discourse.[45] This repertory of political aesthetics continued into the nineteenth century.

Medieval texts, their themes, and vocabulary, and their very appearance were creatively reused and reinvented in the emerging *printed* public sphere (books and journals).[46] Through this aestheticization of philology was finally Arabness articulated in public texts. Print became a carefully controlled aesthetic and material feature of the Ottoman public sphere, accompanied by new flags, rituals, clothing, eating habits, medical practices, and new laws.[47] Patriotic ideas arrived with and through this transformation of the sensorium of the life-world. The discursive side of this transformation was characterized by dialectical continuity with older Muslim grammars of power. The making of modern Muslim memory through print aesthetics entailed that history should become the core narrative shape of patriotism.

Mikhail Bakhtin says that "time, as it were, thickens, takes on flesh" in describing the way literary chronotopos—the time-space connection—works in the novel.[48] The embodiment of time is human flesh on stage. It was in the theater that ancient Arabia, Abbasid Baghdad, and Muslim Andalusia were presented in Arabic first—not as relics of the past, but as means for thinking about the problems of the present. These enlivened *chronotopoi* on stage became standardized in modern Arabic literature.[49] Historicized figures on stage helped the identification with new narratives of the present. Various techniques of surveillance secured the representation of these themes in a manner acceptable to the regime and the ruling groups. Thus historicized Muslim themes were experienced in various locations without being perceived as subversive of the established order.

The architects of patriotism constructed learned Arabic (*al-lugha al-ʿarabiyya al-fuṣḥā*) as a language to achieve a compromise and, in the Egyptian province, to talk to the khedive. They believed that such a language was the key to progress and Arab modernity. This was a language that carried history through the reuse of medieval texts. Most of the works I discuss in the pages that follow are now forgotten. They have been labeled as "neoclassicist literature" or anachronistically described as expressions of a "moral economy" against the colonial power.[50] In making

[45] Chalcraft, "Engaging the State," 304–305.

[46] Al-Bagdadi, *Vorgestellte Öffentlichkeit*; Schwartz, "Meaningful Mediums."

[47] Two crucial books would be soon published by Khaled Fahmy on medicine, and Omar Cheta on merchant law in 1860s Egypt.

[48] Bakhtin, "Forms of Time," 84.

[49] Granara, "Nostalgia, Arab Nationalism."

[50] Khouri, *Poetry and the Making*, 5–36; Noorani, *Culture and Hegemony*, ch. 2.

this argument, I will relegate some well-known nineteenth-century personages to the sideline while placing other, previously marginal figures in positions of prominence.

Audience and Nation

Patriotism is a communal experience—something that is learned in the company of others—as well as an ideology. There is a bidirectional flow between patriotic ideology and practice. Anderson's coinage "unisonality" speaks to this phenomenon. It refers to a sensorial technique of nation-ness in, for example, the experience of collective singing together.[51] I will show that what is regarded today as early patriotic Arabic poetry was in fact composed and set to music for soldiers to sing together. As in Persia, aural patriotism was inserted into the sensorium of nineteenth-century Egypt. [52]

Urbanism transformed the public grammar of the body. There is a relationship between the material transformation of cities, new forms of memory, being public, and new modes of collective experience. Spaces and technologies transformed the value of Arabic language, too. These novelties, by the very widening of what is "public," increased the potential of supervision.

Singing and listening are bodily experiences. The techniques of patriotism included the experience of *physically* being part of an audience. The "citizen audience" was a nineteenth-century global phenomenon.[53] This was made possible by new spaces where individuals could become an audience, for a moment becoming a microcosm of the imagined sons and daughters of the homeland. Theater buildings, café chantants, and bars supplied these spaces and stages. Not all of these were novel. Coffeehouses and public gardens were simultaneously old Islamic and new European spaces of community. In these old-new locations, patriotism became a physical, embodied experience for an audience that was both a target for the entertainment business and a target for ideological inculcation.[54] While in Alexandria and the main countryside cities private stages popped up, in Cairo the government created a number of playhouses for elite use, to which, later, less privileged groups also petitioned for access. This book also unearths the history of the Khedivial Opera House with an eye to how khedives, Arab impresarios, and Ottoman politicians and their audiences used it as a representative public space.

[51] Anderson, *Imagined Communities*, 145.
[52] Chehabi, "From Revolutionary Taṣnīf."
[53] Butsch, *The Citizen Audience*, 26.
[54] Abercrombie and Longhurst, *Audiences*, 37.

Nineteenth-century Arabic theater was a creative innovation that combined old-new Arabic music, poetry, and European acting techniques. Until the 1880s, dominantly Christian Arab impresarios organized troupes while Muslim and Jewish playwrights were active from early on. Similar to the Calcutta musical theater,[55] Arabic music and, specifically, Egyptian singers were crucial in accompanying prose acting on stage.[56] There is a connection between music and collective identity, sound and memory, as Merih Erol shows on the music practices of Orthodox Greeks in late Ottoman Istanbul.[57] From the very beginning of modern Arabic theater in the 1840s, as Ilham Khuri-Makdisi has argued, the bringing of theatrical performers and audiences together had the potential of turning the theater into "a potentially subversive institution."[58] In my interpretation, however, Arabic musical theater was primarily a semibourgeois genre designed to *stabilize* society, even as the genre enabled public discussion of issues relating to justice and solidarity. In khedivial Egypt, this mimetic-acoustic art joined older methods of talking to the sovereign (for instance, Arabic poetry) and, through this talk, established a temporal collectivity. European technologies of the public space and sphere were immediately instrumentalized by intellectuals in an attempt to influence the khedivial regime.

Overview of the Book

Arab Patriotism is composed of three sections. Part I, "The Making of the Khedivate," tackles the paradox of power in the Ottoman Egyptian province. This section focuses on the way the local elites needed to come to terms with the position of Mehmed Ali as a hereditary Ottoman governor and understand this rank in the language of Muslim politics. We shall see how the patriotic idea served a means to negotiate with his successors and for military indoctrination during the Crimean war (1853–1856). We then turn to the Ottoman image of his grandson, Ismail and Ismail's mother Hoşyar (d. 1886) who designed a fundamental, double *compromise* with the rural elites and the Ottoman center in the form of the khedivate. However, Ismail decided that the Ottoman face of Egypt had to be hidden. New public spaces were erected such as the Khedivial Opera House. It was here that Giuseppe Verdi's opera *Aida* premiered in 1871. Far from a simple manifestation of European cultural imperialism,

[55] Chatterjee, *The Black Hole of Empire*, 232.
[56] Sadgrove, "Early Arabic Musical Theatre."
[57] Erol, *Greek Orthodox Music*, 12–13.
[58] Khuri-Makdisi, *The Eastern Mediterranean*, 72–75.

the premiere symbolized the khedivial instrumentalization of European culture through a new political aesthetics.

Part II, "A Garden With Mellow Fruits of Refinement," deals with the question: what is the khedivate? Or, whose is the khedivate? The "gentle revolution," as I call the period between the late 1860s and the mid-1870s, created Arabness as a quality of public patriotism through adjusting language to space. Muslim intellectuals brought *fuṣḥā* Arabic and moral images of being an Arab as a common platform between Ottomans and locals in the khedivate. This civic ideology of Muslim power was largely concerned with education and reform as connected to khedivial power, through a revivalist historicized discourse. As in Russia, the learned came to regard theater as an instrument of public education and refinement, not unlike the schools. But foreign control over Egyptian finances brought unintended consequences. The army and social groups revolted in 1882 in the name of the sultan, and Ismail's son Tevfik (r. 1879–1892) could retain his position only with British help.

Part III, "The Reinvention of the Khedivate," is about the khedivial regime after the British occupation. While Ottomanism became "essentially an instrumentality to the realization of Egypt-centered goals,"[59] this final section describes how patriotism functioned in the restoration, and, I argue, *reinvention* of khedivial power after 1882. After the survey of the relationship between law and public space through the examples of theaters in Egypt, the book concludes between the mosque and the opera. The last chapter reveals the formation of the mixed patriotic-colonial elite through a historical sociology of public codes of elite honor. We discover how the young khedive, Abbas Hilmi II (r. 1892–1914) functioned as a pole of imagined Ottoman-Egyptian sovereignty against the British in the 1890s in the eyes of the young politician, later national icon, Muṣṭafā Kāmil (1874–1908). The story ends before his break with the ruler, as patriotism in late Ottoman Egypt under occupation sang its swan song. It soon gave way to a different ideology: mass Egyptian nationalism struggling for independence against the British.

[59] Jankowski, "Ottomanism and Arabism," 239.

PART I

THE MAKING OF THE KHEDIVATE

> I came to Egypt with the sole goal to provide the Vice-Roy with a new sign of my good will and my special affection, and to inspect this so important part of my empire. All my efforts concern the development of the happiness and well-being of all the classes of my subjects. . . . I am convinced that the Vice-Roy proceeds in the same vein, and following the footsteps of his grandfather, the great man of our nation, he will preserve and perfect his work.[1]

Thus spoke Sultan Abdülaziz (r. 1861–1876), through his foreign minister's French translation, to the consuls and his governor Ismail Pasha in Alexandria in April 1863. This was an extraordinary occasion: no Ottoman sultan had visited the province of Egypt in the three centuries since its conquest by Sultan Selim I in 1517. And in 1863, there were indeed signs of development to be seen in Egypt; Sultan Abdülaziz, for example, traveled by train (for the first time in his life) from Alexandria to Cairo, observed factories, and visited the museum of Egyptology.[2]

The purpose of this part of the book is to make sense of Egypt's Ottoman attachment and to contextualize the interaction of imperial and local patriotisms within the Ottoman Empire. We shall follow the story of how Egypt, a quite independent province in the eighteenth century, became re-Ottomanized by the mid-nineteenth century. While "the great man of our nation" ("nation" meaning the empire here), the governor Mehmed Ali has usually been regarded as the ruler who gained "independence," it fell to his descendants to create a new Ottoman regime-type for the Egyptian province: the khedivate.

[1] Speech cited in letter dated 8 April 1863, from Robert Colquhoun to Foreign Office, FO 78/1754, NA. Gardey, *Voyage de Sultan Abd-Ul-Aziz*, 42.

[2] Cevdet, *Maʾrūzāt*, 57–59. Gardey, *Voyage de Sultan Abd-Ul-Aziz*, 50; 105–106.

CHAPTER 1

The Ottoman Origins of Arab Patriotism

The construction of a new political community as related to a new regime type in Ottoman Egypt can be defined by two problems in the first half of the nineteenth century. The first was the relationship between the Ottoman Empire and its Egyptian province under the rule of Mehmed Ali. The second was the relationship between the governor and the local elites. These problems were interrelated in the legitimacy structure of power, and provided the conditions for the rise of political nation-ness in Arabic.

It was the Crimean war (1853–1856), in which Egypt and other Arab provinces participated, that forcefully brought to the surface patriotism in Arabic as a discursive strategy of constituting political solidarity in public. There were overlapping imagined communities at the imperial and local levels. The idea of the homeland became a means to make sense of new politics through old media: poetry, songs, proverbs, history, and religious treatises. There were new media too, such as the printing press and modern Arabic theater in Ottoman Beirut, which in its inception was connected to solidarity and the Ottoman order.

The Mehmed Ali Paradox

There was a drama of survival at the highest level of Ottoman and Egyptian politics. The key to understanding the logic behind the actions of the self-made governor Mehmed Ali and those of his successors is a simple paradox. Mehmed Ali was neither part of the Ottoman elite, nor was he a local Egyptian or even ethnically Arab. He was not sent from the imperial center to govern, nor was he at the head of a local group in the Nile Valley.

Instead, Mehmed Ali arrived in Egypt in 1801 to fight the French, as an ad hoc commander of an irregular unit of the Ottoman army. He was the unruly nephew of the governor in the Ottoman city of Kavala (today in Greece). He invested in the tobacco trade, but soon joined the Ottoman troops en route to Egypt. After the French evacuation, he seized the governorship of the province by deploying mercenaries, scheming, and expelling the appointed Ottoman governors. One governor, Hüsrev, attempted to introduce novel Ottoman reforms (*Nizam-i Cedid*) much to the chagrin of the sheikhs of al-Azhar. Mehmed Ali commanded the only force capable of maintaining order in Cairo, despite having caused much of the chaos himself. Seeing him as their only means of guarding their financial freedom against Ottoman centralization, the sheikhs made a strategic decision and petitioned the sultan to appoint Mehmed Ali governor. This was a foundational act: lacking an army in Egypt and facing a crisis in Istanbul, the sultan was forced to accede to the request in order to retain the province. The sultanic letter of appointment (a firman) thus arrived in 1805.[1]

Over the next twenty years, Mehmed Ali maintained a loyal connection with the weak imperial center while he eliminated his internal rivals, the neo-Mamluks, the local military elite in Egypt. In their place, he built a new elite composed of Ottoman peoples: his family members and friends from Kavala, Turks, Albanians, Armenians, and Greeks from the Ottoman Mediterranean. He employed local Copts and Syrian Christians in the administration. Then, the pasha created a modern army by forced conscription of Egyptian peasants and employed French, Italian, and Spanish training officers. He monopolized the provincial economy. Finally, Mehmed Ali broke al-Azhar by appointing loyal sheikhs as its leaders. The Ottoman Turkish-speaking elite became known by the Turkish word *zevat* (Arabic *dhawāt*) in Egypt. The *zevat* directed his household government and the army.[2]

Mehmed Ali's actions were crucially informed by his position as an alien in both the Ottoman elite system and the Egyptian province. He was not, like Ali Pasha in Ottoman Greece, of local origin.[3] Aware of precarious position, he always prioritized dealing with the closest threat to his person and rule. Thus, when reforms started in the Ottoman army in the late 1820s, creating the conditions for his removal by force, Mehmed Ali realized his long-cherished plan of acquiring the rich Syrian provinces and gaining more soldiers.[4] He ordered his eldest son Ibrahim to invade the Syrian provinces in 1831. This move upset the Ottoman system in an unprecedented manner.

[1] This paragraph is based on Fahmy, *Mehmed Ali*, ch. 1–3; Scharfe, "Muslim Scholars," ch. 2.

[2] This paragraph is based on Hunter, *Egypt Under the Khedives*; Toledano, *State and Society*; Fahmy, *All the Pasha's Men*; Cuno, "Egypt to c. 1919"; Scharfe, "Muslim Scholars," ch. 6 and 7.

[3] Kechriotis, "Requiem for the Empire," 106.

[4] Fahmy, *All the Pasha's Men*, 47–55.

The Syrian Campaign and Ibrahim's Image in Arabic, 1830s

There were three important consequences of the Syrian campaign from the point of view of Egypt's Ottoman relation and the rise of nation-ness. The first, as Khaled Fahmy underlines, was a homogenizing experience among Egyptian peasant recruits in the army "instilling in them the feeling of hatred of the Ottomans."[5] The second was an Arabic image of Ibrahim. In the 1880s, this image would be incorporated into the ideological restoration of dynastic legitimacy after the British occupation (see in detail in chapter 6); and even later would give rise to speculations about his pro-Arab feelings. The third was the right of Mehmed Ali to the hereditary governance of Egypt, received in 1841—discussed in the next section.

In the Arabic image of Ibrahim appears the first signs of a compromise in Arabic with a Muslim Ottoman ruler who claimed some sovereignty against the Ottoman sultan and caliph, and a vocabulary describing him as an Arab prince. Mehmed Ali also acquired an image in Arabic but it is Ibrahim's that would later become the material of political legitimacy. It is worth noting that we have access to this image in a final form, as it reaches us in printed books, very possibly after careful historical cosmetics. Therefore, it is important to contextualize it briefly in relation to the available historical data. That data, again, are somewhat distorted by the postoccupation period when the Syrian provinces were reintegrated into the empire after 1841.

The Conquest

In 1831 Ibrahim's army, in cooperation with the emir of Mount Lebanon, Bashīr Shihāb II, announced a new balance of power to the Ottoman Syrians. Christians, in particular, seemed to be reconciled with this situation (some even celebrated Ibrahim's entry in Damascus),[6] although they suffered injustices, such as beatings in the first years, and feared they would be forced to wear colored clothes.[7] Nawfal Nawfal (d. 1887), a Syrian Christian in the service of Mehmed Ali who accompanied Ibrahim on his conquest, recalled retrospectively that Mehmed Ali was good to Christians in Egypt, but in Syria "Ibrahim and his men related to the people like the conqueror to the defeated."[8] For instance, Ibrahim's sol-

[5] Fahmy, *All the Pasha's Men*, 268.
[6] Nawfal, *Kashf*, 295.
[7] Letter dated 14 January 1834, 166PO/D11/3, MEAN.
[8] Nawfal, *Kashf*, 295.

diers raped many women, and this, said Nawfal, "will be never forgiven by any [Syrian] Muslim or Christian."[9]

Ibrahim introduced equal taxes and armed some Christians (after he had once disarmed them) against a Druze revolt, as Rustum Bāz, a Maronite courtier of Emir Bashīr, related in his memoirs.[10] Another Christian, the Aleppo-based Catholic school master, Naʿūm Bakhkhāsh, was satisfied with the Egyptians' appointment of a Melkite tax collector,[11] although he also remarked in his diary that the Egyptians "make everyone taste the whip."[12] Yet another Catholic (later Protestant convert), Mīkhāʾīl Mishāqa (1800–1888) from Damascus—whom we will meet again in a later chapter—said of the Egyptian occupiers in a memoir: "right was given where it was due."[13] Ibrahim established a representative council ("with six Turks and six Christians") for juridical purposes, which the French consul in Beirut judged not truly useful.[14] It is not unlikely that Ibrahim acquired some personal friends among Christians; in the late summer of 1837 he stayed for a long time in the house of a certain Sheikh Buṭrus in the Christian village of Ehden (today in northern Lebanon) although it seems that the Maronites generally remained afraid of him.[15]

Loving Ibrahim?

This fear is not detectable in the surviving printed Arabic poetry. Rather, satisfaction and even devotion were expressed in the poems collected by Iskandar Abkāriyūs (d. 1885), a Syrian-Armenian school-teacher and life-long loyalist of the Mehmed Ali family. The poems he published in the early 1880s were written mostly by Christians during the Egyptian occupation in the 1830s.[16] These were not the first expression of admiration in Arabic for the new pashas of Egypt. For instance, when Ibrahim crushed the first Saudi polity in the Hijaz in the 1810s, he was celebrated in the Ottoman Iraqi provinces with Arabic poems by Iraqi Muslim intellectuals.[17] By the Syrian campaign, there had already been discussions in Arabic about the new power in Egypt in the other provinces.

[9] Ibid., 297.
[10] [Bāz], *Mudhakkirāt*, 31; 36–37, n. 2.
[11] Masters, *The Arabs of the Ottoman Empire*, 152–3.
[12] Bakhkhāsh, *Akhbār Ḥalab*, 1:45.
[13] Mishāqa, *Murder, Mayhem, Pillage*, 204.
[14] Letter dated 11 February 1834 and 15 January 1835, 166PO/D11/3, MEAN.
[15] Letter dated 11 September 1837, 166PO/D11/4, MEAN.
[16] Abkāriyūs, *Al-Manāqib al-Ibrāhimīyya*, 94–107.
[17] Al-Wardī, *Lamaḥāt Ijtimāʿiyya*, 2:20.

The poems collected by Abkāriyūs depict a victorious Ibrahim, loved by the people, who accept his "just rule." The poems include a panegyric (*madīḥ*) by the famous intellectual Nāṣīf al-Yāzijī[18] and a praising poem in which every line ends in the letter "l" (*lāmiyya*) by the less famous Amīn al-Jundī, which contains the following lines:

> Indeed it is said Ibrahim arrived as a fighter / and his enemies fell, so they say / he is the lord of ministers, the pearl of their union / such noble virtues dress him up.[19]

Another way to celebrate Ibrahim was through the textual chronogram (*tārīkh*), a popular poetic technique in the eighteenth century in which the numerical values of the Arabic letters provide a number, usually a year (see more on chronograms in the next chapter). Emir Bashīr himself offered the following couplet to commemorate Ibrahim's victory at Acre in a poem printed only in the 1880s. Each hemistich contains the *hijrī* date 1248 (1832) two times. The epigrammatic nature of the chronogram aims to immortalize Ibrahim as a hero of the local community (transliterated here to provide all the letters which have numerical values):

> *Kun bālighān awj saʿdin mā bi-hi ḍarar / aw ghālibān lam yazal fī awwal al-ẓafar*
> 1248 1248 1248 1248
> Be strong even if harmful at the peak of fortune/or a champion always triumphant[20]

Hating Ibrahim?

While poetry, printed later, painted a shining image of Ibrahim, there were abundant signs of dissatisfaction with the occupation at the time—not least because the troops changed the religious and economic fabric of the Syrian provinces. Ibrahim's image must be seen in this context.

The Maronite Christians feared "disadvantages" they might face under Mehmed Ali's rule and asked for renewed French protection in 1835.[21] The poor, regardless of religion, were disadvantaged by the equal taxation.[22] And the Druze did not want to be conscripted in the army.[23]

[18] Abkāriyūs, *al-Manāqib al-Ibrāhīmiyya*, 94–96.

[19] Abkāriyūs, *al-Manāqib al-Ibrāhīmiyya*, 97.

[20] *Al-Laṭāyif* [*Al-Laṭāʾif*], section entitled "al-Taʾrīkh," possibly an appendix to vol. 12 (1886), bound together with the issues, 1–48, at 19.

[21] Letter dated 31 January 1835, 166PO/D11/3, MEAN.

[22] Letter dated 31 October 1837, 166PO/D11/4, MEAN.

[23] Letter dated 21 January 1838, 166PO/D11/4, MEAN.

The Sunni Muslim *ʿulamāʾ* faced something of a quandary. One Muslim sheikh, Ṣāliḥ, noted with horror that Egyptians tore down mosques in order to build stables for the horses.[24] Bruce Masters claims that as an act of resistance another sheikh, Ibn ʿĀbidīn, was among the earliest Arab scholars who recognized Sultan Mahmud II as caliph in the 1830s, and this sheikh argued that Mehmed Ali and Ibrahim revolted against the law of God.[25]

Even the Christian Mīkhāʾīl Mishāqa admitted, in his later writings, that local notables often supported the Ottomans rather than Ibrahim[26] (though such late remarks might be due to his own acceptance of the postoccupation Ottoman order and his class awareness).[27] In Damascus, Christian workers certainly hated the *corvée* they had to do for the fortification of the city.[28] The Christian hostility might have increased by 1840, as a British traveler noted in a private letter in that year: "Ibrahim Pasha is everywhere universally feared, I was about to say, detested."[29] As a reaction to a revolt in July 1840, Mehmed Ali and Ibrahim allowed their soldiers to plunder and burn the Christian mountain villages before they left.[30] Mehmed Ali ordered his troops in Beirut to celebrate the birth of his daughter for seven days; however, to the horror of the French consul, the soldiers used the occasion to sing about raping Christian women and burning villages.[31] These consular reports were possibly a push from "the man on the spot" for intervention. Had the Great Powers, especially Britain, not forced the Egyptian army to evacuate, Ibrahim would have faced more resistance and would have likely responded, in turn, with more cruelty.

Remembering Love

In scholarship, there have been attempts to reconcile the occupation of the Syrian provinces with Egyptian and Iraqi history as the beginning of pan-Arabism. Famously, George Antonius's *The Arab Awakening* (1938) starts with a story about a "false start." Mehmed Ali, says Antonius, sent

[24] Masters, *The Arabs of the Ottoman Empire*, 153–154.

[25] Masters, *The Arabs of the Ottoman Empire*, 154. However, I know of no evidence that sultans had not been recognized as caliphs before.

[26] Mishāqa, *Murder, Mayhem, Pillage and Plunder*, 168–174.

[27] Rogan, "Sectarianism and Social Conflict," 496.

[28] Excerpt from the letter of the French consul in Damascus, dated 9 October 1839, 166PO/D11/4, MEAN.

[29] Letter by Robert Tassel to (his wife?), dated Friday 24 April 1840, in notebook 2, p. 40, GB165-0277, MECA.

[30] Letter dated 14 July 1840, French consul in Beirut to Ambassador in Constantinople, 166PO/D11/4, MEAN.

[31] Letter dated 18 July 1840, French consul in Beirut to Ambassador in Constantinople, 166PO/D11/4, MEAN.

his son Ibrahim to occupy the Syrian provinces "carving out for himself an Arab empire from the sultan's dominions." However, the plan to create an "Arab movement," which would have sustained this empire, failed, Antonius concludes, because the British intervened, Mehmed Ali and Ibrahim were not Arabs, and there was not yet a national Arab consciousness.[32] That Mehmed Ali or Ibrahim would have planned an "Arab empire" was convincingly rejected by Khaled Fahmy.[33] At the peak of Arab nationalism in the 1950s and 1960s, Egyptian historians pointed to the "openness" of the Iraqis after the fall of Davud Pasha, the governor of Ottoman Baghdad, in 1831, to revolt against the Ottomans and to embrace Mehmed Ali and Ibrahim, thus uniting all Arabs under one single power. These claims were rejected by the Iraqi historian ʿAlī al-Wardī as early as the 1970s.[34] Indeed, in 1839, Ali Pasha, the new Ottoman governor of Baghdad, gave a polite but evasive answer to Mehmed Ali's letter about his march to Istanbul to request that the new Grand Vizier Hüsrev Pasha, his arch-enemy, be deposed.[35] On the whole, similar to Syrian sheikhs, the Iraqi Sunni *ʿulamāʾ* decided to support the sultan (the caliph) against the pasha of Egypt.[36] There is no evidence of an attempt to unify the Ottoman Arabs.

There is no need to detail the circumstances in which Ibrahim's occupation ended in the Syrian provinces because of the British bombardment of Beirut and menace of Alexandria in 1840.[37] Mehmed Ali, having no choice, accepted the conditions dictated by the European Powers and the Ottomans in return for the hereditary governorship of Egypt. This was a negotiated solution, representing the interests of all parties: the Powers agreed that the territorial integrity of the Ottoman Empire was key to peace in Europe and received economic and political concessions from the Ottomans in return. Mehmed Ali gained the hereditary governorship, which gave Egypt to him and his family (he had already received the island of Thassos—Taşoz in Turkish—facing the city of Kavala as a personal possession) with Ottoman *and* international guarantees. The Ottoman Empire, for its part, was scratched but remained largely intact.

While military experiences and counterimages are crucial for nationness, for its articulation a structure of governance is needed in which some type of popular sovereignty could appear as a political argument. This transformation was given not by independence; on the contrary, it

[32] Antonius, *The Arab Awakening*, ch. 2.

[33] Fahmy, *All the Pasha's Men*, ch. 6.

[34] Al-Wardī, *Lamaḥāt*, 2: 92–95.

[35] Excerpt from the letter of the French consul in Damascus, dated 9 October 1839, 166PO/D11/4, MEAN.

[36] Al-Wardī, *Lamaḥāt*, 2: 104–105.

[37] Fahmy, *Mehmed Ali*, 94–97.

developed in the context of the centrally produced, imperial Ottoman patriotic ideas.

Ottoman Imperial Patriotism

The origins of imperial patriotism in the Ottoman center were an ideological reaction to disturbance in the provinces, a tool of reintegration, and a device to strengthen the loyalty of the army against external threat. Osmanlılık, "Ottoman citizenship," became the organizing principle of the *Tanzimat*, the reforms to centralize the empire. Law and new taxation were the most powerful tools of this centralization. The attempt to conceptually reframe the Ottoman state can be viewed as a master example of nationalizing an empire[38] earlier than the strategy of playing out "corporate identities," to use the wording of Karen Barkey.[39] These tools were accompanied by songs, chants, slogans, and poetry through which ideology became a physical and sensorial experience. In the late 1840s, the new Arabic theater was born in Ottoman Beirut in this atmosphere, with the first plays demonstrating loyalty to the Ottoman sultan. The peak of imperial aural patriotism was the Crimean War (1853–1856), although certain elements remained in use until the twentieth century.

Patria and the Body of the Sultan

Bernard Lewis claims that in the Ottoman Empire "patriotism was a new discovery, from the French revolution."[40] There was certainly a French moment in early Ottoman and Muslim political thought. It seems, however, that the concept of the *patria* was introduced in a calculated manner into Ottoman imperial ideology.[41]

Patriotism was a discursive ideological device employed by Ottoman elite administrators loyal to the empire rather than the master plan of the dynasty.[42] Ottoman statesmen recognized the value of patriotism in strengthening imperial loyalty at the moment of Mehmed Ali's Syrian conquest. The imperial Education Council considered educating the people in the "love of the homeland" (*ḥubb al-waṭan*, an Arabic expression) in early 1839.[43] The Gülhane Edict (November 1839), generally considered to be the announcement of *Tanzimat*, stated that "it is the

[38] Berger and Miller, eds., *Nationalizing Empires*.
[39] Barkey, *Empire of Difference*, 278.
[40] Lewis, "Watan," 525–526.
[41] The following paragraphs, to some extent, follow Eisenstadt, "Modernization."
[42] Abu-Manneh, "The Islamic Roots"; Findley, *Bureaucratic Reform*, 154.
[43] Quoted in Şiviloğlu, "The Emergence of Public Opinion," 123.

inescapable duty of all the people to provide soldiers for the defense of the homeland [*vatan*].” There was, as Lewis points out, disagreement among the Ottoman elite. A dissenting intellectual, Cevdet Pasha, wrote against the new rhetoric by claiming that “among us, if we say the word *vatan*, all that will come to the minds of our soldiers is their village squares . . . it would not be as potent as religious zeal, nor could it take its place.”[44] This concern failed to hold sway, and statesmen initiated significant changes to fashion the empire as a homeland while they also preserved the importance of religion in public. The Gülhane Edict was translated into Arabic and sent to all Arab provinces, including Egypt.[45]

Two terms were used somewhat casually in the early Ottoman public sphere between the 1830s and the 1860s: *vatan* (“homeland”) and *millet-i Osmanlı* (“the Ottoman nation”). Their relationship is not clear. I propose that at the time the Ottoman nation was defined by identifying imperial territory with the physical and spiritual body of the sultan-caliph (the dynasty).

Ottoman patriotism was expected to be aroused, in part, through the presence and visibility of the ruler. Sultan Mahmud II launched a campaign of visibility that included clothing reform and accessibility. As Hakan Karateke has shown, Muslim religious ceremonies were renewed in the process. After crushing the first Saudi rule in the Hijaz, Mehmed Ali sent the keys of the holy cities to the imperial capital in 1813, where they were displayed publically and, after a city-wide procession, received personally by the sultan at the Imperial Gate.[46] In an extremely rare move, Mahmud II also personally visited the predominantly non-Muslim provinces in the Balkans, where he even donated money for churches.[47] The physical presence of the sultan—a strategy similar to that in other royal modalities—could be also projected via representations and rituals. During the reign of Sultan Abdülmecid (r. 1839–1861), the accession (*cülus*) and birthday (*veladet*) celebrations became formalized all around the empire. Abdülmecid also loved to be present at diplomatic receptions and opera performances. He sent his portraits to the provinces, even to Egypt in 1850,[48] and the portraits of later rulers became part of imperial celebrations until the 1880s. Both Mahmud II and Abdülmecid regularly inspected their troops and personally addressed the imperial soldiers.[49] There was an eminent connection between *vatan*, the sultan, and the army.

[44] Lewis, “Watan,” 528.

[45] Choueiri, *Arab Nationalism*, 71.

[46] Karateke, “Opium for the Subjects?,” 119.

[47] Ibid., 126.

[48] Toledano, *State and Society*, 52.

[49] For example, a visit at the casern of Selimiye and Davud Pasha in 1844, *Journal de Constantinople*, 21 February 1844, 1.

Physical presence and pictorial representation were paired with words that expressed and reaffirmed acceptance of the sovereign. Darin Stephanov has described how Ottoman Christian elites, such as the *voyvoda* of Moldavia, expressed their loyalty to the sultan in this new vocabulary of love. This public discourse seems to have gained momentum in the 1840s. For instance, Abdülmecid was celebrated as a "tsar" during his visit in Rumeli in 1846 with this song:

> Whoever loves the sultan, / Runs to him, / Loves him from the heart, /
> Expends labour for him, / Exhausts life, / Does not leave the Tsar.[50]

These discursive efforts to make the empire a homeland through the person of the sultan were accompanied by a legal distinction between Ottoman (*Osmanlı*) and non-Ottoman subjects. Karen Kern discusses an early 1822 decree that explicitly prohibited marriage between (Sunni, Ottoman) women and (Shīʿī) Iranian men.[51] The 1869 Ottoman Citizenship (also called Nationality) Law (January 1869)[52] clarified that "every person, who was born of an Ottoman father and an Ottoman mother, or only of an Ottoman father, was an Ottoman subject."[53] (Note the echoes of *sharīʿa* concerning the children's religion in a mixed marriage.) The eighth article of the 1876 Constitution reinforced that "all subjects of the Ottoman State, without distinction, are called Ottomans."[54] Ottoman became a legal category: an individual who could be punished only with the sultan's agreement or in accordance with the Ottoman penal law. This legal subjecthood was embodied in a passport.[55]

The Crimean War and Aural Patriotism

I suggest that the peak production of Ottoman patriotism occurred during the Crimean War (1853–1856). The 1850s were the moment when Islam and civic ideas together framed collective loyalty. This is when nationness, boosted by the war atmosphere, appears as a discursive force both at the imperial level in Ottoman Turkish and in Arabic in the Arab provinces.

50 Stephanov, "Minorities, Majorities, and the Monarch,"106.

51 Kern, *Imperial Citizen*, appendix A.

52 Uzunçarşılı and Karal, *Osmanlı Tarihi*, 7:174–178.

53 Cited in Abdel-Malek, *L'Égypte moderne*, 223. Specifically, Parolin, *Citizenship in the Arab World*, 71–74.

54 I quote from the published version in *Basiret*, 8 Dhū al-Ḥijja, 1293 (25 December 1876), 1.

55 Uzunçarşılı and Karal, *Osmanlı Tarihi*, 7:178. Hanssen, Philipp, and Weber, *Empire in the City*, "Introduction," 10.

Ottoman patriotism was a Muslim imperial patriotism, which also meant, as Howard Eisenstadt remarks, that "the nature of public Islam was changing."[56] For instance, *ʿulamāʾ* advocated the war against Russia. The declaration of imperial war, as the older format of Ottomans-going-into-war required, was preceded by a declaration of holy war (*jihād*) by the Sheykh-ül-Islam, the second-highest Muslim authority in the Ottoman system.[57] Yet reflecting the atmosphere and ideology, hundreds of military marches (*harbiye*), patriotic epics (*destan*), and even "folk" songs were written, many of them voicing the call to defend the imperial *vatan*.[58] Unisonality was amply used in wartime Istanbul. Muslim concepts of war and imperial patriotism strengthened each other.

Yusuf Halis, a translator to Arabic in the Translation Office (*Tercüme Odası*), was one of the main producers of patriotic poetry. His poems were printed weekly in the private Ottoman journal *Ceride-i Havadis*, and were published in a small booklet (*Şehname-yi Osmani*) around 1855. In his poems "the love of the homeland" in Arabic (*ḥubb al-waṭan*) is connected to the victorious army, especially in the long and ardently patriotic *Vatan Kasidası* whose every second hemistisch rhymes with the word *vatan*.[59] It is significant, but not surprising, that Ottoman texts used Arabic expressions as patriotic slogans because Arabic had served as a linguistic source of new concepts for Ottoman scholars. In this way, as we shall see below, the Crimean War became a major moment of disseminating Ottoman patriotism in the 1850s in Arabic as well.

Ḥubb al-waṭan 1.0: The Circle of Patriotism

Before Crimea, Ottoman patriotism was already present in Arabic works in the reintegrated Syrian provinces. In general, the Syrian urban elites (*aʿyān*) were empowered by the new system,[60] and wanted to be seen as patriotic Ottomans. For instance, Dana Sajdi shows that the Damascene intellectual Muḥammad Saʿīd al-Qāsimī (d. 1900) edited the text of an eighteenth-century manuscript for publication in a way that reinstated the significance of the state and the sultan together with the urban notables.[61]

The earliest ideological translation of Ottoman patriotism in Arabic that I have been able to find is connected to the making of modern Arabic musical theater. The merchant and intellectual Mārūn Naqqāsh (1817–1855)

[56] Eisenstadt, "Modernization," 436.
[57] Badem, *The Ottoman Crimean War*, 98.
[58] Ibid., 9–11.
[59] Halis, *Şehname*, 23–32.
[60] Masters, *The Arabs of the Ottoman Empire*, 177–183
[61] Sajdi, *The Barber of Damascus*, 180–187.

and his brother Niqūlā (1825–1894) were the first Arab playwrights whose plays were performed between 1847 and 1852 in Beirut. They seem to have written works loyal to the empire, and Mārūn Naqqāsh also praised the Egyptian governor in his poetry. He wrote three musical plays: *al-Bakhīl* (The Miser; staged 1847), *Abū al-Ḥasan al-Mughaffal aw Hārūn al-Rashīd* (Abū al-Ḥasan, the Fool, or Hārūn al-Rashīd; staged 1850), and *al-Salīṭ al-Ḥasūd* (The Vicious and Jealous Young Man; staged 1852).

Since the location of the manuscripts is not known, one must be cautious because the source of our knowledge about the plays is Niqūlā's edited volume, printed in 1869, fourteen years after his brother's death, and at the request of the governor Franco Pasha after the massacres of 1860.[62] Thus the framing of Naqqāsh's Arabic plays may reflect a later constellation of politics than the time of their creation.

In a speech before the performance of his first play in 1847 Naqqāsh introduced the idea of the "love of homeland" (*ḥubb al-waṭan*). This was based on an age-old poetic tradition of the affective use of one's native land (*waṭan*)[63] (see more on this in the next sections) but very possibly also reflected the Ottoman patriotic discourse following the Gülhane Edict, and perhaps Italian politics. Naqqāsh listed selfishness ("everyone among us thinks only about himself") among the reasons for underdevelopment in Arab lands (*al-bilād al-ʿarabiyya*) because the people (*ahl*) abandoned the love of the homeland. Regaining this love and refocusing on "the public good" (*nafʿ ʿāmm*) would help to achieve success through the union of people.[64] In Naqqāsh's thinking, theater was a means to attain patriotism, patriotism was a means to attain solidarity, and solidarity was a means to attain prosperity—in the Arab lands under the Ottoman umbrella. On the model of the famous "Circle of Justice," one may term this idea the "Circle of Patriotism."

Naqqāsh added that he had conceived the idea of Arabic theater during a trip to Alexandria and Italy where he saw the theaters of Milan and Naples.[65] Indeed, he chose "musical theater" (*al-marsaḥ al-mūsīqī*) as the genre of the first play because he liked it more than prose theater and he thought it "would be preferable to my people and kindred."[66] His source of patriotic inspiration was not only Ottoman imperial ideology but also the Italian patriotic movement and its main vehicle, the opera.

[62] Naqqāsh, *Arzat Lubnān*, 3.

[63] Noorani, "Estrangement and Selfhood."

[64] Naqqāsh, *Arzat Lubnān*, 13. Niqūlā Naqqāsh in his introduction remarks that the first performance was arranged in the beginning of 1847 but in the title of the speech 1848 is written.

[65] Ibid., 16; 18.

[66] Naqqāsh, *Arzat Lubnān*, 16, in the translation of Moosa, "Naqqāsh," 110.

Naqqāsh's theater and circle of patriotism was a bourgeois Ottoman intellectual product.[67] His mention of the difference between European and Arab lands did not exclude the imperial context. For the performance of his greatest play, *Hārūn al-Rashīd* (see more about this play in chapter 6), he invited the Ottoman governor, the Ottoman army leaders, and administrative men in Beirut and the European consuls as well.[68] In this play, according to Philip Sadgrove, the praise for the character Jaʿfar, the vizier of the Caliph Hārūn al-Rashīd, was in fact directed at Wāmiq Pasha, the Ottoman governor, who was in the audience.[69] Then, based on this success, the Provincial Council asked the sultan's permission to construct a theater in Beirut, arguing that Arab history was useful in the praise of his glory and empire. It was natural in the context of Ottoman reintegration that they also asked for a *tuğra* (the sultan's calligraphic signature), which they intended to place above the entrance as an expression of their loyalty.[70] Naqqāsh praised the reign of Sultan Abdülmecid in an invocation that was meant to be chanted by all actors at the beginning of his last play:

> He is the light of the sun for the earthly spirits / from the great clan of Osman
> The throne of the caliphate / always advanced by him for eternity[71]

Naqqāsh often expressed Ottoman attachment in his political poetry. Or at least, these were the poems were printed by his brother Niqūlā in 1869. One of the poems celebrating an Ottoman victory during the Crimean war, possibly written in 1854, became so popular in Beirut that, according to his brother, all "the ordinary people sang it, even the children":

> Oh Lord be a guardian / ʿAbd al-Majīd triumphant
> We praise the Lord of the living / the awaited victory arrived
> so rise and say to the frightened / come and shout loudly[72]

Patriotic chants were a way to express imperial loyalty within the everyday sensorium. Naqqāsh simultaneously wrote Arabic panegyrics for Sultan Abdülmecid, for Wāmiq Pasha, and, naturally, for the governors of the Egyptian province.[73] Praise of the sultan and praise of Mehmed Ali's

[67] Khuri-Makdisi, *The Eastern Mediterranean*, 63–64.
[68] Naqqāsh, *Arzat Lubnān*, 11.
[69] Sadgrove, "Early Arabic Musical Theatre," 168.
[70] Permission dated 23 Ṣafar 1267 (28 December 1850), I.MVL 195/5976.
[71] Najm, ed. *Mārūn al-Naqqāsh*, 295.
[72] Naqqāsh, *Arzat Lubnān*, 475–476.
[73] Ibid., 417; 457; 473; 475.

family were not mutually exclusive since both were parts of the Ottoman order after 1841. From time to time the Syrians were reminded of the Egyptian governor's power, as in 1853 when an Egyptian warship arrived in Beirut demanding the extradition of Arab tribal leaders who had escaped from Egypt.[74] Naqqāsh was not alone among the "merchant-littérateurs," as Fruma Zachs calls the Beiruti bourgeois elites,[75] in the production of works that expressed loyalty to both the sultan and the governor of Egypt. But it is now time to look at the post-1841 Egyptian developments.

Elites and the Re-Ottomanization of Egypt

I wish to frame the birth of patriotism in Arabic in Egypt within the context of the specific Beiruti discourse and general Ottoman patriotism. Egypt was, of course, connected to various European countries; and news of nationalist revolutions and patriotic ideas circulated in the Mediterranean in many ways. The Ottoman provinces became part of the world economy through the forced trade agreements with European empires. However, the immediate life-world of the ordinary Egyptian was not much concerned with Europe in the 1840s–1850s. The defining feature was the new constellation of power: the hereditary governorship.

The mid-century, I argue following Toledano, was a period of re-Ottomanization in Egypt. After Mehmed Ali received the firman in 1841, he made some concessions to the imperial center. Next, he established a firm system of rule by loyal elites within Egypt. Externally, after his death, the great question was the direction of reform and Egypt's place within the Ottoman Empire. In this crisis, the contours of the family as a localized imperial dynasty were finalized. This is the situation to which Muslim intellectuals would react through the patriotic idea.

The System of Rule and the Elites: Zevat, Aʿyān, and the Intellectuals

After 1841, Mehmed Ali needed to adopt a sustainable system by appealing to various social groups. He transformed the lands donated to his *zevat* military elite into their permanent properties between 1841 and 1843.[76] He married many of them to slave-girls from his harem.[77] He

[74] Letter dated 12 April 1853, French consul in Beirut to Ambassador in Constantinople, 166PO/D11/10, MEAN.

[75] Zachs, "Cultural and Conceptual," 153.

[76] Barakāt, *Taṭawwur al-Milkiyya*, 71, 101.

[77] Cuno, *Modernizing Marriage*, 26.

told them in 1843 that the time had come to restore the glory of ancient Egypt through good work under his reign.[78] The pasha was profoundly impressed by Egypt's pharaonic past, and by Alexander, Peter the Great, and Napoleon I. His most elaborate instrument to regulate the *zevat* was a new system of law contained in legal codes (*kanunname*). This was an immense change, since independent law-making had been the sultan's prerogative. The most significant administrative project was the first professional census of Egypt undertaken between 1845 and 1848, which gave a precise picture of the subjects to the ruler.[79] These techniques encompassing land, law, and surveillance created a firm basis of dynastic power.

Some local Muslims trained for army purposes or working in the administration came into prominence. These men knew foreign languages, especially Italian and French, medicine, and military engineering, but were also masters of Arabic and Muslim sciences. Some of them received land from Mehmed Ali too. They typically hailed from families considered socially distinguished at the local scale: descendants of the Prophet, rich merchants, and village-headmen (often these three together). Many were Azhar-graduates; and al-Azhar as an institution was bound to Mehmed Ali. The rural elite families were called *aʿyān*, the "notables," and were respected in their communities. This semirural group became a prominent urban folk, enjoyed a close relationship with al-Azhar, and provided many Arabic-speaking intellectuals of late Ottoman Egypt. It is possible that they were regarded together with the *zevat* the "elite" of the province. Mehmed Ali ordered in the 1847 census that the names of "men of high state rank (*al-dhawāt*), the great ulema, the prominent townsmen, and the great merchants" should be recorded first.[80]

The Re-Ottomanization of Mehmed Ali

Although Egypt was not fully reintegrated into the empire, there occurred the re-Ottomanization of the political system and Mehmed Ali himself. For instance, no Ottoman "adviser" was allowed to supervise Egyptian finances,[81] yet Mehmed Ali's monetary regime remained Ottoman.[82] In replying to the edict requesting the *Tanzimat* in Egypt, the pasha answered that he had already introduced most of the demanded reforms,[83] but the Ottoman-

[78] Fahmy, *Mehmed Ali*, 101.
[79] Cuno and Reimer, "The Census Registers."
[80] Cuno and Reimer, "The Census Registers," (appendix III), 214.
[81] Shaw, *History of the Ottoman Empire*, 2:58.
[82] Pamuk, "Interaction between the Monetary Regimes."
[83] Baer, "Tanzimat in Egypt," 30.

British 1838 free trade agreement was implemented in Egypt.[84] The sultan's authority was restored. When Mehmed Ali received the firman in 1841, he thanked the sultan for "this generous bounty" and described that

> All *ʿulamāʾ* and statesmen were present and the text of the firman was read aloud to them. Everyone then sang the sultan's praises and prayed for his long life. In order for all the subjects to enjoy this blessing, the guns were fired in Cairo and in other cities to express our joy and happiness for this event.[85]

All in the province were notified that Mehmed Ali ruled, again, with the support of the empire, backed up by the caliph's authority.

As signs of integration, sexual politics and clothing were crucial. There were important marriages between the imperial elite and Mehmed Ali's family, the most famous of which joined Zeynep, a daughter of Mehmed Ali, and the Ottoman statesman Kiamil Pasha in 1845.[86] Mehmed Ali started to wear the tarbush, the new sartorial sign of being an Ottoman subject.[87] For the first time in his life, the old pasha visited Istanbul in 1846, making a great impression on young Sultan Abdülmecid. The family bought properties along the Bosporus. His successors tried to marry their sons to daughters of the sultan. These moves effectively tied the ruling family to the Ottoman imperial elite through money, clothing, and sexual politics.

Crisis: Making a Dynasty in the Ottoman Shadow

Eventually, the mental capacities of Mehmed Ali declined, and by late 1847 he was unable to govern. The following years were crucial in terms of Egypt's Ottoman position and the *zevat* identity.

The eldest member of the family, Ibrahim, traveled to the sultan to receive the investiture in 1848, but suddenly died upon returning to Egypt. The next-eldest member of the family, Abbas Hilmi (r. 1849–1854) had the privilege to bury his grandfather in May 1849. Three governors of Egypt in three years. This was a serious crisis at an imperial level, and Abbas had to face challenges from the family, too.

Toledano describes the death of Mehmed Ali as provoking "intra-family strife."[88] The main object of disagreement was Mehmed Ali's heritage

[84] Cuno, "Egypt to c. 1919," 86.
[85] Quoted in Fahmy, *Mehmed Ali*, 98.
[86] Mestyan, "Sound, Military Music."
[87] Cuno, "Egypt to 1919," 80.
[88] Toledano, *State and Society*, 100.

(land, money, property),[89] and "the approach to Western-style reform."[90] This familial conflict had important consequences: the forced divorce of Zeynep from Kiamil Pasha (who was exiled to Aswan and finally escaped to Istanbul), the reorganization of the administration, accelerated French-British competition, and in particular the renewed interest of the Sublime Porte in introducing the *Tanzimat* in Egypt.[91] The real fight, it seems, broke out over Egypt's relationship to the Ottoman Empire.

Abbas clashed with the Porte over the introduction of the *Tanzimat* legal code and the Cairo-Alexandria railway. According to Stanford and Ezel Shaw, somewhat unusually, Sultan Abdülmecid met Abbas Hilmi in the island of Rhodes in 1850 to negotiate.[92] Abbas ultimately accepted the code in 1852 but never proclaimed it (that is, never read the firman aloud publically).[93] Yet for the decades to come this was the law (known as *al-Qānūn al-Sulṭānī*) according to which crimes of Egyptians were judged. The frustrated *zevat* and the Egyptians associated with that elite, as Toledano has shown, enacted a classic character-assassination of Abbas Pasha through rumours and accusations. Around 1853 an agreement was struck. The reaffirmation of the Ottoman way of succession and of Abbas personally meant the crystallization of Egypt's dynastic contours.[94] Finally, as a loyal governor, in November 1853 Abbas sent a large contingent of Egyptian troops to help the empire in the Crimean War.[95]

In sum, this period saw an Ottoman reorientation of Egypt, while its internal legal sovereignty was retained.

The Origins of Patriotism in Late Ottoman Egypt

How did Egyptian intellectuals react to Mehmed Ali's power, especially to the 1841 firman, and the creation of a dynasty? In the three previous centuries, Ottoman governors had ruled for short periods only: never was

[89] A French translation of the demands is attachment 3 to Murray to Malmesbury, 3 May 1852, FO 424/7A, NA.

[90] Toledano, *State and Society*, 48.

[91] For the French-British opposition behind the conflict, cf. letter dated 15 February 1851, from Murray to Canning, FO 424/7A, NA.

[92] I have not found any confirmation of this meeting. Shaw, *History of the Ottoman Empire*, 2:83.

[93] Toledano, *State and Society*, 96. Rivlin, "The Railway Question," 377.

[94] Toledano, *State and Society*, 50–67.

[95] Dunn, *Khedive Ismail's Army*, 13–21. Toledano remarks that the Porte requested Egyptian help only in international conflicts after Mehmed Ali's rule. Toledano, *State and Society*, 74. This is not accurate. Ismail's army was involved in Arabia in 1863 and later also in the Cretan war.

there hereditary governorship in Ottoman Egypt. How did the firman transform the local political imagination?

There was a search for a vocabulary in Arabic to describe the novel power of Mehmed Ali and to acknowledge his relationship to Egypt. Next, the idea of *waṭan* as a political means of solidarity gained more currency in Arabic and in Egypt, too, as part of the Tanzimat and during the Crimean War between 1853 and 1856. The military use of the homeland occurred in the conceptual field of *public* speech constrained by absolute power, yet it subtly brought popular sovereignty into the political discourse. Patriotism as a discursive principle developed within the imperial framework in a time of war.

Toledano characterizes the middle decade of the century as riven by "the great social divide" in Egyptian society, which he describes in terms of differences in language, dress, and rights between *zevat* and non-*zevat.* His historical sociology is based on the rediscovery of the elite's Ottoman background, which Toledano uses to establish the complete separation of the ruling class from the ruled. According to him, however, the *zevat* did acquire an "Ottoman Egyptian" identity: the officers of Abbas Pasha in the early 1850s distinguished between Ottoman imperial interests and Egyptian dynastic ones. The governor himself used the expression in Turkish [!] "What comes first for an Egyptian is Egypt" (*Mısrına evvel Mısırdır*).[96]

I propose that the re-Ottomanization, and especially Egypt's participation in the Crimean War, not only created an Ottoman Egyptian elite identity but paradoxically also opened up the possibility of negotiation for Arabic-speaking intellectuals. An attempt was made to bridge the social divide ideologically.

Two features characterize the patriotic Arabic texts in this period: first, many were written as songs to be sung by soldiers or by trained soldier-musicians. The aural features of Arab patriotism and its embodied experience started in the army and only later extended to public musical evenings and theater. Second, the framing of the texts (introductions, titles, postscripts) in the printed or manuscript form appears in a very sophisticated Arabic, fusing the ruler and *waṭan*, the homeland, not only with Ottoman Persian expressions concerning power but also with French ones concerning technology. This educated Arabic, which I term "modern Ottoman Arabic," remained characteristic of public Arabic political texts for the next few decades.

Mehmed Ali in Arabic before 1841

What was Mehmed Ali in the Muslim political imagination? How could his power be translated into the Arabic language of the Ottoman order?

[96] Toledano, *State and Society*, 86–87.

These questions composed a central, conceptual problem for intellectuals. While Mehmed Ali's rule brought general misery to peasants and engendered strong resistance among some religious scholars, surviving texts also indicate an effort by others to accept his rule in public, in print, and in Arabic.

This effort started early, possibly from the 1810s and was accelerated when Mehmed Ali forced the sheikhs of al-Azhar to accept Ḥasan al-ʿAṭṭār (d. 1835), a famous scholar, as Sheikh al-Azhar in 1831.[97] The representative institution of Muslim intelligentsia became closely associated with the government.

In their texts, Mehmed Ali became, first of all, *al-Ḥājj Muḥammad ʿAlī Bāshā*. He was often named as a *wazīr—vezir* in Turkish—since Grand Vizier (*Sadrazam*) was his highest rank in the Ottoman hierarchy. Indeed, he was, after all, only another Ottoman governor. He was also often addressed by the Ottoman Persian titles of the grand vizier: *dāwarī, khidīwī, dustūr*—prince, lord, and authority, respectively. But even these titles, though they suggested his might, indicated his place in the Ottoman hierarchy. Another usual title is *walī al-niʿam/niʿma*, "the benefactor," (literally, "the one who represents the grace") and, the Egyptian everyday title was simply *afandīnā* "our master." (See more on the significance of titles in chapter 2.)

A window into the pre-1841 conceptualization of power is provided by Dyala Hamzah. She shows that as early as 1822 an Arabic panegyric, written by Sheikh Khalīl Aḥmad al-Rajabī at the request of Sheikh al-Azhar, symbolically reconfigured the universe and history to serve Mehmed Ali's power. This seems to have been a counteraction to Sheikh ʿAbd al-Raḥmān al-Jabartī's (d. 1825) highly negative chronicle about Mehmed Ali's reign. Sheikh al-Rajabī praised Mehmed Ali as a *wazīr* who fought against the "infidels" (*kuffār*).[98] There may be similar manuscripts, thus far undiscovered. In addition, a number of poems were produced praising the ruler in official publications, such as in the first Arabic regular periodical in print, *al-Waqāʾiʿ al-Miṣriyya*, from 1828, whose first editor was, again, the loyal Sheikh Ḥasan al-ʿAṭṭār.[99] Al-ʿAṭṭār's student, a young Egyptian sheikh (see below) translated a French poem in 1827 into Arabic that connected the longing for Egypt and praise of Mehmed Ali, and in the introduction called the pasha *wazīr Miṣr* and *walī al-niʿma*.[100] The publications of the government's Būlāq printing house, if we read through the forewords and introductions by the translators,

[97] Scharfe, "Muslim Scholars," 239–241.

[98] Hamzah, "Nineteenth-Century Egypt as Dynastic Locus."

[99] Sheikh al-ʿAṭṭār also wrote poetry on the homeland, in the traditional Arabic vein, which, in Shmuel Moreh's view, represents the birth of Arab nationalism. Moreh quoted in Scharfe, and Sharfe's rejection, "Muslim Scholars," 165.

[100] [Al-Ṭahṭāwī] Réfaha [!], *La lyre brisée.*

provide many clues about how Mehmed Ali was praised in Arabic and Turkish in public.

Sheikh Ḥasan al-ʿAṭṭār helped Mehmed Ali and his administration to address Muslim elites in Arabic. The first part of his writing manual (1834; reprinted at least fourteen times by the end of the century) gives examples of exchange between subjects and rulers, and the second part, to which its overall popularity was due, is about everyday legal deeds (such as marriage and divorce contracts). The sheikh offered the manuscript to the army treasury, which financed its printing. The whole work is dedicated to Mehmed Ali whose praise takes up two full pages. Sheikh al-ʿAṭṭār does not mention anything specifically Egyptian among the titles and deeds: Mehmed Ali is praised as a *wazīr*, a *mushīr* (his Ottoman positions), and foremost as a pious Muslim military conqueror of Mecca, Medina, and the Sudan.[101] Indeed, the samples are ordered according to Muslim hierarchy. First comes an example of a letter to the sultan, praising the Ottoman Empire and the ruler, "the mightiest king and the most gracious sultan."[102] Then come sample letters of requests written to the *sharīf* of Mecca, the sultan of Morocco, the army leader (of the Ottoman Empire? *ṣāḥib juyūsh wa-jihād*), and so on. Does this work in fact insert Mehmed Ali within the Ottoman Arab universe?

Waṭan as Mehmed Ali's Land

In the narratives of Egyptian, and even pan-Arab,[103] nationalism, almost without exception, the founding figure is Rifāʿa Rāfiʿ al-Ṭahṭāwī (1801–1873) who is the young sheikh, student of al-ʿAṭṭār, mentioned above, translating the French poem in Paris in 1827. He hailed from a family of the Prophet's descendants, studied at al-Azhar, was sent as an imam of a student mission to Paris, studied French thoroughly, became director of the Language School between 1837 and 1842, and then directed schools until 1849. He received the high rank "bey" (previously he was either called "efendi" or "sheikh") in 1846.[104] Clearly a man of Mehmed Ali, he was exiled to the Sudan by Abbas Hilmi in 1850, when another young bureaucrat, ʿAlī Mubārak (1823–1893) who had also studied in Paris, became the head of education. Rifāʿa al-Ṭahṭāwī and ʿAlī Mubārak became life-long rivals.[105]

101 [Al-ʿAṭṭār], *Inshāʾ al-ʿAṭṭār*, 4–5.
102 Ibid., 5–6.
103 Chouieri, *Arab Nationalism*, 69–70.
104 Newman, "Life of al-Ṭahṭāwī," 53.
105 Dykstra, "A Biographical Study," 115–139.

In the standard narrative, al-Ṭahṭāwī brought French patriotism to Egypt. Bernard Lewis, for instance, suggests that "he must have become aware of the significance of patriotism in French life";[106] and Albert Hourani imagines that "the idea of the nation too he could have derived from Montesquieu."[107]

The first discursive appearance of political nation-ness in Arabic is connected to making Mehmed Ali part of Egypt. Al-Ṭahṭāwī, in the introduction to one of his Arabic translations, wrote that he translated the book as an exercise in 1829, and because he knew that Mehmed Ali would appreciate it; he described the governor as one who "loves Egypt as his own native land" (*muḥibb li-bilād Miṣr ka-anna-hā waṭanu-hu*).[108] In his speeches at the examination ceremonies at the School of Languages, he regularly emphasized the attachment of Mehmed Ali to Egypt.[109]

Though full of engaging details, al-Ṭahṭāwī's famous description of France (printed in 1834, Ottoman Turkish translation 1839, revised Arabic edition in 1849)[110] does not mention the patriotism of Montesquieu. He highlights the homeland (*al-waṭan*) as a moral truth, among Arabic poems about one's native land, claiming that travel and love for the homeland are not contradictory.

> It is well-known that pearls and musk become precious only when they have left their native land and place of origin. However, none of this belies the fact that *the love of the homeland is from among the branches of faith* [my emphasis]. Travel in the pursuit of discovery or gain does not exclude that a human being is attached to his native land and birthplace since this is instinctive.[111]

It is the poetical, ancient Arab tradition about the place of birth that the young sheikh evokes here, not the French idea of *patrie*. The sentence I emphasize above is a version of a popular Prophetic saying (*ḥadīth*): *ḥubb al-waṭan min al-īmān* ("love of the homeland is part of faith"). I shall discover the curious career of this *ḥadīth* in the next chapter.

Introducing ʿAbd Allāh Abū al-Suʿūd

I suggest that the hereditary governorship was crucial in making the first patriotic texts. Instead of the well-known al-Ṭahṭāwī, in this book we

106 Lewis, "Patriotism and Nationalism," 76.
107 Hourani, *Arabic Thought*, 70.
108 [Depping], *Kitāb Qalāʾid al-Mafākhir*, 3–4.
109 Abū al-Suʿūd, *Kitāb Naẓm al-Laʾālī*, 271–283.
110 Newman, "Life of al-Ṭahṭāwī," 46.
111 I simplified Newman's translation, al-Tahtawi, *An Imam in Paris*, 128–129.

shall follow a forgotten student of his: ʿAbd Allāh Abū al-Suʿūd (1821?–1878). Abū al-Suʿūd was one of the first intellectuals to react to this important change. The School of Languages, training around 142 students-translators by 1842, was the institution where the idea of the homeland was mixed with history and loyalty for the ruler, especially after 1839. It is here that *waṭan* appears as a political principle very similar to the Ottoman patriotism, which, again, used the same word, and same slogans, in Ottoman Turkish, at the same time.

Abū al-Suʿūd wrote a history book in Arabic which further connected Egypt's ancient past to Mehmed Ali's regime. In 1838, his teacher al-Ṭahṭāwī translated a history of ancient Egypt from French for Mehmed Ali. Abū al-Suʿūd, for his part, created a great compilation of French and Islamic history in 1842. The title, *A Necklace of Pearls of Good Manners about French Rulers and Egyptian Kings Before Them*, is a subtle allusion to the revolutionary song the *Marseillaise* in its Arabic translation. Printed in 1842, the book frames Mehmed Ali as a "Great Prince, Mighty *Dustūr* . . . like Khusraw and Caesar, Frederick and Alexander, al-Māʾmūn and Napoleon," who built a mighty Muslim army and "made Egypt a paradise."[112] Abū al-Suʿūd also tells that the book "is full of historical virtues that are connected to our country (*bilādinā*), which is like the bride among the countries, and which, as my teacher . . . Rifāʿa Efendi explained, is the birthplace to us and our ancestors before us."[113] However, as is fitting with nation-ness in a Muslim empire, Abū al-Suʿūd's book contains the history of the caliphate, he praises the Ottoman Empire, and he only ends with Mehmed Ali's rule.

While al-Ṭahṭāwī's description of France did not contain his Arabic translation of the *Marseillaise*, Abū al-Suʿūd's history inserts his teacher's work in his last section on French history (and also the anthem of the July Monarchy, *La Parisienne*). Here are the first critical lines of the *Marseillaise* in French and in al-Ṭahṭāwī's Arabic translation and that translation's English:

> *Allons enfants de la Patrie / Le jour de gloire est arrivé ! Contre nous de la tyrannie / L'étendard sanglant est levé*
>
> Fa-hayyā yā banī al-awṭān hayyā / fa-waqt fakhārikum la-kum tahayyā / ukīmū al-rāyā al-ʿuẓmā sawiyā / wa-shannū ghārat al-hījā milliyyā
>
> Arise people of the homeland arise / the time of your glory is ready for you / Raise the great flag together / Launch the attack and battle untiringly[114]

[112] Abū al-Suʿūd, *Kitāb Naẓm al-Laʾālī*, 3–4.
[113] Ibid., 282.
[114] Ibid., 215–220.

Tyranny is not translated. The lines *Aux armes, citoyens, / Formez vos bataillons / Marchons, marchons !* are translated as "You must take arms, oh my people / and arrange your lines as [a necklace of] pearls"—these last words in Arabic figure in the title of Abū al-Suʿūd's book.

One can explain *not* publishing the *Marseillaise* earlier by the fact that it was banned during Napoleon's reign and the restoration in France, and was only legalized briefly in 1830. It is remarkable that Abū al-Suʿūd printed it, although his teacher did not do so. The song is, after all, against monarchs.

At another place, I have shown that Egyptian soldiers were not enthusiastic about the new military songs, poetry, and European music. Yet the Marseillaise became part of the Egyptian army musical repertoire in the 1820s. There are contradictory reports whether the ordinary soldiers liked this song or not. One Frenchman reports that the soldiers thought it was the song of Napoleon. Possibly this was Mehmed Ali's own understanding since he allowed it to be performed often. It is a cruel irony of fate (or a secret revenge of the translators?) that the soldiers greeted the cruel pasha with this French song against tyranny.[115]

Despite subtle allusions to revolution the production of the Būlāq press was loyalist. Abū al-Suʿūd himself wrote an epic poem in 1847 about the pasha's reign as the Azhari sheikh had done. Next, al-Ṭahṭāwī personally selected Voltaire's *History of Peter the Great* for translation into Arabic, by another student Aḥmad b. Muḥammad ʿUbayd, likely as an allegory for Mehmed Ali or Ibrahim.[116] The 1849 revised edition of al-Ṭahṭāwī's description of France praised the new governor Abbas Hilmi by including several panegyrics by students in the translators' school.[117]

These texts served to naturalize rulers, instead of revolting against them, in Arabic. While there is no direct allusion in these works to *waṭan* as a political idea of solidarity, there is an effort to acknowledge the hereditary governor in the land of Egypt and frame him in comparative histories. Some works, especially Abū al-Suʿūd's do subtly allude to revolution and to diverse political regimes as connected to the French idea of *patrie* as a principle of antimonarchism. The point is that patriotism does not appear as an anti-Ottoman regime force; on the contrary, Ottoman history and the empire are smoothlessly injected into localness in these public texts.

The work of Sheikh al-ʿAṭṭār, al-Ṭahṭāwī, Abū al-Suʿūd, and others mostly occurred in printed form, as opposed to manuscripts. Also, only three of the sixteen history books produced by the Būlāq press between

[115] Mestyan, "Sound, Military Music."
[116] [Voltaire], *Al-Rawḍ al-Azhar*, 3; 347.
[117] Al-Ṭahṭāwī, *Al-Dīwān al-Nafīs* (hijrī 1265 [1849] edition), 220–233.

1822 and 1842 were in Arabic (the rest were in Turkish).[118] The extent to which these works were products of conscious propaganda or parts of a strategy by the *ʿulamāʾ*-turned-efendis to invite the ruler to negotiate, or both, remains to be answered by further researchers.[119]

In all, from the 1820s onward Arabic printed books produced an image of Mehmed Ali as an Ottoman *vezir*, a Muslim conqueror, and a benefactor of Egypt. There is no information about how this printed image effected the perception of the pasha at the time. It certainly conquered the future through the cooperation of the Muslim intelligentia. His successor, Abbas Hilmi, intended to destroy this image by exiling the men, chiefly Rifāʿa al-Ṭahṭāwī, who created it.

Ḥubb al-waṭan 2.0: Unisonality and the Crimean War in Egypt

During the rule of Abbas, and his successor Said, a solid administration in the Egyptian provinces was functioning. In administrative documents, it was called "the local government" (*al-ḥukūma al-maḥalliyya*). The system saw itself not as a state but as a government.

The patriotic idea in Ottoman Turkish and in other Ottoman languages gained momentum in the late 1840s, and it was during the Crimean war (1853–1856) that it appeared as a forceful imperial territorial ideology. This section focuses on how the love of the homeland appeared as the central idea in constructing a new political, imagined community in Egypt. I suggest that the birth of this patriotism was conditioned by the Crimean war and Abbas Hilmi's sudden death, which required a renewed pact between elites and the new governor Said (r. 1854–1863)—first through the military context, and then as a general ideology of politics.

In 1854, the new governor, Said, a son of Mehmed Ali, was reluctant to allow full Ottoman integration, but, again, he tried to act as a faithful subject of the Porte. Yet, the most important text of his reign—the Suez Canal contract—was not submitted to the sultan for approval in 1854.[120] Said restored the *zevat* of Mehmed Ali. He brought back Rifāʿa al-Ṭahṭāwī from the Sudan, and, instead, sent ʿAlī Mubārak to the Crimean War. He abolished the *jizya* tax on Christians (Copts) in 1855 and started to conscript Copts in the Egyptian army.[121] This measure made Egyptian Copts and Muslims equal, at least officially in the spirit

[118] Heyworth-Dunne, "Printing and Translation," 334.
[119] Some answers are provided by Scharfe's dissertation.
[120] For a favorable French description of Said, see Merruau, "L'Égypte."
[121] ʿAfīfī, "Al-Aqbāṭ."

of the Tanzimat, which was one of many conditions for a potential patriotic collectivity.

Said maintained, and even boosted, the Egyptian contingent in the Crimean War: 23,931 Egyptian soldiers had fought there by the end of 1855.[122] Unlike the Syrian campaign against the sultan, where only Mehmed Ali's name was shouted,[123] the participation in the Ottoman Crimean war was justified by patriotic arguments in Arabic, shouting the name of both the governor and the sultan.

During Said's restoration of Mehmed Ali's elite the concept of *waṭan* solidified as a political homeland in learned Arabic. The rehabilitated al-Ṭahṭāwī in Cairo, like Yusuf Halis in Istanbul, wrote military songs called *waṭaniyyāt* (printed 1855, 1856, and later) in which word "the homeland" was instrumentalized to infuse loyalty in the Egyptian soldiers participating during the Crimean War.[124] His student, the poet Ṣāliḥ Majdī (1826?–1881) also wrote fifteen songs called *waṭaniyyāt,* which were set to music for the army.[125] This is the first moment when the homeland and the praise of the ruler were fused within a military context into an embodied, sensorial experience of unity with the help of music.

Unisonality, singing together patriotic songs, served as a form of experiencing a homogenized collectivity. During the Crimean War, unisonality was possibly the defining tool of Arab patriotisms in the empire. In the Egyptian province, the *waṭaniyyāt* of al-Ṭahṭāwī bear a striking similarity to Naqqāsh's rhyming couplet praising Abdülmecid in Beirut, the refrain (*dawr*) of one of them being again the by now familiar Prophetic saying:

> *Li-l-ḥarb hāmū yā shajʿān / ḥubb al-awṭān min al-īmān*
> To war oh brave friends off you go / *the love of the homeland is part of faith*

Thousands of Egyptians were sent to the Crimean War, and it is highly unlikely that there was no interaction between them and the central corps of the Ottoman army, both at a military cooperative, an ideological, and an emotional level.

Unisonality was also appropriated to indoctrinate soldiers with loyalty to the Egyptian governor. Ṣāliḥ Majdī composed *waṭaniyyāt* whose

[122] Badem, *The Ottoman Crimean War*, 112.
[123] Fahmy, *All the Pasha's Men*, 253.
[124] Moreh, *Modern Arabic Poetry*, 18–19.
[125] Majdī, *Dīwān*, 392ff.

primary purpose was the praise of Said. This is possibly the reason why his songs are forgotten today. They insert Said Pasha into the chain of ancient Egyptian and Muslim rulers as a mighty military conqueror and king of the land:

> *Fa-l-khidīwī al-Saʿīd ṣāḥib al-mulk al-ʿamīd / huwa fi-l-hījā farīd wa-muʿādīhi al-ṭarīd*
> The joyful, chief ruler [Said] is the lord of sovereignty / he is unique in war so flees his enemy[126]

Nationalists and Orientalists have jointly obscured the relationship of intellectuals to power and the Ottoman context. During the Nasserite period, after 1952, Egyptian literary scholars were so puzzled by the frequent praise of Said in al-Ṭahṭāwī's *waṭaniyyāt* that they corrected, or purged, the stanzas or simply bracketed praising expressions as if these were mistakes.[127] Another significant question—the Ottoman connection—was denied by Western Orientalists in the formative period of studying Arabic literature in English. The literary scholar Shmuel Moreh reports that when he asked the historian Bernard Lewis in 1965 whether Lewis thought that al-Ṭahṭāwī was "influenced in writing these songs by Turkish patriotic songs, Professor Lewis thought the idea very unlikely."[128]

While it is hard to establish what *exactly* influenced al-Ṭahṭāwī and Majdī to write these patriotic songs, I argue that the Crimean war and Said's love of his army together contributed to writing such songs, whose effects they knew already worked in France, at least in the case of the *Marseillaise*. The similarity between al-Ṭahṭāwī's and Naqqāsh's couplets justifies deeper investigation of *aural* pan-Ottoman propaganda in Arabic during the Crimean War.

Aural Patriotism and the Public Image of Said

The conditions in which the concept of *waṭan* appears during the Crimean War can be further elaborated by considering the system of power. Aural patriotism had to include praise of the governor Said in public. Kenneth Cuno remarks that had the historians of Ismail and of his descendants not written official histories, Said might have been "the founder of modern Egypt."[129] He certainly started to formalize his father Mehmed Ali's

[126] Majdī, *Dīwān*, 413.
[127] Wādī, *Dīwān Rifāʿa al-Ṭahṭāwī*, 89–94.
[128] Moreh, *Modern Arabic Poetry*, 18, n. 24.
[129] Cuno, "Muhammad Ali and the Decline and Revival Thesis," 106.

image and instructed the administration that he could only be mentioned as "Our Master whose Abode is the Paradise" (*Jannat-makān Afandīnā*).

Although only al-Ṭahṭāwī's *waṭaniyyāt* became canonized there was a whole range of loyal Arabic texts during Said's reign. Ṣāliḥ Majdī praised Said's reign not only in his own *waṭaniyyāt* but in a host of other congratulatory poems such as a song celebrating Said's birthday.[130] He also framed the signs of modernity in the conventional Arabic way, such as a panegyrics about a steamship.[131] A forgotten but important intellectual, Sheikh Muṣṭafā Salāma al-Najjārī (d. 1870), composed for Said a whole book of Arabic praising poetry.[132] Another intellectual, the bureaucrat Muḥammad ʿUthmān Jalāl (1829–1898) also dedicated his Arabic translation of the Fables of La Fontaine in 1858 to Said Pasha.[133] These texts show that the Muslim intelligentsia, who were not independent of the system, hoped for some type of cooperation with the pasha (often money, career advancement, land gifts, etc). What resulted was the making of yet another printed image of the governor, this time Said.

The physical aspect of this image was also important. Consider the following occasion of the circumcision ceremony of Said's son, Tusun in 1861. Cairo and the palace Qaṣr al-Nīl were decorated. Tusun was escorted from the Citadel by soldiers, in front of him a music band and notables, mounted on a small horse in a military uniform, with a golden saddle embedded with precious stones. At his sides rode two Ottoman notables, throwing gold to the cheering mass. Said received his son at Qaṣr al-Nīl palace in the company of Kamil (Kiamil) Pasha from Istanbul, with Ismail, Mustafa Fazıl, and Mehmed Ali junior, all in official uniforms. Together they entered the rooms where the *ʿulamāʾ* waited and where the circumcision took place. First the *zevat* went to congratulate, then "some Arabs and foreigners." In the evening Said Pasha drove out to the city in a carriage to "show and share his happiness" with his people. Throughout this day, music was continuous. There was a huge reception in the evening (including 440 *zevat*, 160 men of religion and village headmen, 360 army officers) and giant fireworks.[134]

A particular imagination of martial virtue also framed this governor. Said ordered the biography of Napoleon in Arabic to be distributed among the solders.[135] Napoleon was admired by rulers of the late Ottoman Arab lands: Mehmed Ali's admiration for the French general is well-known, and in the 1840s Aḥmad Bey also decorated his palaces in Tunis

130 Majdī, *Dīwān*, 467.
131 Ibid., 1–2.
132 Al-Najjārī, *Al-Madāʾiḥ al-Saʿīdiyya*, Manuscript, 395 Adab ʿArabī.
133 Jalāl, *Al-ʿUyūn al-Yawāqiẓ*.
134 *Ḥadīqat al-Akhbār*, 26 Rajab 1277 (7 February 1861), 3.
135 Sabry, *La genèse*, 98.

with paintings about Napoleonic battles.[136] Said himself likely found an imagined world in which martial virtues were fused with the homeland to be appealing, since he loved to listen to the adventures of the ancient Arab hero ʿAntar from a man in his entourage, Shaymā Efendi, who was proficient in educated Arabic.[137] (ʿAntar would later become an important character on the patriotic stage of Arabic theater, see chapter 5). Once, when Shaymā described how ʿAntar ordered his soldiers to blow trumpets, Said too ordered trumpets to be blown.[138] The re-acting of the imagined past would become a crucial technique of patriotism. No wonder, that Said was retrospectively described by one of his employees, Iskandar Fahmī, in his private memoirs as an "Egyptian patriot (*waṭanī miṣrī*), in the meaning of the word that he was a just ruler."[139]

Conclusion: Governing Ottoman Egypt in the Global Age of Patriotic Monarchies

This chapter has pointed out the parallelism and connections between the imperial center and Beirut and Cairo during the Tanzimat. In the case of the idea of patriotism, I have underlined similarities and chronological, vertical synchronities. This is a suggestion for a framework, continuing the work of Toledano and Fahmy, and somewhat deromanticizing the picture Ihsanoğlu painted about "the Turks in Egypt." There is much work to be done: tracing Ottoman Turkish-Arabic translations, both cultural works and legal documents; studying payments by Istanbul to local ʿulamāʾ, and reopening the study of military connections.

While Mehmed Ali, once thought to be the "father of modern Egypt," was a fairly ruthless Ottoman pasha, his actions, and not Europe, "awakened" the Arabs of the Ottoman Empire to the possibility of autonomous power—not to an Arab empire, but to a new Muslim power center with great military might outside of the sultan's reach. His rise can be viewed as a belated example of eighteenth-century Ottoman semiautonomous governance, similar to the Husaynids of Tunis and the Phanariots of Wallachia (part of today's Romania). But at his time the empire was centralizing. Thus the pasha and his family became elite Ottomans against the will of the empire. They used creatively the parallel strategies of Ottomanization and localization for political survival.

[136] Brown, *The Tunisia of Ahmad Bey*, 316.
[137] [Iskandar Fahmī], *Mudhakkirāt*, 85, 139.
[138] [Iskandar Fahmī], *Mudhakkirāt*, 139.
[139] Ibid., 63.

In conclusion, I wish to compare the Ottoman Egyptian developments to monarchies in Africa, Asia, and Europe, where similar processes occurred. One instance is the building of internal alliances at the same time in late Ottoman Tunis. In the 1840s, Aḥmad Bey of Tunis wrote in Arabic instead of Turkish, and drew native Tunisian families closer into the system of governance than ever before.[140] In the 1860s, outside of the Ottoman power sphere, in Ethiopia a monarchical system was created with a novel ideology of Ethiopian kingship.[141] In general, mid-century Europe saw a similar moment of re-establishing monarchies, most eminently Napoleon III's Second French Empire in the 1850s. However, the European compromises were achieved between the nationalist bourgeoisie and significantly weakened monarchs, after revolutions,[142] while in Africa and Asia compromises were attempted without revolutions, and the Sunni caliph's legitimacy remained more or less untouched.

Islam remained a central element in politics in the Ottoman world, although there was a contradiction. While Ottoman imperial patriotism contained both Muslim and patriotic ideas, in the case of Egypt the Muslim elements only reaffirmed the subordinated status of the governor to the sultan-caliph. This condition made patriotism in Mehmed Ali's Egypt more open to nonreligious modes of legitimating power. The hereditary governorship opened the possibility for local Christian and Jewish involvement in the patriotic ideology of power.

There was one pasha who did recognize the importance of symbols. It is time to turn to the controversial Ismail, son of Ibrahim, grandson of Mehmed Ali, and the chief creator of the khedivate, during whose rule the love of the homeland would be announced with unprecedented strength, and by unprecedented means, both to his subjects and to the world.

[140] Brown, *The Tunisia of Ahmad Bey*, 210–227.
[141] Orlowska, "The Legitimizing Project."
[142] Osterhammel, *The Transformation of the World*, 750.

CHAPTER 2

The Ottoman Legitimation of Power: The Khedivate

On Tuesday, May 29, 1866, Sultan Abdülaziz received Ismail, the governor of the Egyptian province, at a public reception in Istanbul. He gave him, by his own hand, an imperial edict, which arguably changed the course of history. The letter said: "the imperial edict given to Mehmed Ali Pasha, your grandfather, entrusted the province (*eyalet*) of Egypt to him with the right of inheritance [based on seniority] . . . but henceforth the governor's oldest male son and after him his eldest male son shall become the new governor."[1] This firman changed the rule of succession from seniority to primogeniture. The status of Ottoman Egypt also changed from a province (*eyalet*) to a khedivate (*hidiviyet*) in the next year, and Ismail and his successors could use exclusively the title "khedive."

In the last chapter, we left Said Pasha in the midst of trumpets and songs. His sudden death in January 1863, like all royal deaths, required a renewed pact between the new governor, Ismail, and the local elites. This occurred, I argue in this chapter, through the acknowledgment of the new dynastic order. Royalist historians viewed the codification of the new dynastic order, and the khedivate, as signs of "independence" while nationalists maintained that these were personal follies of a Westernizer.[2] In contrast, I show first the Ottoman face of Ismail, the political role of his mother Hoşyar (d. 1886), and "the Ottoman political culture of conspiracy."[3] This was a unique moment of merging the patriotic idea with the Ottoman-Muslim ideas and symbols of just rule to establish a monarchical order in Egypt. Building on and somewhat upgrading Toledano's theory of Ottomanization/localization, we follow how changes at the imperial level were accepted in the province.

[1] Budak et al., eds., *Osmanlı Belgerelinde Mısır*, 149–151; Letter dated 29 May 1866, from [Ambassador?] to Consul General of France in Alexandria, 166PO/D25/67–68, MEAN.

[2] Di-Capua, *Gatekeepers of the Arab Past*, 164–172.

[3] Riedler, *Opposition and Legitimacy*.

The Ottoman Face of Ismail

When the French consul in 1879 scornfully asked Ismail, who had tried to resort to the authority of the sultan in the face of the financial catastrophe and constant humiliation by Europeans, about how long he had been "a humble servant" of the Ottoman Empire, he replied that "since my birth, monsieur."[4] Indeed, this key figure of modern history, the ideal type of "Westernizer," can be only understood by considering the Ottoman Empire as the backdrop of all his actions.

Showing the Ottoman face of Ismail is not an easy task. Many men and women fabricated and constantly revised the pasha's public image (and counterimages) in Arabic, French, and Italian during and after his rule. We shall see the European image of the pasha in the next chapter. His Ottoman face has been lost, so much so that scholars often write about the Egyptian-"Turkish" relation as a diplomatic one between sovereign rulers and states during his reign.[5] However, this chapter demonstrates that in trying to understand the psyche of this pasha we find that "being Ottoman" was his political strategy during the 1860s.[6]

Like Mehmed Ali, Ismail's actions were dictated by his intermediary position between the empire and Egypt but unlike his grandfather he could count on the sultan. Understanding this support is crucial, since this was what the *zevat* and the *aʿyān* saw when they looked at Ismail in the 1860s.

Making a Sultanic Cousin

There is a striking image in Vienna depicting the fourteen-year-old Ismail (figure 2.1). We see him in proper Turkish clothes, with all the attributes of the Ottoman ruling class: sword, golden belt, golden necklace, and a well-fed, round body. It is unclear whether the young Ismail habitually wore these clothes or whether he was depicted in such fashion by the possibly Orientalizing artist. The painting reflects his social position and conveys the message that he is a confident, powerful, and rich member of the Ottoman elite. This is the image from which Ismail would transform himself into the image of a progressive ruler accepted in Europe.

Death and Islam were in Ismail's name. He was born on January 12, 1830 (17 Rajab 1245) in the Palace of Misafirhane in Cairo[7] as the second

[4] Crabitès, *Ismail*, 286.

[5] Muṣṭafā, *ʿAlāqāt Miṣr*.

[6] Similar studies using psychological arguments: Tagher, "Psychologie du règne"; Tagher, "Portrait psychologique de Nubar Pacha"; Fahmy, *Mehmed Ali*; Sālim, *Fārūq wa-Suqūṭ al-Malakiyya*.

[7] Quoted in Sāmī, *Taqwīm al-Nīl*, part 3, vol. 2, 438. The date of 31 December 1830 is mistakenly given in Zananiri, *Le Khédive Ismail*, 9; al-Rāfiʿī, *ʿAṣr Ismāʿīl*, 1:69. Dating is

FIGURE 2.1. Ismail in 1845
Source: *S.A. Ismael Bey Fils de S.A. Ibrahim Pacha d'Égypte, Nach der Natur gemalt und lith. von Robert Theer. Wien 1845. Gedr. bei Joh. Höfelich.* Bildarchiv, Österreichische Nationalbibliothek, with permission, cat. n. 7346018.

son of Ibrahim. His name was probably chosen to commemorate Ismail, his father's arrogant and daring brother who was burned alive in the Sudan in 1822.[8] The name was a clever choice: in the Koran Ismāʿīl (Ishmael) is the son of Ibrāhīm (Abraham) who builds the Kaʿba, and both

crucial because a December date would mean that Mustafa Fazıl would have the claim to succession. Sammarco, *Le Règne du Khédive*, 2.

[8] Fahmy, *All the Pasha's Men*, 88.

FIGURE 2.2. Ismail after 1867
Source: "The Khedive." Library of Congress, call number: LOT 7741, p. 69 in album "Jerusalem, Alexandria, Cairo, Rome, no. 135."

of them are counted as prophets in Islam. Father and son thus possessed a potential metaphorical parallelism that was often realized in patriotic praises in the 1860s. Not much is known about their actual relationship.

Importantly, baby Ismail was breast-fed by an Arabic-speaking foster mother (a slave-girl married to Dunalı Mustafa Ağa, a soldier of his father Ibrahim) and had thus a foster brother, her son Ismāʿīl Ṣiddīq (1830[9]–1876). Ismāʿīl Ṣiddīq later lived in their countryside estates and acquired local Egyptian manners so much so that he has been thought to be of local peasant origins although he was from among the *zevat*.[10] Ṣiddīq would act as Ismail's Egyptian alter-ego and most trustworthy man.

In the 1860s, retroactive rumours circulated to connect Ismail personally to the sultan. It was said that his mother, Hoşyar (d. 1886) had a sister, Pertevniyal, the mother of Sultan Abdülaziz.[11] How Mehmed II and Mehmed Ali's son Ibrahim acquired two sisters in their harems remains a mystery, but if this story is true, it is unlikely to be a coincidence.

[9] Hunter, *Egypt Under the Khedives*, 145 mistakenly gives 1821 for the birth date.

[10] ʿAbd al-Raḥmān, *Ismāʿīl Ṣiddīq al-Mufattish*, 59–60.

[11] Konrad, *Der Hof der Khediven*, 138; Douin, *Histoire du Règne du Khédive*, 1:205; Lott, *The English Governess*, 167.

Ibrahim certainly knew Istanbul, or at least the Palace, since he was a hostage in the imperial capital in 1806–1807,[12] and he may have met and fallen in love with Hoşyar later in Bebek.[13] What *was* a coincidence was the fact that only a few weeks after Ismail's birth, Pertevniyal gave birth to Abdülaziz, the second son of Sultan Mahmud II, on February 9, 1830. Thus Ismail, the future khedive of Egypt, and Abdülaziz, the future sultan, were of the same age, and said to be cousins.

An invisible (or often visible) competition within the ruling family would define Ismail's reign. His elder half-brother Ahmed Rifaat (1825–1858) died early, but his younger half-brother Mustafa Fazıl (1830–1875) became a crucial political player. Their mothers competed for and through their sons for Ibrahim's attention.[14] Female and male cousins, in addition to uncles and aunts who were even younger than Ismail, such as Abdülhalim (1831–1894) and Mehmed Ali junior (1833–1861) were also influential. Abdülhalim, the longest living son of Mehmed Ali, was a life-long contester of Ismail's legitimacy. These *zevat*—half-brothers, cousins, aunts, uncles, and a foster brother—would compete in and for Ottoman Egypt.

The Family Strife and Ottoman Integration

Unlike his grandfather, Ismail knew the imperial elite. Although he was educated for almost five years (1844–1849) in Vienna and Paris, in the Egyptian Military School, these years may have only given him a personal experience of an aristocratic regime falling to a nationalist revolution in Paris in 1848. The real education occurred after the death of his father Ibrahim in November 1848, when the new governor Abbas Hilmi ordered the "princes" home from Paris in March 1849.[15] This is the moment when the earlier competition fledged into what Toledano names an "intra-family strife"[16] (see chapter 1). As a consequence, Ismail moved to Istanbul where many of the Mehmed Ali family members and elite employees fled. Zeynep, who had been forced to divorce in Egypt, married Kiamil Pasha again in Istanbul around April 1851;[17] in June Mehmed Ali junior announced to the British ambassador that he never would return to Egypt.[18]

[12] Crabitès, *Ibrahim*, 2.

[13] Lott, *The English Governess*, 169.

[14] Al-Ayyūbī, *Tārīkh Miṣr*, 1:375–376.

[15] Unknown to Joseph Hekekyan Bey, 28 March 1849, Vol. XV., MSS/Additional/37462, Hekekyan Papers, BL.

[16] Toledano, *State and Society*, 100.

[17] Canning to Palmerston, 18 April 1851, FO 424/7A, NA.

[18] Canning to Palmerston, 4 June 1851, FO 424/7A, NA.

The young men were integrated into the imperial elite. In June 1851 Ismail and Mehmed Ali junior were both made members of *Şura-ı Askeri* (Military Council of the Ottoman Empire) and promoted to *feriklik* (the rank of general).[19] Abdülhalim was also in the rank of *ferik*. This rank came with a large salary, as was well-known at the time in Egypt.[20] It is possible that at this time Ismail received the title of pasha, together with the rank of the general.[21] Ahmed Rifaat was also promoted to *feriklik* in the same year, although without a salary.[22] In August 1851, Mustafa Fazıl was appointed to the *Meclis-i Ahkam* (the Legislative Council of the Ottoman Empire).[23]

These appointments may reflect the strategy of Mustafa Reşid, the grand vizier. Reşid wanted to utilise the disagreement between the Egyptian Turks to strengthen the Porte's hand over Egypt.[24] The shower of titles indicates that the Porte or the Palace (or together) found it useful to incorporate the young Egyptian "princes" into the imperial hierarchy. Around this time Ismail, Mustafa Fazıl, and Abdülhalim all received the title *vezir* from Sultan Abdülmecid[25] (though in 1856 Mustafa Fazıl was still named a bey in contrast to his brother Ismail who was a pasha).[26] The Mehmed Ali household became firmly accepted as part of the imperial order.

Besides the insertion of the young men in the political elite of the imperial capital, they must have been initiated into the fully fledged *Tanzimat* political and cultural life. This chapter and the next argue that the European cultural infrastructure in khedivial Cairo paradoxically originated, in part, from Abdülmecidian Istanbul. Being close to the entourage of Sultan Abdülmecid, Ismail must have experienced refined Turkish court music, Italian operas, French comedies, circus entertainments, and other pleasures of the Bosporus. There is, however, an opposing Ottoman view: the statesman Cevdet Pasha remembers that the "exiled" Egyptian Turks (especially Zeynep, daughter of Mehmed Ali) "corrupted" the morals of

[19] Letters dated 12 and 20 Shaʿbān 1267 (12 and 20 June 1851), İ.DH. 236/ 14268; scratch, dated 25 Shaʿbān [1267] (25 June 1851), A.}MKT.MHM. 34/3; and 29 Shaʿbān 1267 (29 June 1851), A.MKT.NZD. 38/22, all in BOA.

[20] [Iskandar Fahmī], *Mudhakkirāt*, 68.

[21] In a document dated as early as 29 Shawwāl 1267 (27 August 1851) Ismail is mentioned as a pasha. İ. MVL. 00219/7344, BOA.

[22] Dated 21 Dhū al-Qaʿda 1267 (17 September 1851), İ.MTZ.(05)TAL, 1/38, BOA.

[23] Meclis-i Vālā-ı Ahkām-ı ʿAdliye. Letter dated ? Shawwāl 1267 (? August 1851), A.} DVN.MHM. 9/19, BOA.

[24] Letter from Murray to Palmerston, Cairo, 21 February 1851, FO 424/7A, NA.

[25] In 1861, they are mentioned as vezirs. Letter dated ? Shaʿbān 1277 (? December 1861), A.}DVN.MHM. 32/24, BOA.

[26] *L'Isthme de Suez*, 25 December 1856, 202. In general, see Deny, *Sommaire des Archives Turques*, 35–78.

the capital and the sultan because of their spending and their *alafiranga* ("Frankish," European) lifestyle.[27]

Becoming an Heir

In the order of seniority, Ismail was not considered to be heir of the governorship since Abbas' heir was his uncle Said, and Said's was Ahmed Rifaat. By the 1850s, Ismail had wives and consorts, a number of daughters, and two sons: Mehmed Tevfik (1852–1892) and Hüseyin Kamil (1853–1917). It is not known when Ismail returned to Egypt from Istanbul. He attended the investiture ceremony of Said in July 1854 in Cairo.[28] In November 1854, Ferdinand de Lesseps, rushing to convince Said about the importance of the Suez Canal, had no high opinion about Ismail because he loved pleasures, expensive furniture, and de Lesseps suspected him of already fathering twelve children![29]

At this moment, Ismail was a leading member of the Ottoman Egyptian elite, but without much responsibility. He became a trusted man of Said, perhaps as a measure against his brother, the official heir Ahmed Rifaat. Said sent Ismail to Europe in 1855 on "diplomatic missions," though, according to contemporary Europeans, he spent his time enjoying the luxuries of Paris with Ahmed Rifaat, buying whatever they found.[30] At Said's receptions he was usually present.[31] His palace was full of "furniture heavy and overloaded, bad French taste."[32] An English servant in 1855 gossiped that "nothing is regular in his household."[33] In 1856, Ismail was appointed to head the new *Majlis al-Aḥkām* in Egypt but resigned after a few months.[34]

And then came a change. In May 1858, his brother Ahmed Rifaat died with another *zevat* grandee, Hurşid Pasha in a fatal train accident; only Abdülhalim escaped.[35] Ismail, who had remained in Alexandria, suddenly found himself the heir of the Egyptian governorship in the Ottoman Empire.[36] Rumors remained about Said's or Ismail's hand in the accident, but no proof ever surfaced to prove their involvement.

[27] Cevdet, *Maʿrūzāt*, 7–8.

[28] Al-Rāfiʿī says Ismail returned when Abbas died, *ʿAṣr Ismāʿīl*, 1:69. For the investiture ceremony, note dated 20 July 1854 in vol. VII. MSS/Additional/ 37454, Hekekyan Papers, BL.

[29] Letter dated 25 November 1854, in De Lesseps, *Recollections of Forty Years*, 1:190–191.

[30] Senior, *Conversations*, 2:226–228.

[31] For instance, at a ball on 16 July 1856. *L'Isthme de Suez*, 10 August 1856, 53.

[32] Senior, *Conversations*, 1:137.

[33] Ibid., 2:227.

[34] Sāmī, *Taqwīm al-Nīl*, part 3, vol. 1:194; his resignation: part 3, vol. 1, 225.

[35] Ghali, ed., *Mémoirs de Nubar Pacha*, 181.

[36] Despite the obvious suspicion, there is no proof of Ismail or Said's involvement in the accident. De Leon, *The Khedive's Egypt*, 156–158. Ghali, ed. *Mémoirs de Nubar Pacha*, 182.

According to the conventional narrative, the young man retired to his countryside estates after this incident. He became *le cultivateur modèle*,[37] "an agriculturalist,"[38] so much that even Said mocked him for being a *bakkal* ("merchant" in Turkish).[39] The consul of the Habsburg Empire and an Italian agent also characterized him to their governments as *die Oekonomie ist seine Spezialität*, his only fault being greed (*oikonomia* in the original Greek means running a household).[40] This is how the carefully selected documents of the royalist historians portray him.[41] Said appointed Ismail as regent when he was away on short trips during 1861–1862.[42] Reconfiguring one's self as an "innocent" farmer might rather have been a strategy in response to the fear of assassination.

It is possible that some qualities of his dead brother were transferred to Ismail by courtiers and historians. Ahmed's state salary was certainly transferred to Ismail in 1858.[43] As to his half-brother, Mustafa Fazıl looked for imperial advancement in Istanbul and became the Ottoman Minister of Education in December 1862.[44]

Ismail owned land, houses in Cairo and Alexandria, and at least twenty villages between Minya and Manfalut in middle Egypt along the Nile. Europeans and government employees admired the richness and modernity of his estates, which they saw from the distance.[45] For instance, the poet Ṣāliḥ Majdī (writer of Said's *waṭaniyyāt* as we have seen) wrote an Arabic poem celebrating his establishment of a sugar factory in Rawda in 1861.[46] The state engineer Hekekyan in 1862 watched the *charmantes* factories on Ismail's lands around Minya from his boat on the Nile.[47] From the distance, Ismail seemed to be the ideal model of the Ottoman technocrat.

Meanwhile, Abdülaziz became the sultan in 1861. After the early death of Said in January 1863, this supposed cousin conferred the governorship of Egypt upon Ismail. These two Ottoman masters of Asia and Africa (and

37 Sacré and Outrebon, *L'Égypte et Ismaïl Pacha*, 11.

38 Leon, "Ismail Pacha of Egypt," 742.

39 Ghali, ed., *Mémoirs de Nubar Pacha*, 211.

40 Quoted in Sammarco, *Histoire de l'Égypte Moderne*, 3:6–7, n. 2.

41 It is worth noting that Abdülhalim as an heir second-in-line was also reported to be busy with agriculture. Letter dated 19 September 1865, 166PO/D25/66, MEAN.

42 Sāmī, *Taqwīm al-Nīl*, part 3, vol. 2, 442. It is said that in 1862 Ismail managed to subdue a rebellion in the Sudan without much bloodshed. Al-Rāfiʿī, *ʿAṣr Ismāʿīl*, 1:75; however, Sammarco proves that Ismail did not leave the capital personally. Sammarco, *Histoire de l'Égypte Moderne*, 3:9, n. 3.

43 Sāmī, *Taqwīm al-Nīl*, 3:1: 299.

44 Kuneralp, *Son Dönem Osmanlı*, 6.

45 Cammas and Lefèvre, *La vallée du Nil*, 59–64.

46 Majdī, *Dīwān*, 17.

47 20 February 1862, Vol. IX., MSS/Additional/ 37456, Hekekyan Papers, BL.

Europe to some extent) would have an exceptionally good relationship in the 1860s and 1870s.

Hoşyar: Female Power and the Sultan in Egypt

Ismail's reign started with Abdülaziz's visit in the Egyptian province in 1863. This unprecedented event which opened this part of the book needs explanation. The Ottoman connection was crucial for Ismail, since he was challenged on various fronts: by Mustafa Fazıl, or, as the European press called him, "Prince Mustafa," and by his (younger) uncle Abdülhalim, "Prince Halim," the last surviving son of Mehmed Ali. Ismail was also troubled by Said's widow Melekper, and her son, Tusun, whose protector was Abdülhalim. As in the case of previous successions, the Porte also saw an opportunity to regain control over Egypt. Now there was another candidate for the "throne," Mustafa Fazıl, who had became an imperial Ottoman notable and was cherished in Istanbul.[48] He was promoted to Ottoman Minister of Finance in January 1863.[49]

It was also not clear whether the *zevat* army leaders in Egypt would accept Ismail. His predecessor, Said was not accepted among all the *zevat* when Abbas Hilmi was murdered somewhat mysteriously in 1854; and a brief but crucial power struggle occurred.[50] Finally, upon European and Ottoman intervention, Said became accepted, and he reunited the Turkic elite.[51] This was the second time, after the family strife, when Ismail learned that *zevat*—that is, military—support was crucial for political survival in Ottoman Egypt.

The first clash occurred immediately. In February 1863, Ismail traveled to Istanbul to receive the customary firman of investiture but he refused the hospitality of his half-brother who, in turn, did not show up to say the traditional good-byes to Ismail upon the latter's departure back to Egypt.[52] This was a grave form of public embarassment because Ismail, as the head of the family, was technically the superior of Mustafa Fazıl. It was then "discovered" in Cairo that there was a plan to assassinate Ismail

[48] List dated 13 Ṣafar 1279 (10 August 1862), PVSE, AK.

[49] Kuneralp, *Son Dönem Osmanlı Erkan*, 109.

[50] Toledano, *State and Society*, 47.

[51] According to a rumour, Ahmed Rifaat, Ismail, Mustafa Fazıl, and Ilhami (son of Abbas) petitioned the sultan not to appoint their uncle, which resulted in Said's dislike of his nephews. Senior, *Conversations*, 2:194.

[52] Douin, *Histoire du Règne du Khédive Ismail*, 1:207. McCoan remarks that Ismail was the guest of Mustafa Fazıl for a fortnight and that only after this did their relation deteriorate. McCoan, *Egypt under Ismail*, 24.

by Mustafa Fazıl,[53] or at least some letters "of treasonable nature" were intercepted.[54]

Ismail's mother Hoşyar became a pivotal political figure at this moment. She was one of the few people whom Ismail trusted.[55] Traditionally, mothers played an important informal role within Muslim monarchies. Leslie Peirce shows that the *valide sultan* exercised enormous influence in the affairs of the Ottoman state until the mid-seventeenth century;[56] in Hoşyar we may find an Ottoman-Egyptian example of harem power in the nineteenth century. The female members of Mehmed Ali's harem had already established this precedent,[57] and Said had also been in contact with a lady in the harem of the late Sultan Abdülmecid.[58] During this period, Hoşyar was not alone in this respect; for instance, in Persia Nāṣir al-Dīn Shah's mother Mahd-i ʿUlya interfered in appointments to the Persian army in the 1850s.[59] Pertevniyal, Sultan Abdülaziz's mother (*valide sultan*) was similarly invisible but instrumental in politics. With her son becoming governor, Hoşyar's importance rose accordingly as *wālidat al-bāshā* ("mother of the pasha," in the colloquial *walda bāshā*). Whether or not she was the sister of Pertevniyal, the two mothers cooperated in making a new order in the empire.

Hoşyar did not express her opinion directly in politics; instead, she operated through family members and agents, such as the director of her estates, the powerful and cruel chief eunuch, Khalil Agha.[60] After Khalil's death in 1880, Ibrahim Edhem took his place as the main agent.[61]

The Ottoman face of Ismail involved the manifestation of Muslim power through his mother Hoşyar. To be just to Ismail, in 1865 he also made a large religious endowment (*waqf*) for the maintenance of mosques and other religious buildings;[62] and we shall often see him involving senior *ʿulamāʾ* in decision making, or at least he made efforts to be seen as counting on their opinions. Of Hoşyar's projects the largest was the al-Rifāʿī mosque which she ordered in 1869, exactly at the moment when her son would order an opera house. First, the chief eunuch Khalil Agha was in charge of this dynastic mosque (it was finished only

[53] Douin, *Histoire du Règne du Khédive Ismail*, 1:207.

[54] Letter dated 13 March 1863, FO 78/1754, NA.

[55] Lott, *The English Governess*, 81.

[56] Peirce, *The Imperial Harem*, Preface.

[57] For instance, Mehmed Ali sent his daughter-in-law, Fatma (widow of his son Hussain Kamel), to Istanbul in 1837. Tagher, "La mission de Sarim Bey."

[58] De Lesseps, *Recollections of Forty Years*, 1:164.

[59] Amanat, *Pivot of the Universe*, 145–146.

[60] Fahmy, *Souvenirs du Khédive Ismaïl*, 8; also Rhoné and Herz quoted in Ormos, *Max Herz*, 2:432–3.

[61] Abkāriyūs, *Al-Manāqib al-Ibrāhīmiyya*, 131.

[62] Ghānim, *Al-Awqāf*, 174–175.

in the 1900s).[63] Although Hoşyar later also established a special religious endowment (*waqf*) for the construction, the maintenance of graves, and salaries of the staff,[64] it appears that in fact Ismail's own purse financed this symbolic project.[65]

The Sultan in Egypt: Hoşyar's Plan?

The most effective element in the Ottoman legitimation of Ismail's position was Sultan Abdülaziz's unusual visit in April 1863. This was a message to both the *zevat* and the *aʿyān*. We have seen that even nonhuman agents (or too human ones) helped Ismail's position, like rumours that he was "a cousin of the sultan." Upon her son's accession, Hoşyar sent gifts to the members of the Ottoman Egyptian elite and the *ʿulamāʾ*.[66] At Ismail's accession, there was a rumor that the new rule would be disadvantageous for the Christians, and there were small atrocities against foreigners, including consuls.[67] These rumours may have been magnified by the French consul because of Ismail's intention to renegotiate the terms of the Suez Canal, and the consul indeed explained the injury of French economic interests by religious "fanaticism."[68]

This was, indeed, a moment of reinforcing Ottoman sovereignty in Egypt and affirming the sultan's support of Ismail in various fronts. Abdülaziz's physical presence was an unmistakable sign of Egypt's status as an imperial province. The Ottoman patriotic strategy of making the body of the sultan the symbol of imperial integrity appeared in Egypt, too.

Apart from the sultan's speech to the consuls in Alexandria, Abdülaziz also received the *zevat*, sheikhs, and *aʿyān* in Cairo. He visited the tomb of Mehmed Ali in the Citadel.[69] The pilgrimage to Mecca was launched in the presence of both Abdülaziz and Ismail. This must have been a forceful reminder of the Islamic hierarchy for everyone in late Ottoman Egypt. Re-Ottomanization at this moment also meant the invention of tradition: instead of using the new train and then steamboats, as was the case in the previous years during Said's reign, this time a "traditional" caravan was launched with camels to ʿAqaba.[70]

As to Egyptians, the sultanic entourage saw only signs of joy and respect in the streets. Yet the British consul judged that the Muslim population

[63] Herz, *La Mosquée el-Rifaï*, 17; Ormos, *Max Herz*, 2:430–456.

[64] Ḥujjat al-waqf dated 19 Dhū al-Ḥijja 1296 (4 December 1879), number 1215; in Daftarkhāna, Wizārat al-Awqāf al-Miṣriyya.

[65] Ormos, *Max Herz*, 2:431–2.

[66] Shārūbīm, *al-Kāfī*, 4:177.

[67] Cf. letters in February 1863, especially 16 February 1863, FO 78/1754, NA.

[68] Letter dated 2 February 1863, British consul to Foreign Office, FO 78/1754, NA.

[69] Gardey, *Voyage de Sultan Abd-Ul-Aziz*, 75.

[70] Letter dated 17 April 1863, British consul to Foreign Office, FO 78/1754, NA.

was not enthusiastic for the sultan because they considered "his Majesty's presence as rather destroying the prestige of the Vice-Roy."[71] The reason might have been different, however. The years 1863–1864 brought misery to the country as a whole in the form of epidemics, fire, and poverty. The people of Cairo later thought that the epidemics were brought by the sultan's visit.[72]

Before leaving Egypt, Sultan Abdülaziz joined Ismail within his harem for a dinner.[73] In an extraordinary move, he also bestowed upon Hoşyar the Grand Cordon of Osmaniye.[74] (Later in the century sultans sent more decorations for female members of the khedivial family.) Was it a message from Pertevniyal, the most powerful woman of the empire, through her son, to her possible sister, the most powerful woman in Egypt? Be that as it may, when Ismail in the company of all potential heirs (except Mustafa Fazıl)—Abdülhalim, Tusun, and Ismail junior (Mehmed Ali junior's son)—said farewell to the sultan, Abdülaziz thanked him in public and announced that "I am very satisfied with Egypt and with her noble governor."[75]

The Khedivate as an Ottoman Regime Type

What Mehmed Ali had achieved with his army, Ismail continued with money and the efforts of his mother. The result was the khedivate. The codification of Egypt as a special Ottoman provincial regime was a legal and cultural process during 1866 and 1867. The khedivate was not a simple case of a tributary state. Ismail and Hoşyar reconnected their rule to the sultan's authority in 1863, and they continued to strengthen Ismail's power by the Ottoman universe. They reactivated the quest to change the law of succession.[76] This was to exclude everyone from the dynastic order in favor of Ismail's eldest son, Tevfik. They achieved the new dynastic order of primogeniture in 1866. As a next step, the khedivate was codified in 1867. Together, the two changes constituted a singular strategy and created the framework of a new political order.

Primogeniture, 1866: Harem Diplomacy, Arabic Public Sphere

Nur Yalman suggests that the feature responsible for the course of Ottoman history is the succession order, based on seniority in the house of

[71] Letter dated 17 April 1863, British consul to Foreign Office, FO 78/1754, NA.
[72] Shārūbīm, *al-Kāfī*, Part 4:265.
[73] Lott, *The English Governess*, 127.
[74] Sammarco, *Le Règne du Khédive Ismaïl de 1863 à 1875*, 3:42.
[75] Gardey, *Voyage de Sultan Abd-Ul-Aziz*, 168.
[76] Toledano, *State and Society*, 62–63. Lott, *The English Governess*, 223.

Osman.[77] Sultans Abdülmecid and Abdülaziz certainly wanted to change the order of succession.[78] With regard to Egypt, seniority was a problem and governors wanted to change it to primogeniture. Toledano argues that Ibrahim was "too ill and alienated from Istanbul politics" to gain the privilege for Ahmed Rifaat; Abbas died too early to secure the succession for his son Ilhami (though he had a sort of agreement with the sultan); and Said was not energetic enough to initiate such a negotiation in favor of Tusun (though he discussed this possibility with Napoleon III).[79]

From the moment of the investiture, Ismail and Hoşyar launched a propaganda campaign in Istanbul. As early as February 1863, the sultan's mother, Pertevniyal, arranged for Ismail to meet with Sultan Abdülaziz in private at her palace.[80] In the summer of 1864, Hoşyar traveled to Istanbul to help her son. She arrived with the proposed new heir in question (her grandson Tevfik), lots of money, and arguably the most powerful weapon of all: female diplomacy.[81] The greatest attack they launched started in the spring of 1866. The good offices of the *valide sultan*, Pertevniyal, may have been involved. It was rumored that during these days, Tevhide, the oldest daughter of Ismail, was a guest in the imperial harem and Abdülaziz wanted to marry her.[82]

Ismail also used the growing Ottoman Arabic public sphere to support his requests. *Al-Jawāʾib*, a pan-Ottoman Arabic journal published in Istanbul on behalf of the government, lobbied for him. In fact, as early as 1863 the editor Fāris al-Shidyāq read a panegyric in Arabic in front of Ismail during the latter's visit in Istanbul.[83] Shidyāq then received regular financial support from the khedivial governance; for instance, in 1865 together with the editors of the Ottoman Turkish *Ceride-i Havadis* and the French *Galata Courier* (later *Levant Herald*).[84] French journalists were also in Ismail's pay;[85] such as the editor in chief of the journal *Derby* in Paris,[86] and the pasha paid more to the staff of the French journal

77 Yalman, "The Ottomans and the West," 352–355.

78 Karateke, "Who Is the Next Ottoman Sultan?"

79 Toledano, *State and Society*, 62; 144–145. For Said's negotiations, cf. Sammarco, *Histoire de L'Égypte*, 3:24.

80 Letter dated 6 Ramaḍān 1279 (25 February 1863), from Valide Sultan to Sultan, PVSE, AK.

81 Douin, *Le Khédive Ismail*, 1:206. Lott, *The English Governess*, 248.

82 Douin, *Le Khédive Ismail*, 1:230.

83 *Al-Jawāʾib*, 19 March 1866, 2.

84 Letter dated 13 Rajab ? 1282 (2 December ? 1865), qayd 573, microfilm 99, MST, DWQ.

85 ? Shaʿbān 1282 (end of December 1865), (L. Bertrand, editor of *Dīrkī?*) to Maʿiyya, 186/36, MST, Microfilm 196, DWQ.

86 Letter dated 25 Shaʿbān 1283 (2 January 1867), Ismail Ragib to Maʿiyya, 178/40, MST, Microfilm 199, DWQ.

L'Égypte[87] than to staff of the official Egyptian government bulletin *al-Waqāʾiʿ al-Miṣriyya*.[88] While Ismail waited for the firman in the spring of 1866 *al-Jawāʾib* printed Arabic poems of praise from all over the empire: the support of Ottoman Arab poets such as Ḥāmid Efendi Ālūsī from Baghdad,[89] or Aḥmad Sāmī Efendi from Mosul,[90] suggests that there was wider Arab attention, or at least, an attempt to create the impression of such attention.

The change of the dynastic order for primogeniture was approved. As we have seen, Ismail received the firman personally from the sultan in May 1866. The issue of *al-Jawāʾib* printed on June 5, 1866, was almost solely dedicated to Ismail and his firman.[91] As to Mustafa Fazıl, he bitterly started to support the Young Ottoman movement, Muslim constitutionalism, to challenge the sultan and take revenge for his lost positions from Paris.[92]

The 1866 Firmans and the Romanian Parallel

In the 1930s, the historian al-Rāfiʿī claimed that the money spent on the 1866 firman had had nothing to do with the benefit of the country.[93] This was a shock to monarchist circles at the time. Until then, officially, Ismail's aim had been interpreted as the "independence" of Egypt from the Ottoman Empire.[94]

The 1866 firmans (soon there was another firman regulating the case of regency) contain much more than the modification of succession order and less than independence. In addition to primogeniture, the sultan gave two Red Sea ports to Ismail, allowed the increase of the army, permitted Egypt's own currency, gave the right to nominate civil officers according to the Ottoman system up to the *saniye* (second rank of the first class), and, in return for all of these, set the tribute at 750,000 Ottoman pounds annually. Sultan Abdülaziz justified the privileges as the only means to secure the *bonheur* of Egypt; at least this is how Ali Pasha, the Ottoman foreign minister, explained the changes in his circular to the

87 Letter dated 17 Shawwāl 1283 (22 February 1867), Māliyya to Maʿiyya, 40/318, MST, Microfilm 199, DWQ.

88 Table about yearly expenses dated 26 Rabīʿ al-Ākhir 1284 (27 August 1867), 41/313, MST, Microfilm 200, DWQ.

89 *Al-Jawāʾib*, 22 May 1866, 1.

90 *Al-Jawāʾib*, 15 May 1866, 1.

91 *Al-Jawāʾib*, 5 June 1866, 1–2.

92 Cevdet, *Maʿrūzāt*, 197.

93 Al-Rāfiʿī, *ʿAṣr Ismāʿīl*, 1:79.

94 For example, al-Ayyūbī, *Tārīkh Miṣr*, 1:375.

ambassadors.[95] As compensation Mustafa Fazıl was granted an annuity of 20,000 (British?) pounds.[96] Ismail's victory was complete.

The new privileges did represent a degree of independence. They fashioned Egypt as an Ottoman Arab monarchy, similar to the privileges given to the Ottoman United Principalities of Moldavia and Wallachia (later Romania). In the secret letters addressed to Ismail by his agents in Istanbul, the description of the eastern European princes (including the Serbian one) looking for privileges in Istanbul figures prominently at the time.[97] The sultan invested the Hohenzollern prince Charles, invited by Romanian notables to rule the United Principalities, in October 1866, and he also received the right to his own coinage and army.[98] The eastern European developments informed the political horizon in the Arab provinces as well and can be understood as competing units for the sultanic agreement. Change in the regime type of Ottoman Egypt occurred, however, through the legal upgrading of its governorship.

Looking for a New Rank: ʿAzīz

Sovereignty and the right to borrowing were important preconditions for the integration of Egypt into the world economy,[99] and in this regard, the interest of the dynasty and the interest of foreign bankers intersected. An Ottoman Armenian in the service of the Egyptian pashas, Nubar Nubaryan (1825–1899), later three-time prime minister, at the time the highest diplomatic agent, relays that Ismail was so "sorry" that Egypt had to pay for the new dynastic order that he asked Nubar to suggest something that he could demand from the sultan "for the benefit of the country" as a "compensation for the sacrifice that Egypt made." Nubar suggested the right to Egypt's own customs agreement, analogous to the one enjoyed by the United Principalities.[100]

Among the demands, Ismail also asked for the acknowledgment of the title "Aziz" (*ʿazīz*; "the mighty one"),[101] a ceremonial title that Muslim intellectuals gave perhaps first to the aging Mehmed Ali. This is the title of the pharaoh's governor in the Koran. *ʿAzīz Miṣr* ("the Mighty One

[95] At the suggestion of the French consul, Ismail submitted another request for a detailed regulation in case of a regency (his eldest son Tevfik was fourteen at this moment); thus he received a second firman, dated 15 June 1866. Douin, *Le Khédive Ismaïl*, 1: 218–229.

[96] McCoan, *Egypt under Ismail*, 40.

[97] Regular correspondence from 1865, in 166PO/D25, MEAN.

[98] Jelavich, *The Establishment of the Balkan National States*, 123.

[99] Owen, *The Middle East in the World Economy*.

[100] Ghali, ed., *Mémoirs de Nubar Pacha*, 263–265.

[101] Al-Ayyūbī, *Tārīkh Miṣr*, 1: 386; Douin, *Le Khédive Ismaïl*, 2:394; Ghali, ed., *Mémoirs de Nubar Pacha*, 267.

of Egypt") was an Arabic-Muslim "literary" epitaph, and other Muslim rulers also addressed the governor of Egypt as such in the nineteenth century.[102] The demanded title of *ʿazīz* produced a serious echo in the European and the Ottoman press; some went so far as to claim that he had asked for the title of caliph![103]

Although it may seem only vanity on the part of Ismail, the new title was a crucial demand because it meant a new *rank* within the Ottoman hierarchy. Legally speaking, as a pasha, Ismail had a civil rank; as a *vali* he held a top position in the provincial hierarchy; and as a general and grand vizier he occupied an (empty) position within the Ottoman military system.[104] A new title encompassing a new rank would effectively maneuver him outside the traditional Ottoman hierarchies and would involve a new etiquette, language, chains of order, and, most important, a further step towards legal sovereignty. Furthermore, the suggested title *ʿazīz* would have made a close connection between the ruler, Egypt, and religion. Given the Koranic origin, in Egypt this arrangement would have represented an almost "covenantal" type of symbolism.[105] Similar to the increasingly independent European provinces, the governorship of Egypt could have changed into a symbolic recognition of identity between geography and the governor's power by the title *ʿazīz*. Despite Ismail's cautiously emphasizing his determination to remain within the empire,[106] the new designation would have effectively made the governor not a representative of the empire in the province but rather the province's representative to the empire.

The Ottoman imperial elite understood what is at stake. They also feared that the reigning sultan's name (ʿAbd al-ʿAzīz, Abdülaziz) could have been read in Arabic as the "servant" (*ʿabd*) of *ʿAzīz* Ismail. Grand Vizier Fuad Pasha thus plainly refused the new title in January 1867.

Khedive and Khedivate, 1867

European diplomats and Arab intellectuals helped. Nubar, the negotiator of Ismail, suggested using the foreign ambassadors in Istanbul to bring increasing pressure on the Ottoman leadership.[107] The leading French diplomat, Outrey, supported Ismail's demands, while the Russian ambassador, Ignatieff, remained neutral (which later paid off in secret negotiations

102 Deny, *Sommaire*, 77–78.
103 *Levant Herald*, 4 March 1867, 2; 23 April 1867, 3–4.
104 See the Arabic translation of the firman in *al-Jawāʾib*, 11 March 1863, 1.
105 Smith, *Chosen Peoples*; and idem, *The Cultural Foundations of Nations*.
106 Douin, *Le Khédive Ismaïl*, 1:425–426.
107 Ghali, ed., *Mémoirs de Nubar Pacha*, 269.

between Russia and Egypt).[108] There was again the support of *al-Jawāʾib* in Arabic. For instance, on February 5, 1867, the title page contained a long ode to Ismail.[109] In Egypt, al-Ṭahṭāwī and others continued to write poems of praise that were reprinted in *al-Jawāʾib* in March 1867.[110] In addition, the imperial administration had to engage with Ismail's demands because he had helped to crush the revolt of a tribal leader in Arabia,[111] and had also dispatched Egyptian soldiers to the Cretan War, soldiers the pasha threatened to withdraw in case of further opposition. Finally, the grand vizier offered a number of alternatives, and Nubar chose "khedive."[112] Ismail agreed only at the last moment (perhaps also upon the news about the expected return of Mustafa Fazıl to Istanbul).[113]

Khidīwī in Arabic (*hidiv* in Turkish, *khudaywī* in Egyptian Arabic)[114] is one example of how Arabic used Ottoman terms to address incumbents of power. *Khidew* is a Persian word meaning "king, lord, great prince," and was used in the Ottoman hierarchy as a title of ministers (viziers) and the grand vizier among other Persian titles, such as *dāwar(ī)* ("prince, lord").[115] Nubar should have known that Mehmed Ali's chancellery was already called *dīwān-i khidīwī*, his entourage *maʿiyya khidīwiyya*, and his first official newsletter *Jūrnāl-i Khidīwī*. This title had also been used publically in the Arabic journals in the 1850s and 1860s.[116] Despite the official change, the colloquial Egyptian term for the khedive remained *efendīnā* ("our master"), while the military and official correspondence still often called the governor with the Ottoman epitaph *dhāt-i walā-i walī-niʿmet* ("the supreme ruling benefactor").

The firman dated 8 June 1867, granted the Ottoman title of *Hidiv-i Mısır* to Ismail officially, and his privileges were reaffirmed in 1873. He and his descendants could exclusively use this title,[117] although *ʿAzīz Miṣr* also remained among the customary salutations of the Egyptian rulers up to the twentieth century. European journalists in Istanbul at the time

[108] Butler, *Court Life*, 208–209.

[109] *Al-Jawāʾib*, 5 February 1867, 1–2.

[110] *Al-Jawāʾib*, 26 March 1867, 3.

[111] Al-Rāfiʿī, *ʿAṣr Ismāʿīl*, 1:203

[112] Ghali, ed., *Mémoirs de Nubar Pacha*, 301.

[113] Douin, *Le Khédive Ismail*, 1:426–427. Sammarco, *Histoire de l'Égypte Moderne*, 3: 431–435 (appendix, French translation from the Ottoman Turkish original).

[114] Jean Deny suggests that we should make a distinction between the use of "khedive" before and after 1867. Deny, *Sommaire*, 73.

[115] Deny, *Sommaire*, 69–74. Cf. also Meynard, *Dictionnaire Turc-Français*, 1:691; Ihsanoğlu and Ṣāliḥ, *Al-Thaqāfa al-Turkiyya fī Miṣr*, 358. Sammarco says that the sultans were also addressed by this title, *Histoire de l'Égypte Moderne*, 3:165, n. 2; also Deny, *Sommaire*, 72. However, such a rank never existed in the Ottoman hierarchy. EI2, s.v. "khidīw" [khedive] (P. J. Vatikiotis).

[116] Cf. *Ḥadīqat al-Akhbār*, and *al-Jawāʾib*, 8 May 1866, 1. *Al-Jawāʾib*, 5 February 1867, 1–2.

[117] I owe this observation to Khaled Fahmy.

thought that khedive/khédive, as the word became to be used in English and French, respectively, should be translated as "king."[118] The title also meant the changing of Egypt's legal status from a *vilayet* to a "grand khedivate" (in Ottoman Turkish *hidiviyet-i celile-i Mısrıye*) because it was a new rank (*valilik* changed to *hidivlik*). The main body of the firman addressed the further legal changes that the title included: rights to design the internal legislation of Egypt, to make agreements with foreigners (especially contracting loans), in addition to customs, post, and police privileges, but "always observing the treaties of my [Ottoman] empire in their *status quo*."[119] The khedivate became a distinguished dynastic governorship within the Ottoman Empire.

Patriotism as Compromise: *al-Mamlaka al-Ismāʿīliyya*

It is against Ismail's Ottoman political background that we have to understand the development of patriotism in the province in the 1860s. How did local intellectuals and notables translate and understand the legal changes? What was the khedivate in their eyes? Ismail needed the local elites, too, to support him against the pretenders Mustafa Fazıl and Abdülhalim, to pacify revolting peasants, and to agree to more taxation. In 1864, a huge uprising by bandits and peasants started in Upper Egypt which was cruelly suppressed.[120] The 1866 and 1867 firmans were advantageous moments for intellectuals and rural men of distinction to reaffirm their loyalty and to attempt bridging *zevat* and *aʿyān* worlds by formulating public patriotism. At this moment, their ideology was more "Muslim patriotism" than "Arab": the Koranic history of Egypt supplied concepts to be mixed with political territoriality and dynastic praise.

"Ismail's Empire" and Communal Experiences in Ottoman Egypt[121]

The imperial developments must be contextualized within the renewal of Egyptian military might. In 1865–1866 Ismail's army occupied parts

[118] *Levant Herald*, 25 June 1867, 3.

[119] I.MTZ (05), 20/839, BOA. The originals are reproduced in Budak et al., eds., *Osmanlı Belgerelerinde Mısır*, 124–127. The subsequent translations do not give the document in full. *Levant Herald*, 9 August 1867, 3 gives the first English translation; Douin, *Le Khédive Ismail*, 1:442–443 republishes the French translation of the French embassy in Istanbul; Sammarco, *Histoire de l'Égypte Moderne*, 3:359–360 (appendix), also provides a French translation.

[120] Abul-Magd, *Imagined Empires*, 109–114.

[121] The examples in this section come from a much more detailed analysis in Mestyan, "The Just Prince and the Nation," under review.

of Africa's Red Sea coast (Musawwaʿ, Sawākin) successfully, and these port-cities were given to the governor in the 1866 firman. In fact, when that firman was issued in Istanbul in late May, people discussed rumours in the streets of the Lower Egyptian cities about Ismail's future rule of the Ḥijāz and Ottoman Syria, similarly to his grandfather.[122] Ismail indeed ruled the Sudan, parts of Ethiopia, possessed the island of Taşoz in the Mediterranean, and in the near future would venture into more conquests to build what royalist historians dubbed his "African empire."

In the summer of 1866, there was an official, concentrated effort to frame the change in the succession order as the beginning of a new age in late Ottoman Egypt. The powerful men in the administration, especially provincial governors and inspectors, organized balls, receptions, dinners, celebrations all around the country. During these occasions, Muslim sheikhs, muftis, new efendis, local merchants, *aʿyān*, and diplomats gave numerous speeches and expressions of praise. In these speeches and poems, Egypt as a homeland was identified with Ismail, and everyone celebrated his "success" in bringing about progress and justice.

A crucial figure in these celebrations was Ismāʿīl Ṣiddīq, the foster-brother of Ismail, popularly nicknamed *al-mufattish* because he was the "inspector" of Lower Egypt in the mid-1860s. He had steadily risen through the ranks since the early 1850s, and was trusted by Said; with Ismail as governor he received extra powers and extra gifts of land.[123] During the celebrations of 1866, Ṣiddīq invited Egyptian Arab poets, musicians, and female singers, among them the later-legendary female singer Almaẓ (also written as Almāẓ; d. 1879), to celebrate the new regime in the cities of the Delta, especially in Tanta. He also involved the Egyptian local notables. Some of them, such as Sulaymān Abāẓa of the village of Sharīfa, also invited the singer-dancers Almāẓ and Sakīna for entertainment.[124] Ismāʿīl "al-Mufattish" was the mastermind behind the legitimization of khedivial power in Arabic.

The 1866 summer banquets organized by *zevat* administrators for the *aʿyān* exemplify the physical reality and conceptual difficulty of making sense of the Ottoman legitimation of Ismail's power in Arabic while proposing the idea of the homeland as a common ground. There also occurred a renegotiation of the land tax since the pasha was pressed by

[122] Letter dated 7 Muḥarram 1283 (22 May 1866) from Ismāʿīl Ṣiddīq, 38/29, MST, Microfilm 197, DWQ.

[123] ʿAbd al-Raḥmān, *Ismāʿīl Ṣiddīq*, 66.

[124] Undated letter (around 21 Muḥarram 1283/ 5 June 1866), from Ismāʿīl Ṣiddīq, 111/38, microfilm 197, MST, DWQ. The two singers later were associated with the court of the Pasha and became legendary. It also seems that there were two Almases (or Almāẓ) in the 1860s; one was the famous singer and the other one a beautiful dancer in Upper Egypt; at least according to [Gallini Fahmī], *Mudhakkirāt*, 1: 32.

Said's debts and his own. The cotton boom was not enough to pay for everything, but it was enough to help the notion of capitalism appear in the texts of the time. The imagined community during the celebrations, as felt and constituted through physical togetherness, was also a community of administration and business.

Praise, the Homeland, and Compromise in 1866

A remarkable book contains the poems that were read aloud during these banquets. Sheikh Muṣṭafā Salāma's *A Collection of Beautiful Praise for the Just Prince Ismail* includes texts from the important Egyptian *literati* of the time: Rifāʿa al-Ṭahṭāwī, Abū al-Suʿūd, ʿAlī al-Laythī, Ibrāhīm al-Muwayliḥī, Muḥammad (Jalāl) ʿUthmān, Ṣāliḥ Majdī, Maḥmūd (Sāmī) al-Bārūdī, Muṣṭafā Salāma himself, and many others. Short poems also arrived from less famous countryside judges, teachers in governmental schools, *aʿyān*, and sheiks. Muṣṭafā Salāma (al-Najjārī, d. 1870) was one of the poets who praised Said Pasha extensively in the late 1850s; he also wrote a unique historical text for Ismail in 1863;[125] now in 1866 he was appointed an editor of the Arabic version of the renewed state bulletin, *al-Waqāʾiʿ al-Miṣriyya*.[126] The precursor of these poems is Ṣāliḥ Majdī's praise of Ismail, when he had only been the heir presumptive, for instance in the tribute of 1861.[127]

I argue that though the 1866 celebration was an invited contribution, intellectuals and *aʿyān* did bring their own political vision and vocabulary. The whole book was composed to commemorate what Sheikh Muṣṭafā calls "the Ismailite Kingdom" (*al-Mamlaka al-Ismāʿīliyya*). More than just a collection of panegyrics, the volume embodied various elements of patriotism. First, its title is a chronogram, a literary tool of establishing the *hijrī* year of 1283 (1866).[128] We have already seen this poetical technique in the way Syrian Christians praised Ibrahim in the 1830s. The fact that the title celebrating the new succession order is a year frames that order as a new age.

The book shrewdly depicts the relation of Ismail and the people (*ahl al-waṭan*) as a relation of joy and mutual responsibility. The poems represent, according to some of the poets, the Egyptians as a people. For instance, Sheikh Khalīl al-ʿAzzāzī[129] considers himself and his poem as speaking "in the representation of the people in our Sharqiyya province"

[125] Salāma, *Qiṭʿa min Rawḍ*, manuscript 2389 Tārīkh Taymūr, Egyptian National Library. I am in the process of preparing a publication of this manuscript.

[126] Sadgrove, "The Development of the Arabic Periodical Press," 72.

[127] Majdī, *Dīwān*, 38.

[128] EI2, s.v. "ʿIlm al-Jummal," "Taʾrīkh."

[129] He was an Azharite sheikh and Sufi leader, Hatina, *ʿUlamaʾ*, 60; 67.

(*bi-l-niyāba ʿan ahl wilāyatinā al-Sharqiyya*).[130] The translator ʿAlī Fahmī believes that dynastic praise is "a patriotic service" (*khidma waṭaniyya*).[131] There may have been sceptics such as the translator Muḥammad ʿUthmān [Jalāl], who wrote, with a (perhaps ironic) reference to the *de facto* absolutist rule, the following:

> I have served the homeland for twenty-five years / since I left the School of Languages/
> every time I had a new idea / and I revealed the arbours of my feelings /
> I saw them being concealed in the cautiousness of mannerism [*ḥidhr al-takalluf*] / and they disappeared in the secret of inappropriate language [or oppression, *al-taʿassuf*]
> . . .
> but God sent Ismail from the branch of Ibrahim / made him and his family the heir of sovereignty [*mulk*] generation after generation / . . . and my conditions and compositions improved.[132]

The panegyrics express loyalty but can be read in other ways. For instance, the poet Sheikh ʿAlī al-Laythī in his rhymed prose repeats that the change was the grace of the caliph and that his politics aimed at the progress of the homeland (*taqaddum al-waṭan*), possibly meaning the empire.[133] This was either a gentle reminder that, despite the privileges, Ismail was still the subject of the sultan, or in fact an acknowledgment that Egypt was still ruled by the empire. The poems of provincial notables, such as (Sulaymān) Abāẓa Bey (later Pasha),[134] who was at this time an inspector in the private estates of Ismail, formulated the khedivate before its official codification with terms such as *al-quṭr al-khidīwī*, "the khedivial country."[135] These poems expressed (or had to express) both blessings and hope while navigating between Ottoman loyalty and sovereign claims.

While the role of Ismāʿīl Ṣiddīq remains unclear in soliciting praise from rural *aʿyān*, the role of courtiers can be known. For instance, the notables of Upper Egypt submitted a congratulatory letter to Ismail. The first line, in fact, thanks the Ottoman sultan for the privileges. The letter then expresses patriotic statements, such as "our excessive love for our homeland celebrates you" because Ismail "loves the good and useful

130 [Al-Najjārī], *Majmūʿ*, 25. One of the seven administrative units in Lower Egypt was Sharqiyya with Zaqāzīq as its capital.

131 [Al-Najjārī], *Majmūʿ*, 38.

132 [Al-Najjārī], *Majmūʿ*,18–19.

133 [Al-Najjārī], *Majmūʿ*, 13–14.

134 Hunter, *Egypt under the Khedives*, table 12, 94–95.

135 [Al-Najjārī], *Majmūʿ*, 22.

causes and all of the elite and the ordinary." Yet the letter was composed by ʿAbd Allāh Fikrī, the personal secretary of Ismail, who was asked by the rural notables to help them.[136] In this way, praise circulated: Fikrī wrote in the name of others what he thought the pasha might be pleased with and he may have updated it with his understanding of patriotism. As to Ismāʿīl Ṣiddīq, he was promoted to the general supervisor of both Lower and Upper Egypt immediately after the celebrations.

This unprecedented Egypt-wide production of loyal patriotic expressions reached back to earlier Muslim traditions of talking to the ruler. In many ways, these "invited" poems, speeches, and banquets, which manipulated power as much as promoted the idea of the homeland, became the representation of a new elite political community.

Compromise Embodied: The Consultative Chamber

There were material and legal changes in the status of Egyptian rural notables and bureaucrat-intellectuals in addition to the ideological ones. These mostly included land donations and changes in landowning laws and participation in the administration. Ismail, continuing Said's practice, donated land not only to the *zevat* but also to the *aʿyān* and the few high-ranking efendis, such as ʿAlī Mubārak or al-Ṭahṭāwī, while legal changes also included the participation of civil employees in government-run land sales.[137] This land policy brought some Egyptians close to the Ottoman *zevat*, such as the village notable turned district governor Muḥammad Sulṭān, who became very rich.[138] In fact, in asking for salary raise, Egyptian employees often added in the 1860s that instead they would also accept a few feddans of land.

Law and ideology was institutionalized in an advisory board of legislative functions, the Consultative Chamber of Delegates (*Majlis Shūrā al-Nuwwāb*), in the autumn of 1866, which is often looked upon as a forerunner of a parliament.[139] Ismail, in his order to establish this institution, referred to the beneficial function of the parliament (*majlis al-shūrā*) "in civilized countries."[140] The Chamber contained locally elected rural notables, *ʿumad* and *aʿyān*. Abbas and El-Dessouky consider this representative institution "more like a grant from the khedive to the *aʿyān* than

[136] Fikrī, ed. *Al-Āthār al-Fikriyya*, 203–204.

[137] Abbas and El-Dessouky, *The Large Landowning Class*, 62–63; 64–68.

[138] Hunter, *Egypt under the Khedives*, see tables 19 and 20 about positions and landholdings of Sultan Pasha.

[139] Hunter, *Egypt under the Khedives*, 52.

[140] See the text in Arabic in letter dated 12 Jumādā al-Akhīra 1283 (22 October 1866), to Taftīsh al-Aqālīm, MSA, Microfilm 23, DWQ.

something gained through struggle."[141] Hunter lists and expands the reasons given for its establishment: to check the influence of the Turkish officials, to control the *aʿyān* more closely, that Ismail regarded the Chamber as a means to strengthen Egypt's credit in the eyes of Europeans, to legitimize his land policy, and to help in the administration.[142] It was, I argue, a key political institution of selected local notables and could be regarded as the fulfillment of the negotiation for acknowledgment of the dynastic order and of the new taxes.

Before the establishment of this chamber, possibly encouraged by the celebrations in June 1866 and by Ismāʿīl Ṣiddīq, a number of petitions arrived from the *aʿyān*. For example, Ḥasanayn Ḥamza, a village head and merchant from the Buḥayra district, submitted a very long letter in July 1866 asking for "the complete rights of the homeland" (*wafī ḥuqūq al-waṭan*). He asked for a wholesale reform of Egypt, which he outlined in eight points. He starts with agriculture and suggests that the government should help the peasants in paying their loans; next comes the distribution of lands and workers; then the making and maintenance of canals. Ḥasanayn points out that the engineer and the director of the directorate (both sent from Cairo) do not know what is good for the land—thus the work of cleaning the canals is badly organized; he emphasizes the importance of new agricultural machines; and the establishment of a new state company in which "every subject could participate as a subscriber" (he even makes detailed calculations for the capital needed [*rāʾsmāl*]). He makes explicit the problem that the peasants invest in gold and silver instead of keeping banknotes in villages. Ḥasanayn also requests the establishment of charity houses for the poor and the better distribution of the yearly charity alms (*zakāt*). He requests the granting of extra land and mines to his village, and his final and most important demand is a train line. He offers that the village should pay for it.[143] It should be not a surprise that he was among the first deputies of the Consultative Chamber.

In sum, the change at the imperial level made compromise possible within the province. Along with the festivities, the poems, and the petitions, the Chamber represents a step toward a potential compromise between governor and local elites to share power. One sign of this is that Ismail's inauguration speech on November 25, 1866, was in Arabic and did not mention the sultan. The Chamber met only three months a year, and there were years without any sessions. It could only proceed in matters assigned by the khedive, although the representatives could propose

[141] Abbas and El-Dessouky, *The Large Landowning Class*, 142–143.

[142] Hunter, *Egypt under the Khedives*, 53.

[143] "We pay for the expenses of the train-line" (yakūn takālīf al-sikka ʿalaynā). Letter dated 16 Rabīʿ al-Awwal 1283 (29 July 1866), from Ḥasanayn Ḥamza, 265/38, microfilm 198, MST, DWQ.

projects such as the creation of administrative councils in the countryside (which subsequently became the main power base of rural notables).[144] Later, for instance, in 1871, the phrase *Majlis al-Shūrā al-Waṭaniyya* ("National Consultative Chamber") was used in the (rhyming!) Arabic appointment letters of the "elected" notables, and in these letters particular emphasis was given to the advancement of the homeland.[145] Without a doubt, this institution did not diminish the absolute power of Ismail, but its creation was an important step in making patriotism the ideology of the khedivate.

Muslim Patriotism

I propose to call the ideological sum of the above discourses in 1860s Ottoman Egypt "Muslim patriotism." One may reasonably point out that religious universalism and patriotic particularism exclude each other. Rogers Brubaker, for instance, argues that religion (Islam) and nationalism are incompatible in their twentieth-century forms.[146] Such a logical contradiction, however, was not a problem for Ottoman Arab intellectuals in the nineteenth century.

This ideology was a complex one and occurred as part of Ismail's absolutist system. Here I proceed to explore the idea of the homeland as it became an organizing principle in al-Ṭahṭāwī's *The Paths of Egyptian Hearts in the Joys of the Contemporary Arts* (printed in 1869). Next, I show, through the example of the already quoted saying "the love of the homeland is part of faith," how Islam and the idea of homeland were made compatible at both the imperial level and in the Egyptian province. These are traces of a much wider process that I will further explore in the Second Part of this book.

Al-Ṭahṭāwī and Waṭan

The Paths of Egyptian Hearts was held up first by Albert Hourani as a "theory of politics."[147] However, as Charles Wendell pointedly remarks, it "was not a very veiled eulogy of the Muḥammad ʿAlī dynasty."[148] Crabbs

144 Hunter, *Egypt under the Khedives*, 54; Abbas and El-Dessouky, *The Large Landowning Class*, 143–144.

145 For instance, appointment letter of Maḥmūd al-Sayyid, ʿumdat nāḥiyat Qāw al-tābiʿa li-mudīriyyat Qanā, dated 26 Rabīʿ al-Awwal 1288 (15 June 1871), 138/48 (later in the film), MST, Microfilm 205, DWQ. ʿAbd Allāh Fikrī wrote the general formula of the appointment letter: Fikrī, ed. *Al-Āthār al-Fikriyya*, 73.

146 Brubaker, "Religion and Nationalism."

147 Hourani, *Arabic Thought in the Liberal Age*, 72–83.

148 Wendell, *The Evolution*, 129.

recognizes that this book is dedicated "in remembrance of this nation" and that al-Ṭahṭāwī quotes "a series of ardently patriotic poems."[149] Cole uses this book to characterize Ottoman constitutionalism and loyalty towards the khedivate, and he also discovers in al-Ṭahṭāwī's work, somewhat surprisingly, "a labour theory of value."[150] One must add that while the book is a significant achievement, nothing is known about its readership and reception. Yet the right context is the context of celebrations discussed above.

Al-Ṭahṭāwī uses the patriotic idea for political solidarity. The texts at the opening are presented to prove that patriotism has long been part of the Arabic-Islamic political tradition. The section about *ḥubb al-waṭan* "the love of the homeland" is a historical catalogue of *waṭan* in Muslim tradition and Arabic poetry. It starts with what the second caliph, ʿUmar ibn al-Khaṭṭāb, said about *waṭan*, continues with classical *ʿulamāʾ* and unnamed poets (it is easy to identify them, mostly Abbasid ones). Al-Ṭahṭāwī highlights the mountain tribesman's attachment to his mountains and the settled (*ḥāḍir*) man's relation to his land, and then presents a story about the Umayyad caliph Muʿāwiya hearing a Bedouin's poem about his homeland. Next come poems from emirs, writers, kings, another ʿUmar ibn al-Khaṭṭāb story, a poem about Sicily (with the pointed reminder that it was once under Muslim rule), and the example of the Prophet Muḥammad himself.[151]

In addition to the poetical *waṭan*, there is a justification of monarchical power. Al-Ṭahṭāwī merges the sophisticated legacy of Muslim political thinking with French philosophy. He argues that "monarchical power (*al-quwa al-mulūkiyya*) is the condition of the laws because juridical power itself derives from the monarch (*malik*)."[152] He continues that "the ruler is the leader of his community" (*walī al-amr raʾīs ummatihi*)[153] but "[kings] have obligations for the right of the subjects," though this is not based on the principle of popular representation: because "one privilege of the king is that he is the representative (*khalīfa*) of God in his Earth . . . he is not responsible for his action to any of his subjects."[154] Given that the book was published in the official government press, there is no surprise that rulers have a distinguished place in this patriotic imagination of Muslim power.

[149] Crabbs, *The Writing of History*, 78.
[150] Cole, *Colonialism and Revolution*, 39–44.
[151] [al-Ṭahṭāwī], *Manāhij*, 7–11.
[152] [al-Ṭahṭāwī], *Manāhij*, 232.
[153] Ibid., 235.
[154] Ibid., 236.

Islam and the Patriotic Idea: "Love of the Homeland Is Part of Faith"

In the first pages of *The Paths of Egyptian Hearts*, al-Ṭahṭāwī mentions *ḥubb al-waṭan min al-īmān*, the already quoted tradition attributed to the Prophet Muḥammad: "love of the homeland is part of faith."[155] As we have seen, he had used this *ḥadīth* since the 1820s in various forms: part of a description, as part of *waṭaniyyāt*. Very possibly this slogan circulated in Ottoman intellectual circles as well. By the 1860s, it had become the main slogan of civic Ottoman patriotism with subtle references to constitutionalism. It is a unique clue in understanding the problem of patriotism in the caliphate and to explore the intellectual economy of the Ottoman Eastern Mediterranean.

The saying also appeared in Ottoman Beirut. The Protestant convert Buṭrus al-Bustānī (1819–1883), in his patriotic circulars during the autumn and winter of 1860 (after the massacres in the summer),[156] tells his readers that this tradition from the Prophet Muḥammad prescribes love as the first requirement of being a patriot (*waṭanī*).[157] He introduced the idea of patriot (*waṭanī*) that was to remain a keyword in the next decades in the Arabic press. Al-Bustānī's goal was to achieve a nonsectarian community whose members were connected with inseparable bonds like a family or the human body.[158] He may have meant by the word "family" the educated communities of Beirut, Mount Lebanon, or whole Ottoman Empire. The Ottoman network of Arabic patriotic neologisms connected al-Bustānī in Beirut and al-Ṭahṭāwī in Cairo. Local nation-ness was conditioned by the imperial context.

Although Lewis dismissed the *ḥadīth* as invented and, therefore, unimportant,[159] *ḥubb al-waṭan min al-īmān* had a past. The earliest occurrence is in the thirteenth century, as a fabricated, fictitious (*mawḍūʿ*) Prophetic tradition.[160] It seems that the *ḥadīth* was coined somewhere in the eastern, Persianate domains of Islam.[161] The origin was perhaps in Persian Sufi circles. For these mystics, *waṭan* meant "the heavenly

[155] Ibid., 7. Cf. also Crabbs, *The Writing of History*, 78; and Zachs, *The Making of a Syrian Identity*, 167–168, n. 44.

[156] Zachs, *The Making of a Syrian Identity*, 167.

[157] *Nafīr Sūriyya*, 25 October 1860.

[158] *Nafīr Sūriyya*, 22 April 1861.

[159] Lewis, "Watan," 525.

[160] Al-Ṣaghānī, *Mawḍūʿāt al-Ṣaghānī*, 47.

[161] Perhaps the invention of this ḥadīth was connected to *shuʿūbiyya*, but so far there is no evidence for such a connection.

kingdom."[162] One can also find a version of this sentence in an early fourteenth-century Arabic poem[163] and in a fourteenth-century chronicle, where this *ḥadīth* is uttered by an Ayyubid military commander (*amīr*) from Syria when he encourages an attack against the Egyptian Mamluks. According to the chronicler in this instance, its use meant "that he chose to enter Egypt in any case"—that is, that he was prepared to die for the *waṭan* (here possibly meaning glory as related to the notion of the afterlife in the heavenly kingdom).[164]

This potential was discovered by al-Ṭahṭāwī in Cairo, al-Bustānī in Beirut, and others in Istanbul and in Paris in the mid-nineteenth century. The organ of the Young Ottoman ideology, Namık Kemal's *Hürriyet* also discussed this very same *ḥadīth* in its first issue in 1868. The Young Ottoman group used *vatan* in Turkish in the widest, imperial sense.[165] For them, patriotism served the territoriality of the Ottoman Sunni caliphate, connected to the demand for a constitution.[166] In Egypt, ʿAlī Mubārak categorized the "love of the homeland" as the third type of relationship after love of God and obedience to superiors in an 1868 manual. He also quoted the Prophetic saying and explained that "it not only means that the love of the homeland is a portion, that is, a part of faith, but perhaps it is the faith as a whole and Islam in its entirety."[167]

Intellectuals attempted to make Islam and patriotism compatible through this *ḥadīth.*[168] It became the motto of the Bustānīs's journal *al-Jinān* in 1870 and figured in every single title page. In 1872, it was used to praise Ismail Pasha as a patriot.[169] In 1893, a version was used to praise his grandson Abbas Hilmi II, too[170] (see chapter 8). No wonder the eminent intellectual, the hero of the last chapter of this book, Muṣṭafā Kāmil placed *ḥubb al-waṭan min al-īmān* on the title page of the first issue of his journal *al-Liwāʾ* in the spring of 1900.[171] Even after World War One it became the slogan of the official journal of the short-lived kingdom of the Hijaz (*Barīd al-Ḥijāz*) in 1924. These occurrences reflect an age-old Muslim technique to bring spiritual agreement into materialist politics

[162] EI2, s.v. "Qawmiyya," III. (A.K.S. Lambton). In addition, Bahāʾ al-Dīn al-ʿĀmilī (1547–1621), says that the reader should not understand a city like Damascus or Baghdad by the word *waṭan* but the return to God. al-ʿĀmilī, *Kitāb al-Kashkūl*, 110.

[163] Al-Ṣafadī, *Aʿyān al-ʿAṣr*, 4:553 (W:832).

[164] Al-Ṣafadī, *al-Wāfī bi-l-Wafayāt*, 9:264–265 (W: 1325).

[165] *Hürriyet*, 29 June 1868, 1. Cf. Davison, *Reform in the Ottoman Empire*, 216–219; Campos, *Ottoman Brothers*; Şiviloğlu, "The Emergence of Public Opinion," 90–91.

[166] Davison, *Reform in the Ottoman Empire*, 56 and 195.

[167] Mubārak, *Kitāb Ṭarīq al-Hijāʾ*, 2: 74.

[168] Deringil, *The Well-Protected Domains*, 46–50.

[169] Al-Dasūqī, *Maqāla Shukriyya*, 3.

[170] Yūsuf, *Ayyām al-Janāb al-Khidīwī*, 2.

[171] *Al-Liwāʾ*, 4 April 1900, 1.

by deploying *ḥadīth*. It exemplifies the cultural function of Islam in the construction of political nation-ness.

The Transformation of Life: Arabic Music and Ottoman Power in the Khedivate

Seeing these ideas as part of a physical environment is crucial. Unisonality, through singing *waṭaniyyāt* in the army and reading aloud rhymed verses in Ottoman Arab cities, was an important element of patriotism. However, there was a deeper change that was equally important in creating new conditions of communal experiences. In the mid-century, learned Muslims focused on an art song associated with Muslim Andalusia, the *muwashshaḥ*, which was a genre of infusing poetry and music.[172] This was a dynamic reform of aural communities, a reuse of cultural memory, based on earlier transformations in Greater Syria.[173] The *muwashshaḥāt* had become popular among the Egyptian intelligentsia possibly as early as the late eighteenth century.[174] A collector of songs, the Sufi sheikh Shihāb al-Dīn al-Ḥijāzī defined melody (*laḥn*) as an instrument to create songs out of poetry in its seven genres.[175] From this refined reform-tradition hailed the singer ʿAbduh al-Ḥamūlī (also written as al-Ḥāmūlī; 1830s?–1901) who became the first representative of the Ottoman Egyptian patriotic culture. Like folk music for Greeks, *muwashshaḥ*-culture became a local, educated aural collective form of experiencing the past in Arabic. It became part of the official culture of the khedivate—after some Ottomanization.

The Ottomanization of ʿAbduh al-Ḥamūlī

The career of ʿAbduh al-Ḥamūlī exemplifies the relationship between Ottoman power and Arab music in Egypt. His life, though never explicitly political, connects the symbols of patriotism in the 1860s with the

172 al Faruqi, "Muwashshaḥ."

173 Mishāqa, *al-Risāla al-Shihābiyya*, 56; also Smith, "A Treatise on Arab Music," 212; Maalouf, "Mīkhāʾīl Mishāqā: Virtual Founder"; Gran, *Islamic Roots of Capitalism*, 106–110.

174 Rizq, *Al-Mūsīqā al-Sharqiyya*, 1:41.

175 Neubauer, "Arabic Writings on Music," 382, 369–371. Al-Ḥijāzī, *Safīnat al-Mulk* (1865; 1309), 7–8. It is likely that it is his book that was also advertised in Beirut under the title *Dīwān Shihāb al-Dīn* in 1872, or under the title *Kitāb al-Muwashshaḥāt* al-Andalusiyya. For instance, al-Jinān, back page advertisement "Qāyimat Kutub ṭabʿ Miṣr mawjūda fī-Maṭbaʿat al-Maʿārif," 17 Āb (August 1872), or 15 Ḥazīrān (June) 1872, back page. Faraj shows that such techniques occurred with poems in the colloquial, too. Farāj, "Al-Binya al-Mūsīqiyya wa-ʿAlāqātuhā bi-l-Naṣṣ al-Shiʿrī," 95–121.

increasingly nationalist ones of the 1890s. In royalist historiography and scholarship, he was compared to Verdi,[176] often put in the general context of the *nahḍa*,[177] paired with modernizing Arab poets,[178] and held to be one of the main personalities of the so-called musical *école khédiviale*[179] (the concept itself was derived from the interwar attempt to glorify the memory of Ismail.)[180] Today, ʿAbduh al-Ḥamūlī is often seen as a reformer of Egyptian Arab music, even paralleled with the reformer of Islam, Sheikh Muḥammad ʿAbduh.[181] It is striking that the later popularity of al-Ḥamūlī as the patriotic singer of Egypt in the 1880s and 1890s was made possible by cultural Ottomanization.

Al-Ḥamūlī hailed from the Delta, near Tanta, and was supposedly a pious Muslim. During the late 1850s his amazing voice was discovered, and he joined different *takhts* (Egyptian music ensembles) that performed in Tanta and in Cairo. At the beginning of the 1860s, he sang *muwashshaḥāt*.[182] His *takht* became the most famous one in Egypt.[183] He was summoned by Ismail, who attached him to his entourage. This is a curious event since it has been suggested that this pasha did not appreciate native Egyptian music,[184] yet he liked al-Hamūlī so much that, as an anecdote tells, he allowed him to sing publically *only* with his written permission.[185] There is no exact date of the singer's attachment to the circles of the khedive, but it occurred sometime between 1863 and 1869.[186] Since Ismāʿīl Ṣiddīq invited Almaẓ in 1866 in Tanta, it is possible that al-Ḥamūlī (later the husband of Almaẓ and from around Tanta)[187] was also discovered through Ṣiddīq's good offices.

Al-Ḥamūlī's voice contributed to the legitimation of khedivial power. We first meet al-Ḥamūlī among the performers at the wedding ceremonies

[176] "Fardī," *al-Muqtaṭaf*, 1 March 1901, 193–198, at 197. Cf. Bachmann, "Zwei arabische Verdi-Würdigungen"; Locke, "Beyond the exotic."

[177] Akel, "Hamouli."

[178] Lagrange, "Poètes, intellectuels et musiciens."

[179] Lagrange, "Musiciens et poètes," 64.

[180] Moussali, "L'école khediviale," 175–185. Rizq, *Al-Mūsīqā al-Sharqiyya*, 1:40–51, the personal testimony of Khalīl Bey Muṭrān in vol. 2, 133–142, an anecdote 166–167, his renewal of Arab music, vol. 3: 137–150, another anecdote, vol. 3: 162, ʿAbduh in Istanbul vol. 3: 170, anecdotes vol. 4: 94–100, his marriage with Almaẓ, 105–108. Lagrange, "Musiciens et poètes," 67–71.

[181] Abou Mrad, "L'imam et le chanteur."

[182] Lagrange, "Musiciens et poètes," 67.

[183] Ibid., 68.

[184] Farmer, "Egyptian music: Modern Egypt," quoted in Katz, *Henry George Farmer*, 104, n. 51.

[185] Lagrange, "Musiciens et poètes," 68.

[186] Ibid., 68; Rizq, *Al-Mūsīqā al-Sharqiyya*, 1:49.

[187] Rizq, *Al-Mūsīqā al-Sharqiyya*, 1:66.

of Ismail's daughter, Tevhide Hanım, to Mansur Pasha, in April 1869. The music was continuous: a *takht* composed of al-Laysī [!], al-Ḥamūlī, and al-Qaftānjī (they were his group of musicians) performed in tandem with the female *ʿawālim*, the music group of "Almās" (Almaẓ) and Sakīna (they were also the singers employed by Ismāʿīl Ṣiddīq in 1866). There were also European entertainers. However, an indication of the Ottoman taste is that during this wedding the greatest star was the Turkish Mehmed Şukri, a *ḥāwī* (magician).[188]

The Ottomanization of al-Ḥamūlī occurred through direct contact with the imperial center. He was sent to Istanbul,[189] perhaps numerous times,[190] and also accompanied Ismail on some of his European travels. According to one anecdote, he performed even in the Conservatory of Vienna.[191] The Egyptian singer did not wear an Arab *gilbāb* anymore, but took on an Ottoman *tarbūsh* with a European suit.[192] He presumably translated Turkish songs into Arab and specifically Egyptian musical modalities. His Istanbul stays are mysterious because in fact he did not need to go to Istanbul to study Turkish music since Cairo was full of Ottoman musicians.[193] Al-Ḥamūlī also sang for Abdülhamid II in 1894, but at that occasion, instead of al-Ḥamūlī studying Ottoman music, on the contrary, the sultan ordered one of his own musicians to learn the Egyptian tunes.[194]

The singer became known as the "nightingale of weddings" (*bulbul al-afrāḥ*) in the Arabic press because of his popularity at elite weddings (possibly since Tevhide's in 1869). He usually sang at the weddings of government-associated *zevat* and *aʿyān*'s children.[195] He himself was married first to Almaẓ and, after her death in 1879, he married four more times.[196] His involvement with the khedive, his Ottomanization, made it possible that al-Ḥamūlī was later able to captivate *zevat*, *aʿyān*, and the ordinary people in the 1880s and 1890s (see the last section of this book).

188 *Al-Waqāʾiʿ al-Miṣriyya*, 31 March 1869, 2–3 and *Wādī al-Nīl*, 23 April 1869, 11–12.

189 ʿAbduh was at the head of a "musicians'" mission to Istanbul, which was put together by Hüseyn Kamel (the future Sultan of Egypt). Lagrange, "Musiciens et poètes," 70. It is not clear if al-Ḥamūlī studied in Istanbul (Akel, "Hamouli," 80) or entertained the sultan (and if so, which one?).

190 Lagrange, "Musiciens et poètes," 70.

191 Ibid., 68.

192 Ibid., 68. Rizq, *Al-Mūsīqā al-Sharqiyya*, 1:42–43.

193 Belleface, "Turāth, classicisme et variétés"; Moussali, "l'école khediviale," 175–176.

194 *Al-Ahrām*, 25 September 1894, 3.

195 *Egyptian Gazette*, 22 February 1895, 2.

196 Several letters from 1879, dated 18 Rabiʿ al-Thānī 1296 (11 April 1879), 3002-004512, DWQ, establish the fact that she died on 11 Muḥarram 1296 which is 5 January 1879. Of their love, a famous fictional Egyptian movie was shot in 1950s.

The Soundscape of Zevat *Spaces as an Obstacle to Elite Localization*

Al-Ḥamūlī's association with the entourage of Ismail is curious since the general soundscape of *zevat* culture was high Ottoman in the 1860s. The harem listened to Ottoman Turkish art music.[197] Said nominated the Ottoman Armenian Aleksan as his official lute player, and another Turkish musician, a certain Ali Bey, was also cherished in the entourage.[198] Even the *kānūnci* of Sultan Abdülaziz, Nukhla Matarcı, performed in Cairo.[199] Members of the ruling family literally loved Turkish musicians: Ismail's cousin, Zahra, married the composer Ali Rifaat Catagay, and after his death, the singer Nedim in Istanbul.[200] There were non-Ottoman but non-European musicians too, for instance, Said possessed a special band of thirty-eight Sudanese musician-soldiers, in addition to the ninety-six person "European" military music band.[201]

Zevat culture was Ismail and his mother Hoşyar's private world. This Ottoman culture in her palace, where a thousand slave girls are rumoured to have served,[202] can be seen in the poems of the slave-girl Gülperi who was raised in that palace.[203] Hoşyar had a *yalı* (summer residence) in Istanbul, too.[204] She also possessed a musical troupe of slave-girls who performed Ottoman music. Ismail could talk to his mother only in Turkish or in her Circassan language, and in her palace he was often entertained by Ottoman music; Gülperi also wrote (or had to write) Ottoman Turkish panegyrics about Ismail.[205] The pasha dressed in Ottoman clothes in his private rooms.[206] It seems that "being Ottoman" was not only a political

[197] Under "Ottoman Turkish music," we have to distinguish between a highly refined tradition usually related to the sultan's household ("classical Turkish music," or "Ottoman art music"), religious (Sufi—Mevlevi) music, Ottoman military (janissary, mehter) music, and coffeehouse/gazino/meyhane-music (a secular urban entertainment which often included Italian or French songs too). Bates, *Music in Turkey*, 31–32; 46–48; Shiloah, *Music in the World of Islam*, 90–93; Ayangil, "Turkish Music in the Seventeenth Century," *The Turks*, 4:79–88. In general, cf. *New Grove*, s. v. "Turkey," 19:268–278.

[198] Moussali, "L'école khediviale," 175–176.

[199] Rizq, *al-Mūsīqā al-Sharqiyya*, 1:46.

[200] Moussali, "L'école khediviale," 176.

[201] Jarīdat istiḥqāqāt firqat al-mūzīqa wa- wujāq al-mūzīqiyya al-sūdāniyya tawallī 1863 muwāfiq 1279 (they were also paid in 1862); 2002–003402, DWQ.

[202] Shafīq, *Mudhakkirātī*, 1: 86. During the rule of Ismail, a notable, Muḥammad Sayyid Aḥmad Pasha, owned thirty black and thirty white slave-girls in addition to other male slaves. [Ṣidqī], *Mudhakkirāt*, 6.

[203] İhsanoğlu, *The Turks in Egypt*, 74–79.

[204] Cf. letters dated 29 Dhū al-Ḥijja 1280 (5 June 1864) (in the catalogue the date 1281 is wrong), 7828 0001–00012, TS. MA.d, BOA.

[205] İhsanoğlu, *The Turks in Egypt*, 74–79.

[206] Lott, *The English Governess*, 79.

device but also the everyday, private culture of Ismail. This milieu was not favorable to the use of Arabic entertainment for patriotic experience since there was a discrepancy between high Ottoman language and music on the one hand, and colloquial Arabic songs and mimetic entertainment on the other. As we shall see, there were two strategies to bridge this gap.

The Fear of Death: Abdülhalim, Mustafa Riyaz, and Freemasonry

Before concluding, it is worth noting that, according to Nubar, Ismail "did not like to think about his death."[207] This fear remained despite the victory of Ismail's household. He struck a deal with Mustafa Fazıl in December 1866 to buy all property in Egypt belonging to him, his wife and children, and slaves (*mamālīk*) for 2,000,8000 "lira sterling."[208] Tevfik later reported that his father had "lived in terror of his life and would never allow a stranger or a native to come near him," and after 1866 had Tevfik, the new official heir, watched day and night.[209]

Abdülhalim was now the main challenger in possible cooperation with an important reform-minded *zevat* pasha, Mustafa Riyaz (1834–1911, see more on him in chapter 5). They were involved in freemasonry in 1860s Egypt. Abdülhalim was the representative (president?) of the English freemason grand lodge of *York* in Egypt. Encouraged by his new French secretary, the Marquis de Tard (his real name was Antoine August Papon), Abdülhalim designed a plan to unite all lodges in Egypt in a giant lodge under his presidency. He had a conversation with a certain Dauphin, the president of a French lodge *Les Pyramides* in Alexandria, and Figari Bey, freemason of the Scottish lodge *N. 166*, and secretary of Ismail, sometime in early 1868 in the gardens of the Shubra Palace. He told them that he wanted to use the freemasons for "awakening the people and to change the government," as the French consul wrote in his report. Although Dauphin and Figari showed some enthusiasm, both lodges finally declined to give any support.[210]

Abdülhalim was soon exiled. At the end of the summer in 1868, letters between an Irish mercenary in the Ottoman army and Abdülhalim were intercepted. At this point, Ismail forced his uncle to leave Egypt, and a

[207] Ghali, ed., *Mémoirs de Nubar*, 265.

[208] Letter dated ghāyat Rajab 1283 (December 1866), Qayd 1919, p. 88, and pp. 89 and 107 for the text of the contract, Microfilm 27, MSA, DWQ.

[209] Butler, *Court Life in Egypt*, 204–206.

[210] Letter dated 7 October 1868, from E. Ponjade (consul) to Marquis de Moustier, and undated letter from A. Dobignie (?) to Consul General, and attachments, all in 166PO/D25/70, MEAN.

court was secretly organized in the imperial capital to judge the case. In his note before leaving, Abdülhalim pointedly reminded Ismail that they were both subjects of the sultan and Istanbul was their "shared shelter."[211]

Abdülhalim wanted to achieve political change through patriotic culture. The son of a close supporter of his, Mehmed Arif (or Arifi) Pasha established a Society for Education (*Jamʿiyyat al-Maʿārif*) by buying a printing press in 1868 and publishing a number of *adab* works. Among the society members we find Riyaz, the al-Muwayliḥīs, some members of *Shūrā al-Nuwwāb* (for instance, Ḥasanayn Ḥamza), and Khalīl Yeğen Pasha. The nominal president was Tevfik, son of Ismail. However, in 1869 the society ceased to work and Arif Pasha had to flee to Istanbul because of his association with Abdülhalim.[212] One must note that before the establishment of the society, Riyaz had a huge argument with Khedive Ismail about corruption and was dismissed from his government position in February 1868 (only to be reinstated after eight months).[213] As we shall see, Riyaz and the Yeğen brothers would remain main supporters of reforms and of the claim by "Prince Halim" to Egypt. While the society is celebrated as a literary milestone,[214] its connection through Arif Pasha to Abdülhalim's plans makes it rather a political (and business) enterprise. Ismail finally signed an agreement with Abdülhalim in 1870 in which the latter renounced any claim to the "throne," in exchange of a yearly 60,000 British pounds, paid for forty years.[215] Such was the price of Ismail's khedivate.

Conclusion: A Dinner in Istanbul

It is possible to see the imperial codification of the khedivate and the local unwritten compromise as the end of a process that started with Mehmed Ali. The governors looked for a solution that would secure their position between empire and province, but they could not fully trust either of these parties. Some local Muslim intellectuals, for their part, had made an

211 See the attached copies to the letter of the French consul to the French foreign minister, in a copy addressed to the French ambassador in Istanbul, dated 7 October 1866, 166PO/D25/70, MEAN.

212 Al-Rāfiʿī, *ʿAṣr Ismāʿīl*, 1: 242–244. In another version, he fled from his accumulated debts. Goldziher, "Jelentés," 28.

213 Hunter, *Egypt under the Khedives*, 162–163.

214 DeYoung, *Mahmud Sami al-Barudi*, 188.

215 Contract dated 11 July 1870 (10 Rabīʿ al-Ākhir 1287), referred to in undated note (possibly 1920s), from Muhammad Emad Eddine, wakīl of Said Halim Pasha, to Votre Altesse (?), in 0069–026857, DWQ. The Law of Liquidation in 1881 changed this arrangement.

effort to accept the governors ever since the 1820s. This process came to an end in 1866–1867 when, it seemed, a new age would start.

One can also see the codification of the khedivate as the beginning of a new process. Ismail and selected elites crafted a form of political compromise, as in so many other monarchies, including the Ottoman European provinces, such as Greece, Serbia, or Romania in the 1860s. But unlike in those territories, the quest for the rights given to Egypt was not initiated by local elites. In Egypt, the legal changes were achieved by one household within a localized Ottoman ruling family. There is no information about how Ismail received the patriotic poems, essays, and songs in which he was framed in Arabic. In these texts, the empire recedes into the background, and in its place, Arabness appears. Why did it not work? This is the subject of the following chapters, but a partial answer can already be given: Ismail's Ottoman elite environment prevented the governor from fully accepting his part of the compromise. He would not become an Egyptian.

Look briefly at a moment in the summer of 1867, when tensions were high between Istanbul- and Cairo-based Ottoman elites. In that summer, both the sultan and the new khedive traveled to Paris in June 1867 to attend the Universal Exhibition. The trips were carefully organized so that the two would not meet. A third protagonist, Mustafa Fazıl, hastily left Paris as Ismail approached.[216] Yet, not long after these travels, the khedive dined at his supposed cousin's palace in September 1867 in the Ottoman capital. The press reported that Abdülaziz and Ismail ate together in a most friendly atmosphere. At the same time, Hoşyar threw a dinner in her own palace in the shores of the Bosporus in honor of her supposed sister, Pertevniyal. The *valide sultan* returned the hospitality with an invitation of Ismail's mother to the Dolmabahçe Palace.[217] Thus mother and son reassured the sultan's family that Egypt as a khedivate would remain within the orbit of the Ottoman Empire.

The irreconcilable tension was that the khedivate was not an independent monarchy like post-Ottoman Serbia but continued to be part of the imperial system while aesthetically, and increasingly legally, was represented as sovereign for European audiences. This representation, and the role of Europe, are the subject of the next chapter.

[216] *La Presse*, 15 June 1867, 2.
[217] *Levant Herald*, 9 September 1867, 1.

CHAPTER 3

The European Aesthetics of Khedivial Power

On November 1, 1869, the curtain—emblazoned with images of Ismail Pasha and the French Empress Eugénie—rose in the new Opera House in Cairo. The audience saw yet another image of the ruler: on stage was a bust of Ismail. It was surrounded by eight singers, in costumes, representing eight allegories: Justice, Mercy, Fame, Music (Mélodie), History, Agriculture, Industry, and Commerce. The singers performed a cantata, an Italian ode set to music by Prince Joseph Poniatovski. This work by Napoleon III's favorite musical aristocrat was received with cheers and the shouting of Ismail's name. After immortalizing the khedive in this imperial style, the evening continued with Verdi's *Rigoletto* in a splendid execution. The open-air Suez Canal Opening Ceremony, featuring Ismail, Eugénie, Habsburg Emperor Franz Joseph, and other celebrities, took place sixteen days later at Port Said.[1]

Strikingly different from Muslim patriotism, images of Ismail as a sovereign ruler were created according to western European styles of representation. How was this representation created, and what is its significance? This chapter surveys a global microhistory of Cairo. It focuses on the creation of spaces which brought a new political aesthetics. A system of khedivial theaters started to function and contributed to the reconstitution of the everyday urban sensorium. On the other hand, space and sound built up a new elite experience of power. We shall examine the life of Paul Draneht Bey, who helped to fabricate this "internal Europe"[2] and directed the theaters between 1869 and 1878. The chapter ends with an exploration of the "portrait of the pasha" and the main product of early khedivial culture: Verdi's opera, *Aida*.

[1] *Wādī al-Nīl*, 5 November 1869, 868–869; 12 November 1869, 900–901. Douin, *Histoire du règne*, 2: 470–471.

[2] Barak, "Egyptian Times," 299.

Urban Transformation as Material "Civilization"

European music had functioned as a feature of governance ever since the 1820s. The army of Mehmed Ali employed Italian, Spanish, French, and German musicians who taught military music and possibly some popular opera tunes to Egyptian soldiers. The public representation of the *vali* increasingly included European music through the army.[3] During the Syrian campaign, a European band marched in front of Ibrahim when the Egyptian army passed through Beirut in 1832.[4] During Said's reign, public patriotism was unisonality, fusing Arabic words and European military music; music notation was taught in Arabic in the army;[5] and Said had his own soldier-musicians. By mid-century, the army supplied European symbols for viceregal representation. In this regard, the Khedivial Opera House was a product of the very same utilitarian logic.

As in Istanbul, by the 1860s Italian music had become part of elite entertainment in Cairo. Mehmed Ali had attended Italian opera performances in the 1840s;[6] and visiting musicians performed at weddings and circumcision ceremonies. Said maintained a small summer orchestra of Italian musicians in 1859–1861.[7] Both rulers, Said and Ismail, sponsored the private Zizinia Theater in Alexandria and another one in Cairo in the 1860s with yearly funding,[8] but the Italian opera diva, Adelaide Ristori (1822–1906), traveled to Cairo to sing in only one performance for Ismail in 1864.[9] These early developments were variously perceived in Paris: while the establishment of a French Theater in Istanbul was regarded as a victory over Italian opera,[10] Said's support of the private theater in Cairo in 1862 was ridiculed in the Parisian press. This case is worth noting since Said, before his death, seemingly engaged opera, ballet, and vaudeville troupes and sought to invite, at his own cost, French journalists to attend the opening of the theater in early

[3] Mestyan, "Sound, Military Music."

[4] Letter dated 10 April, from Consul to Ambassador, 166PO/D11/3, MAEN.

[5] Ghārdūn, *Mukhtaṣar.*

[6] Sadgrove, *Egyptian Theatre*, 39–45.

[7] He had a (summer?) theater. Receipts and contracts April–September 1860, in Maḥfaẓa 616, Dīwān al-Khidīwī (Mutafarriqāt), CA, DWQ.

[8] For instance, letter dated 20 Shaʿbān 1282 (8 January 1866), from Muḥammad Sharīf to Maʿiyya, 209/36, MST, Microfilm 196, DWQ.

[9] Papageorgiou, "Adelaide Ristori's Tour."

[10] *La Comédie*, 17 February 1867, 9.

1863 (just before his death).[11] This plan prefigures the grand opening of the Khedivial Opera House in 1869 and may have had an influence on Ismail's own plans.

Cairo's Transformation and al-Azbakiyya

Arguments have been made that Europeans transformed Cairo into a "Paris along the Nile," "a colonial city," and that this occurred after Ismail's visit to the Paris World Exhibition in 1867.[12] The Haussmannization, the division of the city, and the timing are now questioned.[13] Ismail's urban development started immediately in 1863, often with business considerations.[14] The reasons for accelerated urban transformation from 1867 are complex: urban health issues, the extra resources available due to the cotton boom, the experts available from Paris, the opening ceremonies for the Suez Canal (originally scheduled earlier), and the transformation of Egypt's Ottoman status.

New palaces, schools, trains, engines, and steamships had already announced the materially novel governance to ordinary Cairenes. Now new streets, gas-lights, and canals were implemented. The most significant symbolic building was the giant official palace, ʿĀbdīn. The Dolmabahçe Palace of Sultan Abdülmecid—a similarly symbolic project whose construction Ismail saw in Istanbul in 1851–1852—may have served as a model for the one in Cairo. A similar European-style ceremonial building in Ottoman Arab lands was al-Salaḥiyya palace of the ruler Aḥmad Bey in 1850s Tunisia.[15]

Imagined sovereignty materialized in Cairo through five highly visible institutions: a French theater (comédie), a circus, an Italian opera house, a hippodrome, and a new, French-style public garden, which also contained a stage, the later famous garden theater. Four of the new playhouses were built in the district called al-Azbakiyya (or in the colloquial *Izbikiyya*), an elite outskirt of medieval Cairo.[16] This part of the city was a center of life and commerce, including prostitution and crime, because travelers entered Cairo at this location from both the Nile and the new train station. In addition, there were repeated attempts to develop the territory below al-Azbakiyya, today's downtown Cairo. This new district, where Ismail distributed land freely, and where Italian, German,

[11] *Le Ménestrel*, 7 December 1862, 7.

[12] Abu-Lughod, *1001 Years*, 103–105.

[13] Ahmed, "Nineteenth-Century Cairo: A Dual City?"; Fahmy, "Modernizing Cairo"; Elshahed, "Facades of modernity," 30–31.

[14] Letter dated 1 July 1863, from British consul in Alexandria, FO 78/1755, NA.

[15] Brown, *The Tunisia of Ahmad Bey*, 318.

[16] Behrens-Abouseif, *Azbakiyya*.

and French architects built villas and general housing, became known as Ismāʿīliyya ("Ismailtown").

The Public Garden as Arab Refinement and Khedivial Progress

Let us first look at the significance of the public garden in al-Azbakiyya (completed between 1868 and 1872).[17] It is imperative to recognize that the idea of public garden was closely bound to the idea of the khedivate as a potential national monarchy. Public gardens, relating leisure time to public health, were a craze in bourgeois states: the Habsburg, British, and French empires as well as in the United States.[18] The public gardens of Paris and those in Istanbul, such as the new Taksim Garden, may have been among the inspirations.[19]

In the eyes of visitors from Paris, al-Azbakiyya was *haussmannisée*.[20] This refers to the activity of Georges-Eugène Haussmann, the prefect of Paris, who transformed the city by building boulevards and other public spaces, based on aesthetic, hygienic, and security considerations in the 1850s–1860s. Indeed, the European visitor of 1863 to "oriental" Cairo would not have recognized al-Azbakiyya in 1873:[21] the smaller, European, fenced garden contained a little lake, kiosks, a restaurant, and a garden theater.

The new garden with fences was closely monitored. An Arab visitor noted immediately after the first opening in 1871 that "there are individuals who are in charge of safety and order in the garden. They circulate among the groups of visitors in order to prevent any quarrel."[22] Administratively, it became part of the Ministry of Public Works after 1877. It seems that under the British occupation it was less supervised and, as a consequence, by the mid-1890s small stalls, "drinking shops and dancing salons" had been set up. In 1897, the entire staff of the garden was fired, and the establishments were "cleared away" in order that, as a British official emphasized, the "respectable classes of Cairo" could use the space.[23] By 1900, it had become not only a secured privileged space but also an increasingly rentable project. The income the tickets generated had risen to 1,322.080 LE while the expenses of the staff were only 774.192 LE annually. [24]

[17] Delchevalerie, *Le parc public de l'Ezbékieh*, 2.
[18] Rosenzweig and Blackmar, *The Park and the People.*
[19] For Taksim Garden, completed in 1869, Çelik, *The Remaking of Istanbul*, 69.
[20] Pichot, *Les Invités du Khédive*, 16.
[21] De Leon, *The Khedive's Egypt*, 50.
[22] [Sakmānī], *Riḥlat Sakmānī*, 160.
[23] Garstin, *Report upon the Administration* (1898), 38–39.
[24] Garstin, *Report upon the Administration* (1900), 279–280.

By the example of this public garden, we can observe how intellectuals registered the new establishments as signs of "progress." *Adab* and *ẓarf*, the Muslim principles for educated and civilized behavior made possible for the garden to function as a symbol of progress in Arabic texts. Even the introduction of gas in Cairo was celebrated by an Arabic *maqāma* in 1870.[25] The metaphor of "garden" (*ḥadīqa, janīna, junayna*) had been a favorite poetical trope for centuries in Arabic poetry. For instance, in 1866 the Būlāq press reprinted a book entitled *The Garden of Pleasures for the Elimination of Sad Things*.[26] The book contains a rich selection of poets and writers. The powerful Ismāʿīl Ṣiddīq also owned this book.[27] The image of the garden was a metaphor of writers and works—a "garden of texts" in which the seeker of entertainment and knowledge walks (reads) as if among trees.

The new garden of al-Azbakiyya offered an occasion for descriptions in which the earlier trope of the garden could be applied in connection with khedivial power. Muḥammad Rāshid's *The Brilliant Charms of al-Azbakiyya Garden* (1874) framed al-Azbakiyya as the poetical symbol of earthly paradise and praised the gas lamps and the military music in its pavilions.[28] Naturally, the wind that helped the author to wander around this garden of miracles, after praising the refined Egyptians, finally led him to praise the maker of the garden, *ʿAzīz Miṣr*, Ismail Pasha.[29] The court poet Sheikh ʿAlī al-Laythī, during his journey to Vienna and Berlin in 1875, saw a public park (possibly the Belvedere's gardens) in Vienna which reminded him of al-Azbakiyya.[30] We shall see in chapter 4 that the garden and the first Arabic theater in Egypt were so connected in 1872 that a young student included al-Azbakiyya in the title of a play.[31] In one of the first Arabic plays staged in Egypt, a character (possibly ironically) admires how "the governor of Egypt has transformed his kingdom's capital into a garden."[32] The Arabic discourses launched the new material symbols into the metaphysical world.

Non-Egyptian Arabic-speakers also observed the garden. In 1872, a traveler and pilgrim from Zanzibar, Ḥammūd al-Bū Saʿīdī, describes al-Azbakiyya, its music pavilions, and gas lamps with some reservation. He adds that two times a week there was a big (mixed gender) crowd in the

[25] Sīdī Aḥmad, "Allāh Nūr al-Samawāt wa-l-Arḍ," *Rawḍat al-Madāris*, n. 8, 15 Rabīʿ al-Thānī 1287 (15 July 1870), 19–20. For technology and poetry, see Barak, On Time, 245-246.

[26] Al-Shirwānī, Ḥadīqat al-Afrāḥ.

[27] ʿAbd al-Raḥmān, *Ismāʿīl Ṣiddīq*, 62.

[28] Rāshid, *Al-Maḥāsin al-Bahiyya*, 7–9.

[29] Ibid., 12–13.

[30] Al-Laythī, *Riḥlat al-Shaykh ʿAlī*, 82–83.

[31] Al-Miṣrī, *Nuzhat al-Adab*.

[32] Sanua, "Al-Amīra al-Iskandarāniyya," in Najm, ed., *Yaʿqūb Ṣannūʿ*, 167.

garden. This, he thought, "leads all devout men in his faith to disapprove" the garden.[33] In contrast, Iskandar Abkāriyūs, this prime Syrian example of dynastic loyalty, related al-Azbakiyya to the person of Ismail with a touch of transcendence. He wrote in a poem: "[Ismail] ornamented the Garden of al-Azbakiyya / . . . beautified it with musical melodies and all kinds of tunes / and it became similar to the heavenly Paradise."[34]

In addition to these Arabic descriptions, there is also an invisible Turkic story in al-Azbakiyya. This location establishes a botanical connection between Mehmed Ali, the first to order a modern garden in this space, his son, Ibrahim, lover of gardens, and Ismail, lord of public gardens in khedivial Cairo; and all may be reconnected to Emir Özbek, the first Turkic ruler of Mamluk Cairo who used this land for pleasure and ceremony.

Opera and Khedivial Power in Late Ottoman Cairo

Cairo as the khedivial capital contained entertainment institutions at its core whose "gem" was the opera house. These were the spaces where the khedivate and the khedive was destined to be displayed and behind them the poverty of ordinary Egyptians and the Ottoman face of Ismail were to be hidden.

The Operatic State and Theater as "Compensation"

It is necessary to explain here briefly the European theory of opera and its connection to political power. Ruth Bereson characterizes this intersection with the concept "the operatic state." She argues that the opera house "has performed the function of legitimising the power of the state through the use of ceremonial ritual."[35] In addition, theaters, especially a state-owned opera house, represented a social contract between the bourgeois elites and governments in the second half of the nineteenth century. For instance, Charles Garnier, architect of the Paris (Garnier) Opera, explained the necessity of state involvement in building opera houses in 1871 as a "compensation" for the taxing of the citizens.[36] This compensation was perceived to answer the elite demand of freedom, since, as the French historian Jules Michelet remarked once that "the theatre is the most powerful instrument of education; it is the best hope of

[33] [Al-Bū Saʿīdī], *Riḥlat Ḥammūd*, 28–29.
[34] Abkāriyūs, *al-Manāqib al-Ibrāhīmiyya* (1299), 160.
[35] Bereson, *The Operatic State*, 3.
[36] Garnier, *Le Théâtre*, 15–16.

the national renewal."[37] Michelet echoed Victor Hugo's theory about the role a state must fulfill in financing theaters as locations of public education, considered part of the public good.[38] Such views in turn mirrored German aesthetic theories about freedom and the change in human nature that follows from the experience of beauty and art. Friedrich Schiller stated that "art is the daughter of freedom . . . it is through beauty that we arrive at freedom."[39] Thus, at the very depths of the western European arguments for state funding of theaters, and especially the opera house, lingered the freedom of those who had the time, clothes, and money to visit these spaces.

Cultural Transfer from Istanbul, Paris, and Alexandria

For Ismail, the ceremonial aspect became important only gradually. It seems that only a French theater ("Comédie") and the public garden were planned for an early date of the Suez Canal opening, scheduled originally in January 1869. The Comédie was decided upon in September 1868 when Ismail stayed in Istanbul,[40] and a French operetta troupe was invited to "migrate to Cairo" from the imperial capital.[41] The Francophile Seraphin Manasse (1837–1888), an almost forgotten Ottoman Armenian impresario, became the first director of the French theater in Cairo, arriving from Istanbul.

Despite the Istanbul connection, the khedive's private German architect, Julius Franz (1831–1915) designed all the khedivial playhouses in Cairo or at least had a role in their planning.[42] The Comédie was constructed starting at the end of October 1868.[43] Franz built it in the place of the former palace of Ahmed Tahir Pasha and Manasse's French operetta troupe (who lived next to the building), inaugurated it on January 4, 1869. The Comédie was known in Arabic as *maḥall al-malʿab al-musammā bi-l-tiyātrū* ("the building of the playhouse which is called theater") in its first months,[44] and existed until 1887. Franz also designed a circus. Its inauguration took place on February 11, 1869, with the French circus

[37] Quoted in Kruger, *The National Stage*, 36.

[38] Quoted in Gouchard, "De la legalisation du théâtre," 22.

[39] Schiller, *Letters upon the Aesthetic Education of Man*, 1794, II. Letter, online: http://www.fordham.edu/halsall/mod/schiller-education.asp.

[40] Letter dated 22 September 1868 to Kiamil Bey, Maḥfaẓa 80, CAI, DWQ.

[41] *Levant Herald*, 16 October 1868, 2.

[42] Volait, *Architectes et architectures*, 67. Several dispatches during 1285 (1868–69) in daftar 2002–000255 and 2002–000256, DWQ.

[43] *Le Moustique*, 1 November 1868, 2.

[44] *Wādī al-Nīl*, 23 April 1869, 12.

FIGURE 3.1. The Comédie of Cairo, 1869
Source: "Théâtre Français," *Le Monde Illustré*, 6 February 1869, 86. Collection Max Karkégi, with permission from M. Max Karkégi.

company of Théodore Rancy.[45] Mattatias Nahman, a Greek Jewish merchant, bought the building in May 1872, and the "Mattatias-building" was built in its place in 1873.[46] These two buildings of the khedivial infrastructure were the most short-lived.

During the winter and spring of 1869, Seraphin Manasse's position took a quick upward turn. The khedive requested him to arrange a ballet troupe, the only condition being "that the ladies should be pretty." Thus on January 7, 1869, Manasse commissioned Amédée Verger, a dramatic agent in Paris, to contract ballet dancers and to ship them to Egypt. In February 1869, the khedive gave him another order: the recruitment of an opera company. In March, Manasse was in various negotiations and intrigues concerning the singers.[47] A credit of 15,000 Ottoman lire was opened for him in Paris.[48] He may have received another order to

[45] Rancy's troupe arrived on 6 February 1869. *Levant Herald*, 18 February 1869, 4.

[46] Crosnier Leconte and Volait, *L'Égypte d'un architecte*, 63 and n. 53.

[47] This information is from a report in the *Levant Herald*, 24 April 1870, 10, in connection with the later trial of Verger against Manasse. Verger worked with Manasse as early as 1863, *La Comédie*, 9 August 1863, 8.

[48] Undated table with number 66, at the bottom of the page number 81, in Daftar 30, Microfilm 27, MSA, DWQ.

supervise the construction of a planned new Opera House.[49] The news alludes to his being named as superintendent of khedivial theaters.[50]

Opera in Cairo as Global Power

The earliest reference to the construction of an opera house in Cairo is from a consular letter dated February 8, 1869. The French consul reports that "the construction of a theater to perform opera is started" in addition to the two playhouses, and adds that he believes that the khedivial theaters were imitations of European civilization by Ismail in order "to entertain only himself, his harem, some bureaucrats, his entourage, and the Europeans."[51]

It was not only self-entertainment. The construction of an opera house in Cairo must be understood as part of the global opera fever in Paris, Vienna, St. Petersburg, Rio de Janeiro, and Istanbul. At the time, Ismail's lord and "cousin," Sultan Abdülaziz intended to subsidize the Naum Theatre—an Italian Opera House—on a yearly basis in Istanbul. In addition, the sultan planned to build an Ottoman Imperial Theatre.[52] In February 1869, these plans coincided with the invitation of the Italian troupe of the Naum Theatre (an opera company) to Alexandria by a private impresario.[53] The prince and princess of Wales, after a tour in Egypt, departed for Istanbul where they also attended the "Imperial" Naum Theatre to huge press publicity.[54] No direct link can be established between Ismail's decision in Cairo and the developments in the Ottoman imperial capital, but it seems that an aesthetic competition was taking place next to the political one as the world prepared for the opening ceremonies of the Suez Canal. The opera craze, like the telegraph, established global cultural hubs in the Ottoman Eastern Mediterranean.

The Manasse Affair

The prospect of an opera in Cairo reversed the wheels of fortune for Manasse, the Ottoman impresario. On Friday, April 2, 1869, a bomb (*māshīn infarnāl* as a report transliterated the French words into Arabic)

[49] De Vaujany, *Le Caire et ses environs*, 246.

[50] *Le Gaulois*, 31 July 1869, 3. Cf. also *Hayal*, 15 Mayis 1290 (27 May 1874), 1–2.

[51] Letter dated 8 February 1869, French Consul to Ambassador, 166PO/D25/70, MEAN.

[52] *Levant Herald*, 9 February 1869, 3.

[53] *Levant Herald*, 20 February 1869, 3–4; *Levant Herald*, 15 March 1869, 3. The troupe (130 persons!) headed for Alexandria on 10 April 1869. *Levant Herald*, 10 April 1869, 2.

[54] The couple arrived to Alexandria on 4 February 1869 and left for Constantinople on 28 March 1869. *Penny Illustrated Paper*, 13 February 1869, 102, and 3 April 1869, 215. Cf. also *The Times*, 11 March 1869. They visited the Naum in 2 April 1869. *Levant Herald*, 2 April 1869, 2–3.

had been discovered in the khedive's box in the Comédie before he arrived.[55] The news immediately received international media coverage.[56] The always loyal leader of the descendants of the Prophet (*naqīb al-ashrāf*), ʿAlī al-Bakrī, gathered religious scholars in his Cairo home and thanked God that the khedive was safe.[57] The Greek Orthodox community also thanked God.[58] The *aʿyān* and sheikhs of Alexandria also thanked God in the Abū al-ʿAbbās mosque. One sheikh even wrote a poem and recited it publically.[59]

Manasse was arrested and interrogated by the European consuls. He confessed that he had invented the plot, hoping for an additional reward.[60] Soon he and a Greek man were exiled from Egypt forever. The reason for this light sentence is not exactly clear; it is said that a heavier sentence would have "compromised their [the consuls'] dignity."[61] This detail hints to a more critical interest lurking behind the affair. British diplomats reported to London that the khedive believed that his uncle Abdülhalim Pasha was behind the fake plot.[62] Indeed, Ismail did not cease to think that Abdülhalim at least knew about their malicious intentions.[63] Be as it may, Manasse escaped to Marseille and then to Paris with financial compensation![64]

The whole affair was, possibly, a plot against Manasse, to prevent him from being offered the job of superintendent of khedivial theaters.[65] Now that Manasse was out of the khedivial game of political aesthetics, a new man appeared: Paolino Bey, or as he became known in Europe and to Europeans, Paul Draneht Bey.

55 Telegram dated 3 April from Alexandria, *Levant Herald*, 5 April 1869, 2. Cf. Sadgrove, *Egyptian Theatre*, 47.

56 *Levant Herald*, 5 April 1869, 2. The *New York Times* published a telegram from London in its 5 April 1869 number, *Le Figaro* on 6 April 1869. In Ottoman Turkish: *Terakki*, 15 Nisan (April) 1869, 1. The event was, of course, reported in Arabic in *al-Waqāʾiʿ al-Miṣriyya* in 12 April 1869, quoted in Sāmī, *Taqwīm al-Nīl*, part 3, vol. 2:805; and in *Wādī al-Nīl*, 23 April 1869, 12.

57 *Al-Waqāʾiʿ al-Miṣriyya*, 12 April 1869, quoted in Sāmī, *Taqwīm al-Nīl*, part 3, vol. 2:805.

58 Letter dated 26 Dhū al-Ḥijja 1285 (9 April 1869), 425/44, MST, Microfilm 203, DWQ.

59 Letter from the wakīl of the governor of Alexandria, dated 27 Dhū al-Ḥijja 1285 (9 April 1869), 426/44, MST, Microfilm 203, DWQ.

60 Letter dated 7 April 1869, *Levant Herald*, 15 April 1869, 3.

61 Letter dated 19 May 1869, in *Levant Herald*, 27 May 1869, 3–4. Sadgrove, *Egyptian Theatre*, 47. *Al-Waqāʾiʿ al-Miṣriyya*, 13 May 1869, quoted in Sāmī, *Taqwīm al-Nīl*, part 3, vol. 2:815. *Wādī al-Nīl*, 21 May 1869, 134 (based on the news in *al-Waqāʾiʿ al-Miṣriyya*). See also Gellion-Danglar, *Lettres sur l'Égypte*, 241.

62 9 April 1869, from Stanton, Alexandria, FO 78/2092, BA.

63 17 April 1869, from Stanton, Alexandria, FO 78/2092, BA.

64 This compensation is said to be for his "suffering." It is not clear why he deserved this sum. Letter dated 19 May 1869, in *Levant Herald*, 27 May 1869, 3–4; *Le Gaulois*, 2 August 1869, 3, suggests that he received this money in order not to publish a book.

65 *Hayal*, 15 Mayis 1290 (27 May 1874), 1–2.

The Construction of the Khedivial Opera House

Before we explore the life of Draneht Bey, let us survey the construction of the Khedivial Opera House which is another example of how, as Barak says, an "internal Europe" was articulated in late Ottoman Egypt. It is generally believed that Pietro Avoscani, an Italian architect from Alexandria, who also designed the Zizinia Theatre in Alexandria, was the architect of the Khedivial Opera,[66] although the architect Franz Bey may again have had a role in drawing up the plans.[67] The Khedivial Opera House was built in an open space, next to the new garden and close to the French theater and the Circus, and, like all opera houses, it emanated power and organized the city.[68] According to Garnier, only two edifices were designed to host "if not everybody, but the possible greatest number of people: the church and the theater."[69]

The Khedivial Opera House belonged to the theater type *scène classique avec salle classique*[70] (the Naum Theatre in Istanbul was built also in this style, in the late 1840s). This type of theater was designed to make it possible for the audience to see each other at least as much as to watch the stage. It was mainly built of wood, which was widely (re)used in Cairo and in general in Ottoman lands because it was cheap. The technical equipment, scenery, furniture, and instruments arrived from Paris[71] while Italian painters worked on the interior.[72] The construction was financed by the Private Domains of the khedive on "government" (*mīrī*) land. The khedive and Draneht requested detailed reports about the progress of the construction while traveling during the summer of 1869.[73] Avoscani wrote once that the workers (possibly Egyptians) sang while working under the sun but ten workers died during the construction.[74]

[66] ʿAbdūn, *ʿĀyida*, 47; Ulacacci, *Pietro Avoscani*; Balboni, *Gl'Italiani*, 1:294–408; Tagher, "Pietro Avoscani"; Douin, *Histoire du règne*, 470–471; Arnaud, *Le Caire*, 59–61; Pallini, "Italian Architects"; Volait, *Architectes et architectures*, 51, 106. Other names include Franz (Mubārak, Al-Khiṭaṭ al-Tawfīqiyya, 18:241), "Fasciotti and Rossi" (Mostyn, *Egypt's Belle Epoque*, 72 without any further reference); "Avoscani and Rossi" (http://www.cairoopera.org/history.php. Accessed 15 October 2016). Avoscani was certainly the entrepreneur. Letter dated 18 September 1869 to Avoscani from "Nazir de la Daira Hassa," Maḥfaẓa 80, CAI, DWQ.

[67] *Le Ménestrel*, 15 May 1870, 191. Perhaps ʿAlī Riḍā Bey was also responsible. Ismāʿīl, *Tāʾrīkh al-Masraḥ al-Miṣrī*, 53 (without reference).

[68] Donnet, *Architectonographie des théâtres*, 11.

[69] Garnier, *Le Théâtre*, 7–8.

[70] LeBlanc and LeBlanc, *Traité d'aménagement*, 2:4–5.

[71] *Le Ménestrel*, 4 July 1869, 247.

[72] Letter of Avoscani, quoted in an essay of Abdoun (ʿAbdūn) which is annexed to Abdoun, ed., *Genesi dell' "Aida,"* 147–151, under the title "Il Teatro d'Opera del Cairo" nota di Saleh Abdoun, at 148. Repeated by an unknown author, "Histoire de l'Opera du Caire," 54.

[73] Letter dated 9 Ṣafar 1286 (21 May 1869), Qayd 583, p. 11, Microfilm 99, MST, DWQ.

[74] Letter of Avoscani, quoted in Abdoun (ed.), *Genesi dell' "Aida,"* 148. I am indebted to Sara Rosselli for helping with the Italian translation.

FIGURE 3.2. The Khedivial Opera House and the Circus, between 1869 and 1872
Source: Collection Max Karkégi, with permission from M. Max Karkégi.

The building was ready by September 1869,[75] although numerous modifications were made throughout its life—starting in 1872–1873,[76]—until it finally burned down in 1971.[77]

Power was represented in the interior in the Italian modality of political aesthetics. Its interior was accordingly grandiose; the detailed observations of the *New York Times* in 1869 are worth quoting *in extenso*:

> The auditorium is not very large, there being only about 250 seats on the lower floor. The boxes are nineteen in each tier, except the lowest, where the central box gives place to the parquet entrance and there is an amphitheatre above. The viceroyal boxes occupy

[75] On 1 September the building was ready externally. Ismāʿīl, *Taʾrīkh al-Masraḥ al-Miṣrī*, 54. Still, the director of the Private Domains wrote a very unfriendly letter to Avoscani, calling his attention to the terms of contract and demanding the delivery of the House: Letter dated 18 September 1869, to Avoscani from "Nazir de la Daira Hassa," Maḥfaẓa 80, CAI, DWQ. As late as 19 October, a visitor noted that "Le Grand-Théâtre" was not yet ready. Taglioni, *Deux mois en Egypte*, 58.

[76] Letter dated 30 June 1873, from Mohamed Zeki, gouverneur du Caire to Abdelgelil Bey, Istanbul (containing the copy of Mohamed Zeki's letter to De Brunenghi—Consul d'Italie au Caire). Letter dated 7 July 1873 from an unknown person to Chérif Pacha, and letter dated 8 July 1873—Dépêche chiffrée de S. Ex. Zeki Pacha (informing the recipient that the work had resumed), all in. Maḥfaẓa 80, CAI, DWQ.

[77] See the documentary movie about the fire by Abdel Aziz, *Ḥarq Ūbirā al-Qāhira* (2011).

> nearly the whole of the proscenium in heights, and are very broad and spacious, those for his ladies being screened by heavy lace instead of the usual gilded gratings. The public boxes are provided with seats for four only. . . . The Viceroy's own box is hung with magnificent curtains of crimson silk velvet and real ermine, and the rest of the house is upholstered with plush of the same shade. . . . The lightning is by a glass chandelier, candelabra being prepared along the tiers for additional illumination on gala nights. The ceiling is flat, but admirably painted in relief, the panels into which it is divided containing each a medallion, bearing the portrait-bust of a composer upon the ground of dead gold. The busts are remarkably well-done . . . Mercadante, Donizetti, Bellini, Guido-Aretino, Auber, Cimarosa, Verdi, Mozart, Beethoven.[78]

This was the ideal Western European environment to display and to experience the political bonds between the ruler and his elite. Similar to the al-Azbakiyya Garden next to it, the Opera House embodied a new style of class hierarchy.

The Arabic press at the time did not follow the construction. Only the official newspaper *al-Waqāʾiʿ al-Miṣriyya* in June 1869 noted briefly that the construction of *tiyātrū al-ūbirā* had started and that an Italian company from Alexandria was the contractor (Avoscani).[79] *Al-Jawāʾib* in Istanbul mentioned the Opera House only as a part of the Suez Canal Opening Ceremonies,[80] while *Wādī al-Nīl* also only later provided any information. After 1870, however, the Arabic press would be full of news about the theaters in Cairo and the opera house in particular.

Despite the effort to build theaters exactly as in Europe, there was one element that was unique in the khedivial theaters, the so-called harem box. These special boxes were built in the Comédie, the Circus, and the Opera House in Cairo with thin wire (in the opera with "heavy lace") so that no one could see the ladies behind. In Istanbul in the Gedikpaşa Theatre (built 1860), there were harem boxes too and the sultan's box was also wired (in theory, Muslim women were prohibited from visiting theaters for a time in Istanbul).[81] It is possible to interpret this element as the only visible fragment of the Ottoman-Muslim face of Ismail for Europeans.

If we add the Hippodrome constructed in 1870 (designed by Franz, demolished in 1881),[82] and al-Azbakiyya Garden with its small semi-open-air theater (*Théâtre-Concert du Jardin de l'Esbekieh*, presumably again designed

78 *New York Times*, 4 December 1869, 1.
79 *Al-Waqāʾiʿ al-Miṣriyya*, 10 June 1869, 1.
80 *Al-Jawāʾib*, 2 December 1869, 2.
81 Letter dated 15 Jumādā al-Awwal 1276 (10 December 1859), I. MMS 16/691, BOA.
82 Volait, *Architectes et architectures*, 106.

by Franz),[83] it adds up to the impression that Ismail replaced mid-nineteenth-century inland cosmopolitan al-Azbakiyya with a khedivial entertainment district. An order was issued in May 1870 to transfer the buildings from *mīrī* (government) possessions to the city of Cairo, and from 1870 the responsibility for their maintenance also belonged to the Cairo Governorate[84] (see chapter 7 for the legal and administrative history of state and private theaters). The general construction fever also meant that the district of al-Azbakiyya had brought the largest income to the Cairo Governorate from the taxes on houses in the 1870s, for instance, 67,2927.15 LE during 1872–1873.[85]

Spaces of Entertainment in Khedivial Egypt

The new spaces were crucial for new elite communal experiences. There were a number of other stages in Cairo in addition to the khedivial playhouses. Some private theaters functioned already in Alexandria, at their top the Zizinia, next to the many bars and pubs. The khedivial harem could enjoy music and plays in the palace theater in Qaṣr al-Nīl; a stage in Raʾs al-Tīn palace in Alexandria; and later a stage was also built in ʿĀbdīn palace. Italian and French architects designed plans that were never executed.[86] Music and plays were performed in hotels, restaurants, café-chantants, on board ships, and in the open air. For instance, in Cairo in the "Eldorado" in December 1869 operetta songs were performed as figure 3.3 shows. In 1877, Italian entrepreneurs opened a short-lived stage called in French *Théâtre Ismail*.[87] The urban sensorium was transformed by novel spatial organization, which brought a new acoustic field. The spaces of entertainment and leisure provided new ways to spend unappropriated time in public. The very meaning of leisure started to be transformed as, driven by material change, norms of elite visibility and honor were also transformed.

The Curious Life of Draneht Bey

The spaces of entertainment owned by the khedive functioned as a giant workshop for fabricating a new public image of Ismail for the elite audience, and for us, posterity. This system was an injection of Europe in the

[83] Ismāʿīl, *Tāʾrīkh al-Masraḥ al-Miṣrī*, 31, n. 2.

[84] Letter dated 18 Ṣafar 1287 (20 May 1870) to Umur-i Hassa, qayd 583, p. 40, microfilm 99, MST, and letter dated 6 April 1871, from Riaz to Franz Bey, 5013–004133, both in DWQ.

[85] Mubārak, *Al-Khiṭaṭ*, (first edition), 1:94.

[86] The architects Avoscani, Carl von Diebitsch, and Hector Horeau all designed plans of "Arab theaters" for the khedive.

[87] Sadgrove, *Egyptian Theatre*, 70.

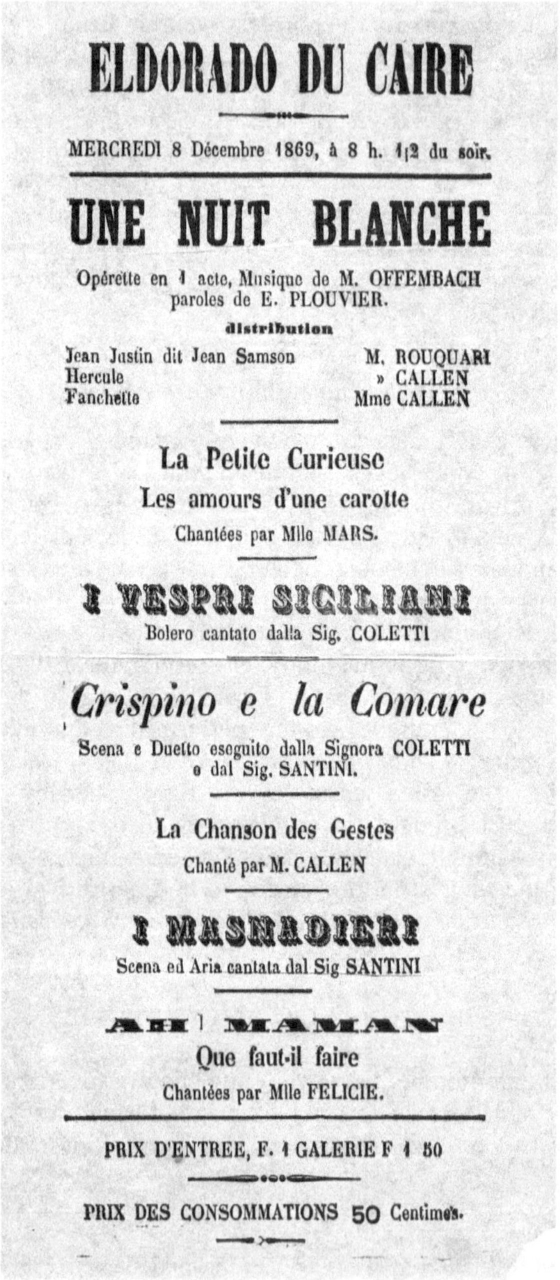

FIGURE 3.3. A poster of Eldorado du Caire, 1869
Source: Poster in Box TCS 70 (Hollis number 012690446), Theater Collection, Harvard University, with permission.

TABLE 3.1. Theatres and Playhouses in Khedivial Cairo, 1868–1879

Name	*Owner*	*Foundation*	*Location*	*Demolition*
Teatro del Cairo	Private	1850s?	al-Azbakiyya	1868?
Comédie	Government*	November 1868	al-Azbakiyya	1887
Circus	Government	January 1869	al-Azbakiyya	1872
Cairo (Khedivial) Opera House	Government	April 1869	al-Azbakiyya	1971
Hippodrome	Government	1869 late summer	Close to al-Azbakiyya	1881
Eldorado	Private	existed in December 1869	?	?
Garden Theatre in Al-Azbakiyya	Government	1872	Al-Azbakiyya Garden	with many transformations, until today
Théâtre Ismail	Private: Filippo Giannona and Clemente Buratti	October 1877	Close to al-Azbakiyya	December 1877

*"Government" refers to the Private Domains or the Cairo Governorate; stages in hotels or pubs and coffeehouses are not counted, neither temporary street stages.

everyday sensorium of Cairo. The man behind this was Paul "Paulino" Draneht Bey who effectively made the system of khedivial theaters work.

Draneht's career gives us a sense about how the loyalty of non-Egyptians was secured for the dynasty: everything that they had become was due to the ruler. They were, in theory, the perfect subjects of the khedivate. Despite their independent outlook, knowledge of languages, and belonging to the educated elite with often large salaries, these men remained servants. They were trained for specific purposes, they served in the function as their master saw fit, they had to request permission to travel abroad, they had to obey orders, and they served their master's will and tastes. If they were shrewd and remained in close contact with the ruler, as Draneht did, they could amass real fortunes which, after

1882, now under British occupation, secured their independence and confirmed their transition to become part of the colonial elite.

From an Ottoman Greek Boy to the Pasha's Pharmacist

The story of the transformation of an Ottoman Greek boy into Mehmed Ali's pharmacist illustrates the patronage system the pasha set up during his reign. Paul Draneht[88] was born in Nicosia, in Ottoman Cyprus, as Pavlos Pavlidis or Pavlos Xristofidis,[89] probably in 1815.[90] His uncle, Logizis Kramvis, was a notable in the city. The Ottoman Greek family (or possibly only young Pavlos and his father)[91] migrated to Egypt around either 1821 or 1827.[92] A Greek merchant in Alexandria introduced the boy to Mehmed Ali, asking the pasha to send him to France to study.[93] Mehmed Ali agreed to finance his studies in medicine on the condition that after returning he would be his personal dentist and pharmacist.[94] This was how the pasha created loyal men; another example from the same period

[88] Apart from numerous short allusions, I located six, sometimes contradictory, short biographies of Draneht. One by his daughter, Despina (Draneht) Zervudachi, was entitled "Twilight memories" privately printed by her son, Mr. Peter Emmanuel Zervudachi. In the 1970s he allowed Hans Busch to use it and he compiled a biography in his Verdi's *Aida*, 631–632. Although the living members of the Zervudachi family did not grant me permission to read this text, I am very grateful to Ms. Manuela Zervudachi, great-great-grand daughter of Paul Draneht, for her efforts in communication; and also to Carol L. Rodocanachi, another great-great-grand daughter of Draneht Bey for her answers. I am also indebted to the website of Samir Rafaat about the history of the Ghezira-palace, http://www.egy.com/zamalek/, accessed 12 July 2011, where I came across the genealogy of the Draneht-Zervudachi family, which also contains a short biography (which is based on his article in *Cairo Times*, 14 October 1999). The third biography is an entry on his name in a Greek lexicon which was translated for me by my colleague, Marios Papakyriacou from Koudounaris, *Biografikon Leksikon*, 137. Saleh Abdoun also published a small biography in Arabic (perhaps based on Draneht's letters in the old Opera House) in ʿAbdūn, *ʿĀyida*, 28. In addition, Abdoun published some letters in his Abdoun, Genesi dell' "Aida." A half-biography was compiled by Sayyid ʿAlī Ismāʿīl who worked from Draneht's pension-dossier in DM, in his *Taʾrīkh al-Masraḥ al-Miṣrī*, 86–92 ; and the sixth one is a long footnote in Politis, *L'Hellénisme*, 1:200, footnote 1.

[89] Pavlos Pavlidis (Busch's data). According to Koudounaris, his father was Xristofakis Pavlidis. It is also backed by Politis, *L'Hellénisme*, 1: 201 who mentions a Ch. (Christoph?) Pavlidis, pouvant beaucoup, among the Cypriots in Egypt.

[90] Draneht was born in 1809 (Koudounaris), in 1815 (Busch, *Verdi's Aida*, 631), or 1817 (ʿAbdūn, *ʿĀyida*, 28). There are arguments for all dates; I choose Busch's version since this is based on information from the family.

[91] Politis, *L'Hellénisme*, 1: 200.

[92] 1821 is given in Koudounaris, *Biografikon Leksikon*, 137. Politis, *L'Hellénisme*, 1: 200, only mentions that they escaped after the massacre in Cyprus during the revolt. The date 1827 is given in Busch, *Verdi's Aida*, 631 with the explanation that the family fled to Egypt because of the "Turkish persecution" in Cyprus.

[93] Politis, *L'Hellénisme*, 1: 200.

[94] Politis, *L'Hellénisme*, 1: 200. Busch, *Verdi's Aida*, 631.

is Joseph Hekekyan, who wrote in his diary, after his father's death, that "I have found another father" in the pasha.[95]

The exact time of Draneht's student period is not known.[96] In Paris, his favorite teacher was the chemist Louis-Jacques Thénard (1777–1857): either Thénard was so proud of the Ottoman student that he "offered him his own name,"[97] or Thénard became a *paternal ami* and Pavlos decided to adopt his name.[98] The boy took on the surname, but spelled it backward, Draneht. Yet, he continued to be known in Egypt as Paulino Bey or Monsieur Paulino;[99] in Arabic *Bāwulīnī/Bāwulīnū Bīk*.[100] He was polyglot, possibly speaking Turkish and Italian in his youth, and later mixing Italian words into his French, typical of a true "Levantine."[101]

The young Paulino started his pharmacist studies in the Abū Zaʿbal hospital, under the Italian botanist Antonio Figari, in September 1831. In Abū Zaʿbal, he took on the rank of *mülazim-i evvel* in the army then rising through *yüzbaşı* (roughly captain) to *sağ kolağası* (senior captain) by 1838. From 1833 (1248) he worked as a pharmacist in the hospital, serving foreigners (*ajzājiyya al-afrank*), and from 1835 (1250), as the supposed agreement with the pasha prescribed, he was ordered to serve as his personal pharmacist. By the death of Mehmed Ali in 1849, Draneht, still in his thirties, reached the senior rank of *kaymakam* (lieutenant-colonel).[102]

[95] Vol 1., p. 172; MSS/Additional/ 37448, Hekekyan Papers, BL.

[96] His pension file does not include this information. Politis, *L'Hellénisme*, 1: 200 states that he was sent with la Mission égyptien. He was not the member of the famous student mission of 1826. He is not indicated in the lists of Heyworth-Dunne, *An Introduction to the History of Education*, 159–163; 170–175; 177–180; and also not mentioned in Silvera, "The first Egyptian student mission." There were three other missions in 1829, 1830, and 1832, cf. Louca, *Voyageurs et écrivains égyptiens*, 46. Perhaps he was in the 1829 mission which contained 34 students. Louca, ibid., 255. It is also possible that he was sent individually. He is not the one who is indicated in Heyworth-Dunne, ibid., 176, footnote 1 as "one student had already been sent to France in order to study medicine" because Heyworth-Dunne refers to ʿAlī Hayba in the mission of 1826 (student n. 30). Thus, either he was sent in 1829 or individually, almost privately.

[97] Busch, *Verdi's Aida*, 632.

[98] Politis, *L'Hellénisme*, 1: 200.

[99] Tagher, ed., *Mémoirs de A-B. Clot Bey*, 373.

[100] *Ḥadīqat al-Akhbār*, 17 Dhū al-Qaʿda 1275 (18 June 1859), p. 3.

[101] Ninet, "Finances et Menus Plaisirs," in *Au pays des khedives*, 279, footnote 1.

[102] This paragraph is based on État de services prêtes au Gouvernement Égyptien par S. E. Paolino Draneht Bey, dated 1 June 1880, and on Kashf Bayān mudad khidmat janāb Bawlīnū Dārānīt Bāshā alladhī kāna bi-Maṣlaḥat al-Tiyātrāt, dated 5 March 1881, both in Dūsiya 7085, Maḥfaẓa 275, ʿAyn 1, Dūlāb 13, DM. Some letters, translated into Arabic, were first published in Ismāʿīl, *Taʾrīkh al-Masraḥ al-Miṣrī*, 87–88. For the establishment of the Abū Zaʿbal hospital, see Fahmy, *All the Pasha's Men*, 212. It must be noted that his name is not mentioned in the comptes rendus of Clot Bey written between 1828 and 1832 about the Medical School of Abū Zaʿbal, neither as a student, nor as a teacher. There was a school

He was trusted by Mehmed Ali, and became a permanent member of his personal staff.[103] The pasha even retained him in his entourage in an inspection tour to the Sudan in 1838.[104] For his services, the pasha endowed him with land in Kafr al-Dawar,[105] and the third of the income of a soap-factory in 1847.[106] Draneht was very close to his person as *ajzājī al-maʿiyya al-khidīwiyya*, the pharmacist of the princely entourage. He attended Mehmed Ali's deathbed as well.[107] This young man must have been intimately aware of the intrigues within the dynasty, including Mehmed Ali's schemes in the 1840s, toying with his heirs, Ibrahim and Abbas Hilmi. After 1848, during the six years of Ibrahim and Abbas's reigns, this knowledge may have been the reason why he continued to receive a *kaymakam*'s salary,[108] and remained in Egypt, but probably without having to carry out his duties.[109]

Said's Factotum

Draneht's career continues, meteorlike, during Said's reign when Mehmed Ali's late elite was restored. For instance, in 1854 Draneht was promoted to the rank of *miralay* (colonel) as *ajzājī bāshā*.[110] Soon, a new Ottoman medal was sent from Istanbul to replace one he had apparently lost.[111] He was said to become a kind of agent, a "factotum" to Said.[112] For instance, at the first, fateful visit of Ferdinand De Lesseps in November 1854 to convince Said to begin the Suez Canal project, during an excursion it was Draneht who brought the Frenchman to attend a dance of *almees* (female entertainers) in the pasha's tent.[113] In 1857 he chatted with the pasha about the Egyptian students in Paris;[114] and never left Said's side during his

---

of pharmacy at this time in the Citadel. Perhaps this was Draneht's first place of work. Clot, *Compte Rendu* (1828, 1829, 1830); and Clot, *Compte Rendu* (1831, 1832).

[103] Enkiri, *Ibrahim Pacha*, 444.

[104] Politis, *L'Hellénisme*, 1:200.

[105] Ibid., 200.

[106] Tagher, ed., *Mémoirs de A-B. Clot Bey*, 375. The soap-factory was divided between three doctors: Clot, Gaëtani (Mehmed Ali's personal doctor), and Draneht.

[107] Ibid., 393.

[108] Kashf Bayān mudad khidmat janāb Bawlīnū Dārānīt Bāshā alladhī kāna bi-Maṣlaḥat al-Tiyātrāt, dated 5 March 1881, Dūsiya 7085, Maḥfaẓa 275, ʿAyn 1, Dūlāb 13, DM.

[109] Politis, *L'Hellénisme*, 1:200.

[110] Kashf Bayān mudad khidmat janāb Bawlīnū Dārānīt Bāshā alladhī kāna bi-Maṣlaḥat al-Tiyātrāt, dated 5 March 1881, Dūsiya 7085, Maḥfaẓa 275, ʿAyn 1, Dūlāb 13, DM.

[111] Letter dated ? 1271 (1854–1855), A.}AMD. 63/78, and letter dated 28 Shaʿbān 1271 (14 May 1855), A.}DVN. 103/98, both in BOA.

[112] Sadgrove, *Egyptian Theatre*, 48. Sadgrove and others may use this phrase after John Ninet who calls Draneht factotum intermédiaire et secrétaire (sans plume) des commandements des Saïd-Pacha. Ninet, *Lettres d'Égypte*, 71.

[113] De Lesseps, *Recollections of Forty Years*, 1:181.

[114] Letter dated 18 April 1857, from Draneht Bey to an unknown person, 3003–041343, DWQ.

visit to Beirut in 1859.[115] In 1857, Draneht was placed on an even higher salary scale (receiving 5,000 *qurūsh* monthly) by the personal order of the pasha.[116] This also meant that he left the military medical service and was attached to the entourage.[117]

Being a pharmacist at the Egyptian court was a very delicate position. Draneht did not sell medicines from a shop. He was constantly close to the aging Mehmed Ali, taking care of his body, knowing his intimate health problems and keeping this perhaps often embarrassing knowledge to himself. This is the key to the confidence in him. He proved himself valuable already in the 1840s. As to Said's particular favor, one has to consider that Said was fluent in French, tutored by a certain François Bravay who became a favorite (and subsequently a millionaire); Draneht knew French and Turkish too, which was definitely an advantage. In addition, Said was almost the same age as Draneht.

Draneht's activity soon expanded to include nonmedical issues. He was sent to Paris to buy "a special item" in 1860. At that time, there was also a negotiation between Said and French bankers (Comptoir d'Escompte-Charles Laffitte) for a major loan. Draneht signed the contract in July 1860 in Said's name.[118] Perhaps he is the one Nubar characterized at this time as *moitié employé, moitié homme d'affairs.*[119] After his return from Paris, Draneht was named the director of Railways (and General Transport, *Mudīr al-Sikka al-Ḥadīdiyya wa-ʿUmūm al-Murūr*) in January 1861, perhaps not unrelated to the fact that one of the bankers in Paris, Laffitte, had great expertise in railway financing.[120] However, despite the government job, he took his salary from the entourage of Said.[121] This was a typical intersection between the government and the entourage employees

[115] *Ḥadīqat al-Akhbār*, 17 Dhū al-Qaʿda 1275 (18 June 1859), 3.

[116] Kashf Bayān mudad khidmat janāb Bawlīnū Dārānīt Bāshā alladhī kāna bi-Maṣlaḥat al-Tiyātrāt, dated 5 March 1881, Dūsiya 7085, Maḥfaẓa 275, ʿAyn 1, Dūlāb 13, DM.

[117] État de services prêtès au Gouvernement Égyptien par S. E. Paolino Draneht Bey, dated 1 June 1880, Dūsiya 7085, Maḥfaẓa 275, ʿAyn 1, Dūlāb 13, DM.

[118] Draneht, et al., *Observations pour Son Altesse*; Landes, *Bankers and Pashas*, 107; Ghali, ed., *Mémoirs de Nubar Pacha*, 191, n. 1. While in Paris, between August and November 1860, Draneht must have bought many objects (for Said) since he received a great number of payment receipts, all in 3003–041344, DWQ.

[119] Ghali, ed., *Mémoirs de Nubar Pacha*, 190.

[120] Sāmī, *Taqwīm al-Nīl*, part 3, vol. 1:367, irāda dated 28 Jumādā al-Ākhira 1277 (11 January 1861). Cf. Hunter, "Egypt's High Officials," 286. Politis, *L'Hellénisme*, 1: 200. For Laffitte's past see Landes, *Bankers and Pashas*, 29, n. 2. Draneht was indicated as the pharmacist of Said Pasha in the *Bulletin de L'Institut Égyptien* 2., no. 4. (1860, printed in 1861), 12. In the satire of Ninet, the khedive says that Draneht was secrétaire des commandements de feu mon oncle et prédécesseur Said. Ninet, "Finances et Menus Plaisirs," in his *Au pays des khedives*, 279.

[121] Kashf Bayān mudad khidmat janāb Bawlīnū Dārānīt Bāshā alladhī kāna bi-Maṣlaḥat al-Tiyātrāt, dated 5 March 1881, Dūsiya 7085, Maḥfaẓa 275, ʿAyn 1, Dūlāb 13, DM. See also letter to Shīmī Efendi, dated 18 Jumādā al-Awwal 1279 (11 November 1862), Qayd 539, MST, Microfilm 99, DWQ.

in mid-nineteenth-century Egypt. Such were the finishing touches of Draneht's final metamorphosis into a French gentleman with a tarbush.

The Agent, 1860s

From this time Draneht acted as a cultural agent for the dynasty. He moved between Paris and Cairo, acquiring French luxury articles, machines, or even books. For instance, he returned to Paris in 1862 to buy four locomotives, with a loan from Comptoir d'Escompte,[122] together with different luxury objects and furniture for Said. His master died in January 1863. Draneht immediately congratulated the new governor, Ismail, adding a note that he needed money for the items already bought.[123]

Ismail too needed the services of Draneht in Paris. In February 1863, there were days when he posted as many as ten packages to Egypt.[124] There is an estimate that the harem of Ismail annually cost 300,000 (British?) pounds, of which one-third was spent on European luxury items,[125] perhaps through Draneht. He was supposed to have real freedom in finances.[126] In the spring of 1868 Draneht negotiated a new, major loan for Ismail.[127] On this occasion, he also bought various agricultural machines and books for Ismail's sons.[128]

From 1864 he also received the record monthly salary of 8,000 *qurūsh* as Director of Railways, which was paid from 1866 by the now separate unit of Public Transport (in 1865 Nubar as Minister of Public Works regained the directorship of the Railways).[129] Draneht's Parisian life was entirely financed by the khedive, with 3,150 francs monthly, and he

[122] Letter dated 10 April 1863, from Draneht to the Minister of Finance. 3003–041345, DWQ.

[123] Letter dated 27 January 1863, from Draneht to Koenig Bey, Maḥfaẓa 80, CAI, DWQ. The letter dated 19 January 1863, Draneht Bey to Koenig Bey, from Paris, asks Koenig to mention to the new pasha, that he had bought four locomotives for 89,333.35 francs. Maḥfaẓa 1/1, CAI, DWQ.

[124] Letter dated 10 January 1863, Draneht to Koenig Bey, Maḥfaẓa 80, CAI, DWQ.

[125] Lott, *The English Governess*, 91.

[126] The Egyptian officials on one occasion thought that Draneht had contracted another loan in Paris, so he had to clarify that he had not, and, that the contract for the second loan was not in his possession. Letter dated 18 June 1863, Paris, from Draneht to Ahmed Rachid Pasha, Minister of Finance, 3003–042627, DWQ.

[127] Letter dated 8 March 1868, French Consul to French Ambassador in Constantinople, 166PO/D25/70, MEAN. Also, Arboit, "L'arme financière," 553.

[128] For the objects, cf. letter dated 17 April 1868, Draneht to Eram Bey. Maḥfaẓa 12, CAI, DWQ. For the princes' education, see letter dated 19 April 1868, Draneht to Khayri; letter dated 28 April 1868, Khayri to Draneht; letter dated 18 May 1868, Draneht to Khayri. Maḥfaẓa 1/2, CAI, DWQ.

[129] Kashf Bayān mudad khidmat janāb Bawlīnū Dārānīt Bāshā alladhī kāna bi-Maṣlaḥat al-Tiyātrāt, dated 5 March 1881, Dūsiya 7085, Maḥfaẓa 275, ʿAyn 1, Dūlāb 13, DM. Also, Ghali, ed. Mémoirs de Nubar Pacha, 184.

received gifts of land again (1,485 feddan),[130] in addition to the lands he already possessed from Mehmed Ali.

In sum, Draneht's career shows a number of transformations, social climbing, acquiring wealth, new languages, and a new name. From an Ottoman Greek boy in the 1820s he changed into a Parisian agent of the khedive in the 1860s. His most valuable quality was his unquestionable loyalty to the rulers of Egypt. During his career, he proved himself trustworthy and able to work as a purveyor of French goods into Egyptian palaces. As a guardian of Mehmed Ali's health, his knowledge established a very unique relation to his masters. This is the prehistory to his surprising appointment in April 1869 as the superintendent of all khedivial theaters. Loyalty was the key in this appointment.

The Administration and Supervision of Public Culture

Why should a superintendent of theaters be loyal to the ruler? The European aesthetics of khedivial power was a double-edged weapon. In addition to serving as personal entertainment, the theaters, and even the opera house, were potential sources of challenging authority *in public*. "Superintendent" means someone who is in charge; typically in the police or in a prison.[131] In the nineteenth century, the superintendent of theaters often was the highest artistic moral authority in a city or in a small state (for instance, in German states). Given the potential critical nature of theater, loyalty to the ruler was crucial in Draneht's position.

Le Grand Maître des Menus Plaisirs

This loyalty included, first and foremost, serving the personal tastes and wishes of Ismail. Draneht had to deal with *all* the French and Italian entertainments of the khedive in Cairo. He sent singers and dancers to Ismail's yacht, to his palaces, and to entertain his guests. In addition, Draneht continued to function as the khedive's agent abroad, contacting French journalists, for instance, and bribing them.[132] There are rumours that he worked as a royal pimp by delivering ladies to Ismail. There is evidence in the documents that Ismail instructed his superintendent to contract beautiful dancers. For instance, in the summer of 1871 Draneht sent photographs of

[130] Draneht sent monthly receipts, at least in 1868. Letter dated 2 December 1868, Draneht to an unknown person (probably to Ismāʿīl Ṣiddīq Pasha, Minister of Finances), 3003–041347, DWQ. Hunter, *Egypt under the Khedives*, 108.

[131] Art. "superintendent," *Oxford English Dictionary*.

[132] Letter dated 21 April 1870, from Draneht to Riaz Pasha, 5013–002701, DWQ.

ballerinas to the khedive who noted that "the dancer Casali is truly beautiful and if her sister is as beautiful as she I think you should not let such a beautiful treasure to escape."[133] No wonder European residents in Egypt described Draneht as *le grand maître des Menus Plaisirs du Vice-Roi.*[134]

Draneht's System

As superintendent, appointed at the end of April 1869,[135] Draneht was the director of a department specializing in representation and entertainment. This department was—or was imagined by Draneht as—a structurally independent unit, outside the Egyptian governmental hierarchy. His (exclusively) French letterheads indicated that this was the *Administration des Théâtres du Khédive d'Égypte.* From November 1870, Draneht himself took his salary from *Muḥāfaẓat Miṣr*, the Cairo Governorate. Within the Governorate there was an administrative unit (possibly on paper only), officially called in Arabic *Maṣlaḥat al-Tiyātrāt* (the Department of Theaters) that existed between 1870 and 1877.[136] This may have been Draneht's administration. From January 1872 this unit became a subunit of the *Service of Roads and Streets* (*Khidmat al-Ṭuruq wa-l-Shawāriʿ*) which was the new name of the City Public Works (*Tanẓīm*), headed by Pierre Grand (1839–1918), an engineer at the Governorate. After April 1877, Draneht again received his salary from the entourage until 1879.[137] Despite the administrative unit's being independent, his position belonged to the Governorate, making him a government employee. There is no evidence to suggest he was responsible for any theater outside of Cairo, or even within Cairo, save the khedivial network. Only during 1869–1870 did he arrange for a circus to perform in Alexandria.[138] Draneht focused on Cairo, on Europe, and on the person of the khedive.

Draneht's "empire," the theatrical infrastructure of khedivial culture, between 1869 and 1873 included the Opera House, the Comédie, the Cirque, the Hippodrome, to some extent the Garden Theater of al-Azbakiyya, the private theater in Qaṣr al-Nīl Palace,[139] and wherever the khedive wanted performances (for instance, on board the yacht

[133] Letter dated 18 August 1871, from Barrot to Draneht, 5013–004133, DWQ.

[134] Ninet, *Lettres d'Égypte*, 73.

[135] *Wādī al-Nīl*, 30 April 1869, 47. Their information comes from *Le Nil.*

[136] Letter dated 18 Jumādā al-Ākhir 1297 (28 May 1880), from Māliyya to Ḍabṭiyya Miṣr, Dūsiya 7085, Maḥfaẓa 275, ʿAyn 1, Dūlāb 13, DM.

[137] Sāmī, *Taqwīm al-Nīl*, part 3, 2:881. Kashf Bayān mudad khidmat janāb Bawlīnū Dārānīt Bāshā alladhī kāna bi-Maṣlaḥat al-Tiyātrāt, dated 5 March 1881, Dūsiya 7085, Maḥfaẓa 275, ʿAyn 1, Dūlāb 13, DM.

[138] Letter dated 21 April 1869, Draneht to Eram Bey, Maḥfaẓa 80, CAI, DWQ.

[139] ʿAbdūn, *ʿĀyida*, 28.

al-Maḥrūsa). These four years were the golden years of Draneht; after 1873 there were financial cuts, and his power was curtailed.

During his intendancy, it was in Draneht's interest to keep all the entertainment institutions under his control, but without being involved in their daily affairs.[140] He only kept the position of director of the Opera House for himself; other positions were subcontracted to various individuals. His was a lucrative position and therefore often challenged.[141] After 1873, with the Cirque demolished and the Hippodrome suspended, Draneht only oversaw the Opera, the Comédie, and the private entertainments.

Draneht's Men: The Staff of the Khedivial Theaters

Who ran the theaters? What did the everyday staff look like? The following short microhistory of the khedivial theaters gives a sense of the conditions and the work of the new material public sphere. In the first years, when Draneht was not in Egypt, Pierre Grand, the chief city planner of Cairo, held the keys of the theaters, literally.[142] Grand was also responsible for the maintenance of the theaters from April 1871.[143] The right-hand man was Léopold Larose, the keeper of costumes from 1872, originally a French actor from Manasse's former troupe.[144] Larose would become Draneht's successor in the early 1880s.

Between 1869 and 1873 the Administration of Khedivial Theaters employed Europeans and Egyptians both temporarily and permanently. Europeans were mostly designated for specialist positions, such as tailors and machinists, while Egyptian men were employed as *farrāsh* (guards, night watchmen, servants). In the autumn of 1869, when the season opened,

[140] When Draneht arrived in Paris in late May 1869, there were rumours that he would appoint Nicole Lablache as administrateur of the Opera and the Comédie. *Le Ménestrel*, 23 May 1869, 199. Lablache was in Cairo in September 1869. Letter dated 29 September 1869, from Antoine Banucci to the Khedive, in 5013–003022, DWQ.

[141] For the Opera, cf. letters dated 22 January 1870, V. Spagnoli to Riaz, and 28 January 1870, V. Spagnoli to Riaz; for the Comédie cf. letter dated 21 April 1870, from Draneht to Riaz, letters dated 19 and 20 January 1871, Rosenboom to Riaz, all in Maḥfaẓa 80, CAI, DWQ. Draneht's argument was that the costumes are shared by the two theaters. Rosenboom got the Azbakiyya Garden Theatre for 3000 francs per year, letter dated 3 April 1871, from Lavasseur to [Barillet ?]. Maḥfaẓa 62, CAI; letter dated 4 April 1871, from Riaz to Monsieur Barillet, 5013–004133, both in DWQ.

[142] Letter dated 8 September [possibly 1870 or 1871], from ? to Riaz. Maḥfaẓa 80, CAI, DWQ.

[143] Attachment to letter dated 1 April 1871, from Franz Bey to Riaz Pasha, 5013–003521, DWQ.

[144] Letter dated 21 June 1872, from Larose to Draneht, in Abdoun, *Genesi dell' "Aida,"* 117. Letter dated 11 September 1872, from Draneht to Larose, in Abdoun, *Genesi dell' "Aida,"* 119–120. Des Perrières, *Un Parisian*, 118, mentions that Larose was among Manasse's actors.

the staff included Madame Ferdinand (Elise) Béroule, costumier;[145] a certain Pravis, decorator; the Frenchmen Lablache and Hostein (two administrators);[146] Alphonse Hébert, *chef magasinier des costumes*, and Jacques Soulet, tailor;[147] and a number of Egyptian guards.[148] At the end of this season, the permanent staff included twelve individuals (tailors, guards, servants) whose total expenses were 2,083 francs.[149] In the next season in 1870, among the Egyptians were Aḥmad Efendi Rāghib (who was the security "supervisor" of the khedivial theaters, *nāẓir al-tiyātrāt*), Muḥammad ʿAlī Muḥyī al-Dīn Qabbānī, Masīḥa Faraj, Sālim Ibrāhīm, and Aḥmad al-Kūmī (we shall meet him again), Muḥammad Ismāʿīl, and many others.[150] There was also a translator, Buṭrus Yūsuf.[151] Most of the visiting Western Europeans were employed on short-term contracts,[152] especially the case during *Aida*'s production in the 1871–1872 season when the Italian Carlo d'Ormeville (1840–1924) was named as poet and *régisseur du théâtre du Caire*.[153]

In 1878, the permanent personnel consisted of nine individuals as table 3.2 indicates. In this table it is not only the high salary of the Europeans compared to the Egyptian guards that is striking (Draneht's salary, see below, was *one hundred* times and Larose's almost *fifty* times more than the Egyptian guards), but also the payment of the Egyptian boss of the *ferraches*, Shāhīn Efendi, which was higher than that of the European tailors. All Egyptian guards were previously employed at khedivial palaces or the Private Domains. Shāhīn Efendi in fact later also served in the

[145] French Note to the Conseil des Ministres from MTP, dated 19 February 1887, 2/1, Niẓārat al-Ashghāl al-ʿUmūmiyya, CMW, DWQ.

[146] Hostein possibly left in December 1869 (though no trace of this was found in the documents). *Le Ménestrel*, 12 December 1869, 15. However, according to the *Revue et Gazette Musicale de Paris* he prolonged his contract for one more year. 10 April 1870, 119.

[147] Case *Jacques Soulet* v. *Alphonse Hébert*, dated April 1870, French consular court, 354PO/3/80, MEAN.

[148] Letter from Rancy to the Police Municipale au Caire, dated 12 November 1869. Maḥfaẓa 80, CAI, DWQ.

[149] Copy of Amr Karīm, dated Ghurrat Ṣafar 1287 (May 1870), in the pension dossier of al-Sitt Farnānd Brūl, Dūsiya 22517, Maḥfaẓa 863, ʿAyn 3, Dūlāb 43, DM.

[150] Daftar, Juzʾ Thānin Jarīdat Istiḥqāqāt bi-Qalam al-Shawāriʿ wa-l-Ṭuruq wa-l-Mutanazzahāt wa-l-Tiyātrāt bi-Muḥāfaẓat Miṣr, Tūtī (Thout) 1587, 2002–003602, DWQ.

[151] Daftar, Juzʾ Thānin Jarīdat Istiḥqāqāt bi-Qalam al-Shawāriʿ wa-l-Ṭuruq wa-l-Mutanazzahāt wa-l-Tiyātrāt al-tābiʿīn li-Muḥāfaẓat Miṣr, Tūtī (Thout) 1588, 2002–003605, DWQ.

[152] Based on the payment daftars of Muḥāfaẓat Miṣr, one can reconstruct the personnel in a detailed way annually: 2002–003604, 2002–003605, DWQ.

[153] *Le Ménestrel*, 2 June 1872, 223. D'Ormeville was an impresario himself. Rosselli, *The Opera Industry in Italy*, 28. In another document of the same year he is mentioned as directeur de la scène while a certain Giovanni Scotta was the régisseur de l'opera. Consular court record, case *Draneht Bey* v. *François Sinibaldi*, 8 December 1871, 354PO/3/81, MEAN.

TABLE 3.2. Personnel du service de l'entretien du matérial, 1878

Nom	*Appointements mensuels*	*Fonctions*	*Age*	*Date de l'entrée du service*	*Temps du service*	*Antécedents de l'employé avant son entrée au service actuel*
Larose Léopold	833 fr = 3,207 piasters	Conservateur du Matériel	38	1871	7	artiste dramatique et régisseur de théâtre
Passotti Joseph	150 fr = 577 piasters	Tailleur costumier	46	1870	8	Tailleur au Collége des Fréres, Caire
Béroule Elise	150 fr = 577 piasters	Couturière	36	1869	9	Néant
Chaïn Efendi	194 fr = 746 piasters	Chef des ferraches, Salle et loges V R	40	1870	8	Chef ferrache au palais de Ras-el-Tin
Mohamet Ismaïl	38.88 fr = 149 piasters	Ferrache Opera	32	1870	8	Ferrache de la Daïra Hassa
Ahmet el-Komi	38.88 fr = 149 piasters	Ferrache Comédie	28	1870	8	Ferrache de Kasr-el-Nil
Aly Ayoub	49.25 fr = 189 piasters	Portefaire	28	1870	8	Néant
Abdallah Awadeine	25.92 fr = 99 piasters	Gardien du nuit Comédie	30	1878		Gaffir au Palais de S. A. Mansour Pacha
Hussein Ibraïm	25.92 fr = 99 piasters	Gardien du nuit Opéra	25	1875	3	Gaffir au service du Gouvernement

Source: Letter dated 30 December 1878, from Léopold Larose to an unknown person (Le Directeur de l'administration de la Voirie?), 4003–037847, DWQ. Original orthography.

army.[154] This means that security was a concern and it was important to employ trusted men. I shall return to questions of control in chapter 7, but now we must have a look into the finances.

Draneht and Money

Ismail's extraordinary spending on entertainment is often legendary. It is indeed certain that between 1869 and 1875 Ismail Pasha spent (sometimes much) more than one million French francs in every year on the theaters.

His spending, apart from vanity, was also due to the fact that Egypt was a province, not a state, thus "official institutions" had to be established by the pasha personally. In 1869, there was no financial framework to which the theaters belonged. The construction was financed by the Private Domains of the khedive, but the Cairo Governorate maintained the buildings. The Private Domains also covered the expenses of the performances and troupes. Only after 1869 did Draneht suggest a financial "system" to the khedive. He proposed that, in order to avoid delays in the payment of the artists and staff, the khedive should open a credit for him at the Anglo-Egyptian Bank or any other bank.[155] Avoiding delays, thus went his argument, was important for the "dignity" of the khedive. This system was not put into effect properly. Payments were made through two channels: either by paying the sums to Draneht by the Private Domains or, mostly, when he was in Europe, credits were opened in different banks but only with previously defined amounts.

Usually, Draneht calculated the approximate cost of the next season and submitted it to the Private Domains. Sometimes, the original calculation had already been exceeded even during the preparation.[156] After every season, he counted and submitted the final cost showing the deficit. Having a deficit was a natural outcome, and this was usually accepted. Sadgrove provides a table with some of the estimated receipts and expenses.[157] For instance, the production of *Aida* alone cost a minimum of 320,000 francs in 1871.[158] These high sums, spent on representation in the form of entertainment, should be regarded in the light of the scarcity of public welfare institutions for the general population.

The first documented trouble with finances occurred in 1875 when Draneht had to return 60,000 francs to the Private Domains, and Ismail

[154] Letter dated 21 Jumādā al-Thānī 1302 (7 April 1885), 0075–027068, DWQ.
[155] Letter dated 27 November 1869, from Draneht to Eram Bey, Maḥfaẓa 80, CAI, DWQ.
[156] Letter dated 11 June 1873, Draneht Bey to Barrot Bey, 5013–003511, DWQ.
[157] Based on Maḥfaẓa 80, CAI, DWQ in Sadgrove, *Egyptian Theatre*, 79.
[158] Calculation dated 12 March 1872, unsigned [Draneht ?], Maḥfaẓa 80, CAI, DWQ.

did not accept the financial plan for the 1875–1876 season.[159] In chapter 7, we shall see that the finances of the khedivial theaters were transferred to the centralized, new government at the end of the 1870s.

The Power of Symbols and *Aida* as a Khedivial Opera

Compared to the symbols of patriotism in Arabic offered to Ismail in the 1860s, the khedivial theaters directed by Draneht offered a way to hide the Ottoman attachment of Egypt. I conclude by highlighting two elements that followed from the use of theaters in the khedivate: the new style of symbolic rule and the opera *Aida*. This also means that the ruler clothed himself in European representation as his public image, literally.

Ismail and his men were not only concerned with his representation but with *his image as the representation of what Egypt would be*. Similar to Peter Burke's observation in the case of Louis XIV, this activity was aimed at Ismail's own urban elite, at foreigners (especially consuls), and posterity, that is, *us*.[160]

The Function of Italian Opera in Khedivial Egypt

The representation of power, as far as the Opera House was concerned and imagined, was Italianized. Within the competition between French and Italian grand operas, it was the Italian language and Italian artists who were the main makers of the European political aesthetics in Egypt. Like Manasse, Draneht also used specialized French agencies to hire "light" operetta artists, for instance, in 1874 Pandolfini,[161] and in 1877 Laugier.[162] In Italy, it was mostly Draneht himself who contracted the most important singers. Draneht also married an Italian woman, Adele Casati (the daughter of a cellist from La Scala) in 1872.[163] For the grand opening (1 November 1869), he contracted the best Italian artists, arranged the scenery, the costumes, paid and asked for payment, lodged the staff, and personally arranged the program of the opening evening. Verdi had been approached to write a hymn for the grand opening in 1869, but he refused the request.[164] An Italian poem was chosen to be set

[159] Letter dated 21 April 1875, Draneht to Barrot, 5013–003511, DWQ.

[160] Burke, *The Fabrication*, 153.

[161] Letter dated 14 February 1875, from Draneht to Barrot, 5013–003511, DWQ.

[162] Letter dated 19 October 1877, from Draneht to Khayri, 5013–003511, DWQ.

[163] Koudounaris, *Biografikon Leksikon*, 137. They married a few months before the premiere of *Aida*. Busch, *Verdi's Aida*, 632.

[164] Letter dated 6 August 1869, Draneht to Riaz, Maḥfaẓa 80, CAI, DWQ.

to music for the opening night as we have seen, and the opera *Rigoletto* was staged.

The Italian *Risorgimento*—the unification of Italy and independence from the Habsburgs—and the popularity of Verdi represented an elite form of patriotism, useful for Ismail, rather than Arabic patriotism, which still could include the Ottoman-Muslim attachment. Also, Italian opera was the choice of Sultan Abdülmecid in the Istanbul of the 1850s. As to the development of global entertainment markets, the Khedivial Opera House became an important Italian location in Egypt within the international network of opera houses. In sum, a new type of political symbolism as "Europe" arrived in the khedivate.

A Portrait of the Pasha

A Muslim religious scholar once complained about the Mixed Courts (introduced in 1876), but perhaps about general Europeanization of Egypt, and Ismail answered: "What can we do now that foreigners live side by side with us, and this is their civilisation?"[165] With the new cultural infrastructure, Ismail acquired the potential to represent his power in the same way Christian monarchs in Europe elaborated their own. European aesthetics has been a means of being accepted in the evolving international order.

Concerning this type of representation, Louis Marin argues that there were three layers of the royal body in France: the physical body, the institution of kingship, and the "semiotic body"—the portrait, a painting of the king—which stood between the physical and the imagined juridico-political institution. Marin states that the self-assured hegemony of Louis XIV could only be complete in representation. "The king is only truly king, that is, monarch, in images."[166] But as it happens, Marin's example, the portrait of the king was not public but is in fact a *description* of the portrait.[167] The description of an image through narration made it possible to talk about the monarch. This aspect of European traditions of kingship was not far from the narrative enunciations of power in Islam. By the eighteenth century, however, most European monarchs had also acquired the opera house for rituals of physical display. An almost bodily connection between culture and sovereignty was established—the "operatic state," to quote again Ruth Bereson. Here the body of the sovereign became an animated representation of imagined territorial sovereignty.

[165] Cook, *Commanding Right and Forbidding Wrong*, 509.
[166] Marin, *Portrait of the King*, 8; 13–14.
[167] Marin, *Portrait of the King*, 207.

FIGURE 3.4. *Allegory of the Joining of the Two Seas*, 1869
Source: Collection Hani Gresh, with permission from M. Hani Gresh.

From the beginning of Ismail's reign, Europeans had manufactured inanimate pictorial and narrative images about this pasha. For instance, Ismail was idealized by Italian merchants in Egypt, and the French photographer Ermé Désiré prepared hundreds of photographs about Cairo, the schools, students, soldiers, by order of the khedive (during 1866-1867).[168] Ismail's own images started to proliferate, in the form of drawings, paintings, photographs, and narrative descriptions. The dynasty even possessed watches with Ismail's portrait (perhaps made for his wives or children).[169] However, by 1869, the iconography of the pasha had included public images that showed him in the contemporary pantheon of imperial monarchs, as in figure 3.4 with Emperor Franz Joseph and Empress Eugénie at the Suez Canal.

In 1870 Ismail ordered the portraits of his children.[170] The Khedivial Opera House itself became a storehouse of dynastic images. In addition to the paintings in the interior and the decorated curtains, Ismail's own

[168] These photos seem to be lost. Bayān al-rusūmāt al-futughrāfiyya, dated 16 May 1867, from Dazīrah Arnī Rassam Futughrāfī, 58/41, MST, Microfilm 200, DWQ.

[169] *The Palace Collections of Egypt*, 199–205.

[170] Jerichau-Baumann, "Egypt 1870."

FIGURE 3.5. A painting of Ibrahim Pasha in the hall of the Khedivial Opera House
Source: Collection Max Karkégi, with permission from M. Max Karkégi.

bust was housed in the building, possibly the one made for the opening ceremony in 1869. His father's, Ibrahim's equestrian statute was placed in front of the Opera, and from 1872 a large painting of the same image hung inside (see figure 3.5).

Ismail's body transformed. All types of public occasions displayed the pasha's body as the animate representation of the khedivate. As early as January 1869, to the astonishment of his minister Nubar, Ismail behaved in the Comédie as a European monarch.[171] At the wedding of Ismail's daughter Tevhide in the spring of 1869 Seraphin Manasse's French operetta troupe also performed. At this occasion, the Egyptian notables sat next to the ruler.[172] Ismail practiced this habitus in Europe a few months later. In the summer of 1869, he visited Le Peletier Opera House in Paris,

[171] Ghali, ed., *Mémoires de Nubar Pacha*, 349–350.

[172] *Al-Waqāʾiʿ al-Miṣriyya*, 31 March 1869, 2–3 and *Wādī al-Nīl*, 23 April 1869, 11–12. *Le Monde Illustré* published an image of this event on its title page on 24 April 1869 and a short description of the Theater of the Harem. This image dated inaccurately as 1873 in Gaultier-Kurhan, *Princesses d'Égypte*, 95 and mistakenly attributed to the marriage of Princess Fatma Ismail. From the Arabic journals, it is clear that it is the marriage of Princess Tevhide (Tawḥīda). Consequently, the date of 1868 as the marriage of Tevhide is also incorrect in Gaultier-Kurhan, *Princesses d'Égypte*, 92–93.

in the company of Draneht and Nubar, and was seated in the loge of the emperor.[173] He was celebrated in London as a curiosity, and a public concert of the works Mendelssohn, Mozart, Rossini, and Costa was organized in his honor by the Sacred Harmonic Society.[174] Though Ismail became an object of curiosity in Europe (similarly to Sultan Abdülaziz in 1867 and the Persian Shah Nāṣir al-Dīn in 1873), he may have been inspired in his use of the Khedivial Opera House under construction in Cairo at that very moment.

In the theaters, the khedive became a member of the audience. His body became visible and approachable. This was radically new in late Ottoman Egypt. As we have seen, architecturally the theaters, especially the opera house, were designed for the gaze to wander freely and to emphasize the presence of the ruler. The auditoriums were built to help that the sheer presence of monarchical bodies pose a physical obligation on their environment. The gaze of the audience had to acknowledge the ruler, who, on his side, also had to acknowledge the presence of his subjects by body language: waving, nodding, and clapping. This mutual acknowledgement of bodily presences should have been the physical confirmation of the bourgeois compromise between the ruler and his (elite) citizens. The break with the Muslim-Ottoman tradition of "absent-present" ruleship, however, was limited to the narrow elite and the European visitors.

This analysis may invite an interpretation of the khedivial theaters as the public extension of a "court culture" following the Western European model.[175] Draneht's career and position, the finances of the theaters, and the way the khedive was framed would endorse such an interpretation. Yet, such a suggestion may draw misleading conclusions about extending the Ottoman style. "Court" is a mistaken concept in connection with the Ottoman style of rule. It is the palace and within it, the public part called *salamlık* and the private, family part called *haramlık* where the body of the ruler was approachable (still from a distance) to selected individuals. These individuals were called the "entourage" (*maʿiyya*). Said Pasha, to some extent, changed this Ottoman mode of dynastic reception and habitation to a more French style.[176] However, the khedivial theaters did not replicate publically what occurred in the "court." In fact, as we have seen in chapter 2 and shall see in the next chapter, Ismail's mode of reign remained largely Ottoman (harem) politics, and the local Muslim elite framed him as a Muslim prince in Arabic.

[173] *Le Moniteur Universel*, 16 June 1869, quoted in Teillais, *La voyage de S. A. le Vice-Roi*, 29–30.

[174] *Illustrated London News*, 10 July 1869, quoted in Warner, *An Egyptian Panorama*, 21.

[175] Ther, *In der Mitte der Gesellschaft*; Bereson, *The Operatic State*.

[176] Konrad, *Der Hof der Khediven*, 379–390.

Aida: Ancient Egypt in the Service of the Khedivate

The peak of the European mode of aesthetic rule is the opera *Aida* and its premiere in December 1871. Its history is well researched,[177] and it became an object of heated debate following Edward Said's critique of it as a colonial opera that portrays an "Orientalized Egypt." Said argues that *Aida* is an example of "an imperial *article de luxe*, purchased by credit for a tiny clientele."[178] Paul Robinson, an opera expert, rejects this interpretation and claims that it is an Italian opera about the ancient Egyptian Empire.[179] According to the Italian literary scholar, Lucia Re, "Khedive Ismail is likely to have seen in Verdi's music a political symbol of the spirit of national independence rather than a means to enslave Egypt . . . to Europe."[180]

I also wish to link *Aida* to the Italian *Risorgimento* as it was understood by the Ottoman elite. The work represents Egypt as an empire. Indeed, khedivial Egypt was an empire-like polity that ruled the Sudan and Ethiopia with links to the Hijaz and Greater Syria. Ancient Egypt was important for Mehmed Ali and Ismail, as we have seen in chapter 2, and the title *ʿAzīz Miṣr*, derived from the Koranic depiction of ancient Egypt, was the way local intellectuals made sense of Ismail's rule. Donald Reid shows that ancient Egyptian symbols were used in state symbolism from the 1820s on and that the science of Egyptology was important for nineteenth-century Egyptians.[181] Ancient Egypt figured as an integral part of the Egyptian popular imagination, as Sandor Fodor argues,[182] although what Michael Cook terms "Hermetic history" popular in the educated circles of mediaeval Egypt may have originated from further east.[183] Be that as it may, Muṣṭafā Salāma al-Najjārī's 1863 history written for Ismail, reactivates this Hermetic tradition as a patriotic one.[184] The khedivate was encouraged to be imagined as a resurrected ancient Egyptian empire since this image was known in Europe as a sovereign state.

Ismail and the Egyptologist Auguste Mariette (1821–1881) conceived *Aida* in order to further enhance this image. This work could be created

[177] Busch, *Verdi's Aida*; Said, *Culture and Imperialism*; Humbert, "Les Expositions universelles de 1867 et 1878"; Weaver, *Verdi—A Documentary Study*; Robinson, "Is Aida an Orientalist Opera?"; Locke, "Beyond the Exotic: How 'Eastern' Is Aida?"; and Re, "Alexandria Revisited," 163–196.

[178] Said, *Culture and Imperialism*, 129.

[179] Robinson, "Is Aida an Orientalist Opera?," 134.

[180] Re, "Alexandria Revisited," 164.

[181] Reid, *Whose Pharaohs?*

[182] Fodor, *Arab legendák*, 104.

[183] Cook, "Pharaonic History," 98.

[184] The manuscript is to be published soon.

only by a European composer, since, except for the military musicians, there was no Egyptian composer trained in polyphony at the time. There was, none the less, a pianist and composer of Egyptian origins, Achille Mansour (d. 1889), in Paris,[185] who could have been asked had Ismail not targeted (Verdi's) fame. The irony is that in 1871, when *Aida* was to be premiered, Mansour in fact composed a *valse* for piano entitled *Patria!* in French.

One important detail may allude to the fact that Ismail, or at least Draneht, understood very well the contemporary elite mechanism of constructing the nation. Draneht explained in a letter to Verdi that Ismail intended to acquire a "national opera."[186] There is no further information about what this meant exactly. The word "national," as used by Draneht, is probably the translation of the khedive's will or a convenient term to convince the maestro. Draneht might have drawn an implicit parallel between Italy revolting against Habsburg rule and Egypt revolting against the Ottoman Empire, as some European journalist mistakenly did.

Aida is about an Ethiopian princess (Aida) who is captured by the Egyptian imperial army. The leader of the Egyptian army (Radames) falls in love with her. He is accused of being a traitor, because the daughter of the pharaoh is also in love with him. Finally, Radames is sent to his death (buried alive) and Aida dies with him. After reading the plot, Verdi wrote that "it shows a very expert hand, accustomed to this craft, and one who knows the theater very well."[187]

The plot was Mariette's, who was also responsible for the set. Yet the Franco-Prussian war caught Mariette with the costumes in Paris in the fall of 1870. This was the moment when Draneht took over from Mariette and negotiated new terms with Verdi.

The premiere in the evening of 24 December 1871 was an apotheosis of the Italian face of the khedivate. It was a physical, somatic, and gendered annunciation of Ismail's power. An eye-witness, Baron de Kusel describes the audience in the following way:

> [T]he Khedive with all the princes were there, and the Khadivah was present, and the Egyptian princesses were in the Royal Harem Boxes, the fronts of which were covered in with thin lattice work, through which one could see, hazily, the forms of the ladies, with their diamonds and precious stones sparkling as they moved to and fro in the large royal box. All the Consul-Generals and their wives were present, the ministers and the Khedival staff officers in their

[185] *Le Ménestrel*, 5 September 1858, 4.
[186] Weaver, *Verdi—A Documentary Study*, 225.
[187] Verdi to Du Locle, 26 May 1870, Busch, *Verdi's Aida*, 17.

> brilliant uniforms while in every box were many lovely women, resplendent with jewels.[188]

As Draneht telegraphed to Verdi immediately after the premiere, it was a "complete success." Not only was the music of Verdi celebrated but also the luxury of the set, to such a point, that—as one French correspondent noted—"when the curtain is raised, we forget Aida and Verdi, the drama and the music, because we are absorbed by the magic of the set."[189] The set prepared by Mariette seems to have amazed the mostly European audience who witnessed "the life of ancient Egypt in a modern theater." The French critic Ernest Reyer congratulated the khedive on the success.[190] Filippo Filippi, the Italian critic similarly remarked that the khedive, not Verdi, was applauded after the performance.[191] *Aida* was, in all accounts, a product of European aesthetics in the service of Ismail's legitimation. We shall see its Arabic translation and performances in the coming chapters.

Let us finish with Paul Draneht. Elevated to the rank of pasha, from 1877 he mostly sent letters from Italy to the khedive. He left Egypt at the end of April 1879 because, as he recounted later, his daughter had fallen ill and the khedive had granted him leave. When Ismail was forced to resign in June 1879, Draneht was asked to receive him in Naples.[192] He remained close to the exiled khedive: for instance, at one occasion he arranged a meeting between Ismail and a young Egyptian nobleman in France in the 1880s.[193] Draneht in fact became a wealthy capitalist in occupied Egypt. He died near Alexandria in 1894,[194] and large estates continued to be known by his name well into the twentieth century.[195]

Conclusion: "Europe" in Ottoman Egypt

There was a difference between Western European aesthetics and local Arabic representation. Muslim patriotism represented Ismail in the old universal order, using the elaborate mixed vocabulary of Persian, Turkish, and Arabic. Yet within that universe he was subordinate not only to

188 Kusel, *An Englishman's Recollections*, 89.

189 *Revue et Gazette Musicale de Paris*, 7 January 1872, 5–6, quoting *Indépendence Belge*.

190 *Journal des Débats Politiques et Littéraires*, 16 January 1872, 5–6.

191 Weaver, *Verdi—A Documentary Study*, 229.

192 Letter dated 9 February 1881, from Draneht to Riaz Pasha, Minister of Interior, in Dūsiya 7085, Maḥfaẓa 275, ʿAyn 1, Dūlāb 13, DM.

193 [Gallini Fahmī], *Mudhakkirāt*, 2:31.

194 I am grateful for this information to the Zervudachi family.

195 Papasian, *L'Égypte économique*, 521.

God but also to the Ottoman sultan and Sunni caliph. In contrast, European political aesthetics offered a symbolic domain free from hierarchies from the point of view of Ismail and Draneht. This representation system was a tool to fabricate the sovereign image of the khedive, to obscure his Ottomanness. The government production of a history of "independence" started at this moment with the instrumentalization of European art.

On the whole, elite Ottomans adopted European public aesthetics in khedivial Cairo. Ismail ordered the buildings from European architects, Draneht (once an Ottoman Greek), at the expense of Manasse (an Ottoman Armenian), brought Italian entertainment. The reason was that they could imagine "civilization" only in terms of a faultless import. They were not Arabic-speaking modern Egyptians and did not want to become ones. For them patriotism was an aesthetic principle of dynastic sovereignty within the international order, à la Europe, and not an expression of local solidarity. The paradox was that this externality occurred *within* Egypt. This internal Europe, a Europe within Egypt—but also a Europe "above" Egypt—extremely close to local intellectuals in the capital, had to be reconciled with Muslim patriotism—the topic of the next part of the book.

PART II

"A GARDEN WITH MELLOW FRUITS OF REFINEMENT"

The great question in the new khedivate was to find out what this regime type was exactly and to whom it belonged. A small group of Muslim intellectuals attempted to manipulate the regime by making patriotism its official ideology. They were constrained by both the Ottoman universe (including Ismail's own Ottoman milieu) and the Western European representations. The spatial transformation required the adjustment of sound and body. They turned to a third solution: a language and a historicity that could compete with the power of European aesthetics and still be acceptable in Muslim-Ottoman terms. This was Arabness, a linguistic and spiritual quality. Muslim patriotism transmuted into a patriotism that now also contained a moral idea of Arabness and a clear Egyptian territorial historical narrative.

In this part of the book, I focus on the relationship of Arabic-speaking intellectuals to power in their efforts to negotiate with the khedive through this complex ideology. Importantly, they were dominantly Muslims. They confidently engaged with the new spaces and technologies. Their work exemplifies a noncolonial moment of Muslim modernity. The social world of khedivial Egypt in this rapidly changing period was similar to what is described in contemporary sociology as an "emergent action field," which is "an arena occupied by two or more actors whose actions are oriented to each other, but where agreement over the basic conditions . . . has yet to emerge."[1] In many ways, the actors did not agree on "what is going on" and could not position themselves. Since patriots defined the interest of the *waṭan* their ideas challenged khedivial authority. From 1876, there was foreign financial control. An unsettled, emergent action field was directed by the logic of stabilizing the political world but finally attained the opposite of this goal. Unintended consequences resulted from making Arab patriotism the ideology of the khedivate.

[1] Fligstein and MacAdam, "Toward a General Theory of Strategic Action Fields," 11.

CHAPTER 4

A Gentle Revolution

On a Sunday evening in February 1870, a young journalist, Muḥammad Unsī, sat in one of the seats of the Khedivial Opera House. He watched the opera *Semiramis*. He immediately grasped that there was a connection between theater, language, and patriotism. "Oh, if such refined works were translated into Arabic successfully," wished Unsī in a review he wrote about the performance, "and they were performed in the Egyptian theaters in the Arabic language as an innovation, that the taste [for theater] may spread among the local (*ahliyya*) groups. Because this is the sum of the patriotic (*ahliyya*) components that facilitated the advancement of the European countries and helped to enhance their internal conditions."[1]

This chapter examines how intellectuals—in the Arabic press and in the Arabic theater—reacted to the spatial and sensorial transformation of Cairo and the work of the khedivate. The intellectual production within or associated with government circles constituted what I term a "gentle revolution."[2] This includes the use of the learned Arabic language (*al-ʿarabiyya al-fuṣḥā*) as official language of the khedivate and the retelling of Muslim history of Egypt as an Arab narrative. The keyword of this process was "the homeland" as a political argument.

A very short, gentle epistemological revolution occurred between the mid-1860s and approximately 1873. As an example of the gentle revolutionaries I follow the activity of ʿAbd Allāh Abū al-Suʿūd in this period, who printed al-Ṭahṭāwī's *Marseillaise* in his 1842 book. His son was

[1] Muḥammad Unsī, "Malʿab al-Ūbira bi-Miṣr al-Qāhira," *Wādī al-Nīl*, 28 Dhū al-Qaʿda 1286 (28 February 1870, 1869 is wrongly printed on the cover page), 1332. Both Sadgrove and Ayalon translate the word *ahliyya* in the subtitle of the journal *Wādī al-Nīl* as "popular" to English. Sadgrove, "The Development," 74; and Ayalon, *The Arabic Press*, 41. I have translated *ahliyya* as "local" but in the second sentence as "patriotic," as a synonym to *waṭaniyya*. I base this on the use of *ahliyya* and *waṭaniyya* as synonyms by ʿAbd Allāh Fikrī in a contemporary letter celebrating the establishment of the journal *Wādī al-Nīl* as al-ṣaḥīfa al-ahliyya al-waṭaniyya. Fikrī, ed., *Al-Āthār al-Fikriyya*, 261.

[2] Juan Cole characterized the period 1852–1882 as "the long revolution." I suggest that time was even more accelerated. Cole, *Colonialism and Revolution*, 110–111.

no one else than Muḥammad Unsī (d. 1885/1886), the journalist in the opera house. Abū al-Su^cūd and Unsī were genuine thinkers and belong to the nineteenth-century vanguard of Arab intellectuals. Their story, and their important printing press and journal *Wādī al-Nīl*, in turn, serve as the backdrop against which we can measure the activity of other intellectuals who became famous despite their actual insignificance, such as the writer James Sanua. The story of Sanua's hasty, failed Arabic theater troupe can be seen as a competing project with Unsī for defining the content, or, *direction* of patriotism. Unsī's was a vertical imagined community while Sanua's was a horizontal construction. These imaginations clashed with each other almost invisibly behind the khedivial façade. Let us first examine the making of vertical patriotism in Egypt.

Fuṣḥā Arabic as the Language of Power

Abū al-Suʿūd and Unsī were parts of a loosely defined group whose activity was related to the khedivial government and should be seen as the first attempt by local intellectuals to use government resources for reform. They are the ones who synchronize the imagined Muslim past with new spaces of power through print, education, sound, and language. What seems to unite these intellectuals was an unspoken but shared belief that educated Arabic, *al-ʿarabiyya al-fuṣḥā*, should become the language of the khedivate. They did not exclude the use of the vernacular for specific functions. But the vernacular was not useful to compete with European aesthetics and for negotiation with a Muslim sovereign because it had no textual historical dimension.

Making Arabic the language of power happened, in fact, officially. True to Benedict Anderson's argument that dynasts adopt "*some* vernacular as language of state,"[3] Ismail declared Arabic (*al-lugha al-ʿarabiyya*, undoubtedly the administrative version of *fuṣḥā* Arabic) the official language of the administration in 1870, instead of Turkish. Turkish remained important: in 1868 Ismāʿīl Ṣiddīq "al-Mufattish" still requested Turkish clerks in the governorates,[4] and army leaders asked for and were granted an exemption in 1870.[5] The administration of the island Taşoz facing the city of Kavala also continued to be conducted in Ottoman Turkish; and this language was taught in (military) schools until the

[3] Anderson, *Imagined Communities*, 85.

[4] Letter dated 8 Dhū al-Ḥijja 1284 (1 April 1868), from Ismāʿīl Ṣiddīq to Maʿiyya, 43/227, MST, Microfilm 202, DWQ.

[5] Letter dated 21 Shawwāl 1286 (24 January 1870) from Shāhīn Kanj, Nazir-i Cihadiye, 411/46, MST, Microfilm 204, DWQ; Sāmī, Taqwīm al-Nīl, part 3, vol. 2: 849.

twentieth century. However, it seems the khedive and Muslim intellectuals agreed in this period that learned Arabic was the official language for the khedivate. Is it possible that this happened because they shared only two features: Islam and the fact that their mother tongue was different? European Orientalists looked at Egyptians as Arabs. For instance, Ignác Goldziher in this period thought that "national literature" in Egypt is "Arab literature." Ismail was happy to satisfy Orientalists by ordering printed editions of Arabic manuscripts.[6] Typically, Arabic-speaking Christians and Jews also favored this language. A rabbi in Alexandria in 1862 thought that Arabic is the purest language.[7] "Pure Arabic" embodied a middle ground since it did not belong to anyone.

Khedivial Education as a Result of Compromise

The making of official Arabic was a common effort by local Muslim intelligentsia. This is where we can see the compromise of the 1860s at work. From the mid-1860s, a number of institutions were created that accorded a special place to the learned Arabic language, and in which its teaching and use were controlled centrally. Between 1867 and 1873, in changing functions, ʿAlī Mubārak dominated the Department of Education (*Dīwān al-Madāris*); Dykstra convincingly suggests that his policies were also influenced by the new Chamber of Representatives.[8]

Mubārak executed, to some extent, the wishes of the *aʿyān* and *shuyūkh*, in the new, small but significant network of government schools (next to the thousands of village Koran-schools [*kuttāb*], which also came under government control after 1867);[9] the Khedivial Library (1868), a new college to train teachers, *Dār al-ʿUlūm al-Khidīwiyya* (1872, in French called the *École normale*); and a school for girls (1873). Yet, most of the specialized government schools trained Egyptians for military or bureaucratic service,[10] with some notable exceptions such as the School of Egyptology. The gentle revolution starts in these spaces.

In the khedivial schools, old sciences such as Arabic grammar, poetry, Muslim theology and law, and new ones, such as engineering and chemistry, formed a plural, hybrid core of modern, patriotic knowledge. Islam remained part of education in a re-Ottomanized form; for instance, only *ḥanafī* law was taught in Dār al-ʿUlūm, which became the dominant *sharīʿa* interpretation in khedivial Egypt (both the House of Osman

[6] Goldziher, "Jelentés," 9.

[7] Hassoun, "Les Juifs," 58.

[8] Dykstra, "A Bibliographical Study," 243–261.

[9] Heyworth-Dunne, *An Introduction*, 362–370.

[10] Heyworth-Dunne, *An Introduction*, 346–347.

and the Mehmed Ali family belonged to the *ḥanafī* school).[11] Azharite sheikhs, however, resisted reforming their curriculum.[12] Islam was important from another point of view as well. ʿAlī Mubārak was also Director of Religious Endowments (*Awqāf*), and it was in this capacity that he collected some *waqf* libraries in Egypt into one central institution, the "Khedivial Library" (*Dār al-Kutub al-Khidīwiyya*; often called in rather Ottoman Arabic *al-Kutub-khāna al-Miṣriyya* [the Egyptian Library]).[13] Although the library also received donations from abroad, its foundations were the *waqf* libraries; books (manuscripts and prints) that the wealthy in Ottoman Egypt had collected and donated for education. While centralization represented an intervention in Islamic law (*waqf* is nonalienable), at the same time, because the central library served educational purposes, and was open to "everyone," it preserved at least the donors' intentions. Yet as a result, the supervision of knowledge passed into the hands of the government.

As for the students, a government publication in 1873 mentions 2665 schools in which a total of 96,141 students studied, out of which only 3,699 studied in the new "civil" schools. In this calculation "civil" includes military schools and primary schools as well.[14] There is another estimate that 4,817 schools functioned in Egypt in 1875, of which 4,685 were the traditional Koran-school (*kuttāb*) and only *nine* were graduate, "civil" college-like schools,[15] but in addition to military and missionary schools, the student missions in Europe, and the mosque-university al-Azhar. There were new styles of learning too, such as a lecture hall ("amphitheater") open for public lectures in the main "hub" of education, the Department of Education (the former palace of Mustafa Fazıl, called Darb al-Jamāmīz);[16] the first khedivial library, in the same building, was also open to the public. Young Azhari students were attracted to new knowledge through these lectures.[17]

Fuṣḥā *Arabic for Khedivial Praise in Schools*

The few but significant schools—even in the 1890s only 4.8 percent of the total population could read and write[18]—were sites of an unprece-

[11] On Hanafization see Hatina, *ʿUlamaʾ, Politics, and the Public Sphere*, 36–38; Cuno, *Modernizing Marriage*, 123–125.

[12] Hatina, *ʿUlamaʾ, Politics, and the Public Sphere*, 32–36.

[13] Cf. letter dated 5 Dhū al-Hijja 1286 (8 March 1870), from ʿAlī Mubārak, Nāẓir al-Awqāf, 468/46, Microfilm 204, MST, DWQ.

[14] *Programme de l'enseigemment*, 11.

[15] Heyworth-Dunne, *An Introduction*, 376.

[16] *Rawḍat al-Madāris*, "Iʿlān," 15 Ṣafar 1288, 3.

[17] Heyworth-Dunne, *An Introduction*, 376–377.

[18] Fahmy, *Ordinary Egyptians*, 32–33.

dented experiment with education in the Egyptian province. It would be unjust to reduce the fascinating production of knowledge, the sensitive balance between Muslim sciences and Western technology, and the openness of Muslim intellectuals in this period to the story of patriotism in Arabic. The first Copts as public figures also appear at this time. Nonetheless, the teachers and students had to participate in the praise of the absolute ruler, as they had during the reign of Mehmed Ali.

The makers of patriotism cherished *fuṣḥā* Arabic both as a patriotic and as a moral value. ʿAbd Allāh Fikrī, the Arabic teacher of Ismail's sons, his secretary for Arabic correspondence, and later director of education, wrote in these years that "the best language in the world and the most brilliant one in which the human race ever talked . . . is the language of the Arabs."[19] This is perhaps not surprising if we note that he hailed from a noble family of *ʿulamāʾ*.[20] He became subdirector in 1871 at *Dīwān al-Madāris* and later its minister. Indeed, one wonders whether it was due to ʿAbd Allāh Fikrī's hidden influence on Ismail that Arabic became the official language of the administration.

The schools essentially served as the prime sites through which patriotism became an ideological tool that accompanied the acquisition of knowledge in Arabic. ʿAlī Mubārak's department of education employed Ṣāliḥ Majdī (who was the *wakīl* of the ministry), and old al-Ṭahṭāwī himself, both writers of *waṭaniyyāt*. The exams and end-of-the-year celebrations were public occasions attended by the "princes" (often Tevfik, the heir presumptive),[21] where, as ʿAlī Mubārak once wrote to the khedive, "the students can demonstrate in front of the noble *zevat*, the most learned *ʿulamāʾ*, and the esteemed merchants what they have learned from the sciences and arts in the shadow of his Highness the Khedive."[22] On these occasions, al-Ṭahṭāwī and others gave speeches in *fuṣḥā* Arabic, as had been the habit in the 1840s. The printed speeches[23] attributed success to both divine providence and Ismail, as in the declaration that "God opened the gates of knowledge by the khedive of Egypt."[24]

At the same time, however, multilingualism continued in everyday life. The teachers spoke versions of Egyptian Arabic as their mother tongue, and they often knew some Italian and French, as well. In addition,

[19] Fikrī, *Rasāʾil al-Inshāʾ*, Manuscript, 5115 Adab.

[20] Fikrī, ed., *Al-Āthār*, 4–5.

[21] Shafīq, *Mudhakkirātī*, 1:8.

[22] Letter dated 31 Ramadan 1288 (14 December 1871), from ʿAlī Mubārak, Mudīr Dīwan al-Madāris to al-Maʿiyya, 447/48, MST, Microfilm 205, DWQ.

[23] For instance, the issue of Ghāyat Shaʿbān 1288 (14 November 1871) contains only speeches.

[24] "Ṣūrat al-Khuṭba allatī Iftataḥa bi-hā Imtiḥān Maktab al-Marḥūma Wālidat al-Marḥūm ʿAbbās Bāshā," *Rawḍat al-Madāris al-Miṣriyya*, Ghāyat Shaʿbān 1294 (9 September 1877), 8–9.

elites close to the khedivial household, such as ʿAbd Allāh Fikrī or Ismāʿīl Ṣiddīq, were fluent in Ottoman Turkish. Alongside the official projection of monolingualism, then, there was everyday multilingualism in all social circles.

Print Enterprises and Muslim Aesthetics

Besides new spaces and pictorial images, the khedivial government used first the *non-Egyptian* press for the pasha's public image. This image was designed as an external one. We have seen that Said and Ismail in the 1850s and 1860s financially supported *Ḥadīqat al-Akhbār* in Beirut, *al-Jawāʾib*, Turkish, and French journals in Istanbul (*Ruzname-i Ceride-i Havadis* received yearly support even in 1870; the editor of *Basiret* in 1877; and the *Levant Herald* throughout the 1870s), and a number of French journals in France. This shows that the pashas in Egypt, like the Ottoman imperial administration, were aware of international (and imperial Ottoman) public opinion as a powerful means in politics.[25]

Within the province, in 1866, a Press Office (*Jurnāl Kalamı* in Ottoman Turkish) containing five censors (including a Turkish officer) and led by a certain Trabi Efendi was established in the Department of Foreign Affairs.[26] It was established in that department because at the time permissions to start journals were given mostly to foreign subjects. There were Italian, Greek, and French private journals and presses.[27] The private Arabic lithographic and printing presses in Cairo and Alexandria were supervised by the governorates and the Interior Ministry, and sometimes asked the opinion of the grand mufti, but those presses did not produce periodicals at the time.[28] (See more in chapter 7 on later censorship.) These measures were part of a general effort in the 1860s to assert control over European activity in late Ottoman Egypt.

At this time, a new "national" printing press was also imagined. There is an unsigned proposal in French in the Egyptian Archives possibly from 1866 that proposes an *Imprimerie Nationale Égyptienne*, the main purpose of which was to emphasize sovereignty and save money for the government (which had documents printed in various languages by firms in England or France), reasoning that "a government cannot trust its projects on a private printing press." The project contains the unification of

[25] Şiviloğlu, "The Emergence of Public Opinion."

[26] Letter dated 15 Jumādā al-Ukhrā 1283 (25 October 1866), from Ismail Ragib to Khedive, 374/39, and letter dated 23 Rajab 1283 (1 December 1866), from Khārijiyya to Khedive, 63/40, both in MST, Microfilm 199, DWQ.

[27] Sadgrove, "The European Press," 114–117.

[28] Schwartz, "Meaningful Mediums."

the French press of Antoine Mourès in Alexandria (after purchasing it) and the press of the État-Major (Department of War) in the Citadel, and suggests a staff of fifty-one persons. Even the text of a contract between Mourès and the government was prepared regarding the acquisition of machines and typefaces, and appointing him as director.[29] There is no evidence that the press was ever established.

The Muslim Press and Arabness in Egypt, 1866–1873

The early Arabic press is often considered to have been, exclusively, a means of social mobilization that helped the ʿUrābī revolution.[30] In contrast, others, such as Ami Ayalon, suggest that Ismail used the first Arabic journals in Egypt for propaganda.[31] Here, I rethink these contradictory claims by examining early Arabic journalism as both a business enterprise and part of the complex mechanism of Arab patriotism. The periodicals functioned as interfaces between khedivial interests and interests of Arabic-speaking intellectuals.

Between 1866 and 1873, there were only three regular Arabic periodicals printed in Egypt: *Wādī al-Nīl* (The Nile Valley, 1867–1872?), *Rawḍat al-Madāris al-Miṣriyya* (The Garden of Egyptian Schools, 1870–1877), and the government bulletin *al-Waqāʾiʿ al-Miṣriyya* (Egyptian Events, 1828–today).[32] There were some ephemeral private Arabic periodicals. In May 1870, a short-lived commercial periodical, *al-Munbih al-Tijārī al-Miṣrī* (The Egyptian Commercial Gazette) was printed in Italian and partly in vernacular Arabic in Cairo (see below). Another commercial publication was *Jūrnāl ʿUmūmī li-Kāfat al-Iʿlānāt*, printed by the Castelli Press in 1872. The elite Egyptian Ibrāhīm al-Muwayliḥī also printed, with his own press, the journal *Nuzhat al-Afkār* (The Promenade of Ideas) in August 1870; it was discontinued (possibly banned) after only two

[29] Undated, unsigned note Projet de création d'une Imprimerie Nationale Egyptienne présenté à son Excellence Chérif Pacha Président du Conseil des Ministres; and undated, unsigned [Contract] Entre le Gouvernement Egyptien d'une part et Antoine Mourès, Imprimeur, domicilié à Alexandrie, d'autre part. These are next to a letter dated 11 August 1866, and therefore I believe this is the right year; 5013–002616, DWQ.

[30] Cole, *Colonialism and Revolution*, ch. 4. Fahmy, *Ordinary Egyptians*, 7–8.

[31] Ayalon, *The Arabic Press*, 19.

[32] The only governmental periodical was *al-Waqāʾiʿ al-Miṣriyya*, which was intermittently published, and in Ottoman Turkish as well. This journal published dynastic praise in addition to official and some local news regularly since the 1830s. Next was a scientific circular for doctors in Arabic, *Yaʿsūb al-Ṭibb*, which was printed in the governmental Būlāq press from 1865, and a military periodical, but the distribution of these journals was not public.

issues, which are now lost. These were all Cairo-based periodicals. From 1873 on, the center of Arabic journalism moved to Alexandria due to new Ottoman Syrian enterprises.

The primary goal shared by the early Cairo journals was the dissemination of old and new types of knowledge, including a great concern with *fuṣḥā* Arabic and Islam, and government propaganda, as opposed to the later more capitalist underpinnings of the Arabic press.[33] Some of these early journals, like *Wādī al-Nīl*, were also part of printing businesses which aimed at profit. Yet they were not "journals" in the sense that we think of them today as a means to transmit news to the public as an economic activity and as a check on governments. They rather represent an intermediate stage between old and new regimes of public knowledge; their activity created a form of modern Muslim memory through printing and serializing selected medieval works. They created classics and themselves became classics.

I contextualize and rethink the activity of the two core Muslim periodicals *Wādī al-Nīl* and *Rawḍat al-Madāris* in this section. Their distribution was limited (a couple of hundred copies each), but given the oral culture in Egyptian streets, they may well have reached a much wider audience. A German traveler in 1870–1871, for instance, noted that *Wādī al-Nīl* was read aloud among groups of men "in the coffeehouses, at public fountains, and in the mosques" and had an "influence."[34] Reading journals aloud in streets is a familiar trope that is often repeated later. The papers also represent much wider projects than a journal. I call them "enterprises."

The Wādī al-Nīl *Enterprise*

The first private Egyptian Arabic periodical, *Wādī al-Nīl* (The Nile Valley), was published in July 1867, through its own Arabic printing press, just a few weeks after the Ottoman firman of the khedivate. Some believe that it was the khedive's instrument.[35] Ibrāhīm ʿAbduh, the great press historian, ambivalently judges that "the idea for its establishment was the loyal service of the khedive" but adds that "it was the first national and popular periodical in Egypt."[36] Sadgrove differs, arguing that it was an "independent newspaper,"[37] Cole suggests that government donations "did keep subscription and newsstand prices down,"[38] and Barak terms it "semiprivate."[39]

[33] Barak, *On Time*, 130.
[34] Stephan, *Das heutige*, 174, 325.
[35] Sabry, *Le Genèse*, 113; Ayalon, *The Arabic Press*, 41.
[36] ʿAbduh, *Taṭawwur*, 60–61.
[37] Sadgrove, "The Development," 73.
[38] Cole, *Colonialism and Revolution*, 127.
[39] Barak, *On Time*, 117.

In fact, ʿAbd Allāh Abū al-Suʿūd funded the journal at great sacrifice without government involvement. The khedivial secretary ʿAbd Allāh Fikrī hoped that Ismail Pasha would help Abū al-Suʿūd since, Fikrī argued in a letter to the khedive, this first popular (*ahliyya*) journal furthered patriotic progress.[40] The government bulletin celebrated its private "sister" journal, *Wādī al-Nīl*.[41] Ayalon's claim that Abū al-Suʿūd was "hired by Khedive Ismail to edit a government newspaper"[42] seems to be incorrect. As a response to Fikrī's request, Ismail may have encouraged the journal, which later did rely on government resources and which was indeed loyalist, as this was the condition of public speech.

The journal *Wādī al-Nīl* must be seen as part of a larger printing business enterprise and a quite successful one. The printing house of the same name was a major producer of *fuṣḥā* texts. Abū al-Suʿūd and his son Muḥammad Unsī were both the editors of the journal and the directors of the press; the typeface was owned by Unsī;[43] the whole printing house was owned by his father.[44] Unsī had earlier owned, with his brother Aḥmad, a printing machine with Latin and Arabic typefaces in Cairo; the brothers' only surviving publication is an archaeological essay in Italian in 1865, which contains images of half-naked female Greek sculptures.[45] He also had a lithograph and published popular mystical and theological texts in 1867.[46]

As table 4.1 shows, the printing press under Abū al-Suʿūd's and Unsī's direction published around fifty titles, often in multivolume formats, and four journals, over approximately eleven years (the majority between 1867 and 1873). This is an estimate. Some military and economic manuals, so far unlocated, must also be added to this number, and serialized books in the periodicals. The journal *Wādī al-Nīl* worked in symbiosis with its printing press: it often advertised the books and their prices.[47] There was also a bookshop, run by Muḥammad Unsī and Mourès, where the journal could be contacted, and where the press moved in 1869 for a few years.[48] The press printed and sold selected linguistic and *adab* works (some of them were published in a serialized format in the journal); and

[40] Fikrī, ed., *al-Āthār al-Fikriyya*, 261–263.

[41] *Al-Waqāʾiʿ al-Miṣriyya*, 18 and 25 July 1867.

[42] Ayalon, "Sihafa," 269.

[43] Sadgrove, "The Development," 74.

[44] The final colophon says that the press is owned by Abū al-Suʿūd in al-Harawī, *Al-Talwīḥ* (1285 [1868]).

[45] Vassalli, *D'una rappresentazione di Sirene*. Muḥammad Unsī's brother is known from a hand-written note at the end of the manuscript "Tarjamat al-Fāḍil ʿAbd Allāh Abī al-Suʿūd Afandī," manuscript, Tārīkh Taymūr 1098.

[46] Like Dardīr, *Ḥāshiyat*; Al-Nasafī, *Kitāb Kanz al-Daqāʾiq*.

[47] For instance, *Wādī al-Nīl*, 25 Dhū al-Ḥijja 1287, 7–8. It also advertised other publishers, such as the government's Būlāq press, or the publications of Ibrāhīm al-Muwayliḥī.

[48] Physically, the press was moved between Bāb al-Shaʿriyya neighborhood in Cairo where Abū al-Suʿūd lived and Kawm al-Shaykh Salāma neighborhood in al-Mūskī.

TABLE 4.1. Publications of the Wādī al-Nīl Printing Press, 1867–1878*

Author	*Title*	*Publication Year*	*Remarks*
Journal	*Wādī al-Nīl*	July 1867–1872 (?)	Re-published in 1875?
ʿAlī Mubārak	*Kitāb Ṭarīq al-Hijāʾ wa-l-Tamrīn ʿalā al-Qirāʾa fī al-Lugha al-ʿArabiyya* 3 vols.	Vol. 1: no date, Vol. 2: Beginning of Ramaḍān 1285 (December 1868)	2 vols. in 1. Third volume is promised
Qūrtanbīr al-Firansāwī (translated by ʿAbd Allāh Abū al-Suʿūd)	*Kitāb al-Dars al-Mukhtaṣar al-Mufīd fī ʿIlm al-Jughrāfiya al-Jadīd*	1286 (1869–1870) on title page	First translated during Mehmed Ali's reign; school book; first in installments in the journal *Wādī al-Nīl* before April 1869
Shihāb al-Dīn Aḥmad b. Muḥammad al-Dimashqī al-Anṣārī (Ibn ʿArab-Shāh)	*Kitāb ʿAjāʾib al-Maqdūr fī Akhbār Taymūr*	1286 (1869–1870)	Title page: 1285; first in installments in the journal *Wādī al-Nīl* from April 1869 (Muḥarram 1286)
Abū Isḥāq Ibrāhīm b. Ismāʿīl b. ʿAbd Allāh al-maʿrūf bi-Ibn al-Ajdābī al-Ṭarābulusī	*Kifāyat al-Mutaḥaffiẓ wa-Nihāyat al-Mutalaffiẓ*	1286 (= March 1869-March 1870)	Announced in journal *Wādī al-Nīl*. Second edition in 1287
ʿAbd al-Laṭīf al-Baghdādī	*Kitāb al-Ifāda wa-l-Iʿtibār fī al-Umūr al-Mushāhada wa-l-Ḥawādith al-Muʿāyana bi-Arḍ Miṣr*	1286 (= March 1869-March 1870)	No exact month given in colophon
Heinrich Brugsch	*Taʿrīb al-Khuṭba allatī Khaṭaba bi-hā al-Muʿallim Hinrī Brūksh*	1286 (= March 1869–March 1870)	Translated by Abū al-Suʿūd Efendi, no exact month given in colophon

Auguste Marriette	*Furjat al-Mutafarrij ʿalā al-Antīqa-khāna al-Khidīwiyya al-Kāʾina bi-Būlāq*	1869	First in installments in the journal *Wādī al-Nīl* between June and September 1869. There is also a Paris edition in which the Arabic text is bound with a French preface.
Ibn Baṭṭūṭa	*Kitāb Riḥlat Ibn Baṭṭūṭa—Tuḥfat al-Nuẓẓār fī Gharāʾib al-Amṣār wa-ʿAjāʾib al-Asfār*	Vol. 1: End of Rajab 1287 (October 1870) Vol 2: middle of Jumādā al-Thānī 1288 (September 1871)	2 vols. in 1. Also in installments in the journal *Wādī al-Nīl*
Masʿūd b. ʿUmar al-Taftazānī	*Kitāb al-Niʿam al-Ṣawābigh fī Sharḥ al-Kalim al-Nawābigh li-l-Ustādh al-Zamakhsharī*	Ghurrat Rajab 1287 (September 1870)	1286 on title page
Journal	*Rawḍat al-Madāris al-Miṣriyya*	1870–1871	From 1871 published by the Department of Schools's printing press
	Six books serialized in *Rawḍat al-Madāris al-Miṣriyya*	During 1287 (1870–1871)	
Rifāʿa Bey (al-Ṭahṭāwī)	*Al-Qawl al-Sadīd fī al-Ijtihād wa-l-Tajdīd*	1287 (1870–1871)	On behalf of *Rawḍat al-Madāris al-Miṣriyya*; no precise date; 24 pages
Shihāb al-Dīn Abū Muḥammad ʿAbd al-Raḥmān b. Ismāʿīl ibn Ibrāhīm al-Maqdisī al-Shāfiʿī	*Kitāb al-Rawḍatayn fī Akhbār al-Dawlatayn*	Vol. 1: end of 1287 (February 1871); end of Rajab 1288 (October 1871)	2 vols. in 1

(*Continued*)

TABLE 4.1. (*Continued*)

Author	*Title*	*Publication Year*	*Remarks*
Dumas, Alexandre (trans. Bashāra Shadīd Taqawwaʿī)	*Qiṣṣat al-Kūnt Dū Muntū Kristū*	1288 (1871–1872)	Translation finished 8 August 1869; printed at the expense of the translator; on title page: 1287
Muḥammad b.Ibrāhīm b. ʿAbbād al-Nafzī al-Rundī	*Sharḥ ʿalā matn al-Ḥikam li-l-Imām al-muḥaqqiq Abī al-Faḍl Aḥmad ibn Muḥammad ibn ʿAbd al-Karīm ibn ʿAṭāʾ Allāh al-Sikandarī* Bound together with *Sharḥ al-muḥaqqiq Shaykh al-Islām al-Shaykh ʿAbd Allāh al-Sharqāwī*	1288 (1871–1872)	?
Antonio Ghislanzoni (Verdi's librettist)	*ʿĀyida* (translation of *Aida*'s libretto)	1288 (December 1871, before the premiere)	Translated by ʿAbd Allāh Abū al-Suʿūd by the order of Khedive Ismail
Eugène Scribe and Émile Deschamps (librettists of Meyerbeer)	? (translation of *Les Huguenots*)	1871	Translated by ʿAbd Allāh Abū al-Suʿūd by the order of Khedive Ismail
ʿAbd Allāh Fikrī	*Al-Maqāma al-Fikriyya fī al-Mamlaka al-Bāṭiniyya*	1289 (1872?)	Mentioned as printed first in the press Wādī al-Nīl in 1289 in Fikrī, *Al-Āthār*, 276.

Shams al-Dīn Abū ʿAbd Allāh Muḥammad b. Qāsim al-Ghazzī	*Fatḥ al-Qarīb al-Mujīb ʿalā al-Kitāb al-Musammā bi-l-Taqrīb*	Beginning of Muḥarram 1289 (March 1872)	1288 on title page; second edition after the 1281 Būlāq print; at the expense of Sheikh Manṣūr Shabbāna and ʿAṭiyya Qamr; corrected by Abū al-Suʿūd
Abū Sahl Muḥammad b. ʿAlī Harawī; ʿAbd al-Laṭīf al-Baghādī	*Kitāb al-Talwīḥ fī Sharḥ al-Faṣīḥ—Faṣīḥ Thaʿlab al-Mashhūr* Bound together with *Kitāb Dhayl al-Faṣīḥ li-Thaʿlab*	*Kitāb al-Talwīḥ*: 20 Rabīʿ al-Ākhir 1289 (27 May 1872); *Kitāb Dhayl al-Faṣīḥ* no date given, only 1289 on the title page	No exact month given in colophon; 1285 on title page; 2 books in 1.
ʿAbd Allāh Abū al-Suʿūd (d. 1878)	*Kitāb al-Dars al-Tāmm fī al-Tārīkh al-ʿĀmm—al-Mulakhkhaṣ min Kutub al-Tawārīkh al-Urūbiyya wa-l-ʿArabiyya fī al-Sāḥa al-Khidīwiyya li-Qaṣd Tadrīsihi li-Ṭalbat al-ʿIlm bi-Madrasat Dār al-ʿUlūm al-Miṣriyya*	1289 (possibly spring 1872)	No date because no colophon (all copies abruptly end)
Al-Shaykh Muḥammad al-Mahdī b. Aḥmad b. ʿAlī b. Yūsuf al-Fāsī	*Kitāb Muṭāliʿ al-Masarrāt bi-Jalāʾ Dalāʾil al-Khayrāt*	15 Shaʿbān 1289 (18 October 1872)	Corrected and printed by Abū al-Suʿūd at the expense of Sheikh Manṣūr Shabbāna and Sheikh ʿAtiyya Qamr
Felix [?] (translated by ʿAbd Allāh Abū al-Suʿūd)	*Kitāb Tarqiyat al-Jamʿiyya fī al-Kīmiyāʾ al-Zirāʿiyya*	15 Ramaḍān 1289 (16 November 1872)	

(*Continued*)

TABLE 4.1. (*Continued*)

Author	*Title*	*Publication Year*	*Remarks*
Muḥammad b. Abī Bakr al-Rāzī	*Kitāb Mukhtār al-Ṣiḥāḥ al-Mashhūr fī Mustaʿmal al-Lugha wa-l-Ḥadīth al-Maʾthūr*	Middle of Dhū al-Qaʿda 1289 (14 January 1873)	In his afterword Abū al-Suʿūd mentions he saw manuscripts in the library of Paris; internal title page: 1287
ʿAbd al-Raḥmān al-Ṣafawī	*Nuzhat al-Majālis wa-Muntakhab al-Nafāʾis*	Beginning of Rabīʿ al-Awwal 1290 (April-May 1873)	2 vols. in 1
Aḥmad b. al-Shaykh Muḥammad al-Ḥaḍrāwī	*Kitāb al-ʿIqd al-Thamīn fī Faḍāʾil al-Balad al-Amīn*	Beginning of Rabīʿ al-Awwal 1290 (April–May 1873)	On title page: 1289
ʿAlī Mubārak	*Kitāb Taqrīb al-Handasa li-Istiʿmāl al-ʿAskariyya al-Miṣriyya*, vol. 1	Middle of Rabīʿ al-Thānī 1290 (12 June 1873)	Second edition (!); by the order of Dīwān al-Jihādiyya; on the title page 1289
M.(uḥammad) ʿ.(Uthmān) J.(alāl)	*Al-Shaykh Matlūf*	Beginning of Jumādā al-Thānī 1290 (July 1873)	Egyptianization of Molière's *Tartuffe* ; on title page also with Latin characters : *Le Tartuffe—Poésie Arabe*
[anonymous]	*Fihrist al-Kutub al-Mawjūda bi-Kutub-khāna al-Khidīwiyya al-Miṣriyya al-Kubrā al-Kāʾina bi-Sarāy Darb al-Jamāmīz al-ʿĀmira bi-Miṣr al-Qāhira*	End of Shaʿbān 1290 (23 October 1873)	On title page 1289; possibly Ṣāliḥ Majdī is the author

Journal	*Jarīdat Arkān Ḥarb al-Jaysh al-Miṣrī*	1873–1874	From 1874 by the army's own printing press
Tāj al-Dīn b. ʿAṭāʾ Allāh al-Iskandarī	*Tāj al-ʿArūs al-Ḥāwī li-Tahdhīb al-Nufūs*	Beginning of Rajab 1291 (August 1874)	Printed at the expense of Abū Ṭālib b. ʿAbd Allāh al-Yamanī
Muḥammad Unsī	*Al-Qirāʾ wa-l-Kitāba al-ʿArabiyya wa-l-Turkiyya wa-l-Fārisiyya*	1291 (1874–1875)	
Muḥammad Unsī	*Al-Juzʾ al-Thānī min Talṭīf al-Uslūb wa-Takhfīf al-ʿArabiyya ʿalā al-Qulūb aw al-Mutaʿallam li-Ḥājat al-Taʿlīm wa-l-Taʿallum fī al-Naḥw*	1291 (1874–1875)	(first and third part too were printed in the press; not found)
Journal	*Rawḍat al-Akhbār*	1874	Until 1878?
Muḥammad Unsī	*Uslūb Jadīd wa-Ikhtirāʿ Mufīd li-Tashīl Taʿlīm Fann al-Kitāba al-ʿArabiyya*	1292 (1875–1876)	
Niẓām al-Dīn Abū Yaʿlā Muḥammad b. Muḥammad al-ʿAbbāsī al-Hāshimī al-maʿrūf bi-l-Habbādī	*Kitāb al-Ṣādiḥ wa-l-Bāghum*	Beginning of Rabīʿ al-Thānī 1292 (May 1875)	Selected from *Kashf al-Ẓunūn* possibly by Abū al-Suʿūd
ʿAbd al-Mālik ibn ʿAbd al-Wahhāb al-Fattānī (Patanī?)	*Sharḥ Khulāṣat al-Farāʾiḍ—Naẓm Matn al-Sirājiyya*	11 Ṣafar 1293 (8 March 1876)	on title page 1292

(*Continued*)

TABLE 4.1. (*Continued*)

Author	*Title*	*Publication Year*	*Remarks*
ʿAbd Allāh Abū al-Suʿūd	*Mukhtaṣar Tārīkh Miṣr bi-Muddat al-Marḥūm Muḥammad ʿAlī Bāshā*	1294 (1877–1878)	Sadgrove, "The Development," 94. The original manuscript, dated Ṣafar 1263 (February 1847), is in the Egyptian National Library; possibly printed in early 1877.
Mehmed Mukbil (Muḥammad Muqbil)	*Kitāb al-Durr al-Thamīn fī Asmāʾ al-Banāt wa-l-Banīn*	8 Rabīʿ al-Awwal 1294 (23 March 1877)	In Ottoman Turkish; names; the author was the chief of the Turkish office in the Foreign Affairs Department.
ʿAlāʾ al-Dīn b. ʿAlī al-Irbilī	*Kitāb Jawāhir al-Adab fī Maʿrifat Kalām al-ʿArab*	15 Jumādā al-Awwal 1294 (28 May 1877)	Correctors: Sheikh ʿAlī Nāʾil and Ḥasan b. al-Shaykh Abī Zayd
ʿAbd al-Ḥāfiẓ ʿAbd al-Ḥaqq al-Ḥujājī	*Kitāb Yuwāqīt al-Taṣānīf al-Abniyya wa-l-Naṣārīf*	1295 (1878)	With the approval of al-Azhar sheikhs; no month is given.
Ibn Hishām al-Anṣārī	*Sharḥ Shudhūr al-Dhahab fī Maʿrifat Kalām al-ʿArab*	1295 (1878)	Corrector: Ḥasan b. Abī Zayd Salāma
ʿAlī Riyāḍ	*Al-Azhār al-Riyāḍiyya fī al-Mādda al-Ṭibbiyya*; vol. 1.	1296 (1878–1879)	No month given on colophon; second part 1297
Amīn Fikrī	*Jughrāfiyat Miṣr*	1296 (1878–1879)	No month given on colophon

*The list may be amended in light of new material; the press, sold to the brothers Muḥammad Rafʿat and Maḥmūd Fāḍil around 1878, continued to publish books until 1882.

religious texts such as Koran interpretations. It also published calendars.[49] It printed various materials: an Arabic primer,[50] the translations of the Egyptian Museum catalogue in 1869[51] and of the librettos of the operas *Les Huguenots*[52] and *Aida* in 1871,[53] all by Abū al-Suʿūd; and a romantic Arabized novel, and the Arabic translation of Dumas's *The Count of Monte Cristo*.[54] The printing press, the journal, and the bookshop were elements of a real enterprise serving the owners' own interests, as well as orders from the government and from private individuals.

In addition to its own journal, this press published three periodicals in the early 1870s: *Rawḍat al-Madāris al-Miṣriyya*, the official journal of the Ministry of Education, between 1870 and 1871 (this journal lasted until 1877),[55] *Jarīdat Arkān Ḥarb al-Jaysh al-Miṣrī*, the official journal of the General Staff of the Egyptian army in 1873 (it then was printed at another press until 1879); and Unsī's new journal *Rawḍat al-Akhbār* from December 1874.[56]

Evidence of the entrepreneur spirit is that Unsī and Mourès owned another press (or a typeface) together in 1869 that could print with French characters.[57] The enterprise at the beginning seems to have been sufficiently successful that, in September 1868, a certain De Morely asked permission to establish an Arabic press in Alexandria and to similarly publish an Arabic *revue* (he was not granted permission).[58] In early 1870, Unsī's French typeface was destroyed in a fire, and he suspected that this "devilish act" (*faʿliyya shayṭāniyya*) was intentional, committed either by a foreigner or by a local Egyptian, possibly for business reasons or against the journal itself.[59]

The Wādī al-Nīl enterprise was close to the government. In 1869–1870 they printed librettos in Arabic at Draneht's personal order.[60] One should

[49] Barak, *On Time*, 118–119.

[50] Schwartz, "Meaningful Mediums," 425–428.

[51] [Mariette,] *Furjat al-mutafarrij*.

[52] Letter dated 31 January 1872, from Draneht to Khayri Pasha, in Abdoun, *Genesi dell' "Aida,"* 109–110.

[53] [Ghislanzoni], *Tarjamat al-Ūpīra* [!] *al-Musammā bi-Ism ʿĀyida*.

[54] Schwartz, "Meaningful Mediums," 304, n. 184.

[55] The printing press of the journal changes to Maṭbaʿat al-Madāris al-Milkiyya bi-Darb al-Jamāmīz in Cairo; starting at vol. 2., n. 4 (Ghāyat Ṣafar 1288 = 22 May 1871).

[56] Sadgrove, "The Development," 93.

[57] De-Marchi, *La fiesta dei Khalidj in Cairo* printed by "Imprimerie Onsy et Mourés au Mouski" in 1869. It is unclear whether the "Imprimerie Onsy et Mourés" and the earlier "Imprimerie franco-arabe Onsy frères" were identical with Maṭbaʿat Wādī al-Nīl.

[58] Letter dated 19 September 1868, from Charles François Antoine De Morely to the Khedive, 192/44, MST, Microfilm 203, DWQ.

[59] *Wādī al-Nīl*, 3 Rabīʿa 1287, 2–4.

[60] However, the first translation of Offenbach's *La belle Hélène* (*Hīlāna al-Jamīla*) was printed at the Būlāq press. Perhaps because it was not Abū al-Suʿūd's translation.

not forget Abū al-Suᶜūd's job in the Translation Office. This press may even have been shrewdly conceived as a private business, which awaited official orders to gain extra profit in the private printers' competition for Arabic publications.[61] Or was it a consequence of the draft project for an Egyptian National Press in 1866? Is this the reason why it also printed *Jarīdat Arkān Ḥarb* and books for the army? Abū al-Suᶜūd and Unsī had access to news over the telegraph through the government, and thus their journal was the first to publish telegrams in Arabic. In 1870, their press also printed at least six books for the Department of Education, serialized in *Rawḍat al-Madāris*. It continued to work at a smaller scale until around 1878 when it was taken over by new owners.[62]

The journal *Wādī al-Nīl* contributed to patriotism in various ways, first of all by framing government news within a literary context in *fuṣḥā* Arabic. As fitting nation-ness, the title—the Nile Valley—alluded to a territorial attachment without defining exactly the borders or announcing a polity. In its available issues,[63] it regularly published news related to the khedive, such as his attendance in the khedivial theaters, the marriage of his daughter in 1869, his movements, his charities, or even the public sale of khedivial horses. It also reported on *Majlis Shūrā al-Nuwwāb*; published the train schedule and announcements from the khedivial post service; and often repeated those news items from *al-Waqāʾiᶜ al-Miṣriyya* that the editors considered "patriotic" (*ahlī, waṭanī*), such as the results of school exams. The journal never printed critical reports from the foreign language press, although the editors regularly borrowed news from Italian and French papers.

Its title page carried the first human images in Arabic journalism. An example from 1869 (figure 4.1) tells of an effort to bring together visually the various histories and features of khedivial modernism. We can see Ismail Pasha, presumably, on a camel, between two pyramids (pyramids had already been present in the title image of *al-Waqāʾiᶜ al-Miṣriyya*), framed by two palm trees. At the front sits a man with two camels. At the base of the palm trees there are various instruments on both sides: on

[61] More on the private printers in Schwartz, "Meaningful Mediums."

[62] In the colophon of Mubārak, *Kitāb Nukhbat*, the owners are two brothers Muḥammad Rifᶜat and Maḥmūd Fāḍil. It is possible that the press was taken over by them after the death of Abū al-Suᶜūd in 1878. Ibn Nujaym's *Kitāb al-Ashbāh wa-l-Naẓāʾir* was printed at Maṭbaᶜat Wādī al-Nīl at the end of Ramaḍān, 1298 (August 1881); and Ibn Miskawayh's *Tahdhīb al-Akhlāq* at the end of Shawwāl 1299 (August 1882); its multazim (contractor) was a rival printer, Aṣlān Bey Kāstilī (Castelli), which may indicate that the press was no more profitable. For the Castellis see Schwartz, "Meaningful Mediums," 293–325. There is a later *Wādī al-Nīl* press and journal in the early twentieth century that should not be confused with this one.

[63] Two volumes between April 1869 and March 1871 (corresponding to 1286 and 1287 hijrī years). However, Sadgrove had access to the first issue in 1867.

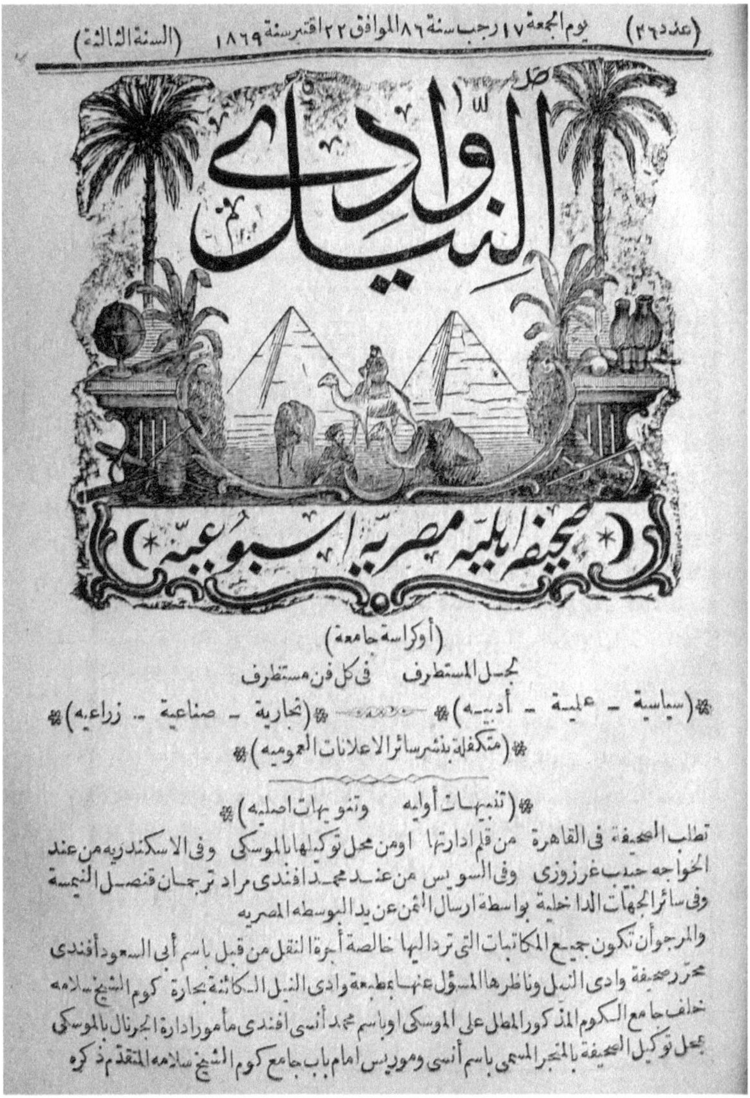
(عدد ٢٦) يوم الجمعة ١٧ رجب سنة ٨٦ الموافق ٢٢ اقتبر سنة ١٨٦٩ (السنة الثالثة)

وادى النيل

صحيفة اهلية مصرية اسبوعية

(أو كراسة جامعة)

لجل المستطرف في كل فن مستطرف

(سياسية - علمية - أدبيه) (تجارية - صناعية - زراعيه)

(متكفلة بنشر سائر الاعلانات العموميه)

(تنبيهات أوليه وتنويهات اصليه)

تطلب الصحيفة في القاهرة من قلم ادارتها اومن محل توكيلها بالموسكى وفي الاسكندريه من عند الخواجه حبيب غرزوزى وفي السويس من عند محمد افندى مراد ترجمان قنصل النيمسة وفي سائر الجهات الداخلية بواسطة ارسال الثمن عن يد البوسطه المصريه

والمرجوأن تكون جميع المكاتبات التي ترد اليها خالصة أجرة النقل من قبل باسم أبي السعود أفندى محرر صحيفة وادى النيل وناظرها المسؤل عنها بمطبعة وادى النيل الكائنة بحارة كوم الشيخ سلامه خلف جامع الكوم المذكور المطل على الموسكى اوباسم محمد أنسى افندى مأمور ادارة الجرنال بالموسكى بمحل توكيل الصحيفة بالمتجر المسمى باسم أنسى وموريس امام باب جامع كوم الشيخ سلامه المتقدم ذكره

FIGURE 4.1. Title page of *Wādī al-Nīl* journal, 22 October 1869
Source: author's photograph.

the one side perhaps representing agriculture and at the other possibly tools of navigation (technology). The great calligraphic title, *Wādī al-Nīl*, looms over the image.

Wādī al-Nīl could be bought in all the Ottoman Arab provinces, in theory even in Baghdad, while in Egypt in Cairo, Alexandria, Suez, and anywhere through the khedivial post. First, it was a weekly, then it was published two times a week, and from 1871 again weekly (appearing every Friday).[64] In 1869 the yearly subscription was 100 *qirsh* (36 francs), and one issue was 4 *qirsh* (1.25 francs); in 1871, when it changed back to a weekly, the price was lowered to 3 *qirsh*. These prices made the journal available to the readers of Arabic with modest income but certainly not to peasants and workers; although oral dissemination may have reached them. It was often quoted by *al-Jawāʾib* in Istanbul. *Wādī al-Nīl* was part of the Ottoman Arabic public sphere.

This patriotic product was a Muslim journal and represented a new form of Muslim cultural memory through careful selections. While the use of news from the telegraph brought epistemological confusion by the parallelism of the Hijri-Gregorian calendars this novelty may not vindicate Barak's judgment that the journal "became one of the technologies that formed the worldview of the colonial subject."[65] *Wādī al-Nīl* created rather a new, aesthetic sense of Muslim culture in print, which was influenced by new communication systems and European practices. It carried on its title page a motto that it "contains a great selection from all elegant arts" (*jāmiʿa li-jull al-mustaṭraf fī kull fann mustaẓraf*), which was an allusion to the medieval *adab* collection of entertaining stories and poems spiced with *ḥadīth* and Koranic verses, by Shihāb al-Dīn al-Ibshīhī (d. 1446), who wanted to collect all *fann ẓarīf*, "the elegant and witty arts."[66] The surviving issues do not contain congratulatory poems or other forms of direct dynastic praise; rather, the journal's main activity was delivering news and serializing *adab* works. It also published Unsī's articles, such as the one about the opera with which we began this chapter. Certainly, Abū al-Suʿūd and Unsī's patriotism was not a secular one—Muslim scholarship and the Koran figured prominently in their activity, as Koran interpretations were printed in their press. Their journal highlights the co-existence of Muslim ideas and nation-ness together as intertwined textual traditions.

Abū al-Suʿūd and Unsī did not perceive their activity to be an exclusive form of linguistic dominance via print-based patriotism. This much is clear from their reaction to the Italian–vernacular Arabic *al-Munbih al-Tijārī al-Miṣrī* in 1870. They noted that, although it is not in "correct" Arabic, nor in the "pure" Ḥijāzī Arabic [!], "it is not without benefit and elegance." As Barak points out, they approved of the printed vernacular as useful in terms of providing the speed needed for commercial

[64] Cf. the announcement in *Wādī al-Nīl*, 25 Dhū al-Ḥijja 1287, 2.
[65] Barak, "Outdating," 23.
[66] Al-Ibshīhī, *Al-Mustaṭraf*, 1.

transactions.[67] Their press also printed the vernacular translation of *Tartuffe* by Muḥammad ʿUthmān Jalāl (though with a *fuṣḥā* introduction). The ultimate purpose of *Wādī al-Nīl* was self-refinement—to make one's self *ẓarīf*, an educated and entertaining gentleman by both Muslim Arab and contemporary French standards. One may also detect some European Orientalist influence here in the selection of serialized texts. Still, in this project vernacular products could be fitted in if their subject or goal was considered useful. Overall, the press made a spectacular production of texts and journals, and thus their forgotten owners, Abū al-Suʿūd and Unsī, had much more importance at the time than the many "great men" who were later canonized.

It seems that the journal *Wādī al-Nīl* was suppressed by the order of the government in 1872.[68] Sadgrove suggests that it was only suspended for a time, and continued to be published at least in 1875.[69] Abū al-Suʿūd worked as a senior translator at the Translation Bureau, but in 1872 he was appointed the leading history teacher at the newly established Dār al-ʿUlūm, and was also promoted to head the Translation Bureau.[70] He received the one-time sum of 280 LE in 1872, an extraordinarily high amount.[71] His son Unsī's new journal certainly also received financial support from Ismail in 1875.[72] The historian Mohamed Sabry remarks that Abū al-Suʿūd defended Khedive Ismail until he died in 1878.[73] As we shall see below, the journal's suspension and Abū al-Suʿūd's appointment in 1872 were perhaps connected. The press itself was taken over by others after 1878, and after 1882 there is no publication in its name.[74]

The Rawḍat al-Madāris *Enterprise: Cairo as Abbasid Baghdad*

The second enterprise clearly included an effort to make patriotism the ideology of the khedivate in schools. *Rawḍat al-Madāris al-Miṣriyya* was a government publication, appearing first on April 16, 1870, to be distributed among teachers and students in both the reformed schools and the new ones. For this reason, it featured more khedivial praise than

[67] *Wādī al-Nīl*, 3 Rabīʿ al-Awwal, 1287, 5–6.

[68] "Tarjamat al-Fāḍil ʿAbd Allāh Abī al-Suʿūd Afandī," manuscript, Tārīkh Taymūr 1098, Microfilm 12979, Dār al-Kutub al-Miṣriyya. Al-Rāfiʿī, *ʿAṣr Ismāʿīl*, 1: 250.

[69] Sadgrove, "The Development," 76.

[70] "Tarjamat al-Fāḍil ʿAbd Allāh Abī al-Suʿūd Afandī," manuscript, Tārīkh Taymūr 1098, Microfilm 12979, Dār al-Kutub al-Miṣriyya.

[71] Cole, *Colonialism and Revolution*, 127.

[72] ʿAbduh, *al-Taṭawwur*, 66.

[73] Sabry quoted in Heyworth-Dunne, *An Introduction*, 345.

[74] However, the early 1880s publications of *al-Maṭbaʿa al-ʿIlāmiyya* use very similar fonts to the *Wādī al-Nīl* fonts.

Wādī al-Nīl.[75] Edited by ʿAlī Fahmī, al-Ṭahṭāwī's son, it was the organ of the new system of education, and connected with the new Khedivial Library,[76] about which both Fahmī and ʿAlī Mubārak wrote in the first issue. Mubārak in his article connected the library to the "freedom" that Egyptians now enjoyed under Ismail's reign.[77] Soon it was printed by the Department of Education's own printing press, which also published educational texts for school use. This project was a government branch's enterprise for the distribution of knowledge and patriotism.

Rawḍat al-Madāris played a crucial role in connecting intellectuals in the new schools, and outside of them, by distributing information and organizing intellectual contests around puzzles. It often framed its articles as being in "the service of the homeland." Among its authors were Copts who seized upon the forum to step onto the stage as patriotic intellectuals. It was more scientifically and technologically conscious than *Wādī al-Nīl*. Its history is well-known;[78] Hoda Yousef highlighted its significance for rethinking the construction of the categories "modern" and "traditional" knowledge.[79] Here I point out the way it framed the khedive as part of official nation-ness.

The first issue was centrally concerned with presenting itself to the khedive and convincing him of the publication and its authors' absolute loyalty. In addition to the aforementioned articles, it also featured panegyrics by Ṣāliḥ Majdī and the student Aḥmad Naẓmī, which were greetings sent to the ruler on the occasion of the new *hijrī* year (the issue was published in Muḥarram, the first Muslim month) and which also contained chronograms (the *hijrī* year 1287). As before, Muslim concepts remained part of Arab patriotism. Aḥmad Naẓmī thanked God for Ismail because he was "the khedive of Egypt and its Mighty One / its owner [or king: *malīk*] and sum of its pure gold, the scion of [its earlier] lover" (possibly Mehmed Ali).[80] Subsequent issues also contained instances of such direct praise.

Rawḍat al-Madāris published diverse articles, some of which were quite personal, such as the short, moving eulogy written by ʿAlī Fahmī after

[75] It was related to that journal in several ways. It was printed on its press in the first year, it was supervised by al-Ṭahṭāwī until 1873, who was Abū al-Suʿūd's teacher, and Abū al-Suʿūd himself published articles in this journal.

[76] Letter dated 5 Dhū al-Ḥijja 1286 (8 March 1870), from ʿAlī Mubārak (Nāẓir al-Awqāf), 468/46, MST, Microfilm 204, DWQ.

[77] ʿAlī Bāshā Mubārak, "[untitled letter]," *Rawḍat al-Madāris al-Miṣriyya*, 15 Muḥarram 1287 (16 April 1870), 7–10.

[78] Ḥasan and Dusūqī, *Rawḍat al-Madāris*.

[79] Yousef, "Reassessing Egypt's Dual System of Education."

[80] Aḥmad Naẓmī, introduction to the greeting poem, *Rawḍat al-Madāris al-Miṣriyya*, 15 Muḥarram 1287 (16 April 1870), 14.

his father's death.[81] Yet even some of the more professional topics were connected to khedivial authority. Abū al-Suʿūd, for instance, translated a treatise on education from French, in which he praised Ismail for establishing Dār al-ʿUlūm (in the article mentioned as *Dār al-Muʿallimīn*).[82] This happened after the legendary closure of his own journal in 1872. In fact, the entire end of Dhū al-Ḥijja 1290 (February 1874) issue was dedicated to Ismail, with Abū al-Suʿūd's essay followed by Tādrus Bey Wahbī's panegyrics celebrating three marriages within the dynasty and ʿAlī Fahmī's poem for that occasion (see below).

The revival and reinvention of the Muslim past as an Arab one, connected to a strong sovereign, was central to making discursive nationness. Through the dissemination of loyal patriotic speeches *Rawḍat al-Madāris* contributed to a general sense of cultural revival. The cultural life of Baghdad in the ninth and tenth centuries, during the Abbasid Empore, seems to have served as a reference point. The speeches of al-Ṭahṭāwī usually contained poems; for example, there was this speech in June 1870: "And after giving thanks to God: indeed the progress / is firmly established in Egypt / arts make Ismail happy / he renewed an age, the time of trust! / and by him indeed Egypt became Baghdad / but the sciences of the Egyptian age are more / the beauty of Paris and the pride of London / the rich and the mighty traveled to Egypt." [83] The poem actually announced the first Abbasid symbol of Egyptian modernization.

In sum, the available information suggests that the gentle revolution attempted to build patriotic culture *through* the government. When we look at the attention of Egyptians in high positions (ʿAbd Allāh Fikrī and ʿAlī Mubārak) to the needs of Abū al-Suʿūd, his press, and *Rawḍat al-Madāris*, we see not some kind of khedivial plan, but an effort on the part of learned bureaucrats to convince the khedive of their "patriotic service."[84] This was a clever manipulation of khedivial needs for a preemptive response to the critical European press.[85]

Democracy in the Khedivate

History teaching, like the Arabic press, presented both a blessing and a curse for the regime. History was the core of nation-ness and was also one of the primary ways in which the ruler could be bound together

[81] *Rawḍat al-Madāris al-Miṣriyya*, 15 Ramaḍān 1290 (6 November 1873), 3.
[82] *Rawḍat al-Madāris al-Miṣriyya*, Ghāyat Dhū al-Ḥijja 1290 (19 February 1874), 3–7.
[83] *Rawḍat al-Madāris al-Miṣriyya*, Ghāyat Rabīʿ Awwal 1287 (1 June 1870), 3–6, here 4.
[84] Fikrī, ed., *Al-Āthār*, 262.
[85] Sadgrove, "The European Press."

with the notion of the homeland through narration.[86] History, however, facilitated regime-type comparisons that could potentially undermine authority. Indeed, I suggest that comparative history caused the fall of Abū al-Suʿūd and the closure or suspension of the journal *Wādī al-Nīl*.

Abū al-Suʿūd was appointed as teacher of history in Dār al-ʿUlūm in 1872. He immediately wrote and printed *The Complete Course in Universal History* because there were no books to teach history (he does not seem to notice al-Ṭahṭāwī's earlier work). Abū al-Suʿūd was arguably the ideal person for this task, as a devoted Muslim who had studied at al-Azhar, but who also translated Mariette's ancient Egyptian history, *Aida*'s libretto, and French geography. His book is a mixture of translations from European histories and original passages from Arabic books "in the khedivial courtyard," as the subtitle adds in large characters. The book is humbly credited as "collected and Arabized" by Abū al-Suʿūd. The intended audience was mostly Muslim students from al-Azhar who were the student body in Dār al-ʿUlūm.[87]

The Complete Course in Universal History was an original achievement. The book mixes French historical theory and Egyptology with Arabic linguistics, *ḥadīth*, medieval Muslim historians (Ibn al-Athīr, Ibn Khaldūn, et al.), Arabic poetry, and Abū al-Suʿūd's own ideas. He certainly followed al-Ṭahṭāwī's earlier discussions of European political forms and likely had first-hand experience in Paris (he visited the city, but it is not clear when). The book had to serve as both his own and his graduates' teaching material. This is the reason why there are exam questions on the content following each chapter. *Al-Dars al-Tāmm* could function as a teach-yourself-how-to-teach-history manual.

At Dār al-ʿUlūm the subject was *histoire universelle*, as opposed to other schools.[88] This time, the homeland is clearly the Nile Valley. Abū al-Suʿūd wanted to write a history of the Egyptian nation (*al-umma al-miṣriyya*) within a universal history, comparing Egypt to other nations, with a special place for the dynasty. He praises the amazing power of electricity and the telegraph. Ismail is evoked in the preface with the usual praise; for example, he is described as "the first missionary (*dāʿin*) leading in the path of civilization and happiness."[89] The khedive also figures among the definitions of the word *tārīkh* ("date," "history") when Abū al-Suʿūd shrewdly describes the use of chronograms with the example written to celebrate the change of the succession order in 1866: "'Ismail's clan

[86] Although there are a number of studies of Egyptian historiography, these early years are typically left out. For instance, Di Capua, *Gatekeepers*.

[87] Abū al-Suʿūd, *Kitāb al-Dars al-Tāmm*.

[88] *Programme de l'enseigemment*, 7.

[89] Abū al-Suʿūd, *Kitāb al-Dars al-Tāmm*, 3.

inherits Egypt' makes the year 1284" (*yarith Miṣrā* [!] *Āl Ismāʿīl sanat 1284*).[90] This is the only indication of Egypt's Ottoman attachment.

However, we do not know how he would have written about Egypt's place in the Ottoman Empire. *Al-Dars al-Tāmm*, despite the obvious effort to please the khedive, seems to have been censored. Only the theoretical introduction and six chapters of ancient history remain out of the planned twelve chapters. All surviving copies that I was able to access stop abruptly at the beginning of chapter 7, third part, on page 400. We do not even know whether the book was actually taught in Dār al-ʿUlūm, although the truncated text was printed in several copies.

The introduction is a general methodology of history with a theory of politics, surpassing al-Ṭahṭāwī's canonized earlier work. It contains the comparison of three regime-types: monarchical (*mulūkiyya*), aristocratic (*al-ḥukūma al-aʿyāniyya*), and popular (*al-ahliyya*) government. This last one Abū al-Suʿūd calls democratic (*dīmūkrāsiyya*): "[in this regime type] the administration of the resources of the community (*milla*) is in its own hands, I mean, it rules itself without the control of a king, a sultan, or a group of notables."[91]

Abū al-Suʿūd also explains that, theoretically, a country's regime expresses its "system of sovereignty or power" (*niẓām al-mulk aw al-sulṭān*), and constitutes, together with the laws and customs of the people, its "civilization." He draws a distinction between two subtypes of monarchical government (*al-ḥukūma al-mulūkiyya*): absolute and constitutional (*al-muqayyada aw al-qānūniyya*). He then briefly adds another distinction, noting that a monarchy can be inherited in a family or be based on *election*.[92] This sentence provides the first direct clue that Egyptian intellectuals saw the consequences of changing the succession order in 1866. The notion of election, in fact, was not new: there were texts in Arabic about election of kings, and Salāma Muṣṭafā al-Najjārī's 1863 history also contained the notion of elected kings. After all, it was well known that the first caliphs of Islam were elected, too.

Abū al-Suʿūd's work has a strikingly different approach to power than the short booklet of al-Ṭahṭāwī for disciplining students published in the same year in the *Wādī al-Nīl* press. Al-Ṭahṭāwī there explains that rulers in theory should obey the *sharīʿa* and the consensus of the *ʿulamāʾ* "but in reality, the order of the ruler (*ḥākim*) is compulsory."[93]

90 The extra alif is needed for the numerical value of the year. Abū al-Suʿūd, *Kitāb al-Dars al-Tāmm*, 7.

91 Abū al-Suʿūd, *Kitāb al-Dars al-Tāmm*, 13.

92 Abū al-Suʿūd, *Kitāb al-Dars al-Tāmm*, 12.

93 [Al-Ṭahṭāwī], Rifāʿa Bey, *Al-Qawl al-Sadīd*, 20.

We should not forget that in France the Second French Empire fell, the Commune was defeated, and a new republic emerged in 1871–1872. Abū al-Suʿūd (as al-Ṭahtāwī) was fluent in French and had access to such news; he may have visited Paris in this period. I suspect that this book and the general turbulence in France was the reason his journal *Wādī al-Nīl* was shut down in 1872. An additional reason may be that Abū al-Suʿūd was attacked by some *ʿulamāʾ* for his translation of a French geography, published in serial format in *Wādī al-Nīl*, which described the Earth as round.[94] His son Muḥammad Unsī, as we shall see soon, had his own fight in 1872, although on a different front.

Marriage and Poetry: Ismail as "The Father of Arabs"

While the press and history carried potential subversion, poetry and rhythmic prose continued to fuse dynastic praise with patriotism. Sheikh ʿAlī al-Laythī took over the role of the leading poet from the deceased Muṣṭafā Salāma al-Najjārī in 1870. Al-Ṭahṭāwī and Majdī continued to regularly praise Tevfik,[95] and Ismail[96] in poetry, but we do not find poems from Abū al-Suʿūd. Fikrī was responsible for the khedive's correspondence in Arabic with Arab sovereigns such as the sultan of Morocco or the leader of the Sanūsī order, and, of course, also composed congratulatory poems.[97]

Arabic poetry was featured on dynastic occasions such as the reception of sultanic firmans, marriages, and circumcision ceremonies. With regard to marriages specifically, there were two particularly noteworthy occasions of multiple weddings in 1869 and in 1873. The first was the wedding of Tevhide, the favorite daughter of Ismail, and Mansur Yeğen Pasha in the spring of 1869; at approximately the same time, the marriage of Zübeyde (a cousin of Ismail) and a rich *zevat* Ali Celal Pasha was also arranged. The second occasion was a giant dynastic union, four marriages in three weeks in 1873. Three sons of Ismail (Tevfik, Hüseyin, Hasan) and his daughter Emine married their cousins. As Kenneth Cuno argues, the introduction of endogamy—not an Ottoman custom—into the ruling family also imposed monogamy on the males since the marriage to a "princess ruled out the additional wives due to her standing."[98]

The reason of dynastic monogamy was political. Ismail had already expressed to the French consul in 1866 that "it is dangerous to have many

[94] Fikrī, ed., *Al-Āthār al-Fikriyya*, 221–239.

[95] *Rawḍat al-Madāris al-Miṣriyya*, Ghāyat Rabīʿ Thānī 1287 (1 July 1870), 18–19; in competition with ʿAbd Allāh Fikrī and ʿAlī Fahmī: Ghāyat Jumādā al-Ūlā 1287, 290–293.

[96] *Rawḍat al-Madāris al-Miṣriyya*, 15 Jumādā al-Ūlā 1287 (13 August 1870), 3.

[97] Fikrī, ed., *al-Āthār*, 15.

[98] Cuno, *Modernizing Marriage*, 21.

children of the same age. It would be important to prevent the rivalries of the harem." Therefore, reports the consul, Ismail "started to look for men who know the Koran well and thus can help to create a new law by which he could force his children to have only one legitimate wife." A committee of twelve religious scholars in Cairo declared that monogamy was not contrary to the Koran. A similar committee was to be formed in Alexandria and, if they also approved Ismail's plan, the approvals were to be signed by all sheikhs and then presented to the sultan. The move to monogamy was regarded by the French consul as a step forward in "civilization." [99] Although no such law was finally drawn, it is noteworthy that Ismail consulted the religious establishment and intended to have the approval of the local Egyptian notables *and* the sultan. This reflects the nature of the khedivate, and the imagined compromise between khedive and subjects. Yet, instead of legal means, the 1873 weddings were occasions for such public approval by symbolic ones.

ʿAlī Fahmī published a long congratulatory poem on the khedivial marriages in 1873,[100] as well as a short booklet of patriotism, *Tasting the Branch in Its Root through the Love of the Homeland and its People*,[101] which celebrated yet another firman reaffirming the privileges of Ismail in the same year. In Fahmī's wedding poem, Ismail, the Ottoman governor, is described as "the father of Arabs" (*Abū al-ʿArab*).[102] As to the celebration of the 1873 firman, using ample chronograms, Fahmī thanks God for giving Ismail and his sons to Egypt and prescribes gratefulness to Ismail for every "sensible person" since "the Ismailite state of the Mighty One" (*al-dawla al-ʿazīziyya al-Ismāʿīliyya*) was reaffirmed "in the light of the greatest caliphate" for "both general and individual benefit."[103] This small poem together with al-Ṭahṭāwī's Baghdad-Cairo parallel intended to naturalize the khedivate and Ismail in an "Arab" romantic revivalism.

There were other individuals who were not connected to the patronage systems, such as one young man of extraordinary literary talent, ʿAbd Allāh Nadīm (1843–1896), who worked as a telegrapher in the palace of Hoshyar Hanım, Ismail's mother, during the gentle revolution. He would later go on to have a much more important role in the ʿUrābī revolution. But during the spring of 1873, perhaps at the last moment when Egyptian intellectuals may have seen Ismail as a potential monarch, Nadīm wrote a long *fuṣḥā* poem celebrating the khedivial weddings. Nadīm sent the long poem to the editor of the official bulletin, with the title "To Serve

[99] Letter dated 30 July 1866, from French consul in Alexandria to Direction Politique (French Ministry of Foreign Affairs), 166PO/D25/67–68, MEAN.

[100] Fahmī, *Mazdūja*.

[101] Fahmī, *Qudwat*.

[102] Ibid., 9.

[103] Ibid., 4.

Kings Is to Praise Kings" (*Khidmat al-Mulūk Fī Tahānīʾ al-Mulūk*) but only a few strophes were printed.[104]

Finally, the first significant *zevat* poet in Arabic publically appeared in the person of Sāmī al-Bārūdī (1835–1904) who, next to his military appointments, also praised Ismail Pasha in Arabic in the 1860s. He undoubtedly recognized his power in panegyrics, in one especially addressing the pasha he wrote: "you have been blessed with kingship."[105] His and Nadīm's further political actions, which contradict to their early poems, are discussed in the next chapter. In sum, in the early 1870s an extraordinary production of printed texts aimed at fabricating an Arabic image of Ismail Pasha, while patriotism gained solid territorial contours.

Space and Language: Performing Patriotism

How could ideas become a communal experience and feeling? While patriotic projects identified the khedive and the homeland in print Arabic, Ismail and Draneht built a very different spatial aesthetics of power (see chapter 3). Muḥammad Unsī's demand for Arabic plays in the khedivial theaters in February 1870 is the first public sign of the recognition of the discrepancy between the two projects. Space and language had to be synchronized.

Unsī demanded Arabic translations of plays and not original works. The reason for this is possibly the acknowledgment that (Ottoman) Arab mimetic entertainment was not efficient for learning modern patriotism, since it lacked the historical dimension. Farces and *karagöz* (in Egyptian Arabic *arāghūz*) were oral, vernacular genres that typically mocked the powerful or criticized society and had no engagement with heroic narratives.[106] Patriotism needed modern, historical plays that could be presented to the khedive. While *Aida* was intended by Ismail and Draneht to be a "national" opera in Italian, local intellectuals sought to create their own form of patriotic Arabic theater. One example is Muḥammad ʿUthmān Jalāl's "Egyptianization" of *Tartuffe,* which, in fact, starts with a few *fuṣḥā Arabic* lines remarking that "plays (*tiyātrāt*) are made for learning and refinement" and, after the vernacular play, ends with the compulsory *fuṣḥā* praise of the khedive.[107]

The educated Muslim vision of theater is perhaps best characterized by the didactic novel *ʿAlam al-Dīn* by ʿAlī Mubārak which was written in the

[104] Nadīm, ed., *Sulāfat al-Nadīm*, 1:37–38.

[105] DeYoung, *Mahmud Sami al-Barudi*, 66–88; the quotation is from 79. For another poem: Al-Bārūdī, *Dīwān*, 1: 517–531.

[106] Cf. examples in Bahjat, *Al-Arājūz al-Miṣrī.*

[107] J[alāl], *Al-Shaykh Matlūf*, 86–87.

early 1870s (but published only in 1882).[108] He drew a clear distinction between "obscene and dull" traditional entertainment (*awlād Rābiya* and singers) and the civilizing effects of European theaters. This difference is explained, in the conversation between a British Orientalist and an Egyptian sheik, by the fact that the European (or British) actors and opera singers are trained and educated while the Egyptian street entertainers are not. The Orientalist explains that theater could be also useful for the rule of law (*sharīʿa*) and religion (*diyāna*), because it helps people to imagine "hell." The sheikh does not find this point extremely convincing.[109]

ʿAlī Mubārak, through these characters, emphasizes the teaching function of theater: "it is a channel that stretches between the members of the nation (*umma*) and in which the water of science and scholarship flows from top to down, from the scholars and the elite to the ignorant and the ordinary."[110] This understanding of the modern theater, resembling the Syrian bourgeois theory of entertainment, articulated an elite turn away from street entertainment. But it did not exclude the use of the vernacular for characterization. ʿAlī Mubārak himself suggested the use of *ʿāmmiyya* in the first "Egyptianized" play of Jalāl. In Molière's *Le médicin malgré lui* Jalāl had Egyptianized both the language (using an unrhymed Cairene dialect) and the plot (giving Arab names, etc.) because ʿAlī Mubārak had "instructed" him to do so.[111]

Importantly, theater needs both cultural and financial capital. A troupe needs actors to be trained, texts to be written, and stages to be created. These were not provided by Draneht's cultural system, which imported all its elements from abroad except for the security guards. Unsī's first solution was translation, and as a next step, as we shall see, the very logical demand for a school of acting. But someone else hastily created an Egyptian troupe, without training, relying on the tradition of Egyptian farces and Italian comedies instead of the learned *adab* tradition.

Marginalizing James Sanua

This was James Sanua (Yaʿqūb Ṣanūʿ, 1839–1912), who applied for government funds for a vernacular theater, almost completely misunderstanding the nature of the khedivial regime. Sanua's comedies embody a type of patriotism that did not grow out of Muslim Arab traditions, directed by learned men, but imagined instead an urban vernacular culture as a horizontal community. It was doomed to failure and was a quite

108 Dysktra, "A Biographical Study," 2: 405

109 Mubārak, *ʿAlam al-Dīn*, 2:404–410.

110 Mubārak, *ʿAlam al-Dīn*, 2:419.

111 Quoted in Bardenstein, *Translation and Transformation*, 105.

marginal enterprise compared to the projects by Abū al-Suʿūd and many others loosely associated with the government. Notwithstanding Sanua's mistakes in many respects, however, his troupe did provide a platform that could be used by more sophisticated playwrights.

Sanua's education was financed by Mansur Yeğen Pasha in the 1850s (Mansur Yeğen would marry Ismail's daughter in 1869). In the 1860s, he worked as a language teacher and a poet, a typical middleman or "cultural creole," to borrow Julia Clancy-Smith's term.[112] He wrote poems in Italian and was an Italian subject (his father was an Italian Jew from Livorno), but also spoke vernacular Arabic, while calling himself "James" instead of Yaʿqūb. In the late 1860s he became a member of a Masonic society in Cairo and, possibly through the Yeğen household, eventually became a partisan of Abdülhalim Pasha.[113] In 1878, he started a satirical political journal, *Abū Naẓẓāra* (*Abū Naḍḍāra* in the vernacular) and was almost immediately exiled. Until his death, he published various journals in Arabic and French in Paris, confessing himself an Egyptian patriot, and an enemy of the British.[114]

I have already argued that Sanua's troupe was an isolated, short-lived project that sought khedivial patronage and wanted to be seen as loyal.[115] Here, I modify my interpretation to some extent. Although no information survives regarding the acting of the troupe, I suggest that Sanua's comedies (but not the full repertoire of his troupe) may have been interpreted as subversive, even if this was not his intention. Thus the performances, partly in vernacular Arabic, may have posed a potential challenge to khedivial absolutism, especially in 1872, when Abū al-Suʿūd also printed a historical theory about various types of government. However, such a reading only makes sense when understood against the backdrop of the earlier engagement with theater in the gentle revolution.

Theater in the Khedivate, 1869–1872

Sanua's troupe developed out of the theater craze in Cairo caused by the new khedivial theaters. Draneht sent *libretti* for Arabic translation and printing during the summer of 1869.[116] Translations were also made, in larger numbers, into Ottoman Turkish, and even from Italian to French.[117]

[112] Clancy-Smith, *Mediterraneans*, 8.

[113] The Yeğen boys' political role in the early 1870s is not clear. There are references that they conspired against Ismail but he never punished them; possibly because the oldest Manṣūr was the husband of his favourite daughter.

[114] Ettmüller, *The Construct of Egypt's Nation-Self*.

[115] Mestyan, "Arabic Theater in Early Khedivial Culture."

[116] Sadgrove, *Egyptian Theatre*, 48.

[117] *Aida* was translated to Turkish from Arabic. Original French letter published in Abdoun, ed., *Genesi dell' "Aida,"* 101, and its English translation in Busch, Verdi's Aida, 266.

The khedive paid for the journalist of *Wādī al-Nīl* to have a seat at the Opera among the European journalists during the first season (1869–1870). The journalist was Unsī, who later called for Arabic plays, as we have seen, in February 1870. In November the same year, Donizetti's *La Favorite* and Rossini's *Il Barbiere di Siviglia* were printed in Arabic by the press of Ibrāhīm al-Muwayliḥī[118] and were sent to *Wādī al-Nīl* for distribution with an informal letter from the chief of police, allowing them to be printed. In the introduction, theater is held up as a means of civilization and progress. No translator is credited, so *Wādī al-Nīl* assumed it was Muḥammad ʿUthmān Jalāl.[119] It is possible that this remarkable Egyptian translator and poet was thought to be the translator because of his previous association with al-Muwayliḥī (they co-edited the short-lived journal *Nuzhat al-Afkār*) and because his translation of La Fontaine's tales was reprinted the same year.[120]

At the same time, in 1870, young Egyptians in Cairo wanted to stage a play entitled *Alexandre dans les Indes*, which had been translated into Arabic. We know this from the French report of a secret agent who called himself Agent Z. The agent attributed the desire of "the population" for theater in Arabic to a combination of recent events: a book of Arabic dramas printed in Beirut (probably Niqūlā Naqqāsh's edition of Mārūn's plays, *Arzat Lubnān*, 1869); a speech about Arab theater buildings delivered in Cairo's New Hotel (probably by the architect Hector Horeau); and Arabic translations of *libretti* ("*Don Juan, Moïse, Barbier du Seville*"). One of these was among the *libretti* that al-Muwayliḥī sent to *Wādī al-Nīl*. The Qaṭṭāwī family, an Egyptian Jewish banker dynasty, also wished to stage Arabic dramas in their own house, possibly employing the same young Egyptians mentioned above, but had to postpone their patronage due to a family tragedy. Agent Z suggested to the government that it

---

A bilingual Italian-French edition of the libretto was also printed in 1871. [Ghislanzoni], *Aida—Opera in 4 atti e 7 quadri.*

118 Ibrāhīm al-Muwayliḥī's press, al-Maṭbaʿa al-Wahbiyya, was established in 1868 according to El Mouelhy, "Les Mouelhy en Égypte," 319; however, there are books available in library catalogues printed in this press earlier, from hijrī year 1281 (1864–5).

119 *Wādī al-Nīl*, 20 Shaʿbān 1287 (15 November 1870), 2–3. Sadgrove, *Egyptian Theatre*, 58–59; 100, accepts that the translator was ʿUthmān Jalāl and calls *Tartuffe* and *Le malade imaginaire* "operatic libretti." However, these are not operas (although *Le malade imaginaire* contains musical interludes). Bardenstein rejects the idea that Jalāl translated libretti. Bardenstein, *Translation and Transformation*, 36.

120 Since Jalāl in his autobiography relates his difficulties with finding a publisher in the 1850s and leaves the impression that he printed the book at his own expense, it has been commonly thought that it was published for the first time in 1870. Moreh and Sadgrove, *Jewish Contributions*, 20; Bardenstein, *Translation and Transformation*, 32, n. 20. But the book was first printed in August 1858 (Dhū al-Ḥijja 1274) (Cairo: Maṭbaʿat al-Ḥajar, 1274); copies could even be bought in Beirut, *Ḥadīqat al-Akhbār*, 12 Muḥarram 1276 (11 August 1859), 4. It was reprinted in June 1870 (Rabīʿ al-Awwal 1287) (Cairo: al-Maṭbaʿa al-Kāstīliyya [Castelli], 1870).

should support theater in Arabic with a view to educating the masses, by erecting a national theater building and *une école filodramatique et musicale*, as well as by introducing a copyright law [!]. In this suggestion, no distinction was made between *fuṣḥā* and vernacular Arabic. The project suggested by Agent Z would have served to "enlighten" the people, luring ordinary Egyptians to the theater rather than leaving them to "sing obscene songs" in the cafes. Thus, it was argued, theater in Arabic would usher in a new morality to khedivial Egypt.[121]

It is important to note that Unsī's public Arabic and Agent Z's secret French suggestions both framed Arabic theater as an instrument of progress. Both intended to reach the ears of the khedive. Their suggestions fit well with the imagination of Abū al-Suʿūd, Mubārak, and their colleagues. The belief in progress and in ethical purification through theater indicates that these suggestions were part of a general worldview. Unsī believed that theater in the "national" language was a key to progress in Europe and wanted the same to be established in Egypt. These utterances, from an educated Egyptian, and from a secret agent, highlight the connection between nation-ness and "progress" in learned patriotism.

Sanua himself was possibly encouraged by the fact that in the spring of 1871 the interregional Arab press also seemed, in different ways, to seek to convince the khedive of the necessity of an Arabic-language theater.[122]

Sanua's Troupe as Part of Khedivial Culture, 1871–1872

In early 1871, James Sanua organized a theater troupe with some of his students. In all likelihood, their first public performance took place somewhere in Cairo on July 8, 1871, before a large audience. *Al-Jawāʾib* remarked that the Cairenes chose *al-Qawwās*, "an Englishman's play," despite the fact that Arabic plays from Beirut were available to them.[123] On July 27, the troupe performed in front of Ismail in Qaṣr al-Nīl palace. They started with short pieces in vernacular Arabic written by Sanua, followed by the performance of two longer, more refined plays, *al-Bakhīl* and *al-Jawāhirjī*.[124] The evening was arranged under the direction of *Jamʿiyyat Taʾsīs al-Tiyātrāt al-ʿArabiyya* (Society for the Establishment of Arabic Plays). James Sanua was the only member of this society mentioned in the press. There is no evidence as to whether the society was

[121] Letter dated 27 January 1871, Agent Z to M. Nardi, 5013–003022, DWQ.

[122] *Al-Jawāʾib*, 12 April 1871, 2. *Al-Jinān* as quoted in *al-Jawāʾib*, 10 May 1871, 2.

[123] *L'Égypte*, 9 July 1871, and L'Avvenire *d'Egitto*, both quoted in Tagher, "Les débuts," 206. *Al-Jawāʾib* only later reports on the "first night" of the theater, in its issue of 16 August 1871, 2.

[124] *Wādī al-Nīl*, quoted in *al-Jawāʾib*, 27 August 1871, 3; Sadgrove, *Egyptian Theatre*, 98.

the same as the theater troupe that staged the performances. This evening performance before the khedive may have been a test: was theater in Arabic eloquent enough to be included among the arts of the khedivate?

In October 1871, Sanua's troupe again performed short comedies/operettas in Arabic, this time in the al-Azbakiyya Garden.[125] Meanwhile, Verdi's *Aida*, the main cultural project of Ismail and Draneht, premiered on December 24, 1871, in the Opera House. Parallel to the Italian product for the khedivate, by January 1872 the Arabic theater in al-Azbakiyya had become popular among Egyptians,[126] but then ceased for some time. This theater was a potential space for new communal experiences, and it later indeed became a center of learned patriots.

First, it seemed that the khedivate finally would have an Arabic stage. Ismail entrusted the arrangements for an Arabic theater to Sanua, who planned to reopen it on April 10, 1872, in the al-Azbakiyya Garden.[127] By April, the Arabic theater (*al-malhā al-ʿarabī*) was indeed popular among the "modern and idle people," first with dancing girls from Beirut, then without them. The troupe prepared to perform in the Comédie on April 22, which was the first occasion of an Arabic performance in a khedivial theater.[128] The Azbakiyya Garden was crowded that month as a result of rumors that tickets would soon be introduced, replacing the system of free entrance.[129] In May, the advertisement of an Arabic drama, known as *Laylā*, by the Azhari student Muḥammad ʿAbd al-Fattāḥ al-Miṣrī, mentioned "the Arabic theater [troupe]" (*al-tiyātrū al-ʿarabī*) "now performing in the garden of al-Azbakiyya."[130] In the preface of this drama, the author thanks his friend, "the esteemed director James," for his advice. He also hails James as a pioneer and dedicates the play to Ismāʿīl Ṣiddīq ("al-Mufattish"), at that time minister of finance.[131] ʿAbd al-Fattāḥ al-Miṣrī considered Sanua and Ismāʿīl Ṣiddīq as his patrons or at least as supporters of Arabic theater.

The troupe performed *Laylā* at least twice in June or July 1872. The first performance was probably part of the garden's inauguration.[132] *Le Nil* reported that in the theater of "M. James" the audience thought that the actors had actually killed each other during the performance and,

[125] *L'Avvenire d'Egitto*, 10 October 1871, quoted in Tagher, "Les débuts," 206.

[126] *L'Avvenire d'Egitto*, 4 January 1872, quoted in Tagher, "Les débuts," 206.

[127] *Al-Jawāʾib*, 28 March 1872, 2.

[128] *Al-Jawāʾib*, 11 April 1872, 2.

[129] *Al-Jawāʾib*, 17 April 1872, 2.

[130] *Al-Waqāʾiʿ al-Miṣriyya*, 7 May 1872, as translated in Sadgrove, "Leyla," 167–168; this article was also reprinted in Najmi's introduction to al-Miṣrī, *Luʿbat Laylā*.

[131] al-Miṣrī, *Luʿbat Laylā*, 3; Sadgrove, "Leyla," 164; idem, *Egyptian Theatre*, 107–108.

[132] Sadgrove, "Leyla," 168; Goldziher, "Jugend- und Strassenpoesie," 609, n. 3.

when reassured to the contrary, demanded an *encore*.[133] This is the last contemporary report available on the theater of Sanua.

Draneht, Unsī, and the Question of Language

How did Draneht, the master of early khedivial culture, react to Sanua's Arabic troupe? More important, how did Muḥammad Unsī react, who demanded Arabic plays earlier? Draneht had already made some efforts to publicize opera in Arabic. In the summer of 1869, he hed opera libretti translated into Arabic to "instruct the audience."[134] The prices of the boxes in the Opera House were communicated in Arabic in the journal *Wādī al-Nīl*, together with a report about the first show.[135] But the program of the Opera House in the first season, unlike the Circus of Rancy, was not advertised in Arabic. Only in February 1870 was the opera *Semiramis* announced in *Wādī al-Nīl*, together with a definition of the genre of opera, and Muḥammad Unsī's call for Arabic performances.[136] Draneht likely disapproved of the staged amateur, local, and satirical comedies.[137] He preferred and always opted for "dignified" or professional Italian or French musical theater. But because Draneht spent the summer of 1871 in Italy (mostly in Milan) and France, dealing with the arrangements for *Aida*,[138] he had no direct control over what happened in Cairo. It was in this context that Sanua's troupe made its debut and performed in front of the khedive himself in July 1871. Sanua's later recollections testify that Draneht, upon his return, was not supportive of Sanua's project.[139]

Neither was Muḥammad Unsī, for his part, happy with the first Arabic troupe in Egypt. He had initially supported Sanua's troupe,[140] but it seems that he soon changed his mind. Together with the French teacher Louis Farrugia (d. 1886), who worked at the École des Arts et Métiers,[141] Unsī proposed a rival Arabic theater enterprise to the government. They

[133] *Le Nil*, 9 July 1872, quoted in Sadgrove, *Egyptian Theatre*, 108.

[134] Letter dated 27 July 1869 Draneht to Khayri, Maḥfaẓa 80, CAI, DWQ. Cf. Sadgrove, *Egyptian Theatre*, 48.

[135] *Wādī al-Nīl*, 5 November 1869, 868–869: report about the ode for the khedive and the prices. *Wādī al-Nīl*, 12 November 1869, 900–901: report about the opera *Rigoletto*.

[136] *Wādī al-Nīl*, 17 February 1870 (1869 is wrongly printed on the title page), 1285.

[137] Sadgrove, *Egyptian Theatre*, 105. Sanua later severely criticized Draneht's attitude. Moosa, *The Origins*, 45 and Moosa, "Yaʿqūb Ṣanūʿ," 407–408. Sanua depicts Draneht as one of his greatest enemies, but also adds that he managed not to provoke him to anger. Apart from his testimony we have no other sources that would testify to Draneht's attitude.

[138] Draneht left for Milan on 29 April 1871 and arrived back in Cairo around 10 October; Busch, *Verdi's Aida*, 154 and 236.

[139] Moosa, *The Origins*, 45; and Moosa, "Yaʿqūb Ṣanūʿ," 407–408.

[140] *Wādi al-Nīl*, quoted in *al-Jawāʾib*, 27 August 1871, 3.

[141] Dossier of Louis Farrugia, 354PO/2/34, MEAN.

submitted their project in April 1872, when the popularity of Sanua's theater was at its zenith and seemed to be institutionalized by Ismail Pasha. They argued that "the experiment" had not reached a "good result."[142] Their own project, written in French and proposed quite clearly to counter Sanua's project, was personally recommended to the khedive by Draneht several times, and through the intermediary of Khayri, the khedive's secretary.[143] But why did Draneht support the idea of an Arabic theater project at all?

The imagined Arabic theater of Unsī and its school [!] were planned as a part of Draneht's administration. Unsī proposed a troupe called the *Théâtre National* in which young Egyptian boys and girls would be trained to become professional singers and actors. It would use the "Kiosque" of the Garden Theater in al-Azbakiyya, and sometimes the Comédie. The troupe would perform in *fuṣḥā* and would draw upon the great medieval pool of Arabic texts. Unsī suggested in French that "the Arabic language is amazingly applicable in the art of drama and in the intellectual amusements."[144]

Importantly, Unsī's competition with Sanua does not seem to have been motivated by envy. Rather, Unsī was deeply concerned about the style of official patriotic entertainment. We have seen that his printing press published *adab* works, journals, and language manuals. The way Sanua realized Arabic theater, mostly in *ʿāmmiyya* (by April 1872 *Laylā* was not yet staged), was likely not viewed by Unsī as contributing to the progress of Egypt. In the following years Unsī composed at least four books on Arabic language in his capacity as a language teacher. The first was a language book of Arabic for foreigners, the second a new method in reading Arabic for elementary schools, the next taught *fuṣḥā* for beginners, and finally he published a new Arabic grammar for elementary schools in three volumes. These works were all printed by his press, perhaps at the order of ʿAlī Mubārak, for the new khedivial schools.[145] It was this educational attitude and engagement with the learned Arabic language, coupled with a respect for *adab*, that informed Unsī's theater project. We see here the intellectual's desire to shape modern culture according to his own tastes, representing possibly the whole educational spirit at the time. Unsī's proposal was backed by Draneht because doing

142 Sadgrove, *Egyptian Theatre*, appendix 3.

143 Sadgrove, *Egyptian Theatre*, 93; Moosa, *The Origins*, 47.

144 Letter dated 20 April 1872, from Draneht to Khayri. He attaches the (French) project for the Arab théâtre, dated 15 March 1872, which was published by Sadgrove in *Egyptian Theatre*, appendix 3, 186–196; for analysis, 105–106.

145 "Bayān Mā Ṭubiʿ bi-Maṭbaʿat Wādī al-Nīl fī Taʿlīm al-Lughāt li-Muḥammad Unsī," in Unsī, *Al-Juzʾ al-Thānī min Talṭīf al-Uslūb*. There was a planned third part. Cf. idem, *Uslūb Jadīd*.

so offered the latter a way to control theater in Arabic, in addition to the European troupes. However, no reply to the proposal survives from the khedive or the government. Instead of Unsī or Sanua, intellectuals from Ottoman Syria took advantage of the momentum to create Arabic theater for the khedivate in the 1870s.

The Repertoire of Sanua's Theater and Patriotism

Before concluding, since Sanua's theater was the first enterprise to create a communal experience in the modern Arabic theater in Egypt, it is worth mentioning the images of the patriotic community presented in the performed works. Did these plays conform to the dominant technique of musical theater, that is, history and historicization? Were they comparable to *Aida*, and could they compete with it?

ʿAbd al-Fattāḥ's *Laylā* is a historicized Arab love story resulting in a blood bath between proud tribal Arab leaders in the desert. The trope was based on ancient Arabic epics. The tragedy, with its educated language (though some vernacular words, such as *ashūf*, are interspersed), including a quotation from the ancient poet ʿAntara b. Shaddād, evoking a moral concept of Arabness. For instance, the father Amīr Zaydān warns the hero Ḥasan not to employ any trick against his rival because "treason is not an Arab or heroic quality" (*al-khiyāna laysa hiya min sha*ʾ*n al-*ʿ*arab wa-l-fursān*).[146] When the rival lover, Amīr ʿImrān, plays false, Amīr Zaydān accuses him of not being an Arab because "Arabs do not act in this way, tell me, did you go mad?"[147] The drama contained the same intellectual principles that were expressed in Unsī's proposal: the use of *fuṣḥā* and tribute to the great Arab literary heritage. The early Egyptian formulation of moral Arabism in this tragedy fit in with the ideal form of a national drama, and indeed it was written, as ʿAbd al-Fattāḥ remarked, "for the sons of the homeland" (*abnā*ʾ *al-waṭan*).[148] Another indication of this intention was *Laylā*'s immediate publication (in contrast to Sanua's plays in vernacular Arabic, which remained in manuscript form). ʿAbd al-Fattāḥ's tragedy represented an early patriotic Egyptian Arabic play.

There was no historical core similarly grounding Sanua's works, which were written in colloquial Arabic (mixed with French, Italian, Greek, and *fuṣḥā* Arabic). These can be reconstructed as approximately twelve texts with songs; seven of them were printed posthumously.[149] The humor

[146] Al-Miṣrī, *Luʿbat Laylā*, 33.

[147] Ibid., 44.

[148] Ibid., 4.

[149] This is similar to the number given by ʿAbd al-Fattāḥ, who wrote that his friend composed "more than twelve plays." Al-Miṣrī, *Luʿbat Laylā*, 3; Sadgrove, "Leyla," 164. An often mentioned lost play is *Patrie et Liberté* or *al-Waṭan wa-l-Ḥurriyya* (for instance, Moosa,

of the plays relies on language mistakes and mutual misunderstandings. There are no heroes, no battles, no myths. A short dialogue ridicules an English tourist. Six comedies are about love and marriage. The main characters are urban Syrians and Egyptians, members of modestly wealthy Arabic-speaking merchant families, interacting with Frenchmen, Greeks, and Englishmen. The play *al-Ḍarratayn* is an exception; its male protagonist is a hashish addict, and its theme is polygamy. In general, however, the Egyptian characters do not mention subversive ideas; this is especially true of the servants (there are also two European maids), who are portrayed neutrally.[150] In contrast, the comedy *al-Ṣadāqa* praises the government for encouraging foreign investment.[151] An Egyptian character in *al-Amīra al-Iskandarāniyya* asserts that he would give up his status as a French protégé to become a subject of the khedive again. Another character admires the fact that "the governor of Egypt transformed his kingdom's capital into a garden."[152] These texts, contrary to Moreh and Sadgrove's interpretation, are not concerned only with "themes far from politics."[153] They ridicule ignorance while praising the khedive. This is why their staging had the potential for irony—even if unintentional irony. In 1872, the lines "The governor of Egypt transformed his kingdom's capital into a garden" could be made into a barbed joke with the right body language and intonation.

Most important, Sanua did not understand, or could not use, historicization, the principal vehicle of patriotic imagination. Nor did he recognize the *fuṣḥā* modernity in the works of Abū al-Suʿūd, Unsī, and others. But the Azhari student ʿAbd al-Fattāḥ did use a historicized plot in *fuṣḥā* Arabic in *Laylā*. Had the theater troupe survived longer, it might have performed more plays using historical or historicized themes. The troupe had the potential to become a forum for other playwrights in Arabic and thus a vehicle of patriotism. But Sanua misread the horizon of possibilities, looking for fame and money from Ismail, without securing the cooperation with Abū al-Suʿūd, Unsī, and ʿAlī Mubārak, or even the

"Yaʿqub Sanuʿ," 408; and Moreh and Sadgrove, *Jewish Contributions*, 23) but so far nothing substantiates its existence or performance. The play *Mūlyīr Miṣr* (1912) must be excluded from the performed works during 1871–72. Badawi, "The Father of the Modern Egyptian Theater," 143; Sadgrove, *Egyptian Theatre*, 113; Levy, "Jewish Writers in the Arab East," 161. Because they were not published, it is not certain that Sanua's works in manuscript were performed and vice versa. The printed works include *Mūlyīr Miṣr* and six comedies with one short dialogue (manuscripts discovered by Lūqā, published by Najm, 1963). A number of theatrical texts appeared in Sanua's various journals; ʿĀnūs collected these in *Yaʿqūb Ṣanūʿ*; see also Ettmüller, *The Construct*, 101.

150 Sadgrove, *Egyptian Theatre*, 114, repeats Moosa, "Yaʿqub Sanuʿ," 430.

151 Al-Ṣadāqa, in Najm, *Yaʿqūb Sannuʿ*, 128.

152 Al-Amīra al-Iskandarāniyya, in Najm, *Yaʿqūb Sannuʿ*, 154, 167.

153 Moreh and Sadgrove, *Jewish Contributions*, 22.

aggressive Europeanizer Paul Draneht. The form of discursive nationness that the Muslim intellectuals created was contradictory to Sanua's vernacular imagination as expressed in his plays.

The idea of a nation without history was unacceptable in early khedivial culture, and realism coupled with irony was not welcomed. In a way, Sanua not only faced the khedive but also the intellectuals who were busy with making *fuṣḥā* Arabic the language of the khedivate. Ismail did not grant financial help, and the troupe dissolved in the summer of 1872. Sanua tried twice to return to the stage: in 1873 and next in 1876 with a comedy in Italian. In 1877, the inauguration of Théâtre Ismail was advertised with his participation (with the "Egyptian Molière"). The audience did not receive his comeback well.[154] At this point the disappointed Sanua joined the circles of the political thinker, Jamāl al-Dīn al-Afghānī. Their activity and the next group of theater-makers are the subjects of the next chapter.

Conclusion: The Invention of Muslim Memory and the Lack of Capital

The gentle revolution was an attempt to make patriotism the official ideology of the khedivate. This involved the formulation of a language and a historical imagination based on selected cultural motives. This new Muslim memory had to compete with and conform the European aesthetics of Ismail and the actual Ottoman belonging of Egypt. Spatial transformation brought politics to be performed in front of the powerful. Thus the language as a public representation had to be adjusted.

In this period, the Ottoman attachment of Egypt recedes in the background and the Nile Valley is clearly the content of the idea of *waṭan*. Abū al-Suʿūd, for instance, writes in a well-commented translation in 1872 that he wants to "substitute the details of the French Kingdom's description, which is the author's beloved homeland, with the details of Egypt's geography, God willing, since she is our beloved homeland" (*waṭanunā al-ʿazīz*).[155] This switch of national homelands clearly indicates the territorial meaning of *waṭan*.

Note that the adjective of "homeland" in Arabic is often *ʿazīz* which is exactly the title given to Ismail in official Arabic texts, and what he demanded from the sultan in vain. The khedive was discursively identified with the land of Egypt. *Fuṣḥā* Arabic transplanted the physical body of the pasha into a patriotic symbol by identifying personhood and geography.

[154] Sadgrove, *The Egyptian Theatre*, 116–120.
[155] Qūrtanbīr, *Kitāb al-Dars*, 193.

The learned language, and the new textual pool associated with it, helped the appearance of Arabness as a moral and communal category. The failure of vernacular modernity as an accepted official representation (though it would eventually be the main language of the entertainment market)[156] was partly due to the un-historicity of the vernacular language(s). The religious status, the historical corpus, and the reinvented tradition made *fuṣḥā* Arabic the perfect candidate for a common ground between khedive, Muslim intellectuals, European Orientalists, and as we shall see soon, Arabic-speaking Christians, with which no version of vernacular Arabic could compete.

The common feature of Unsī's and Sanua's enterprises is the lack of capital. Ismail spent hundreds of thousand francs for Italian opera, but gave very limited support to patriotic education and press. The manipulation of absolutist rule by patriotic means in Arabic was thus limited by the absence of funding. Why did Abū al-Suʿūd, Unsī, and even Sanua not apply for private support from Egyptian merchants and *aʿyān* is a complicated question and needs further research. What did the *aʿyān* do in this period when they were, in fact, involved in administration through the Consultative Chamber?

Around 1873, it thus became obvious that the khedivate as a regime type is no more than the allocation of some possibilities for *aʿyān* capitalism through the Consultative Chamber. Ismail started to appoint again more *zevat* in administrative positions. ʿAlī Mubārak was reduced to being a simple supervisor in 1872. In the coming years, the Ottoman Empire forcefully returned as another homeland in Egypt as we shall see in the next chapter.

[156] Armbrust, *Mass Culture and Modernism*; Fahmy, *Ordinary Egyptians.*

CHAPTER 5

Constitutionalism and Revolution: The Arab Opera

How did the uncodified compromise between the khedive and local notables and intellectuals break down? Why couldn't they agree in basic principles? The period from the mid-1870s to 1882 is an extremely complex one. There was a financial crisis, European takeover of the khedivate's fiscal politics, social mobilization, and army revolt: the ʿUrābī revolution in 1882.

This chapter, instead of a linear progress to revolution, highlights two traits: the return of Egypt's Ottoman attachment in public texts and the relationship of intellectuals to power. The ambivalent use of the word *waṭan* reappeared, denoting both the Ottoman Empire and Egypt. Ismail could still rely on the fragile support of local notables and intellectuals. But after he was deposed in 1879, his son Tevfik was unable to maintain this support. Importantly, all parties attempted to use Ottoman sovereignty for local change.

In this period, large groups of society were alienated, and traditional client-patron relations were broken. The *ʿulamāʾ* at al-Azhar disagreed over reforms and formed opposing alliances. The khedive and European controllers introduced new taxes, and reduced the number of soldiers in the army (94,000 troops in 1871 to 36,000 in 1879, 18,000 planned for later).[1] The too knowledgeable Ismāʿīl Ṣiddīq was arrested and murdered in 1876 possibly by the order of Ismail. New political figures appeared: the anti-British Persian thinker Jamāl al-Dīn al-Afghānī (1838–1897), living on a government pension in Cairo, found useful allies in Ottoman Syrians to fight European imperialism.

The events, and the role of General Aḥmad ʿUrābī, were immediately the subject of ideological readings.[2] Scholars look at this period and the revolution as "proto-nationalist,"[3] others as a double movement

[1] Reid, "The ʿUrabi revolution," 220.

[2] Mayer, *The Changing Past*; Di Capua, *Gatekeepers*, 172–174.

[3] Reid, "The ʿUrabi Revolution," 218.

of a "struggle among social classes" and "regional patriotism."[4] Landau suggests considering the role of freemasonry and the conspiracies of Abdülhalim (Ismail's uncle);[5] Berque, Sālim, Schölch, and Cole prove the wide social basis of the movement with differing interpretations;[6] EzzelArab refocuses the role of the elite and constitutionalism;[7] and recently Khuri-Makdisi and Fahmy channel the cultural production of the period into the history of radicalism, and Egyptian vernacular nationalism, respectively.[8]

Through the intersection of patriotism and theater this chapter also explores how revolutionary culture informed the forgotten origins of Egyptian stardom. Salāma Ḥijāzī (1852–1917), the first Egyptian singer to sing in the Khedivial Opera House, appears during the turbulent spring of 1882 with the impresario Sulaymān Qardāḥī (1854?–1909). Egyptian stardom origins in a trans-Ottoman Arab enterprise: Ḥijāzī became a national star in the 1880s through his associations with Syrian troupes. We start with the Syrians, the new cultural entrepreneurs of Arab patriotism in Egypt.

Khedivial Syrians

Ottoman Syrian migration to Egypt in the 1870s was a potential source of loyal subjects in the khedivate. In the grand narratives of resistance, some of these individuals are destined to be revolutionaries. In contrast, I look upon their cultural activity as initially loyal to Ismail. Their behavior could change into public criticism because of their independent capital and their protection by rival pashas and European powers.

The Beirut-Cairo Connection

As we have seen in chapter 1, Ottoman Syrians remained aware of the power of the Mehmed Ali family after the 1830s occupation. There had also been small but important Syrian Christian trading communities in Egypt since the eighteenth century.[9] Prompted by the changing economy of the Lebanon mountain, and Ottoman efforts of reintegration,

[4] Cole, *Colonialism and Revolution*, 268.

[5] Landau, "Prolegomena."

[6] Sālim, *Al-Quwa al-Ijtimāʿiyya*; Schölch, *Egypt for the Egyptians*; Cole, *Colonialism and Revolution*.

[7] EzzelArab, *European Control*; see his other articles in the following notes.

[8] Khuri-Makdisi, *The Eastern Mediterranean*, 115–116; Fahmy, *Ordinary Egyptians*, 55–60.

[9] Philipp, *The Syrians in Egypt*, 17–25.

Syrians migrated in larger numbers all around the world. Egypt was an attractive location, since no passport was needed for them and the ticket was relatively cheap (at least it was remembered as such in the Syrian diasporas).[10]

The image of khedivial Egypt in the Syrian Arabic public sphere was certainly attractive. We have discussed Said's relations with the Beiruti elite, and Ismail further advanced the image of Egypt and his own rule by financing *Ḥadīqat al-Akhbār*, the most important journal, and the projects of the intellectual Buṭrus al-Bustānī in Ottoman Beirut.[11] In *Ḥadīqat al-Akhbār*, and in al-Bustānī's journals *al-Jinān* and *al-Janna*, Egypt was often described in the most extravagant words. But there was no need for khedivial money: according to *al-Najāḥ*, yet another Christian Arab journal in Beirut, which had no proven connection to Ismail, the khedivate of Egypt was "the most advanced country in the East" in 1871.[12]

As part of the growing public sphere in a city of merchants, there was a revival of Arabic theater in late Ottoman Beirut. In a new school for patriotic education, *al-Madrasa al-Waṭaniyya*, opened by Buṭrus al-Bustānī in 1863, teachers such as Nāṣīf al-Yāzijī encouraged theater activities,[13] or wrote plays, such as al-Sayyid Salīm Ramaḍān and Ibrāhīm al-Aḥdab.[14] The book *Arzat Lubnān*, publicizing Mārūn and Niqūlā Naqqāsh's ideas and plays, was published in 1869, prompted by the Ottoman governor's request.[15] Coincidently, this was the year when the Comédie and the Opera House were constructed in Cairo. As we have seen, in 1871 plays were sent to Cairo from Beirut,[16] and *al-Jinān* asked the khedive to establish Arab theaters.[17] Perhaps *al-Jinān*'s correspondent made another proposition, because the correspondent of the Istanbul paper *al-Jawāʾib* ridiculed him (and the editor, al-Bustānī) for asking the khedive to "create a theater in which he can bring dancers and dancing girls to perform."[18] There is no known reaction from Beirut to Sanua's theater

[10] Letter dated 16 March 1984, AAC.

[11] Al-Khūrī received 1,000 wīntū, order dated 18 Jumādā al-Akhīra 1281 (18 November 1864), Sāmī, *Taqwīm al-Nīl*, part 3, 2:579. The subsidy for *al-Jawāʾib* and *al-Jinān* was reduced to 300 pounds in 1879, thus these journals must have received a larger amount before that date. Letter dated 20 January 1879, Maḥfaẓa 1, Juzʾ 2, Niẓārat al-Dākhiliyya, CMW, DWQ.

[12] *Al-Najāḥ*, 9 *Kānūn al-Thānī*, 1871, 11–12; next number, 29–30, next number 43–45, next number 60–61 (khedivial music), next number 76–77; then 221–222.

[13] Hanssen, *Fin de siècle Beirut*, 168.

[14] Moreh and Sadgrove, *Jewish Contributions*, 68.

[15] Sadgrove, "Syrian Theatre," 273.

[16] As Agent Z reported in his letter dated 27 January 1871 to Mr. Nardi, the Inspector of Police in Cairo in 5013–003022, DWQ.

[17] *Al-Jinān* as quoted in *al-Jawāʾib*, 10 May 1871, 2.

[18] *Al-Jawāʾib*, 27 March 1872, 2.

troupe in Cairo. And after that amateur troupe dissolved in 1872, the floor was open for the more professional Syrians.

In the 1870s, Ottoman Syrians were already professionally instrumentalizing the past for community building. Luke Leafgren shows that Salīm al-Bustānī, editor of *al-Jinān*, used the phrase *al-umma al-ʿarabiyya* (the Arab community or nation) both in 1870 in his journal (which also had *ḥubb al-waṭan min al-īmān* – "the love of the homeland is part of faith" as its title slogan) and in 1874 in a historical novel about the Muslim conquest.[19] In 1875, *Al-Jinān* also mentioned Arabic plays as helping *al-umma al-ʿarabiyya.*[20] William Granara argues that Jurjī Zaydān's later novel about Muslim Andalusia (1904) established the literary use of Andalusia as a chronotope in Arabic literature—a compressed past time and space that may be resurrected in the present.[21] We shall see that Muslim Andalusia started to develop earlier in the Arab historical-political imagination as a topos in theater, connecting patriotism and dynastic loyalty.

A Patriotic Migration

The migration of the playwright, translator, and impresario Salīm Khalīl Naqqāsh (1850–1884) from Beirut represents a calculated migration pattern. It was a conscious decision that was preceded by contact and the survey of possibilities. Salīm was the nephew of Mārūn and Niqūlā Naqqāsh, the merchants-poets-playwrights. He studied French and Italian, and worked at the Customs in the Beirut port, perhaps as a protégé of his uncle (Niqūlā also worked at the Customs).[22] He wrote and printed his Arabic tragedy *Mayy* or *Mayy wa-Ḥūrās* using elements from Corneille's *Les trois Horaces et les trois Curiaces* in 1868 (perhaps translated earlier in 1866) and enriched it with songs.[23] It is not known whether Salīm was involved in the performances of the 1860s.[24] In 1874, he reprinted his *Mayy* with an introduction in which he praised Khedive Ismail and with a special dedication to a merchant in Alexandria. As a next step, in early 1875 Salīm Naqqāsh traveled to Egypt to look for better prospects.

[19] Leafgren, "Novelizing the Muslim Wars of Conquests," 51–52.

[20] [Al-Bustānī], "Al-Riwāyāt al-ʿArabiyya al-Miṣriyya," 443.

[21] Granara, "Nostalgia, Arab Nationalism," 57–73.

[22] Shaykhū, *Taʾrīkh al-Ādāb al-ʿArabiyya*, 106.

[23] Sadgrove, *Egyptian Theatre*, 130; Najm, *al-Masraḥiyya*, 204–206. It is unclear when it was staged; it was produced together with his uncle's play *al-Bakhīl*. An anonymous article in *al-Jinān* (Salīm al-Bustānī?) states that it was staged "after Salīm Efendi arrived from the mountain," in "Al-Riwāyāt al-Khidīwiyya al-Tashkhīṣiyya," *al-Jinān*, 1 Tishrīn al-Awwal (October) 1875, 694–696. Moosa believes that it was in 1868, Moosa, *The Origins*, 33; Sadgrove states it was in 1875, Sadgrove, *Egyptian Theatre*, 130.

[24] Sadgrove supposes that the young man aided his uncle Niqūlā in performances. Sadgrove, "Syrian Theatre," 283.

The young man was charmed by khedivial Cairo, which seemed to him much more advanced than Beirut. In addition, he hoped to find financial patronage. He later explained to his Beiruti audience that "our city's material means became too few for what I needed [for my theater], so I decided to realize my aims somewhere else . . . I saw that people enter [Egypt] as if it were the Paradise," remarking also that Ismail had financed Salīm al-Bustānī.[25] Likely through *al-Jinān*'s new local correspondent, Edward Ilyās,[26] Salīm Naqqāsh contacted the superintendent Draneht, and watched a performance of *Aida* at the Opera House in the early spring of 1875. He discussed theater with Draneht, who was "satisfied with his [Naqqāsh's] competence." Sadgrove states that Naqqāsh persuaded Ismail Pasha "through the offices of Draneht" to support Arabic theater,[27] which possibly included the establishment of two specifically designed buildings for Arab troupes, one in Cairo and one in Mansura.[28] It is unclear who persuaded whom: the superintendent who recognized the value of a professional, and loyal, Arab Thespian in the service of the khedivate or the young Beiruti intellectual who needed financial support from a government. Be that as it may, Naqqāsh and Draneht exchanged ideas, which resulted in the khedive's issuing an decree (*irāda*) that Naqqāsh should prepare Arabic plays for late-Ottoman Egypt.[29] Naqqāsh framed this as a means that would help him to advance the social body and *al-umma al-ʿarabiyya* (the Arab nation).[30]

Preparations: The Arabic Aida *and Isḥāq*

Now there was a chance to include Arabic theater in khedivial culture. Salīm Naqqāsh undoubtedly prepared for an Arabic theater as part of the khedivial system or at least did everything possible to become acceptable. Unlike James Sanua in 1871–1872, this young man understood the requirements of the regime. Upon his return to Beirut, he immediately translated "parts of" the opera *Aida* into Arabic. It was the second translation of the libretto, the first having been undertaken by Abū al-Suʿūd in 1871. He dedicated the text again to Khedive Ismail and published it before July 1875 in Beirut.[31]

[25] Naqqāsh, "Fawāʾid al-Riwāyāt aw al-Tiyātrāt," 519–520.

[26] Letter dated 10/22 June 1871, from Salīm al-Bustānī to Zaki Pasha, attachment to 219/48, Microfilm 205, MST, DWQ.

[27] Sadgrove, *Egyptian Theatre*, 130. Moosa, *The Origins*, 34.

[28] *Revue de Constantinople*, 13 June 1875, 594. It cites *Phare d'Alexandrie* as a source. Sadgrove refers to *al-Jawāʾib*, 16 June 1875.

[29] [Al-Bustānī], "Al-Riwāyāt al-ʿArabiyya al-Miṣriyya," 423.

[30] Naqqāsh, "Fawāʾid al-Riwāyāt aw al-Tiyātrāt," 520.

[31] Abul Naga, *Les sources françaises*, 110; Garfi, *Musique et Spectacle*, 222.

Naqqāsh's *ʿĀʾida* is in five parts but the original *Aida* has only four acts. When later this Arabic *Aida* was performed, the original music and singing were also changed to "Eastern melodies."[32] The earlier translation of Abū al-Suʿūd was not for public distribution or performance. By retranslating *Aida*, the main work of early khedivial culture, into *ʿĀʾida* to be performed, and printing it for sale as a booklet, Naqqāsh fulfilled an important service to spread khedivial taste and its preferred historical imagery in Arabic.

His second activity was the training of a company with another theater-loving customs officer, the even younger Adīb Isḥāq (1856–1884). Isḥāq, born in Damascus, was a Greek Catholic *Wunderkind* of the Beiruti literary circles. By 1874, he had written poetry and a play, *The Chinese Incident*, which was staged in Beirut. In 1875, when he was only nineteen, he translated Racine's *Andromaque* into Arabic, possibly as a preparation for serving the khedive. In accordance with the musical theater tradition, the young playwright recommended the use of several Turkish tunes in the performance of this play.[33] He also translated Offenbach's *La Belle Hélène* into Arabic, possibly in this year,[34] which was the favorite operetta of Ismail. Naqqāsh and Isḥāq assembled seventeen actors and actresses and put on rehearsals in Beirut. They rehearsed *al-Bakhīl* and the Arabic *Aida*. We should not forget that such training was impossible in Cairo for Muḥammad Unsī or even for James Sanua four years earlier. Although the Beiruti troupe was ready by August 1875,[35] an outbreak of cholera postponed their arrival for more than a year.

"Actors of the Khedivial Plays:" Music, Fuṣḥā, *Nation-Ness*

The 1875 summer and autumn articles in *al-Jinān* suggest that Naqqāsh's goal was to serve Arabic plays for Khedive Ismail and Draneht Bey. The khedivate was a favorable regime for Ottoman Arabism. At this moment, Beiruti merchant culture was ready to join the production of patriotism in khedivial Egypt. The construction of an Arab cultural patriotism in which the khedive figured as a benevolent ruler also became the work of Syrians. The previous preference for *fuṣḥā* among Egyptian intellectuals gained an additional importance for the Christian Syrians since it was a means that subjected everyone equally regardless of religion or origin. Naqqāsh noted that the Egyptian and Syrian vernaculars are different

[32] Najm, *Salīm Naqqāsh*, page b.

[33] Sadgrove, Egyptian *Theatre*, 133. Kedourie, "The Death of Adib Ishaq," 81–100.

[34] Isḥāq, ed., *Al-Durar*, 10.

[35] "Al-Riwāyāt al-Khidīwiyya al-Tashkhīṣiyya," *al-Jinān*, 1 Tishrīn al-Awwal (October) 1875, 694–696.

and he decided to "perform Arabized plays in pure Arabic" (*ʿarabiyya ṣaḥīḥa*).[36]

The Naqqāsh-Isḥāq troupe reached Alexandria only in November 1876. This delay was critical because meanwhile, in response to Khedive Ismail's suspending the payment of the enormous interest on foreign debt, his creditors, backed by the French and British governments, forced the ruler to accept a Debt Commission to control the finances of the province. The commission cut the expenditure of the government, and by 1878 had compelled the members of the khedivial family to transfer most of their estates to the government.[37]

The agreement between Draneht and Naqqāsh and the khedive's order was known in Egypt. *Rawḍat al-Madāris* republished an article of *al-Jinān* about the history and modernity of Alexandria, in which the anonymous author speculated that the Syrian actors might first reach an understanding with the European actors in Alexandria, with whom they would share the same theater (perhaps the Zizinia). In the article the troupe is called "the actors of the khedivial plays" (*mushakhkhiṣū al-riwāyāt al-khidīwiyya*).[38] Was this a hint that the Syrian troupe was intended to be an official, khedivial enterprise?

The would-be khedivial actors arrived in an Alexandria where the Syrian community was already large. They had help. Syrian journalist-capitalists, the Taqlā-brothers had just established their journal, *al-Ahrām* in the summer of 1876; there were Christian schools; and soon a number of Syrian Christian charity societies. The troupe of Naqqāsh also received help from Ömer Lutfi Pasha (the governor of Alexandria, perhaps the same man who had supported Sanua four years before), possibly from the khedive, and press support from *al-Ahrām*, the bookshop-owner Ḥabīb Gharzūzī, and the press-owner and journalist Salīm Ḥamawī. Upon their arrival, *Al-Ahrām* immediately praised the Naqqāsh troupe in an article. The paper reminded the public that theater was "one of the primary means to fuse society together" and that "all civilized countries give this matter the utmost consideration" therefore attendance at the performances was an obligation.[39] In a later article, Isḥāq remembered that, like Jalāl and Mubārak earlier, they were indeed convinced that "theatre [was] one of the reasons for the progress of human society."[40]

As we have seen, popular mimetic entertainment in Egypt was a vernacular one, and Sanua also tried a vernacular theater. In contrast, the

[36] Naqqāsh, "Fawāʾid al-Riwāyāt aw al-Tiyātrāt," 520.

[37] Hunter, *Egypt under the Khedives*, 181–189.

[38] *Rawḍat al-Madāris*, 18 November 1876 (Ghāyat al-Shawwāl 1293), 9–12; also in Ismāʿīl, *Taʾrīkh al-Masraḥ al-Miṣrī*, 130.

[39] Sadgrove, *Egyptian Theatre*, 128–136.

[40] In Sadgrove's translation, *Egyptian Theatre*, 137.

Syrian plays were written mostly in *fuṣḥā* Arabic and were mostly historical or historicized (the staging, however, must have contained some vernacular). This made nation-ness the matter of an educated imagination. The Syrians employed local music to facilitate their acceptance. Mārūn Naqqāsh at the end of the 1840s had already chosen opera as the format of his first play, because he thought that musical theater would entertain "his people."[41] Salīm Naqqāsh and Adīb Isḥāq, twenty-eight years later, used music as a means to make the Beiruti troupe acceptable to the Egyptian audience. Naqqāsh deliberately favored "Arabic songs" (*anghām ʿarabiyya*) as opposed to "European" (*afranj*) ones in the plays. He argued that there is difference in taste.[42] There was an additional reason. A Syrian in Alexandria, Buṭrus Shalfūn, taught Egyptian tunes to the members of the troupe, so that Egyptian music might sweeten the *fuṣḥā* of the plays and make the audience forgive their *shāmī* colloquial.[43] We shall see that soon Egyptian singers would be involved in Syrian troupes establishing a pattern that would define Arab entertainment history up to the present. These developments, especially music, were important conditions in the communal experience of aural patriotism.

The Naqqāsh-Isḥāq troupe performed in Alexandria from late December 1876 until February 1877, for less than three months. They staged translated or Arabized French and Greek dramas (*Mayy, al-Kadhūb, Andrūmāq, Sharlumān,* perhaps *Fidrāʾ*), original Arabic plays (Mārūn Naqqāsh's *Hārūn al-Rashīd, al-Salīṭ al-Ḥasūd,* Salīm Naqqāsh' *al-Ẓalūm*) but possibly not *ʿĀyida*.[44] These plays in *fuṣḥā* Arabic embodied either a translated version of European myths or an Arab historical imagination, or in fact, a mixture of both. This repertoire suggests a very different idea about patriotic Arabic culture from that of James Sanua's vernacular comedies. The plays would likely have been approved by Muḥammad Unsī and ʿAbd Allāh Abū al-Suʿūd, had they ever seen the performances. The plots were on historical or historicized topics, conforming to educated patriotic conditions, and the use of *fuṣḥā* made them fit for presentation in front of the khedive.[45]

In order to fulfill the agreement, Salīm Naqqāsh traveled to Cairo in the summer of 1877, with the aim of finally arranging evenings for his troupe in one of the khedivial theaters. By that time, Isḥāq had already left Alexandria and the troupe, and set up a press in Cairo, which

[41] Naqqāsh, *Arzat Lubnān*, 16.

[42] Naqqāsh, "Fawāʾid al-Riwāyāt aw al-Tiyātrāt," 520.

[43] Buṭrus Shalfūn, "Al-Tamthīl al-ʿArabī," *al-Hilāl*, 1906, in NM1, 157–158, and Sadgrove, *Egyptian Theatre*, 127.

[44] Najm, *al-Masraḥiyya*, 94–101; Sadgrove, *Egyptian Theatre*, 125–138.

[45] It is often said that the play *al-Ẓalūm* (The Tyrant) angered Khedive Ismail but in fact there is nothing in the content of the play that would be offensive.

published a journal, *Miṣr* (Egypt), from July 1877. He immediately supported Naqqāsh in an article in *Miṣr* in his aim to perform within the frames of khedivial culture. Isḥāq wrote that "it has been the intention of [Naqqāsh] Efendi to let this [troupe] perform in Cairo in the service of the noble khedive."[46]

However, no performance was arranged. From 1877 Draneht was mostly in Italy; Ismail seemingly lost interest in financing a loyal Arabic troupe. Even *Rawḍat al-Madāris* ceased to be published in 1877. Naqqāsh then left the troupe in Alexandria and joined his friend at the journal *Miṣr*; he then published the periodicals *al-Maḥrūsa* (1877), *al-Tijāra* (1878), and *al-ʿAṣr al-Jadīd* (1880). This was good business since soon Naqqāsh could afford a house worth of French Fr 16,000 in Alexandria.[47] The young men (Isḥāq was only twenty-one in 1877) became vocal in criticizing foreign intervention through their periodicals, expressing a strong Ottomanism.[48] While it might be striking that in his first visit in early 1875 Naqqāsh was blind to the autocratic nature of Ismail's rule, it is equally striking how quickly he and Isḥāq switched from loyal theater to critical journalism. This was due to their meeting with Jamāl al-Dīn al-Afghānī.

An Emerging Action Field: Ottoman Constitutionalism in Egypt

We leave briefly the construction of patriotism in order to survey ideas deriving from Egypt's Ottoman context. Excellent studies discuss the activity of the thinker al-Afghānī and his followers in khedivial Egypt: Landau and Kudsi-Zadeh stressed the role of the secret societies in political activity,[49] and Cole added new sources about "the ideology of dissent" at the time.[50] Here I further contextualize al-Afghānī within the Ottoman universe of the late 1870s. This context was defined by the Ottoman constitution, the Russian-Ottoman war, the 1878 Congress of Berlin, and the still-ongoing competition within the ruling *zevat* family of Egypt.

In my interpretation, efforts were directed at the repair of the khedivial system, not at its demise. However, there was no agreement on the diagnosis of the roots of crisis and on a coordinated solution. Hence the emergent social actions, although aimed at stabilization, unintentionally

[46] Quoted in Sadgrove, *Egyptian Theatre*, 137.
[47] Cole, *Colonialism and Revolution*, 128.
[48] Cole, *Colonialism and Revolution*, 141–147.
[49] Landau, "Prolegomena"; Kudsi-Zadeh, "Afghānī and Freemasonry in Egypt."
[50] Cole, *Colonialism and Revolution*, 133–163.

challenged the incumbents of power. Almost all "challengers have sold themselves on some collective identity to justify their position as challengers,"[51] and this collective identity was mostly patriotism at the time. The clash, or failed synchronization, between interests and ideas of the main actors, however, is the subject of this subsection as much as it was related to our main topic: the Ottoman context and the relationship of intellectuals to power. Let us see the central figure in the master narratives of revolution—as an Ottomanist.

Al-Afghānī as an Ottomanist

Jamāl al-Dīn, a Shīʿī Muslim and a *sayyid* (descendent of the Prophet), widely traveled between Persia, Afghanistan, India, and Istanbul in the period 1857–1869. British imperialism had a thorough impact on his political views. He advised an Afghan emir against the British in 1867–1868 and may have developed relations with Russia.[52] Then he arrived in Istanbul in 1869. Due to his networking skills, and magnetic personality, concealing his Shīʿī origins (calling himself "al-Afghānī," though later in Egypt he signed his letters as Jamāl al-Dīn al-Ḥusaynī[53]), in February 1870 this unknown sheikh could give a speech at the opening ceremony of the first Ottoman university (*Darülfünun*), in which he urged the Islamic *milla* to be open to Western science.[54] A later talk of his was, however, used by the Ottoman *ʿulamāʾ* to crack down on the new educational institution.[55] This traveling figure of Western Asia resonates with the image of a wandering Sufi challenging the established men of religion.

The context of al-Afghānī in the 1860s was the so-called New Ottoman ideology, and his and his associates' activity in 1870s Egypt was a late continuation of that Ottomanism. A loose association of intellectuals, statesmen, and Ottoman aristocrats, called New Ottomans (*Yeni Osmanlılar*), preached Muslim reforms in order to strengthen the Ottoman Empire in the 1860s. At the center was the demand for a constitution, which would help imperial regeneration. The sidelined Mustafa Fazıl, half-brother of Ismail, was their main supporter, and, in fact, staged himself as their representative in 1867–1868.[56] After his death in 1875, Abdülhalim, who may have been involved earlier (his 1868 schemes in Egypt,

[51] Fligstein and MacAdam, "Toward a General Theory," 18.

[52] Keddie, *Sayyid Jamāl ad-Dīn*, 25, 27, 31, 41, 43, 47.

[53] Letter dated 8 Ramaḍān 1296 (26 August 1879), Jamāl al-Dīn al-Ḥusaynī to Tashrīfātjī, an attachment to letter dated 9 Ramaḍān 1296 (27 August 1879) from Muḥammad Rāʾif to Tashrīfātjī Khidīwī, 5016–001542, DWQ.

[54] Ibid., 63–64.

[55] Ibid., 78–79.

[56] Davison, *Reform*, 200–208.

especially *Jamʿiyyat al-Maʿārif*, resembled their program [see chapter 2]) continued to demand reforms. Al-Afghānī maintained his Istanbul contacts during his stay in Egypt.[57]

Mustafa Riyaz, the chief treasurer of Ismail at the time, invited the sheikh, who arrived in Cairo sometime in late March 1871.[58] They may have already known each other from as early as 1866.[59] Riyaz served in various government positions from the 1850s, and had accumulated large estates, but lived modestly. He was a devoted Muslim, of possibly Jewish origins, believing in the importance of Muslim revival, but was also impressed by modern technology. He was a fierce guardian of monarchical hierarchy and wanted just government, like the New Ottomans.[60] In 1873–1874 he became Director of Education and maintained the work of ʿAlī Mubārak. Riyaz may have been a secret supporter of Abdülhalim (he was a member of *Jamʿiyyat al-Maʿārif* in 1868). The ideas of Riyaz and al-Afghānī seem to be in accordance for a long time. They only fell out after the establishment of the Nubar government (August 1878). Riyaz considered the reforms to be beneficial for just administration, even at the price of European ministers and high-salaried employees, while al-Afghānī thought allowing Europeans to control would lead to the colonization of the province.[61] In December 1878, Riyaz Pasha was still mentioned as "the friend" of al-Afghānī.[62] It is certain that al-Afghānī until this time enjoyed Riyaz's protection.

The summer of 1877 was an Ottoman moment in Egypt. The Russian-Ottoman war started. After the deposition of Sultans Abdülaziz and Murad, the new sultan Abdülhamid II was forced to declare the constitution in December 1876, and in 1877 elections were held in all provinces, but not in Egypt or in Tunis. Despite poor beginnings, which even involved the beating of his first Egyptian follower Muḥammad ʿAbduh by Azhari students,[63] by this moment in 1877 al-Afghānī was able to attract a number of followers: Syrian Christians, Muslim notables, Azhari students, even some Europeans.

This group instrumentalized print technology and capital professionally for bringing Ottomanism back in Egypt. ʿAbduh started to publish articles in the new journal *al-Ahrām*. The once "khedivial actors" Adīb and Naqqāsh also engaged in journalism in the summer of 1877, expressing

[57] Note dated 15 Shaʿbān 1296 (4 August 1879), 5016–001542, DWQ.

[58] Hunter, *Egypt under the Khedives*, 192.

[59] Al-Hilbāwī, *Mudhakkirāt*, 70.

[60] Hunter, *Egypt under the Khedives*, 165, 191.

[61] Al-Hilbāwī, *Mudhakkirāt*, 72.

[62] Letter dated 12 December [18]78, Adīb Isḥāq to Jamāl al-Dīn al-Afghānī, 5016–001542, DWQ.

[63] Al-Hilbāwī, *Mudhakkirāt*, 53.

Ottomanism. Adīb wrote an article in his journal *Miṣr* entitled "The King and the Subjects" (*Al-Malik wa-l-Raʿiyya*) in which he praised constitutional government, both the Ottoman and the khedivial ones! In the atmosphere of the Ottoman-Russian war, he compares the "wise, constitutional" (*al-ḥakīma, al-shūrawiyya*) Ottoman government to the backward, unconstitutional, Russian autocracy. He also announces that different regime types fit different peoples: for instance, the "republic" (*jumhūriyya*) is not fit for China and "despotic kingship" (*malakiyya istibdādiyya*) is not fit for England. In his wording, *waṭan* (the homeland) means the Ottoman Empire at this time—in Egypt.[64] Al-Afghānī may have had the same opinion at the time, and after the Ottoman defeat he started a six-month period of mourning.[65]

Thinking about reforming Ottoman politics functioned as an umbrella ideology. It is unclear who benefited most in this network of intellectuals: al-Afghānī, a spiritual leader, instrumentalizing the young Muḥammad ʿAbduh and the Syrian actor-journalists in a sect-like atmosphere (Adīb especially uses magnificent Sufi titles for Afghānī [*mawlānā*]),[66] or the young men utilizing al-Afghānī's connections for permissions to establish journals as business enterprises (in 1878 his patron Mustafa Riyaz Pasha became minister of the interior). All these possibilities may have been true. Keddie and Cole's suspicion about al-Afghānī preferring philosophical and political over Islamic teachings in these years can be corroborated by the memoirs of his student Ibrāhīm al-Hilbāwī (1858–1940). Al-Hilbāwī remembers that the lectures were "mixed with politics in which he took up those issues that concerned Egypt, India, Afghanistan, and Turkey."[67] This direction made his teaching acceptable for Christians as well as Muslims. The Ottoman Empire was used as a principle of solidarity in Egypt in a moment of war and defeat.

Freemasonry and Societies

How did these progressive Ottomanists in Egypt network? The most important format for socializing was freemasonry, which was an almost public institution. Freemasonry was related to household politics. Ismail, Tevfik, and other *zevat* were all freemasons for political reasons. Abdülhalim remained in contact with freemasons in Egypt after his exile in 1868 to Istanbul.[68] (In 1868, Sanua was also a member of a lodge.)

[64] Isḥāq, ed., *Al-Durar*, 93–97.

[65] Sabry, *La genèse*, 126.

[66] For instance, letter dated 11 February [18]79, Adīb Isḥāq to Jamāl al-Dīn al-Afghānī, 5016–001542, DWQ.

[67] Al-Hilbāwī, *Mudhakkirāt*, 113.

[68] Landau, "Prolegomena," 149–150.

Al-Afghānī himself was in contact with French and Italian lodges from 1875 on, and in December 1877 he was elected to the Star of the East Lodge 1355,[69] although from time to time he was invited to other lodges, such as La Concordia.[70] The Star of the East was established by a British diplomat and until 1875 was secretly chaired by Abdülhalim from Istanbul.[71] Next to Christian Syrians the membership also included Egyptian notables such as ʿAbd al-Salām al-Muwayliḥī, ʿUthmān and Sulaymān Abāẓa, ʿAbd Allāh Fikrī, Buṭrus Ghālī, and some Egyptian army officers. Even the sidelined Muḥammad Unsī, the intellectual demanding Arabic plays in the previous chapter, was a member.[72]

Freemasonry connected journalism and Ottomanism: the journal *Ḥaqīqat al-Akhbār* (The Truth of News) was printed in Cairo from April 1877 with freemason symbols on its title page. This was a pro-Ottoman, private periodical, edited by a certain Anīs Khallāṭ, bringing news of the Ottoman-Russian war, including translations of articles from the Istanbul-based Ottoman journals. The fact that Khallāṭ could use telegraphs extensively indicates that significant capital or government connections were involved. In this journal, *waṭan* clearly meant the empire, and "interior news" meant news from the empire, including Egypt but not only Egypt.

The Egyptian *aʿyān* and village headmen joined Syrian merchants and were also active as Ottomanists to some extent. In 1878 there was an effort to re-establish fragile ties especially between Lower Egyptian notables and Ismail Pasha through Ottomanism. In January 1878, a patriotic society was funded in Tanta. This city was the center of the 1860s alliances designed by Ismāʿīl Ṣiddīq (assassinated in 1876). In January 1878, *al-Ahrām* reported that local notables and merchants in Tanta had established a society out of "patriotic fervor and Arab defense" to help the injured Egyptians fighting in the Ottoman army and invited Ismail to a celebration (*laylat al-uns*) in February. The khedive accepted the invitation, and all members of his entourage, and hundreds of village headmen joined the occasion. Many singers sang, the government military band performed, and the evening ended with fireworks. Ismail distributed Ottoman medals to the local consuls (mostly Syrian Christians) and to many village headmen. Like the 1866 celebrations in the same city, this was organized or encouraged by the government, since Shāhīn Pasha, the

[69] Cole, *Colonialism and Revolution*, 139.

[70] Invitation dated 7 January 1879 to R.L. La Concordia, 5016–001542, DWQ.

[71] ʿAn Bayān al-taʿrīfāt allatī ḥaṣalat min al-Shaykh Jamāl al-Dīn, 5 Ramaḍān [12]96 (23 August 1879); 5016–001542, DWQ.

[72] Bayān al-awrāq alladhī [!] ṣāra ḍabṭu-hā min manzil al-shaykh Jamāl al-Dīn: summary of approximately seventy-five documents confiscated from the apartment of al-Afghānī, without date (must be August 1879), 5016–001542, DWQ.

mufattish now, oversaw the preparations together with the rich merchant Dimitri Duhhan (the German consul in Tanta) and ʿAbd al-ʿĀl Bey who was the president of the Gharbiyya provincial council and who were all the founding members of the society. The celebration was enacted again as a moment of affective community of vertical togetherness during which the local village headmen paid respect to the khedive. *Al-Ahrām* invited all "sons of the homeland" to participate in order to help the (Ottoman) army to defend the homeland (that is, the Ottoman Empire).[73] Again *waṭan* in the moment of war becomes a transparent idea, an imagined territory, through which one can see both Egypt and the empire.

Al-Afghānī's Opinion of the Khedivate

What was al-Afghānī's opinion about Ismail personally and his khedivate? Cole attributes an unsigned, unpublished essay from 1877 to al-Afghānī in which the author blames the Ottomans for Muslim decline but praises the Egyptian reforms and Ismail's government.[74] In February 1879, he called for the reform of the regime in his first public, enigmatic article entitled "Despotic Government" (*al-Ḥukūma al-Istibdādiyya*) in the journal *Miṣr*. This was perhaps influenced by a public letter of Ismail's rival Abdülhalim in 1878.[75] Al-Afghānī elaborates the topic of despotism, which, as we have seen, by that time had been a trope in Arabic thought. In this article al-Afghānī categorized the khedivial regime as an "enlightened despotism" but an "inexperienced one" which leads to ruining the people. Al-Afghānī thought that a professional enlightened despotism—a wise one—was necessary for "the sons of the East."[76] In a police interrogation al-Afghānī maintained that he was a supporter of Ismail and his son Tevfik, as we shall see below.

The "Patriotic Party" and The Fall of Ismail and Afghānī

While the spring of 1879 is characterized as a "spring of discontent" by Cole, strong voices supported, or at least recognized, Ismail Pasha in exchange for representation and protection of rights. In March, a significant group of notables, many of the members of *Majlis Shūrā al-Nuwwāb*, proposed an alternative fiscal plan and demands for a constitution to the khedive. This has been called "The National Program" (*Lāʾiḥa Waṭaniyya*)

[73] *Al-Ahrām*, 13 January 1878, 1 and 3 March 1878, 1.
[74] Cole, *Colonialism and Revolution*, 149.
[75] Landau, "Prolegomena," 151–152.
[76] Cole, *Colonialism and Revolution*, 150–151, based on Kenny's translation in 1966.

in scholarship.[77] The document, emerging from "the politics of notables," to use Albert Hourani's concept, was shrewdly shown by Ismail to the European controllers as a sign of support from the "Patriotic Party" (often translated as the "National Party," *al-Ḥizb al-Waṭanī*). In this "party," many notables saw the khedive as a legitimate ruler who should represent their interests. However, under European pressure, Sultan Abdülhamid II deposed Ismail on 26 June 1879.

After the deposition of Ismail, al-Afghānī was also deposed from the presidency of the lodge with the accusation of "despotism [!] and intervening in political issues contradictory to the codes" on 1 July 1879;[78] and was soon exiled from Egypt. He also broke up completely with Riyaz Pasha (Riyaz would be also briefly exiled). In a police interrogation before he left, al-Afghānī described a break in his freemasonry lodge over who would be the right successor of Ismail. He said that he preferred Tevfik while the earlier leaders of the lodge, and "some Syrians," preferred Abdülhalim. While he denounced "some Syrians" during his interrogation, a devoted Syrian follower, Salīm al-Bustānī in fact showed up at the police station, ready to support him.[79] Given that Tevfik indeed became the khedive, al-Afghānī's claim must be handled cautiously. He referred to himself and his followers as from *al-Ḥizb al-Waṭanī* (The Patriotic Party; possibly in contradistinction to the Abdülhalim supporters).

"Patriotic," or "National" as it is often translated, in the name of the party must have meant that the members were supporters of the constitutional proposal and regarded Ismail and Tevfik as legitimate rulers. Certainly there are overlaps among Afghānī's supporters in the lodge and the signatories of the National Program, starting with ʿAbd al-Salām al-Muwayliḥī.[80] Despite a much later recollection of Muḥammad ʿAbduh about discussing the assassination of Ismail,[81] the evidence above suggests that, compared to European rule, al-Afghānī considered the khedive, and his son, the lesser evils.

Postscriptum to al-Afghānī and Riyaz

No coherent collective action emerged during the coming years after the summer of 1879. The important intellectual institution Al-Azhar was

[77] EzzelArab, "The Fiscal and Constitutional Program."

[78] Letter dated 1 Tammūz 1879 (1 July 1879) from Niqūlā Sakrūj, ʿAbd al-Raḥīm Mīkhāʾil, Jibrān Qudsī, Niqūlā ʿAraqjī (all of them raʾīs sābiq) to Jamāl al-Dīn, Raʾīs Lūj Kawkab al-Sharq n. 1355, 5016–001542, DWQ.

[79] ʿAn Bayān al-taʿrīfāt allatī ḥaṣalat min al-Shaykh Jamāl al-Dīn, dated 5 Ramaḍān [12]96; 5016–001542, DWQ.

[80] The resignation letters of his followers (all dated 10 and 11 July 1879) are registered in 5016–001542, DWQ.

[81] Sedgwick, *Muhammad Abduh*, 26.

divided. Patriotic ideas among the *ʿulamāʾ* were connected to the defense of religion.[82] In the autumn of 1881, when, shaken by cuts and the French occupation of Tunisia, the army demonstrated, the blind Sheikh Ḥusayn al-Marṣafī underlined the connection between the community—*umma*, often translated as "nation," could be unified by language, location, or religion—and the geographical territory of living (*waṭan*) but this did not make him a patriot in the sense of giving priority to territorial community over Muslimness.[83]

Others, like the editors of *al-Ahrām*, cooperated, or were forced to cooperate, with the government, and it is possible that Salīm Naqqāsh also did so. For instance, al-Hilbāwī, the student of al-Afghānī, after the exile of his teacher, published an article in Naqqāsh's journal *al-Tijāra* about the misuse of power in the countryside. He was arrested for this, and brought to the Interior Ministry in 1880. There he saw the original manuscript—that he sent by post to the editor—in the hands of the meanwhile reinstalled Riyaz Pasha, prime minister and minister of the Interior.[84] Free speech did not necessary bring misery: after a short imprisonment, al-Hilbāwī in fact was given an editorship at the state bulletin *al-Waqāʾiʿ al-Miṣriyya*, which was headed by Muḥammad ʿAbduh at the time (1880–1881). This was a result of Riyaz's renewed scheming, through the Egyptian pupils of al-Afghānī. He is also said to have protected the French journal *L'Égypte* in 1880–1881.[85] Political change was accompanied by quickly changing ideas about solidarity, mixed with personal and business interests.

The Invention of Hārūn al-Rashīd: Arabic Theater and Loyalism

I propose to further explore political events through cultural history. This gives us the freedom to detect changes in ideology before they are manifest in social action. Between 1878 and the summer of 1882, there were performances of plays in Arabic that reflected these changes. These were performed for a relatively small and often a rather upper-middle-class or elite audience. The performances—apart from their economic or artistic goals—can be regarded as means of communication similarly to petitions. They asked for justice and solidarity from the ruler.

[82] Hatina, *ʿUlamaʾ, Politics, and the Public Sphere*, ch. 4.

[83] Al-Marṣafī, *Risālat al-Kalim al-Thamān*, 1–29. Cf. Wendell, *The Evolution*, 135–140; Delanoue, *Moralistes et politiques musulmans*, 2: 357–359; Mitchell, *Colonizing Egypt*, 131–137.

[84] Al-Hilbāwī, *Mudhakkirāt*, 69.

[85] Goldziher, "Muhammadan Public Opinion," 109.

The Beiruti actors, left alone in Alexandria by Adīb and Naqqāsh, had to establish themselves in that city. One of them, Yūsuf Khayyāṭ, took over the leadership of the troupe.[86] He was able to gain more popularity and even khedivial support in 1878–1879. This second Arab impresario instrumentalized a new means to build audience in Alexandria and Cairo, one that neither Sanua nor Unsī could make any use of in 1871–1872 in Cairo. This was *charity*.

The bourgeois connection between charity societies and theater had already been experimented with in Beirut. Now in Alexandria, this middle-class culture was further enhanced: for instance, on 10 January 1878 the Syrian troupe performed for the benefit of the Patriotic Society for Aid (for the injured in the Ottoman-Russian war) at the Zizinia Theatre. The growing number of Syrian migrants helped Khayyāṭ since they transferred their philanthropic activities to Alexandria and Cairo. We shall see in the next chapters that a working relationship developed between charity societies and Arabic theater in the 1880s.

Second, Khayyāṭ and the future Arab impresarios never gave up the pursuit of what had originally been agreed between Draneht and Naqqāsh about khedivial support. In the atmosphere of growing discontent in 1878, Ismail hastily turned to all available means to gain popularity: his interest now was to become truly the "father of Arabs." This did not mean proper financing, only symbolic occasions were arranged. Khayyāṭ thus was able to collect on the agreement between Draneht and Naqqāsh.

Khayyāṭ's troupe performed an Arabic piece in the Khedivial Opera House in February 1878 in the presence of Ismail. This was the first Arabic play staged in this symbolic space. The performance was Mārūn Naqqāsh's *Abū al-Ḥasan al-Mughaffal aw Hārūn al-Rashīd* (1849), one of the most sophisticated Arabic musical plays in the nineteenth century. It is a musical comedy based on the 1001 Nights tale of *al-Nāʾim wa-l-Yaqẓān* usually translated as "The Sleeper Awakened." It is a love story about Abū al-Ḥasan, a foolish older drunkard in Baghdad who is tricked by the caliph by making him believe that he rules Baghdad, although for only one day. The confused and petty Abū al-Ḥasan just brings disaster on himself. Hārūn al-Rashīd reappears at the end, reveals himself, explains the trick, and generously gives him money.[87]

The play contains references to the Ottoman context. At the end, Hārūn al-Rashīd is called a *sulṭān* and *amīr al-muʾminīn* and is portrayed as a generous and just ruler who helps the lovers, forbids the wrong, and rewards loyalty. At the time of its first staging in 1849, the Beiruti elite, as we have seen in chapter 1, could read the character of Hārūn al-Rashīd as a

[86] Sadgrove explored his activity in detail, and I summarize his findings in the following. Sadgrove, *Egyptian Theatre*, 138–143.

[87] Najm, *Mārūn Naqqāsh*, 69–192 (with list of songs).

reference to Sultan Abdülmecid. However, in February 1878 in Cairo, in the Khedivial Opera House, the character of this caliph might have been a symbol for both the khedive and the sultan. This character would serve as the central hero of Arab patriotism in the khedivial opera in the 1880s. But even if it was a metaphor of the Ottoman sultan, an independent, strong, but benevolent ruler sent a clear message to the Ottoman Egyptian audience in early 1878 when the Ottoman-Russian war was being fought and the Debt Commission challenged the khedive's power.

The performance of *Hārūn al-Rashīd* was the second instance of Ismail's recognition of Arabic theater after Sanua's briefly encouraged enterprise, at a time when Draneht lived abroad. Compared to Sanua, Khayyāṭ's troupe was professional. This professionalism meant the use of *fuṣḥā*, well-chosen historical topics, and learned performance techniques.

Khedive Ismail and Arabic Theater

Khayyāṭ toured Cairo once more, first performing at the Comédie in front of Ismail Pasha, then at the Opera House, where the main attraction of his repertoire was again *Hārūn al-Rashīd*, attended again by Ismail, his family, and a number of ministers on 21 January 1879.[88] These performances mean that Ismail and his elite considered Khayyāṭ and the troupe as appropriate, and, most importantly, loyal to the khedivate.

Al-Afghānī appeared also in the theater audience in the spring of 1879. This is the moment when Syrian artists further developed the idea of Mārūn Naqqāsh in musical theater by not only studying Egyptian tunes but in fact also involving Egyptian singers. This meant the recognition that Egyptian tunes had to be performed by an Egyptian, with proper Egyptian pronunciation, and, perhaps most important, by someone with a wonderful voice. In May 1879 in Alexandria, when Salīm Naqqāsh, in a momentary return to the theater, put on a play in the Zizinia, the famous female singer al-Sayyida Bazāda took part in the performance. This is the first known instance of the involvement of an Egyptian (female) singer in an Arabic theater performance. The performance was attended by Jamāl al-Dīn al-Afghānī and the governor of Alexandria, Mustafa Fahmi Pasha.[89] Was this a belated gesture, showing al-Afghānī's support for the khedive?

However, the overthrow of Ismail and the closure of khedivial theaters thwarted Yūsuf Khayyāṭ's plans. The troupe, or at least Khayyāṭ, remained mostly inactive until 1881. The period saw the development of three features, which will remain characteristic of Syrian intellectuals and actors in Egypt: their ability to reach the khedive (but unsuccessful

[88] Sadgrove, *Egyptian Theatre*, 141.
[89] Ibid., 143.

institutionalization), their cooperation with Egyptian singers, and their attempts to achieve an Arabic historical repertoire to unite the audience through the celebration of a past hero.

The Play Homeland*: Theater as a Means of Patriotic Petition*

As Avriel Butovsky emphasized, "when Tawfiq came to power, new ways of thinking about the relationship of the khedive to society and the process of social change had come into the public sphere."[90] The break-up of Khayyāṭ's troupe does not mean that there were no more occasions for communal experiences and communications to the khedive through Arabic performances. In fact, from around 1879, Arabic theater became an integral part of public patriotism. Between 1879 and 1882, Egyptian playwrights offered new imaginative representations about the community. They were, unlike the Ottoman Syrians, explicit about *waṭan* being "Egypt;" and it was an Egypt inhabited by "Arabs." The new ruler Tevfik was attentive at the beginning.

The first Egyptian play that can be considered a petition was the work of ʿAbd Allāh Nadīm, a former telegrapher and poet once in the service of Hoşyar Hanım. In 1879 he established the first patriotic Muslim Egyptian society for teaching the poor in Alexandria, and there he also created a dramatic society and group. Nadīm, a man of linguistic virtuosity, a "literary bohemian,"[91] wrote a play entitled *al-Waṭan wa-Ṭāliʿ al-Tawfīq* ("The Homeland and the Star of Success," a pun on Tevfik's name). The play was first staged in April 1880 in Nadīm's school, then in July in the Zizinia Theatre before Tevfik and a number of dignitaries, including ʿAlī Mubārak. The school and the society had a record income on this occasion: Tevfik alone donated 100 LE and an additional total of 350 LE was raised.[92] Compare this with the monthly sum of 8 LE, the relatively high salary of Ibrāhīm al-Hilbāwī, as an editor of the official bulletin in this year.[93] Seemingly, *al-Waṭan* and the cause of the school attracted support.

The reason for this success is that the play discloses a patriotic conception in which the ruler and the poor are united. There are hints that this union is against the European Dual Control (called in Arabic *kumsūn*, "commission")[94] or against the rich (*al-aghniyāʾ*). The play calls for general education and for the establishment of patriotic societies. Contrary to the later female gendered images of Egypt as a woman,[95] in this first

[90] Butovsky, "Reform and Legitimacy."
[91] Wendell, *The Evolution*, 140–141.
[92] Sadgrove, *Egyptian Theatre*, 145–146.
[93] Al-Hilbāwī, *Mudhakkirāt*, 73–74.
[94] Al-Nadīm, "Shadhra min Riwāyat al-Waṭan," in *Sulāfat*, 2:40.
[95] Baron, *Egypt as a Woman*.

theatrical anthropomorphization the Homeland is an old man. He sits on stage and listens to the dialogues between various representatives of the people, such as peasants, hashish addicts, or urban educated individuals. They do not recognize *Waṭan* as the Homeland (in a funny moment one character says *būnū suwār yā Musyū al-Waṭan*—"bon soir Monsieur Homeland").[96] He tries to open their eyes, at one point crying out: "where are my people, where are my children, where are my men, I have become lost in my cause, I do not know what may happen to me";[97] or, "you are my people and you left me."[98] Some recognize him and his message; one character confirms "I say to God oh brothers . . . that we all belong to one homeland."[99] While the poor complain about food and scarcity of resources, *Waṭan* condemns them for their ignorance and says that if they would unite their forces ("if you would agree on one word") and turn to the government or "the greatest leader" (*al-raʾīs al-akbar*) they would surely receive help.[100] Finally, the representative character of the educated patriots, ʿIzzat Efendi, who works at an embassy and knows foreign languages, decides to establish a school by gathering support and donating a small amount in "the age of success" (or "age of Tevfik," *ʿaṣr al-tawfīq*, again a pun on the name of Tevfik).[101] When even idle and poor characters decide to send their children to this school with the support of *Efendīnā* (the khedive), the play turns into a celebration of Tevfik. Its last sentences wish "a happy khedivial day" (*yawm al-khidīwī saʿīd*) and warns that all should turn to "look at the prince."[102] We can imagine the effects of these last words in the theater where the ruler was present.

Compared to the theatrical fashion of the time, *al-Waṭan* is exceptionally ahistorical and without music, but it is didactic and evokes the khedive. It is, as if it was written directly to teach the use of nation-ness to the ruler, almost in the mode of a medieval mirror for princes or a petition. Nadīm masterfully characterizes the protagonists with their dialect,[103] but *Waṭan* and the Arab (Bedouin) talk mostly in pure *fuṣḥā*. This work poses a problem to teleological histories of national revolt and is usually left out;[104] even Samah Selim, who analyzes the play for its image of the peasant, remarks that "the play begins and ends with an extended

[96] Al-Nadīm, "Shadhra min Riwāyat al-Waṭan," in *Sulāfat*, 2:48.
[97] Ibid., 2:34.
[98] Ibid., 2:44.
[99] Ibid., 2:39.
[100] Ibid., 2:35.
[101] Ibid., 2:51.
[102] Ibid., 2:55.
[103] Selim, *The Novel and the Rural*, 55–56.
[104] For instance, it is not in Fahmy, *Ordinary Egyptians*, 39–60.

dialogue between them [Homeland and the peasants]."[105] But this is not the case. The play ends with a praise sang by girls to the khedive and the calling of all the "Arabs" to watch the prince.[106]

There were other attempts to involve the ruler in patriotic activities related to education and theater. Copts also put on a school play at the Zizinia and at the al-Qubārī school in the presence of Tevfik, both in August 1880. There were other school plays in Alexandria, in the Qardāḥī-school (see below). These were also the years when ʿAlī Mubārak published his novel *ʿAlam al-Dīn* with the chapter praising the theaters that was already quoted. The Jewish Charitable Society asked Yūsuf Khayyāṭ to help in staging the play *Ḥifẓ al-Wudūd* at the Opera in April 1881. This performance might have increased the value of Arabic theater for nurturing nonsectarian patriotism. This time Khayyāṭ also submitted a request to use the Comédie in Cairo in the coming theater season. This was granted, but the financial aid—Khayyāṭ asked for 6,000 LE[107]—was refused.[108] The lack of financial support especially hurt because the government subsidized the foreign troupes in the Opera and the Comédie with 225,000 francs in the 1880–1881 season.[109] However, adding these to Nadīm's theater activity there was a remarkable interest in theater.

Exactly at the moment when Khayyāṭ's sponsorship was rejected, Tevfik asked ʿAbd Allāh Nadīm to restage *al-Waṭan* in the Zizinia in July 1881. This proved a dismal failure because the enemies of Nadīm, perhaps at the instigation of Riyaz Pasha, did their utmost to discourage the audience. There is no clue why Riyaz opposed Nadīm when he had previously supported dissent as in the case of al-Afghānī, ʿAbduh, and al-Hilbāwī. Nadīm the next day resigned from the school and the Islamic Charitable Society.[110] This event may have contributed to Nadīm's turning to the rebellious army officer Aḥmad ʿUrābī, who asked him to travel in the countryside to deliver patriotic speeches in his support in the following spring.[111]

Arabizing the Egyptian army

A political crisis accompanied the cultural stirrings. The Egyptian army, led by colonel Aḥmad ʿUrābī, demanded the restoration of their pensions and the sacking of the European advisers. The summer of 1881 continued

[105] Selim, *The Novel and the Rural*, 56.
[106] al-Nadīm, "Shadhra min Riwāyat al-Waṭan," in *Sulāfat*, 2:63.
[107] *Al-Jinān*, 15 June 1881, 359.
[108] Sadgrove, *Egyptian Theatre*, 151–152.
[109] Compte Général, dated 5 April 1881, 4003–037847, DWQ.
[110] Sadgrove, *Egyptian Theatre*, 152–153.
[111] Shārūbīm quoted in Fahmy, *Ordinary Egyptians*, 56.

with a troubled autumn. On 23 September 1881, the army openly demonstrated in front of the Abdin Palace against French and British control and against their pay cuts. The army became the central force to unite all dissenting challengers, and created "a coalition" of forces which is a condition of an action field.[112]

Now the government made a more conscious effort to collect support through the Arabic public sphere. Although journalism is often counted as a revolutionary activity in the period, the government in fact paid 2505 subscriptions in 1881 to various journals (*al-Ahrām* 336, *al-Waṭan* 265, *al-Burhān* 232, *al-Maḥrūsa* 235), which was possibly both support and control.[113]

In addition, Tevfik received Yusūf Khayyāṭ at a private audience and allowed him to perform at the Comédie from November 1881 to January 1882. Now ʿAbd Allāh Nadīm once more tried to reach the khedive, by giving a speech when Khayyāṭ's troupe staged again the play *Hārūn al-Rashīd* in front of Tevfik. However, the attendance was poor.[114] In January 1882 Khayyāṭ's troupe dissolved, and Nadīm eventually turned into the "orator of the revolution."

The army then entered the public sphere. Nadīm started to print a satirical journal, *al-Tankīt wa-l-Tabkīt*, between July and October 1881; and now was editing *al-Ṭāʾif* (from November 1881 to the summer of 1882). In these journals he called ʿUrābī a "hero" (*fāris*) and ridiculed the efendis who imitated the European life-style. An explicitly pro-military journal was *al-Ḥijāz* (July-November 1881), edited by a certain Ibrāhīm Sīrāj al-Madanī, a Muslim scholar from Medina, who bought his press in Cairo on money from the officers of the 3rd Infantry in the Citadel.[115] It was known as "the journal of the colonels" and finally was suppressed by the government. *Al-Ḥijāz* praised the new laws after the army demonstration in September 1881 by employing Muslim symbols and figures of speech both in prose and in poetry. Al-Madanī advertised a favorable Muslim Arab image of the army: "our army places the claims of humanity and the state above personal interests," and even praised Tevfik's (in reality Riyaz's) economic measures. There were articles about Arab greatness in Andalusia, the past Arab empires, the British in India, and the contemporary French occupation of Tunis and Algeria. The editor also published the letter of the Azharite Sheikh Ḥasan al-ʿIdwī to the sultan which accompanied his book-gift to Istanbul in 1881. Al-Madanī connected Islam, moral and racial categories whose embodiment he found

112 Fligstein and MacAdam, "Toward a General Theory," 6.

113 Note dated 8 January 1882, Maḥfaẓa 1/2, Niẓārat al-Dākhiliyya, DWQ.

114 This paragraph draws on Sadgrove, *Egyptian Theatre*, 145–156.

115 Goldziher, "Muhammadan Public Opinion," 114, n. 39.

in the Egyptian army within the Ottoman frames.[116] This ideological description made the army the representative of patriotic defense, the ideal symbol of nation-ness constituted by Islam and empire.

The Arab Opera

The experience of patriotism occurred in the theater again. The general discontent and the army grievances prompted Tevfik to appoint a new government in February 1882 led by the poet and soldier Maḥmūd Sāmī al-Bārūdī, and in which Aḥmad ʿUrābī became minister of war (in reality he was the strong man in the government).[117] ʿAbd Allāh Fikrī became minister of education and his undersecretary was ʿAlī Fahmī. That spring saw increased struggle between the European controllers, ʿUrābists, the khedive, and constitutionalist *zevat* and *aʿyān*. Tevfik approved an Organic Law for the Assembly of Deputies in February 1882 which brought all legislation and contracts of Egypt to the power of the Assembly. While it has been regarded as a constitution, it does not regulate the status of the ruler, his dynasty, nor does it announce popular sovereignty, or deal with the status of Egypt as an Ottoman province.[118]

There was a conflict within the army between the "Turks" (or "Circassians") in leading positions and the "Egyptians." In this closing section, we continue following intellectuals and artists and their relation to power in an increasingly unstable atmosphere.

The Patriotic Munshid*: Salāma Ḥijāzī*

Revolutions are lucrative periods for the arts. The career of the most important singer-actor in fin-de-siècle Egypt starts during the spring of 1882. Unlike ʿAbduh al-Ḥamūlī, whom we met in chapter 2, Salāma Ḥijāzī lacked the khedivial touch; he is not known to have sung for the khedive, or to have been exposed to late Ottoman culture. In contrast to ʿAbduh al-Ḥamūlī, "the nightingale of weddings," Ḥijāzī was later often described as "the village headman" (*ʿumda*) of the Arabic theater. He was fully immersed in nonofficial Egyptian Muslim culture. He was a *munshid*, a half-religious half-entertaining singer from Alexandria. His career gives a model of patriotic entertainment through local Muslim traditions.

Ḥijāzī's father died early, and the child, raised by a barber, was supported by a leader of a Sufi order (the *Raʾsiyya*). He participated in Sufi

[116] Citations in Goldziher, "Muhammadan Public Opinion," 120–132.

[117] Fahmī (al-Muhandis), *al-Baḥr al-Zākhir*, 210.

[118] Blunt, *Secret History*, appendix III.

ceremonies and *festivals*, and also knew the Koran by heart at the age of eleven. He was taught by Aḥmad al-Yāsirjī, Khalīl Muḥarram (the leading singer in Cairo, ʿAbduh al-Ḥamūlī was once in his troupe), and Kāmil al-Ḥarīrī, all famous *munshidīn* of the time. He became the leader of the Raʾsiyya at a young age, and, although he was not trained, Ḥijāzī announced regularly the morning prayer in a neighborhood mosque in Alexandria. At the age of twenty-two he married a girl named ʿĀʾisha and soon Muḥammad their first child was born, who died early. Perhaps because of the need to finance his family he formed a *takht*, a group of musicians, with whom he performed in popular celebrations and marriages.

There is uncertainty, even by those biographers who knew him in person, how Ḥijāzī transitioned from a *munshid* in the 1870s into a theater star in the 1880s.[119] This uncertainty, I suggest, is deliberate. Oftentimes the narratives emphasize that Salāma Ḥijāzī stepped on stage after the ʿUrābī revolution (1882). He himself remembered once that he had made up his mind about musical theater only around 1884 and after a discussion with al-Ḥamūlī and his musicians in the presence of Khedive Tevfik.[120] This memory was an attempt to connect his rise to a politically loyal setting. Yet Ḥijāzī had already performed for Aḥmad ʿUrābī in Cairo during the spring of 1882.

Ḥijāzī must have been performing even earlier. It is said that, being in Alexandria, Ḥijāzī first thought that the modern theater was a condemnable innovation (*bidʿa*) and rejected the first enquiries from Naqqāsh or Khayyāṭ in the late 1870s.[121] In his earliest biography, his first role was Horace (Kūriyās) in Salīm Naqqāsh' *Mayy*, arranged by his "teacher" of acting, Sulaymān al-Ḥaddād, yet another Syrian intellectual.[122] There was one performance of *Mayy* by Sulaymān al-Ḥaddād on 4 June 1881 in Alexandria,[123] which may have been Ḥijāzī's first performance. He in fact remained attached to the Ḥaddād family through his life.[124] This attachment did not prevent Ḥijāzī from "forgetting" his performances in front of ʿUrābī, for which the explanation must be the fear of punishment after the failed revolution. We shall see in the next chapter that in the 1880s he actively participated in rebuilding an Arabic façade for Khedive Tevfik. His origins, education, and social setting contributed to his public patriotic image and leading role in the musical theater.

119 Sadgrove, *Egyptian Theatre*, 157, based on al-Ḥifnī; Fatḥ Allāh, *Salāma Ḥijāzī*, 24–25; Fāḍil, *Al-Shaykh Salāma Hijāzī*, 23–26.

120 Fāḍil, *Al-Shaykh Salāma Hijāzī*, 28.

121 Fāḍil, *Al-Shaykh Salāma Hijāzī*, 10–18; Fatḥ Allāh, *Salāma Ḥijāzī*, 21.

122 Al-Zayyāt and al-Kutubī, *Bulbul al-Suʿūd*, 2.

123 Sadgrove, *Egyptian Theatre*, 152.

124 When Amīn Ḥaddād, son of Sulaymān and a playwright, died in 1913, Salāma Ḥijāzī paid for the publication of his selected works. Al-Ḥaddād, *Muntakhabāt*, pages ṭāʾ, yā.

FIGURE 5.1. Sheikh Salāma Ḥijāzī, possibly in 1913
Source: al-Ḥaddād, *Muntakhabāt*, unnumbered [2].

Qardāḥī and the Establishment of the Arab Opera

Sulaymān Qardāḥī's life, by contrast, is an example of mobility in the eastern Mediterranean, or better to say, in the whole world, since he lived for a short time even in South America (see next chapter for his later years). Qardāḥī was born in Dayr al-Qamar in Mount Lebanon into a Christian Arab family.[125] He was already an orphan in 1860 at the

[125] His name is transliterated as "al-Qurdāḥī" in Mohamed Garfi, *Musique et spectacle*, 223, and also as "Kourdeghi Efendi," in Beckman, "Le théâtre arabe moderne." In Moosa, *The Origins*, 35 his name is transliterated as "al-Qirdahi," as in Fahmy, *Ordinary Egyptians*,

time of the bloody conflict in Mount Lebanon and Damascus. The young Sulaymān was then educated in France.[126] It is not known when he returned to Beirut or when he migrated to Egypt from there. He may have participated in Naqqāsh and Khayyāṭ's troupes and was possibly related to another actor, Sulaymān Ḥaddād, the first acting "teacher" of the singer Ḥijāzī.[127] Christine Qardāḥī, Sulaymān's wife, established a "Patriotic School for Girls" (*Madrasat al-Banāt al-Waṭaniyya*) in Alexandria in the late 1870s. Sulaymān Qardāḥī worked for the journal *al-Ahrām* in 1879.[128] He also put on plays in Arabic and French with the pupils (girls) at the end of the school-year celebrations in 1879 and 1880.[129] However, as opposed to Adīb, Naqqāsh or even Ḥijāzī, he had no creative talent: he was not a translator, playwright, or a singer. His talents seemingly were acting and, foremost, management.

Qardāḥī involved women in his theater troupe. In February 1882 he established a troupe in Alexandria with two women: his wife, Christine, and an actress or singer, called Ḥunayna who may also have been a relative.[130] He himself took to the stage, and Anṭūn Khayyāṭ, the brother of Yūsuf, may have also have been a member of the troupe.[131] His greatest addition was the singer Salāma Ḥijāzī, who in association with Qardāḥī would become a widely known artist. Other, presumably Egyptian, singers (Sheikh Maḥmūd and Sheikh ʿAlī) also performed with them. Music defined the new troupe: it became known as the Arab Opera *(al-Ūbira* [!] *al-ʿArabī)*.

The Arab Opera and Politics

The alliance of Syrian actors and Egyptian singers in the production of patriotic entertainment was an answer to the ʿUrābist atmosphere. During February and March 1882, under the Bārūdī-government, in Cairo and

---

126. However, based on a letter, dated 21 April 1887 in Maḥfaẓa 2/1, Niẓārat al-Ashghāl al-ʿUmūmiyya, CMW, DWQ, where his name is transliterated by the Egyptian Ministry of Public Works as "Cardahi," and another written by the Ministry to the Conseil des Ministres, dated 24 February 1887, Maḥfaẓa 2/1, Niẓārat al-Ashghāl al-ʿUmūmiyya, CMW, DWQ, it is sure that mostly his name was pronounced as Qardāḥī. His name is also transliterated as such ('al-Qardāḥī') in Sadgrove, *Egyptian Theatre*, 127; and in Halima, *Un demi-siècle*, 39. His family members use Cordahi in French today, AAC. Since he and the contemporary Arab press did not use his name with an article (al-), I write his name as Qardāḥī.

[126] Letters 2 and 5, AAC. In the Beiruti house of one Ḥabīb Qardāḥī, the performance of Ṭannūs al-Ḥurr's *al-Shābb al-Jāhil al-Sikkīr* took place in 1863. Najm, *Al-Masraḥiyya*, 57. Was Ḥabīb Qardāḥī related to Sulaymān?

[127] In this paragraph, information is summed up from letters 2 and 5, AAC.

[128] *Al-Ahrām*, 6 March 1879, 4.

[129] Sadgrove, *Egyptian Theatre*, 143. Ismāʿīl, *Taʾrīkh al-Masraḥ al-Miṣrī*, 140.

[130] *Al-Ahrām*, 15 April 1882, 2. Cf. also Najm, *al-Masraḥiyya*, 107.

[131] *Al-Jinān*, 1 May 1882, 264.

Alexandria societies and notables held gatherings and evenings, where the two central Muslim figures, ʿAbd Allāh Nadīm and Muḥammad ʿAbduh, gave patriotic speeches and demanded constitutional government (*al-ḥukm al-qānūnī*). In this tense political atmosphere, an advertisement appeared in the Arabic press in 28 March 1882, calling the patriotic notables of Cairo to the performances of the Arab Opera:

> An Arab Opera will be presented in the capital's Opera [House] in the middle of April [18]82, under the leadership of its director, Sulaymān Qardāḥī. [This troupe] consists of twenty-five individuals who are the most famous singers with pleasant voice and with perfect declamation and theatrical abilities. . . .
>
> I [Sulaymān Qardāḥī] proceeded with this theatrical art whose joyful excellence and educative (*adabiyya*) advantage is not hidden from you. Thus I have arranged an Arab troupe with a special consideration for the performing skills of the participants, their pleasant voice, and their perfect declamation. I have also chosen good and gentle plays for this art, sacrificing money, working day and night in order to perfect it.[132]

The Arab Opera's guest evenings in Cairo may have not been entirely Qardāḥī's idea. There must have been an informal connection between Qardāḥī and the military engineer Maḥmūd Fahmī, the minister of public works, who was legally responsible for the Opera House (see chapter 7). Qardāḥī's official request for the free use of the Opera House is dated 25 March 1882, yet the previous day *al-Ahrām* had already published the news that the troupe had received permission to use the Opera House *gratis*, from Maḥmūd Fahmī, who even promised to pay for the gas lighting.[133] Qardāḥī in his written request asked for eight evenings, the necessary equipment, and the gas.[134] The ministry granted the request, however, on condition that he "should conform to the current regulations."[135]

This was the first Arabic "season" in the Khedivial Opera House. Qardāḥī emphasized the political utility of theater. In his application, he argued that his troupe was a patriotic (*waṭanī*) enterprise. He wrote to the minister of public works that "I have started to teach some Arabic plays to an Egyptian troupe," although it may have contained more Syrians

[132] *Al-Ahrām*, 28 March 1882, 2–3.

[133] *Al-Ahrām*, 24 March 1882, 3. The journal expressed its gratitude to the Minister for letting the group use the Opera without payment and for paying for the lighting, 27 March 1882, 3.

[134] Arabic letter dated 25 March 1882, from Sulaymān Qardāḥī to MTP, 4003–037847, DWQ.

[135] Letter dated 30 March 1882, Guy Lussac (Comité des Théâtres) to MTP; 4003–037847, DWQ.

than Egyptians. The Arab Opera was considered in the Syrian-owned Arabic press as an expression of patriotism (*waṭaniyya*), mostly in the journals *al-Ahrām* and *al-Maḥrūsa*.[136] On the other hand, the Egyptian-owned periodicals in print during the spring 1882 (*al-Kawkab al-Miṣrī, al-Burhān, al-Ittiḥād al-Miṣrī, al-Mufīd, al-Muntakhab, al-Najāḥ*, Nadīm's *al-Ṭā'if, al-Zamān, al-Waṭan*) either do not mention Qardāḥī's troupe or are not available today. This silence remains curious. Was there a competition between Syrian and Egyptian intellectuals for representing patriotism?

ʿUrābī and ʿAntar

Since there was an irreconcilable political tension between the khedive, the foreign advisers, and the Egyptian army officers, *public* events carried extra weight during the spring of 1882. It seems that there were moments of temporary balance. The equilibrium was expressed in cultural terms through the public performances of Qardāḥī. This is the time when a new hero replaced Hārūn al-Rashīd. This is ʿAntar, an ancient pre-Islam warrior and poet, who would serve as a symbol for Aḥmad ʿUrābī. The warrior replaced the caliph as symbol of unity.

The Arab Opera performed in the Khedivial Opera House altogether on seven evenings and one public rehearsal (Qardāḥī advertised only six performances but gave one encore).[137] Their repertoire consisted of four plays: *Tilīmāk* (*Telemachus*), *Fursān al-ʿArab* (*The Arab heroes*), *Zifāf ʿAntar* (*The wedding of ʿAntar*), *al-Faraj Baʿd al-Ḍīq* (*The release from suffering*). Three of these plays feature a hero: Tilīmāk (Telemachus) and the legendary ʿAntar. ʿAntar (or ʿAntara) b. Shaddād was a pre-Islamic poet and warrior in Arabia whose life and battles (*Sīrat ʿAntar*) were enshrined in oral and written poetry. Arab coffeehouse culture had cherished storytellers who read aloud the manuscripts of "The Life of ʿAntar."[138]

The hero ʿAntar (on stage portrayed by Salāma Hijāzī) and Colonel ʿUrābī offered a potential symbolic pair. In my interpretation, both ʿAntar and ʿUrābī represented fighters who resisted oppression and injustice. It is worth remembering that Said Pasha also loved the story of ʿAntar,

136 *Al-Ahrām*, 15 April 1882, 2.

137 After rehearsals in Alexandria the Arab Opera travelled to Cairo in early March. Now Larose's troupe moved to Alexandria to perform in the Zizinia Theatre. *Al-Maḥrūsa*, 15, 18 and 24 April 1882, at all dates on page 2. *Al-Ahrām*, 24 March 1882, 3; 27 March 1882, 3; 28 March 1882, 2–3; 11 April 1882, 3; 15 April 1882, 3 and throughout April-May scattered news. *Al-Ahrām*, 2 May 1882, 2. Sadgrove provides a detailed description of the plays: Sadgrove, *Egyptian Theatre*, 156–159. See also Ismāʿīl, *Ta'rīkh al-Masraḥ al-Miṣrī*, 140, although he, for some reason, is not concerned with these performances in 1882 unlike Najm in his *Al-Masraḥiyya*, 107–108.

138 Kruk, "Sīrat ʿAntar ibn Shaddād."

and Said's time was a good period for the young ʿUrābī.[139] The portrayal of the martial virtues of an Arab warrior must have been well received among the army officers in the government.

The political context, however, alludes to a more complex understanding of the image of the hero. April 1882 started with a strike of coal heavers in Port Said, one of the first modern workers' strikes in Egypt.[140] Though possibly unconnected, the first performance of the Arab Opera was delayed for a week and coincided with yet another important event. This was the discovery of a presumed plot against ʿUrābī Pasha on 11 April 1882. Most of the men arrested were of Circassian or Turkish origin. Salīm Naqqāsh in his pro-dynastic chronicle, written just after the revolution, remarked that the people in Cairo were terrified when the news arrived.[141] A military committee investigated the issue, while, according to the memoirs of Maḥmūd Fahmī, the ʿUrābists tortured the accused officers in the prison of the Citadel.[142] Finally, forty-two officers were condemned to death. Khedive Tevfik, however, intervened and changed the sentence to exile to the Sudan.[143] While the performances of the Arab Opera were cheered in the Opera House during April, this trial was possibly the major talk of the town as we can see in table 5.1.

The performance of *Zifāf ʿAntar* on 23 April was especially successful: the audience was so enthusiastic that they demanded the repetition of the third act with Salāma Ḥijāzī. The journals highlighted the bravery of ʿAntar and the gentleness of the acting and voice of Sheikh Salāma. Other actors, especially Christine Qardāḥī, were also praised. *Al-Maḥrūsa*, Naqqāsh's journal, did not miss the opportunity to underline that this art was so far the privilege of Europeans and expressed hope for more government support for Arab acting. Meanwhile, the military investigation proceeded, and more suspects were arrested, now numbering to 48, but there were rumours that as many as 150 officers had been taken into custody.[144]

The bravery of ʿAntar, a black slave turned tribal hero, embodied by Ḥijāzī, had the potential of a powerful political allegory for the new leader. The last performance of the Arab Opera, *Fursān al-ʿArab* (The Arab heroes) took place on 30 April 1882. This was yet another play about ʿAntar, the hero. Since ʿUrābī Pasha was also called a hero (*fāris*) in the periodicals of ʿAbd Allāh Nadīm, this play can be seen as a subtle statement to support him. On this evening, the actors were cheered

[139] Fahmī, *Mudhakkirāt*, 85.
[140] Beinin and Lockman, *Workers on the Nile*, 29–30.
[141] Al-Naqqāsh, *Miṣr li-l-Miṣrīyyīn*, 4: 264.
[142] Fahmī, *al-Baḥr al-Zākhir*, 211.
[143] Reid, "The ʿUrabi revolution," 229.
[144] *Al-Ahrām*, 21 April, 1882, 2.

TABLE 5.1. Political Events and the Performances of the Arab Opera, April 1882

Performances of the Arab Opera, 1882	*Political Events in Cairo, 1882*
13 April—*Tilīmāk*	11 April—arrest of Circassian/Turkish soldiers
16 April—*al-Faraj baʿd al-Ḍīq*	
(19 April a private rehearsal)	around 20 April—trial
20 April—*Fursān al-ʿArab*	
23 April—*Zifāf ʿAntar*	around 22 April—sentence to death (khedive intervenes)
28 April—*Tilīmāk*	28 April—sentence to exile in the Sudan
30 April—*Fursān al-ʿArab*	30 April—public announcement of exile

and continuously asked for encores by a clapping audience. This was the day when news of the exile of the forty-eight army officers to the White Nile was released. After the performance, Qardāḥī, as the director of the group, stepped on stage and greeted ʿUrābī and thanked him for the support of the government. This was an important gesture, because so far the khedive had been thanked by impresarios (Sanua, Naqqāsh, Khayyāṭ), even if he had not done anything. And in fact, not ʿUrābī, but Maḥmūd Fahmī, minister of public works, had provided the support for the troupe. Furthermore, other statesmen in more elevated positions were present in the Opera, such as the president of the National Assembly (*Majlis al-Umma*), but they were not mentioned in Qardāḥī's speech, or, at least, not in the reports.[145]

THE *UMMA* AND THE *SHAʿB*: "A GARDEN WITH MELLOW FRUITS"?

Before concluding with the well-known story of the 1882 summer events, the revolution that led to the British occupation, it is worth highlighting a competition that discloses two ways of imagining an Egypt without a khedive. Two petitions for the concession of the Opera House and the

[145] *Al-Ahrām*, 2 May 1882, 2. For more details of this season see Sadgrove, *Egyptian Theatre*, 156–160.

Comédie contain these unique patriotic proposals. The petitions were prompted by the fact that the Bārūdī government had decided upon a 9,000 LE subsidy for the following theater season (1882–1883).[146] The petitions highlight a possible trajectory of the non-khedivial state culture in Egypt and a competition between Arab theater directors.

The first one arrived from Yūsuf Khayyāṭ and ʿAbd Allāh Nadīm from Alexandria. This unexpected couple submitted a request in April 1882 for the free use of the Comédie. They wanted to offer forty evenings during five months in the following theatrical year. The Syrian Christian impresario and the Egyptian Muslim intellectual requested the costumes, the building, and the right that during their concession no one else would stage theatricals in Cairo without their prior consent. This last element may well have been due to the competition between Arab troupes. The theater monopoly, requested by Khayyāṭ and Nadīm, entails a regulation of the market with help from the state.

In the Khayyāṭ-Nadīm short proposal, theater, "the art of representing historical events" (*fann tashkhīṣ al-waqāʾiʿ al-taʾrīkhiyya*), is "among the enlightened means [to produce] ever-circulating ideas." In their view, education in advanced states is conducted through scenes "about their own history, in the language of their people, including some events of the other nations;" so "as a result understanding [theater] is easy because their people already possess the capacity to grasp the essence of the play." In this conception, before using theater as an educational means, it has to match the people's language (no reference to which form of Arabic) and history. The keyword is *umma* or *umma miṣriyya* (translated here as "people"). Khayyāṭ and Nadīm add that until this moment "no Egyptian troupe was formed among the Egyptian people that would conform to their own language and their own manners." This later remark implies that these two intellectuals did not consider the troupes of Sanua, Naqqāsh, Khayyāṭ's own, and Qardāḥī's as Egyptian or conforming to Egyptian manners, or, at least, they wanted to convince the government of this.[147] It is remarkable that Khayyāṭ and Nadīm professionally highlighted the main components of patriotism: language and history.

Another request arrived from the victorious impresario Sulaymān Qardāḥī. With the encouragement of the minister Maḥmūd Fahmī, he proposed to perform fifteen different theatrical pieces in Arabic, with thirty actors and fifteen actresses in the Comédie in the next season.

[146] Later this subsidy was cancelled, leaving only the option of the free concession of the Opera House and the Comédie with its costumes and scenery. Letter dated 18 March 1882, From Présidence du Conseil des Ministres signed Mahmoud [Maḥmūd Sāmī] to Mahmoud Bey Fehmy MTP, 4003–037847, DWQ.

[147] Letter without date, (sealed as 10 April 1882, transferred to the Comité des Théâtres 13 April 1882), from ʿAbd Allāh Nadīm and Yūsuf Khayyāṭ to MTP, 4003–037847, DWQ.

Qardāḥī described his efforts and losses that he sacrificed to establish the "Patriotic Arab Troupe" (*al-Jawq al-ʿArabī al-Waṭanī*), another name for the Arab Opera. This remarkable letter is not simply another offer for the government to promote theater as a means of education but is also a personal expression of devotion to theater in Arabic:

> Indeed, a strong zeal for this fine art has taken me to try to use it in Arabic until we will be able to [perform plays] in our language perfectly and we won't need [theater] in foreign languages anymore. . . . I was sure that if I asked the Exalted Government it would give a helpful hand when I notify the leaders about my zeal in refined education (*adab*) and my passion for the renewal of this useful project.

In this letter Qardāḥī understood theater as a "garden with mellow fruits," providing knowledge to which *everyone* has access. He also requested money for the translation of "historical and scientific books." Coming from a school environment, based on the Beiruti tradition, similar to Khayyāṭ-Nadīm, to his thinking theater was an instrument of education. But in contrast to Khayyāṭ-Nadīm, Qardāḥī deployed other ideas to describe the people who are to be educated: they are not *umma*, but they are *shaʿb* (people) or *ahl al-bilād* (the locals) or *jumhūr* (the public). None of these words have religious connotations. Thus his theater would not only educate the people, but this education would also contain a sense of nonreligious equality. His main intention was to produce "well selected plays which suit the taste of the people and are useful for the public." In locating the taste(s) (*adhwāq*) of the Egyptians, Qardāḥī found music indispensable: he wanted to improve performances through the study of Arabic singing, and have more actors and actresses, with musicians. To boost the troupe, he requested financial support from the government, though he also expected the "wealthy" of the country to contribute. In his words, this was a musical enterprise that would result in "public benefit" (*fāyida* [*fāʾida*] *ʿumūmiyya*).[148]

The khedive is missing from the submissions of Khayyāṭ-Nadīm and Qardāḥī—this would have been unimaginable even a year earlier. There is no mention of dynastic support; they presented patriotic conceptions only to the government. Both petitions assume a concept of community, and both imagine this community to be taught by the government through the theater. The proposals themselves were already part of education, explaining the meaning of theater to Maḥmūd Fahmī, the minister, who was a military engineer. The use of *umma* and *shaʿb* distinctively

[148] Undated letter, (sealed as 3 May 1882, transferred to the Council of Ministers 7 May 1882), from Sulaymān Qardāḥī to MTP, 4003–037847, DWQ.

does not disclose major differences at this moment, though Qardāḥī's *shaʿb* has no religious connotations. While Khayyāṭ-Nadīm thought language and history to be the main features of patriotism, Qardāḥī emphasized the role of music to match "the taste" of the people. These Arabic submissions were never answered.

The Last Act

At about the time when Qardāḥī and Ḥijāzī left Cairo in May 1882, at a gathering of Egyptian notables (many of them from the Consultative Chamber), the army officers demanded to depose Tevfik and to ask for a new khedive from Sultan Abdülhamid II. The notables declined first, preferring a compromise.[149]

The political tension resulted in a riot in Alexandria. The events accelerated with foreign intervention invited by Tevfik. After the British bombardment of Alexandria on 11 July, the khedive, who had secretly urged the bombing,[150] declared ʿUrābī a rebel on 24 July.[151] A few days later, an assembly of notables and army leaders announced that Tevfik had "deviated from the rules of God's noble law and the sublime law [of the sultan]" (*kharaja min qawāʾid al-sharʿ al-sharīf wa-l-qānūn al-munīf*) and requested a new khedive from the sultan.[152] Within the army, the decision was explained that "the khedive had betrayed the nation" (*al-khidīwī fī khidāʿ al-umma*) and "he sided with the British instead of returning to our Exalted [Ottoman] State which entrusted him with this glorious emirate." The leaders asked that the decision be passed on to all soldiers and "every single member of the Egyptian nation (*umma*)."[153] Empire was an argument for Egyptian nation-ness at this moment.

The 24 July decision, signed by learned patriots such as ʿAbd Allāh Fikrī and ʿAlī Fahmī, indicates the complete breakdown of Tevfik's authority but not the breakdown of the Ottoman khedivate as an institution. On the contrary, the rebels claimed that they were supporting the Ottoman caliph. Abdülhamid II suspected, though, that ʿUrābī was paying only lip service to his authority (the sultan seems to have favored Abdülhalim as a new khedive at the time).[154] Finally, the sultan denounced

[149] Schölch, *Egypt for the Egyptians*, 241–242; Reid, "The ʿUrabi revolution," 231.

[150] Galbraith and Al-Sayyid-Marsot, "The British Occupation of Egypt."

[151] Broadly, *How We Defended*, 94.

[152] Proclamation dated 13 Ramaḍān 1299 (29 July 1882), attachment to letter dated ? Ramaḍān 1299 (July-August 1882), to the Mudīr of Danqala, 5016–000005, DWQ.

[153] Letter dated ? Ramaḍān 1299 (July-August 1882), to the Mudīr of Danqala, 5016–000005, DWQ.

[154] Schölch, *Egypt for the Egyptians*, 244, 246, 257.

the Egyptian general as a rebel.[155] Qardāḥī and his family rushed back to Beirut with other migrants, including Naqqāsh and Khayyāṭ. Hijāzī with his family hid in Rashīd (Rosetta) to become a muezzin in the Zaghlūl mosque.[156] The Arab Opera dissolved. The British army occupied the province of Egypt.

Conclusion: The Return of the Empire

There were competing visions of what the khedivate was. Local intellectuals nurtured various ideas, of which the defining one was that it was a polity whose official language is *fuṣḥā* Arabic and whose history is plural. The majority seems to have thought that it was a Muslim state with attachments to the Ottoman caliph. For Ismail himself, the khedivate was all of these but most importantly a security measure against pretenders. Critical thinking typically aimed at the improvement of the khedivial system, to achieve an "enlightened despotism" to use the words of Adīb and al-Afghānī. Politically, the main breaking point seems to have been the acceptance or rejection of British and French controllers vis-à-vis khedivial authority. The Ottoman Empire became important again for intellectuals in Egypt.

There are traces of a discursive competition for talking to the khedive in the name of the nation. Arabic-speaking nonlocal Ottomans and locals such as Nadīm used patriotism. A continuous communication in culture occurred through works addressed to the ruler. It is this effort that resurrected two powerful characters as symbols of justice and power: Hārūn al-Rashīd as an allegory of the khedive and ʿAntar as an allegory of ʿUrābī. Didactic works, such as Nadīm's *al-Waṭan*, targeted the ruler and called for solidarity. Through these efforts, the discursive Arabization of the khedive developed further. In sum, the various representations, staging, and performance of Arabness point at a moral quality offered also to the Ottoman elite to be included.

The Egyptian army's intervention into the affairs of governance made it possible to formulate national images in which the khedive no longer figured. In his place ʿUrābī appears as leader of the homeland. This change symbolizes a break in ideology, or, in the learned imagination about the army, since legally the khedive remained the leader of the army but his loss of control had already been expressed on the Arabic stage. This was an unprecedented development: a radical change in the realm of ideas before the actual revolt.

155 Deringil, "The Ottoman Response," 15; 17.
156 Fāḍil, *Al-Shaykh Salāma Ḥijāzī*, 16.

PART III

THE REINVENTION OF THE KHEDIVATE

> The Khedive's open encouragement of popular demonstrations in his favour by ostentatious attendance at prayers in the Mosque and performances in the Opera House has had the effect of greatly increasing the excitement among the natives. . . . The anti-English demonstration planned for the occasion of the Khedive's visit to the Opera House was frustrated only by the rigorous measures of the authorities and the strong police force present.[1]

Thus did the *New York Times* describe the popularity of the young khedive, Abbas Hilmi II (r. 1892–1914) in 1893. How could this Ottoman governor become so popular when a general revolt had occurred against Tevfik, his father, only eleven years before? And how could he use both the mosque and the opera for attracting attention?

The British intervention and the Ottoman declaration that the ʿUrābīsts were rebels against the caliph removed the immediate threat to the khedivial regime, yet re-establishing the authority of that regime was another matter. This required an elaborate politics of memory since the khedivate now hinged upon the interpretation of the revolution, Ottoman approval, and actual British support.

The final three chapters of this book explore how the culture of patriotism functioned to re-establish, in fact, reinvent the khedivial regime in the postrevolutionary period. I restrict the period of study to the 1880s and early 1890s, with occasional excursions to the 1900s. Abbas Hilmi II in 1893 was seen as the delegate of the province at the empire and *not* as a delegate of the empire to the province. How did this happen?

[1] *New York Times*, 23 January 1893, 5.

CHAPTER 6

Hārūn al-Rashīd under Occupation

In September 1898, a petition in Arabic arrived at the Egyptian Ministry of Public Works. It requested the privilege of performing in the Khedivial Opera House in front of the German Emperor who was expected to visit Cairo. The petitioner emphasized that the performance would be in Arabic, "the language of the nation." He reminded the minister that "your servant was the first one to take the initiative and the first to receive privileges for reviving the art of Arabic theater in the East in general and in this beloved homeland in particular. His Highness the Khedive was favorably disposed towards your humble servant and allowed him to perform in the Qubba Palace. . . . Furthermore, the Exalted Government has helped him for more than twenty years with resources and funds." The petition was signed by Sulaymān Qardāḥī.[1]

This chapter argues that post-1882 Arab patriotism served simultaneously to reconfigure and reinvent the khedivial regime. The impresario Qardāḥī, as we have seen in the previous chapter, featured Salāma Ḥijāzī in the role of ʿAntar as a metaphor for ʿUrābī in April-May 1882. His petition sixteen years later in 1898, written to Tevfik's son and successor, Abbas Hilmi II, reveals the same appeal to become an accepted provider of official culture. Only in this instance, Qardāḥī now seems to be on intimate terms with the ruler. Indeed, this Syrian Christian impresario, together with Ḥijāzī, helped to further the Arabization of the khedive on stage during the first decade of the British occupation. With the support of Tevfik, their "Arab Patriotic Troupe" had unprecedented success between 1886 and 1889 in the Khedivial Opera House. The second half of the 1880s is the period of an Arabic theatrical boom. By tracing the otherwise unknown story of Qardāḥī and Ḥijāzī in the late 1880s, we shall also follow the rivalry between Arab theater directors, the development of Arab stardom, and the way Arabic theater became a private enterprise in the late Ottoman Mediterranean. By examining these performances, we can chart the ways in which the patriotic imagination was

[1] Petition, undated, a note at the side: "Nessim, please, put this into English, 20 September 1898," 4003–037914, DWQ.

synchronized in Ottoman Arab cities by the 1900s. In this way, we explore a foundational aspect of the cultural network between Arab imagined communities.

In occupied Egypt, the defining feature of the late 1880s was the hope for British evacuation. An Ottoman High Commissioner, Ahmed Muhtar Pasha (1839–1919), arrived in Cairo in December 1885. However, the negotiations, later moved to Istanbul, failed in 1887. It is crucial to bear in mind the ongoing Ottoman-British negotiations in the 1880s while telling the story of khedivial restoration.

Retroactive Justice in Arabic

While there are eminent studies about the various aspects of the British occupation,[2] the postrevolutionary relationship of local elites to khedivial power has rarely been discussed.[3] The decade after 1882 remains a black hole in historical scholarship.[4] It was indeed an embarrassing period for all actors involved. In 1882, ʿUrābī and Tevfik accused each other of treason, some elite groups denounced the khedive, Syrian Christians fled Egypt, everybody betrayed the sultan-caliph, who, in turn, declared the Egyptian soldiers rebels, and finally many were killed and thirty thousand men were arrested—and still Egypt remained an Ottoman khedivate now under British rule. This was a paradox to be solved. Retroactive history, a form of memory politics, was the solution.[5]

The Logic of the Early Occupation

In the winter of 1882–1883, administrative chains of command, offices, and ministries—now with British advisers—were quickly re-established. Members of the prerevolution *zevat* elite (most of them Circassian), like Mustafa Riyaz, Mehmet Zeki, Ismail Ayyub, and ʿAlī Mubārak, represented continuity in government. The army was put under a British commander, and expenditure was strictly controlled. Notables were grouped in three consultative bodies (Legislative Council, General Assembly, provincial councils), based on the colonial model in British India. New courts were set up, in addition to the already complex legal system. The Arabic press continued to be dominated by Syrian Christian cultural entrepreneurs, but soon Egyptians also started enterprises in press capitalism.

[2] See cited works of Tignor, Al-Sayyid, Berque, and Barak.
[3] Butovsky, "Reform and Legitimacy," 108–109.
[4] With the exception of articles in Booth and Gorman, eds., *The Long 1890s in Egypt*.
[5] Rév, *Retroactive Justice*.

For the British, the logic of the early occupation was defined by the goal of evacuation until 1887. The occupiers saw stability and order as resting on the monarchical principle.[6] The colonial officials remembered the Indian revolt in 1857, and so Consul-General Evelyn Baring upheld the importance of "traditional" power in 1883; Lord Salisbury wanted evacuation in 1885.[7] Yet, by mid-1887, British-Ottoman negotiations had failed, due in part to Baring's opposition, the Mahdist revolt, and French-Russian interference.[8] From 1888 onward, the principles underlying the British occupation shifted towards a long-term colonial policy.

The Remaking of Tevfik

What role did Tevfik himself play in repairing his public image? The historiographical image of Tevfik is that of a puppet in the hands of British colonizers; the usual phrase is that "he reigned, not ruled." In the fall of 1882, he wanted ʿUrābī to be executed but had to concede to the British who opted to impose exile instead.[9] Tevfik would never allow ʿUrābī to return. He showed signs of extreme fear. He stopped his own nephew from becoming the secretary of his half-brother Hasan when Hasan was briefly appointed the governor of the Sudan in 1885. Tevfik feared that a new family faction was being built up against him.[10]

To be sure, the khedive had much to fear. In Istanbul, his great-uncle Abdülhalim continued scheming. Even his own father Ismail (also ending up in Istanbul) attempted return from time to time. Masonic lodges also remained active in Ottoman Egypt; in 1890 there were twelve, including *Kawkab al-Sharq*. Tevfik continued to struggle against Abdülhalim; it is worth noting that the official representatives of Abdülhalim's estates in Egypt in the 1880s were ex-students of al-Afghānī: Saʿd Zaghlūl and Ibrāhīm al-Laqānī.[11] Abdülhalim was considered several times by the British and the French as a potential ruler. The British found "Prince Halim" useful as a sort of stick with which Tevfik could be threatened.

Like his father, Tevfik and his men encouraged positive reports in the European press about his modernizing rule.[12] New patriotic rituals were invented (imitating the sultan) such as the celebration of the birthday of the khedive, and more formalized *ʿĪd al-Fiṭr* and *ʿĪd al-Aḍḥā* receptions. Sultan Abdülhamid II's accession to the Ottoman throne was also

[6] Tignor, *Modernization and British Colonial Rule*, 52.
[7] Ibid., 66–68; 82; 91.
[8] Al-Sayyid, *Egypt and Cromer*, 49.
[9] Tignor, *Modernization and British Colonial Rule*, 67–68.
[10] Al-Hilbāwī, *Mudhakkirāt*, 89–92.
[11] Al-Hilbāwī, *Mudhakkirāt*, 105.
[12] Cuno, *Modernizing Marriage*, 39–40.

celebrated, announcing that Egypt was an Ottoman province. "The Palace" appears now as political center, separate from the government. It advertised Tevfik's joint appearances together with his wife Amina—appearances that Kenneth Cuno argues publicly connected monogamy to national regeneration.[13] Amina was often mentioned by the title "Mother of Charitable Persons" (*Umm al-Muḥsinīn*) in the Arabic press since, like Hoşyar, she established religious endowments and donated money for the poor. Tevfik also engaged in the protection of Islamic monuments. This activity, it is suggested, may have aimed at differentiating Egypt from the Ottomans in architecture[14] but certainly helped to repair the khedive's pious image. Tevfik continued to tour the countryside each year, providing occasions for rural notables to affirm their loyalty. He pardoned imprisoned intellectuals involved in the ʿUrābī movement, such as ʿAbd Allāh Fikrī,[15] who wrote a long poem asking for his grace, and for the reinstallment of his pension.[16] Fikrī made the pilgrimage in 1884, perhaps as part of penitence, and published a patriotic moral manual in which, as Abū al-Suʿūd had done in his 1872 history book, he cleverly explained the meaning of "date" (*tārīkh*) by the example of the start of Tevfik's governorship.[17] Even Muḥammad ʿAbduh was pardoned in 1889.[18] But, of course, there was no pardon for ʿUrābī.

Who Is the Traitor?

The repair of khedivial authority was effected through the interpretation of the revolution as an illegitimate break in the divine order that had led to catastrophe. Tevfik's legitimacy hinged on the depiction of ʿUrābī and the ʿUrābists as having caused the British occupation which, in turn, was connected to Tevfik's own image as a brave leader in the face of chaos. Creating this image involved an elaborate restructuring of the immediate past.

There was an accusation that Tevfik had sought refuge on board a British ship during the bombardment of Alexandria on 11 July 1882; some historians have even taken this accusation as fact.[19] If true, it would mean

[13] Ibid., 41.

[14] Ormos, *Max Herz Pasha*, 1: 49–50; 54; 179.

[15] "Tarjamat al-Marḥūm al-Amīr ʿAbd Allāh Bāshā Fikrī," in Yūsuf, *Muntakhabāt al-Muʾayyad*, 1:491–495.

[16] Fikrī, ed., *Al-Āthār*, 22–24.

[17] Fikrī, *Kitāb al-Fawāʾid al-Fikriyya*.

[18] Ṣāliḥ, *Al-Shaykh ʿAlī Yūsuf*, 1:77.

[19] Berque, *L'Égypte*, 108, states that the khedive's being on the shore was a fabricated tale implying that he was on a British ship. Tevfik's flight to a British warship is explicitly stated in Galbraith and al-Sayyid-Marsot, "The British Occupation of Egypt," 486; repeated in Al-Sayyid-Marsot, *A History of Egypt*, 88; but it is curiously missing from the earliest work of Al-Sayyid, *Egypt and Cromer*, 25–26.

that the ruler left his army and his people; he would be a traitor. However, all available sources suggest that Tevfik was in Ramleh Palace on both the 11th and 12th of July.[20] He did, however, collude with the British in other ways. Most pro-khedivial texts emphatically deny Tevfik's flight, but the fact that they felt the need to do so indicates the extent to which such a rumor must have been circulating in the late 1880s. This rumor, extracted by "reading against the grain," was the ultimate argument for deposing the khedive, and only an equally strong argument could fight against it. This counterargument was that, on the contrary, Aḥmad ʿUrābī had caused a disruption in Muslim unity by betraying his ruler. This argument reached back to the role of the khedive as representative of the caliph and mobilized Islamic principles. Ironically, it was usually Syrian Christians and Ottomans who fabricated this argument.

The narrative of ʿUrābī's immorality began to be produced through the Arabic press. As early as mid-August 1882, *al-Ahrām* called the activity of the ʿUrābists "oppression" (*ṭughyān*) and published the congratulatory poem of Muḥammad Munīb (a captain in the cavalry) to the khedive on the Festival of Breaking the Ramadan Fast.[21] Journalists quickly produced prodynastic histories that portrayed ʿUrābī as a traitor and Tevfik as a brave ruler. Salīm Naqqāsh himself compiled the first officially endorsed history of the revolution with the title *Egypt for the Egyptians* (*Miṣr li-l-Miṣriyyīn*) in 1884. Its publication was allowed by the Ministry of Interior.[22] Naqqāsh described ʿUrābī as a rebel, and his followers as *ahl al-fitna* (revolting people). He quoted an observer who stated that the khedive left Rāʾs al-Tīn only on the morning of 12th July.[23] According to Naqqāsh, ʿUrābī gave fifty thousand franks to the soldiers to kill everyone in Ramleh Palace after the bombardment of Alexandria, but Tevfik bravely negotiated with these soldiers.[24] Finally, Naqqāsh quoted prokhedivial articles arguing that ʿUrābī "clearly left the necessary obedience to the Exalted Khedive therefore he also clearly left the obedience owed to the Commander of the Faithful [the Ottoman caliph]."[25]

20 *British and Foreign State Papers*, 74: 515.ʿUrābī himself states also this in his first memorandum: Ahmed Arabi the Egyptian, "Instructions to my Counsel," The Nineteenth Century (July-December 1882), 969–996, at 983; fully published as [ʿUrābī], *The Defense Statement*, 35. See also Chaillé-Long, *The Three Prophets*, 146. Shafīq, *Mudhakkirātī*, 1: 163–165; al-Rāfiʿī, *Al-Thawra al-ʿUrābiyya*, 324–325; and Schölch, *Egypt for the Egyptians*, 259.

21 *Al-Ahrām*, 18 August 1882, 1.

22 Internal correspondence dated 11 May 1884, Maḥfaẓa 1/1, Dīwān al-Dākhiliyya, DWQ. The first three parts were not published, if ever written (in these Naqqāsh would have told the modern history of Egypt from Mehmed Ali to 1879).

23 Naqqāsh, *Miṣr li-l-Miṣriyyīn*, 5:59.

24 Ibid., 5: 72–76.

25 Ibid., 5: 189.

The young journalist, and later famous writer, Jurjī Zaydān (1861–1914), who migrated to Egypt in 1883, announced in his history textbook in 1889: "it seems that the insistence of ʿUrābī was the cause of the final decision because the English government had no intention to occupy this country."[26] Another journalist (and lawyer), Yūsuf Āṣāf, in 1889 described the crucial moment before the bombardment of Alexandria: "[the envoy of the British admiral] officially announced the decision of the admiral to the Exalted Honorable Ruler to bombard the fortresses of Alexandria on the morning of Tuesday, 11 of the month [July], and urged him to leave Raʾs al-Tīn and seek shelter in the Palace of Raml and he did so fortunately."[27] In 1890, Āṣāf described Tevfik's first three years of reign as a just and free period that was interrupted and brought to catastrophe by ʿUrābī and his followers,[28] and the crucial day of 11 July 1882 with the same words as in the publication a year before.[29] In a widely-circulating obituary collection after the death of Tevfik in 1892, ʿAzīz Zand emphasized that the khedive "did not go to the British ships of war."[30]

Such coverage can be explained by the fact that the interior ministry was still controlled by the khedivial regime until 1890, and so Arab journalists could be rewarded for their cooperation with the "Palace." Indeed, the Syrian press owners demanded financial compensation for their journals that had been suspended or for contracts not paid during the revolution or afterward. In 1883, Salīm Taqlā, the owner of *al-Ahrām*, received compensation of 2,292 francs.[31] For a brief suspension in 1884 Taqlā was again able to request compensation in 1886.[32] In April 1883, Salīm Naqqāsh also requested compensation for his journals *al-Maḥrūsa* and *al-ʿAṣr al-Jadīd*, which were suspended in 1882.[33] The Egyptian government continued to pay a stipend to Aḥmad Fāris al-Shidyāq, the editor of *al-Jawāʾib* in Istanbul, and also to the (Coptic) editors of *al-Waṭan* in Egypt, in addition to the yearly subscriptions. In 1883, the government paid *al-Jawāʾib* for 328 subscriptions while it subscribed to *al-Ahrām* for only 200 copies; the government subscribed altogether to twenty-two

[26] Zaydān, *Kitāb Tārīkh Miṣr*, 307.

[27] Āṣāf and Naṣr, *Dalīl Miṣr li-ʿĀmmay 1889–1890*, 108.

[28] Āṣāf, *Dalīl Miṣr, 1890–1891*, 177–186.

[29] Āṣāf, *Dalīl Miṣr*, 1890–1891, 185.

[30] Zand, *Al-Qawl al-Ḥaqīq*, 198. Berque, *L'Égypte*, 108, quotes Zand in something of a free translation.

[31] Letter dated 23 December 1883, from Direction Generale de la Comptabilité de l'État to the Président de Conseil, Maḥfaẓa 1/3/m; Dīwān al-Dākhiliyya, DWQ.

[32] Letter dated 19 August 1884, attached to ? 1886, from Taqlā to Minister of Interior, Maḥfaẓa 1/3/m, Dīwān al-Dākhiliyya, DWQ.

[33] Letter dated 24 April 1883, from Salīm Naqqāsh to Minister of Interior, Maḥfaẓa 1/2, Dīwān al-Dākhiliyya, DWQ.

journals.[34] Only in 1887 did the government decide to reduce the number of subscriptions and grants.[35]

Next to journalists, poets also worked to restage the legitimacy of the khedive. This meant that not only the events of the revolution but the whole nineteenth-century reign of the Mehmed Ali family was retold. As early as 1882, the Armenian Syrian Iskandar Abkāriyūs published the now familiar poetic history of Ibrahim, Tevfik's grandfather, and his conquest of Ottoman Syria. He collected poems by Syrians written to Ibrahim (see chapter 1). The images of Ibrahim as a "just" ruler and his supposed goal of uniting the Arabs during the 1830s created a sense of legitimacy and aimed at the restoration of the postrevolutionary regime. This work was reprinted several times until the interwar period.

Elite poetry also commented on the immediate past. In 1883, Abkāriyūs published another poetry book,[36] this time featuring a congratulatory poem to Tevfik upon his re-entering Cairo "after breaking the thorn of the rebels' stick."[37] The book is a poetic affirmation of the dynasty. After the praise for Tevfik came praise for his grandmother Hoşyar, brothers Hasan and Hüseyin, then Ismail, other family members, leading *zevat*, and well-known personalities.[38] Others wrote poems about the fate of Alexandria and the war. The last line of the Ottoman Mustafa Subhi's long poem about the ʿUrābīsts' treason against Tevfik is a chronogram: "everyone follows [the example of] Mehmed Tevfik" makes the *hijrī* year of 1300 (1882/1883). Adīb Isḥāq's emotional (and censored) eulogy was perhaps a last cry; the Ottoman Kudri Bey's two poems commemorated Alexandria; and an unknown poet's short work was a sign of a nostalgia for the "old" Alexandria and its wealth.[39]

It is unclear whether or to what extent these works, mostly by Syrian Christians, were consciously planned; whether the authors simply conformed to the supposed expectations of the regime; or whether they actually believed that ʿUrābī had caused the occupation and that Tevfik had not colluded with the British.

In contrast, while many Egyptians, like Ibrāhīm al-Hilbāwī (who was imprisoned by the ʿUrābists),[40] may have agreed with the interpretation

[34] Undated (1883) table, Maḥfaẓa 1/2, Dīwān al-Dākhiliyya, DWQ.

[35] Letter dated 4 December 1887, from the President of the Council to Mohamed Zeki Pasha, Ministre des Finances, Maḥfaẓa 1/2, Dīwān al-Dākhiliyya, DWQ.

[36] Abkāriyūs, *Dīwān Nuzhat al-Nufūs*.

[37] Ibid., 7.

[38] Both books of Abkāriyūs were supported financially by Muḥammad Mikāwī, the ex-director of the estates of the murdered Ismāʿīl Ṣiddīq Pasha.

[39] Al-Naqqāsh, *Miṣr li-l-Miṣriyyīn*, 5:237–247. In 1898, Shārūbīm in volume four of his *al-Kāfī* republished these and other poems.

[40] Al-Hilbāwī, *Mudhakkirāt*, 81–82.

of ʿUrābī's excess as the cause of the occupation, they also condemned Tevfik. But the Palace erased such views that threatened to complicate the khedivial narrative. The special notes that al-Hilbāwī wrote soon after the revolution were requested by Ahmed Khayri in the khedivial entourage and were never returned to the author.[41] ʿUrābī's self-defense appeared in Cairo soon after 1882, but his accusations regarding the khedive's treason were omitted.[42] Maḥmūd Fahmī, the minister of public works in the Bārūdī government, called his former colleague ʿUrābī a "traitor" (*khāʾin*) in his world history written during their years of exile.[43]

As we shall see, the rewriting of history and memory was also enacted in the theater of the 1890s. It became the monarchical narrative, taught in schools. As late as the interwar period, the official school textbook emphasized that the main mistake of ʿUrābī was his rise against the legitimate ruler.[44]

The Return of Mehmed Ali Pasha

The historical "euphemism," to use Berque's word,[45] was not a solution chosen by the old and new local patriots. In their subsequent works, the ʿUrābī revolution was typically simply omitted. Instead, writing histories about Mehmed Ali as "the father of modern Egypt," I argue, became the main Egyptian intellectual strategy to avoid dealing with the recent past and to prove, in the face of the British occupiers, the "sovereign" past of late Ottoman Egypt.

My explanation differs from scholars who have understood this image as an invention around 1901–1905, when the centenary of Mehmed Ali's reign was celebrated.[46] Yoav Di-Capua names the image as "the founder paradigm" and understands its formation as a general attempt to introduce "the rise" of Egypt as an independent nation-state as hinged on "the decline" of the Ottomans in the 1890s.[47] I go further and argue that the image of this pasha as "founder of modern Egypt" in Arabic essentially emerged as a second compromise—a compromise between a ruler with broken authority and Egyptian intellectuals under occupation in the 1880s.

Before we proceed to histories written by male writers, it is worth noting the poetry by a *zevat* lady and her subsequent novel about just Islamic governance. Ayşe Ismet, the daughter of Ismail Pasha Teymur (1840–1902)—better known as ʿĀʾisha Taymūriyya in Arabist

41 Ibid., 77.
42 "Introduction," in [ʿUrābī], *The Defense Statement*, 2.
43 Mayer, *The Changing Past*, 7.
44 Ibid., 13–17.
45 Berque, *L'Égypte*, 107–108.
46 Cuno, "Muhammad Ali."
47 Di Capua, *Gatekeepers*, 61.

scholarship—wrote poems in Turkish, Persian, and Arabic. In her first book of poetry (1886), containing only Arabic poems,[48] panegyrics were written to Ismail, Tevfik, and other children of Ismail, also celebrating the birth of Tevfik's son, Abbas.[49] For our purposes here, the most remarkable is a poem written for the return of Tevfik after the revolution. In this poem Teymur writes that Tevfik's (*ʿazīzunā*) return is the return of order and security in Egypt; she both describes the whole population as celebrating and uses couplets to call for celebration.[50] While the poems in Arabic might be understood as a literary device of a *zevat* lady to include herself within the imagined nation, the publication also strengthened the image of Tevfik as the legitimate ruler. Next, she published a didactic novel (1888) again in Arabic, which told a symbolic story of the education of an Abbasid prince. According to Mervat Hatem, the book deals with the principles of just Islamic governance and, at the end, shows the prince's return as sanctified by the *ʿulamāʾ*, the army, and the general population. In Hatem's words, Ismet suggested that "Islamic dynastic government was the only legitimate type of government."[51]

Muḥammad Durrī (al-Ḥakīm) attempted to popularize the dynasty's reign and modernity. His 1889 book was intended to be an expression of gratitude for "the deliverance from the darkness of vileness and ignorance to the lights of knowledge and refinement." The author—a doctor educated in one of the student missions—believed that the one who renewed Egypt was Mehmed Ali in the "path of civilization" (*sabīl al-ʿumrān*), and therefore it was a "duty" and "service to the Egyptian public" to praise the ruling dynasty. Durrī illustrated the book with portraits of the rulers (he received "real images" of the dynasty and sent them to Paris to be drawn for the book) for youth who had never known the past rulers in person; in fact, he named this supply of imagery as his main goal.[52] Durrī omitted the British occupation from his biography of Tevfik;[53] only briefly mentioning that Tevfik pardoned ʿUrābī and his associates. The latter were described as those who "hated Egypt and wanted to have a free hand," but after a "civil war" (*fitna*) and "revolution" (*thawra*), the khedive generously pardoned everyone.[54] Durrī's omissions annoyed one reader so much that in one of the copies I have read there is a short addition in Arabic handwriting at the end: "During his reign occurred the unfortunate (*mashʾūma*) ʿUrābī revolution which resulted in the British

[48] Hatem, *Literature, Gender, and Nation-building*, concerning politics: 171–180.
[49] Taymūriyya, *Al-Dīwān al-Muḥyī*.
[50] Taymūriyya, *Al-Dīwān al-Muḥyī*, 21–23.
[51] Hatem, *Literature, Gender, and Nation-Building*, 85–87.
[52] Durrī, *Kitāb al-Nukhba*, 2–5, 49.
[53] Ibid., 38–45.
[54] Ibid., 43.

bombarding Alexandria in 11 July 1882 and their soldiers entered Egypt and occupied her."[55]

The greatest work sanctifying Tevfik's public image was entitled *The New Tevfikian Survey* (*al-Khiṭaṭ al-Tawfīqiyya al-Jadīda*, printed 1888–1889). The "author" was aging ʿ Alī Mubārak who represented continuity as the minister of public works until 10 January 1884, and again from June 1888 as minister of education in the government of Mustafa Riyaz. His monumental work is renowned by scholars for its wealth of information on Egyptian urbanism, history, popular practices, and so on.[56] It also depicted Ottoman rule as a dark age and that of Mehmed Ali as an enlightened one.[57] Mubārak had started this enterprise in the 1870s, with a team of scribes and researchers, in the spirit of the gentle revolution. Khedivial revivalism—the idea that the princely world of medieval Arabic textual production was to be revived under Ismail—was also a motivating factor behind this work. Mubārak's model here was al-Maqrīzī's (d. 779/1378) *Khiṭaṭ* ("Survey"), and this is why, when Mubārak's book was finally published in 1888, it was entitled *The New Tevfikian Survey*. The corrector, or rather censor, of the book of the Būlāq press, Muḥammad al-Ḥusaynī (he appears in several prodynastic publications in 1880s, including Durrī's[58]) provided an introduction, in which he described Tevfik as a just and pious ruler who led a revival of ethics, and praised his support of arts and Islamic monuments.[59] Tevfik's rule was connected to the renewal of Alexandria—arguably even in contradistinction to Ismail's urbanism in Cairo—but most significantly, the British bombardment in 1882 was not even mentioned.[60] In Mubārak's autobiography, the revolution is mentioned as a *fitna* and strongly condemned.[61]

Printed history in Arabic, in short, became a strategy to repair the khedivate. The young lawyer (later nationalist leader) Muḥammad Farīd (1868–1919) published a history of Mehmed Ali (1890) that framed him as "the civilizer of Egypt"; the narrative was, yet again, accompanied by poetry and praise by Muḥammad al-Ḥusaynī.[62] Even in a history of the Egyptian postal service, printed in the same year, Mehmed Ali was mentioned as the one who re-established order in the country, making possible, in turn, the development of the modern postal service. The author, Nuʿmān Anṭūn, praised Mehmed Ali for attaching Egypt to the imperial

[55] Ibid., 45. This copy was from Princeton Library 2269.2994.368.

[56] Until today, the best discussion in English of the Khiṭaṭ is Dysktra's dissertation, "A Biographical Study," 418–439.

[57] Reimer, "Egyptian Views of Ottoman Rule."

[58] Durrī, *Kitāb al-Nukhba*, 50–52.

[59] Mubārak, *al-Khiṭaṭ al-Tawfīqiyya*, 1: 1–4 (separate folio).

[60] Mubārak, *al-Khiṭaṭ al-Tawfīqiyya*, 10: 82–84.

[61] Dykstra, "A Biographical Study," 1: 314–316.

[62] Farīd, *Kitāb al-Bahja al-Tawfīqiya*.

Ottoman post.[63] It is no surprise that the book on the post ended with the poet Asʿad Ṭrād's four-page praise of Tevfik, written at the request of Nuʿmān Efendi.[64] In early October 1894, Zayn Zayn, a teacher of Arabic in a Jesuit school, wrote the first play about Mehmed Ali Pasha, which he offered in a beautiful manuscript to the young Abbas Hilmi II.[65]

Despite these efforts, old men like the railroad-employee Iskandar Fahmī remembered Mehmed Ali only as the "founder of the Egyptian government" (*muʾassis al-ḥukūma al-miṣriyya*).[66]

Pro-Khedivial Press

Finally, one should note the role of the press. The administration controlled agitation: for instance, the journal *al-Qāhira* (*al-Ḥurra*) was closed down in 1886. Next to the regular dailies, there were specialized journals in prokhedivial propaganda. In 1882 September, immediately after the occupation the journal *Al-Zamān* started to be printed, with praise of Tawfīq, on its full title page.[67] Such was also the mission of the magazine-journal *al-Nūr al-Tawfīqī* ("The Tevfikian Light," edited by Dīmitrī Maskūnās) which in 1888 brought together Arabic poetry, the portraits of the Mehmed Ali dynasty, and historical anecdotes in its pages.

One can place in this category the periodical *al-Muʾayyad* ("The Supported," or, "The Confirmed [Truth]"). *Al-Muʾayyad*, as its title shows, associated Egyptian sovereignty with Islam and, ultimately, with the khedive and the sultan. Its editor, Sheikh ʿAlī Yūsuf (1863–1913), a poor Muslim boy from Upper Egypt, studied for some time at al-Azhar, and in the mid-1880s wrote poetry, served as the editor of various journals, such as *al-Qāhira*, and ran his own literary journal *al-Ādāb*. In 1889, supported by the capital (100 LE) of a certain Sheikh Aḥmad Māḍī, he established *al-Muʾayyad*, very possibly as a countermeasure to the pro-British periodical *al-Muqaṭṭam*. There are a number of individuals who are said to have encouraged the sheikh to start the periodical: Mustafa Riyaz, Latif Salim, Saʿd Zaghlūl, Ibrāhīm al-Hilbāwī, Muḥammad Farīd, and others who may have formed a secret elite anti-British society.[68] Informal connections certainly existed between most of these individuals: al-Hilbāwī asked Latif Salim's wife to be his matchmaker,[69] and he worked with Saʿd Zaghlūl (they knew each other already from

[63] Anṭūn, *Kitāb al-Ṭāʾir al-Gharīd*, 170.
[64] Anṭūn, *Kitāb al-Ṭāʾir al-Gharīd*, 210–216.
[65] *Al-Ahrām*, 5 October 1894, 3.
[66] [Fahmī, Iskandar], *Mudhakkirāt*, 44.
[67] *Al-Zamān*, 25 September 1882, 1.
[68] EI2, "ʿAlī Yūsuf" (Peri Bearman); for the various legends about the establishment Ṣāliḥ, *Al-Shaykh ʿAlī Yūsuf*, 1:69–71.
[69] Al-Hilbāwī, *Mudhakkirāt*, 102.

al-Azhar and al-Afghānī's circle), while Riyaz, the minister of interior, knew everyone.[70]

In the 1890s *al-Muʾayyad* shored up support behind the young khedive Abbas Hilmi II as a Muslim prince against the British occupiers. The first issue announced that it was a political and patriotic daily newspaper (*jarīda waṭaniyya*) for "the service of homeland's sons"; the editors asked for the help of God and announced that "people are two kinds: ruler and ruled."[71] In 1890 the journal sold 800 copies daily, the following year this went up to 1200, and by the end of the 1890s was around 12,000,[72] which made it one of the most popular papers of the time.

Through these texts, reform was discursively reattached to the dynasty. The European idea that the dynasty was not the generator but the obstacle of reform did not gain currency in the public sphere in the late 1880s.[73] The memory of Khedive Ismail, as the young Muḥammad Farīd notes in 1891, was cursed because of his disastrous finances,[74] but the khedivial system itself became a symbol of anti-British sovereignty.

The Arab Patriotic Troupe

The connection between the reinvention of the khedivate and patriotism can be seen clearly through the unprecedented success of Sulaymān Qardāḥī and Salāma Ḥijāzī in the second half of the 1880s. Their performances in Alexandria, Cairo, and the countryside helped the spread of patriotic ideas and through these communal experiences to synchronize intellectual products with popular emotions.

Theater-going became a popular urban pastime in the late 1880s. The European community took the reopening of the Opera House in December 1882 as a sign of pacification.[75] By 1885 there were three main Arabic theater troupes in Egypt. Next to them there were dozens of small amateur theater groups performing in Arabic in Alexandria and Cairo in the late 1880s and 1890s. Below I shall focus on the performances by Qardāḥī and Ḥijāzī because they exemplify both the political use of theater in projecting a secular image of Muslim power on stage, as fitting nation-ness, and the making of an entertainment market.

[70] While Farīd as a young man may have supported *al-Muʾayyad*, he was too young at this moment (1889) to participate in any organized action.

[71] "Fātiḥa," in Yūsuf, *Muntakhabāt al-Muʾayyad*, 1: 1–5.

[72] Ṣāliḥ, *Al-Shaykh ʿAlī Yūsuf*, 1: 115.

[73] Butovsky, "Reform and Legitimacy."

[74] Farīd, *Mudhakkirāt*, 55.

[75] *Egyptian Gazette*, 30 November 1882, 2.

Al-Ḥamūlī's Restart

In addition to texts, sound helped the khedivial restoration by the public appearance of the singer ʿAbduh al-Ḥamūlī, whom we left in chapter 2 singing for Khedive Ismail. Arabic theater, after a shocked pause of two years,[76] restarted in 1884, and now al-Ḥamūlī magnetized masses in Alexandria and Cairo.

Al-Ḥamūlī was employed by the first postoccupation Arab theater director, who was new to Egypt. The Damascene impresario Abū Khalīl al-Qabbānī (183?—1902) arrived in Alexandria in the summer of 1884. Unlike previous Arab impresarios, he was Muslim and supposedly did not know French or Italian. Neither was al-Qabbānī particularly well versed in history. Instead, the man was a musician, a pure entertainer. He began to stage musical plays in Damascus but was chased away. Upon his arrival in Egypt, he immediately hired al-Ḥamūlī, with whom he may have become acquainted when the latter visited Ottoman Syria. Al-Ḥamūlī sang between the breaks of al-Qabbānī's performances in Alexandria in the summer of 1884.[77] Such cooperation helped the actors since the ex-khedivial singer was already a celebrity. It seems that ʿAbduh never stepped on stage as an actor. He only sang between the acts or after the play. Like Naqqāsh in 1876, al-Qabbānī used Egyptian music to popularize his Syrian troupe in 1884. As for al-Ḥamūlī, his career runs parallel to Arabic theater in the 1880s–1890s since he too used theater stages for musical performances as we shall see.

The Return of Qardāḥī: The Arabic Entertainment Market

Soon other impresarios returned, who saw Egypt as a market worthy of competition. Yūsuf Khayyāṭ reorganized his troupe in late 1884 with Salāma Ḥijāzī as the main star. Sulaymān Qardāḥī appeared in Egypt in the early months of 1885 and applied for the concession of the Khedivial Opera House for the spring season of 1886,[78] but his request was rejected.[79] At the time, Italian impresarios (Santi Boni and Soschino) received the concession of the Opera House; an Ottoman (Armenian) operetta troupe from Istanbul achieved unusual success performing in Turkish in Alexandria and in al-Azbakiyya theater; and to top this, the Ottoman Armenian impresario, the first director of the Comédie, Seraphin Manasse (who was

[76] School plays might have been performed in Arabic. *Al-Ahrām*, 1 February 1884, 3.

[77] Karachouli, "Abu Halil al-Qabbani," 88.

[78] He requested four months first, then only two months. Letters dated 7 April 1885, and 7 May 1885, Soliman Cardahi to Rouchdy, both in 4003–037911, DWQ.

[79] Draft dated 21 May 1885, to Manasse (representative: Mougel Bey), Khayat (Alexandrie), Kardahi (Alexandrie), from Ministry, informing them of the refusal. 4003–037911, DWQ.

supposed to be banished from Egypt) arrived to negotiate a contract for his French operetta troupe.

Qardāḥī cooperated with the singer Mūrād Romano (*Rūmānū*) in 1885, and they were usually mentioned in the press as the "group of Qardāḥī Efendi and Rūmānū Efendi,"[80] thus highlighting the equal leadership between the actor-impresario and the singer. This troupe has been also called the Qardāḥī-Ḥaddād troupe[81] (it is possible that Sulaymān Ḥaddād, the "teacher" of Salāma Ḥijāzī, was also a member), but it became known "The Arab Troupe" (*al-Jawq al-ʿArabi*).

A French theater expert visiting Egypt at this time mentioned the *spéculateur habile*, Qardāḥī ("Kourdeghi Efendi") who established a patriotic [!] troupe against the Syrian "occupation" of the Egyptian scene.[82] Seemingly, he did not know that Qardāḥī was an Ottoman Syrian. Soon, Qardāḥī's troupe in Cairo was challenged by the arrival of al-Qabbānī's troupe,[83] and they returned to Alexandria.[84] In this season, Qardāḥī's repertoire consisted of the 1882 plays (*Tilīmāk*, *ʿAntar* plays, *al-Faraj baʿd al-Ḍīq*) and some new ones (*Zanūbiyā*, etc.). Their greatest success was an ʿAntar play (*ʿAntara al-ʿAbsī*), featuring this now familiar Arab hero who rose against oppressors, that they performed only in Alexandria.

They changed the name of the troupe to "The Arab Patriotic Troupe" (*al-Jawq al-ʿArabī al-Waṭanī*),[85] which was a name that Qardāḥī had already used for the Arab Opera, too, in 1882. This old-new name had more than stylistic significance. *Waṭanī* emphasized that the troupe was patriotic, that is, political (possibly vis-à-vis al-Qabbānī and Khayyāṭ) and invites the audience for "patriotic" experience. It also meant a change in the composition of the troupe: Mūrād Romano left,[86] and, to complete the *waṭanī* image, the singer Salāma Ḥijāzī rejoined Qardāḥī's troupe in early 1886. The patriotic ideology of theater troupes also served as a potential commercial tool for attracting larger audiences and to request khedivial patronage.

The Khedive and the Arab Patriotic Troupe, 1886

In this section, I unearth the forgotten story of the Arab Patriotic Troupe, starring Ḥijāzī and run by Qardāḥī, which was central in repairing the

[80] For instance, *al-Ahrām*, 27 October 1885, 3 or 15 January 1886, 2. Ismāʿīl, *Taʾrīkh al-Masraḥ al-Miṣrī*, 141.

[81] Fāḍil, *Al-Shaykh Salāma Hijāzī*, 30–32.

[82] Beckman, "Le Théâtre arabe moderne," 87. Beckman obviously did not know that Qardāḥī was Ottoman Syrian.

[83] *Al-Ahrām*, 13 November 1885, 2–3; 16 November 1885, 3.

[84] *Al-Maḥrūsa*, 9 November 1885, 2; *al-Ahrām*, 4 December 1885, 3), by January they had became popular. *Al-Ahrām*, 2 January 1886, 2; 4 January, 3; 15 January, 2; 18 January, 3; 22 January, 3; 25 January, 3.

[85] *Al-Ahrām*, 17 March 1886, 2.

[86] *Al-Ahrām*, 25 January 1886, 3.

khedivial image and staging sovereignty for elite audiences in Arabic in the late 1880s. It seems that the performances for ʿUrābī in 1882 were either forgotten or pardoned. Between 1886 and 1889, until a mistake of Qardāḥī, the troupe was accepted, even supported, by Tevfik.

Qardāḥī's performances during the spring of 1886 were provided for in the Italian impresarios Santi Boni and Soschino's extended contract in the Khedivial Opera House.[87] By that time, Arabic theater in the post-occupation Opera House was not a novelty, since in January 1885 al-Qabbānī's troupe[88] and in April 1885 Khayyāṭ's troupe[89] had performed there. However, while in 1882 Qardāḥī had been able to contract easily with Léopold Larose, in 1886 Santi Boni and Soschino asked for (and received) 300 francs for every evening in the Opera.[90] This was expensive, but the unexpected success helped.

In achieving success Qardāḥī employed his now familiar techniques: the press, music, and charity. He held rehearsals in Alexandria at the beginning of 1886 and then moved to the capital. In February 1886, he published an advertisement for the Arabic-reading audience in Cairo. "It is our honour to announce to the public that we are heading to the capital and we wish to summon all the literate and gracious, because we have started again our theatrical activities."[91] Qardāḥī's timing was similar to what he had done in the spring of 1882 when he stepped on stage in the Khedivial Opera House in a tense political atmosphere. Now in the spring of 1886 there was an expectation that the British would evacuate Ottoman Egypt.

Tevfik, the Ottoman representative Ahmed Muhtar, and many (Ottoman) Egyptian high functionaries listened to Qardāḥī's call. In an unusual move, Tevfik often attended the Arabic performances. He personally encouraged Qardāḥī at the end of his lease to submit a request for the following year (1887), which the impresario immediately did.[92] The success was so great that three additional evenings were held for the benefit of the actors and actresses, with the attendance of the khedivial

[87] They originally included al-Qabbānī, not Qardāḥī. Letter dated 10 August 1885, from Santi Boni to Rouchdy, 4003–037912, DWQ.

[88] *Al-Ahrām*: 10, 12, 20, 24, 31 January 1885.

[89] *Al-Ahrām*: 14, 17, 18, 20, 25 April 1885; 5, 7, 9 May 1885.

[90] Undated letter in Arabic, from Sulaymān Qardāḥī to Raʾīs Majlis al-Nuẓẓār (President of the Council of Ministers), Maḥfaẓa 2/1, Niẓārat al-Ashghāl al-ʿUmūmiyya, CMW, DWQ.

[91] Ismāʿīl, *Taʾrīkh al-Masraḥ al-Miṣrī*, 142, cited from *al-Qāhira*, 16 February 1886.

[92] On 24 March, the khedive was in the Opera, and Qardāḥī's letter was dated (by Sayyid ʿAlī Ismāʿīl) to 25 March 1886 thus a strong connection might be supposed between the two events. Ismāʿīl, *Taʾrīkh al-Masraḥ al-Miṣrī*, 143–144. I have also seen the original letter, but in my notes there is no date, just as there is no date indicated in the photocopy that Sayyid ʿAlī Ismāʿīl published. It is the undated letter in Arabic, from Sulaymān Qardāḥī to the Raʾīs Majlis al-Nuẓẓār (President of the Council of Ministers), Maḥfaẓa 2/1, Niẓārat al-Ashghāl al-ʿUmūmiyya, CMW, DWQ.

family.[93] Subsequently, the khedive ordered that in the next spring season (1887) Qardāḥī should be granted a two-month concession of the Opera House.[94] This was generally looked upon as a gift from the khedive, and the press thanked him.[95] The greatest fan of the Arab Patriotic Troupe was in fact not the khedive but the Ottoman High Commissioner Ahmed Muhtar, who requested repetitions of the plays.[96] (See chapter 8 on his presence in the Opera.)

The Syrian-owned Arabic newspapers (especially *al-Qāhira* and *al-Ahrām*) did their utmost to support Qardāḥī. Perhaps the most interesting praise came from the freshly arrived (from Beirut to Cairo) and otherwise art-blind scientific monthly, *al-Muqtaṭaf*. Its article "Arab Acting" (*al-Tamthīl al-ʿArabī*) explored the art of theater "scientifically" by presenting its history from the inherent "acting" nature of man to the ancient Greeks and Romans to the great French, English, and German playwrights. The anonymous author incorrectly remarked that Arabs had not been active in theater until Qardāḥī's performances and that the Khedivial Opera House was "the first building that was built in Arabic countries for the dramatic art."[97] Although the author mentioned that the "Orientals" (*al-sharqiyyīn*) conformed to, rather than competed with, foreign works, he still appreciated the use of the noble Arabic language—that is, *fuṣḥā*—in theater and congratulated Qardāḥī, hoping that the khedive and the elite would support him.[98] In this way, *al-Muqtaṭaf* contributed to the formation of the discourse through which progress and reform were related to the dynasty.

Singing the Nation: Musical Theater and Charity, 1886

It seems that Qardāḥī's troupe was considered to be "the" Egyptian troupe in 1886. But why was it considered more "patriotic," more "Egyptian" than al-Qabbānī's or Khayyāṭ's? How was it able to please the khedive, Ahmed Muhtar, *zevat*, and *aʿyān* alike? The answer lies in the combination of timing, aesthetic form, charity, and the content of the plays.

With regard to aesthetics, Egyptian music, especially the singing of Salāma Ḥijāzī, further helped to garb the troupe in patriotic colors. In addition, the troupe—apart from employing the comedian Muḥyī al-Dīn to perform a popular pantomime after the plays (see below)—included a

[93] Announcement in *al-Ahrām*, 24 April 1886, 2.

[94] *Al-Ahrām*, 1 April 1886, 2; 24 April 1886, 2; *al-Qāhira* and *al-Zamān* in Ismāʿīl, *Taʾrīkh al-Masraḥ al-Miṣrī*, 144, footnote 5; *al-Ḥuqūq*, 8 May 1886, 91.

[95] *Al-Ahrām*, 22 April 1886, 2.

[96] *Al-Ahrām*, 10 March 1886, 2.

[97] The editor, Fāris Nimr, was present in October 1884 at al-Qabbānī's theater and gave a supporting speech. *Al-Ahrām*, 24 October 1884, 2–3.

[98] *Al-Muqtaṭaf*, 1 April 1886, 339–440.

full Egyptian band (*takht*) of "the most famous masters in the art of music that one can find in the land of Egypt."[99] The journal *al-Ahrām* highlighted the Egyptianness of the actors/singers ("most of them are Egyptians with the most pleasant voices").[100] The scenes were interspersed by the Egyptian *takht*; the press especially celebrated the *ʿūd*-player, Aḥmad al-Laythī,[101] and Salāma Ḥijāzī in the limelight.

Social networks were essential too. Continuing the earlier civic practice, Qardāḥī's troupe performed for charity during their stay in the Khedivial Opera. For instance, they staged a play for the Free Schools. They also performed *Ḥifẓ al-Widād* ("Faithfulness") for the Tevfik Charitable Society (*Jamʿiyyat al-Tawfīq al-Khayrī*).[102] Charity helped the actors to attach their activity directly to social justice and progress. In addition, it is also possible that family members of Qardāḥī were employed by some of the Syrian periodicals, which in turn provided extra press attention.

The Repertoire: Hārūn al-Rashīd 2.0

It is important to emphasize the expectations that were attached to the evacuation and to the return of Egypt to the Ottoman Empire. This political background is crucial to contextualize Qardāḥī's repertoire and, indeed, to understand how the performances of his troupe could inspire patriotic emotions through lived experience in public. The imagined community as an audience was constructed through the imagined defense of the homeland. This experience was made possible by the identification of historical or historicized heroes on stage. To quote Bakhtin again, the past became flesh on stage and this physical connection helps emotional identification.

In his 1885 spring proposal, Qardāḥī listed twenty plays, five times more than the number presented by the troupe in 1882.[103] These twenty plays, mostly translations or adaptations of classical topics, were not staged in

[99] *Al-Maḥrūsa*, 16 March 1886, 3. *Al-Ahrām*, 5 March 1886, 2.

[100] *Al-Ahrām*, 10 March 1886, 2.

[101] *Al-Ahrām*, 17 March, 1886, 2. We have no clues as to the identities of these musicians and singers, but they were regarded as Egyptians by the public press.

[102] *Al-Ahrām*, 5 (page 2) and 9 March 1886, 3.

[103] This unique list was written in French (here it is given with the original orthography): "1. Télémaque, trajédie 2. Joseph vendu par ses frères, trajédie 3. Mariage d'Antar, comédi 4. Les Chevaliers Arabes, trajédie 5. Jephté, trajédie 6. Costhon, trajédie 7. Eustache, drame 8. Ce que sont les femmes, comédi 9. Auguste-César, trajedi 10. Mérope, trajedi 11. Pygmalion et Astarbé, trajedi 12. Zénobie, trajedi 13. Alexandre le Grand, drame 14. L'Amoureuse de Léla (Roman Arabe) 15. Phédre, trajedi 16. L'Avare, comedi 17. Geneviève, trajedi 18. Les deuse Dianes, comedi 19. Clémence des Mois, drame et plusiers autres pièces sous composition dont entre eux: Cléopâtre, reine d'Egypte." Letter dated 7 May 1885 to Rouchdy from Soliman Cardahi, 4003–037911, DWQ.

their entirety during the season in March–April 1886. The most frequently performed work (*Hārūn al-Rashīd*) is in fact missing from the list. Also, in the Arabic announcement of the approved plays, some variations occurred (seventeen titles),[104] and ultimately only fourteen plays were performed. I compare these three lists (the 1885 French proposal, the 1886 Arabic advertisement, and the actual 1886 performances) in table 6.1.

As we will see, these titles remained the backbone of Qardāḥī's repertoire, with one important addition in the following next year (1887): *ʿĀyida*. Never was Arabic musical theater presented in the Khedivial Opera House in such a professional way and for such a long time. This was, as the press reports testified, a unique sign of Arab cultural strength (translated and genuine works) at a crucial political moment.

Tilīmāk was a translation of Fénelon's *Les Aventures de Télémaque*, a didactic, satirical novel published in 1699 about Odysseus' son Telemachus. He is accompanied in his travels by Mentor, his teacher, who finally turns out to be the Goddess Minerva. It was a very popular text in the Ottoman Empire (there were Armenian, Greek, Ottoman Turkish, and many Arabic translations);[105] those who studied French at the time often read this text in school. Rifāʿa Bey's printed Arabic translation (1867) was available at Muḥammad Unsī and Mourès' bookshop in Cairo and Ḥabīb Gharzūzī's bookshop in Alexandria in 1869 (together with a printed *Qiṣṣat ʿAntar*).[106] Even the young Jurjī Zaydān made a translation as a school exercise in 1881.[107] The story was especially adaptable to stage, since it contains short sections involving a relatively small number of protagonists around the central characters of Telemachus and Mentor. Both the Arabic and the Ottoman Turkish theatrical versions were set to music,[108] as were the European examples (the most famous of those are Gluck's "drama per musica" *Telemaco, ossia L'isola di Circe* [1765]). It is not known which Arabic translation was used by Qardāḥī's troupe—possibly that of Saʿd

[104] In the beginning of Qardāḥī's two months, another list was published in *al-Ahrām* that was "approved by the Commission of the Opera": Tilīmāk [Telemachus], *Bīkmāliyūn* [Pygmalion] aw *Astarba* [Astarbe], *Mīrūbā* [Merope] aw ʿAlā'l-Bāghī Tadūr al-Dawāʾir, Yūsuf al-Ḥasan, *Fīdr* [Phèdre] *aw Nakth al-ʿUhūd, Istīr* [Esther], *Hārūn al-Rashīd aw Gharām al-Mulūk, Zanūbiyā—Malikat Tadmur, al-Jāhil al-Muṭabbib* [should be al-Mutaṭabbib], *Maḥāsin al-Ṣudaf, Salīm wa-Asmā aw Ḥifẓ al-Widād, al-Murūʾa wa-l-Wafāʾ, Andrūmak* [Andromaque], *Dhāt al-Khidr, Iṣṭāk, ʿAntara al-ʿAbsī, al-Bārīziyya al-Ḥusnāʾ* [La belle parisienne]. *Al-Ahrām*, 10 March 1886, 2.

[105] Strauss, "Who Read What?," 49–50 and n. 105. See also Hill, "Utopia and Civilisation in the Arab Nahda"; Cachia, "Translations and Adaptations," 27; and Sadgrove, *Egyptian Theatre*, 143.

[106] Advertisment in *Wādī al-Nīl*, July 1869, 437.

[107] "Ḥawādith Tilimāk (tarjama ḥarfiyya—al-kitāb al-awwal)," in Undated school notebook, Box 2, AA.6.2.26.1, Jurjī Zaydān Papers, AUB Special Collections.

[108] And, *Türk Tiyatrosu*, 462.

TABLE 6.1. Comparison between the French Proposal, the Advertised Arabic Program, and the Staged Plays of al-Jawq al-Waṭanī in the Khedivial Opera House, March–April 1886

Title of performed play, based on al-Ahrām *and Ismāʿīl,* Tārīkh *(largely based on* al-Qāhira*)*	*Date(s) of performance, spring 1886**	*Title in Arabic announcement,* al-Ahrām, *10 March 1886, 2.*	*Title in French proposal, dated 7 May 1885.*
*Zanūbiyā/Zaynūbiyā, Zanūbiyā—Malikat Tadmur**	11, 30/31 March	*Zanūbiyā—Malikat Tadmur*	*Zénobie*
Yūsuf	12 March	*Yūsuf al-Ḥasan*	*Joseph vendu par ses frères*
Ḥifẓ al-Widād aw Asmā wa-Salīm†	15 March	*Salīm wa-Asmā aw Ḥifẓ al-Widād*	?
Iṣṭāk‡	18 March	*Iṣṭāk*	*Eustache*
Istīr	20 March	*Istīr*	*Esther?*
Hārūn al-Rashīd wa-l-Ṣayyād / Hārūn al-Rashīd "al-Ṣayyād"§	14 March, 17 April	?	
Harūn (!) *al-Rashīd*	24 March, 3 April	?	?
Gharām al-Mulūk aw Hārūn al-Rashīd	1 May	*Hārūn al-Rashīd aw Gharām al-Mulūk*	?
Mīrūbā aw ʿalā al-Bāghī Tadūr al-Dawāʾir	25 March	*Mīrūbā aw ʿalā al-Bāghī Tadūr al-Dawāʾir*	*Mérope*
Tilīmāk	28 March	*Tilīmāk*	*Télémaque*
ʿIffat al-Nafs	29 March, 6 April	*Geneviève?*	

(*Continued*)

TABLE 6.1. (*Continued*)

Title of performed play, based on al-Ahrām *and Ismāʿīl,* Tārīkh *(largely based on* al-Qāhira*)*	*Date(s) of performance, spring 1886**	*Title in Arabic announcement,* al-Ahrām, *10 March 1886, 2.*	*Title in French proposal, dated 7 May 1885.*
*Maḥāsin al-Ṣudaf***	1 April, 15 April	*Maḥāsin al-Ṣudaf*	
Ghāʾilat al-Makr wa-l-ʿĀqibat al-Ghadr / Dalīlat al-Muḥtāla	13 April		
al-Jāhil al-Muṭabbib / al-Ḥakīm al-Jāhil	20 April	*al-Jāhil al-Muṭabbib*	*Le médicin malgré lui* (at least three translations in the 1880s)
Dhāt al-Khidr††	22 April	*Dhāt al-Khidr*	?
al-Faraj baʿd al-Ḍīq	24 April		
five acts from *Tilīmāk, Zanūbiyya, al-Ṣayyād, Ḥusn al-Ṣudaf* [!], *Iṣṭāk* [*Istākiyūs*]‡‡	27 or 28 April		

*According to Ismāʿīl, this play was compiled by Jūrj Mirzāʾ, the editor of *al-Ittiḥād.* Ismāʿīl, *Taʾrīkh al-Masraḥ al-Miṣrī*, 144.

†Sadgrove, *Egyptian Theatre*, 151.

‡This play had already been performed in Beirut, possibly written by Salīm al-Bustānī, Najm, *al-Masraḥiyya*, 54–55.

§Written by Maḥmūd Wāṣif.

**Written by Maḥmūd Wāṣif.

††"This is a play consisting of selected Egyptian manners, written by Saʿīd Efendi al-Bustānī." *Al-Ahrām*, 22 April 1886, 2.

‡‡*Al-Ḥuqūq*, 1 May 1886, 81–82.

Allāh al-Bustānī (1870). *Tilīmāk* remained a standard piece on the Arabic stage until the 1900s.

Some observers focused on how Qardāḥī's theater taught history through translated/Arabized Greek tragedies. For instance, in the journal *al-Ḥuqūq*, the journalist described the plots of *Andrūmāk*, *Tilīmāk*, and *Pīkmāliyūn* and asked for the support of the audience.[109] This periodical was important since it was the official Arabic journal of the Popular Courts in Egypt, and it often highlighted the importance of (French) historical knowledge in Arabic. After the last performance of the Arab Patriotic Troupe, the journalist remarked that the actors had performed so well that he felt as if the past scenes were actually in the present.[110]

But when it came to the heroes of the historical imagination, the central figure was Hārūn al-Rashīd. Jokes about Hārūn al-Rashīd were circulating among ordinary intellectuals in the 1880s (possibly nothing to do with *The Arabian Nights* stories),[111] and there were at least ten printed Arabic editions of *The Arabian Nights* (in which Hārūn al-Rashīd is a central figure) by the time, so his reappearance on the Arabic stage should not be surprising. As we have seen, a Hārūn al-Rashīd play (written by Mārūn Naqqāsh in Beirut) had been performed for Khedive Ismail in 1878 and 1879, and for Tevfik in 1881.[112] It seems that this caliph had become a symbol of the just ruler in the learned Arab imagination: there were at least four Hārūn al-Rashīd plays on the Arabic stage by the 1890s,[113] and this figure remained part of the theatrical repertoire well into the twentieth century, embodying justice in the popular imagination.[114]

The play staged in 1886 was a Hārūn al-Rashīd musical comedy, entitled *Khalīfa, the Fisherman, with Qūt al-Qulūb and Hārūn al-Rashīd*, by the Egyptian playwright Maḥmūd Wāṣif.[115] If the versions of *Hārūn al-Rashīd* were one single piece, then this play was Qardāḥī-Ḥijāzī's most popular

[109] Anonymous, "Gharāʾib Akhbār wa-Nawādir Aʿṣār," *al-Ḥuqūq*, 17 April 1886, 65–66.

[110] *Al-Ḥuqūq*, 1 May 1886, 81–82.

[111] See the Hārūn al-Rashīd anecdotes in Saʿd, *Tuḥfat Ahl al-Fukāha*.

[112] Sadgrove, *Egyptian Theatre*, 139–141.

[113] Apart from Naqqāsh and Wāṣif's plays, there are two other Hārūn al-Rashīd plays associated with the name of Abū Khalīl al-Qabbānī.

[114] Al-Ḥakīm, *Min Dhikriyyāt al-Fann*, 43–44.

[115] The play was published in an anonymous and undated form. Its introduction mentions that it was printed sometime after the play was performed in the Khedivial Opera House. [Wāṣif], *Riwāyat Harūn* [!] *al-Rashīd maʿ Qūt al-Qulūb*, 1. The title of the book on the title page and the title given in the introduction are different. Ismāʿīl states that in an 1895 publication Maḥmūd Wāṣif wrote that this play was his, but that it was printed without his permission. Ismāʿīl, "Masraḥiyyāt lahā Taʾrīkh 5—Hārūn al-Rashīd," *al-Jumhūriyya*, 19 December 2010. Maḥmūd Wāṣif was the author of the play *Maḥāsin al-Ṣudaf* as well. In the 1900 edition that I consulted, Wāṣif writes that it was so successful in the Opera House and

one, performed five times (once by special khedivial order) out of the twenty-three evenings.[116] The plot is as follows: Hārūn al-Rashīd loves the beautiful slave girl Qūt al-Qulūb. His jealous wife, Queen Zubayda, drugs her and sells the unconscious girl in a huge box in the market. Meanwhile Hārūn al-Rashīd goes to hunt and fish (in disguise) and befriends the fisherman Khalīfa. Their scenes are full of jokes because it is funny that in the presence of Hārūn, *amīr al-muʾminīn*, the caliph, someone else is called a *khalīfa* (albeit throughout the play Hārūn is called *malik* [king] by both his courtiers and the writer in his instructions). When Hārūn returns to his palace he learns that Qūt al-Qulūb is dead. Khalīfa, the fisherman arrives to claim his money from the courtiers, because they ate his fish. There is another humorous scene (a cruel one: the fisherman is humiliated by the courtiers), but finally Khalīfa leaves without much compensation. He goes to the market, buys the huge box, and at home he finds out that inside is the hungry Qūt al-Qulūb. She writes a letter to the king, delivered by Khalīfa, and Hārūn al-Rashīd happily discovers that his favorite slave is alive and forgives everyone. This play remained popular in Egypt, could pass censorship, and was on stage even in the 1920s.[117]

Wāṣif's comedy provides clues to the ways in which patriotism negotiated khedivial power and channeled Egyptian popular entertainment into elite culture. The central technique is again parallelism. There are direct allusions that ninth-century Baghdad was an allegory for late nineteenth-century Cairo. The liveliest character is Khalīfa, who uses Egyptian vernacular expressions and is often the butt of the humor on stage. The other characters speak and sing in *fuṣḥā* Arabic. The context also seems to be a direct allusion to Egypt. In the beginning of the play, the servants sing an ode in which they ask their lord to "preserve the honour of Egypt" (*iḥfaẓ majd Miṣr*).[118] This is certainly strange in a play set in Baghdad. At the end, Hārūn al-Rashīd orders his vizier Jaʿfar to "embellish the city of Baghdad, gather groups among the servants, set free the prisoners and pardon the sinners."[119] If the play was put on stage with these words in 1886 it was very hard to miss the allusion to the ʿUrābists in prison, in exile, or in silence. The character of the benevolent Arab caliph offered a convenient symbol for Khedive Tevfik, or for Sultan Abdülhamid II himself. At this moment, with the instrumentalization of Ottomanism, the khedive's public image relied more on the sultan than ever before in occupied Egypt.

---

the khedive liked it so much (likely referring to Tevfik) that he felt obligatory to print it. Wāṣif, *Riwāyat Hārūn al-Rashīd*, 2.

[116] *Gharām al-Mulūk* is a different Hārūn al-Rashīd story.

[117] Cf. letters in the printed play, n. 2306, MQMFSH.

[118] [Wāṣif], *Riwāyat Harūn* [!] *al-Rashīd maʿ Qūt al-Qulūb*, 3.

[119] Ibid., 44.

It is appropriate to remark that soon such Hārūn al-Rashīd plays were viewed by learned elites less favorably. In al-Muwayliḥī's late 1890s didactic novel, a character remarks that such plays, portraying well-known Muslim heroes and rulers, are in fact insults of Islam:

> Nor is it any part of Islamic practice that we should be portraying its history and that of its caliphs and holy men, devising various plots, making up stories, and placing them in amorous situations. By so doing, we make them say things they never uttered and put them in unreal situations. Even so, that is what many non-Muslims are daring to do these days in our country. What can you possibly say about the Caliph Hārūn al-Rashīd singing, his vizier Jaʿfar al-Barmakī playing the flute, and al-Faḍl ibn al-Rabīʿ dancing? Without the slightest doubt it's an insult to our ancestors and a distortion of history.[120]

The Arabic Aida: *Culture and Legitimacy*

The Arabic stage became even more crowded with history. In the following season in 1887 Hārūn al-Rashīd was joined by an Ethiopian princess, ʿĀyida, in the celebration of elite patriotism in occupied Egypt. The opera *Aida*, as I have previously discussed, was conceived as part of the Italian representation of the khedivate. We have seen that Abū al-Suʿūd translated first the libretto into Arabic in 1871; in the 1880s, however, the 1875 translation of Salīm Naqqāsh provided continuity with Ismail's experiment and added an additional (imperial) symbol to the patriotic imagination. In this way, a European product ordered for an Ottoman governor entered learned Arabic culture.

The Arabic season of the Khedivial Opera House in the spring of 1887 was yet another triumph of the Qardāḥī-Ḥijāzī enterprise. The performances were elite political occasions representing the Ottoman attachment of Egypt. By the order of the khedive, Qardāḥī received an independent concession of two months. Fortunately for him, the original owners of the concession, the two Italian impresarios, went bankrupt in December 1886, and the Egyptian government had to ship their artists back to Europe.[121] The money thus spent was judged as "regretful" by the

[120] Allen's translation of the original article in *Miṣbāḥ al-Sharq*. Al-Muwaylihi, *What ʿIsa Ibn Hisham Told Us*, 2:175. The names are changed in the book-edition, although the tone is even harsher. Al-Muwaylihi, *A Period of Time*, 374.

[121] Letter dated 28 December 1886 (from the Président du Conseil des Ministres to Rouchdy Pacha, Min. Trav. Pub.), Maḥfaẓa 2/1, Niẓārat Al-Ashghāl al-ʿUmūmiyya, CMW, DWQ. The events were reported in *al-Qāhira al-Ḥurra*, 14 December 1886, 2 (based on the *Bosphore Égyptien*). Previously, at the end of November, Santi Boni asked if his name could

journalists who asked the government to help the Arab actors as it had the Europeans, since "to help the first is better than to help the second,"[122] but, admitted later that, "it is not proper to the honour of Egypt to leave the [European] actors in distress."[123] An administrator (perhaps Minister Rushdī) then decided that Qardāḥī's promised two months should start sooner, in February 1887—a decision that *al-Ahrām* praised as wise.[124] Indeed, the troupe arrived in Cairo at the end of February and immediately began to perform on February 25, 1887, putting on the play *al-Murūʾa wa-l-Wafāʾ*.[125] They advertised thirty evenings, four (Thursday, Saturday, Sunday, Tuesday) in every week for approximately two months.

The troupe's staff and its preparation were largely identical with the one in the year before. With Sheikh Salāma Ḥijāzī in the limelight, the troupe had performed in the Politeama in Alexandria in January and February 1887, as preparation for their grand Cairo visit.[126] In this period they were variously called, again, "The Patriotic Troupe" or simply "Qardāḥī Efendi's troupe." This year the leading actors and singers included Ḥijāzī, Aḥmad Abū al-ʿAdl, ʿIzzat [Abū al-ʿAdl], Sulaymān Ḥaddād (he was also the "artistic director" [*mudīr mushakhkhiṣīn*]),[127] actress Kātrīn (Qardāḥī's wife, Catherine), and an actress called Hānūlā[128]; in April the (Syrian) actor Iskandar Sayqalī also joined them for two nights. It seems that the khedive's support followed Qardāḥī everywhere. Already in Alexandria the troupe was given assistance; for instance, they performed *ʿĀyida* there on February 9, 1887, and received unspecified "important things" (*muhimmāt*) from Cairo (possibly from the Opera House). An Egyptian military band and soldiers helped in the staging as well.[129] Furthermore, Qardāḥī remained unchallenged by competitors: Khayyāṭ wisely toured in the countryside (Zaqaziq, Mansura, Tanta),[130] while Santi Boni and al-Qabbānī vanished from Egypt.

---

be deleted from the contract, al-*Ahrām*, 26 November 1886, 2. Cf. also *al-Ahrām*, 17 December 1886, 2 and *al-Ahrām*, 26 December 1886, 2.

[122] *Al-Qāhira al-Ḥurra*, 26 December 1886, 3.

[123] *Al-Qāhira al-Ḥurra*, 28 December 1886, 3.

[124] *Al-Ahrām*, 18 January 1887, 2.

[125] *Al-Qāhira al-Ḥurra*, 27 February 1887, 2. *Al-Ahrām*, 28 February 1887, 2.

[126] Najm, *al-Masraḥiyya*, 109; Ismāʿīl, *Taʾrīkh al-Masraḥ al-Miṣrī*, 146; and the numbers of *al-Ahrām* through January and February 1887.

[127] *Al-Ahrām*, 19 April 1887, 2. Sulaymān Ḥaddād sold theater tickets in the shop of Ḥabīb Gharzūzī in the summer of 1884, when ʿAbduh al-Ḥamūlī returned to the stage in the Zizinia Theatre. *Al-Ahrām*, 28 July 1884, 3. In a later letter in 1894, Ḥaddād remembers that he started working in theater seventeen years before, which makes it possible that he was part of the original troupe of al-Naqqāsh, arriving from Beirut in 1876. Letter dated 12 December 1894, from Haddad to the Président (du Conseil des Ministres), Maḥfaẓa 2/1, Niẓārat al-Ashghāl al-ʿUmūmiyya, CMW, DWQ.

[128] *Al-Ahrām*, 2 April 1887, 2.

[129] *Al-Ahrām*, 10 January 1887, 3.

[130] *Al-Ahrām*, 28 February 1887, 3.

Given these favorable conditions, Qardāḥī's Arab Patriotic Troupe had the most successful theatrical season in the Opera House in Cairo, entertaining Khedive Tevfik and other Egyptian dignitaries in the audience in the spring of 1887.[131] They performed plays for charity too, for instance, for the benefit of the Society of Acquiring Education (*Jamʿiyyat Iqtibās al-Ādāb*),[132] the Maronite Charitable Society,[133] and for the Egyptian Brotherly Union (*al-Ittiḥād al-Akhawī al-Miṣriyya*).[134] During this term other charity balls were also organized in the Opera House, once even with the singer ʿAbduh al-Ḥamūlī who sang for the benefit of the Jewish Free Schools (*Écoles Gratuites Israélites du Caire*).[135]

With the addition of *ʿĀyida*, the 1887 repertoire largely consisted of the same works as in 1886. They performed an ʿAntar-play, too; seemingly Tevfik did not (or did not want to) remember its presumed association with ʿUrābī because after the performance he received the impresario and showed signs of joy.[136]

ʿĀyida was staged three times during the 1887 season in the Khedivial Opera House. The translation of Salīm Naqqāsh (1875) was performed by al-Qabbānī in Alexandria in 1884, then by Khayyāṭ in May 1885 in the Opera House starring Ḥijāzī.[137] For its first known performance by Qardāḥī's troupe in the Khedivial Opera House, on 7 March 1887, numerous dignitaries attended including Ahmed Muhtar, the Ottoman High Commissionaire, and Nubar, the prime minister.[138] On 8 March and 2 April 1887 *ʿĀyida* was repeated to popular acclaim. Seemingly, Qardāḥī deliberately chose this play as an update in his repertoire, rehearsed it in Alexandria, and received permission from the khedive to use the military music band. He continued to employ this band in the Opera House performances. Although they also performed *Hārūn al-Rashīd*, this time *ʿĀyida* was the gem of the season.[139]

131 *Al-Ahrām*, 3 March 1887, 2. Cf. Najm, *al-Masraḥiyya*, 110 and Ismāʿīl, *Taʾrīkh al-Masraḥ al-Miṣrī*, 146.

132 *Al-Ahrām*, 8 March 1887, 3.

133 *Al-Ahrām*, 9 March 1887, 2.

134 *Al-Qāhira al-Ḥurra*, 13 April 1887, 2.

135 Note dated 10 Mars 1887 from MTP to the Président, Maḥfaẓa 2/1, Niẓārat al-Ashghāl al-ʿUmūmiyya, CMW, DWQ. Cf. *Al-Ahrām*, 24 March 1887, 2. *Al-Qāhira al-Ḥurra*, 21 March 1887, 3. Cf. the information about permissions to Sheikh Dasūqī Badr (director of the Alexandrian school of al-Najāḥ al-Tawfīqiyya), and to Les Sociétés de Bienfaisance Copte et Grecque Catholique, La Société Maronite de Bienfaisence, Écoles Gratuites Israelites du Caire. Letters dated 6, 14, and 17 March 1887, to Tanzim from Chef du Service Administratif, 4003–036990, DWQ.

136 *Al-Ahrām*, 3 March 1887, 2.

137 *Al-Ahrām*, 9 May 1885, 2.

138 *Al-Ahrām*, 9 March 1887, 3. Ismāʿīl gives 11 March, *Taʾrīkh al-Masraḥ al-Miṣrī*, 147.

139 *Al-Ahrām*, 12 March 1887, 2.

The press was full with praise for Qardāḥī and Ḥijāzī. The latter sang the role of Ramsis in *ʿĀyida*. Even ʿAbduh al-Hamūlī joined the troupe once, and introduced one of their last evenings in the Opera House for the benefit of an actor (who received the evening's whole income).[140] The last performance in the capital was on 6 May.[141] *Al-Ahrām* was bursting with praise, and thanked the khedive, the audience, the troupe, and Qardāḥī in particular for advancing Arabic theater.[142] Their success was so great that Rushdi Pasha, the minister of public works, suggested that the Council of Ministers offer a financial award. Only 400 LE from the budget of the theaters remained (which was enough only for the lighting), so he wanted to give at least this quite large sum to Qardāḥī.[143] *Al-Ahrām* announced that "it was decided that 400 LE will be given to him [Qardāḥī] from the subsidy of the theatres."[144] Khedive Tevfik again received Qardāḥī at a private audience,[145] which confirms that he approved of the Syrian impresario's troupe and his version of patriotism.

Khedivial support was not limited to the guest performances in the capital but was extended to the troupe's tour in the countryside. It continued in the summer of 1887 when Qardāḥī performed in Asyut and Alexandria, and was able to use the military music band in *ʿĀyida* in the summer.[146] By this time, major Egyptian cities such as Tanta, Asyut, Zaqaziq, Suez, and others, had acquired cafés-chantants, small theaters, clubs, and other stages. The guest plays and tours helped to spread the repertoire and strengthened the textual production of patriotism in the Arabic press, history books, and schools. In this way, the standardization of patriotic culture, fueled by various sources of narrative identification, was beginning.

Popularizing Patriotism? Economy and Markets

In this last section, I explore the business side of Qardāḥī's enterprise in the late 1880s and explain why his success has been forgotten. Why did Qardāḥī not refer to this period in his 1898 letter to Abbas Hilmi II? The

[140] *Al-Ahrām*, 25 April 1887, 2.

[141] *Al-Ahrām*, 7 May 1887, 3.

[142] *Al-Ahrām*, 7 May 1887, 3.

[143] Letter dated 21 April 1887 from MTP to the Président, Maḥfaẓa 2/1, Niẓārat al-Ashghāl al-ʿUmūmiyya, CMW, DWQ. Its Arabic translation is published in Ismāʿīl, *Taʾrīkh al-Masraḥ al-Miṣrī*, 147–148.

[144] *Al-Ahrām*, 6 May 1887, 2. Repeated *al-Ahrām*, 7 May 1887, 3.

[145] *Al-Ahrām*, 7 May 1887, 3.

[146] *Al-Ahrām*, 21 and 22 July 1887, 3; *Al-Ahrām*, 3 August 1887, 3.

strengthening of khedivial authority *together* with renewed patriotism occurred parallel with the commercialization of Arabic musical theater. Chapter 8 will provide a more detailed discussion of the economics of entertainment and the audience, but a short overview is in order here.

The Economy of Arabic Theater Performances at the End of the 1880s

Arab impresarios had to look upon theater as a business enterprise. The actors had to be fed, the scenery and the rent had to be paid for. Impresarios toured the countryside (typically Mansura, Tanta, Asyut, Suez, and al-Mahalla al-Kubra) partly in response to the small audiences in Alexandria and Cairo. The success of Qardāḥī's troupe in the Khedivial Opera House in the spring did not translate into a steady income during the year.

By the end of the 1880s Arabic theater troupes could make significant income if they combined their performances with the marketing force of a charitable society or a singer. ʿAbduh al-Ḥamūlī alone could earn 80 LE for a concert.[147] For instance, the Arab Patriotic Troupe's performance of *ʿĀyida* in March 1887 for the benefit of the Maronite Charitable Society in the Opera House resulted in 6,000 francs (around 230 LE).[148] As noted earlier, Qardāḥī paid 300 francs (around 11.5 LE) rent for every night in the Opera in 1886, which means that the receipts for every performance must have far exceeded this amount: in twenty-two evenings he paid 6600 francs (around 240 LE), or one charity night's full income, just for rent. If at least half the house was full each night, and tickets were the same price as a charity evening, this would mean that over its twenty-two nights of performance in 1886, the troupe made 2,640 LE or 68,640 francs.

As a comparison, in 1885, the cheapest bottle of wine was three to four francs, a first-class hotel room for a night was between fifteen and twenty francs,[149] and a short donkey ride in Cairo was one to two piasters (0.01 LE; 0.2 francs).[150] In 1886–1887, 5 piasters was the price of a line of an advertisement and 96.5 piasters (around 1 LE) was a yearly subscription to the journal *al-Ḥuqūq*. The cost of a locomotive was 390 LE in 1898.[151] All in all, Arabic musical theater, at least for Qardāḥī in the late 1880s, was an occasionally lucrative enterprise, but it could not provide a stable income for the actors-singers or for the impresario.

[147] Lagrange, "Musiciens et poètes," 152.
[148] *Al-Ahrām*, 12 March 1887, 2.
[149] *Baedeker's Lower Egypt*, 5, 17.
[150] Ibid., 233.
[151] Letter dated 18 July 1898, Arthur Koppel (Cairo) to De Martino Pasha, HIL 158, AHP.

Qardāḥī's Third Patriotic Troupe (1888–1889)

Qardāḥī's activity had a global scope. Despite his success, or perhaps because of it, he left Egypt for Ottoman Syria in 1887.[152] In his absence, Yūsuf Khayyāṭ's "Patriotic Arab Troupe" (*Jawq ʿArabī Waṭanī*) performed during the autumn of 1887 in Alexandria.[153] It is almost impossible to tell whether Khayyāṭ simply took over Qardāḥī's troupe or created a new one with the same name. Qardāḥī returned to Alexandria in April 1888[154] and established a new troupe.[155] It is again not clear if this was an entirely new troupe or the re-creation of the previous one, but Sheikh Salāma Ḥijāzī again joined him. First, the troupe performed in Alexandria (in the Zizinia in November 1888[156] because the Politeama was too small for the large audience).[157] Qardāḥī contracted a new singer or actress, called Laylā.[158] *Al-Ahrām* now mentioned his group as "the Egyptian Patriotic Troupe" (*al-Jawq al-Waṭanī al-Miṣrī*), perhaps in contrast to Khayyāṭ's "Arab Patriotic Troupe."

This time Qardāḥī may have had less success,[159] although *al-Ahrām* still praised the company. The troupe even had to compete with Sarah Bernhardt, who arrived for a tour in Egypt;[160] and they shared the Khedivial Opera House in the spring of 1889 with ʿAbduh al-Ḥamūlī, who could also contract for a few evenings.[161] Ḥijāzī and the singer Laylā were the main stars, but Laylā sang *after* the actual play (as al-Ḥamūlī had done previously in association with al-Qabbānī), or between the acts. For instance, while Ḥijāzī acted and sang the title role of *Mūnghūmirī* (*Montgomery*) with the actress Ms. *Lūna* (?), Laylā connected the acts with her songs.[162] Ḥijāzī was again praised because "[his] skill of acting surpassed the cream of the European actors and the diversity of songs was even more marvelous."[163] If we consider that in March ʿAbduh

[152] It is called by Najm a riḥla tamthīliyya ("a theatrical journey," I presume he means a tour), Najm, *al-Masraḥiyya*, 110. I have no information about the tour. Sayyid ʿAlī Ismāʿīl believes that Qardāḥī's absence is proof of failure. Ismāʿīl, *Taʾrīkh al-Masraḥ al-Miṣrī*, 148.

[153] *Al-Ahrām*, 25 November 1887, 3.

[154] *Al-Ahrām*, 30 April 1888, 3.

[155] Najm, *al-Masraḥiyya*, 110.

[156] *Al-Ahrām*, 8 November 1888, 3; *al-Qāhira al-Ḥurra*, 16 November 1888, 2.

[157] *Al-Ahrām*, 16 November 1888, 3.

[158] Najm, *al-Masraḥiyya*, 110.

[159] Ismāʿīl, Taʾ*rīkh al-Masraḥ al-Miṣrī*, 148 quotes *al-Qāhira* (*al-Ḥurra*), 19 November 1888. My notes indicate that *al-Qāhira al-Ḥurra* published this article on 16 November 1888, 2, and the journal itself republished this critique from *al-Ittiḥād al-Miṣrī*.

[160] For instance, *al-Ahrām*, 22 December 1888, 2.

[161] *Al-Ahrām*, 4 March 1889, 2–3.

[162] *Al-Ahrām*, 4 March 1889, 3.

[163] *Al-Ahrām*, 7 March 1889, 3.

al-Ḥamūlī also performed in the Opera House,[164] then an unprecedented demonstration of modern Arab-Egyptian cultural wealth was displayed in the main symbolic space of the occupied khedivate.

At least according to *al-Ahrām*, the popularity of both the patriotic troupe and of al-Ḥamūlī himself rose to exceptional heights: "the audience was much more numerous than in the preceding nights. People who stood on foot surrounded the already packed sitting places. Never had such a thing happened to any Arab or foreign troupe in Cairo!"[165] An Egyptian notable expressed his joy at one of ʿAbduh al-Ḥamūlī's evenings with the following words: "How wouldn't I be happy . . . when here I see only the people of the East; there is not even a European cap among us, the same in the lodges, and this proves us the most liberal (*aryāḥiyya*) people of the East."[166] The performances delivered, at least in the press, peak moments of patriotic unity. Next, Qardāḥī's troupe moved to Tanta to tour in the countryside with the same plays.[167]

Cultural Transfer Reversed: A Mistake in Paris

The pursuit of economic success, however, led to a serious rupture in Qardāḥī's shining career, when he went to the World Exhibition in Paris to stage a commercial Orientalized production in 1899. This French adventure is an important detail in the nineteenth-century history of Mediterranean entertainment business. It is an example of a reverse cultural transfer, from Egypt to Europe.

Seymour Wade, an Englishman and owner of *Le Théâtre International*, a showcase theater at the World Exhibition, contacted Qardāḥī during the summer of 1889, and his offer seems to have been good enough that the Arab impresario arranged a special troupe for the Exhibition. They arrived in Paris on 24 August and started the performances on 31 August 1889. The troupe was *not* the theater troupe usually employed in Egypt. It did not contain Ḥijāzī or any of the celebrated Egyptian singers. And instead of historical Arabic musical dramas, the troupe apparently performed an Oriental(ized) show.

The French critics recognized the contrast with the Vietnamese theater, which "was presented to us as a reflection on the habits, the civilization, the customs, and the intellectual tendencies" of that country, while Qardāḥī's was only "a spectacle of pure curiosity" in Egyptian colors. It remains a question whether this Orientalized show was ordered by

[164] *Al-Ahrām*, 4 March 1889, 2.
[165] *Al-Ahrām*, 18 March 1889, 2.
[166] *Al-Ahrām*, 3 March 1889, 3.
[167] *Al-Ahrām*, 2 April 1889, 3.

Wade or was staged by Qardāḥī for the French and international audience. Their repertoire contained "pictures" and "scenes," although the "tableaux" may have included extracts of the Arab theatricals. Perhaps to make these Orientalized performances more official, the troupe also performed some *hymnes au Khédive*.[168] Wade advertised Qardāḥī as the director of the Khedivial Opera House, performing with the personal approval of the ruler.[169]

Unfortunately for Qardāḥī, the news reached Khedive Tevfik. Santerres des Boves, the editor of the Egyptian *Journal Officiel*, published an open letter in *Le Figaro* denying that Qardāḥī was the director of the Opera House. He also denied that Qardāḥī performed with the blessing of the khedive. Such commercial business was not appropriate for the khedive's dignity, wrote Boves Bey.[170] And so, after approximately ten days of performing in Paris, the khedivial benevolence that this Arab impresario had so diligently built up over the preceding four years was completely lost.

Qardāḥī sued Wade for dishonoring him. He demanded 150,000 francs in indemnity, but a French court judged that Wade advertised the theater based on the information that Qardāḥī himself had supplied. Thus, the Arab impresario even had to pay the court costs.[171] To his dismay, his Parisian adventure proved to the khedivial court that Arabic theater was not yet ready or not yet respectable enough for official representation.

Alexandria and the Tours: Abbas Hilmi II's Impresario?

The later activity of Qardāḥī suggests that he was ultimately pardoned but could never regain the favor of the khedives. Instead, he developed an entertainment business in Alexandria. He became famous among the non-Arabic-speaking communities in Egypt as well, and he always wrote his name as Soliman Cardahi in French. A French journal even portrayed him in a little poem which ended with these words: *Chantons donc; Vive Cardahi / Ha, ha, ha, ha ! Hi, hi, hi hi !*[172] *(Let us sing; Viva Cardahi / Ha, ha, ha, ha! Hi, hi, hi, hi!).*

According to family memory, after the fiasco in Paris, Qardāḥī traveled with his family (perhaps running away from the expenses of the

168 Pougin, *Le théâtre à l'Exposition universelle*, 100–103. Such as Tableau 1: Les Arabes se vengent du grand héros Antare; Tableau 2: La chanson d'amour par Zénabe et sa compagnie, at 101. Pougin first published his article in *Le Ménestrel*, 1890, 4 May, 1890, 139–141.

169 *Le Figaro*, 24 August 1889; *Le Ménestrel*, 1 September 1889, 8.

170 *Le Figaro*, 14 September 1889, 2.

171 *Journal des Débats Politiques et Litteraires*, 5 Décembre 1890, 4.

172 *La Correspondance Egyptienne*, 2 December 1894, 7. I thank Alexandre Cordahi for sending me this article.

FIGURE 6.1. The troupe of Sulaymān Qardāḥī in Paris, 1889
Source: "Danseuses du ventre et musiciens de la troupe Seymour Wade," by Nadar (atelier), NA 237 01069; Médiathèque de l'architecture et du patrimoine, Paris, with permission.

court case) to Argentina where his wife, the actress and school mistress Christine, started a successful enterprise.[173] But the remarkably mobile artist did not stay in Argentina because "he received a pardon from the khedive through his friends at the court."[174] He returned to Egypt as early as November 1891.[175]

In his absence, the theater market changed again. Salāma Ḥijāzī established his own troupe. Ḥijāzī saw the need for "the patriotic taste" (*al-dhawq al-waṭanī*) in the Arabic theater.[176] The Damascene Abū Khalīl al-Qabbānī also returned and was now popular in Egypt. Qardāḥī established himself in Alexandria, and from here he started to tour the Egyptian countryside[177] and the Mediterranean. Gradually, he again became a serious player in the entertainment market. During the summer of 1893,

[173] Letter dated 16 March 1984, AAC.
[174] Ibid.
[175] Najm, *al-Masraḥiyya*, 110.
[176] *Al-Ittiḥād al-Miṣrī*, 7 April 1890, 3.
[177] Ismāʿīl, *Taʾrīkh al-Masraḥ al-Miṣrī*, 149.

his troupe performed in Cairo and in the Azbakiyya Garden with success,[178] then moved between Alexandria and Cairo. In 1894, he built his own theater building, the *Théâtre Cardahi*, with municipal backing at the seaside in Alexandria.[179] He went back to Ottoman Syria the same year,[180] and at the end of that year, after returning to Egypt, he allied with yet another Egyptian singer, Ḥasan al-Miṣrī.[181] His theater building in Alexandria also functioned as a host institution to Italian troupes.

"The Palace" still needed his service. The young khedive Abbas Hilmi II invited Qardāḥī's troupe for the wedding party of one of his sisters in the al-Qubba Palace in Cairo in 1895. According to a piece of news in *al-Ahrām*, Abbas Hilmi personally gave Qardāḥī seven (perhaps Egyptianized) plays by Muḥammad ʿUthmān Jalāl, and ordered Qardāḥī to teach these to his troupe.[182] The troupe performed for two nights—once for the ladies of the harem and once for the male guests.[183] In his 1898 petition to entertain the German Emperor—quoted at the beginning of this chapter—Qardāḥī referred to this event.[184]

In 1899 Qardāḥī established a new troupe with his old companion, and possibly family-relation, Sulaymān Ḥaddād. They may have performed again in Paris in 1900. In this year, his theater in Alexandria was closed, and Qardāḥī petitioned Lord Cromer for help in gaining a lot or a building in Azbakiyya as a compensation or, if it is not possible, the Garden Theatre itself, or financial compensation.[185] No reply to this petition has survived. He toured the countryside with two Egyptian comedians, the famous mimic Aḥmad al-Fār and Muḥammad Najī in 1906–1907.[186] Qardāḥī's last enterprise was a tour in North Africa in 1908–1909, in the years of the Young Turk revolution. It is said that this adventure was intended as the first phase of an international tour in Europe and Latin America,[187] but he died in Tunisia at the beginning of May 1909.[188] To

[178] Ibid.

[179] *Annuaire des artistes*, 782.

[180] Najm, *al-Masraḥiyya*, 111.

[181] Ibid.

[182] *Al-Ahrām*, 2 February 1895, 4.

[183] *Al-Ahrām*, 25 January 1895, 2.

[184] Petition, by Sulaymān Qardāḥī, transmission date 20 September 1898, 4003-037914, DWQ.

[185] Landau, *Studies*, 69; Undated letter from Soliman Cardahi to Lord Cromer (on the margins: 1900), FO 141/357, NA.

[186] Fahmy, *Ordinary Egyptians*, 69.

[187] Halima, *Un demi-siècle*, 39, footnote 4, without source.

[188] Halima, *Un demi-siècle*, 41–44. Charfeddine published the necrology in *Deux siècles de théâtre*. Qardāḥī arrived in Tunis in November 1908, following another Egyptian theater group, the group of ʿAbd al-Qādir al-Miṣrī, Halima, *Un demi-siècle*, 35. See Halima's footnotes about the confusion of his name. Charfeddine, *Deux siècles de théâtre en Tunisie*,

this day Tunisians regard him as the father of Arabic theater in their country.[189] A relative (who wrote his name as A. Kordahi) owned the Zizinia Theater during World War One. In Egyptian cultural memory, Sulaymān Qardāḥī was ironically portrayed by the writer Tawfīq al-Ḥakīm as having a heavy *shāmī* accent and preferring artificial movements on stage; and being very stingy with his actors.[190]

A Last Word on the Memory of ʿUrābī: The Murderers of Egypt

Having traced the reparation of the khedive's image in history and in theater, weaving together Ḥijāzī and Qardāḥī's stories with political and economic history, it is appropriate to finish this chapter by noting, nonetheless, that such a memory politics was never fully accepted, nor did it manage to truly transform the popular perception of 1882. It was far from easy to forget ʿUrābī and the revolution in the 1890s when the main figures returned in Egypt. ʿAbd Allāh Nadīm, "the orator of the revolution" was discovered in 1891 (he was disguised in dervish clothes in a village), and, after a brief exile,[191] he was pardoned in 1892, and returned to Egypt. Muḥammad ʿAbduh, as we have seen, was also pardoned, and became the Grand Mufti of Egypt in 1899. Even ʿUrābī's return was discussed time to time.

One evening in early April 1900, during an Arabic play in the private "New Theatre" (*al-Masraḥ al-Jadīd*) in Cairo, the audience started to whistle and shout at each other and the actors. At first the troupe of Abū Khalīl al-Qabbānī continued the performance. But soon chairs were thrown, and members of the audience began fighting. The police closed down the theater and arrested one individual. The audience's animation could be easily explained. Even the title of the performed work—*Maqātil Miṣr—Aḥmad Bāshā ʿUrābī*—was controversial; the vocalization *maqātil Miṣr* means "the murderers of Egypt" while *muqātil Miṣr* is "the warrior of Egypt." The plot concerned the ʿUrābī revolution, especially the events of Alexandria in July 1882. The play was written in 1897 by a certain

242–244. Some Tunisian journals commented on his arrival as if the troupe had been recommended to the Bey of Tunis by the khedive, but the Egyptian journals rejected this. Halima, *Un demi-siècle*, 40, footnote 2. In January-February 1909 his troupe performed in Tunis, Bizerte, and Kairouan. Qardāḥī stopped in Tunis in order to prepare for a tour in Algeria. He was decorated by the Bey of Tunis. Najm, *al-Masraḥiyya*, 112; Halima, *Un demi-siècle*, 44.

189 Halima, *Un demi-siècle*, 44; Charfeddine, *Deux siècles de théâtre en Tunisie*, 239.

190 Al-Ḥakīm, *Min Dhikriyyāt*, 29–31.

191 Shārūbīm, *al-Kāfī*, 4:591.

Muḥammad al-ʿIyyādī in Alexandria who also paid for its printing, and, awaiting success, secured the rights to its performance as well. At the beginning of the play, the allegory of Egypt, a female character (note that ʿAbd Allāh Nadīm's *Waṭan* was a male character), talks to Tevfik, assuring him of his right to rule her. Egypt calls him *ʿazīzī*, a pun on the familiar title *ʿAzīz Miṣr* "the Mighty One," thus transforming it into "my dear." In the crucial scene before the British bombardment, the khedive—or, here, the male "partner" of a female Egypt[192]—clarifies the situation to one courtier: "your lord does not want to leave, your lord is not afraid, your lord only uses fair means, and your lord did not stir the rebels."[193]

This was a clear theatrical expression of the argument about ʿUrābī's treason as the cornerstone of khedivial authority. By this time, ʿUrābī's bad reputation seems to have been established among patriotic intellectuals.[194] Yet the fight that broke out in the theater suggests that the narrative was not accepted among larger circles of ordinary Egyptians or that, at the very least, the population was polarized. Two short reports were published in the journals *al-Ahrām* and *al-Muqaṭṭam*, and al-Qabbānī's troupe hastily left Cairo.[195] The play continued to be staged and supported by the authorities, and it continued to cause controversy in subsequent years.[196] In the following year, 1901, the scene was set for an even bigger clash about the meaning of Mehmed Ali's reign and the ʿUrābī revolution in national memory when the broken Aḥmad ʿUrābī in fact returned in Cairo.[197]

Conclusion: Audience and Nation

After 1882, the Ottoman Empire became important in the Arabic public sphere while an attempt was made to repair Tevfik's image through patriotic ideology. Crucially, this activity occurred in a very different constellation of power from the gentle revolution between 1866 and 1873. Tevfik had no absolute power, the khedivate was under occupation, and an independent legal system had emerged under British control. It is,

[192] For the gendering of Egypt see Baron, *Egypt as a Woman.*

[193] Al-ʿIyyādī, *Riwāyat Maqātil Miṣr*, 53.

[194] Di Capua, *Gatekeepers*, 35. Omar, "'And I Saw No Reason," 300.

[195] *Al-Ahrām*, 11 April 1900, 2. There was no news about this event in *al-Muʾayyad*, *al-Ittiḥād al-Miṣrī*, or *al-Liwāʾ*. For al-Qabbāni's leave see *al-Liwāʾ*, 9 April 1900, 3. Also, Najm, *Al-Shaykh Aḥmad Abū al-Qabbānī*, 410, and for *al-Muqaṭṭam*'s article (12 April 1900) see ʿAwaḍ, *Ittijāhāt Siyāsiyya*, 17.

[196] Ramsīs ʿAwaḍ hypothesizes that there was another play or plays entitled *ʿUrābī Bāshā*, which was composed with the opposite intention. ʿAwaḍ, *Ittijāhāt Siyāsiyya*, 19–20.

[197] Di Capua, *Gatekeepers*, 32.

thus, not entirely clear whether the renewed production of (Ottoman) Arab patriotism truly occurred in order to restage the khedive as a symbol of sovereignty, or whether the old elite simply used the khedive's name to mobilize the public against the threat of losing their own privileges to increased colonial control. The point, however, is that patriotism again took on the work of achieving an uncodified compromise between elites and the khedive.

During this period the full-fledged practice of civic patriotism in Arabic was firmly established. The two collectivities of audience (a physical experience) and nation (an imagined community) began to overlap. The understanding of the audience as a closed and private group in the Muslim entertainment tradition (for instance, when a Sufi *munshid* sang for the brethren of his *ṭarīqa,* or singers at wedding parties)[198] transmuted into the understanding of the audience as a public community. Ultimately, the audience stood for the collective of the homeland; sometimes simply expressed as "the people of the East." The cooperation of Egyptian singers with Syrian actors and writers was decisive in the popularization of Arabic musical theater; the patriotism they expressed often appealed not so much to territorial unity but to a higher idea of Arab solidarity in Ottoman colors to gain imagined sovereignty against the British.

As for the cultural spaces, in particular the symbolic Khedivial Opera House, foreign impresarios were contracted for the winter seasons with subsidies, and Arab impresarios, Qardāḥī in particular, performed during the spring without subsidies. This system granted the same space to foreigners and Arabic-speakers, but not with the same conditions. Who decided such conditions, and how was Arabic entertainment perceived in the state administration? What was going on behind the scenes of all these displays of patriotism in Arabic theater?

[198] Waugh, *The Munshidīn* of Egypt, 10, 37–38.

CHAPTER 7

Behind the Scenes: A Committee and the Law, 1880s–1900s

On 25 January 1885 the impresario Abū Khalīl al-Qabbānī and the singer ʿAbduh al-Ḥamūlī received a letter in Arabic. They had been performing together in the Khedivial Opera House, having had access to the building for around a month. The short note informed them that their troupe's behavior was unacceptable, because they were making coffee using small lamps while the performances took place on stage. In addition, they smoked in the theater, posing a great threat to the wooden building. They were warned if this happened one more time, the Opera House would be closed, and they would lose the concession. The letter was signed by the *Comité des Théâtres du Khedive* (the Committee of Khedivial Theatres).[1]

This chapter surveys the legal background of theatres in late Ottoman Egypt. I start with a microhistory of the Comité des Théâtres. Its administrative history highlights the work of the colonial government and the limited way the khedives' wishes were accepted in the Opera House. Next, I focus on private theaters and their legal environment. How were theaters legal in a predominantly Muslim land? This question takes us outside of government-funded culture and provides insight into the evolving concept of *public space*, including a look at censorship. I explore the way non-Islamic and Islamic norms of public morals were articulated. The institutions surveyed here can be also regarded as the predecessors of both the interwar monarchical propaganda and the post-1952 Ministry of National Guidance, today's Ministry of Culture.

[1] Letter dated 25 January 1885, Comité des Théâtres to ʿAbduh Afandī al-Ḥamūlī and al-Shaykh Aḥmad Abū Khalīl; and letter dated 24 January 1885, Félix Thome to Léopold Larose, both in 4003–022541, DWQ. For the permission, cf. note dated 24 December 1884, MTP to Conseil des Ministres, Maḥfaẓa 2/1, Niẓārat al-Ashghāl al-ʿUmūmiyya, CMW, DWQ.

The Comité des Théâtres

Between 1881 and 1900, an interministerial unit, called *Le Comité des Théâtres du Khédive* (in Arabic *Lajnat al-Tiyātrāt al-Khidīwiyya*, in French sometimes misleadingly called *Comité des Théâtres au Caire*), supervised the Opera House, the Comédie, and the Azbakiyya Garden Theatre. It was operated by the two key British-controlled units: the Finance and the Public Works Ministries. It had no authority over private or municipal theaters in Cairo or elsewhere. It was not related to the police or to the Interior Ministry. Like the cultural system directed by Paul Draneht (see chapter 3), the Comité was concerned with official representation. Financial supervision was their source of power. The purpose was to maintain and guard the government's most symbolic space, the Opera House, and to provide entertainment for the colonial and Ottoman Egyptian elite.

The Transfer to the Ministry of Public Works

The conditions for government supervision arose from transforming a khedivial asset into a government one. We left the administrative history of the khedivial theaters when Draneht's administration dissolved around December 1878. As early as April 1877, his post had been abolished at the Cairo Governorate (his salary was now paid from the civil list of the khedivial entourage).[2] At first, the responsibility for the staff and their salaries passed temporarily to the Cairo City Public Works (*Tanẓīm*), headed by Pierre Grand.

This unit soon became a part of the Ministry of Public Works.[3] In the background was the activity of French and British controlers who aimed at the centralization of control over government expenditure to regulate the Egyptian floating debt.[4] The parallel structure of *dāʾira* (dynastic estates) and government expenditure had to be abolished in order to gain full control over the Egyptian economy in order to pay the debt; and this meant the transfer of many assets considered "khedivial" to the government budget. Although legally the maintenance of the khedivial theaters were transferred already to the Cairo Governorate in 1870,[5] when the structure of the new Ministry of Public Works was created in

[2] Letter dated 18 Dhū al-Ḥijja 1297 (21 November 1880), from Māliyya to Ḍabṭiyyat Miṣr, and Kashf min Jarāʾid Istiḥqāqāt al-Maʿiyya al-Saniyya ʿanhu bi-Ism Saʿādat Dranīt Bāshā, undated, Dūsiya 7085, Maḥfaẓa 275, ʿAyn 1, Dūlāb 13, DM.

[3] Letter dated 7 January 1879, Directeur de l'administration de la Voirie to MTP, 4003–037847, DWQ.

[4] Owen, *The Middle East in the World Economy*, 130–132.

[5] Letter dated 18 Ṣafar 1287 (20 May 1870) to Umur-i Hassa, qayd 583, p. 40, microfilm 99, MST, DWQ.

December 1878 they became the responsibility of its General Administrative Department (together with the railways and the Egyptian Museum [*Antīqkhāna*]).[6] This move made the buildings government property.

It seems to have been decided that not only should the government take over the buildings but that the Khedivial Opera House, at least, should also receive a yearly subsidy, in addition to the cost of maintenance. This decision accounts for the character of the Ministry of Public Works as a pseudo–cultural ministry, perhaps reflecting the preferences of Ernest-Gabriel de Blignières (1834–1900), the minister of public works, or ʿAlī Mubārak who was a superminister in charge of Education and Religious Endowments, perhaps nominally also minister of public works[7] in the government headed by Nubar (until April 1879).

The budget (subsidy and maintenance) of the theaters within the ministry represented an obscure niche. From 1887, the gas and the water supply to the Opera House were taken care of by a subdivision called the Office of the State Buildings (*Qalam al-Mabānī al-Mīriyya*, Bâtiments de l'État).[8] In 1891, the Opera was classified under the "General Direction of Cities and Buildings" as a subsection.[9] From 1898 to 1905 and possibly later, the subsidy and salaries of the staff (between 5,300 and 7,300 LE yearly) and the cost of maintenance (steadily growing from around 500 LE to 1,700 LE yearly) were paid from the budget of the Central Office of the Public Works Ministry.[10] It was only in the interwar period that government subsidies were given to some privately owned Egyptian theaters, while the Opera House kept its central role in the official culture of the monarchy. The Ministry of National Guidance (established November 1952)—later National Guidance and Culture—continued the maintenance and supervision of these and other theaters along ideological lines.[11] In sum, the foreign control of official culture was a consequence of debt management and became normalized as the everyday work of the newly created, occupied state structure.

The Making of a Committee

The origin of the body that managed the khedivial theaters in the 1880s and 1890s is difficult to understand. In 1879 Grand wanted to get rid

[6] Amr ʿĀlī dated 31 December 1878 in Jallād, *al-Qāmūs al-ʿĀmm*, 1:97.

[7] Rizq, Taʾrīkh *al-Wizārāt al-Miṣriyya*, 57; *Taʾrīkh Ḥayāt al-Maghfūr lahu ʿAlī Mubārak*, 45–46.

[8] Letter dated 13 December 1887, to M. Legros (Ingénieur en chef en Service de la Ville), 4003–036990, DWQ.

[9] AE (1891–1892), 48.

[10] See W. E. Garstin's reports between 1898 and 1905, published in Cairo by the National Printing Office (cf. bibliography).

[11] Nasīra, *Wizārat al-Thaqāfa*, 14–15.

of the additional burden of setting the theater employees' salaries. In the political crisis of the summer of 1879 (when Ismail was forced to abdicate and Tevfik became khedive), ʿAlī Mubārak remained Minister of Public Works, under Prime Minister Mustafa Riyaz, and continued to influence cultural matters from the autumn of 1879 until September 1881.[12] It was during his tenure, when the economy was still invisibly overseen by Evelyn Baring (later Lord Cromer) and de Blignières,[13] that a committee called in French the *Comité du Théâtre* (in the singular!)—also referred to as the *Comité de l'Opéra*—was created within the Finance Ministry in December 1880.[14] It appears to have been a short-lived entity, meeting only a few times to decide the amount allocated for the maintenance and staff of the Opera House. The members were Gerald Fitzgerald, director general of Public Accounts at the Ministry of Finance[15] and Jules-Ferdinand Gay-Lussac, the later director of the state company *al-Dāʾira al-Saniyya*.[16] They represent the British-French dual control at the time. But they were not the only ones who worried about the theaters' finance; in fact, Khedive Tevfik also ordered an investigation into the budget in 1880.[17]

The committee finally took the title *Le Comité des Théâtres du Khédive* when two other members joined them in the spring of 1881. A perhaps more apt title was the original one, *Comité théâtral de surveillance* (Theatre Oversight Committee).[18] Their legal existence was established by a short note from Prime Minister Riyaz.[19] The 1881 government budget provided a total of 121,520 LE for the khedivial theaters, covering salaries, maintenance, and some extra costs.[20] This committee was responsible only for the government theaters (though, for instance, in 1896 incorporating the Zizinia Theatre in Alexandria within the committee's purview was considered[21]).

[12] Rizq, *Taʾrīkh al-Wizārāt*, 73–85.

[13] Owen, *Lord Cromer*, 124–126.

[14] Memorandum dated 23 December 1881, Comité des Théâtres to MTP, and letter dated 27 December 1881, FitzGerald (Comité des Théâtres) to Ismail Pacha Ayoub, 4003–037847, DWQ.

[15] Hourani, "The Middleman in a Changing Society," 116.

[16] AE (1891–92), 53.

[17] Letter dated 11 May 1880, Goudaire in the name of the khedive to Riyaz Pacha, Maḥfaẓa 2/1, Niẓārat al-Ashghāl al-ʿUmūmiyya, CMW, DWQ.

[18] Cf. Guy-Lussac's appointment letter, dated 18 May 1881, mentioned in Catherina and Bourdillaud, eds. Fonds Gay-Lussac, under number 36 J 24.

[19] Letter dated 12 May 1881, Riaz Pasha to Ministre des Travaux publiés [*sic*], Maḥfaẓa 2/1, Niẓārat al-Ashghāl al-ʿUmūmiyya, CMW, DWQ.

[20] Letter dated 1 July 1881, signed d'Ornstein, Gay-Lussac; 4003–037847, DWQ.

[21] *La Réforme (L'Égypte)*, 23 February 1896, 2.

The Members of the Comité: Ornstein

In 1881, the Comité des Théâtres consisted of four members: Gay-Lussac, Fitzgerald, Ornstein, and possibly Grand.[22] They were not really known to the public, though sometimes their names were published, even outside Egypt.[23] Ornstein in the next decade or so, would sign most of the letters in the name of the committee, usually only as "[D']Ornstein" (twice in 1886 he was addressed as the "president of the Committee of Theatres").[24] Therefore it is important to have a look at the background of this man who decided over the use of the representative space of the khedivate.

John (Jean) Maurice Isidor Ornstein was born in post-Ottoman Iași (Jassy, in Romania) in 1852. His father was Austrian (or Austro-Hungarian), and his mother Russian, very possibly of a Jewish family. He studied in Dresden, then in England. Upon his father's death the young Ornstein returned to Bucharest in 1874 and became the private secretary of Sir Hussey Crespigny Vivian (1834–1893), a British diplomat. Vivian was next appointed British Consul General in Egypt in 1876; Ornstein accompanied him. In 1878, Vivian helped Ornstein to gain British citizenship.[25] For unclear reasons, Ornstein remained in Egypt when Vivian was appointed to his next post in Switzerland in 1879.[26] Ornstein became the secretary of the Egyptian Control (of the British Occupation) in September 1882.[27] In August 1882, after the occupation, a British general described a certain d'Ornstein, a "private secretary," who spoke English well, among the "lazy court officials" of Khedive Tevfik. He thought that d'Ornstein was a Hungarian Jew from Budapest. The khedive said that Ornstein knew Egypt well.[28] For his services, Ornstein was subsequently

[22] For instance, cf. letter dated 9 April 1881, Khalīl Linant (ʿAlī Mubārak) to Fitzgerald, 0075–033141, DWQ; cf. also Sadgrove, *Egyptian Theatre*, 151.

[23] *Al-Jinān*, 15 June 1881, 359.

[24] Letter dated 26 February 1886, Santi-Boni to J. D'Ornstein (Président du Comité des Théâtres au Caire), 4003–037912, DWQ. Also letter dated 29 November 1886, Ministre des Finances, Note pour M. Ornstein (Président du Comité des Théâtres), in Dūsiya 24653, Maḥfaẓa 1020, ʿAyn 1, Dūlāb 50, Milaffāt Khidma, DM.

[25] See the correspondence, including the letter of Ornstein to Vivian, dated 5 October 1878 and support letter of Vivian dated 28 October 1878, HO 45/9469/78581, A2748 (naturalization issued 4 November 1878), NA.

[26] The private letters of Vivian do not provide any hint. GB165–0294, Vivian, MECA. Ornstein was not part of the Austro-Hungarian community in Egypt. His name does not figure in Agstner, *Die österreichisch-ungarische Kolonie in Kairo*, nor Komár, "Az Osztrák-Magyar Monarchia."

[27] *London Gazette*, 29 September 1882, 1.

[28] Vetch, *Life, Letter, and Diaries*, 226–227. It is possible that this British general mixed up names, and he met Julius Blum (1843–1919), an Austro-Hungarian Jew who was indeed born in Budapest. Ronall, "Julius Blum Pasha (1843–1919)," 101.

knighted by the queen, and granted the Ottoman Mecidiye Order two times by the khedive. Finally, Ornstein moved to Alexandria possibly in 1889,[29] where in 1891 he worked as the sub-director-general of the Egyptian Customs.[30]

Ornstein's membership and the existence of the committee before and after the summer of 1882 indicates that the British military occupation formalized a system already in place. His example shows that the khedivial theaters were supervised by men with little to no attachment to Arabic or Egyptian culture.

Later, other members joined the Committee. In 1888, for instance, it was composed of Ornstein, Tigrane, Keller, Barois;[31] in 1889 Ornstein, Blum, Barois, Figari;[32] in 1890 they even had a subcommittee whose task was to lobby for the introduction of electricity in the Opera (composed of Blum [who very soon after left Egypt], Ferrnich, Bisch, Grand, and the new superintendent Pasquale Clemente; see below).[33] In 1892 the body included Barois, Le Chevalier, Elwin Palmer, Boghos Nubar, Henry Settle;[34] in 1893 Palmer signed letters; in 1896, Palmer still was a member.[35] The engineer Julien Barois (1849–1937) was secretary general in the Ministry of Public Works; later he was appointed the director of the Egyptian Railways. Elwin Palmer (1852–1906) served as the Financial Adviser of the Khedive between 1889–1898, oversaw the conversion of the public debt, and finally became the first president of the National Bank of Egypt.[36] Some of these men, like Barois, served on other state artistic committees too.[37]

Most members of the Comité des Théâtres resigned in 1900. The Ministry then suggested to the government that there was no need for a committee; instead, it was enough to continue financial supervision with one delegate from the Ministry of Public Works and one from the Finance

[29] Letter dated 11 December 1889, Scott Moncrieff to President Conseil des Ministres, 0075–034491, DWQ.

[30] AE (1891–92), 160; cf. *London Gazette*, 20 May 1880; 28 April 1891.

[31] Undated letter (for 1888–1889), concerning the request of Santini, about the reduction of the rent of the Azbakiyya Garden Theatre, signed by Tigrane, Keller, Ornstein, Barois. Maḥfaẓa 2/1, Niẓārat al-Ashghāl al-ʿUmūmiyya, CMW, DWQ.

[32] Letter dated 20 March 1889, "Copie d'une lettre adressée par les délégues du Gouvernement du Théâtre de l'Opéra à Son Excellence le Ministre des Travaux Publics," 4003–022543, DWQ.

[33] Letter dated 4 September 1890, Muhammed Zeki to Conseil des Ministres, Maḥfaẓa 2/1, Niẓārat al-Ashghāl al-ʿUmūmiyya, CMW, DWQ.

[34] Letter dated 7 May 1892, Comité des Théâtres to ?, Maḥfaẓa 2/1, Niẓārat al-Ashghāl al-ʿUmūmiyya, CMW, DWQ.

[35] Amonasro, "La question des théâtres," *La Réforme* (*L'Égypte*), 1 March 1896, 6–7.

[36] Owen, *Lord Cromer*, 242, 247, etc.

[37] Ormos, *Max Herz Pasha*, 1:52, 90–91.

Ministry.[38] At this point, the Comité ceased to exist but control over the Opera House naturally continued since it remained a state institution.

Pension as a Sign of Hierarchy

At first, the payment of employees was the only responsibility of the Comité. They mediated between the Ministry of Finance and the staff of the theaters until 1884.[39] In addition, the Comité had to deal with any enquiries related to retirement pensions. The matter of a pension was the key administrative distinction between non-Egyptian and Egyptian employees, with the former receiving pensions and the latter not.

Sometimes the Comité or Ornstein showed favor towards the European employees. For instance, the costumier Elise Béroule, with whom we have already met, the employee who was longest in service (she entered service in 1869 and retired in 1904) was helped by the Comité. In 1886 the government abolished her post. Ornstein suggested to the Financial Committee and to Scott Moncrieff, the adviser of the Ministry of Public Works, that Béroule was in fact an *écrivain magasinier* and thus she should be included in the retirement scheme.[40] In contrast, none of the Egyptian *farrāshīn* were entitled to pensions. Although Shāhīn Shāhīn, the boss of the *farrāshīn*, asked for an increase in his salary, I could not locate any request for a pension from Egyptian employees to the Comité. Shāhīn was entitled to a pension later only because of his army service. The administrative classification of employees thus embodied a mixture of hierarchical notions of expertise, race, and class.

Fire and Electricity

A significant concern of the committee was the protection of the buildings. It is fair to say that the members were obsessed with the risk of fire, given the history of fires in Cairo, Istanbul, and European capitals. They also financed the repair of al-Azbakiyya Garden Theatre. In their twenty-some years of existence, an ocean of official letters addressed to the Finance Ministry, the police, and the Council of Ministers dealt with such issues. As early as 1881 Ornstein sent a request, following a fire at the Ring Theatre in Vienna, for a secure system of oil lighting to be installed in the Opera building.[41]

[38] Note dated 26 November 1900, ? to Conseil des Ministres, 0075–033188, DWQ.

[39] Various letters in 4003–036765, DWQ.

[40] Compiled from the pension dossier of al-Sitt Farnand Brul, Dūsiya 22517, Maḥfaẓa 863, ʿAyn 3, Dūlāb 43, Milaffāt Khidma, DM, especially letter dated 31 December 1887, Ornstein to Abdarrahman Pasha Rouchdy, MTP.

[41] French letter dated 23 December 1881, les Membres du Comité des Théâtres (Ornstein) to MTP, Maḥfaẓa 2/1, Niẓārat al-Ashghāl al-ʿUmūmiyya, CMW, DWQ.

The Opera was a prominent location in the electrification of Cairo. A particular concern, as early as 1887, was the introduction of electricity in the building.[42] In an 1890 letter, the Comité (Keller) argued that electric lighting was safer than gas lighting, which had caused fires; they had already requested tenders.[43] Soon a separate subcommittee to "reduce the risk of fire in the Opera House" was set up.[44] Electricity was finally installed in 1894–1895.[45]

Decision Making

It was the Comité rather than the minister that decided which theater group or charitable society should have access to the Opera House, and who could receive financial support in addition to the free concession. The Comité's administrative decisions provide a window onto the logic of bureaucrats who are not citizens of the country where they are employed.

The usual administrative process was as follows. An artist, impresario, or private society would petition the Ministry of Public Works or the Cabinet of the Khedive with a request for the concession of a given period in the Opera House or the Comédie. The letter would almost automatically be transferred to the Comité and, if it was in Arabic, it would be translated into French. The Comité would either agree or not (quite explicitly accepting or rejecting the proposal). If the case was not easy to decide, the Comité would ask for the opinion of other ministries or the Council of Ministers. They would then make a "recommendation" to the minister of public works, who would sign off on it. Finally, the decision would be communicated to the applicant by the ministry. In the case of agreement, a contract was signed between the minister, representing the government (the owner of the Khedivial Opera House), and the impresario. Often a clause was included mentioning that the impresario was responsible to the Comité des Théâtres.[46] In the case of rejection, there was no further authority to which an applicant could appeal.

How did the Egyptian ministers react to this system? When in spring 1882 the minister of public works in the Bārūdī-government, Maḥmūd Fahmī, agreed to help Qardāḥī's Arab Opera as we have seen, by this small decision he overstepped the mark. But the Comité, possibly due

[42] Note dated 8 October 1887, Scott Moncrieff to Conseil des Ministres, 4003–036990, DWQ.

[43] Letter dated 18 May 1890, Comité des Théatres to MTP. Maḥfaẓa 2/1, Niẓārat al-Ashghāl, CMW, DWQ. See also similar requests in 0075–033144, DWQ.

[44] Note dated 4 September 1890, Muhammed Zekil, MTP, to Conseil des Ministres, Maḥfaẓa 2/1, Niẓārat al-Ashghāl al-ʿUmūmiyya, CMW, DWQ.

[45] Letter dated 5 September 1894, MTP to President, Conseil des Ministres. Maḥfaẓa 2/1, Niẓārat al-Ashghāl al-ʿUmūmiyya, CMW, DWQ.

[46] For instance, contract dated 3 March 1888, 4003–036990, DWQ.

to the patriotic atmosphere, did not oppose the ministerial decision.[47] The postoccupational ministers understood the power hierarchy or at least I have not found documents suggesting any major disagreement. Ministers ʿAlī Mubārak (1882–1884), ʿAbd al-Raḥmān Rushdī (1884–1888), Mehmed Zaki (1888–1894), Ḥusayn Fakhrī (1894–1895), Aḥmad Maẓlūm (1895–1907), Ismāʿīl Sirrī (1908–1917) had little to say about the concession of the Opera House or financial help for visiting impresarios. The most they did, especially Minister Rushdī, was giving recommendations to the Comité.

A New Superintendent and Regulation

After Draneht's system was abolished, no one was given the title "superintendent." Though Léopold Larose took care of the everyday matters (from 1878), his official title remained keeper of costumes (*Conservateur du Matériel*). Larose was granted the concessions for the full seasons between 1880 and 1883 and became an impresario himself. Like Draneht, he brought companies from Italy and France to perform in Cairo but only with limited authority, on a one-term contract and budget. After 1883, Larose only carried out his everyday tasks as the keeper of costumes. In 1885, he again submitted a plan for the concession but was turned down,[48] and in January 1887 he retired.[49] His activity is not known to have included censorship.

The superintendence was re-established in the winter of 1886, partly as a reaction to Larose's planned retirement. Other factors were a steady rise of applications from impresarios, the bankruptcy of two inglorious Italian impresarios in December 1886 (Santi Boni and Soschino), and the establishment of the state pension scheme. This latter transformation also regulated the status of the theater employees. From now on, their salaries were paid directly from the yearly budget of the ministry. Since the Comédie was about to be demolished and the Azbakiyya Theatre was on a permanent lease, the regulation only affected the personnel of the Opera House. The Comité included the post of the superintendent in the new pension scheme.[50]

They put forward Pasquale Clemente (1842–191?) for the post of superintendent. He was an Italian pianist from Naples and possibly a music

[47] Letter dated 30 March 1882, Guy Lussac (Comité des Théâtres) to MTP, 4003–037847, DWQ.

[48] Letter dated 9 April 1885, Larose to Rouchdy, 4003–037911, DWQ.

[49] Note au Conseil des Ministres, dated ? December 1886, 4003–037911, DWQ.

[50] Letter dated 15 December 1886, MTP (Rouchdy [Rushdī]) to Cons. des Min. Maḥfaẓa 2/1, Niẓārat al-Ashghāl al-ʿUmūmiyya, CMW, DWQ.

teacher.[51] He had already been awarded the Mecidiye medal and was a *chevalier de la couronne d'Italie*.[52] There is no information about why he was given these decorations or why the Comité chose him. Clemente was designated as superintendent of the Khedivial Theatres in November 1886 on a temporary basis and appointed officially on 19 January 1887. His accountant was Victor Bellour,[53] who had already worked with Larose, and with whom the Comité had been very satisfied. Clemente's post represented continuity with Draneht's system: it was again called the *Administration des théâtres du khédive d'Égypte*.[54] His first job was to supervise the transmission of materials from the Comédie during 1886–1887. The Comédie, once seen as the most convenient space for Arab theater, was to be demolished due to the damage inflicted by the horses of the British army.

A (rather belated) ministerial decree stated that the Comité's responsibilities in 1887 covered: 1. any requests concerning the concession or the budget decided by the accountant for the theaters; 2. any requests concerning the appointment and retirement of the staff; 3. issuing regulations for the administration of the theaters; 4. any request and contract of concessions and the submission of these to the minister; 5. any one-off requests such as those from charitable societies; and 6. the formulation of terms of contracts either for a theatrical season or for a ball or any other such event.[55] Accordingly, the Comité drew up a new rule concerning the concession of the khedivial theaters. It contained six points, the most important of which was the request of a deposit from the candidates for the concession.[56] For example, Ottoman Armenian impresarios paid a deposit of 1,100 francs (around 50 LE) in 1888 for a guest season.[57] Arab impresarios, who rarely had capital, were certainly disadvantaged by this requirement.

Importantly, the regularized salary and pension system, and the new superintendent made the existence of the Comité *unnecessary* from an

[51] Sessa, *Il melodramma italiano*, 121. Clemente was hired first instead of the aging Larose, as a keeper of costumes. *Al-Ahrām*, 11 November 1886, 2. For his birth date, certificate dated 1 September 1909 of the Italian Consulate in Cairo, Dūsiya 24653, Maḥfaẓa 1020, ʿAyn 1, Dūlāb 50, Milaffāt Khidma, DM.

[52] Undated État de service (1887), Dūsiya 24653, Maḥfaẓa 1020, ʿAyn 1, Dūlāb 50, Milaffāt Khidma, DM.

[53] Attachment to letter dated 17 February 1887, Dūsiya 24653, Maḥfaẓa 1020, ʿAyn 1, Dūlāb 50, Milaffāt Khidma, DM.

[54] Letter with printed letterhead, dated 10 November 1887, from Clemente to Inspecteur du Tanzim, 4003–036990, DWQ.

[55] Jallād, *al-Qāmūs al-ʿĀmm*, 1:527.

[56] "Ikhtiṣāṣāt Lajnat al-Tiyātrāt al-Khidīwiyya," *al-Qāhira al-Ḥurra*, 7 June 1887, 3.

[57] Letter dated 20 February 1888, Comité des Théâtres to Abdul Rahman Pacha Rouchdy, 4003–037874, DWQ. They did pay this amount as evidenced by letter dated 22 May 1888, to Direction Générale du Tanzim, 4003–036990, DWQ.

administrative point of view from 1886. Their continuation for fourteen more years until 1900 can be only explained by a distrust in the system, the lack of a cultural ministry, and the personal interest of the highest financial officers of the occupation.

The Global Entertainment Market and the Staff of the Opera House

Clemente with his expertise in Italian music represented a manager of elite culture in occupied Egypt. He maintained a convenient schedule much like that of a colonial officer. During his summer vacations, he collected troupes from France and Italy. For instance, he went for an official summer trip in 1890 in Italy,[58] and during this time the well-known impresarios Victor Ulman and Octave Dupont were contracted, who then brought a troupe (received government subsidy of 100,000 francs for the season of 1890–1891).[59] In December of the same year, Clemente went to Paris to contract the next impresario.[60] When he was away, Bellour took charge of affairs. After the abolition of the Comité in 1900, Pasquale Clemente remained the superintendent (often called director) of the Opera House until 1911, accompanied by his faithful accountant, Bellour (who retired in 1913).[61] In 1911 Albert Baroche, a French theater-director, was appointed as the director of the Opera. Clemente's twenty-three years in office reconnected Cairo to the French and Italian cultural markets and made the global circulation of opera possible again.

Unlike Draneht, Clemente was a state employee, not a khedivial courtier. He had no authority over the budget and mostly acted as an executive. He does not seem to have received the title bey or pasha. Nevertheless, Clemente also knew the khedives personally, at least Abbas Hilmi II, who in September 1894 summoned him to Milan to give a report about his work[62] and remained in contact with him afterwards. By 1904, Clemente's personnel of the Opera House included eighteen individuals as shown in table 7.1.

[58] Letter dated 4 May 1890 in the pension dossier of Pasquale Clemente, Dūsiya 24653, Maḥfaẓa 1020, ʿAyn 1, Dūlāb 50, Milaffāt Khidma, DM.

[59] *L'Art Musical*, 15 June 1890, 94 and 31 July 1890, 110.

[60] Letter dated 6 December 1890, MTP to President (Conseil des Ministres), Maḥfaẓa 2/1, Niẓārat al-Ashghāl al-ʿUmūmiyya, Majlis al-Wuzarāʾ, DWQ (old system).

[61] Though Clemente was required to retire in 1908 because he had reached the age of sixty-five, an extension was granted. Letters dated 15 March 1911, and 24 March 1908, Dūsiya 24653, Maḥfaẓa 1020, ʿAyn 1, Dūlāb 50, Milaffāt Khidma, DM. As to Bellour's retirement, cf. letter dated 31 March 1913, ? to Néghib Bey Courgi, Secrétaire du Comité des Finances, 4003–023154, DWQ.

[62] Letter dated 20 September 1894, A. Rouilly to Clemente, Dūsiya 24653, Maḥfaẓa 1020, ʿAyn 1, Dūlāb 50, Milaffāt Khidma, DM.

TABLE 7.1. État nominatif du personnel de l'Opéra pour le mois de janvier 1904, dated 25 January 1904

Noms	*Fonctions*	*Appoint. LE M*	*Total LE M*
Personnel classé (Chap. 5—Art. I):			
Clemente Pasquale	Intendant	58.333	
Bellour Victor	Sécrétaire—comptable	22	80.333
Art. II: Magasins et accessoirs:			
Bruno Fortunato	Magasinier	9	
Furmat Adrien	Taillet—Cons.	9	
Talamos Elena	Ouvrière	4.100	
Coussa Adèle	Ouvrière	4.100	
Francestini Léontine	Ouvrière	4.100	
Mille Césarine	Ouvrière	4.100	
Isard Arnaud	Ouvrière	4.100	38.500
Art. 3. Agents hors cadres:			
Mansour Ghanem	Moaven	12	
Granato Alphons	Moulahiz	8	
Ahmed el-Komy	Farrach	2.700	
Mahmoud Ahmed	Farrach	2.700	
Mohamed Aly	Farrach	1.980	
Abdalla Saïd	Farrach	1.980	
Ahmed Aly	Farrach	1.800	
Mohamed Aly	Gaffir	1.950	
Hassan Moussa	Gaffir	1.950	

Source: Pension file of Alphonso Granato, Dūsiya 24774, Maḥfaẓa 1030, ʿAyn 3, Dūlāb 50, DM. Original orthography.

The mini-security system of the opera reflects the history of control in khedivial Egypt. The *farrāsh* Aḥmad al-Kūmī, the employee with the longest record of service (he looked after the Opera House for more than twenty-six years), earned 150 piasters monthly, while Larose earned 3,210 piasters, twenty times as much in the early 1880s.[63] In 1904, as the table above shows, Clemente the director earned almost thirty times more than al-Kūmī the guard. It appears that al-Kūmī did not receive a pension (and so it is not known when he finally left his job). In contrast, the Italian *farrāsh*, Alfonso Granato (1849–19?), who arrived from the City Police, and was in charge of the keys of the Opera House from 1899, guarded the doors, and ensured that employees signed a sheet upon leaving, was awarded a pension upon retirement.[64] Granato also reported to the police.[65] In 1902 he was promoted to the position of *surveillant*, from which he retired in 1911. The cosmopolitan entertainment market in the opera was guarded by an equally cosmopolitan staff.

Privatisation? La Société Théâtrale et Artistique du Caire

The administrative nationalization of khedivial theaters occurred at a moment when wealthy Europeans and educated individuals could claim cultural authority. For instance, there was another committee of (private) theaters in the 1890s in Alexandria composed of Luigi Stagni, N. Abet, Mario Colucci, C. Penazzi, and Fred W. Simond. There was a plan to merge the two committees in 1896, which proved to be unnecessary.[66]

The Khedivial Opera House was also looked upon as a space that might be privately run. First, in 1888, the Council of Ministers wanted to abolish the subsidy of the visiting foreign troupes (yearly 3,500 LE). They suggested opening a public subscription and promised that the state would match the amount raised.[67] Nonetheless, there are examples of continued subsidies for the troupes in the subsequent years. Second, in 1897 *The Egyptian Theatrical Company* was established mostly by rich

[63] See Jarīdat Māhiyāt al-Antik-khāne [!] wa-Abū Qīr wa-l-Tiyātrū 1881, 4003–001063; Juz᾿ Thānī Istiḥqāqāt Ḥiraf al-Antīq-khāne [!] wa-l-Tiyātrāt bi-Dīwān al-Ashghāl 1882, 4003–001064; Juz᾿ Awwal Istiḥqāqāt al-Antīk-khāne [!] wa-l-Tiyātrū bi-Dīwān al-Ashghāl 1883, 4003–001065, DWQ.

[64] Letter dated 16 August 1911, MTP to l'Intendant des théâtres, Dūsiya 24774, Maḥfaẓa 1020, ʿAyn 2, Dūlāb 50, Milaffāt Khidma, DM.

[65] Cf. letter dated 23 October 1899, signed C. Caprara and D. I Chapman, Dossier 24774, Maḥfaẓa 1020, ʿAyn 2, Dūlāb 50, Milaffāt Khidma, DM.

[66] *La Réforme (L'Égypte),* 23 February and 1 March 1896, 6–7.

[67] Note dated 26 April 1888, 0075–006682, DWQ.

Greek and Austro-Hungarian citizens. In 1899, another company called the *Société Théatrale et Artistique du Caire* was established by seven rich men, the most well-known the bankers Moses Cattaoui (Qaṭṭāwī) and Raphael Suarès. This society came to life with the purpose of renting the Khedivial Opera House,[68] but there is no further information about the nature and future of this enterprise. It reflects the increasing capitalist spirit in the entertainment business.

Winter and Spring Seasons: Dividing Culture

Against this background, how could Sulaymān Qardāḥī have managed to be successful in the second half of the 1880s, as we saw in the previous chapter? We have seen that he was supported by the khedive. How did the incorporation of theaters into the colonial state inform dynastic interests?

The split between "European" (Italian and French) and Arabic elite culture was reflected in chronological terms in official public space. The schedule at the Opera consisted of a winter season from October to February, during which foreign troupes performed. This was then followed by approximately one month of performances in Arabic during the spring in the 1880s and early 1890s. The main difference between the two periods was that Arab impresarios typically did not receive any subsidy from the government, not even the complimentary gas for the lighting. The tension between Arab and non-Arab troupes was normalized into everyday bureaucratic processes.

The post-1882 Arab impresarios (al-Qabbānī, Qardāḥī, Khayyāṭ, Ḥaddād, later Ḥijāzī, Faraḥ, Abyaḍ) actually never submitted a request for a full season in the Opera. The longest season of Qardāḥī was approximately one and a half months. Even George Abyaḍ (1880–1959), the first "professional" Arab actor, trained in France, requested a maximum of two months in the Khedivial Opera House for his troupe in the years immediately before 1914. In the mid-1880s, contracts with an Italian or a French impresario often included the right of the ministry (the Comité) to arrange performances in Arabic and concerts at the Comédie (until 1887) or special evenings in the Opera. However, by the 1890s such clauses were missing from the contracts because the Comédie had been demolished and Clemente had taken over the daily business.

[68] Acte préliminaire à la constitution d'une Société Anonyme sous la dénomination de "Société Théâtrale et Artistique du Caire," dated 5 May 1899, 0075–008620, DWQ.

The Comité and the Khedive's Arab Impresarios

How did the Comité decide among proposals from the Arab impresarios? Let us look at the spring of 1885 when five proposals arrived for the concession of the Opera House. This moment is important because the decisions made established a pattern that was followed in the following years.

The five applicants were the Italian impresarios Santi Boni and Soschino; the returning Khayyāṭ; the returning Qardāḥī; Larose, the Keeper of Costumes; and finally another returning cultural entrepreneur, our old friend Seraphin Manasse from Istanbul. Since Manasse's proposal was forwarded by Nubar, prime minister at the time, Nubar's attention was also on the matter.[69] Nubar advised the Ministry of Public Works that no subsidy should be given, and expressed his preference that "the performance evenings should be equally distributed among the various Arab, European and Turkish troupes."[70] Despite Nubar's wish, Rushdī, the minister of public works transmitted the proposals to the Comité with a recommendation in favor of the Italians and Khayyāṭ only.[71] But the Comité refused Manasse, Larose, Qardāḥī, and even Khayyāṭ,[72] and decided to contract only Santi Boni and Soschino.[73] The reason behind this decision is not entirely clear. The Italians' primacy may have been due to the fact that they were already performing with their troupe at the Opera and it seems that they accepted the fact that there was to be no further subsidy.[74] But the issue was not yet finished.

In July 1885, Khayyāṭ again submitted a request, asking for only two months of Arabic theater *after* Santi Boni's season, with the same conditions. However, Rushdī earmarked the request with a note to the Comité: "I do not think now that we can agree to the requested permission."[75] Sensing the possible competition, Santi Boni and Soschino now submitted a new proposal to the ministry. They wanted to bring an Arab and a Turkish theater troupe for the two additional months (March and April

[69] Letter dated 22 March 1885, Ministre des Affaires Etrangères to Rouchdy, and letter dated 22 March 1885, Manasse to Nubar Pasha, 4003–037911, DWQ.

[70] Undated letter (in its Arabic translation 26 April 1885), Président du Conseil des Ministres (Nubar) to MTP, 4003–037911, DWQ.

[71] Letter dated 11 May 1885, Rouchdy to Comité des Théâtres, 4003–037911, DWQ.

[72] Unsigned draft dated 21 May 1885, 4003–037911, DWQ.

[73] "Grand Théâtre Khédivial de l'Opéra—Projet pour la saison 1885–86, sous la direction Santi Boni et G. Soschino du 1 novembre 1885 au 1er mars 1886," dated 18 May 1885, 4003–037912, DWQ.

[74] Letter dated 2 May 1885, S. Boni et Soschino to Abdel-Rahman Rouchdy, MTP, 4003–037911, DWQ.

[75] Letter dated 28 July 1885, Joseph Kaiat to MTP, 4003–037912, DWQ.

1886). The proposed Arab troupe was Abū Khalīl al-Qabbānī's, and the Turkish one may have been Séropé Benlian's Ottoman Operetta troupe. The ministry, perhaps Rushdī himself, transferring their request to the Comité, noted "I would like to call your attention that the Turkish troupe would please the Court as well as the notables in this country as the Arab performances would in general please the indigenous population."[76] The Comité accordingly agreed to the extension of Santi Boni's contract and rejected Khayyāṭ for the second time.[77] This was due to Khedive Tevfik's dislike of Khayyāṭ's performances.[78] As we have seen, it was finally Qardāḥī who performed in the Opera House in 1886 (and had to pay rent to Santi Boni); and there was no "Turkish" company. In this cultural deliberation, the Comité's decisions were informed by the minister's recommendation and khedivial preference.

The khedive's wishes and taste were usually taken into consideration—though these concerned minor, indeed sometimes ridiculously minor, matters. For instance, Tevfik could order that one society's ball would replace another's to match his schedule. Sometimes, the minister noted that impresarios were "approved by the khedive." In other cases, especially involving money, Tevfik's will was not easily accepted. When he ordered to make a payment to Qardāḥī in 1887 this was received with opposition from the Comité, because there was no money in the budget for uncalculated expenses, only the amount for the gas.[79]

Following the wish of Abbas Hilmi II, Sulaymān Ḥaddād was allowed to use the Opera House in the spring of 1893, and the ministry paid the cost of the gas too;[80] although in 1895 he was refused.[81] Abbas Hilmi II also used Arabic performances to boost his popularity. In 1893, the Egyptian playwright and lawyer Ismāʿīl ʿĀṣim's (1840–1919) request for an Arabic theatrical evening at the Opera (with Iskandar Faraḥ's troupe), was also underscored by the minister's comment: "H.H. the Khedive would like to attend."[82] The khedives also had their favorites among the Italian and French companies and plays. Like Ismail, his grandson Abbas Hilmi II personally approved the Italian program at the Opera House.[83]

[76] Letter dated 13 August 1885, MTP to Comité des Théâtres, 4003–037912, DWQ.

[77] Letter dated 10 October 1885, Barois to Santi Boni et Soschino, 4003–037912, DWQ.

[78] Undated letter (1886 winter?), from Rouchdy to President, Conseil des Ministres, Maḥfaẓa 2/1, Niẓārat al-Ashghāl al-ʿUmūmiyya, CMW, DWQ.

[79] Note dated 21 April 1887, MTP to Conseil des Ministres, Maḥfaẓa 2/1, Niẓārat al-Ashghāl al-ʿUmūmiyya, CMW, DWQ.

[80] Letter dated 10 January 1893, MTP to Suleiman Haddad, 4003–022553, DWQ.

[81] Note dated 5 January 1895, Maḥfaẓa 2/1, Niẓārat al-Ashghāl, CMW, DWQ.

[82] Undated (1894?) letter, M. Zeki Ministre to Comité des Théâtres, 4003–037803, DWQ.

[83] Letter dated 5 September 1913, Cherif Seddik to Albert Baroche, 5013–005406, DWQ.

Selection or Censorship?

Both the khedive and the Comité had a say about the plays that were staged. A copy of the repertoire was enclosed within most applications and accompanied all contracts. It had to be verified (and sometimes chosen) by the Comité.[84] Often it was also sent to the khedive's cabinet. For instance, in 1887, Qardāḥī's Arabic repertoire was "approved."[85] A French impresario, Meynadier, had to pay a 14,000 francs deposit in 1889 for the concession on condition that his performances would be inspected in Italy by the Comité (perhaps Clemente) and in case they were not approved, he would lose his money. This is indeed what happened, and the Finance Ministry refused the repayment arguing that "it should be an example for future directors."[86] (However, in 1891 the khedive granted the repayment.)[87]

In sum, the Comité, through financial control, ran the government institution according to their tastes. They allowed the wishes of the khedives to be fulfilled if there was no cost attached and very rarely granted small rewards to favored Arab impresarios. The prefiltering of the program had the effect that only loyal plays could be staged, which the Arab impresarios understood, in a form of self-censorship.

Regulating and Policing Theaters

Now I would like to extend the discussion to the legal framework of both government and private theaters in nineteenth-century Egypt before and after the British occupation. There are three central issues: the laws concerning the establishment of a theater building (or a stage); the laws of censorship and the act of censoring or banning plays; and the police supervision of performances. With the analysis of the legal measures, we move our focus from government bureaucracy to the private sphere. Muslim religious scholars, from the 1890s, voiced negative opinions about public behavior in the theaters and thus could ask for official intervention into such matters. The history of theater censorship in Egypt, despite the efforts of Ramsīs ʿAwaḍ, Sayyid ʿAlī Ismāʿīl, Ilham

[84] Contract dated 2 June 1886, between Santi Boni, Graziadio Soschino, and MTP. Maḥfaẓa 2/1, Niẓārat al-Ashghāl al-ʿUmūmiyya, CMW, DWQ.

[85] *Al-Ahrām*, 10 March 1886, 2.

[86] Note dated 27 April 1890, MTP to Conseil des Ministres. Maḥfaẓa 2/1, Niẓārat al-Ashghāl al-ʿUmūmiyya, CMW, DWQ.

[87] Letter dated 4 April 1891, Secrétariat de Khédive to Riaz Pacha, and letter dated 11 April 1891, President Conseil des Ministres to Finance Ministry, Maḥfaẓa 2/1, Niẓārat al-Ashghāl al-ʿUmūmiyya, CMW, DWQ.

Khuri-Makdisi, and Ziad Fahmy (and Juan Cole, concerning the general censorship in the pre-1882 period), has not been adequately explored. My contribution to this topic also remains fragmented because of the limited access to sources.

Here I argue that a new concept of public space evolved as a moral domain to be supervised by the government. European entertainment spaces in late Ottoman lands serve as eminent examples through which we can study the interaction of European and Islamic legal and moral codes, including honour and visibility. The precondition of these changes was a new spatial epistemology, which was based on extensive urbanization, new technologies, new building materials, and new energy sources. The material transformation of late Ottoman cities (and the countryside) was coupled by state centralization and, after 1882, in Egypt by the British occupation. These material and political changes impacted social norms and spiritual beliefs.

One must note that besides legal and police measures, there was also communal-informal and educational disciplining. That is, the neighborhood, the family, or friends also expressed their opinions about acting. Second, despite the learned perception that theater is useful for morals (but by the late 1890s opposed by al-Muwayliḥī), the Ministry of Education issued a prohibition of acting for senior students as early as February 1888.[88] Such measures indicate that acting had become widespread in the late 1880s (see the next chapter for amateur theatrical societies) and that the government considered this activity illegitimate for students.

Supervision, Censorship, Crime and the Khedivial Theaters

What was the role of police in relation to the khedivial spaces? In the late 1860s and 1870s the main concerns were the security of Ismail, the behavior of (and intelligence about) the audience and the artists, and the content of the plays. The location of the public buildings made control easy because the theaters in Azbakiyya were designed conveniently within a small area. The Comédie actually faced the police station. Khedivial public spaces were designed to be supervised.

Theaters, in particular, have been dangerous public buildings for political leaders. For instance, the President of the United States, Abraham Lincoln, was assassinated in a theater in Washington, DC, in 1865. Theaters in Alexandria had already been under police supervision. Yet there is no data about similar measures in Cairo. After 1869 a regulation at the Opera and the Comédie prohibited smoking and loud shouting. At least eight policemen were seated among the audience in the Comédie

[88] Landau, *Studies*, 80.

and in the Opera House in the first season of 1869–1870,[89] though the police could not enter the loges of the harem, not even during the British occupation.[90] The prefect of the police owned his own seat both in the Comédie and in the Opera.[91] It is said that Ismail also kept a fire steam engine "always at the side of the [Opera] house ready for instant use."[92] By adding eight policemen to the six Egyptian *farrāsh* and to the khedive's personal guard, it seems that Ismail's physical safety was heavily protected.

Secret agents also screened the theaters. The khedivial police chief directed agents to collect information about the general atmosphere among the resident Europeans. Often they received reports by voluntary informants. For instance, a certain Antoine Banucci during the construction of the Opera House asked the khedive to intervene on behalf of the ballerinas who were badly treated by the administrator Nicole Lablache.[93] In 1871, a secret agent, Agent X, reported on the two political factions among the Italian musicians in the orchestra,[94] noting that the divide was causing disturbances even among the dancers. Agent X also reported about a planned boycott of the Opera.[95] Egyptians were also spied on. We have already seen the report of Agent Z about the first planned and failed Arabic play in Egypt. It is worth noting that there are no reports about James Sanua's experiments in 1871–1872.

The security system was adjusting to a new area of responsibility at the end of the 1860s. There was some confusion about who exactly should exercise control over the new spaces. For instance, the al-Azbakiyya Garden was supposed to be open in the daytime only. In October 1869 the Cairo police (*Ḍabṭiyya*) refused to send extra policemen to protect the garden from the entry of "rebellious" elements (*al-māridīn*). It advised the Tanzim to appoint four of its own fourteen *qawwās* to the task.[96] In

[89] Letter dated 14 January 1870, Draneht to "la Daira des affaires particuliers de Son Altesse le Khédive," Maḥfaẓa 80, CAI, DWQ.

[90] Letter dated 28 September 1887, from the Commandant of Police Cairo City, to H.E. the Inspector General of Police Headquarters, 4003–036990, DWQ.

[91] Letter dated 14 January 1870, from Draneht to "la Daira des affaires particuliers de Son Altesse le Khédive," Maḥfaẓa 80, CAI, DWQ.

[92] Dye, *Moslim Egypt and Christian Abyssinia*, 14.

[93] Letter dated Le Caire le 29 December 1869, to the Khedive from Antoine Banucci, 5013–003022, DWQ. Lablache was the administrative director of the Opera House, La Revue musicale de Paris 36 n. 21, 23 May 1869, 174.

[94] Letter dated 11 January 1871 from Agent X to M. Nardi Inspecteur de Police au Caire. 5013–003022, DWQ. These factions very likely debated the unification of Italy in 1871.

[95] Letter dated 29 January 1871. From Agent X to Inspecteur de Police au Caire, M. Nardi. 5013–003022, DWQ.

[96] Letter dated 24 Jumādā al-Thānī 1286 (1 October 1869), daftar 2003–000355, p. 117, DWQ.

addition, there must have been many more secret reports that are now lost, uncatalogued, or at unknown locations.

Examining police involvement in the construction of the khedivial theaters enriches our understanding of the khedivial state before occupation. If there was a disputed question of payment to a foreigner worker, the *Ḍabṭiyya* mediated between the Private Domains and Pietro Avoscani's company and the consulates, as in the case of a certain Mr. Pawlawoski (?, Fablafūskī), a French citizen, or in the case of three Austro-Hungarian carpenters (who worked "in the theater" in October 1869; possibly the Opera House still under construction).[97] In the case of Mr. Pawlawoski (?), the police withheld a part of his salary because a lady had filed a legal case against him.[98] It is remarkable that the police meddled into payments of the theater staff in 1869. Branches in the khedivial government interacted with each other and, even in the case of protected foreigners, could execute legal action.[99]

Between 1869 and 1878 the program was filtered by Paul Draneht directly and indirectly. Only two plays are known to have been directly censored. The first was a pantomime in the Circus, entitled *Un invité*, which mocked the khedive's guests at the Suez Canal Opening Ceremonies. It depicted a European gentleman who did not want to pay for anything, replying always: "I am invited." This was immediately suppressed by Draneht, and he ensured that his objection was shown to the khedive.[100] In November 1870, Ismail himself censored the program: a play entitled *Quinze jours de siège* was planned in the Comédie but he found it "uninteresting" and asked Draneht to suppress the play.[101] His reaction must have been related to the Prussian siege of Paris at the time. Otherwise, censorship was indirect. There is no evidence, as discussed in chapter 4, that the troupe of Sanua in 1872 was banned explicitly. Direct censorship might have been viewed as a proof of autocracy in the eyes of the international community and was avoided.

Yet, spatially, crime remained connected to entertainment in al-Azbakiyya, just as it had been in the 1850s and 1860s. For instance, a French woman, Madame Geraldine, who worked "in the theater" and lived around al-Azbakiyya, was robbed in her flat by two Greeks. They

[97] Letter to al-Dāʾira al-Khāṣṣa dated 12 Jumādā al-Awwal 1286 (20 August 1869), p. 31; letter to [al-Dāʾira] al-Khāṣṣa undated (possibly 1 Rajab 1286 [7 October 1869), p. 98; letter to [al-Dāʾira] al-Khāṣṣa, 3 Shaʿbān 1286 (8 November 1869), p. 126; 2003–001827, DWQ.

[98] Letter dated 2 Rajab 1286 (8 October 1869), to [al-Dāʾira] al-Khāṣṣa, and another of the same date, p. 98, 2003–001827, DWQ.

[99] Kozma, *Policing Egyptian Women*, 121.

[100] Letter dated 26 December 1869, Draneht to [Rancy], Maḥfaẓa 80, CAI, DWQ. See also Sadgrove, *Egyptian Theatre*, 50.

[101] Letter dated 22 November 1870, from Pini Bey? to Draneht Bey, 5013–004133, DWQ.

stole items to the value of 955 francs but were caught and jailed.[102] Another French employee in the theaters (B-t-r-ī Jān), a *sardjī* (prop man) accused Ḥusayn Sulaymān and Farḥāt al-Māyis of stealing from him. They were found guilty and sent to jail.[103] Inside the theaters there was petty crime. In 1870, items were stolen from the costume storage room. Draneht was informed that a Frenchman called Soullier (? S-ū-l-ī-a) was suspected, but had been apprehended; another Frenchman, Alphonse, an employee of the theater, was summoned (through the French consulate) to testify to the police.[104] In 1874, Draneht himself was robbed by his maid and her lover. The couple ran away but were caught.[105] In the same year, the European technicians of the khedivial theaters had discussed sabotage, but, after the police warned their consulates, they dropped the issue.[106] There must have been more small disturbances.

Documentation of the activity of secret agents between 1879 and 1882 is missing, although we know that Tevfik inherited some of his father's trusted agents.[107] Abbas Hilmi II set up his own small secret agency around 1895—entrusted with spying on the British, Ottoman Egyptian notables, and Egyptian patriots—that provided reports about the general atmosphere. They rarely reported about theatrical activities. In the beginning of the 1900s, for instance, an agent reported that in al-Azbakiyya Garden there was a gathering of about 500 men, including journalists, patriots, and Ismāʿīl Ḥāfiẓ Pasha. They watched an Arabic play and listened to Arabic poems.[108] Al-Azbakiyya's garden theater became the regular stage of patriotic societies by that time. The khedivial intelligence gathering aimed less at the suppression of these activities than at detailed knowledge about their conduct and participants.

While the Comité des Théâtres was principally occupied with the Opera House, in the 1900s the al-Azbakiyya Garden Theatre came under closer government control. From 1903 its director, the widow Madame Santini, had to request the approval of the ministry for every contract,

[102] Letter dated 15 Muḥarram 1287 (17 April 1870), to French Consulate, 2003–002068, p. 68, DWQ.

[103] Letter dated 1 Rabīʿ al-Awwal 1287 (1 June 1870), to French Consulate, 2003–002068, p. 167, DWQ.

[104] Letter dated 17 Muḥarram 1287 (19 April 1870), to French Consulate, 2003–002068, p. 70; letter dated 18 Ṣafar 1287 (20 May 1870), to French Consulate, 2003–002068, p. 135; letter dated 21 Ṣafar 1287 (23 May 1870), to French Consulate, 2003–002068, p. 139, DWQ.

[105] Letters dated 29 March 1874, Burichetti (Cabinet de Directeur de Police) to Hairy Pacha (Chef du Cabinet du Khedive), both in 5013–003022, DWQ.

[106] Letters dated 6 and 9 September 1874, Burichetti (Cabinet de Directeur de Police) to Hairy [Khayrī] Pacha (Chef du Cabinet du Khedive), both in 5013–003022, DWQ.

[107] See undated letter and its mention of dafātir sirriyya, in 28/7, HIL/28/1–190, AHP.

[108] Undated letter, possibly around 1902, 28/31, HIL/28/1–190, AHP.

despite the fact that she was running a private business.[109] The contracts contained a clause that reserved seats for the government.[110] It is possible that this increased attention was in line with the post-1890s new regulation ("cleaning up") of al-Azbakiyya Garden that I have mentioned in chapter 3; it certainly reflected the growing number of patriotic anti-British activities from the 1890s.

On the other hand, the official police force, controlled by the British, acted according the legal codes set up by the colonial administration.[111] These laws and ordinances provide the legal concept of public space in its evolution.

Islamic and Colonial Laws: The Legal Concept of "Public Space"

How did theaters become *legal* in a predominantly Muslim territory with no prior tradition or history of such buildings before the nineteenth century? The khedivial decrees did not establish a legal framework into which these entertainment spaces would fit. A public space of leisure owned by a private individual was not a new phenomenon in Ottoman Egypt (since the coffeehouse had functioned in exactly this way), but such spaces were increasingly viewed as entities that ought to be controlled centrally. The reason for this was the shifting understanding of what the "public" was and the growing distrust in the "neighborhood gaze."[112]

Sharīʿa might consider theaters immoral, but I have found no evidence so far of significant religious opposition to such spaces (there is one Egyptian and one Syrian example, see below), or any related legal case in a *sharīʿa*-court in the nineteenth century. I have not found a single fatwa concerning theaters among the decisions of Sheikh Muḥammad al-ʿAbbāsī al-Mahdī (d. 1897), the Grand Mufti of Egypt between 1848 and 1897;[113] nor among the published *fatāwā* of Sheikh Muḥammad Muḥammad al-Bannā (1828–1896) who briefly replaced him as Grand Mufti between 1887 and 1889.[114] Sheikh al-ʿAbbāsī approved the destruction of the sculptures in al-Azbakiyya (presumably Ibrahim's statue) at the end of August 1882, in the midst of the ʿUrābī revolution, and suggested the closure of pubs and coffeehouses that served alcohol,[115] but theater

[109] Various letters between 1903 and 1907, in 4003–038633 and 4003–038635, DWQ.

[110] Draft dated 7 April 1903, MTP to Mme. Veuve Santini, 4003–038635, DWQ.

[111] Tollefson, *Policing Islam.*

[112] I learned this expression from Avner Wischnitzer at a conference at the British Institute at Ankara in April 2015.

[113] Al-Mahdī, *Al-Fatāwā al-Mahdiyya*; Peters, "Muḥammad al-ʿAbbāsī al-Mahdī."

[114] Mūsā, *al-Iftāʾ al-Miṣrī*; Hatina, *ʿUlamaʾ, Politics, and the Public Sphere*, 74.

[115] al-ʿAbbāsī al-Mahdī, *Al-Fatāwā al-Mahdiyya*, vol. 5: 299–300.

buildings were not affected. The first known *fatāwā* in relation to Arabic theater are those of Sheikh Rashīd Riḍā in the 1900s, following Muḥammad ʿAbduh's general *fatwa* about images in 1904. It is worth noting that Riḍā's two theater rulings were responses to Russian and Syrian Muslim requests, not to Egyptian enquiries.[116]

One possible explanation is that until the 1860s, and possibly even later, from a legal point of view (be that *sharīʿa*, Ottoman sultanic law, or Egyptian governor's law) the private buildings, possessed by (Christian) foreign subjects (though perhaps on rented land), were considered extraterritorial business enterprises and thus under the effect of the Capitulations (the contracts of European states with the Ottoman Empire for trade and for the consular jurisdiction of their subjects). In fact, the early theaters were not buildings but rather stages in storehouses, bars, and brothels (*kara-khāna*). The first real theater building, the Zizinia theater in Alexandria (built in 1862), was the property of Count Zizinia (d. 1865), who was not only a foreign subject but also the consul of Belgium.

There may have been an "understanding" in the ranks of the *ʿulamāʾ*, and in the government departments, at least until the 1860s, that either these spaces or their audiences could be excluded from regulation and moral supervision because they were neither Egyptian nor Ottoman nor Muslim. Potential proof for such official regard can be found in the first known official initiative to regulate theaters in late Ottoman Egypt. This was a circular in Italian by Artin Bey, Mehmed Ali's secretary for foreign affairs, to the foreign consuls in 1847, written in order to discipline the (non-Egyptian) audiences of an Alexandrian theater. Artin Bey considered this theater to be under the jurisdiction of the Alexandria municipality, yet he considered the audience outside of Egyptian jurisdiction because he wrote the letter in Italian to the consuls. Eight Egyptian policemen were stationed close to the theater in case of trouble.[117]

No documentation has been located thus far about the regulation of the private bars and theatrical activities in al-Azbakiyya in the 1850s and early 1860s or the growing number of theaters in Alexandria. In theory these spaces were under the authority of the provincial governorates. Growing concern is reflected in an 1866 agreement between the government and the consuls, which gave khedivial policemen the right to enter "cafés, restaurants, cabarets" owned by foreign subjects and thus

[116] Ramadan, "The Aesthetics of the Modern," ch. 1 and appendix 1. For Riḍā's opinions see Al-Munajjad, ed., *Fatāwā al-Imām Muḥammad Rashīd Riḍā*, 549–554, 1090–1093.

[117] This text was published first in Tagher, "Les débuts du théâtre"; then Najm, *al-Masraḥiyya*, 21–22 (with wrong date and mistranslation); finally Sadgrove, *Egyptian Theatre*, appendix 1, 169–171.

protected by the Capitulations.[118] In October 1877, a private theater was set up in Cairo but again nothing is known about its license.[119]

In 1880 a police regulation gave detailed instructions about what should be involved in the sphere of official action concerning public spaces, although it omitted the explicit mention of theaters. It warned against Egyptian popular weddings celebrated in the streets during which people might become drunk and dance publicly; against prostitution; against the mixing of genders at small coffee shops belonging to women who make coffee during the *mawālīd*; against the drunkenness of female singers in cafes; and against public dancers (*khawalāt*), street singers and street musicians, and the homeless who sleep on the street, and so on. The measures were to be communicated through neighborhood sheikhs to their communities. The reasons cited were moral (and religious), public safety, or health arguments. The law prescribed permissions for the opening of all kinds of shops, coffeehouses, taverns, and so on, from the *Ḍabṭiyya*, the health ministry, and the Ornato (the committee for urban improvement); theaters were only implicitly included ("and what is of this kind," art. 49). Though the 1880 law does not contain the word "public space" in Arabic, every issue is concerned with urban public behavior and morals. [120]

The British occupation crystallized the laws describing police responsibilities. They mirror the new attention to public space as the responsibility of the government, rather than religious or neighborhood authority. In 1883, the ministry of the interior in a series of regulations was concerned with public activities, such as the charmers of snakes, or other keepers of dangerous animals in streets, and so on;[121] and also prohibited the stoning of trains in rural areas.[122] The Penal Code of 1883 did not contain a specific point concerning theaters or public establishments.[123] A detailed police law appeared in November 1891. It defined public establishments (in French *établissements publics*) by naming the types of institutions: pubs, theaters, clubs, or anything similar. It detailed how public enterprises could be opened: the request had to be submitted to the government in writing and should contain the personal information of the director, the nature of the enterprise, and the address of the building

[118] See the text of the agreement, dated 26 April 1866, [Ministère de l'Intérieur], *Législation de police*, 484, n.1.

[119] Sadgrove, *Egyptian Theatre*, 70.

[120] Jallād, *Qāmūs al-ʿĀmm*, 3: 215–221.

[121] Letter dated 16 Rabīʿ al-Awwal 1300 (25 January 1883), Niẓārat al-Dākhiliyya to all provinces, *al-Manshūrāt wa-l-Qarārāt al-Ṣādira fī Sanat 1883 Afrankiyya*, 10.

[122] 14 Shaʿbān 1300 (20 June 1883), Niẓārat al-Dākhiliyya to all in charge, *al-Manshūrāt wa-l-Qarārāt al-Ṣādira fī sanat 1883*, 55–56.

[123] *Codes égyptiens* (1883), 427–507.

in which the proposed enterprise was to be opened. The wording of the law made it clear that these obligations were new, as the owners of already existing pubs, theaters, and so on, had thirty days to show their *certificat d'inscription* and change it into the new license (art. 2). The *certificat d'inscription* alludes to the fact that there was an older method of registration. Temporary celebrations, theaters, and pubs could obtain permissions from the local authorities (art. 7). The regulation prescribed that all such institutions should close at midnight in the winter and at 1 am in the summer (art. 13). Policemen had the right to enter theaters, circuses, and public balls to maintain the order, regardless of status of their owner.[124] The selling of alcohol needed extra permission, although as an exception the permission of the establishment included the license of selling alcohol by default in the "European districts of Cairo, Alexandria, Port Said, Ismailia, and Suez."[125] This code defined the basic duties of the police, and by extension, the state control of public spaces in most respects until the interwar period.

In 1896, 1899, and 1900 smaller modifications of the police law were applied.[126] In the 1890s there was a French form issued by the ministry of interior for *Autorisation pour un établissement public provisoire*, which was still used in the 1900s.[127] In 1904, the 1891 rules were updated and extended; for instance, the application for opening a public establishment now had to be approved first by the police, and the consumption of hashish was explicitly forbidden.[128]

Municipalities also began to regulate theaters. The only known regulation so far was drawn by the Alexandria Municipality (in the 1890s it had already been sponsoring theaters, such as the Zizinia, or Qardāḥī's theater). In 1901, it allocated 500 LE yearly support for "European theaters."[129] Khuri-Makdisi quotes a 1904 resolution which stated that "all shows and all representations of an immoral nature will be formally forbidden" and that "no theatre could be erected without the municipality's previously written authorization."[130] This law is quite a late development

[124] Sayyid ʿAlī Ismāʿīl states that this law prescribed that policemen had to be present during the theater performances, but I have not found any trace of this. Sayyid ʿAlī Ismāʿīl, "Tārīkh al-Raqāba wa-l-Taṭawwuruhā," http://kenanaonline.com/users/sayed-esmail/posts/119149, accessed 9 March 2014.

[125] [Ministère de l'Intérieur], *Législation de police*, 477–485.

[126] Lantz, *Répertoire général de la jurisprudence égyptienne*, 500–501 (art. 9360–9364).

[127] Cf. permission for Sayyid Ḥamūda to opening a theater in 1909. http://modernegypt.bibalex.org/DocumentViewer/TextViewer.aspx?w=1418&h=778&type=document&id=33302&s=2, and many others in BA.

[128] Lamba, *Code Administratif Égyptien*, 183–193.

[129] [Commission Municipale], *Budget pour l'exercice 1901*, 14.

[130] Quoted in Khuri-Makdisi, *The Eastern Mediterranean*, 76.

compared to the situation in Istanbul, where municipality regulations of theaters had already been written in the 1850s, or, after 1867.[131] The 1904 Alexandria regulation discloses a growing concern about the content of staged plays, which leads us to the question of censorship.

The Legal Background of Censorship, Muslim Morals, and Arabic Theater

The institution of censorship in the Ottoman Empire in general, and in the Ottoman Arab lands in particular, was an administrative mechanism to protect the dignity of the ruler, public morals, and the unity of the realm by suppressing the articulation of dissent and subversive political ideas. Censorship established a connection between the three principles: dignity, morals, and unity. In the khedivate of Egypt, censorship initially had the same goals: to protect the dignity of the khedive and the sultan, the public morals, and peaceful rule. After 1882, however, censorship was designed primarily to prevent too fervent pro-Ottoman, revolutionary, or anti-British ideas from appearing in public. The laws regulating printing and journalism included printed plays in theory, but only at a later date can any information be found suggesting that plays were banned from performance. There was no coherent control of printed or staged plays until the 1910s.

The censorship of *printed plays* was not mentioned explicitly in the laws concerning printed material (books, periodicals, pamphlets). The Ottoman laws of 1857 (on printing presses) and 1865 (on journals) have no separate entries about printed plays (these laws were not fully implemented in Egypt anyway);[132] the penal code in the 1870s contained only the punishment of the unauthorized opening of a printing press and the printing of obscene drawings.[133] The 1881 Egyptian law on printed products omitted the mention of plays (though drawings, *rusūmāt*, were included, possibly because of James Sanua's *Abū Naḍḍāra*).[134] The 1883 penal code contains measures against unauthorized presses, and prescribing the punishment of printing or distributing texts containing insults to the ruler, the government, or the representatives of public authority (art. 170), or, again, that contained obscene drawings (art. 172).[135] The absence of special rules for plays is not surprising, however, given that that the performances by Naqqāsh, Khayyāṭ, Qardāḥī, and Nadīm were

131 Mestyan, "A Garden with Mellow Fruits," 384–385.
132 Cioeta, "Ottoman Censorship," 168. Also Cole, *Colonialism and Revolution*, 223–224.
133 *Projet de code pénal* (1871), 35; *Codes égyptiens* (1875), 484.
134 Naqqāsh, *Miṣr li-l-Miṣriyyīn*, 4:194–197. Fahmy, *Ordinary Egyptians*, 58.
135 *Codes Égyptiens* (1883), 466–467.

not subversive, and that until the 1890s Arabic plays were printed only in small numbers in Beirut and not in Cairo, with very few exceptions.

The relationship between *printed plays* and their *performances* is not clear in the early decades of the British occupation. The key to understanding this lack of regulation is that modern Arabic plays were written for performance and not for reading. The theater historian Sayyid ʿAlī Ismāʿīl calls attention to the fact that if plays had been printed in the 1880s, in theory the printing press would have had to indicate the permission given by the press office (*Qalam al-Maṭbūʿāt*) in the interior ministry.[136] Yet plays printed in this period lack any indication that they received permission.[137] Ramsīs ʿAwaḍ, Sayyid ʿAlī Ismāʿīl, and Ziad Fahmy provide a number of plays "censored" in the period starting from the late 1890s. Ismāʿīl mentions an Arabic play—according to him, the earliest—which was stamped, interestingly in Turkish, to indicate the permission of its staging by a censor in 1897 (it was *al-Ifrīqiyya* [the Arabized version of Meyerbeer's opera *L'Africaine*] to be performed by the troupe of Iskandar Faraḥ).[138] In this copy, the censor deleted the Arabic words "king" (*malik*) and "kingly" (*mulūkī*) and substituted with more Ottoman *mīr* and *ʿālī*.[139] The censor must have been an Ottoman member of the censorship office within the interior ministry, not a separate officer responsible for staged performances. During World War One there was a British theater censorship committee in Cairo.

There are examples of banning a performance while the same play in print was relatively freely distributed: in 1906 the play written about the Dinshaway incident (when Egyptian peasants clashed with British soldiers in a village and were harshly punished) was banned from being staged but was then printed under the title *Ṣayd al-Ḥamām* ("Pigeon Hunt") and sold openly in the streets.[140] Such discrepancies suggest the government lacked, as yet, an overarching mechanism to control the public or that there was no need at the time for such a mechanism.

The censorship or banning of plays from *performance* possesses a history that is distinct from that of *printed material*, precisely because many plays were not printed but remained in manuscript. As I have argued above, the Comité des Théâtres and their 1887 regulation could be considered an administrative device for indirect censorship, but this committee did not include a censorship office, especially not one with reference to private theaters.[141] With regard to private theaters, Sayyid ʿAlī Ismāʿīl

[136] Ismāʿīl, "Tārīkh al-Raqāba wa-Taṭawwuruhā."

[137] Such was [Wāṣif], *Riwāyat Harūn al-Rashīd maʿ Qūt al-Qulūb*; see chapter 6.

[138] Ismāʿīl, "Tārīkh al-Raqāba wa-Taṭawwuruhā."

[139] MQMMFS, play n. 129 (an 1897 print of *al-Ifrīqiyya*); p. 14.

[140] Fahmy, *Ordinary Egyptians*, 93–94.

[141] Sayyid ʿAlī Ismāʿīl states that Ḥifẓ al-Tiyātrāt (the Comité) in 1879 was a body for censorship, and also gives its internal legislation of 1887 as the legal constitution of

has collected a number of cases when *performances* were prevented by the police. The earliest case in 1893 was the performance of a play entitled *Yūsuf* (Joseph) that was prevented by the police in Damietta. The police intervention was requested by the local *ʿulamāʾ* in order to prevent a "massacre" (*madhbaḥa*). This seems to be the first case in Egypt when religious opposition, requesting government intervention, prevented a theater performance. In 1896, another play, *Mutaʿaṣṣiba Shanʿāʾ* (The Ugly Bigot Lady), was prevented from being performed in Alexandria, and on that occasion, the government (possibly the interior ministry) asked a member of the Municipality to read all plays before staging. (There is nothing known about this affair.) In 1898 the performance of the play *Edhem Pasha* was prevented in the Abbas Theatre in Alexandria.[142] These individual cases indicate that performances of potentially subversive plays were banned by the authorities on a one-by-one basis.

The 1893 case in Damietta makes it explicit that although no indication of opposition survived from Muslim religious scholars, modern Arabic theater was seen by some *ʿulamāʾ* as a morally intolerable practice. There is an as-yet-unconfirmed anecdote that al-Qabbānī's first theater in Damascus was closed down because of the hostile *ʿulamāʾ*.[143] In Egypt, in July 1894, possibly out of newly found Muslim moral concern, the government banned public dancing in cafes and public spaces. However, since non-Egyptian subjects could still dance, the dancing girls quickly married (were married?) to Algerian Muslim men since these individuals typically were under French jurisdiction.[144] The occasional bans indicate the popularity of such leisure practices.

As opposed to older forms of popular mimetic entertainment, modern theaters—the buildings, troupes, and stages—represented a rupture in practices of public entertainment. There was a need for creating historical arguments for compatibilities. For instance, the young leader of all Egyptian Sufi orders Muḥammad Tawfīq al-Bakrī (1870–1932) sometime in the 1890s explained in a talk that "something similar to the representation of events which is known now as theater" was practiced among Arabs (al-ʿArab) during early Islam. His insistence reflects an argument according to which theater (and many other practices, like balls, paintings etc.) was not known before the European influence. Whether this argument came from European Orientalists or Muslim reformists, al-Bakrī clearly thought theater is permissible because there were ancient mimetic traditions in Muslim societies.[145] Sheikh Rashīd Riḍā's fatwa in

censorship, but there is no proof that the Comité had any power outside of the state theaters. Ismāʿīl, "Tārīkh al-Raqāba wa-Taṭawwuruhā."

[142] Cf. the references in Ismāʿīl, "Tārīkh al-Raqāba wa-Taṭawwuruhā."

[143] Karachouli, "Abu Halil al-Qabbani," 87.

[144] Farīd, *Mudhakkirāt*, 173.

[145] Al-Bakrī, *Ṣahārīj al-Luʾluʾ*, 258–259.

1907 to the question of a Russian Muslim schoolteacher was also not about theater per se. It was about the presence of women on stage and in the audience. Riḍā examined Arabic performances in Egypt in person and found that the only benefit was that ordinary people could listen an elevated Arabic language on stage whose "level" he placed somewhere between *fuṣḥā* and *ʿāmmiyya*.[146] He judged that while women should not dance with men and not adorn themselves with jewelry in public, acting itself could carry some benefits. A few years later in 1911, answering questions from Syrian students, Riḍā affirmed that acting could be used for the representation of historical events.[147]

Next to Islamic morals, technology and the spread of subversive ideas also made entertainment more political. Ziad Fahmy describes the effects of innovations, such as the gramophone and a mass printing industry, with the term "media-capitalism," which he believes started around 1907.[148] On the political side, the unjust sentences and executions after the Dinshaway scandal in 1906, the revolutions in St. Petersburg (1905), Tehran (1905–1907), Istanbul (1908–1909), the new Ottoman constitution (1908), the death of the patriotic leader Muṣṭafā Kāmil in 1908, the rise of the workers movement, the spread of revolutionary ideas, the assassination of Prime Minister Buṭrus Ghālī in 1910, and the new mass-participation in politics all prompted the British officials and traditional elites to resort to stronger measures of control.

From 1906, an increasing number of plays were banned by the interior ministry from performance, such as the one about ʿUrābī or the Dinshaway play.[149] In 1910, a journal reported that policemen were to be sent to every performance in every single Arab theater.[150] Though this piece of news likely exaggerated, the concern of colonial authorities with public entertainment was unprecedented in this turbulent period. Two specific laws were proclaimed about public spaces and texts. The first in 1909 revived the 1881 press law.[151] Next, proclaimed in July 1911, was a Law on Theatres (*Lāʾiḥat al-Tiyātrāt*), which is the best-remembered law on theater in Arabic.[152] This specialized law did not change the conditions of establishing a theater, but added three important restrictions: that the program and a new troupe had to be approved first by the police, that in every city "a theater committee" was to be created (chaired by the police

[146] Al-Munajjad, ed., *Fatāwā al-Imām*, 549–554.
[147] Ibid., 1093.
[148] Fahmy, *Ordinary Egyptians*, 96–97.
[149] ʿAwaḍ, *Ittijāhāt Siyāsiyya*, 19 and 21.
[150] Quoted in Ismāʿīl, "Tārīkh al-Raqāba wa-Taṭawwuruhā."
[151] Fahmy, *Ordinary Egyptians*, 103–104.
[152] For instance, http://www.e-socialists.net/node/4538, accessed 19 February 2014.

prefect), and that in every theater a special seat for a policeman must be maintained.[153] This legal act explicitly assumed the subversive potential of public acting. The police regulations and the continued censorship in the Interior Ministry established the legal framework and mechanisms that would supervise the rebellious Egyptian public after the proclamation of the British protectorate in 1914.

Conclusion: Law and Space

This chapter has traced the process by which khedivial theaters became state institutions overseen financially and administratively by the Comité des Théâtres. I have shown that financial experts expressed cultural preferences through indirect censorship of the program within the Opera House. The preferences of the khedives were also taken into consideration, when and if there was no cost involved, and some favored Arab impresarios could use the Opera House. In this way, patriotism in Arabic was staged in the stage of the symbolic Opera House within the colonial frames. As a consequence, "culture" attained a double function as both legitimizing and mirroring elite power.

The analysis of laws concerning private theaters and plays has shown that the theater buildings, which at the beginning were extraterritorial entertainment locations, came to be increasingly controlled by the government. Some *ʿulamāʾ* requested police intervention to ban performances from the 1890s onwards. However, the early Muslim jurists judged the theater permissible on the whole. The institutionalization of government censorship was the disciplinary response to the increased anticolonial activity in the 1910s.

"Being public" was associated with elaborate economic and legal norms. Instead of material change and capitalism creating a civil society to control politics, in khedivial-colonial Egypt being public meant the shrinking scope of free activity both in print ("the public sphere") and in the new spaces such as theaters. The constant adjustment to an imagined discipline, pushed by civilization discourses, colonial police, and Muslim reformists, resulted in the elite appropriation of the dominant modes of public presence. Not everyone was accepted as a patriot. The new codes of public spaces had to be learned and performed correctly. In the next and final chapter, I examine the ways in which elite social norms changed through the new spatial epistemology and the way patriotism peaked and transformed in the 1890s.

[153] *Al-Waqāʾiʿ al-Miṣriyya*, 17 July 1911, republished in Ismāʿīl, *al-Raqāba*, 30–33.

CHAPTER 8

Distinction and Patriotism: Muṣṭafā Kāmil and the Making of an Arab Prince

> Sunday evening the prince went to the khedivial playhouse which is known as the Opera to watch a great play. When the audience saw him they all stood up in admiration and greeted him with clapping and shouting. The music band played four times his greeting while the clapping and shouting continued. The playhouse was full with locals and all kinds of foreigners but only a few British employees and administrators were present. And this was a sign for Lord Cromer about the feelings of the foreigners towards the prince after he knew the feelings of the locals.[1]

Thus did Mīkhāʾīl Shārūbīm, a Coptic judge, describe the presence of Abbas Hilmi II in the Khedivial Opera House sometime in January 1893. His Arabic account confirms the *New York Times* article with which this part of the book started. He reveals a mixed audience in the official theater of the khedivate, the mastery with which the young khedive used publicity, and an old-new Arabic title: the prince (*amīr*).[2]

In this chapter, we follow the peak and end of Arab patriotism in Ottoman Egypt. The sudden death of Tevfik in 1892 helped to complete the restoration of khedivial legitimacy. However, patriotic intellectuals retained an uneasy relationship with khedivial authority. The symbolic figure of this relationship was Muṣṭafā Kāmil who was to become the first Egyptian nationalist politician. Another forgotten, tragic figure is the Sufi leader Muḥammad Tawfīq al-Bakrī (1870–1932). The three men—the khedive, the sheikh, and the politician—were of roughly the same age. Here I focus on Abbas Hilmi and Kāmil only.[3] Their entrance into politics

[1] Shārūbīm, *al-Kāfī*, Part 5, 1:1: 177–178.

[2] The full evaluation of Abbas Hilmi II's reign—the difficulty of which is best captured by the clash between the memoirs of Evelyn Baring (Lord Cromer) and Abbas' own—is not the task of this chapter. However, it is worth noting that compared to the essays about Baring and Kāmil, no serious academic work has been written about Abbas Hilmi II, the third powerful actor of the era.

[3] Al-Bakrī's ideas and complex position should be the subject of a separate study.

defines the end of patriotism and opens a contested era of anticolonial nationalism.

The young Kāmil imagined the young khedive (they were of the same age) as a compatriot Muslim Arab ruler who represented both the imagined nation and the Ottoman caliph. Ottomanism and khedivial authority are sometimes identical in this period. The men and women who shared or accepted this imagination—the audience of patriotism—belonged to the upper strata of Egyptian society, mixed with colonial elites, and were characterized by distinct cultural markers. This is the period in which the elite generation of interwar Egypt was formed and norms became established which have been governing Arab eliteness until today.

The early 1890s was also characterized by a theatrical boom in Arabic. Female writers, such as Zaynab Fawwāz (d. 1914), appeared not only as playwrights but also as critics in journals. There were more private stages, and the first theater building in Cairo was also built for performances exclusively in Arabic. As the playwright Maḥmūd Wāṣif wrote in his introduction to a 1900 edition of *Hārūn al-Rashīd,* there was an "Arab revival in Egypt" (*nahḍa ʿarabiyya fī Miṣr*) "in the shadow of his Highness the Khedive."[4] Plays were translated and composed in Arabic, which challenged public norms and textual standards. This chapter cannot pay justice to the richness of Arabic production and staging of plays in various settings. I only follow here the peak of patriotism through elite figures in order to catch the governing norms and framework of politics during the first years of Abbas Hilmi II's reign.

Markers of Distinction

How should we define the patriotic elite in late Ottoman Egypt? In this section, I draw on the sociologist Pierre Bourdieu's theory of distinction and various forms of capital in order to paint a picture of the elite audience, and in general, to describe late-nineteenth-century Egyptian urban society.[5] Bourdieu argues that "cultural capital" is a form of accumulated knowledge, convertible into economic capital, but which also represents an investment by external wealth into the personal habitus.[6] While the embodied symbolic value within an individual's personality is usually called "refinement" and "urbanity" (the original meaning of Arabic *adab* and *ʿumrāniyya*) its function is more than a convertible asset. Shared norms and shared knowledge establish a *solidarity* between the

[4] Wāṣif, *Riwāyat Hārūn al-Rashīd,* 2.
[5] Bourdieu, *Distinction.*
[6] Bourdieu, "The Forms of Capital," 48.

possessors of the same cultural capital. In turn, solidarity and markers establish a community of norms. This imagined community of norms was discursively bound by the idea of the homeland. Yet, while the patriotic collectivity was imagined as everyone's nation, in practice it was the possession of the few who shared these norms.

I connect cultural capital to elite class formation.[7] I use the term "class" here as derived from Arabic discourses in the 1890s regarding economically distinct groups. The Arabic word for "class" is *ṭabaqa*, literally, the "layer" of society; it has been used to denote various groupings of peoples and things, the typical example being the individuals who belong to one profession (like the poets) or to one generation (like ninth-century scholars). *Ṭabaqa* from the 1890s started to denote also "classes" of society in Arabic. A new, French-inspired sociological taxonomy replaced the old social categories, such as ruler and ruled, or the distinct elites of *zevat* and *aʿyān*, with that of one single patriotic elite, the middle class, and the poor.

Poor, Not Poor, and the Middle

A discussion arguing that "the rich" had a *political* responsibility towards "the poor" in Egypt started as early as the 1870s, as we have seen in the theater play of ʿAbd Allāh Nadīm in chapter 5. (The ancient Muslim pious obligation is not discussed here.) Two decades later, in the 1890s, articles in the journal *Miṣbāḥ al-Sharq* with titles such as "The Sons of Princes" condemned the increasingly lavish lifestyle of the sons of *zevat*.[8] Theoretical articulation of the new social taxonomy was perhaps first expressed by Aḥmad Fatḥī Zaghlūl, the brother of the later nationalist Saʿd Zaghlūl in 1899.[9] In the Arabic works of the time, the word "middle" (*wasaṭ*) denoted an imagined social layer between rich and poor. An often quoted work, *The Present of Egyptians* (*Ḥāḍir al-Miṣriyyin*, 1902) by a certain Muḥammad ʿUmar underlined the importance of the middle layer (*al-ṭabaqa al-wusṭā*) in patriotism. He thought "they are the blossom of the nation" (*zahrat al-umma*).[10] ʿUmar understood the middle mostly in terms of *function* and *institutions*. The institutions include those–which, at that time, were related around the world to bourgeois patriotic activities—al-Azhar (a university), courts,

[7] Egyptian and non-Egyptian historians often use the category of class to describe workers and middle class formation. Beinin and Lockman, *Workers on the Nile*; and Lockman, "Imagining the Working Class."

[8] Mestyan and Volait, "Affairisme dynastique."

[9] [Demolins], Dīmūlān, *Sirr Taqaddum*, 18–31.

[10] ʿUmar, *Kitāb Ḥāḍir al-Miṣriyyīn*, 83. Cf. the interpretation of Roussillon, "Réforme sociale."

the trade, and Arabic journals.[11] The destiny of the middle class, according to ʿUmar, was patriotism (*waṭaniyya*), which was to be produced by the knowledge learned in these institutions; furthermore, only this *ṭabaqa* could overcome religious divisions and achieve independence through national unity.

As Ryzova shows, Egyptians born in the 1890s in the countryside often used the category of the middle class, or at least a perceivable difference between their family and both the poor and the elite, to describe their background in hindsight.[12] Rural notables, however, were often aware of their high social status and wealth. For instance, the later politician, ʿAbd al-Raḥmān ʿAzzām (1893–1976), who was born in an *aʿyān* family, realized that he was from one of the "highest families."[13] The British occupation was generally favorable for the local landowning elite by further securing their lands and rights gained earlier. Ultimately, it was the *aʿyān* disguised as middle class that would lead the national independence movement.

Egyptian intellectuals, often from *aʿyān* background, used literature to define themselves. Rising Egyptian novelists, Samah Selim argues, expressed themselves as distinct from the poor: "The narrative representation of this class's social environment (*al-wāqiʿ al-ijtimāʿī*) was one of the mechanisms by which this process of self-reflection unfolded. The *fallāh* provided the raw material for the new nationalist literary imagination, while also figuring as an archetypal narrative other for the cosmopolitan, urban subject."[14] Michael Gasper affirms "the power of representation" through various texts in the 1890s in which peasant characters talk about progress and politics, and argues that "the new Egyptian [was] defined . . . by a new kind of social consciousness."[15]

Nation-Ness, Religion, and Charity

An Arabic journal remarked in 1893 that "the [charitable] societies are the strength of the nation (*umma*)."[16] The wealth and changing culture of the rural and urban elite was articulated in public rituals of solidarity. The interplay of charitable societies and Arabic theater performances provide a window into this articulation. Patriotism and philanthropy were connected as a religious *and* class activity in order

[11] ʿUmar, *Kitāb Ḥāḍir al-Miṣriyyīn*, 188.
[12] Ryzova, *The Age of the Efendiyya*, 59.
[13] Coury, *The Making of an Egyptian Arab Nationalist*, 64.
[14] Selim, *The Novel and the Rural*, 5.
[15] Gasper, *The Power of Representation*, 127.
[16] *Al-Farāyid*, 15 May 1893, 174.

to finance education and welfare services since the government did not provide enough.[17]

The most visible charitable society was the Syrian Orthodox Society (*al-Jamʿiyya al-Sūriyya al-Urthūdhuksiyya*), established in 1875 or 1876 in Alexandria. This organization had attracted 34,000 subscribers by 1880. In 1881, Armenians in Egypt also established their own charitable society (*al-Jamʿiyya al-Khayriyya al-Armaniyya*).[18] Muslim Egyptians grouped in two main societies in late 1870s Cairo: the Society of Benevolent Intentions (*Jamʿiyyat al-Maqāṣid al-Khayriyya*) and the Muslim Charitable Society (*al-Jamʿiyya al-Khayriyya al-Islāmiyya*). In 1880, Sheikh Muḥammad ʿAbduh underlined the usefulness of such organizations for Muslim Egyptians and asked for government support.[19] ʿAbd Allāh Nadīm, in his play *al-Waṭan* (1879), also suggested the charitable society as the best social form for (nongovernment) education.[20] Such societies were important sites of political discussion before the ʿUrābī revolution. Later, among the post-1882 societies, in addition to the Syrian Orthodox, we find the Orthodox Coptic Charitable Society, under the presidency of Buṭrus Ghālī, and the Roman Catholic Charitable Society, with president Bishāra Taqlā, while the Muslim charity organization of the 1880s was the Tawfīq Charitable Society, under the honorary presidency of heir presumptive Abbas Hilmi.[21] In the 1890s, the most politically important Muslim society was the Islamic Charitable Society (*al-Jamʿiyya al-Khayriyya al-Islāmiyya*), established in 1893 by mostly *aʿyān*-origin lawyers whose main goal was to finance education. They often used both the al-Azbakiyya Garden and the Opera House for charitable performances.[22]

The emerging bourgeoisie displayed itself according to religious lines during charity performances in the Opera House, al-Azbakiyya, and in the Zizinia theater in Alexandria—though these lines could also be crossed. As discussed in chapter 6, the cooperation with charitable societies for Arabic theater troupes was often crucial in order to gain more visibility and a larger audience. This included a few cross-sectarian interactions. In 1885, the Muslim singer ʿAbduh al-Ḥamūlī was asked by the Greek Catholics' Charitable Society to contribute to a charity evening in the Opera House.[23] However, finally, instead of ʿAbduh, the troupe of

[17] No historical work has been written about these crucial organizations, their function in society, or their economics from the late 1870s; only a short introduction can be given here.

[18] *Al-Ahrām*, 17 May 1881, 2.

[19] Republished in ʿAbduh, *al-Aʿmāl al-Kāmila*, 2:5–7. Originally *al-Waqāʾiʿ al-Miṣriyya*, 19 October 1880.

[20] Sadgrove, *Egyptian Theatre*, 145.

[21] Āṣāf, *Dalīl Miṣr li-ʿĀmmay 1889–1890*, 163.

[22] Al-Hilbāwī, *Mudhakkirāt*, 118–119, Farīd, *Mudhakkirāt*, 186, etc.

[23] *Al-Ahrām*, 26 February 1885, 2.

Yūsuf Khayyāṭ performed the play *al-Ẓalūm* (The Tyrant) starring another Egyptian Muslim singer, Salāma Ḥijāzī, who "won a complete victory over the hearts" of the audience.[24] ʿAbduh al-Ḥamūlī sang in Alexandria for the benefit of *Jamʿiyyat al-Tawfīq al-Khayriyya* in 1886.[25] One year later, he repeated this in the Cairo Opera House for the benefit of the Free Jewish Schools (*al-Madāris al-Isrāʾīliyya al-Majāniyya, Écoles Gratuites Israélites du Caire*), and *al-Ahrām*, run by Christian Arabs, thanked his benevolence.[26] These instances have often been considered as proofs of liberal cosmopolitanism or nationalist unity. However, the occasions are rare, and served class socialization.

Theatrical Societies and Charity

The self-educative aspect of the intersection of charity and theater must be also highlighted. Najm enumerates dozens of "theater societies" (*jamʿiyyāt al-tamthīl*) from the 1880s until World War One.[27] These were clubs and groups of men (and perhaps women) who did not earn their living as actors but considered theater an important passion or social duty. The earliest, the Society of Refined Education (*Jamʿiyyat al-Maʿārif al-Adabiyya*), was established in 1885 by officials of the Train and of the Post Companies and lasted until 1908. It had the explicit aim of bringing "Egyptian taste" into theater as opposed to the taste of Europeans and Syrians. In the 1890s dozens of such amateur, often ephemeral, theatrical associations were established: *Jamʿiyyat al-Ibtihāj al-Adabī* (1894), *Jamʿiyyat al-Taraqqī al-Adabī* (1894), *Jamʿiyyat al-Sirāj al-Munīr* (1895), *Jamʿiyyat al-Ittifāq* (1896), *Jamʿiyyat Nuzhat al-ʿĀʾilāt* (1897), *Jamʿiyyat Muḥibbī al-Tamthīl* (1899), and so on.[28] These amateur clubs and groups entertained relations with the more influential charitable societies. Most important, the society-troupes represented a middle-class form of engagement with self-refinement and solidarity, somewhat independent from the large landowner elite and *zevat* aristocracy.

Prices and Salaries

It is time to talk money. The acquisition of cultural capital is typically conditioned by economic factors and by transmission. The economic factors in the case of theater performances can be measured through the

[24] *Al-Ahrām*, 17 April 1885, 2.

[25] *Al-Ahrām*, 12 April 1886, 3.

[26] *Al-Ahrām*, 24 March 1887, 2.

[27] Following Najm, Ismāʿīl, *Taʾrīkh al-Masraḥ al-Miṣrī*, 233–262 also lists a number of societies. Al-Dasūqī, *Al-Taʾrīkh al-Thaqāfī*, mostly repeats Ismāʿīl's work concerning the theaters.

[28] Najm, *al-Masraḥiyya*, 176–182.

ticket prices. The Opera House was described by English journals as the space of "the richer classes" in December 1882.[29] The writer Tawfīq al-Ḥakīm quotes in a semifictional note an actor who started his career in 1882 and who "remembers" that at the time the ticket was only 1 piaster for an ordinary performance but for a Qardāḥī-Ḥijāzī performance in the Opera the cheapest was 4 piaster so they could watch it only once![30] Who had the money to watch a play in the theater? And who had the clothes to attend the Opera?

In its first years, the entrance fee to khedivial theaters, for simple seats, was indeed expensive for the ordinary. In 1869 the cheapest ticket for a third floor seat in the opera was two francs (around 8 piasters), but the first floor best loges cost 75 French francs.[31] In December 1869, the best places in the Cirque were five francs, three for the second rank and one and a half francs for the cheapest seats.[32] Yet despite the cheap tickets, the expenses were not calculated for the income at the gate: Draneht's system, as we have seen, always operated at a deficit.

Compare the 1869 prices with the salary of Aḥmad al-Kūmī, the *farrāsh* of the Opera House. In the middle of the financial crisis, in 1877 he earned monthly 38.88 francs (149 piasters), as shown in table 3.1. Al-Kūmī, a man who received relatively low pay, could visit the Circus by spending approximately one day's salary on the cheapest ticket or two days' salary for the cheapest ticket in the Opera (provided, of course, that he already owned the appropriate clothes). If he ever wanted to rent the best loge in the Opera, he would have had to spend two months' salary for a single evening. (However, since he was the *farrāsh* of the Opera he could watch the plays for free.)

Yet in fact, al-Kūmī's salary in 1877 was still double that of the average worker's wage. The average daily wage of an unskilled worker or peasant was two piasters (the price of a load of bread, approximately 0.5 franc), that is, monthly around 60 piasters (around 15 francs). Given this, one can also measure the significance of the amounts donated by some pashas to the French and Italian artists. For instance, in 1870 for the *caisse des secours* of the actors Ali Pasha Şerif donated 505.5 francs, Sefer Pasha 500 and "La Princesse Said Pacha" 757.50 francs.[33] This last donation is almost twenty times more in one sum than al-Kūmī's monthly salary, and more than forty times more than an unskilled worker's monthly pay. The favorite musician of Khedive Ismail, ʿAbduh al-Ḥamūlī, is said

[29] *Egyptian Gazette*, 30 November 1882, 2.

[30] Al-Ḥakīm, *Dhikriyyāt*, 21.

[31] *Wādī al-Nīl*, 5 November 1869, 869. The advertisment says 120 or 1.20 "British pounds" as equivilant of 75 francs, but this seems to be a miscalculation.

[32] *Wādī al-Nīl*, 3 December 1869, 972.

[33] Draneht to Riaz, 21 February 1870, Maḥfaẓa 80, CAI, DWQ.

to have received the handsome 15 LE (375 francs) and Almāẓ 10 LE (250 francs) monthly salaries in the 1870s.[34] It is worth remembering that the Private Domains paid 320,000 francs alone for *Aida*'s production in 1871, an almost unimaginable sum compared to the salary of workers and even bureaucrats in the khedivate.

Later theater, even the Opera House, became more accessible. In the 1880s–1890s the Egyptian pound was relatively stable, fluctuating around 25–26 francs. One franc was 4 piasters. In the spring of 1882, the impresario Paravey calculated 180 LE (4680 francs) for the whole season and 4 LE (104 francs) per performance for a first-class box; 65 LE (1690 francs) for a second class box and 2 LE (52 francs) per performance; and a simple seat's annual subscription 20 LE (520 francs) and 8 francs [!] per evening; and in the amphitheater 2.5 francs per evening without subscription.[35] Compare this with Saʿd Zaghlūl's salary of 8 LE (208 francs) monthly as the assistant editor of the official bulletin in 1881.[36] He could easily watch the Ḥijāzī-Qardāḥī performances, which were presumably cheaper, in the ʿUrābist spring of 1882.

Ryzova quotes that the young ʿAbd al-ʿAzīz Fahmī in 1889 was very happy to be appointed in a job with 8–12 LE (208–312 francs) monthly salary, since the average was 5 LE (130 francs). She adds that in the early 1900s, a rural household of five lived on 3 LE (78 francs) monthly. Two *feddan* of land could yield 25–30 LE (650–780 francs) yearly, approximately 2 LE (52 francs) monthly.[37] The high officials of the government earned comparatively generous amounts: for example, Yūsuf Shakūr was appointed the head of the Alexandria municipality council in 1892 with 100 LE (2500 francs) monthly;[38] while Fayzi Pasha was appointed governor of the Gharbiyya province with 125 LE (3125 francs) monthly salary in 1893.[39] One must note again that ʿAbduh al-Ḥamūlī is said to have received yearly 180 LE from Khedive Tevfik, too, in the 1880s.[40] It was good to be an Ottoman Arab star.

The young Ismāʿīl Ṣidqī (1875–1950; prime minister in the interwar period) earned only 5 LE (130 francs) monthly in 1894 and envied his friend ʿAbd al-Khāliq Tharwat, who was one year ahead, earning 15 LE (390 francs) at the same time.[41] Ismāʿīl Ṣidqī would have had to spend

[34] Lagrange, "Musiciens et poètes en Égypte," 73.

[35] Letter dated 18 March 1882, Paravey to MTP, Maḥfaẓa 2/1, Niẓārat al-Ashghāl, Majlis al-Wuẓarāʾ, DWQ.

[36] Al-Hilbāwī, *Mudhakkirāt*, 73.

[37] Ryzova, *The Age of the Efendiyya*, 115, 135.

[38] Farīd, *Mudhakkirāt*, 102–103.

[39] Ibid., 117.

[40] Lagrange, "Musiciens et poètes en Égypte," 152.

[41] Badrawi, *Ismaʿil Sidqi*, 3.

almost his whole monthly salary for a first-class box in the Opera House for one evening, but he could have regular access to a simple seat if he wished so and had the proper clothes. He could participate, and likely did so, in the patriotic charity occasions of the Islamic Charitable Society in the late 1890s, which asked 10 piasters (0.1 LE, 2.5 francs) for the ticket in al-Azbakiyya Garden but 50 piasters (0.5 LE, 12.5 francs) for an ordinary seat in a charity evening in the Opera House and finally 5 LE (the entry-level monthly salary of bureaucrats) for a first-class box![42]

Comparatively, in 1895 in the private Abbas Hilmi Theatre in Alexandria (it was called khedivial, but it was a business enterprise) tickets for an Italian production were the following: the best box was 1 LE (100 piasters, 25 francs this time) for one performance, which included the entry of three individuals, a numbered seat went for 8 piasters, and a simple entry was 5 piasters.[43] Compare this with the 292.20 piaster monthly salary of Saʿd Zaghlūl's cook in 1901.[44]

Based on this data, there were hierarchies between theater buildings, performances, and within the theater itself. Access varied according to income. A simple seat for an ordinary performance in a private theater in the 1880s–1890s was affordable for bureaucrats, small merchants, teachers, or even for a cook in fin-de-siècle Egypt. A middle-income bureaucrat could join the audience by buying simple seats even in the Opera House—if he had the proper clothes. Sartorial politics and interest, however, were possibly defined by the family background. Ṣidqī, for instance, came from an assimilated, elite Turco-Egyptian family in government service, and thus possibly had a suit as part of his social background. In general, the above data means that the Arabic reports we have followed about performances in the Opera reflect the experience, emotions, and ideology of the wealthier segments of Egyptian society.

Language and Moral Distinction: The Educated Nation

Language also became a marker of distinction and a central characteristic of the patriotic idea of community. I have already argued that public patriotism had to occur in *fuṣḥā* Arabic because of its historical depth and because of the difference between Syrian-Egyptian vernaculars. The space of the theater and the opera house in particular helped to transform the earlier mode of addressing the ruler into a new mode of speech, still in Arabic, but this time addressing the imagined community. There seems to have been an understanding among educated Arab intellectuals

[42] Al-Hilbāwī, *Mudhakkirāt*, 118–119.
[43] *Egyptian Gazette*, Supplement, 17 January 1895, 1.
[44] Zaghlūl, *Mudhakkirāt*, 1:160.

that only those who know *fuṣḥā* Arabic could speak in the name of the nation (*umma*). Language use further emphasized the distinction between poor and not poor in cultural terms.

However, this distinction was not clear cut. I have already tackled the question of language in plays and poetry. With the exception of Sanua and Jalāl, we have seen a preference for *fuṣḥā* Arabic in plays (Nadīm uses *ʿāmmiyya* for characterization). Naqqāsh, Khayyāṭ, Qardāḥī, and al-Qabbānī in the 1880s and 1890s mostly staged or composed *fuṣḥā* plays in which *ʿāmmiyya* was often used for articulating humorous situations. A particular example in chapter 6 was the play *Hārūn al-Rashīd* by Maḥmūd Wāṣif, staged by Qardāḥī's troupe. Intellectuals such as the writer Muḥammad ʿUmar, and the journalist and politician Muṣṭafā Kāmil, also preferred *fuṣḥā* in public speech.[45]

Wafā Muḥammad, the guardian of books in the Khedivial Library, published his opinion about the vernacular and *fuṣḥā* Arabic in 1892. He emphasized that the ordinary speaker had no conscious knowledge about language but that educated speakers were special because "only they can be called rightly by the name 'nation' (*umma*) [because their] books are written in the *fuṣḥā* language in which there is no distinction between Muslim and Christian, only between Eastern and Western [ways of writing]."[46] It was no surprise that he considered "the unity of language . . . a condition for the unity of the nation" and asserted that "the speakers of Arabic in all territories are all possessors of the same connection: the Arabic language."[47] According to Wafā Efendi, the young khedive Abbas Hilmi II was especially intent on teaching *fuṣḥā* in Egyptian schools.[48] This employee connected educated Arabic to dynastic praise *and* patriotic (here: pan-Arab) unity. We may also note that in 1892 an Academy of Arabic Language (*Mujtamaʿ/Majmaʿ al-Lugha al-ʿArabiyya*) was established in Egypt—a development that did not please every Egyptian.[49] It was also in these years that patriots such as the young Muḥammad Farīd remarked that the use of French in official occasions should be replaced by "the noble Arabic language."[50]

The use of language in theater developed into an expression of social distinction. An example is the writer and actor Faraḥ Anṭūn (1874–1922), yet another fervent Ottomanist from Beirut. His play *New and Old Egypt* was accompanied by an explanation about the play itself and about "the problem of language." The problem was the language registers, and the

45 Fahmy, *Ordinary Egyptians*, 89.
46 Muḥammad, *Muqaddimat Kitāb al-Tuḥfa*, 4.
47 Ibid., 6–7.
48 Ibid., 16.
49 *Al-Ustādh*, 7 March 1893, 673–686.
50 Farīd, *Mudhakkirāt*, 165.

fact that *fuṣḥā* was not used in everyday exchange. Anṭūn believed that one had to use *fuṣḥā* Arabic if the play was a translated one, because the original language in which the characters spoke was foreign (*aʿjamiyya*). The problem of register arose when the play was in Arabic and related events and activities that in life happened in *ʿāmmiyya*. What would the audience think, asks Anṭūn with horror, if "they would hear the ladies of dancing cafes, the [street] sellers of the newspapers, the female and male servants, the Nubians (*barābira*), the drunken and the negligent or even the ladies in their private rooms talk in *fuṣḥā*?" But if the author would use *ʿāmmiyya* in general he would commit an even more horrible mistake, namely, that of weakening pure Arabic, thus harming "those who tasted the pleasure of this language." His solution was that the elite characters should talk in *fuṣḥā*, because their education made doing so their "right" (*ḥaqq*), while the ordinary characters would talk in *ʿāmmiyya*. In order to avoid situations in which one person might ask in *fuṣḥā* and the other answers in *ʿāmmiyya* he sometimes allowed elite characters to talk in *ʿāmmiyya*, even a pasha.[51] But the socially inferior would never use *fuṣḥā*. Such social valorisation of language here was a literary trick but mirrored the deeper relationship between *fuṣḥā* and power.

In addition, language is a complex operation of somatic communication, especially in the theater. For instance, Qardāḥī once performed the role of Othello with an Italian company in Alexandria and while they spoke Italian, he "embodied the role in an Arabic way" (*yumaththil tamthīlān ʿarabiyyān*) on stage.[52] This might have meant his use of the Arabic language or a somatic movement characteristic of Arab actors or simply that he was regarded as an "Arab."

Elites and Public Entertainment as Honorable

Ryzova points out that between the wars middle-class Egyptian families held up their respectability by enjoying entertainment in private.[53] The valorization of leisure, however, occurred with the opposite value among the wealthy. Being publicly entertained in official spaces became in itself a social marker of distinction. This change transpired through an interplay between cultural, gender, and economic codes. Being publically entertained and being an elite male individual were connected. In khedivial theaters, there was also the sense that through sheer bodily presence Ottoman Egyptian dignitaries were displaying sovereignty.

[51] Anṭūn, *Miṣr al-Jadīda*, pages bā–dāl.
[52] *Al-Ahrām*, 31 October 1894, 4.
[53] Ryzova, *The Age of Efendiyya*, 195 and 204.

Dignity and Elite Theater

In the early period of khedivial culture Ismail financed a number of loges through *al-Dāʾira al-Khāṣṣa*, both in the Opera and in the Comédie for the members of his entourage (in French *Suite de Son Altesse*). However, not everyone's seat was covered automatically. For instance, Ismail's son "Prince" Hüseyin did not pay for his loge in December 1869, and Draneht had to ask for the payment from the Private Domains. There is no information revealing whether the "princesses" of the harem ever paid for their special loges. For instance, in the contract with Meynadier in 1871, the boxes of the khedive and his harem were included free of charge in the Comédie. Thus, in the 1870s a number of Ottoman Egyptian dignitaries attended the theaters in Cairo, because it was free for them, and, possibly, because they were interested.[54]

The children of elite families were certainly interested. The khedivial children as early as in 1870 were brought to the Circus with the female members of the harem by Zurayb Bey, the doctor of Ismail.[55] Aḥmad Shafīq (Ahmed Şefik), an important member of Abbas Hilmi II's court, recollected that his brother and the schoolmates were desperate to attend the performances in the Opera during Ismail's reign. They employed a trick. They bought two tickets, and two of them entered the building. Then one came out with the two tickets and two again entered and so on. Their passion may also have been fueled by the fact that every year Ismail sent free tickets to the best student group in that school.[56] This anecdote evokes again the idea of "internal Europe" in Egypt and alludes to the fact that the acquisition of high European culture started in childhood for the new elite generation *within* Egypt before they studied in France or England.

An anecdote underscores that the Opera House became very important—arguably even ridiculously important—for the "princes" of the ruling dynasty. Mehmed Ali, the younger brother of Abbas Hilmi II, and his uncle Fuad (the later King Fuad) initially shared a box in the 1890s. Only Mehmed Ali used it because Fuad gave up his share. In 1897 Mehmed Ali failed to respond to inquiries regarding whether he wanted to keep the box, therefore, Fuad was given full ownership. Mehmed Ali became furious and, though apologies were made, he decided he now wanted a box of his own.[57] A box at the Opera was by this

[54] This paragraph is based on various letters between 1869 and 1878 in Maḥfaẓa 80, CAI, DWQ. For the ruler as a patriarch within the dynasty, cf. Konrad, *Der Hof der Khediven*, 168–170.

[55] Jerichau-Baumann, "Egypt, 1870," 281.

[56] Shafīq, *Mudhakkirātī*, 1: 57–58. This supposes that the tickets were not checked or marked at the entrance.

[57] Harrison, *The Homely Diary*, 50–52.

time understood as a prime space for practicing one's modernizing habitus and was included in the symbolic hierarchy of elite honor.

We have seen examples of educated Arabic- and Turkish-speakers who celebrated the theater as an appropriate public space. Amīn Fikrī (son of ʿAbd Allāh Fikrī), for instance, during his visit to the Orientalist Congress in Stockholm in 1889 found nothing objectionable at a reception about the dancers of the Swedish Opera in Egyptian costumes.[58] In 1896, the young Muṣṭafā Kāmil gave his first political speech in Arabic in the Abbas Theatre in Alexandria to an audience of eight hundred people, including some Egyptian notables (*aʿyān*).[59] The theater building served as a space that staged him *as* a public figure.

There were less dignifying venues such as the Garden Theatre in al-Azbakiyya, which nonetheless counted as proper for khedivial representation. On the occasion of the performances by an Ottoman Armenian troupe in 1885, the Turkish-speaking ladies of Cairo attended this small theater; at their head was Madame Nubar—and Khedive Tevfik.[60] There were also charity balls held in al-Azbakiyya. Sometimes, such as in 1895, the famous Egyptian singers ʿAbduh al-Ḥamūlī, Muḥmmad ʿUthmān, and Sheikh Yūsuf sang together for the attendees, including the khedivial family, ministers, and Lord and Lady Cromer.[61] The Garden Theatre was also important to governmental employees. In 1897 ʿAbd al-Karīm Mūsā, an employee at the Ministry of Public Works, complained that he did not receive the free place there that was granted to the staff of the ministry. He was seated in a first-class chair, but he had to move to a less prestigious seat, and so after the first part of the play he left in anger.[62] This example shows that employees in lesser positions also thought that they had a right to free seats in theaters owned by the government.

Private theaters also served as spaces of elite entertainment. In Alexandria, the Zizinia Theatre from its inception served as an embodiment of (resident Italian, Greek, French, later Syrian) bourgeois wealth and power. Here rulers and statesmen also regularly appeared, and the khedive had his own box. We have seen that between 1879 and 1882 Tevfik participated in Arabic performances in this private theater. In the 1880s, the prefect of the city and the Cairo-based pashas on holiday also

[58] Fikrī, *Irshād al-Alibbā*, 2: 713–714. Reid, *Whose Pharaohs?*, 250 states that *Aida* was also performed, but I do not find any trace of this. See also *La Turquie*, 28 September 1889, 2 in which the (possibly French) journalist mocks the Egyptian delegation.

[59] Kāmil, *Miṣr wa-l-Iḥtilāl al-Inklīzī*, 130–151 (with the ensuing debate about the dukhalāʾ).

[60] *Al-Ahrām*, 16 March 1885, 2.

[61] *Egyptian Gazette*, 14 January 1895, 3.

[62] Letter dated 19 September 1897, from ʿAbd al-Karīm Mūsā to Minister, 4003–036055, DWQ.

attended performances. Zülfikar Pasha, for instance, in 1888 supported the charity organization of the Roman Catholics by attending a performance in the Zizinia.[63] In 1896, Ismāʿīl Ṣabrī attended the Greek community's evening in the Zizinia, occupying the loge of the khedive.[64] Muṣṭafā Kāmil, as noted, entered the public sphere physically in this building.

Entertainment as Dishonorable—and the Military Occupation

Stages that served a purely commercial function, such as café-chantants, revues, and cabarets, were criticized through a specific moral (and gendered) discourse from the 1890s. There were voices that government-financed spaces were also immoral. In the already quoted novel of Muḥammad al-Muwayliḥī the resurrected character, Ahmed Pasha al-Manakli, becomes angry upon seeing the statute of Ibrahim (once his friend and military leader) in front of the Opera House. His companion, ʿĪsā ibn Hishām comments that the Opera "does more harm than good."[65]

The discourses of dishonor, however, rarely crossed into official territory. There are no instances of ballet performances in the Opera House being criticized, for example, even though there was frequent criticism of dancing girls in bars around al-Azbakiyya. The café chantants in the neighborhood offered roulette games where Egyptians spent, and too often lost, their money as early as the 1870s.[66] As discussed in chapter 7, immoral dancing in cafes was prohibited in the early 1890s. Musicians cursed the music halls as "caves of demons," and al-Azbakiyya itself was decried as a "square of debauchery and immorality."[67]

The British military occupation facilitated the opening of shops with alcohol licenses and the creation of more entertainment spaces for soldiers in the 1880s. There were special theaters to entertain British soldiers. The main space in Cairo, apart from the Club, was the Azbakiyya Garden where a British military band performed in the afternoons. Several plays in English or French were staged during the late 1880s and 1890s, often in temporary army theaters; there was even one in the Citadel. Officers frequented al-Azbakiyya, but were apparently quite loud (for instance, in June 1886 British military music was forbidden here for a period, out of respect for the death of Hoşyar Hanım).[68] Another private

63 *Al-Qāhira (al-Ḥurra)*, 22 May 1888, 3.
64 *La Correspondance Égyptienne illustrée*, 1–8 April 1896, 4–5.
65 al-Muwayliḥī, *A Period of Time*, 299.
66 Zádori, *Éjszakafrikai útivázlatok*, 95.
67 Al-Khulaʿī, *Al-Mūsiqā al-Sharqī*, 172, n. 1.
68 *Al-Ahrām*, 29 June 1886, 2–3.

theater that the British officers often visited was a Politeama building in Cairo, where General Stephenson was celebrated once.[69] In general, they—together with some Egyptian army officers—drank and looked for women in the new pubs and cafes around al-Azbakiyya.[70]

Occupiers and Ottomans in the Khedivial Opera House

The game of empires served as the backdrop for Cairo high society in the 1880s. Since the doctrine of the territorial integrity of the Ottoman Empire and the costs of occupation pushed the British towards early evacuation, a new agreement was planned. In 1885 an Ottoman-British agreement specified that two high commissioners should be sent to Egypt as direct representatives of both governments, in addition to de facto rulers: the British consul-general and the khedive. From the British side Sir Henry Drummond Wolff (1830–1908) and from the Ottoman side Gazi Ahmed Muhtar Pasha (1839–1919) were chosen. Their task was to negotiate the evacuation and the future size of the Egyptian army. This goal was never achieved. Among the reasons for the failure were the unstable British politics, changing public opinion, Baring's opposition, and the Mahdi's revolt in the Sudan.[71] Wolff was recalled in 1887, but Muhtar Pasha remained in Egypt for two decades.[72]

This was the political context for the revival of elite patriotism, as we have seen in chapter 6. After surveying distinction based on economic and social capital, let us now focus on the way politics and distinction were connected in the main, symbolic khedivial space: the Khedivial Opera House.

Occupiers and Subscribers

Special evenings were arranged for the senior army officers and members of the British resident community, for instance, in April 1884 in the Opera House.[73] The colonial administrators, however, in general were not fond of opera performances. George Boyle, one of the British administrators who spent the longest time in colonial Egypt, wrote to his

[69] *Al-Qāhira (al-Ḥurra)*, 5 January 1887, 2.

[70] Cf. various letters in AHP.

[71] Hornik, "The Mission of Sir Henry Drummond-Wolff."

[72] Peri, "Ottoman Symbolism"; Hirszowicz, "The Sultan and the Khedive"; Deringil, "Ghazi Ahmed Mukhtar Pasha"; Owen, *Lord Cromer*, 217.

[73] *Al-Ahrām*, 30 April 1884, 3.

mother in 1904 that he went to the Opera, "a thing I seldom do."[74] A senior military officer, Lord Cecil, described the opera as "nothing else on Earth except a concert of cats."[75] Nonetheless, Cromer had to attend performances, even the Arabic ones, to counterbalance the presence of the khedive. (Naturally, Cromer and his wife also gave "almost weekly parties" at the embassy for their own British community.)[76] Wolff, the British High Commissioner, regularly attended the Opera House while in Cairo, and an American diplomat also loved to go to the Opera at the end of the 1890s.[77] In this way, the Khedivial Opera House served as an unofficial space for imperial diplomacy, too. How can we define the wealthy and official audience in the 1880s and 1890s?

The government provided a definition. In 1886 they wanted to suppress the sponsorship of the winter seasons. They expected that individuals who were described as "a class" of foreigners economically "benefitting directly from their stay in Cairo" should provide at least half of the expenses for bringing foreign troupes.[78] The definition of a "class" of "those who profit directly from their stay in Cairo" can be further qualified by a subscription list from the same year, 1886, as given in table 8.1.

The 230 names were registered by the impresarios to support their request for the next season's concession in 1886–1887, and this purpose must be taken into consideration. These names comprise the core of what we might think of as the myth of a cosmopolitan elite in Cairo. It includes individuals whose profession could be regarded as elite at the time: diplomats, bankers, senior military officers, lawyers, doctors, and directors of companies. Mostly Italian, French, British, Greek, and few local (such as the Qaṭṭāwīs) names figure in the list. Notable are the Russian consuls at the very end (who may have been added in haste). Names such as Izzet Bey, Camougli, Farrag Bey, A. Nassif, Moussally allude to individuals of Ottoman background who were interested in Italian opera. The list includes men of distinction, and perhaps men who wanted to be seen as such. Despite the fact that these are all male names, it is more likely that whole families rented boxes. Since Sir Wolff, the British Imperial Commissioner, headed the list, let us turn now to his operatic counterbalance, the Ottoman representative Ahmed Muhtar Pasha.

[74] Letter dated 20 February 1904, Boyle to his mother, File 2, Box C, Gordon, GB165–0120, MECA.

[75] Cecil, *The Leisure of an Egyptian Officer*, 146.

[76] Quoted in Owen, *Lord Cromer*, 253.

[77] Harrison, *The Homely Diary*, 49.

[78] Note dated 26 April 1888, 0075–006682, DWQ.

TABLE 8.1. List of 230 Subscribers to the Seasons of Santi Boni and Soschino in the Khedivial Opera House, 1885–1886 (original order, original orthography)

1. S. E. Sir H Drummond Wolff
2. Le Général J. Stephenson
3. Le Général Clery
4. Lord Waux of Harrowden
5. Lord Dunmore
6. Gerald M. Portal
7. S. E. Izzet Bey
8. Major C. M. Macdonald
9. Jacques Cattaoui
10. J. Oppenheim
11. B. Bitter
12. V. Krikunmann?
13. J. Schnitzler
14. Ch. Kazenstein
15. L. A. Hope
16. W. C. Cartwright
17. Ch. T. Bruce
18. J. Suarès
19. Joseph Cattaoui
20. J. S. Coronel
21. N. Giro
22. J. Kthanassaky
23. Berthy
24. Art. Tito Tigani
25. De Sterliek
26. M et Mde Du Port Bey
27. Victor Gallichi
28. P. Pagnon
29. Pomphée Parvois
30. Joseph Parvois
31. U. Prinoth
32. A. Krieger
33. J. Brassem
34. Ambrose Sinadino
35. Le docteur Comanos
36. Le col Hallam Parr Bey
37. Le général Lothrab Pacha
38. Le colonel Ardagh
39. Le colonel Saint-Leger
40. Le Major Mouey [? Money?]
41. Le cap Murray (Royal Artillery)
42. Le Doc Loverds
43. Le doct N. Apergis
44. L'avocat Manusardi
45. L'ingénieur J. Battigelli
46. P. Roumoli
47. Emm. Severy
48. Klaus Hery Bey
49. J. Gianola et famille
50. L. A. Horn
51. N. Sabbay
52. A. Hailund
53. M. Sager
54. Le docteur Richter
55. Cesar de Farro
56. Davio de Farro
57. Auguste de Farro
58. R. Sternous
59. H. Cosi
60. M. J. Santini
61. A. Rossano
62. M. Georges LeChavalier
63. Charles Gravier
64. Arillat
65. Bertrand
66. M. Belleville
67. J. A. Perichon
68. L'avocate Cecconi
69. D. Chiarisoli
70. Pierre Bianchi
71. A. Bourgiae
72. Camougli
73. Tourneaux
74. H. Maujeand
75. Jauve
76. L. Désiré
77. V. Sabadini
78. Sinibaldi
79. J. S. Sinibaldi
80. E. Mattey
81. J. Francés
82. Lauteire
83. H. Belon
84. J. Belon
85. Paschal et Comp
86. H. Bengé
87. Le colonel Campbell
88. Avocat Manusardi
89. Le colonel J. H. Sandwitch
90. C. S. Mobuch
91. A. Steheglow
92. A. Ismalum
93. Le Colonel W. J. Myers
94. Le Captain Rouielly
95. A. Larahudi
96. Major A Crawford
97. Major W. Palmer
98. Valle (direction de la Poste)
99. Farag bey (chef de gas)
100. Avocat Dilberoglu
101. Le major Maletta
102. C. Galano
103. L'avocat Molteni
104. A. Jattucci
105. G. Cerranova
106. A. Nassif (jeune)
107. Victor Hancy
108. M.J.M. Rancy (inspection de gas Gouv.)
109. M. Mugard
110. J. Kantilly
111. G. Houres
112. P. J. Loukas
113. Lieut J. W. Shalhum
114. J. Leon
115. J. Jabbu
116. S. Madane
117. E. Montobbu
118. S. di A Miely

119. E. J. Beusehitt
120. J. B. Cantarutti
121. A. Pierini
122. L. Alimentano
123. E. Dello Sholago
124. M. and A. Miely
125. Roberto Jatta
126. Dante Montobbio
127. Rossamo e Morpurg[o?]
128. A. Oppi
129. P. Pilagatti
130. A. Oswald
131. G. Huggi Basilion
132. H. Vildamare
133. N. Apergis
134. L. Ricci
135. D. Casiragh
136. L. Jay
137. G. Penasson
138. A. de Sylla
139. Joa fréres
140. N. Gerassimo
141. S. Craves
142. A. Hopper
143. G. Roth
144. E. Bondy
145. J. Santarelly
146. G. Oubia
147. C. Bonnard
148. L. Santarelli
149. E. Romoly
150. G. Clava
151. A. Lauzone
152. Ar. C. Viligardi
153. M. Bajocchi
154. Leopardi
155. M. Stagni
156. U. Lucchesi
157. Cecchi
158. De Sterlich
159. C. Rosenzweig
160. C. Augiohm
161. Blattner
162. E. Dettorelly
163. Saponiader
164. C. Giordano
165. A. Runaldi
166. G. Gai
167. R. Bracci
168. A. Papadaky
169. M. Adamy
170. Auge Cerny
171. A. Montecarboli
172. J. Archivollte
173. A. Chelmys
174. H. Belon
175. Montopha [Mustapha?] Fréres
176. A. Petrini
177. E. Maneim (peintre)
178. E. Boccara
179. Dr G Gherardi avocat
180. Ingeneiur Caubruggi
181. Doct Sconomopoulo
182. J. Crovaioli
183. R. Hubner
184. J. Amatoury
185. B. Watson
186. J.K.D. Beek V.S.E.A.
187. S. Moussally
188. Doct. Jatron
189. L. Pagoni
190. R. Engelard
191. J. Kouphodonti
192. L. Rivalta
193. A. Spagnouli
194. M. De Colucci
195. A. Glavaris
196. G. Roth
197. M. Lucchezi
198. E. Janni
199. R. Dalli
200. J. Bortologgi
201. R. Khunberry maison de Stein
202. E. de la Bruyère
203. A. Fontini
204. A. Hausselem
205. M. Cicurel la maison Harmaux
206. A. Pini ingenieur
207. Albert Dupuis
208. Joseph D'Avrial [?]
209. A? Mayer
210. L. Gauchy
211. Em. Bopsoural [?]
212. G. Valassaki
213. J. Marmola Iploral
214. C. de P. Ceccarelli
215. C. di Lorenzo
216. H. Buccianti
217. O. Dakovich
218. J. Condom
219. A. de Tullion
220. G. Angioli
221. R. Cioni
222. V. Cartonie
223. V. Bigazzi
224. Ch. Verdi
225. Ch. Goethe
226. E. Mattier
227. L. Sinibaldi
228. A. Savioggi
229. Kitrovo Consul General de Russie
230. Ivanoff attaché au Consulat de Russie

Source: Letter dated 27 March 1886, 0075–008613, DWQ.

Ottomans and the Arabic Theater in the Opera

The Khedivial Opera House was instrumental for proclaiming Ottoman sovereignty in the late 1880s. This was an unexpected function given, as we may recall from chapter 3, that the theaters were constructed to hide the Ottoman face of khedivial Egypt.

Ahmed Muhtar arrived in Cairo in December 1885. The Ottoman Imperial High Commissioner was a remarkable man. A warrior and general of the Ottoman army, he fought the Russian army in 1877–1878 (hence the title *Gazi*). The presence of an Ottoman war hero aroused pro-Ottoman sentiments in British-occupied Cairo.[79] Muhtar was also a man of science, interested in time-keeping. He published a piece in Turkish on this theme immediately after his arrival in Cairo,[80] and also a Turkish-Arabic bilingual book (the Arabic translation was done by Şefik Mansur Yeğen, the nephew of the khedive).[81] It was well received among the local intelligentsia, who seem to have used the publication to introduce Ahmed Muhtar to the Egyptian elite.[82] In the light of On Barak's analysis of the general transformation of temporality in Egypt, it is remarkable that an Ottoman general was so concerned with time and periodization.[83] As the representative of the sultan, the liege-lord of the khedive, Muhtar lived in one of the most beautiful palaces, the Ismailiyya Palace. He also married his son to Khedive Ismail's youngest daughter, thus properly joining to the Ottoman Egyptian *zevat*.[84]

In occupied Egypt, the Ottoman Empire now provided the framework for patriotism in Arabic. Ahmed Muhtar faithfully upheld the Ottoman colors in Cairo, despite having only symbolic means, secret agents, and his own bodily presence to express Ottoman sovereignty. For instance, his presence forced the khedive to celebrate the *Cülus-i Hümayun* (the anniversary of the sultan's accession to the throne).[85] The symbolism was displayed in the Khedivial Opera House too: soon after Muhtar's arrival the first proper Arabic season in the Opera by Qardāḥī-Ḥijāzī's Arab Patriotic Troupe offered a convenient moment to start a symbolic competition with Sir Wolff. *Al-Ahrām* and other Arabic journals took up a pro-Ottoman position this time. Muhtar Pasha subscribed to all performances of Qardāḥī's troupe and promised his personal attendance. This

[79] Peri, "Ottoman Symbolism," 104.

[80] Muhtar, *Riyaz ül-muhtar*.

[81] Muhtar, *Işlāḥ al-Taqwīm*.

[82] *Al-Ḥuqūq*, 10 July 1886, 173–175.

[83] However, Barak does not mention him in *On Time*.

[84] Uçarol, *Gazi Ahmed Muhtar*, 180–285. Tugay, *Three Centuries*, 7–32; Ihsanoğlu, *Mısır'da Türkler*, 221.

[85] Peri, "Ottoman Symbolism," 111.

was made an example by *al-Ahrām,* and, as usual, the notables (*zevat* and *a*ʿ*yān*) were summoned to support Arabic theater.[86]

Ottoman Egyptian notables attended the performances with Muhtar often. For instance, on 16 March 1886 the khedive, his harem, Osman Galib, together with Muhtar *and* Wolff, attended the performance of *Ḥifẓ al-Widād.*[87] A few days later, the khedive and Khayri Pasha, the old supporter of Arabic theater, with Muhtar *and* Wolf watched together Wāṣif's *Hārūn al-Rashīd.*[88] Tevfik, as we have seen, encouraged Qardāḥī to apply for the next year's concession, and Muhtar requested the repetition of the whole performance. He liked *Hārūn al-Rashīd,*[89] possibly because the character of the caliph could be read as an allegory of the sultan-caliph. *Al-Ahrām* announced later that this play would be repeated due to "popular demand."[90]

In an occupied land, Muhtar's role was to represent the continued protection of the Ottoman Empire for its subjects. He had a special relationship with the Ottoman subjects in Egypt. In particular, the Syrian Maronites often asked him to be the patron of their charity evenings. In this way, for instance, in 8 March 1887 under his patronage *ʿĀyida* was performed in Arabic in the Opera for the benefit of the Maronite community.[91] This evening was considered to be a celebration, of course, in honor of Sultan Abdülhamid II.[92] Similarly, in the last triumphant season of Qardāḥī and Ḥijāzī in the Opera House in 1889, it was under Muhtar's auspices that the Maronite Charitable Society organized a charity evening. On this particular night, the secretary of the Society gave two speeches: the first praised the sultan and identified the Maronites in Egypt as Ottomans (*ʿuthmāniyyūn*) while the second paid tribute to the khedive.[93] In this very subtle way Muhtar Pasha was able to radiate the authority of the Ottoman Empire upon its subjects in occupied Egypt.

Muhtar's relationship with Abbas Hilmi II was complicated. Abdülhamid II demanded the acknowledgment of full Ottoman suzerainty in Egypt and his rights as the caliph of all Muslims; this entailed an almost compulsory yearly visit by Abbas Hilmi II to Istanbul.[94] At first, Abbas happily made this visit since the Ottoman umbrella was useful to rebond Egyptian loyalty in the 1890s as we shall see below. Also, Muhtar posed

[86] *Al-Ahrām*, 10 March 1886, 2.
[87] *Al-Ahrām*, 17 March 1886, 2.
[88] *Al-Ahrām*, 25 March 1886, 2.
[89] *Al-Ahrām*, 1 April 1886, 2.
[90] *Al-Ahrām*, 16 April 1886, 2.
[91] *Al-Ahrām*, 3 March 1887, 2.
[92] *Al-Qāhira (al-Ḥurra)*, 12 March 1887, 2.
[93] *Al-Ahrām*, 26 March 1889, 2–3.
[94] Peri, "Ottoman Symbolism," 108.

as a respectable fatherly figure to the young khedive, playing an instrumental role in his appointment ceremony, and generally masterminding a surge of Ottomanism.[95] In the mid-1890s Abbas and Muhtar often attended Muslim ceremonies and opera performances together. Nonetheless, Abbas wrote in his memoirs that he thought that "it is necessary to handle him [Muhtar] with care."[96] Their goals against the British were connected but Muhtar, a devoted man of the Ottoman Empire, attempted to curb khedivial authority.

Arabizing the Khedive 2.0: Muṣṭafā Kāmil and the Patriotic Imagination

Ottoman Arab patriotism reached its peak during the first years of Abbas Hilmi II's reign. The best example of this ideological and emotional peak is the early thought of Muṣṭafā Kāmil. For the first time, the racial definition of the community appeared also among religious, linguistic, and imagined territorial concepts. In this final section, I explore Kāmil's student years in the late 1880s—at the moment of the restoration of khedivial authority by old Egyptian intellectuals, his early relationship to Abbas Hilmi II, and his drama *The Conquest of Andalusia* (*Fatḥ al-Andalus*, 1893). This play exemplifies the emergence of an imagined form of patriotic unity with a strong (pan-)Arab favor, reconfiguring yet again the khedive as Ottoman representative.

Kāmil's Posthumous Image

It is not easy to gain access to a "historical" figure in history. In the same way that royalist historians formulated the image of Khedive Ismail as a magnificent modernizer, the nationalist counterstroke created Muṣṭafā Kāmil as the heroic model of the patriotic Egyptian man rising against the old regime. Already in the interwar period, fathers were consciously forming their sons according to Kāmil's life narrative.[97] This model of the ideal efendi included knowledge of good Arabic and good French, education in the law school, the pilgrimage to Europe (Paris), and early signs of being a genius. The social value of "youth" was also the result of this model.[98]

[95] Shārūbīm, *al-Kāfī*, Part 5, 1:1: 81–86.

[96] Sonbol, trans., *The Last Khedive of Egypt*, 99.

[97] Ryzova, *The Age of Efendiya*, 95, 96, 153.

[98] Baron argues that Muṣṭafā Kāmil himself produced an image of the nation, and after his death he became one image of the nation. Baron, *Egypt as a Woman*, 62–67. See also Di Capua, "Embodiment of the Revolutionary Spirit."

The first codifier of Kāmil's image as part of the national pantheon was Kāmil's older brother, ʿAlī Fahmī Kāmil (1870–1926). He published nine volumes of collected writings with recollections and photographs with the narrative of "the great man," soon after his younger brother's death.[99] Next, the historian al-Rāfiʿī contextualized this image in the 1930s within nationalist teleology, framing Kāmil as the "one who resurrected the national movement."[100] The extent to which Muṣṭafā Kāmil was tied to khedivial culture as a member of a wealthy Egyptian family and his early years as a dynastic patriot were suppressed. Equally suppressed was the function of Abbas Hilmi II and his old supporters, such as Riyaz, ʿAlī Mubārak, or even ʿAbd Allāh Nadīm, in generating a new wave of patriotism, thus leaving only Kāmil as the dynamic center of change.

For al-Rāfiʿī, it was crucial to prove that Muṣṭafā Kāmil started his patriotic activity prior to Abbas Hilmi II's reign. Chronology was important to ensure that "national history" and "political (dynastic) history" were two separate narratives[101] and to discredit any claim the khedive might have had in launching, or having a share in, the politically organized national movement. Abbas Hilmi II, to his credit, did not claim that Kāmil was his creation; he writes in his memoirs that "Mustafa Kamel belonged to no one but himself."[102] The following sections investigate the relationship between the old elites, the young khedive, and the young intellectual.

The Mosque and the Opera: The Peak of Patriotism

Abbas Hilmi was studying in the Theresianum in Vienna when his father Tevfik unexpectedly died in January 1892. The death spurred a certain amount of chaos, as the death of an Ottoman *vali* always did in Egypt. And now there was the British occupation. At first, Abbas assumed governing powers without an Ottoman firman (there was only a telegram from Abdülhamid II acknowledging his rights). There was, for the first time, a border issue connected to his appointment as khedive.

The solution that emerged called on multiple sources of support. First, there was the Egyptian army. In this moment of transition, an unprecedented event occurred: the army—including both the Egyptian and the British officers—took an oath of allegiance to the new ruler in his presence on January 26, 1892. The Egyptian officers did so in Arabic, swearing on a copy of the Koran (which was in the hand of the Sheikh

[99] Kāmil, ed., *Muṣṭafā Kāmil.*
[100] Al-Rāfiʿī, *Muṣṭafā Kāmil*, 23.
[101] Ibid., 342.
[102] Sonbol, trans., *The Last Khedive of Egypt*, 139.

al-Azhar), and on their own honor, that they would obey the khedive and "defend the rights of the country."[103] After this, it seems logical that Abbas Hilmi II changed his personal guards from English to Egyptian soldiers.[104]

Next came Ottoman recognition and an appeal to Egyptian patriots. After a long delay, he received the firman. On British insistence, the ceremony took place in a new environment, at Abdin square, rather than in the Citadel, making it a public event.[105] Then the khedive and his men consciously prepared a new beginning. He ordered a decrease in the price of salt and pardoned prisoners. He organized dinners with Alexandrian notables. Next, in the autumn of 1892, he declared general amnesty for the remaining ʿUrābists, including ʿAbd Allāh Nadīm, excluding only ʿUrābī and his fellow exiles in Ceylon. Nadīm called him "Abbas, the Compassionate."[106] It seemed that patriotic elites and the khedive were ready for a new compromise, yet again.

The result was a peak in Arab patriotism as related to the khedive. "Our prince" was described by the intellectual Aḥmad Zakī as "the best model and the perfect ideal, because he is the first in engaging with the advancement of the beloved homeland to the peak of pride and the tribune of honour."[107] This warm welcome should be understood in light of the ongoing restoration of the khedivate since the late 1880s, the amnesties, and new appointments (Aḥmad Zakī himself was promoted in 1892).[108]

The symbolic test of restored trust was a political clash, which, although it resulted in the defeat of Abbas Hilmi II, in fact brought him a magnificent victory in the public sphere. The khedive clashed with Consul-General Baring over the discharge of Prime Minister Mustafa Fahmi in January 1893; Abbas appointed a new government, but Baring forced him to change it: the negotiated result was the return of Mustafa Riyaz as prime minister. The khedive received support and thanks from even countryside *ʿumad* and *aʿyān*, who seem to have hated Mustafa Fahmi.[109] In Shārūbīm's description, when the khedive prayed in the al-Ḥusayn mosque one Friday in early 1893, the crowd wanted to pull his carriage instead of the horses, and during this celebration a young Copt gave an effusive speech.[110] The people of Cairo shouted, "Viva the prince, down with the occupiers!" As quoted at the beginning of the chapter,

[103] Farīd, *Mudhakkirāt*, 90.
[104] Shārūbim, *Al-Kāfī*, Part 5, 1:1: 145.
[105] Farīd, *Mudhakkirāt*, 99.
[106] *Al-Ustādh*, 14 March 1893, 722–723.
[107] Zakī, *Al-Safar ilā al-Muʾtamar*, 43.
[108] Farīd, *Mudhakkirāt*, 97, 122.
[109] Shārūbim, *Al-Kāfī*, Part 5, 1:1: 165.
[110] Shārūbim, *Al-Kāfī*, Part 5, 1:1: 169.

and in the beginning of this part, he then went to the Opera for a performance, where the audience celebrated his presence.[111]

The peak in popularity in the first years of Abbas's reign can be corroborated from a number of other sources. The demonstration of sympathy in January 1893, when, by the way, the khedive watched *Aida* in the Opera, is remarked upon also by Muḥammad Farīd.[112] He further gives an account of Abbas' tour in Upper Egypt, during which cities were elaborately decorated in order to celebrate the khedive (this was, admittedly, a standard way of expressing loyalty that was also enacted for his less popular ancestors). The young khedive (or perhaps more likely, his advisors), effectively deployed both traditional and nontraditional symbols in his first years. Abbas Hilmi II regularly went to the mosque to pray publically and also attended the Opera House. In fact, sometimes these were connected. Consider this piece of news from 1895:

> H.H. the Khedive visited the Citadel Mosque on Tuesday evening to attend the ceremonies on the anniversary of "Leylat el Mearag" [!], or the night of the Prophet's miraculous ascent to heaven . . . Ghazee Moukhtar Pasha, with a great number of high functionaries, assisted at the proceedings, and a large number of tourists were also present. His Highness left about nine o'clock and drove to the Khedivial Opera House, when Donizetti's *Favorita* was performed.[113]

A few weeks after this occasion, during Ramadan, the khedive went to break the fast with the *ʿulamāʾ* and then similarly attended the opera *Le Petit Duc* in the Khedivial Opera House.[114] Abbas Hilmi II resorted to the simultaneous use of religious and nonreligious symbols. The presence of the British occupiers helped to stage him as the representative of both the Muslim-Ottoman and the national community in the face of foreign intrusion, while his young age boosted popular sympathy.

Elite Anti-Abbasism

This popularity rested on the restoration of the khedivial image. Old khedivial patriots, such as ʿAlī Mubārak or Mustafa Riyaz, and new Syrian loyalists were instrumental in this restoration. It also relied heavily on the narrative of Mehmed Ali as regenerator of Egypt. Before we see the old men in their relationship with the young khedive and Muṣṭafā Kāmil, the differing opinions should be pointed out.

[111] Shārūbim, *Al-Kāfī*, Part 5, 1:1: 177–78; *New York Times*, 23 January 1893, 5.
[112] Farīd, *Mudhakkirāt*, 116. Shafīq, *Mudhakkirātī*, 2: 62.
[113] *Egyptian Gazette*, Supplement, 24 January 1895, 1.
[114] *Egyptian Gazette*, 1 March 1895, 2.

The salon of "Princess" Nazlı (185?–1914), the daughter of the pretender Mustafa Fazıl, in fin-de-siècle Cairo was less than friendly towards the new ruler. This legendary great-aunt of Abbas Hilmi II was a supporter of the ex-ʿUrābists, and may also have been associated with Said Halim, the son of the pretender Abdülhalim in Istanbul. Nazlı, at the center of the dynastic conspiracy, hosted a number of politically active and culturally elitist individuals and handsome British officers. She herself, according to the memoirs of Muḥammad Farīd, "was among the supporters and lovers of the British" and "always wrote against the Egyptians."[115] Members of her wide circle, such as Sheikh Muḥammad ʿAbduh, heavily opposed the Ismailite line and the dynastic historical ideology that located Mehmed Ali in its center as "the founder of modern Egypt," even at the price of being more friendly to the British occupiers. [116] A few other significant members of the Muslim intelligentia soon clashed with the khedive, such as the leader of Sufi orders, Muḥammad Tawfīq al-Bakrī, who already in 1895 seems to have a major disagreement with the khedive and this cost him his position as the "leader of the Prophet's descendents" (*naqīb al-ashrāf*).

The Student and the Prince

Let us now examine patriotism as the imagined Ottoman nation-ness of khedivial Egypt. Muṣṭafā Kāmil, in 1897, addressed a letter to Abbas Hilmi II in which he offered to write a book about "the real reasons of the ʿUrābī revolution," "guarding jealously the dignity of your name in history." He addressed the khedive, however, in an entirely new way in Arabic: *ḥaḍrat al-sayyid al-jalīl wa-ibn al-waṭan al-ʿazīz* which can be translated in at least three different ways into English: "the great lord and son of the homeland, the Mighty One" or "the great lord and mighty son of the homeland" or "the great lord and son of the dear/mighty homeland."[117] The ambiguity of whose adjective goes with *al-ʿazīz*, regardless of its conscious or unconscious use, indicates the transferability of khedivial attributes to the homeland and vice versa. Be this as it may, Kāmil clearly addresses the khedive as a member of the imagined Egyptian nation.

There is no exact information about the moment the two teenagers met for the first time. As noted earlier, dating Kāmil's start of politics before the reign of Abbas Hilmi II was a crucial historical tool to write a national

[115] Quoted in Allen, "Writings of Members of the Nazlī Circle," 79.

[116] ʿAbduh, "Āthār Muḥammad ʿAlī."

[117] Letter dated 16 April 1897, Paris, from Muṣṭafā Kāmil to Abbas Hilmi II, HIL 4/1–4/3, AHP.

history devoid of the monarchical regime after 1952. The khedive visited the Law School in November 1892, as part of a tour that visited all schools, and Muṣṭafā Kāmil was among those who greeted him. [118] This may have been the first time they met in person. Yet I argue that the date is not actually that crucial: whenever Muṣṭafā Kāmil started to think along ideological lines, he publicly imagined the khedive as the first man of the nation, as an Arab prince. And he was prepared for this imagination.

Kāmil's family background, social networks, education, and skills are all responsible for his strikingly early embedding in the highest political circles. He was born in 1874 into a prestigious local family in Cairo, which drew on both a traditional and a modern (army) education. His father ʿAlī Muḥammad (1816–1887), from a rich Tanta-based merchant family, was educated in the Tora school and in the Khānka camp during Mehmed Ali's reign. The family bought a house for ʿAlī Muḥammad's mother next to the Tora school, in order to see her son when she wished. They also arranged for ʿAlī Muḥammad to be able to leave the school whenever he wanted. This unusual freedom reflected their social network and wealth. ʿAlī Muḥammad became a military engineer, was attached to the entourage of Said Pasha in the 1850s, and finally retired from service from the Ministry of Public Works in 1877. He had two wives, seven sons, and two daughters. His second wife Ḥafīẓa—Muṣṭafā's and ʿAlī Fahmī's mother—hailed from a family who could trace back their origins to Ḥusayn, the Prophet's grandson. There is no indication of the family's involvement in the ʿUrābī-revolution, and later Kāmil accepted its interpretation as a disaster that caused the British occupation. After their father's death in 1887, Muṣṭafā and ʿAlī Kāmil inherited a large amount of money, as well as much gold and silver jewelry. Relatively rich, the young boys continued to be educated under the guardianship of their eldest brother.[119]

Muṣṭafā Kāmil started his secondary education in the Khedivial School and when he was around fifteen (1889) he established a student society, *Jamʿiyyat al-Ṣalība al-Adabiyya*, where he gave speeches every Friday. The young Kāmil's eloquence in Arabic caught the attention of ʿAlī Mubārak, who was minister of education at this time again, and who personally tested the knowledge of the few students. Mubārak must have personally known Kāmil's father, too. There are anecdotes that Kāmil became a frequent visitor in Mubārak's salon. It is possible that even Prime Minister Riyaz Pasha met the young student there.[120]

[118] Farīd, *Mudhakkirāt*, 110. Fahmy, Ordinary Egyptians, 67.

[119] This paragraph and the next one summarize Kāmil, ed., *Muṣṭafā Kāmil*, 1:54–137; al-Rāfiʿī, *Muṣṭafā Kāmil*, 31–35; Steppat, "Nationalismus und Islam bei Muṣṭafā Kāmil," 241–246; Schüller, *Muṣṭafā Kāmil* (1874–1908), 33; Moghira, *Moustapha Kamel*; and al-Rāfiʿī, *Muṣṭafā Kāmil*, 46.

[120] Dykstra, "A Biographical Study," 360–362.

Since the pardoned ʿAbd Allāh Fikrī was also a visitor at Mubārak's salon in the late 1880s, the ideology of these old intellectuals can be explored in Fikrī's last book published in his lifetime (printed December 1888). It is a short moral manual for Muslim boys. Fikrī starts with useful knowledge: times, calendars, and measures, followed by sections on "Love of God," "Affection for the Prophets," the duties of a child to his parents and family, and moral codes of behavior such as speaking softly, not sleeping with other boys, not cursing, and so on. Fikrī finishes the book with a long section on "The Love for the Homeland" (*Maḥabbat al-Waṭan*), the main message of which is that "your service [to the homeland] is in fact to serve yourself"; he emphasizes that knowledge is the only remedy against absolute rulers, the adverse effects of foreigners' rule on the people's rights in the patria, and the importance of cooperation and mutual respect (through the example of bakers). Yet Fikrī also adds that the community needs a ruler (*ḥākim*) who stops "the strong from oppressing the weak," provides justice, and organizes the country, "since it is not possible that all people of the homeland would come together." This idea of just kingship in the late 1880s reflected the earlier ideas during the gentle revolution, partly generated by Fikrī himself at the time. Fikrī likely expressed his ideas in Mubārak's salon to the student Kāmil (at one point he actually addresses the reader: "thou, celebrated genius boy, *al-kāmil*").[121] We should not forget either that the orphaned Kāmil may have also found (grand)father-like figures among these old intellectuals.

In addition to Mubārak and Fikrī, the young Kāmil had connections to other pro-khedivial Egyptians. He came into contact with Sheikh ʿAlī al-Laythī, the Sufi court poet of ex-Khedive Ismail. And, after 1892, there was the pardoned ʿAbd Allāh Nadīm who may have become more than simply a pardoned rebel, since he later wrote secret reports to the young khedive from Istanbul.[122] The platforms of expression of Nadīm and Kāmil (journalism, societies, oratory, plays) are often compared and evaluated as if Kāmil had learned these from Nadīm.[123] Kāmil did establish a journal, *al-Madrasa* (*The School*, 18 February 1893—December 1893), which is said to have reached 24,000 subscribers in eight months.[124] Journalism probably facilitated his acquaintance with Nadīm, who printed his journal *al-Ustādh* (*The Teacher*, from August 1892) in the same printing house (*al-Maḥrūsa*).[125] Nadīm listed Muṣṭafā's journal among the new Egyptian periodicals in his own organ[126] and, as befits the editor of *al-Ustādh*, may

[121] Fikrī, *Kitāb al-Fawāʾid al-Fikriyya*, 64–73.
[122] Letters 9/31–78, AHP.
[123] Al-Jumayʿī, *ʿAbd Allāh al-Nadīm*, 199–225.
[124] Kāmil, ed., *Muṣṭafā Kāmil*, 1: 185.
[125] Kāmil, ed., *Muṣṭafā Kāmil*, 1: 184.
[126] *Al-Ustādh*, 28 February 1893, 666.

have given advice to the young man for his *al-Madrasa*. Their relationship would establish a symbolic connection between the first discontents of European intervention and the new patriotic generation.[127] Since Nadīm's historiographical image as the "orator" of the ʿUrābī revolution made him a perfect hero for post-1952 nationalism, Kāmil's supposed relationship with him was the subject of much more speculation than his likely more decisive informal education among the old khedivial patriots in Mubārak's salon.

The cooperation between Abbas Hilmi II and Kāmil is first documented in the summer of 1895, but it must have started earlier: possibly Kāmil's 1894 summer trips and his autumn law exam in France were financed by the khedive.[128] By this time, as figure 8.1 shows, young Muṣṭafā Kāmil could dress as a perfect French bourgeois. While Abbas Hilmi II acquired the image of an Arab prince, Kāmil's acquisition of the dominant modality of European culture as a patriot was complete. He was ready to launch both an international and a national campaign in the name of Egypt, independently of the khedive, but secretly supported by him in the second half of the 1890s. The details of this process, the eventual fallout between the khedive and Kāmil in 1904, the way mass nationalism rose, and the khedive's changing image belong to another book. Instead, I would like to finish this book by going very close to young Muṣṭafā Kāmil's world.

Ḥubb al-waṭan min al-īmān *Yet Again*

The identification of homeland and the khedive was successful in public in 1893. Now the Ottoman khedive was seen as an Arab prince, not delegated by the sultan-caliph to rule Egypt but empowered by the people of Egypt to represent the sultan in Egypt. This interplay of patriotic collective imagination and religious community produced a moment of imaging Muslim power in the early 1890s. There was no clash between religious and patriotic concepts of power yet, because the (reinvented) Ottoman caliphate functioned as the ultimate source of sovereignty.

Kāmil's first truly significant experience of patriotic solidarity was the demonstration that the school students (headed by the Law School students) organized in January 1893 in favor of Abbas Hilmi II against the British and against their mouthpiece journal *al-Muqaṭṭam*.[129] A generation

[127] Al-Rāfiʿī, *Muṣṭafā Kāmil*, 37, thought that Nadīm "informed him about the secrets of the ʿUrābī revolution" (ʿarafa min aḥādīthihi asrār al-thawra al-ʿurābiyya). Steppat, "Nationalismus und Islam bei Muṣṭafā Kāmil," 245.

[128] Fahmy, "Francophone Egyptian Nationalists," 193.

[129] Kāmil, ed., *Muṣṭafā Kāmil*, 1: 145.

مصطفى كامل باشا
فى التاسعة عشرة من عمره

FIGURE 8.1. Muṣṭafā Kāmil in 1893
Source: Kāmil, ed. *Muṣṭafā Kāmil*, 2: 148.

of educated Egyptians, such as Ismāʿīl Ṣidqī, also name this occasion as their first true experience of patriotic unity. This is also the moment when Abbas was celebrated both in the mosque and in the opera. At this time, Kāmil published his first article in *al-Ahrām*, entitled "Patriotic Advice" (*Naṣīḥa Waṭaniyya*), which was a fierce attack on the Syrian supporters of the British. His own journal *al-Madrasa* regularly published pro-khedivial patriotic poetry, possibly written by Muṣṭafā Kāmil himself. Consider these verses from November 1893, which were published in the "Section of Patriotic Hymns" (*Bāb al-Anāshīd al-Waṭaniyya*):

> You are the sons of the merry Nile / full of pride and great value
> Defend it with seriousness / since you built it rightly guided
> You are her sons but do not / raise what has been destroyed
> The ruler of Egypt is in front of you / our Abbas the strong fortress
> This is the Prince in his best / and in his love for his country[130]

This political song represents an aural imagination in which the homeland and religion intermingle. In my interpretation, the term "prince" (*amīr*) in this context represents the relationship to the Ottoman caliph. This is also the title that contemporaries, like Shārūbīm, used for Abbas Hilmi II most frequently and, at least in Shārūbīm's use, it served to reaffirm Egypt's Ottoman allegiance. The ancient caliphs had emirs who fought on behalf of their empires, and this image was resurrected in the 1890s and applied to Abbas Hilmi II.

It is also possible to interpret this moment in 1893 as transferring the Hamidian ideology of the reinvented caliphate for internal Egyptian politics.[131] Muhtar Pasha's presence in the late 1880s had already enforced the sense of symbolic Ottoman authority; he increased his activity in 1892, and then, in the summer of 1893 the khedive, accompanied by scores of Egyptian *ʿulamāʾ* and notables, traveled to Istanbul to request (in vain) an Ottoman army contingent to come to Egypt.[132] When they returned in August 1893, the welcoming crowd in Alexandria, according to Shārūbīm's account, sent the message to the British that "the country that you occupy is Ottoman and its prince still belongs to the Ottoman throne."[133] The editor, Sheikh ʿAlī Yūsuf, updated readers about the visit in Istanbul throughout the summer, emphasizing in particular the ceremonial receptions, the friendly welcome of the sultan at Yıldız Palace, and the special dinner in honor of the Egyptian delegation, where all notables were invited.[134] Abbas Hilmi II was called emir and khedive, and Abdülhamid II caliph and "commander of the faithful." The sultan even sent his own band to entertain the young khedive.[135] Abbas also met the Abdülhalim and Fazıl branches of the dynasty, and his grandfather, Ismail, all of whom were living in exile

130 Kāmil, ed. *Muṣṭafā Kāmil*, 1: 297.
131 Deringil, *The Well-Protected Domains*, 22–26.
132 Al-Sayyid, *Egypt and Cromer*, 118–119.
133 Shārūbīm, *Al-Kāfī*, Part 5, 1:1:219.
134 Yūsuf, *Ayyām al-Janāb al-Khidīwī*, 40–41, 45, 47–48, 64–67, etc.
135 Ibid., 50.

in Istanbul.[136] Yūsuf later published the articles in a book, which was introduced by a modified version of the slogan "the love of the homeland is part of faith,"[137] the familiar patriotic slogan, and sent the book to thousands of *al-Muʾayyad* subscribers. Being young and having more Ottoman colors, the title "prince" (*amīr*) emphasized belonging to the reinvented Ottoman caliphate.

Egypt in Andalusia

The romanticized image of Abbas Hilmi II is reflected in Muṣṭafā Kāmil's drama *The Conquest of Andalusia.* He was not the only Egyptian to write a political play as a young man; Salāma Mūsa remembers that he too wrote a play as a teenager.[138] Egyptians joined the ranks of Arab playwrights: Maḥmūd Wāṣif, Ismāʿīl ʿĀṣim, and many others wrote original Arabic plays in the 1890s. For Kāmil, the Ottoman Arab patriot, theater remained important throughout his life. Even in the first issues of his political journal, *al-Liwāʾ*, in 1900 he wrote about theater as producing refinement and moral progress.[139]

The young Kāmil wrote the drama "in the manner" of a Belgian journalist who composed a play about the Belgian revolt against the Netherlands.[140] The incentive for writing can be also attributed to the previously surveyed patriotic atmosphere in the streets, cafes, and the Opera House in Cairo. The drama, announced in December 1893,[141] is not analyzed here for its importance as a popularizing instrument (it was perhaps never performed), but for what it tells us about its young writer's political imagination at the peak of dynastic patriotism and for what it indicates about the imminent demise of this peak.

The most important feature of this drama is the historical element. It adds medieval Muslim Andalusia, another chronotrope, to the repertoire of the learned Arabic historical imagination. By the 1890s, Andalusia was a symbol in Ottoman imagination, as testified by Ziya Pasha's translation of Louis Viardot's *History of Andalusia,* which was printed in Istanbul as early as 1859.[142] But unlike its later use as a symbol of religious tolerance in the Arab, Ottoman, and Orientalist imagination, Kāmil's play embodies the opposite: Andalusia stands for the conquest, the power of Islam, and its moral superiority over Christianity. As I read it, and as possibly

136 Ibid., 43, 47.
137 Ibid., 2: ḥubb al-waṭan la-min al-īmān.
138 Musa, *The Education of Salama Musa*, 23.
139 Quoted in Al-Jumayʿī, *ʿAbd Allāh al-Nadīm*, 217.
140 Kāmil, ed., *Muṣṭafā Kāmil*, 2: 165.
141 *Al-Muʾayyad*, 18 December 1893, 4.
142 Ziya, *Endülüs Tarihi.*

Kāmil intended,[143] the play embodies a youthful allegorical, moral vision of Abbas Hilmi II, an emir of a caliph, in the struggle against the British. Contrary to previous interpretations, I analyze this work as a peculiar instance of patriotism that appropriates Arab-Muslim history for Egyptian politics.[144]

The image of the nation in *The Conquest of Andalusia* is characterized by an interplay between the racial and religious categories. Kāmil composed the play in order "to show to my people (*qawmī*) the intrigues of the interlopers (*dukhalā*ʾ) among the nations who wear their clothes and talk in their language" because "they are like poison in the body."[145] It seems, as also attested to by Muḥammad Farīd's memoirs, that there was a growing awareness among Egyptians that the British-ruled government favored Syrians for high administrative positions. Kāmil's concept of "interlopers" referred to these Syrians in Egypt. However, the words may reflect also the anti-Semitic discourse in France where the trial of Captain Dreyfus had just begun in November 1894 and where talk of "treason" was circulating everywhere, at the same time that Kāmil was finishing his exams. But the reader should not be misled. While the plot of the drama suggests an act of treason as the quality of race (the *rūmī* people, possibly Byzantines), and by extension the formulation of a morally superior "Arab nation" (*al-umma al-ʿarabiyya*), I argue in the following that its invisible problem is the political relationship between the ruler (an Arab prince) and his men.

The plot is set in 711 as the Muslim army prepares to launch an attack against the tyrant King Roderick (Ludhrīq) in Hispania. The dramatic conflict occurs between the emir Mūsā ibn Nuṣayr (the ruler of the Maghrib in the name of the Umayyad caliph), his vizier ʿAbbād of *rūmī* (perhaps Byzantine) origin, ʿAbbād's *rūmī* love Maryam, and the *rūmī* friend Nasīm. Maryam and Nasīm ask ʿAbbād to find a means to stop the conquest and, thus, to betray Mūsā. After some consideration, ʿAbbād commits the treason, not only because he is of *rūmī* origin but also because he loves Maryam. He and Nasīm devise a plan in which they will send a letter reporting the death of the military leader Ṭāriq ibn Ziyād, compelling Emir Mūsā to call back the army. They plan then to kill the soldier who delivers their message. All unfolds as planned, until a letter arrives from Ṭāriq to

[143] *Al-Muʾayyad*, 18 December 1893, 4. The announcement says that Ḥusayn Efendi Kāmil, the editor of *al-Madrasa*, wrote a play about the conquest of Andalusia as an allegory of good and bad values at the time.

[144] Dennis Walker analyzed the play in a somewhat general fashion and contextualized it as an early instance of Arabism. He argued that the tyrant Roderick stood "for a potentiality within Abbas." Walker, "Egypt's Arabism," 65. I provide a very different interpretation.

[145] Kāmil, ed. *Muṣṭafā Kāmil*, 2: 167.

the emir, reporting that he has conquered Andalusia and killed Roderick. The spy ʿĀrif confirms that ʿAbbād had sent a forged letter, thus making his treason known. In the final scenes, Mūsā and Ṭāriq meet in Andalusia at the head of the victorious armies, discuss the glory of Arabs and Muslims, and send ʿAbbād and his companions to prison.[146]

The drama is an allegory of an ideal Ottoman Egyptian (Muslim) Arab monarchy, that is, the khedivate. The play presents a prince who rules in the name of the caliph but is betrayed by his Christian grandee. The Muslim Arabs of lower ranks come to the ruler's help. Apart from the French background of the Dreyfus Affair, it is hard not to find a similarity with the situation of Abbas Hilmi II in 1893. He was officially the caliph's representative in Egypt, viewed as betrayed by the Syrian Christian editors of *al-Muqaṭṭam* and the old Nubar Pasha, but supported by the army and the students. Emir Mūsā symbolizes the khedive not only because of his position as an emir, but also because, by the end of play, he has come to function more like a national arbitrator. For instance, he turns to his "brothers, teachers of the nation, and scholars of the people" (*ikhwānī asātidhat al-umma wa-ʿulamāʾ al-shaʿb*) to compare the prudence of Ṭāriq and the treason of ʿAbbād.[147] If we push the symbolic parallelism further, that is, if the character of Mūsā embodies Abbas Hilmi II, then Ṭāriq embodies Muṣṭafā Kāmil, preparing to conquer France for his prince. In the final scene, when both the *ʿulamāʾ* and the non-*ʿulamāʾ* of the people (*qawm*) are summoned to witness the sentencing of ʿAbbād, emir Mūsā delivers a speech in which he extolls the superiority of the Muslim nations (*al-umam al-islāmiyya*), summarises the moral of ʿAbbād's treason (the power of love and women) and the dangers of the *dukhalāʾ*, and announces that Ṭāriq is "the exemplary hero of all times."[148] The emir does not forget to add that a state must be built on the firm basis of leading men. *Fatḥ al-Andalus* is thus a didactic work, or an expression of wishful thinking, in which the (Muslim) Arab nation is presented as capable of advancing only if powerful men remain loyal to the ruler. This was the lesson of patriotism in the imagination of Kāmil, a law student, in 1894.

Two contradictions run throughout the play. The first is the confusing message that ʿĀrif's character sends, as spying is not morally positive. The author solves the contradiction by saying that, in this instance, spying is "an act of revenge" (*intiqām*) and "a service to Islam." ʿĀrif notifies Ṭāriq about the treason in order to teach ʿAbbād a lesson, so he would "burn in hell."[149] Still, the constant spying is not truly justified by the

[146] Ibid., 2: 169–240.
[147] Ibid., 2: 223.
[148] Ibid., 2: 237–238.
[149] Ibid., 2: 194–195.

plot. Second, this work is distinct from the earlier plays that set parallels between the khedivate and past empires in that it valorizes being an Arab and Muslim at the expense of others. The contradiction is between the moral use of the Arab past and Arabness, and the rejection of community with the *dukhalāʾ* "who speak the same language."

While ʿAbd al-Fattāḥ al-Miṣrī's 1871 play or even Maḥmūd Wāṣif's 1886 comedy described Arabs as honest men without an "Other," Muṣṭafā Kāmil's drama contains a hierarchy similar to the French dominant discourse. For instance, ʿAbbād first considers an Arab to deliver his message. But he recognizes that "Arabs are famous among the nations (*umam*) for their strong attachment to the interests of their country and the devotion to their homelands (*awṭān*), because Arabs are very clever and smart people," so he sends instead a Berber soldier who is easier to deceive and kill.[150] The word and concept of "intruders/interlopers" would remain in the political vocabulary of Muṣṭafā Kāmil in his future speeches.[151]

The ideological landscape mirrored by *The Conquest of Andalusia*, a drama written by an enthusiastic twenty-year-old during the peak of learned patriotism, is an indication of the way national and revelation-based elements co-existed in this moment of symbolic uprising against the occupiers. The signs of a racial definition of the nation and the quest for a sovereign state are apparent. These elements indicate a new ideological direction. In the following years Muṣṭafā Kāmil would become the face of anti-British Egyptian nationalism, still an Ottoman, but no more a khedivial patriot.

Conclusion: The End of Patriotism?

This chapter has surveyed the markers of distinction produced by economic and political transformation. The ideological product of this elite Arab Ottoman intellectual culture was a blend of patriotism, dynastic loyalty, Ottomanism, history, and Islam. I have analyzed this blend as Arab patriotism in the khedivate. We stop at this high moment of patriotism in the 1890s, without following the khedive and Muṣṭafā Kāmil's eventual falling out, or the rise of anti-colonial nationalism lead by intellectuals such as Kāmil or Aḥmad Luṭfī al-Sayyid in 1900s Egypt. Various elements of Ottomanism remained strong until World War One.

150 Ibid., 2: 202.

151 It was still part of his March 1896 speech in Alexandria. He had to explain himself in public on the meaning of dukhalāʾ. Quoted in Kāmil, ed., *Muṣṭafā Kāmil*, 4:173–176; and Kāmil, *Miṣr wa-l-Iḥtilāl al-Inklīzī*.

We stop here in the 1890s because patriotism gave way to vernacular mass nationalism against the British, as well as to new ideologies, such as socialism, exemplified by revolutionary plays about social injustice. Muṣṭafā Kāmil died prematurely, and the khedivate's last decade saw the crystallization of a new political force and vision, often independent of the khedive: territorial nationalism demanding the end of occupation, limitation of absolute power (new constitutionalism), and increasing reluctance to return to the Ottomans. In 1914, the British government abolished the khedivate and established a direct British Protectorate over Egypt. A new political pact had to be made.

CONCLUSION

The Ottoman Origin of Arab Nationalisms

This book has reflected on the problem of what the Ottoman context of Egypt means for its nationalism. What were the consequences of the imperial embedding for a well-established national narrative? The revision made it necessary, first, to theorize an Ottoman network of Arab imagined communities, second, to reflect on the special place of Egypt within these communities due to its specific geography and power structure (the khedivate), and, lastly, to bring Islam back into the discursive formation of national identity. A network-based theory of Arab patriotism seemed to encompass all these three points, and it also served to reject the application of the distinct Western categories of the "religious," "territorial," and "ethnic/linguistic" in the Ottoman nineteenth century.

The empire was mediated by the khedives in the Egyptian province. The khedivate's main feature was that its governors had no dependence on the imperial infrastructure in order to rule. They married in the imperial elite but established their own Ottoman-Egyptian subsystem. The findings of this book have suggested that selected local groups were ready to make a compromise with them. Intellectuals, though with opposing ideas, attempted to make Arab patriotism the ideology of the khedivate. The Ottoman Empire meanwhile served as a guarantee for all parties involved, since there remained a mutual distrust. The main consequence of telling the story of Egypt through its Ottoman attachment is the articulation of the non-European, local power structure before and even during direct European rule. While this local-imperial system used amply European techniques and technologies the attribution of change to colonial (i.e., European) agency, reducing the khedives and their men to puppets, or identifying emerging new subjectivities as only semi- or fully colonial ones, are ahistorical and inaccurate. It leads to false conclusions concerning the nature of power in post-Ottoman Egypt and the Arab world, even today.

The same criticism that Elie Kedourie directed against Albert Hourani's *Arabic Thought in the Liberal Age* can be applied against my study. Kedourie argued in the 1960s that there was a difference between public and private views in khedivial Egypt. He hinted that the difference was one between belief and nonbelief, implying, for instance, that the private attitude of the famous pan-Islamist al-Afghānī was in fact one of "religious unbelief." However, Hourani thought that the real criticism of his book was not this but that he should have emphasized "continuity rather than a break with the past."[152] I would add as criticism of my own narrative that, despite the network theory, it is very much Cairo-based and it is the history of the educated groups.

I have tried to answer both Kedourie's observation and Hourani's self-criticism. The possible discrepancy between public and private can be explained by the khedivial and Ottoman (later British) regime of power. But there is a much more important angle of being public as a new political form in itself. Material and ideological changes transformed the codes of public behavior. Space and language synchronized. Second, I have looked at continuity, especially within the Muslim-Ottoman universe. That "continuity" was a strategic reuse of older Muslim tropes and modules to talk about an ideal just order. The translation of political change occurred through pre-existing Muslim notions in Arabic. As to my own critical remarks, patriotism has always been an urban and learned ideology and practice. I hoped to show that change occurs from the interaction of interests from above and from below.

The common feature of patriotic enterprises in the khedivate is the lack of capital and the demand for government resources or khedivial support. This can lead us to question why the enterprising cultural patriots from Abū al-Suʿūd, Unsī, Sanua to Qardāḥī, Ḥijāzī, and young Kāmil did not look for funding from the rural notables and urban merchants. For, while the government monopolized certain means of production, there was much private wealth related to the local notables in the khedivate. Such private wealth is essential in creating conditions of new communal experiences by building public spaces (theaters, museums, etc.) or financing journalism. Explanations for the lack of private capitalist mobilization include the ability of the khedives to stage themselves as cultural players, the character of public political enterprises (anything not connected to the khedives could be viewed with suspicion), and the novelty of public entertainment and texts as political forms among local elites. From the late 1870s on, private capital was channeled into patriotism, but it was often owned by Ottoman Syrians, not by Egyptian *aʿyān*. Where were they? The history of capitalism as connected to Arab histories of nation-ness is yet to be written.

In many ways, this book was intended to provide a new framework and to challenge existing notions in canonized histories of the modern Middle East. It looked at the making of nation-ness as a dirty process of

[152] Hourani, Preface to the 1983 re-issue of *Arabic Thought*, viii.

negotiation and an impure cultural construction. It is an invitation to think through, deromanticize, and recalibrate the Ottoman background of Arab nation-states. It is high time to study the way the patriotic experience constructed in physical spaces in the cities of the Syrian and Iraqi provinces, too, where the empire was much closer and without khedivial mediation. It is high time to survey the ways Islam—various Islams—served as cultural memory and transmuted into religion and modern political-sectarian practices.

Based on the interpretation in this book, one may also open a new enquiry about the relationship of patriotism in Arabic to the two major kinds of national ideologies that defined the twentieth century. The emergence of these ideologies—"pan-Arab nationalism" (that all Arabs should live in one state) and territorial nationalism, such as that of Egypt—was related to a new situation just before and after World War One.

What precisely is the relationship between nineteenth-century patriotism and twentieth-century nationalisms? There have already been vague explanations of genealogies. As to pan-Arab nationalism, Ernest C. Dawn has famously suggested that "the theory of Arab nationalism . . . grew out of modernist diagnosis of Moslem decline and prescription of Moslem revival." Dawn thought that there were "Arab modernists" and "Ottoman modernists," but in the same essay he also maintained that "Arabism grew out of modernist Ottomanism."[153] Next, Al-Azmeh has claimed that "early Arab nationalism is a by-product of Ottoman civic nationalism," and that an Ottoman Arab *Bildungsbürgertum* "drifted unconsciously into Arab nationalism" because "the same political and public outlook was brought on public affairs."[154] Keith Watenpaugh has confirmed the almost "unconscious" transition of the middle class as a "cultural construct" based on his research on early-twentieth-century Aleppo.[155] These arguments suppose a smooth, genealogical evolution from Ottoman Arab patriotism to Pan-Arabism in the former Syrian and Iraqi provinces of the Ottoman Empire.

Patriotism was not the effect of the diagnosis of Muslim decline. It was the ideological and cultural effect of imperial-local interaction in which various Muslim concepts were also used. The life-world of urban Ottoman Arabic-speaking communities, including Egyptians, could quite smoothly transform into a nation-state frame since patriotism had already created some of the basic conditions: public institutions, communal experiences, and everyday symbolism of localness around the political idea of the homeland. The cultural world of nation-ness in the empire arguably

[153] Dawn, *From Ottomanism to Arabism*, 394, 397.
[154] Al-Azmeh, "Nationalism and the Arabs," 73–74.
[155] Watenpaugh, *Being Modern in the Middle East.*

carried the potentials of sovereign state culture. I hope to have shown that in Ottoman Egypt there was a cultural life-experience of patriotism in Arabic. However, the transition from patriotism to nation-state nationalism is more problematic in the realm of political ideas.

Is this relationship truly genealogical? Is Arab patriotism and its Ottoman context the *origin* of both pan-Arabism and particular Arab territorial nationalist ideologies? And what does an "origin" mean in the case of ideologies? In the following I consider possible ways to think about this relationship.

One line of reasoning regarding the relationship of the Egyptian version of Arab patriotism and twentieth-century pan-Arabism might focus on the power and image of the khedives among Ottoman and non-Ottoman Arabs. Their conceptualization as Muslim Arab princes offered an occasion for experiencing sovereignty in a moment when there was no independent and self-consciously Sunni Muslim "Arab state" (with the exception of Morocco). Their unique positionality as neither imperial nor local also invited a larger following among Copts and Syrian Christians. The body of an Arab king could become a representation of sovereignty. The monarchical idea of such a religious-secular Arab sovereignty would have continued to the twentieth century, and, even without the Egyptian rulers, may have fueled continuing notions of unity under a single power. (Abbas Hilmi II's schemes of his own "Arab" caliphate are still largely unexplored.) Such monarchism might also have been the origin of the narrative George Antonius constructed in the 1930s for the Hashemite family. It is worth remembering that new, colonial Arab nation-states, with the exceptions of Lebanon and Syria, were monarchies until the 1950s.

Another argument can be made about the relationship as only a *discursive* one between Ottoman Arab patriotisms and all kinds of Arab nationalist ideologies. It is possible to see the educated textual production of patriotism as a pool of texts and concepts in Arabic that would serve as resources for later ideologies. Ideas and habits also traveled through aural means: due to the gramophone and the tours Salāma Ḥijāzī became a pan-Arab star by the 1910s,[156] and Sulaymān Qardāḥī died in Tunis on a tour. The reuse of these ideological and emotional fragments was made possible by the fact that the concept of the homeland in Ottoman Arabic was a flexible one, prone to ideological appropriation. This argument would imply, however, that the "genealogical" connection between Arab patriotism and twentieth-century nationalisms was a relatively empty one of borrowing vocabulary, since the new ideologies gave new meanings to earlier concepts—such as the new goal of the sovereign nation-state. The definition of sovereignty changed. From this perspective, one

[156] [Jawhariyya], *The Storyteller of Jerusalem*, 40–41.

might interpret the last Arab patriots in Ottoman Egypt, such as the young Muṣṭafa Kāmil, as crafting a form of new nationalism that used a pre-existing patriotic vocabulary but deployed it for a very different goal. Ottomanism was "instrumental" for him, but it was based on a pre-existing religious and political bond.

A third, easier argument can be made about the relationship between Arab patriotism in Egypt and twentieth-century Arabism in Egypt. In most of the early Arabic musical plays, with the exception of Sanua's comedies, there are allusions to Egyptians as Arabs and/or to the Arab Islamic past as significant for Egyptian history. The pride, self-esteem, and good morals of Arabs became principles present in most bourgeois Arabic performances after 1882, when such principles provided spiritual reinforcement against the occupiers. "Arabs" should be understood not as nomads (the usual meaning of the word that time) but as a reference to an imagined, glorious past of "Arab" caliphates or to a longing for ethical purity. In this sense, being "Arab" was a somewhat later innovation than the political use of nation-ness in Arabic. The extent to which Arab communal ideas and feelings formed an integral part of patriotism in Egypt and their survival needs further study. But at the very least, it seems clear that Egyptians expressed Arabic-Islamic collective notions of cultural unity more in the nineteenth century than was previously supposed.

Overall, the theory of patriotism may serve as an explanation of the religious potential that silently impregnated secularist Arab nationalisms in the twentieth century, both at the level of ideas and at the level of social life. A network of imagined communities existing among Ottoman peoples of various faiths without the loss of faith sustained this ideology. Keep in mind that Syrian and Iraqi Christian denominations and Copts are religious communities, too. Nation-ness, to repeat, had to share the time of history with other principles of collectivity that were revelation-based. And this impure, crowded time has obstructed and will continue to frustrate the making of Western-type homogeneity.

Finally, I wish to end with a word about the role of Europe in late Ottoman Egypt and the way Muslim thinkers thought about this role. Throughout this book I have made a distinction between the way "Europe" functioned as a model for literary and material production within Egypt and the way external European imperial interests caused political change. There are various roles: we can see even a thin, almost invisible thread of European Orientalism in the cultural construction of Arabic patriotism. "Europe" (including Russia) was unquestionably a model of development both in Egypt and all around the late Ottoman Empire. That imagined "Europe" meant the imperial metropolises, their technology, and elite culture—Ottomans and Egyptians were not truly interested in, for example, Danish villages. And despite all the imperial interventions, and informal imperialism, European power did not *directly* define the life-world of everyday Ottomans and Egyptians until the 1880s. The generation of intellectuals who were the makers of Arab patriotism were confidently open to European novelties, and they invented their own ones as much as their own order of power allowed. They were civic Muslims without a liberal age.

Acknowledgments

It was a long journey to translate my obsessions into an academic language. Those who made it possible or taught me how to do this are the following in chronological order: István Ormos; Nadia Al-Bagdadi; Anna Selmeczi; László Kontler; Marsha Siefert; Mercedes Volait and the staff of EN VISU (INHA); Khaled Fahmy; Philipp Ther; Selim Deringil; Philip Sadgrove; Ralph Bodenstein; Ahmad El-Bindari and his family; Emad Helal; Aziz Al-Azmeh; Edhem Eldem; Georges Khalil; Ola Seif; Alia Mosallam; Nariman Youssef; Ulrike Freitag; Nora Lafi; Georges Khalil, Michael Allan and my EUME-fellows in 2011–2012; Esra Akcan; Nelly Hanna; the late Max Karkegi; Manuela Zervudachi; Yasmine El Dorghamy; Eugene Rogan; Avi Shlaim; Walter Armbrust; Lucie Ryzova; Mohamed Salah-Omri and colleagues at Oxford's Oriental Institute; Abbas Hilmi and the Mohamed Ali Foundation; my fellow Junior Fellows at the Harvard Society of Fellows, especially my indefatigable partner of conversation Abhishek Kaicker, and Ya-Wen Lei, Daniela Cammack, Christopher Rogan, Marta Figlerowicz, Alma Steingart, Alexander Bevilacqua, and Andrew Ollett; Alexandre Cordahi—I remain grateful for his family letters, our discussions, and for calling my attention to the images of Cardahi's troupe in Paris; Roger Owen; Cemal Kafadar; Sreemati Mitter; Noora Lory; Dana Sajdi; Raph Cormack, Kathryn Schwartz, and special thanks to Noah Feldman for the help and Khaled Fahmy again for the final push. I thank Nadia Mustafa and the staff in the Egyptian National Archives (DWQ); the staffs in CEU's History Department, Dār al-Maḥfūẓāt al-ʿUmūmiyya, Dār al-Kutub al-Miṣriyya, IDEO, BOA, Atatürk Kitaplığı, İSAM, İRCICA, BL, NA, BnF, MEC Library in St Antony's in Oxford, AUC library, the Special Collections at Durham University, MEA in Nantes, AUB Special Collections; András Riedlmayer and the Harvard Widener staff; the Österreichische Nationalbibliothek; Diana Morse, Kelly Katz, and Yeşim Erdmann at the SoF; the support of László Vida, István Zimonyi, László Tüske, Renáta Kovács (four succeeding directors of the Hungarian Cultural Institute in Cairo); the staff in IFAO and the research project *Architecture Cosmopolite*; the Milton Fund of Harvard University; Ilse Lazaroms, Gábor Danyi, Elena Sahin, and Deniz Turker who copied books or documents for me in various cities; and Lina Mounzir and

George Taylor for patiently correcting my English. Peter Hill graciously read the whole manuscript hunting for transliteration mistakes and saved me from two grave mistranslations. Finally, it was a pleasure to prepare this book for publication while in residence at IFAO and I thank Nicolas Michel, its most generous staff, and the good people of Munīra.

Kim Greenwell rescued me with the best editing coaching that one could ever wish. This is partly her book. My special thanks also go to the fantastic reviewers at Princeton University Press and to Jay Boggis for the wonderful copyediting. The reviewers, critical remarks shaped very much the final argument. The Dean's Publication Subsidy at Trinity College, Duke University, helped with the expense of indexing the book. I thank Fred Appel at Princeton University Press for his encouragement, editing, and the professional help during the publication process. Friends in the Kuwait circle—you know who you are—were of constant inspiration. Without Ya-Wen's love I would have not been able to finish. I dedicate this book to my mother, Edit Alföldi, and my grandmother, Edit Wolf, while I thank my grandfather, Lajos Alföldi, for never giving up his faith in me.

I have incorporated materials from two earlier articles of mine ("Music and Power in Cairo," *Urban History* and "Arabic Theatre in Early Khedivial Culture," IJMES) with the permission of Cambridge University Press.

Translations, unless indicated otherwise, are mine. And all mistakes remain mine alone.

Abbreviations

AAC	Archive Alexandre Cordahi, Paris
AE (year)	*Annuaire Égyptien* (year of edition)
AHP	Abbas Hilmi II Papers, Durham
BA	Bibliotheca Alexandrina
BL	British Library
BOA	*Başbakanlık Osmanlı Arşıvı* (The Prime Ministry's Ottoman Archive, Turkey)
DM	*Dār al-Maḥfūẓāt al-ʿUmūmiyya* (Archive of the Finance Ministry, Egypt)
DWQ	*Dār al-Wathāʾiq al-Qawmiyya* (The National Archives of Egypt)
EI2	*Encyclopaedia of Islam*, Second Edition
IJMES	*International Journal of Middle East Studies*
MEAN	Ministère des Affaires Étrangères, Archives Diplomatiques, Nantes
MECA	Middle East Centre Archive, St Antony's College
MQMMFS	*Al-Markaz al-Qawmī li-l-Masraḥ wa-l-Mūsīqa wa-l-Funūn Shaʿbiyya* (National Center for Theatre, Music, and Popular Arts, Egypt)
MSA	*Al-Maʿiyya al-Saniyya ʿArabī* archival unit in DWQ
MST	*Al-Maʿiyya al-Saniyya Turkī* archival unit in DWQ
MTP	Ministère/Ministre des Travaux Publics (*Niẓārat/Nāẓir al-Ashghāl al-ʿUmūmiyya*, Ministry/Minister of Public Works, Egypt) in DWQ
MM (numbers)	*Al-Masraḥ al-Miṣrī* series of MQMMFS (years)
NA	The National Archives of the United Kingdom
NM1 or NM2	al-Khaṭīb, *Naẓariyyāt al-Masraḥ*, vol. 1. or vol. 2.
ZDMG	*Zeitschrift der deutschen morgenländischen Gesellschaft*

Works Cited

Archival Sources

Egypt

DWQ DĀR AL-WATHĀʾIQ AL-QAWMIYYA (EGYPTIAN NATIONAL ARCHIVES), CAIRO

In 2009 an electronic catalogue system was introduced in DWQ. This change included a new archival taxonomy as opposed to the earlier handwritten catalogues. For instance, the old archival unit called *ʿAhd Ismāʿīl* is now included in the new *Usrat Muḥammad ʿAlī* unit in the electronic catalogue. I provide here the main electronic catalogue headings (the first number of the archival code) that I have used in this book:

0069	Wathāʾiq ʿĀbdīn (The papers of the ʿĀbdīn Palace)
0075	Majlis al-Nuẓẓār wa-l-Wuzarāʾ (The Council of Ministers)
2002	Muḥāfaẓat Miṣr (The Cairo Governorate)
2003	Ḍabṭiyyat Miṣr (The Cairo "Police")
3002	Bayt Māl Miṣr (The Cairo Treasury)
3003	Dīwān / Wizārat al-Māliyya (The Ministry of Finance)
4003	Dīwān /Wizārat al-Ashghāl al-ʿUmūmiyya (The Ministry of Public Works)
5013	Usrat Muḥammad ʿAlī (The Mehmed Ali Family)
5016	Al-Zuʿamāʾ al-Miṣriyyīn (The Egyptian "Leaders")

Sijillāt al-Maʿiyya al-Saniyya (ʿArabī and Turkī; The Records of the Khedivial Entourage, Arabic and Turkish) registers and documents are on microfilm.

For the archival units based on the old catalogues, which are mostly in boxes (*maḥāfiẓ*), I use the following abbreviations:

CA	Collection ʿĀbdīn
CAI	Collection ʿAhd Ismāʿīl
CMW	Collection Majlis al-Wuzarāʾ (Majlis al-Nuẓẓār)
CWM	Collection al-Waqāʾiʿ al-Miṣriyya
DK	Dīwān al-Khidīwī

DM DĀR AL-MAḤFŪẒĀT AL-ʿUMŪMIYYA (REGISTRY AND ARCHIVE OF THE EGYPTIAN FINANCE MINISTRY), CAIRO

Milaffāt Khidma (Pension dossiers of state employees)

DAFTARKHĀNA, WIZĀRAT AL-AWQĀF (REGISTER-LIBRARY, MINISTRY OF RELIGIOUS ENDOWMENTS)

Ḥujjat Waqf 1215

MQMMFS AL-MARKAZ AL-QAWMĪ LI-L-MASRAḤ WA-L-MŪSĪQĀ WA-L-FUNŪN AL-SHAʿBIYYA, WIZĀRAT AL-THAQĀFA (THE NATIONAL CENTER FOR THEATRE, MUSIC, AND POPULAR ARTS, CULTURAL MINISTRY)

Play n. 2306
Play n. 129

BA BIBLIOTHECA ALEXANDRINA

http://modernegypt.bibalex.org/DocumentViewer/TextViewer.aspx?w=1418&h=778&type=document&id=33302&s=2, accessed 22 January 2015

Turkey

BOA T. C. BAŞBAKANLIK DEVLET ARŞIVLERI GENEL MÜDÜRLÜĞÜ (REPUBLIC OF TURKEY, STATE ARCHIVES OF THE PRIME MINISTRY, GENERAL DIRECTORATE)—OSMANLI ARŞIVI (OTTOMAN ARCHIVE), ISTANBUL

The Grand Vezier's Office:

A} AMD	Bāb-i ʿĀlī Sadāret Evrāki, Sadāret Āmedī Kalemi Defterleri
A} DVN	Bāb-i ʿĀlī Sadāret Evrāki, Sadāret Divan Kalemi
A} DVN.MHM	Bāb-i ʿĀlī Sadāret Evrāki, Sadāret Divan Kalemi, Mühimme Kalemi
A} MKT.MHM	Bāb-i ʿĀlī Sadāret Evrāki, Mektubi Kalemi, Sadāret Mektub Mühimme Kalemi
A.MKT.NZD	Bāb-i ʿĀlī Sadāret Evrāki, Mektubi Kalemi, Nezaret Devair Giden Defteri

Decrees:

İ.DH	Dahiliye İradeleri (Decrees, Interior Ministry)
İ.MMS	Meclis-i Mahsus İradeleri (Decrees, Sultanic Privy Council)

İ.MVL	Meclis-i Vala İradeleri (Decrees, Legislative Council)
İ.MTZ	Eyālāt-ı Mümtāze İrādeleri (Decrees, "Distinguished Provinces")

PVSE, AK PERTEVNIYAL VALIDE SULTAN EVRAKI, ATATÜRK KITAPLIĞI (PAPERS OF THE SULTAN MOTHER PERTEVNIYAL, ATATÜRK LIBRARY)

France

AAC ARCHIVE ALEXANDRE CORDAHI, PARIS

Private papers, by courtesy of Mr. Alexandre Cordahi. Mostly letters from his grandfather, "Farid," Alfred Paul Elias Cordahi (1888–1986), written in the early 1980s about their family history. Farid's father, Paul and his uncle Buṭrus (Pierre) were cousins of Sulaymān Qardāḥī, and for a while Paul worked in Sulaymān's theater troupe.

MAEN ARCHIVES DIPLOMATIQUES, MINISTRE DES AFFAIRES ÉTRANGÈRS, NANTES (DIPLOMATIC ARCHIVES OF THE FRENCH FOREIGN MINISTRY, NANTES)

166PO/D11	Beirut Consulate to Embassy in Constantinople
166PO/D25	Alexandria Consulate to Embassy in Constantinople
354PO/2	Cairo Consulate, dossiers of deceased
354PO/3	Cairo Consulate, consular court records

Lebanon

ARCHIVE AND SPECIAL COLLECTIONS OF THE AMERICAN UNIVERSITY IN BEIRUT

AA.6.26.1	Jurjī Zaydān Papers

United Kingdom

AHP ABBAS HILMI II PAPERS, MOHAMED ALI FOUNDATION, ARCHIVE AND SPECIAL COLLECTIONS, DURHAM UNIVERSITY LIBRARY, DURHAM

HIL/4
HIL/28
HIL/158

MECA MIDDLE EAST CENTRE ARCHIVE, ST ANTONY'S COLLEGE, OXFORD

GB165–0294 (Vivian)
GB165–0120 (Gordon)

NA NATIONAL ARCHIVES OF THE UNITED KINGDOM, KEW, LONDON

Foreign Office: FO/78/1754, FO/78/1755, FO/424/A
Home Office: HO/45/9469/78581, A 2748

BL BRITISH LIBRARY, LONDON

Hekekyan Papers

United States of America

HOUGHTON LIBRARY, HARVARD UNIVERSITY

Eli Smith Papers
Theater Collection

MANUSCRIPTS

Dār al-Kutub al-Miṣriyya (Egyptian National Library)

Abū al-Suʿūd, ʿAbd Allāh b. ʿAbd Allāh. *Minḥat Ahl al-ʿAṣr*. 44 Jalāl al-Ḥusaynī, microfilm 56561.

Fikrī, ʿAbd Allāh. *Rasāʾil al-Inshāʾ*. 5115 Adab, microfilm 32046.

Al-Najjārī, Muṣṭafā Salāma. *Al-Madāʾiḥ al-Saʿīdiyya fī Amjad al-Dawla al-Khidīwiyya*. 395 Adab ʿArabī.

Al-Najjārī, Muṣṭafā Salāma. *Qiṭaʿ min Rawḍ Madīḥ Ismāʿīl*. 2389 Tārīkh Taymūr, microfilm 28637.

[?],"Tarjamat al-Fāḍil ʿAbd Allāh Abī al-Suʿūd Afandī," manuscript, Tārīkh Taymūr 1098, Microfilm 12979.

FILM

Ḥarq Ūbirā al-Qāhira (The Burning of the Cairo Opera), Kamal Abdel Aziz, 2011.

ONLINE NON-ARCHIVAL SOURCES

Cairo Opera House. http://www.cairoopera.org/history.php. Accessed 18 July 2011.

Catherine, Marcel et François Bourdillaud, eds. *36 J Fonds Gay-Lussac—Archives Familiales (1800–1914)*. PDF document. Archives Départmental de la Haute Vienne, 1995. http://archives.haute-vienne.fr/_depot_ad87/_depot_arko/articles/723/consulter-l-instrument-de-recherche-archives-_doc.pdf Accessed 23 December 2015.

Ismāʿīl, Sayyid ʿAlī. "Tārīkh al-Raqāba wa-Taṭawwuruhā." http://kenanaonline.com/users/sayed-esmail/posts/119149. Accessed 9 March 2014.

Rafaat, Samir. http://www.egy.com/zamalek/. Accessed 18 July 2011.

Schiller, Friedrich. *Letters upon the Aesthetic Education of Man*, 1794, II. Letter, online: http://www.fordham.edu/halsall/mod/schiller-education.asp. Accessed 1 October 2013.

Printed Non-Archival Sources

Encyclopaedias (dictionaries are not given)

EI2 *Encyclopeadia of Islam, New Edition.* 11 Vols. and Supplement. Leiden: Brill, 1986–2002

The New Grove Dictionary of Music and Musicians, Second Edition. 29 Vols. London: Macmillan Publishers Limited, 2001.

Periodicals

Abū Naẓẓāra, 1878
Al-Ahrām, 1876–1898
Basiret, 1876
Bulletin de l'Institut Égyptien, 1866
Al-Burhān, 1881
Bosphore Égyptien, 1885, 1887
La Comédie, 1863, 1867, 1872
La Correspondance Égyptienne, 1894
La Correspondance Égyptienne illustrée, 1896
The Egyptian Gazette, 1895
Al-Farāyid, 1893
Le Figaro, 1869, 1889
Le Gaulois, 1869
Ḥadīqat al-Akhbār, 1858–1864
Hayal, 1870, 1874
Hürriyet, 1868
Al-Ḥuqūq, 1886
L'Isthme de Suez, 1856
Al-Ittiḥād al-Miṣrī, 1890
Al-Jawāʾib, 1863–1874
Journal de Constantinople, 1844
Journal des débats politiques et litteraires, 1869, 1872, 1890
Al-Jinān, 1870–76, 1881–82
Al-Jumhūriyya, 2010
Al-Laṭāyif [*al-Laṭāʾif*], 1886
The Levant Herald, 1867–70
Al-Liwāʾ, 1900
The London Gazette, 1880, 1882, 1891
Al-Maḥrūsa, 1882, 1886
Le Ménestrel, 1835, 1862, 1868–1870, 1872, 1889
Le Monde Illustré, 1869
Le Moustique, 1868
Al-Muqtaṭaf, 1876–1901
Nafīr Sūriyya, 1860–1861
Al-Najāḥ, 1871
The New York Times, 1869, 1893
The Nineteenth Century, 1882

Al-Nūr al-Tawfīqī, 1888
Penny Illustrated Paper, 1869
La Presse, 1867, 1882
Al-Qāhira (al-Ḥurra), 1886–88, 1890
La Réforme (L'Égypte), 1896
Rawḍat al-Madāris al-Miṣriyya, 1870–1877
Revue de Constantinople, 1875
La Revue musicale de Paris, 1866, 1869
Revue et Gazette musicale de Paris, 1872
Al-Riyāḍ al-Miṣriyya, 1889
The Times, 1869
Le Théâtre Illustré, 1869
La Turquie, 1888–1889
Al-Ustādh, 1892–1893
Al-Zamān, 1882
Wādī al-Nīl, 1869–1871
Al-Waqāʾiʿ al-Miṣriyya, 1830s–1911

Books, Articles, and Theses

(*ʿAyn* and *hamza* are not considered as distinct letters here—ʿUrābī is at U; *al-*, de, d' etc. are not considered—al-Naqqāsh is at N, de Amacis at A (but Elshahed is at E); authors without family names are indicated by their first name—Osman Bey is at O; ç and ch is at C; ḥ is at H; kh is at K; ph is at P; ş and sh are at S; titles [bey, efendi, pasha] are omitted.)

PUBLICATIONS WITHOUT INDICATED EDITOR OR AUTHOR

Annuaire des Artists de l'Enseignment Dramatique et Musical et des Sociétés Orphéoniques de France et de l'Etranger. Paris: Montorier, 1895.
Annuaire Égyptien—1891–1892, Administratif et Commercial. Cairo: G. Teissonière, 1891.
Baedeker Egypt—Handbook for Travellers. London: Karl Baedeker, 1885.
Baedeker's Lower Egypt. London: Dulau, 1885.
British and Foreign State Papers 1882/1883. Vol. 74. London: William Ridgway, 1900.
[Commission Municipale], *Budget pour l'exercice 1901*. Alexandria: Imprimerie générale A. Mourés & Cie, 1901.
Codes égyptiens, précédé du réglement d'organisation judiciaire. Alexandrie: Française A. Mourès, 1875.
Codes égyptiens précédés du règlement d'organisation judiciaire. Cairo: Moniteur Égyptien, Barbier et Cie, 1883.
[Ministère de l'Intérieur]. *Législation de police de l'Égypte*. Cairo: Imprimerie Nationale, 1894.
Al-Manshūrāt wa-l-Qarārāt al-Ṣādira fī Sanat 1883 Afrankiyya. Cairo: Maṭbaʿat Būlāq, 1303 [1885–86].

The Palace Collections of Egypt—Catalogue of the Highly Important Collection of Works of Art in Precious Metals—A 1954 March Sale in the Koubbeh Palace. [Cairo?]: Sotheby and Co., 1953.

Projet de code pénal. Alexandria: Mourès, 1871.

Programme de l'enseigemment donné dans les Écoles civiles du Gouvernement Égyptien. Cairo: Delbos-Demouret, 1873.

Taʾrīkh Ḥayāt al-Maghfūr lahu ʿAlī Mubārak Bāshā. Cairo: al-Maṭbaʿa al-Ṭibbiyya, 1894.

PUBLICATIONS WITH AUTHOR OR EDITOR

Abbas Hilmi. *The Last Khedive of Egypt: Memoirs of Abbas Hilmi II.* Translated by Amira Sonbol El Azhary. Cairo: American University in Cairo Press, 2006.

Abbas, Raouf, and Assem El-Dessouky. *The Large Landowning Class and the Peasantry in Egypt, 1837–1952.* Syracuse, New York: Syracuse University Press, 2011.

ʿAbd al-Raḥmān, Jamāl. *Ismāʿīl Ṣiddīq al-Mufattish—Rajul al-Azamāt—Ḍaḥiya al-Wishāya.* Cairo: Dār al-Faḍīla, 2004.

Abdel-Malek, Anouar. *L'Égypte moderne—Idéologie et renaissance nationale.* 1975; repr., Paris: L'Harmattan, 2004.

ʿAbduh, Ibrāhīm. *Taṭawwur al-Ṣiḥāfa al-Miṣriyya 1798–1981.* 4th ed. Cairo: Muʾassasat Sijill al-ʿArab, 1982.

ʿAbduh, Muḥammad. *al-Aʿmāl al-Kāmila.* 5 Vols. Cairo: Dār al-Shurūq, 1993.

ʿAbduh, Muḥammad. "Āthār Muḥammad ʿAlī." In *Taʾrīkh al-Ustādh al-Imām Muḥammad ʿAbduh.* Edited by Rashīd Riḍā, 2:414–420. Cairo: Maṭbaʿat al-Manār, 1324 [1906–1907].

Abdoun, Saleh, ed. *Genesi dell' "Aida," con documentazione inedita,* Quaderni dell'Istituto di Studi Verdiani 4, 1971.

ʿAbdūn, Ṣāliḥ. *ʿĀyida wa-Miʾat Shamʿa.* Cairo: al-Hayʾa al-Miṣriyya al-ʿĀmma li-l-Kitāb, 1975.

———. *Khamsūn ʿĀmman min al-Mūsīqā wa-l-Ūbirā.* Cairo: Dār al-Shurūq, 2000.

Abercrombie, Nicholas, and Brian Longhurst. *Audiences.* London: Sage, 1998.

Abkāriyūs, Iskandar. *Al-Manāqib al-Ibrāhīmiyya wa-l-Maʾāthir al-Khidīwiyya.* 1299 [1882]; Homs: Maṭbaʿat Ḥimṣ, 1910.

———. *Dīwān Nuzhat al-Nufūs wa-Zīnat al-Ṭurūs.* Cairo: Maṭbaʿat Jarīdat al-Zamān, 1883.

Abou Mrad, Nidaa. "L'imam et le chanteur: reformer de l'interieur—une mise en parallèle de Muhammad ʿAbduh et ʿAbduh al-Hâmûlî." *Les Cahiers de l'Orient* 24 (1991): 141–150.

Abu-'Uksa, Wael. *Freedom in the Arab world—Concepts and Ideologies in Arabic Thought in the Nineteenth Century.* Cambridge: Cambridge University Press, 2016.

Abul-Magd, Zeinab A. *Imagined Empires: A History of Revolt in Egypt.* Berkeley, CA: University of California Press, 2013.

Abul Naga, El Saïd Atia. *Les sources françaises du théâtre egyptien, 1870–1939.* Alger: SNED, 1972.

Abu-Lughod, Janet. *1001 Years of the City Victorious.* Princeton, New Jersey: Princeton University Press, 1971.

Abu-Manneh, Butrus. "The Islamic Roots of the Gülhane Rescript." *Die Welt des Islams*, n.s., 34, no. 2 (1994): 173–203.
Abū al-Suʿūd, ʿAbd Allāh. *Al-Dars al-Tāmm fī al-Tārīkh al-ʿĀmm*. Cairo: Maṭbaʿat Wādī al-Nīl, 1289 [1872].
———. *Kitāb Naẓm al-Laʾālī fī al-Sulūk fī-Man Ḥakama Firānsā wa-Man Qābalahum ʿalā Miṣr min al-Mulūk*. Būlāq, Miṣr : [s.n.], 1257 [1842].
Abercrombie, Nicholas, and Brian Longhurst. *Audiences*. London: Sage, 1998.
ʿAfīfī, Muḥammad. "Al-Aqbāṭ bayn ʿAhd al-Dhimma wa-ʿAqd al-Waṭaniyya," *Al-Ijtihād* 8, 30 (1996): 89–102.
Agstner, Rudolf. *Die Österreichisch-Ungarische Kolonie in Kairo vor dem Ersten Weltkrieg—Das Matrikelbuch des k.u.k. Konsulates Kairo 1908–1914*. Schriften des österreichischen Kulturinstitutes Kairo, Band 9. Cairo: Österreichisches Kulturinstitute, 1994.
Ahmed, Heba Farouk. "Nineteenth-Century Cairo: A Dual City?" In *Making Cairo Medieval*. Edited by Nezar AlSayyad, Irene A. Bierman, and Nasser Rabbat, 143–172. Lanham, MD: Lexington Books, 2005.
Akel, Samia. "Hamouli—La voix royale de la Nahda." *Arabies* (1991): 78–83.
Allen, Roger. "Writings of Members of the Nazlī Circle." *Journal of the American Research Center in Egypt* (1970): 79–84.
Amanat, Abbas. *Pivot of the Universe—Nasir al-Din Shah and the Iranian Monarchy*. 1997; London: I. B. Tauris, 2008.
Al-ʿĀmilī, Bahāʾ al-Dīn. *Kitāb al-Kashkūl*. [Cairo?]: al-Maṭbaʿa al-Kubrā al-Ibrāhīmiyya, 1288 [1871–1872].
And, Metin. *A History of Theatre and Popular Entertainment in Turkey*. Ankara: Forum Yayınları, 1964.
———. *Osmanlı Tiyatrosu*. 1976; Ankara: Dost Kitabevi, 1999.
———. *Tanzimat ve İstibdat döneminde Türk Tiyatrosu (1839–1908)*. Ankara: Türkiye İş Bankası Kültür Yayınları, 1972.
Anderson, Benedict. *Imagined Communities*. Rev. Ed. 1983; London: Verso Books, 2006.
Antonius, George. *The Arab Awakening*. 1939; Safety Harbor: Simon Publications, 2001.
Anṭūn, Nuʿmān Afandī. *Kitāb al-Ṭāʾir al-Gharīd fī Waṣf al-Barīd*. Cairo: Maṭbaʿat al-Muqtaṭaf, 1890.
Anṭūn, Faraḥ. *Miṣr al-Jadīda wa-Miṣr al-Qadīma*. Cairo: Maktabat al-Taʾlīf, [1913?].
ʿĀnūs, Najwa Ibrāhīm. *Yaʿqūb Ṣanūʿ, al-Luʿbāt al-Tiyātriyya*. Cairo: al-Hayʾa al-Miṣriyya al-ʿĀmma li-l-Kitāb, 1987.
Applegate, Celia. *A Nation of Provincials: The German Idea of Heimat*. Berkeley, CA: University of California Press, 1990.
Arboit, Gérald. "L'arme financière dans les relations internationales: l'affaire Cernuschi sous le Second Empire." *Revue d'histoire moderne et contemporaine* 46, no. 3 (1999): 545–559.
Armbrust, Walter. *Mass Culture and Modernism in Egypt*. Cambridge: Cambridge University Press, 1996.
Arnaud, Jean-Luc. *Le Caire—mise en place d'une ville moderne 1867–1907*. Arles: Actes Sud, 1998.

Asad, Talal. "The Construction of Religion As an Anthropological Category." In Talal Asad, *Genealogies of Religion: Discipline and Reasons of Power in Christianity and Islam*, 27–54. 1982; Baltimore, MD: Johns Hopkins University Press, 1993.

Āṣāf, Yūsuf. *Dalīl Miṣr, 1890–1891*. Cairo: al-Maṭbaʿa al-Amīriyya, 1890.

Āṣāf, Yūsuf, and Qayṣar Naṣr. *Dalīl Miṣr li-ʿĀmmay 1889–1890*. Cairo: al-Maṭbaʿa al-ʿUmūmiyya, 1889.

ʿAshmāwī, Sayyid. *Al-ʿAyb fī al-Dhāt al-Malikiyya—Inhiyār Haybat Ḥukm al-Fard al-Muṭlaq (al-Khidīw—al-Sulṭān—al-Malik)*. Cairo: Al-Hayʾa al-Miṣriyya al-ʿĀmma li-l-Kitāb, 2002.

ʿĀṣim, Ismāʿīl. *Ḥusn al-ʿAwāqib—Hanāʾ al-Muḥibbīn—Ṣidq al-Ikhāʾ*. Edited by ʿAlī al-Rāʿī. [Cairo]: Wizārat al-Thaqāfa, [1996?].

[Al-ʿAṭṭār, Ḥasan]. *Inshāʾ al-ʿAṭṭār*. Cairo: Dār al-Ṭibāʿa al-ʿĀmira, 1277 [1860–1861].

Audouard, Olympe. *Les mystères de l'Égypte dévoilés*. Paris: E. Dentu, 1865.

ʿAwaḍ, Ramsīs. *Ittijāhāt Siyāsiyya fī al-Masraḥ qabla Thawrat 1919*. Cairo: al-Hayʾa al-Miṣriyya al-ʿĀmma li-l-Kitāb, 1979.

Ayalon, Ami. *The Press in the Arab Middle East—A History*. New York: Oxford University Press, 1995.

———. "'Sihafa': The Arab Experiment in Journalism." *Middle Eastern Studies* 28, no. 2 (1992): 258–280.

Ayangil, Ruhi. "Turkish Music in the Seventeenth Century." In *The Turks*. Edited by Hasan Celal Güzel, C. Cem Oğuz, Osman Karatay, 4:79–88. 4 Vols. Ankara: Yeni Türkiye, 2002.

Al-Ayyūbī, Ilyās. *Taʾrīkh Miṣr fī ʿAhd al-Khidīw Ismāʿīl Bāshā min Sanat 1863 ilā Sanat 1879*. 2 Vols. 1923; Cairo: Maktabat Madbūlī, 1996.

Al-Azmeh, Aziz. *Muslim Kingship—Power and the Sacred in Muslim, Christian and Pagan Polities*. 1997; London: I.B. Tauris, 2001.

———. "Nationalism and the Arabs." In *Arab Nation, Arab Nationalism*. Edited by Derek Hopewood, 63–78. Houndmills: MacMillan Press, 2000.

Bachmann, Peter. "Zwei arabische Verdi-Würdigungen aus dem Jahre 1901." In *Musikalische Quellen—Quellen zur Musikgeschichte: Festschrift für Martin Staehelin zum 65. Geburtstag*. Edited by Ulrich Konrad with Jürgen Heidrich and Hans Joachim Marx, 439–447. Göttingen: Vadenhoeck and Ruprecht, 2002.

Badawi, M. M. "The Father of the Modern Egyptian Theatre: Yaʿqūb Ṣannūʿ." *Journal of Arabic Literature* 16 (1985): 132–145.

———, ed. *Modern Arabic Literature*. Cambridge: Cambridge University Press, 1992.

Badem, Candan. *The Ottoman Crimean War (1853–56)*. Leiden: Brill, 2012.

Badrawi, Malak. *Ismaʿil Sidqi (1875–1950)—Pragmatism and Vision in Twentieth Century Egypt*. Richmond: Curzon, 1996.

Baer, Gabriel. "Tanzimat in Egypt—The Penal Code." *Bulletin of the School of Oriental and African Studies* 26, no. 1 (1963): 29–49.

Al-Bagdadi, Nadia. *Vorgestellte Öffentlichkeit*. Wiesbaden: Reichert Verlag, 2010.

Bahjat, Nabīl. *Al-Arājūz al-Miṣrī*. Cairo: al-Majlis al-Aʿlā li-l-Thaqāfa, 2012.

Bakhtin, Mikhail M. "Forms of Time and of the Chronotope in the Novel." In *The Dialogic Imagination: Four Essays by M.M. Bakhtin*. Edited by Michael Holquist, 84–258. Austin: University of Texas Press, 1981.

Bakhkhāsh, Naʿūm. *Akhbār Ḥalab*. 3 Vols. Aleppo: Maṭbaʿat al-Iḥsān, 1985.
Al-Bakrī, Muḥammad Tawfīq. *Ṣahārij al-Luʾluʾ*. Cairo: Muḥammad Maḥmūd Ḥujjāj, 1906.
Balboni, L. A. *Gl'Italiani nella Civiltà Egiziana del Secolo XIX*. 2 Vols. Alexandria: Penasson, 1906.
Barak, On. "Egyptian Times: Temporality, Personhood, and the Technopolitical Making of Modern Egypt, 1830–1930." Ph.D. diss., New York University, 2009.
———. *On Time—Technology and Temporality in Modern Egypt*. Berkeley: University of California Press, 2013.
———. "Outdating: The Time of Culture in Colonial Egypt." *Grey Room* 53 (2013): 6–31.
Barakāt, ʿAlī. *Taṭawwur al-Milkiyya al-Zirāʿiyya fī Miṣr 1813–1914*. Cairo: Dār al-Thaqāfa al-Jadīda, 1977.
Bardenstein, Carol. *Translation and Transformation in Modern Arabic Literature—The Indigenous Assertions of Muhammad ʿUthman Jalal*. Wiesbaden: Harrassowitz Verlag, 2005.
Barkey, Karen. *Empire of Difference—The Ottomans in Comparative Perspective*. Cambridge: Cambridge University Press, 2008.
Baron, Beth. *Egypt as a Woman: Nationalism, Gender, Politics*. Berkeley, CA: University of California Press, 2005.
Al-Bārūdī, Maḥmūd Sāmī. *Dīwān*. 4 Vols. Beirut: Dār al-ʿAwda, 1992.
Bates, Eliot. *Music in Turkey: Experiencing Music, Expressing Culture*. Global Music Series. New York: Oxford University Press, 2011.
Bayly, Christopher. *The Birth of the Modern World, 1780–1914*. Malden-Oxford: Blackwell Publishing, 2004.
———. *Origins of Nationality in South Asia—Patriotism and Ethical Government in the Making of Modern India*. Delhi: Oxford University Press, 1998.
[Bāz, Rustum]. *Mudhakkirāt Rustum Bāz*. Beirut: Manshūrāt al-Jāmiʿa al-Lubnāniyya, 1955.
Beckman, Joseph Doïmo. "Le théâtre arabe moderne." *Revue d'Art Dramatique* 24, (1890): 80–93.
Behrens-Abouseif, Doris. *Azbakiyya and Its Environments from Azbak to Ismail, 1476–1879*. Cairo: Institut français d'archéologie orientale (IFAO), 1985.
Beinin, Joel, and Zachary Lockman. *Workers on the Nile—Nationalism, Communism, Islam, and the Egyptian Working Class, 1882–1954*. Princeton, NJ: Princeton University Press, 1987.
Belleface, Jean-François. "Turāth, classicisme et variétés: les avatars de l'orchestre oriental au Caire au début du XXe siècle." *Bulletin d'Études Orientales* 39–40, 1987–1988 (1989): 39–65.
Bereson, Ruth. *The Operatic State: Cultural Policy and the Opera House*. London: Routledge, 2002.
Berger, Stefan, and Alexei Miller, eds. *Nationalizing Empires*. Budapest: Central European University Press, 2015.
Berque, Jacques. *Egypt: Imperialism & Revolution*. London: Faber, 1972.
Blickle, Peter. *Heimat: A Critical Theory of the German Idea of Homeland*. Rochester, NY: Camden House, 2002.

Blunt, Wilfrid Scawen. *My Diaries—Part One: 1888–1900*. New York: Knopf, 1922.
———. *Secret History of the English Occupation of Egypt*. New York: Alfred A. Knopf, 1922.
———. *Al-Tārīkh al-Sirrī li-Iḥtilāl Injiltirā Miṣr*. Cairo: Maktabat al-Adab, 2008 = *Secret History of the English Occupation of Egypt*. New York: Alfred A. Knopf, 1922.
Booth, Marilyn, and Anthony Gorman. *The Long 1890s in Egypt—Colonial Quiescence, Subterranean Resistance*. Edinburgh: Edinburgh University Press, 2014.
Bourdieu, Pierre. *Distinction—A Social Critique of the Judgement of Taste*. Cambridge, MA: Harvard University Press, 1984.
———. "The Forms of Capital." In *Handbook of Theory and Research for the Sociology of Education*. Edited by J. E. Richardson, 241–258. New York: Greenwood, 1984.
Broadly, A. M. *How We Defended Arabi and His Friends*. London: Chapman and Hill, 1884.
Brown, L. Carl. *The Tunisia of Ahmad Bey, 1837–1855*. Princeton, NJ: Princeton University Press, 1974.
Brubaker, Rogers. *Grounds for Difference*. Cambridge, MA: Harvard University Press, 2015.
———. "Religion and Nationalism: Four Approaches." *Nations and Nationalism* 18, no. 1 (2012): 2–20.
Budak, Mustafa, et al. (eds.). *Osmanlı Belgerelerinde Mısır*. Istanbul: BOA, 2012.
Budden, Julian. *Verdi*. New York: Vintage Books, 1987.
Burke, Peter. *The Fabrication of Louis XIV*. New Haven, CT: Yale University Press, 1992.
[al-Bū Saʿīdī, Ḥammūd]. *Riḥlat Ḥammūd al-Bū Saʿīdī, 1872, al-Ḥijāz—Miṣr—al-Shām*. Damascus: al-Takwīn, 2009.
Busch, Hans. *Verdi's Aida—The History of an Opera in Letters and Documents*. Minneapolis, MN: University of Minnesota Press, 1978.
[Al-Bustānī, Salīm]. "al-Riwāyāt al-ʿArabiyya al-Miṣriyya." *Al-Jinān*, 1 Tammūz 1875, 442–444.
Butsch, Richard. *The Citizen Audience*. New York: Routledge, 2008.
Butler, Alfred J. *Court Life in Egypt*. London: Chapman and Hall, 1887.
Butovsky, Avriel. "Reform and Legitimacy: The Egyptian Monarchy." In *Entre réforme sociale et mouvement national*. Edited by Alain Roussillon, 103–112. Cairo: CEDEJ, 1995.
Cachia, Pierre. *Popular Narrative Ballads of Modern Egypt*. Oxford: Clarendon Press, 1989.
———. "Translations and Adaptations," in *Modern Arabic Literature*. Edited by M. M. Badawi, 23–35. Cambridge: Cambridge University Press, 1992.
Cammas, Henri, et André Lefèvre. *La vallée du Nil—impressions et photographies*. Paris: L. Hachette et Cie, 1862.
Campos, Michelle U. *Ottoman Brothers: Muslims, Christians, and Jews in Early Twentieth-Century Palestine*. Stanford, California: Stanford University Press, 2011.
Cecil, Lord Edward. *The Leisure of an Egyptian Officer*. London: Hodder and Stoughton, 1921.

Çelik, Zeynep. *The Remaking of Istanbul: Portrait of an Ottoman City in the Nineteenth Century*. Berkeley, CA: University of California Press, 1993.
Cevdet, Ahmed. *Maʿrūzāt*. İstanbul: Çağrı Yayınları, 1980.
Chaillé-Long, Charles. *The Three Prophets: Chinese Gordon, Mohammed-Ahmed (el Maahdi)*. New York: D. Appleton and Company, 1884.
Chalcraft, John. "Engaging the State: Peasants and Petitions in Egypt on the Eve of Colonial Rule." *International Journal of Middle East Studies* 37, n. 3 (2005): 303–325.
Charfeddine, Moncef. *Deux siècles de théâtre en Tunisie*. Tunis: Editions Ibn Charaf, Société Tunisienne des Arts Graphiques, [2001?].
Chatterjee, Partha. "Anderson's Utopia." *Diacritics* 29, no. 4 (1999): 128–134.
———. *The Black Hole of Empire—History of a Global Practice of Power*. Princeton, NJ: Princeton University Press, 2012.
———. *The Nation and Its Fragments: Colonial and Postcolonial Histories*. Princeton, NJ: Princeton University Press, 1993.
Chehabi, Houchang. "From Revolutionary *Taṣnīf* to Patriotic *Surūd*: Music and Nation-Building in Pre–World War II Iran." *Iran* 37 (1999): 143–154.
Cheta, Omar. "Rule of Merchants: The Practice of Commerce and Law in Late Ottoman Egypt, 1841–1876." Ph.D. diss., New York University, 2014.
Choueiri, Youssef M. *Arab Nationalism—A History*. Oxford: Blackwell, 2000.
———. *Modern Arab Historiography – Historical Discourse and the Nation-State* Rev. ed. London: Routledge, 2003.
Cioeta, Donald J. "Ottoman Censorship in Lebanon and Syria, 1876–1908." *International Journal of Middle East Studies* 10, no. 2 (1979): 167–186.
Clancy-Smith, Julia A. *Mediterraneans: North Africa and Europe in an Age of Migration, 1800–1900*. Berkeley, CA: University of California Press, 2011.
Clot, Antoine-Barthélémy (Clot-Bey). *Compte Rendu de l'École de Médecine d'Abou-Zabel (Egypte), 1828, 1829, 1830*. Marseilles: Feissat Ainé, 1830.
———. *Compte Rendu des Travaux de l'École de Médecine d'Abou-Zabel (Egypte), 1831, 1832*. Marseille: Feissat Ainé, 1832.
Cohen, Joshua, and Martha C. Nussbaum, eds. *For Love of Country: Debating the Limits of Patriotism*. Boston, MA: Beacon Press, 1996.
Cole, Juan R. *Colonialism and Revolution in the Middle East—Social and Cultural Origins of Egypt's ʿUrābī movement*. Princeton, NJ: Princeton University Press, 1993.
Colla, Elliot. *Conflicted Antiquities—Egyptology, Egyptomania, Egyptian Modernity*. Durham, NC: Duke University Press, 2007.
Cook, Michael. *Commanding Right and Forbidding Wrong in Islamic Thought*. Cambridge: Cambridge University Press, 2010.
———. "Pharaonic History in Medieval Egypt." *Studia Islamica* 57 (1983): 67–103.
Coury, Ralph M. *The Making of an Egyptian Arab Nationalist—The Early Years of Azzam Pasha, 1893–1936*. Reading: Garnet, 1998.
Crabbs, Jack A., Jr. *The Writing of History in Nineteenth-Century Egypt*. Cairo: The American University in Cairo Press, 1984.
Crabitès, Pierre. *Ibrahim of Egypt*. London: George Routledge and Sons, Ltd., 1935.
———. *Ismail—The Maligned Khedive*. London: George Routledge and Sons, Ltd., 1933.

Crosnier-Leconte, Marie-Laure, and Mercedes Volait. *L'Égypte d'un architecte—Ambroise Baudry (1838–1906)*. Paris: Somogy Édition, 1998.

Cuno, Kenneth M. "Egypt to c. 1919." In *The New Cambridge History of Islam*. Edited by Francis Robinson, vol. 5: 79–106. Cambridge: Cambridge University Press, 2010.

———. *Modernizing Marriage—Family, Ideology, and Law in Nineteenth- and Early Twentieth-Century Egypt*. Syracuse, NY: Syracuse University Press, 2015.

———. "Muhammad Ali and the Decline and Revival Thesis in Modern Egyptian History." In Raouf Abbas, ed., *Reform or Modernization? Egypt under Muhammad Ali*, 93–119. Cairo: Al-Majlis al-Aʿlā li-l-Thaqāfa, 2000.

Cuno, Kenneth M., and Michael J. Reimer. "The Census Registers of Nineteenth-century Egypt: A New Source for Social Historians." *British Journal of Middle Eastern Studies* 24, 2 (1997): 193–216.

Daly, Martin W, ed. *The Cambridge History of Egypt*. 2 Vols. Cambridge: Cambridge University Press, 1998.

Dardīr, Aḥmad. *Hādhihi Ḥāshiyat al-ʿĀlim al-ʿAllāma al-Baḥr al-Ḥabr al-Fahhāma al-ʿĀrif bi-Allāh al-Niḥrīr Abī al-Barakāt al-Ustādh al-Shaykh Aḥmad al-Dardīr ʿalā Qiṣṣat al-Miʿrāj li-l-ʿAllāma al-Humām Barakat al-Anām Najm al-Dīn al-Ghayṭī*. Cairo: Maṭbaʿat Muḥammad Unṣī, 1284 [1867].

Al-Dasūqī, Wāʾil Ibrāhīm. *Al-Tārīkh al-Thaqāfī li-Miṣr al-Ḥadītha—al-Muʾassasāt al-ʿIlmiyya wa-l-Thaqāfiyya fī al-Qarn al-Tāsiʿ ʿAshar*. Cairo: Dār al-Kutub wa-l-Wathāʾiq al-Qawmiyya, 2012.

Al-Dasūqī, Ibrāhīm ʿAbd al-Ghaffār. *Maqāla Shukriyya li-l-Ḥaḍra al-Ismāʿīliyya ʿalā Inshāʾ Dār al-Warrāqa Dhāt al-Bahja wa-l-Ṭalāqa*. Cairo: Dār al-Ṭibāʿa, 1288 [1871].

Davison, Roderic H. *Reform in the Ottoman Empire (1856–1876)*. Princeton, NJ: Princeton University Press, 1963.

Dawisha, Adeed. *Arab Nationalism in the Twentieth Century: From Triumph to Despair*. Princeton, NJ: Princeton University Press, 2003.

Dawn, Ernest C. *From Ottomanism to Arabism: Essays on the Origins of Arab Nationalism*. Urbana, IL: University of Illinois Press, 1973.

Delanoue, Gilbert. *Moralistes et politiques musulmans dans l'Égypte du XIXe siècle (1798–1882)*. Vol 2 (livres IV et V). Cairo: Institut français d'archéologie oriental, 1982.

Delchevalerie, G. *Le parc public de l'Ezbékieh au Caire*. Ghent: C. Annoot-Braeckman, 1897.

De-Marchi, F. A. *La fiesta dei Khalidj in Cairo ossia la vergine del Nilo—episodo del poema la Valle del Nilo*. Cairo: Imprimerie Onsy et Mourés au Mouski, 1869.

Deny, J. *Sommaire des Archives Turques du Caire*. Cairo: Institut français d'archéologie orientale, 1930.

[Depping, Georg-Bernhard], Al-Khawāja Dabbingh (Depping), *Kitāb Qalāʾid al-Mafākhir fī Gharīb ʿAwāʾid al-Awāʾil wa-l-Awākhir*. Būlāq: Dār al-Ṭibāʿa al-ʿĀmira, 1249 [1833].

Deringil, Selim. "Ghazi Ahmed Mukhtar Pasha and the British Occupation of Egypt." *Al-Abḥāth* 34 (1986): 13–19.

———. "The Ottoman Response to the Egyptian Crisis of 1881–82." *Middle Eastern Studies* 24, no. 1 (1988): 3–24.

———. *The Well-Protected Domains—Ideology and the Legitimation of Power in the Ottoman Empire*, 1876–1909. London: I.B. Tauris, 1998.

DeYoung, Terri. *Mahmud Sami al-Barudi—Reconfiguring Society and the Self*. Syracuse, NY: Syracuse University Press, 2015.

Di Capua, Yoav. "Embodiment of the Revolutionary Spirit: The Mustafa Kamil Mausoleum in Cairo." *History and Memory* 13, no. 1 (2001): 85–113.

———. *Gatekeepers of the Arab Past*. Berkeley, CA: University of California Press, 2009.

Dīmūlān, Idmūn [Demolins, Edmond]. *Sirr Taqaddum al-Inkilīz al-Saksūniyyīn, tarjamahu min al-lugha al-Faransiyya Aḥmad Fatḥī Zaghlūl*. Cairo: Maktabat al-Taraqqī, 1899.

Donnet, Alexis. *Architectonographie des théâtres de Paris ou parallèle historique et critique de ces édifices*. Paris: De Lacroix-Comon, 1857.

Douin, Georges. *Histoire du règne du Khédive Ismail*. Rome: Nell'Istituto poligrafico dello Stato per reale società di geografia d'Egitto, 1934.

Draneht Bey, Ad. Crémieux, and Jules Favre. *Observations pour Son Altesse Le Vice-Roi d'Égypte*. Paris: E. Thunot, 1862.

Dunn, John P. *Khedive Ismail's Army*. London: Routledge, 2005.

Duri, A. A. *The Historical Formation of the Arab Nation—A Study in Identity and Consciousness*. Translated by Lawrence I. Conrad. London: Centre for Arab Unity Studies, Croom Helm, 1987.

Durrī, Muḥammad. *Kitāb al-Nukhba al-Durriyya fi Maʾāthir al-ʿĀʾila al-Muḥammadiyya al-ʿAlawiyya*. Būlāq: al-Maṭbaʿa al-Kubrā al-Amīriyya, 1307 [1889–1890].

Dye, William McEntyre. *Moslim Egypt and Christian Abyssina, or Military Service under the Khedive*. New York: Atkin and Prout, 1880.

Dykstra, Durrell. "A Biographical Study in Egyptian Modernization: ʿAli Mubarak (1823/4–1893)." Ph.D. diss., University of Michigan, 1977.

Eisenstadt, Howard. "Modernization, Imperial Nationalism, and the Ethnicization of Confessional Identity in the Late Ottoman Empire." In *Nationalizing Empires*. Edited by Miller and Berger, 429–459.

Ellis, Matt. "King Me: The Political Culture of Monarchy in Interwar Egypt and Iraq." M.Phil. thesis, University of Oxford, 2005.

Elshahed, Mohamed. "Facades of Modernity—Image, Performance, and Transformation of the Egyptian Metropolis." Master's thesis, MIT, 2007.

Enkiri, Gabriel. *Ibrahim Pacha*. Cairo: Imp. Française, 1948.

Erol, Merih. *Greek Orthodox Music in Ottoman Istanbul: Nation and Community in the Era of Reform*. Bloomington, IN: Indiana University Press, 2015.

Ettmüller, Eliane Ursula. *The Construct of Egypt's Nation-Self in James Sanua's Early Satire and Caricature*. Berlin: Klaus Schwarz Verlag, 2012.

EzzelArab, AbdelAziz. *European Control and Egypt's Traditional Elites—A Case Study in Elite Economic Nationalism*. New York: Lewiston, 2002.

———. "The Fiscal and Constitutional Program of Egypt's Traditional Elites in 1879—A Documentary and Contextual Analysis of 'al-Lāʾiḥa al-Waṭaniyya' ('The National Program')." *Journal of the Economic and Social History of the Orient* 52 (2009): 301–324.

Fāḍil, Muḥammad. *Al-Shaykh Salāma Ḥijāzī*. Damanhūr: Maṭbaʿat al-Umma, 1932.

Fahmī, ʿAlī. *Mazdūja Mawsūma bi-ʿArūs al-Afrāḥ*. Cairo: Maṭbaʿat al-Madāris al-Milkiyya, 1290 [1873].

———. *Qudwat al-Faraʿ bi-Aṣli-hi fī Ḥubb al-Waṭan wa-Ahli-hi*. Cairo: Dār al-Ṭibāʿa al-Khidīwiyya, 1290 [1873–1874].

Fahmī, Amal. *Al-ʿAlāqāt al-Miṣriyya al–ʿUthmāniyya ʿalā ʿAhd al-Iḥtilāl al-Briṭānī*. Cairo: Al-Hayʾa al-Miṣriyya al-ʿĀmma li-l-Kitāb, 2002.

[Fahmī, Gallini Pasha]. *Mudhakkirāt Qillīnī Fahmī Bāshā*. 2 Vols. Cairo: Maṭbaʿat Miṣr, 1934.

[Fahmī, Iskandar]. *Mudhakkirāt Iskandar Bāshā Fahmī*. Alexandria: Dār al-Wafāʾ li-Dunyā al-Ṭibaʿa wa-l-Nashr, 2002.

Fahmī, Maḥmūd. *Al-Baḥr al-Zākhir fī Tārīkh al-ʿĀlam wa-Akhbār al-Awāʾil wa-l-Awākhir*. 1894–95 in 4 Vols.; repr. Cairo: Dār al-Kutub wa-l-Wathāʾiq, 2007 (a reprint of a part of the original vol. 1.).

Fahmy, Gallini. *Souvenirs du Khédive Ismail au Khédive Abbas II*. Cairo: La Patrie, [1935].

Fahmy, Khaled. *All the Pasha's Men. Mehmed Ali, his Army and the Making of Modern Egypt*. 1997; Cairo: AUC Press, 2002.

———. *Mehmed Ali—From Ottoman Governor to Ruler of Egypt*. Oxford: Oneworld, 2009.

———. "Modernizing Cairo: A Revisionist Narrative." In *Making Cairo Medieval*. Edited by Nezar AlSayyad, Irene A. Bierman, and Nasser Rabbat, 173–200. Lanham, MD: Lexington Books, 2005.

Fahmy, Ziad. "Francophone Egyptian Nationalists, Anti-British Discourse, and European Public Opinion, 1885–1910: The Case of Mustafa Kamil and Yaʿqub Sannuʿ." *Comparative Studies of South Asia, Africa and the Middle East* 28, no. 1 (2008): 170–184.

———. *Ordinary Egyptians—Creating the Modern Nation through Popular Culture*. Stanford, CA: Stanford University Press, 2011.

Farāj, Yāsmīn. "Al-Binya al-Mūsīqiyya wa-ʿAlāqātuhā bi-l-Naṣṣ al-Shiʿrī fī Ashkāl al-Ghināʾiyya al-Miṣriyya Ibbān al-Qarn al-Tāsiʿ ʿAshar." In *al-Tārīkh wa-l-Mūsīqā*. Edited by Muḥammad ʿAfīfī and Naḥla Maṭar, 95–121. Al-Haram: ʿAyn li-l-Dirāsāt wa-l-Buḥūth al-Insāniyya wa-l-Ijtimāʿiyya, 2013.

Fargues, Philippe. "Family and Household in Mid-Nineteenth Century Cairo." In *Family History in the Middle East: Household, Property and Gender*. Edited by Beshara Doumani, 23–49. New York: State University of New York Press, 2003.

Farīd, Muḥammad. *Kitāb al-Bahja al-Tawfīqiyya Fī Tārīkh Muʾassis al-ʿĀʾila al-Khidīwiyya*. Būlāq Miṣr: al-Maṭbaʿa al-Amīriyya, 1890.

———. *Mudhakkirāt Muḥammad Farīd—Tārīkh Miṣr min Ibtidāʾ Sanat 1891*. Cairo: Dār Nahḍat al-Sharq, 2002.

Al-Faruqi, Lois Ibsen. "Muwashshaḥ: A Vocal Form in Islamic Culture." *Ethnomusicology* 19, no. 1 (1975): 1–29.

Fatḥ Allāh, Īzīs. *Salāma Ḥijāzī*. Cairo: Dār al-Shurūq, 2002.

Fauser, Annegret. *Musical Encounters at the 1889 Paris World's Fair*. Rochester, NY: University of Rochester Press, 2005.

Fikrī, ʿAbd Allāh. *Kitāb al-Fawāʾid al-Fikriyya li-l-Makātib al-Miṣriyya*. Cairo: al-Maṭbaʿa al-Mīriyya, 1302 [1884–1885].

Fikrī, Amīn Muḥammad. *Irshād al-Alibbā ilā Maḥāsin Urubbā*. 2 Vols. Al-Haram [Giza]: ʿAyn l-il-Dirāsāt wa-l-Buḥūth al-Insāniyya wa-l-Ijtimāʿiyya, 2008.
Fikrī, Amīn Muḥammad, ed. *Al-Āthār al-Fikriyya*. Cairo: al-Maṭbaʿa al-Kubrā al-Amīriyya, 1897.
Findley, Carter V. *Bureaucratic Reform in the Ottoman Empire—The Sublime Porte, 1789–1922*. Princeton, NJ: Princeton University Press, 1980.
Fleischer, Heinrich. "Fortsetzung des wissenschaftlichen Jahrberichtes für das Jahr 1847 bis Ende des Jahres 1849." *Zeitschrift der Deutschen Morgenländischen Gesellschaft* 4 (1850): 434–504.
Fligstein, Niel, and Doug MacAdam. "Toward a General Theory of Strategic Action Fields." *Sociological Theory* 29, no. 1 (2011): 1–26.
Fodor, Sándor. *Arab legendák a piramisokról*. Budapest: Akadémiai Kiadó, 1971.
Galbraith, John S., and Afaf Lutfi al-Sayyid-Marsot. "The British Occupation of Egypt: Another View." *International Journal of Middle East Studies* 4 (1978): 471–488.
Gardey, L. *Voyage de Sultan Abd-Ul-Aziz de Stamboul au Caire*. Paris: E. Dentu, 1865.
Garfi, Mohamed. *Musique et spectacle—Le théâtre lyrique arabe, esquisse d'un itinéraire, 1847–1975*. Paris: L'Harmattan, 2009.
Garnier, Charles. *Le Théâtre*. Paris: Hachette et Cie, 1871.
Garstin, W. E. *Report upon the Administration of the Public Works Department for 1898*. Cairo: National Printing Office, 1899.
———. *Report upon the Administration of the Public Works Department for 1900*. Cairo: National Printing Office, 1901.
———. *Report upon the Administration of the Public Works Department for 1905*. Cairo: National Printing Office, 1906.
Gasper, Michael Ezekiel. *The Power of Representation: Publics, Peasants, and Islam in Egypt*. Stanford, CA: Stanford University Press, 2009.
Gaultier-Kurhan, Caroline. *Princesses d'Égypte*. Paris: Riveneuve Editions, 2009.
Geertz, Clifford. *Negara—The Theatre State in Nineteenth-Century Bali*. Princeton, NJ: Princeton University Press, 1980.
Gellion-Danglar, Eugène. *Lettres sur l'Égypte contemporaine, 1865–1875*. Paris: Sandoz et Fischbacher, 1876.
Gellner, Ernest. *Nations and Nationalism*. Ithaca, NY: Cornell University Press, 1983.
Gendzier, Irene. *The Practical Visions of Yaʿqub Sanuʿ*. Cambridge, MA: Harvard University Press, 1966.
Gershoni, Israel. "The Evolution of National Culture in Modern Egypt: Intellectual Formation and Social Diffusion, 1892–1945." *Poetics Today* 13, no. 2 (1992): 325–350.
Gershoni, Israel, and James Jankowski. *Egypt, Islam, and the Arabs: The Search for Egyptian Nationhood, 1900–1930*. New York: Oxford University Press, 1986.
Ghali, Mirrit Butrus ed. *Mémoirs de Nubar Pacha*. Beirut: Librairie du Liban, 1983.
Ghānim, Ibrāhīm al-Bayyūmī. *Al-Awqāf wa-l-Siyāsa fī Miṣr*. 1968; Cairo: Dār al-Shurūq, 1998.
Ghārdūn, *Mukhtaṣar Yataḍamman Qawāʿid Aṣliyya min ʿIlm al-Mūsīqā Muʾallaf fī Khuṣūṣ Jamīʿ al-Muwaysīqāt al-Mutaʿalliqa bi-l-ʿAsākir al-Miṣriyya bi-ʿAhd Ḥaḍrat al-Khidīwī al-Aʿẓam Muḥammad Saʿīd Bāshā*. [Cairo]: Maṭbaʿat Būlāq, 1272 [1855].

[Ghislanzoni, Antonio]. *Aida—Opera in 4 atti e 7 quadri, parole di A. Ghislanzoni, musica del Comm. G. Verdi.* Cairo: Tipografia francese Delbos-Demouret, 1871.

[Ghislanzoni, Antonio]. *Tarjamat al-Ūpīra al-Musammā bi-Ism ʿĀyida, maṣnaf-hu bi-Amr Saʿādat Khidīwī Miṣr—taʿrīb al-ʿabd al-faqīr Abī al-Suʿūd Afandī, Muḥarrir Ṣaḥīfat Wādī al-Nīl.* Cairo: Maṭbaʿat Jurnāl Wādī al-Nīl, 1288 [1871].

Ginzburg, Carlo. "Clues: Roots of an Evidential Paradigm." In *Myths, Clues and the Scientific Method.* Translated by John and Anne C. Tedeschi, 96–125. London: Hutchinson Radius, 1990.

Goldziher, Ignácz. *Jelentés a Magyar Tudományos Akadémia Könyvtára számára a Keletről hozott könyvekről tekintetettel a nyomdaviszonyokra Keleten.* Értekezések a Nyelv- és Széptudományok köréből, vol. 4. Budapest: Atheneum, 1874.

———. "Jugend- und Strassenpoesie in Kairo." *Zeitschrift der Deutschen Morgenländischen Gesellschaft* 33 (1879), 608–630.

———. "Muhammadan Public Opinion." Translated by Jerry Payne and Philip Sadgrove. 1882; *Journal of Semitic Studies* 37, 1 (1993): 97–133.

Gouchard, Albert. "De la legalisation du théâtre à Rome et en France." Ph.D. diss., Université de France, Lille, 1880.

Gran, Peter. *Islamic Roots of Capitalism: Egypt, 1760–1840.* 1979; repr., Syracuse, NY: University of Syracuse Press, 1998.

Granara, William. "Nostalgia, Arab Nationalism, and the Andalusian Chronotope in the Evolution of the Modern Arabic Novel." *Journal of Arabic Literature* 36, no. 1 (2005): 57–73.

Al-Ḥaddād, al-Shaykh Amīn. *Muntakhabāt.* Alexandria: Maṭbaʿat Jurjī Gharzūzī, 1913.

Al-Ḥadīdī, Fatḥī Ḥāfiẓ. *Dirāsāt fī al-Taṭawwur al-ʿUmrānī li-Madīnat al-Qāhira.* Cairo: al-Hayʾa al-Miṣriyya al-ʿĀmma li-l-Kitāb, 2010.

Al-Ḥakīm, Tawfīq. *Min Dhikriyyāt al-Fann wa-l-Qaḍāʾ.* Cairo: Dār al-Maʿārif, 1953.

Halima, Hamadi Ben. *Un demi-siècle de théâtre arabe en Tunisie (1907–1957).* Tunis: Publications de l'Université de Tunis, 1974.

Halis, Yusuf. *Şehname-yi Osmani.* Istanbul: s. n. [after 1271/1854].

Hamzah, Dyala. "Nineteenth-Century Egypt as Dynastic Locus of Universality: The History of Muhammad ʿAli by Khalil ibn Ahmad al-Rajabi." *Comparative Studies of South Asia, Africa and the Middle East* 27 (2007): 62–82.

Hanssen, Jens, Thomas Philipp, and Stefan Weber, eds. *The Empire in the City—Arab Provincial Capitals in the Late Ottoman Empire.* Beirut: Orient Institut, 2002.

Hanssen, Jens. *Fin de siècle Beirut: The Making of an Ottoman Provincial Capital.* Oxford: Clarendon Press, 2005.

al-Harawī, Abū Sahl. *Al-Talwīḥ fī Sharḥ al-Faṣīḥ.* Cairo: Maṭbaʿat Wādī al-Nīl, 1285 [1868].

Harrison, Thomas Skelton. *The Homely Diary of a Diplomat in the East.* Boston: Houghton Mifflin Company, 1917.

Ḥasan, Muḥammad ʿAbd al-Ghanī, and ʿAbd al-ʿAzīz Dasūqī. *Rawḍat al-Madāris: Nashʾatuhā wa-Ittijāhātuhā al-Adabiyya wa-l-ʿIlmiyya. Dirāsa Naqdiyya Taḥlīliyya.* Cairo: al-Hayʾa al-Miṣriyya al-ʿĀmma li-l-Kitāb, 1975.

Hassan, Mona. *Longing for the Lost Caliphate: A Transregional History* (Princeton, NJ: Princeton University Press, forthcoming).

Hassoun, Jacques. "Les Juifs, une communité contrastée." In *Alexandrie 1860–1960—Un modèle éphémère de convivialité : Communautés et identité cosmopolite*. Edited by Robert Ilbert and Ilios Yannakakis, 50–67. Paris: Autrement, 1992.

Hatem, Mervat Fayez. *Literature, Gender, and Nation-building in Nineteenth-century Egypt: The Life and Works of 'Aisha Taymur*. New York: Palgrave Macmillan, 2011.

Hatina, Meir. *ʿUlamaʾ, Politics, and the Public Sphere—An Egyptian Perspective*. Salt Lake City, UT: University of Utah Press, 2010.

Herz, Max. *La Mosquée el-Rifaï au Caire*. Milan: Imp. Humbert Allegretti, 1912.

Heyworth-Dunne, James. *An Introduction to the History of Education in Modern Egypt*. 1939; repr., London: Cass, 1969.

———. "Printing and Translations under Muḥammad ʿAlī of Egypt: The Foundation of Modern Arabic." *Journal of the Royal Asiatic Society of Great Britain and Ireland* 3 (1940): 325–349.

Ḥijāzī, Āmina. *Al-Waṭaniyya al-Miṣriyya fī al-ʿAṣr al-Ḥadīth*. Cairo: Al-Hayʾa al-Miṣriyya al-ʿĀmma li-l-Kitāb, 2000.

Al-Ḥijāzī, Muḥammad b. Ismāʿīl b. ʿUmar Shihāb al-Dīn. *Safīnat al-Mulk wa-Nafīsat al-Fulk*. 1865; Cairo: Maṭbaʿat al-Jāmiʿa bi-Shāriʿ ʿĀbdīn, 1309 [1891–92].

Al-Hilbāwī, Ibrāhīm. *Mudhakkirāt*. Cairo: al-Hayʾa al-Miṣriyya al-ʿĀmma li-l-Kitāb, 1995.

Hill, Peter. "Utopia and Civilisation in the Arab Nahda." Ph.D. diss., Oxford University (expected in 2016).

Hirschkind, Charles. *The Ethical Soundscape: Cassette Sermons and Islamic Counterpublics*. New York: Columbia University Press, 2006.

Hirszowicz, L. "The Sultan and the Khedive, 1892–1908." *Middle Eastern Studies* 8 (1972): 287–311.

Hornik, M. P. "The Mission of Sir Henry Drummond-Wolff to Constantinople, 1885–1887." *The English Historical Review* 55, no. 220 (1940): 598–623.

Hourani, Albert. *Arabic Thought in the Liberal Age, 1798–1939*. 1962; repr., Oxford: Oxford University Press, 2002.

———. "The Middleman in a Changing Society: Syrians in Egypt in the Eighteenth and Nineteenth Centuries." In idem, *The Emergence of the Modern Middle East*, 103–123. Berkeley: University of California Press, 1981.

Huizinga, Johan. "Patriotism and Nationalism." In *Men and Ideas—History, the Middle Ages, the Renaissance*, 97–155. New York: Meridian Books, 1959.

Humbert, Jean-Marcel. "Les Expositions universelles de 1867 et 1878 et la création d'*Aïda*: l'image de l'Égypte transmise par Auguste Mariette." In *La France & l'Égypte: à l'époque des vice-rois 1805–1882*. Edited by Daniel Panzac et André Raymond, 289–309. Cairo: Institut français d'archéologie orientale, 2002.

Hunter, F. Robert. "Egypt's High Officials in Transition from a Turkish to a Modern Administrative Elite, 1849–1879." *Middle Eastern Studies* 19, no. 3 (1983): 277–300.

———. *Egypt under the Khedives: From Household Government to Modern Bureaucracy*. 1984; repr. Cairo: The American University in Cairo Press, 1999.

Al-Ibshīhī, Shihāb al-Dīn Muḥammad b. Aḥmad. *Al-Mustaṭraf fī Kull Fann Mustaẓraf*. Beirut: Dār Maktabat al-Ḥayāt, 1988.

İhsanoğlu, Ekmeleddin. *Mısır'da Türkler ve Kültürel Mirasları*. Istanbul: Research Centre for Islamic History, Art and Culture (IRCICA), 2006.

———. *The Turks in Egypt and their Cultural Legacy: An Analytical Study of the Turkish Printed Patrimony in Egypt from the time of Muhammad 'Ali with Annotated Bibliographies*. Translated by Humphrey Davies. Cairo: The American University in Cairo Press, 2012.

Ihsanoğlu, Ekmeleddin, and Ṣāliḥ Saʿdāwī Ṣāliḥ. *Al-Thaqāfa al-Turkiyya fī Miṣr*. Istanbul: Research Centre for Islamic History, Art and Culture (IRCICA), 2003.

Isḥāq, ʿAwnī, ed., *Al-Durar wa-hiya Muntakhabāt al-Ṭayyib al-Ḍhikr al-Khālid al-Athar al-Kātib wa-l-Shāʿir wa-l-Khaṭīb al-Marḥūm Adīb Isḥāq*. Beirut: al-Maṭbaʿa al-Adabiyya, 1909.

Ismail, Annelies. *Alexandria Was Our Destiny: Based on the Memories of Marie-Luise Nagel*. Alexandria: Bibliotheca Alexandria, 2012.

ʿIsmat, ʿĀʾisha [Taymūriyya, ʿĀʾisha]. *Al-Dīwān al-Muḥyī Rufāt al-Adab al-Bāligh Min Funūn al-Balāgha Ghāyat al-Arab al-Muḥtawī min Ḥusn al-Barāʿa ʿalā Mā bi-hi Imtāz al-Musammā Ṭibqan li-Maʿnā-hi bi-Ḥilyat al-Ṭirāz*. Cairo: al-Maṭbaʿa al-Sharafiyya, 1892 [1886].

Ismāʿīl, Sayyid ʿAlī. *Ismāʿīl ʿĀṣim fī Mawkib al-Ḥayāt wa-l-Adab*. Cairo: Maktabat Zahrāʾ al-Sharq, 1996.

———. "Masraḥiyyāt lahā Taʾrīkh 5—Hārūn al-Rashīd." *al-Jumhūriyya*, 19 December 2010.

———. *al-Raqāba wa-l-Masraḥ al-Marfūḍ*. Cairo: al-Hayʾa al-ʿĀmma al-Miṣriyya li-l-Kitāb, 1997.

———. *Taʾrīkh al-Masraḥ fī Miṣr fī al-Qarn al-Tāsiʿ ʿAshar*. 1997; Cairo: Maktabat al-Usra, 2005.

Issawi, Charles. *An Economic History of the Middle East and North Africa*. New York: Columbia University Press, 1982.

Al-ʿIyyādī, Muḥammad. *Riwāyat Maqātil Miṣr—Aḥmad Bāshā ʿUrābī*. Alexandria: Maṭbaʿat al-Kāmil, 1897.

Al-Jabartī, ʿAbd al-Raḥmān. *ʿAjāʾib al-Āthār fī al-Tarājim wa-l-Akhbār*. 5 Vols. Cairo: Maktabat Madbūlī, 1997.

Jacob, Wilson Chako. *Working Out Egypt: Effendi Masculinity and Subject Formation in Colonial Modernity, 1870–1940*. Durham, NC: Duke University Press, 2011.

J[alāl], M[uḥammad] ʿ[Uthmān]. *Al-Shaykh Matlūf*. Cairo: Maṭbaʿat Wādī al-Nīl al-Miṣriyya, 1290 [1873].

Jalāl, Muḥammad ʿUthmān. *Al-ʿUyūn al-Yawāqiẓ fī al-Amthāl wa-l-Mawāʿiẓ*. Cairo: Maṭbaʿat Ḥajar, 1858.

Jallād, Fīlīb. *Al-Qāmūs al-ʿĀmm li-l-Idāra wa-l-Qaḍāʾ*. Vols. 1 and 3. Alexandria: Maṭbaʿat Yanī Lāghūdāks, 1890 and 1899.

Jankowski, James. "Ottomanism and Arabism in Egypt, 1860–1914." *The Muslim World*, 70, no. 3–4 (1980): 226–259.

[Jawhariyya, Wasif], ed., Salim Tamari. *The Storyteller of Jerusalem—The Life and Times of Wasif Jawhariyyeh, 1904–1947*. Northampton, MA: Clockroot Books, 2013.

Jelavich, Charles, and Barbara. *The Establishment of the Balkan National States, 1804–1920*. Seattle, WA: University of Washington Press, 1977.

Jerichau-Baumann, Elisabeth. "Egypt 1870." *Victorian Literature and Culture* 38 (2010): 267–284.

Jerrold, Blanchard. *Egypt under Ismail Pacha*. London: Samuel Tinsley, 1879.

Al-Jumayʿī, ʿAbd Al-Munʿim Ibrāhīm al-Dasūqī. *ʿAbd Allāh al-Nadīm wa-Dawru-hu fī al-Ḥaraka al-Siyāsiyya wa-l-Ijtimāʿiyya*. Cairo: Dār al-Kitāb al-Jāmiʿī, 1980.

———. *Al-Khidīw ʿAbbās al-Thānī wa-l-Ḥizb al-Waṭanī, 1892–1914*. Cairo: Dār al-Kitāb al-Jāmiʿī, 1982.

Jundī, Jurj, and Jāk Tājir, eds. *Ismāʿīl—Kamā Tuṣawwiru-hu al-Wathāʾiq al-Rasmiyya*. Cairo: Maṭbaʿat Dār al-Kutub al-Miṣriyya, 1947.

Kallander, Amy Aisen. *Women, Gender, and the Palace Households in Ottoman Tunisia*. Austin, TX: University of Texas Press, 2013.

Kāmil, ʿAlī Fatḥī, ed. *Muṣṭafā Kāmil Bāshā fī 34 Rabīʿān*. 9 Vols. Cairo: Maṭbaʿat al-Liwāʾ, 1908–1910.

Kāmil, Muṣṭafā. *Fatḥ al-Andalus—al-Naṣṣ al-Kāmil li-l-Masraḥiyya al-Waḥīda allatī Katabahā*. Cairo: Maṭābiʿ al-Hayʾa al-Miṣriyya al-ʿĀmma li-l-Kitāb, 1973.

———. *Miṣr wa-l-Iḥtilāl al-Inklīzī aw Majmūʿat Aʿmāl Muṣṭafā Kāmil Muddat ʿĀm Wāḥid min Māyū 1895 li-Māyū 1896*. [Cairo?]: Maṭbaʿat al-Ādāb, 1313 (1896).

Karachouli, Regina. "Abu Halil al-Qabbani (1833—1902)—Damaszener Theatergründer und Prinzipal." *Die Welt des Islams* 32, no. 1 (1992): 83–98.

Karateke, Hakan T. "Legitimizing the Ottoman Sultanate." In *Legitimizing the Order—The Ottoman Rhetoric of State Power*. Edited by Hakan T. Karateke and Maurus Reinkowski, 13–52. Leiden: Brill, 2005.

———. "Opium for the Subjects? Religiosity as a Legitimizing Factor for the Ottoman Sultan." In *Legitimizing the Order—The Ottoman Rhetoric of State Power*. Edited by Hakan T. Karateke and Maurus Reinkowski, 111–129. Leiden: Brill, 2005.

———. "Who Is the Next Ottoman Sultan? Attempts to Change the Rule of Succession during the Nineteenth Century." In *Ottoman Reform and Muslim Regeneration—Studies in Honour of Butrus Abu-Manneh*. Edited by Itzhak Weismann and Fruma Zachs, 37–54. London: I. B. Tauris, 2005.

Katz, Israel. *Henry George Farmer and the First International Congress of Arab Music*. Leiden: Brill, 2015.

Kayalı, Hasan. *Arabs and Young Turks—Ottomanism, Arabism, and Islamism in the Ottoman Empire, 1908–1918*. Berkeley, CA: University of California Press, 1997.

Kechriotis, Vangelis. "Requiem for the Empire: "Elective Affinities" Between the Balkan States and the Ottoman Empire in the Long 19th Century." In *Beyond the Balkans: Towards an Inclusive History of Southeastern Europe*. Edited by Sabine Rutar, 97–122. Vienna: Lit, 2014.

Keddie, Nikki R. *Sayyid Jamāl Ad-Dīn "al-Afghānī": A Political Biography*. Berkeley: University of California, 1972.

Kedourie, Elie. "The Death of Adib Ishaq." In idem *Arabic Political Memoirs and Other Studies*, 81–100. London: Cass, 1974.

Kern, Karen M. *Imperial Citizen: Marriage and Citizenship in the Ottoman Frontier Provinces of Iraq*. Syracuse, NY: Syracuse University Press, 2011.

Khalidi, Rashid. "Arab Nationalism: Historical Problems in the Literature." *The American Historical Review*, 96, no. 5 (1991): 1363–1373.

Khalidi, Rashid et al., eds. *The Origins of Arab Nationalism*. New York: Columbia University Press, 1991.

Al-Khaṭīb, Muḥammad Kāmil, ed. *Naẓariyyāt al-Masraḥ*. 2 Vols. Damascus: Manshūrāt Wizārat al-Thaqāfa, 1994.

Khouri, Mounah A. *Poetry and the Making of Modern Egypt*. Leiden: Brill, 1971.

Al-Khulaʿī, Muḥammad Kāmil. *Kitāb al-Mūsīqā al-Sharqī*. [around 1904]; Cairo: Maktabat Madbūlī, 2000.

Khuri-Makdisi, Ilham. *The Eastern Mediterranean and the Making of Global Radicalism*. Berkeley, CA: University of California Press, 2010.

Komár Krisztián. "Az Osztrák-Magyar Monarchia és Egyiptom kapcsolatai, 1882–1914." Ph.D. diss., Szegedi Tudományegyetem (University of Sciences in Szeged), 2006.

Konrad, Felix. *Der Hof der Khediven—Herrscherhaushalt, Hofgesellschaft und Hofhaltung, 1840–1880*. Würzburg: Ergon Verlag, 2008.

Koudounaris, Aristeidis. *Biografikon Leksikon Kyprion (1800–1920)*. Nicosia: Pierides Foundation, 1989.

Kozma, Liat. *Policing Egyptian Women: Sex*, Law and Medicine in Khedivial Egypt. Syracuse, NY: Syracuse University Press, 2011.

Kruger, Loren. *The National Stage—Theatre and Cultural Legitimation in England, France, and America*. Chicago, IL: The University of Chicago Press, 1992.

Kruk, Remke. "Sīrat ʿAntar ibn Shaddād." In *Arabic Literature in the Post-Classical Period*. Edited by Roger Allen and D.S. Richards, 292–306. Cambridge: Cambridge University Press, 2006.

Kudsi-Zadeh, Albert. "Afghānī and Freemasonry in Egypt." *Journal of the American Oriental Society*. 92, no. 1 (1972): 25–35.

Kuneralp, Sinan. *Son Dönem Osmanlı Erkan ve Ricali (1839–1922)*. Istanbul: Isis, 1999.

Kusel, Baron de. *An Englishman's Recollections of Egypt, 1863–1887*. London: John Lane, [1915].

Lagrange, Frédéric. "Musiciens et poètes en Égypte au temps de la *Nahḍa*." Ph.D. diss., Université de Paris VIII à Saint Denis, 1994.

———. "Poètes, intellectuels et musiciens." *Les Cahiers de l'Orient* 24 (1991): 151–173.

Lamba, Henri. *Code Administratif Égyptien*. Paris: Librairie de la Société du Recueil Sirey, 1911.

Landau, Jacob M. "Prolegomena to a Study of Secret Societies in Modern Egypt." *Middle Eastern Studies* 1, no. 2 (1965), 135–186.

———. *Studies in the Arab Theater and Cinema*. Philadelphia: University of Pennsylvania Press, 1958.

Landes, David S. *Bankers and Pashas*. London: Heinemann, 1958.

Lantz, Milt. *Répertoire général de la jurisprudence égyptienne mixte et indigène*. Brussels: P. Weissenbruch, 1907.

Al-Laythī, al-Shaykh ʿAlī. *Riḥlat al-Shaykh ʿAlī al-Laythī bi-Bilād al-Nimsā wa-Almāniyā*. Beirut: Dār al-Bashāʾir al-Islāmiyya, 2011.

Leafgren, Luke Anthony. "Novelizing the Muslim Wars of Conquests: The Christian Pioneers of the Arabic Historical Novel." Ph.D. diss., Harvard University, 2012.

LeBlanc, Louis, et Georges LeBlanc. *Traité d'aménagement des salles de spectacles*. 2 Vols. Paris: Vincent, Fréal and Cie Éditeurs, 1950.
Leon, Edwin de. "Ismail Pacha of Egypt." *Harper's New Monthly Magazine* 39, n. 233 (1869): 739–749.
———. *The Khedive's Egypt; or, The Old House of Bondage under New Masters*. New York: Harper and Brothers, 1878.
Lesseps, Ferdinand de. *Recollections of Forty Years*. 2 Vols. London: Chapman and Hall, 1887.
Levy, Lisa Lital. "Jewish Writers in the Arab East—Literature, History, and the Politics of Enlightenment, 1863–1914." Ph.D. diss., University of California, Berkeley, 2007.
Lewis, Bernard. "Patriotism and Nationalism." In *The Middle East and the West*, 71–98. New York: Harper & Row, 1964.
———. "Watan." *Journal of Contemporary History* 26 (1991): 523–532.
Locke, Ralph P. "Beyond the Exotic: How "Eastern" Is Aida?" *Cambridge Opera Journal* 17, no. 2 (2005): 105–139.
Lockman, Zachary. "Imagining the Working Class: Culture, Nationalism, and Class Formation in Egypt, 1899–1914." *Poetics Today*, 15, no. 2 (1994), 157–190.
Lott, Emmeline. *The English Governess in Egypt: Harem Life in Egypt and Constantinople*. London: Richard Bentley, 1867.
Louca, Anouar. *Voyageurs et écrivains égyptiens en France au XIXe siècle*. Paris: Didier, 1970.
Maalouf, Shireen. "Mīkhāʾīl Mishāqā: Virtual Founder of the Twenty-Four Equal Quartertone Scale." *Journal of the American Oriental Society* 123, no. 4 (2003): 835–840.
Al-Mahdī, Muḥammad al-ʿAbbāsī. *Al-Fatāwā al-Mahdiyya fī al-Waqāʾiʿ al-Miṣriyya*. 7 Vols. Cairo: al-Maṭbaʿa al-Azhariyya, 1301 [1303; 1885–1886].
Mainardi, Patricia. *Art and Politics of the Second Empire: The Universal Expositions of 1855 and 1867*. New Haven, CT: Yale University Press, 1989.
Majdī, Ṣāliḥ. *Dīwān*. Būlāq: al-Maṭbaʿa al-Amīriyya, 1311 (1893).
Mardin, Şerif. *The Genesis of Young Ottoman Thought—A Study in the Modernization of Turkish Political Ideas*. 1962; Syracuse, NY: Syracuse University Press, 2000.
[Mariette, August,]. *Furjat al-Mutafarrij ʿalā l-Antīqah-khāna al-Khidīwiyya al-Kāʾina bi-Būlāq Miṣr al-Maḥmiyya wa hiya ʿIbārat ʿan Waṣf Nukhbat al-Āthār al-Qadīma al-Miṣriyya al-Mawjūda fī Khazīnat al-Tuḥaf al-ʿIlmiyya al-Miṣriyya*. Translated by ʿAbd Allāh Abū al-Suʿūd]. Cairo: Maṭbaʿat Wādī al-Nīl, 1286 [1869].
Marin, Louis. *Portrait of the King*. Minneapolis: University of Minnesota Press, 1988.
Al-Marṣafī, al-Shaykh Ḥusayn. *Risālat al-Kalim al-Thamān*. Cairo: al-Maṭbaʿa al-Sharīfiyya, 1298 [1881].
Masters, Bruce. *The Arabs of the Ottoman Empire, 1516–1918—A Social and Cultural History*. Cambridge: Cambridge University Press, 2013.
Mayer, Thomas. *The Changing Past: Egyptian Historiography of the Urabi Revolt, 1882–1983*. Gainesville, FL: University Presses of Florida, 1988.
McCoan, James Carlile. *Egypt under Ismail: A Romance of History*. London: Chapman and Hall, 1889.

Merruau, Paul. "L'Égypte sous le gouvernement de Muhammad-Said Pacha." *Revue des deux mondes* (1857): 323–366.
Mestyan, Adam. "Arabic Lexicography and European Aesthetics." *Muqarnas* 28 (2011): 69–100.
———. "Arabic Theatre in Early Khedivial Culture: James Sanua Reconsidered." *International Journal of Middle East Studies* 46 (2014): 117–137.
———. "A Garden with Mellow Fruits of Refinement—Music Theatres and Cultural Politics in Cairo and Istanbul, 1867–1892." Ph.D. diss., Central European University, 2011.
———. "The Just Prince and the Nation." Under Review.
———. "Sound, Military Music, and Opera in Egypt during the Rule of Mehmet Ali Pasha (1805–1848)." In *Ottoman Empire and European Theatre*. Vol. 2. Edited by Michael Hüttler and Hans Ernst Weidinger, 631–656. Vienna: Hollitzer Wissenschaftsverlag, 2014.
Mestyan, Adam, and Mercedes Volait. "Affairisme dynastique et dandysme au Caire vers 1900: Le Club des Princes et la formation d'un quartier du divertissement rue ʿImād al-Dīn." *Annales Islamologiques* 50 (2016): forthcoming.
Mishāqa, Mīkhāʾīl. *al-Risāla al-Shihābiyya fī al-Ṣināʿa al-Mūsiqiyya*. Cairo: Dār al-Fikr al-ʿArabī, 1996.
———. *Murder, Mayhem, Pillage and Plunder—The History of the Lebanon in the Eighteenth and Nineteenth Century*, trans. W.M. Thackston. Albany, NY: State University of New York Press, 1988.
Al-Miṣrī, ʿAbd al-Fattāḥ. *Luʿbat Laylā—Nuzhat al-Adab fī Shajāʿat al-ʿArab al-Mubhija li-l-Aʿyun al-Zakiyya fī Ḥadīqat al-Azbakiyya*. 1872; Beirut: Dār Ṣādir, 2002.
Mitchell, Timothy. *Colonising Egypt*. 1989; Berkeley, CA: University of California Press, 1991.
Moghira, Mohamed Anouar. *Moustapha Kamel L'Égyptien (1874–1908)*. Paris: L'Harmattan, 2007.
[Montesquieu] Mūntiskyū. *Uṣūl al-Nawāmīs wa-l-Sharāʾiʿ*. Vol.1. Cairo: al-Maṭbaʿa al-ʿUmūmiyya, 1891.
Moreh, Shmuel. *Modern Arabic Poetry*. Leiden: E. J. Brill, 1976.
Moreh, Shmuel, and Philip Sadgrove. *Jewish Contributions to Nineteenth-Century Arabic Theatre. Journal of Semitic Studies*. Supplement 6. New York: Oxford University Press, 1996.
Moosa, Matti. "Naqqāsh and the Rise of the Native Arab Theatre in Syria." *Journal of Arabic Literature* 3 (1972): 106–117.
———. *The Origins of Modern Arabic Fiction*. 2nd ed. Boulder, CO: Lynne Rienner Publishers, 1997.
———. "Yaʿqūb Ṣanūʿ and the Rise of Arab drama in Egypt." *International Journal of Middle East Studies* 4, no. 4 (1974): 401–433.
Mostyn, Trevor. *Egypt's Belle Epoque: Cairo and the Age of the Hedonists*. 1989; repr., London: Tauris Parke Paperbacks, 2006.
El Mouelhy, Ibrahim Pacha. "Les Mouelhy en Égypte." *Cahiers d'Histoire Égyptienne* (1949–1950): 313–328.
Moussali, Bernard. "L'école khediviale." *Les Cahiers de l'Orient* 24 (1991): 175–185.

Mubārak, ʿAlī. *ʿAlam al-Dīn.* 2 Vols. Alexandria: Maṭbaʿat Jarīdat al-Maḥrūsa, 1882.
———. *Al-Khiṭaṭ al-Tawfīqiyya al-Jadīda.* 20 Vols. 1886–89; repr., Cairo: Dār al-Kutub wa-l-Wathāʾiq al-Qawmiyya, 1980–2007.
———. *Kitāb Nukhbat al-Fikr fī Tadbīr Nīl Miṣr.* Cairo: Maṭbaʿat Wādī al-Nīl, 1297 [in fact, Ṣafar 1298; January 1881].
———. *Kitāb Ṭarīq al-Ḥijāʾ wa-l-Tamrīn ʿalā al-Qirāʾa fī al-Lugha al-ʿArabiyya.* Vols. 1–2. Cairo: Maṭbaʿat Wādī al-Nīl, 1285 [1868–1869].
Muḥammad, Al-Sayyid Wafā. *Muqaddimat Kitāb al-Tuḥfa al-Wafāʾiyya fī al-Lugha al-ʿĀmmiyya al-Miṣriyya.* Cairo: al-Maṭbaʿa al-Mīriyya, 1310 [1892].
Muhtar, Gazi Ahmet Paşa. *Iṣlāḥ al-Taqwīm.* Cairo: Muḥammad Efendi Muṣṭafā, 1307.
———. *Riyaz ül-Muhtar, Mirat ül-Mikat ve-l-Edvar.* 2 Vols. in 1. Bulak: Bulak Matbaası, 1303 [1885].
Al-Munajjad, Ṣalāḥ al-Dīn, ed. *Fatāwā al-Imām Muḥammad Rashīd Riḍā.* Beirut: Dār al-Kitāb al-Jadīd, 1970.
Murray, John. *A Handbook for Travellers in Egypt.* London: Murray, 1875.
Mūsā, Nīfīn Muḥammad. *al-Iftāʾ al-Miṣrī fī al-Qarn al-Tāsiʿ al-ʿAshar (Qirāʾa fī Fatāwā al-Shaykh Muḥammad al-Bannā).* Cairo: Dār al-Kutub wa-l-Wathāʾiq al-Qawmiyya, 2013.
Musa, Salama. *The Education of Salama Musa.* Leiden: Brill, 1961.
Muṣṭafā, Aḥmad ʿAbd al-Raḥīm. *ʿAlāqāt Miṣr bi-Turkiyya fī ʿAhd al-Khidīw Ismāʿīl.* Cairo: Dār al-Maʿārif, 1967.
Al-Muwayliḥī, Muḥammad. *A Period of Time.* Translated by Roger Allen. Oxford: Ithaca Press for The Middle East Centre at St. Antony's College, 1992.
———.*What ʿIsa Ibn Hisham Told Us.* 2 Vols. Translated by Roger Allen. New York: New York University Press, 2015.
Nadīm, ʿAbd al-Fattāḥ, ed. *Sulāfat al-Nadīm fī Muntakhabāt al-Sayyid ʿAbd Allāh al-Nadīm.* 2 Vols. Cairo: Maṭbaʿa Hindiyya, 1914.
al-Nadīm, ʿAbd Allāh. "Shadhra min Riwāyat al-Waṭan wa-Hiya Riwāya Tashkhīṣiyya al-Gharaḍ min-hā al-Ḥithth ʿalā al-Taʿāwun (li-Inshāʾ al-Madāris al-ʿIlmiyya wa-l-Ṣināʿiyya)." In *Sulāfat al-Nadīm*, 2 Vols. 2:33–63. Cairo: Maṭbaʿat Hindiyya, 1901.
[Al-Najjārī], al-Shaykh Muṣṭafā Salāma. *Majmūʿ al-Thanāʾ al-Jamīl li-Dāwar al-ʿAdl Ismāʿīl.* [Cairo, 1867?].
Najm, Muḥammad Yūsuf. *Al-Masraḥiyya fī al-Adab al-ʿArabī al-Ḥadīth.* Beirut: Dār al-Thaqāfa, 1985 (1956).
———, ed. *Mārūn al-Naqqāsh.* Beirut: Dār al-Thaqāfa, 1961.
———, ed. *Al-Shaykh Aḥmad Abū al-Qabbānī.* Beirut: Dār al-Thaqāfa, 1963.
———, ed., *Yaʿqūb Ṣannūʿ.* Beirut: Dār al-Thaqāfa, 1963.
———, ed. Salīm al-Naqqāsh. Beirut: Dār al-Thaqāfa, 1964.
Najm, Zayn al-ʿĀbdīn Shams al-Dīn. *Miṣr fī ʿAhday ʿAbbās wa-Saʿīd.* Cairo: Dār al-Shurūq, 2007.
Naqqāsh, Mārūn. *Arzat Lubnān.* Edited by Niqūlā Naqqāsh. Beirut: al-Maṭbaʿa al-ʿUmūmiyya, 1869.
Naqqāsh, Salīm Khalīl. "Fawāʾid al-Riwāyāt aw al-Tiyātrāt aw Nisbat al-Riwāyāt ilā Hayʾat al-Ijtimāʿ." *Al-Jinān*, 1 Āb (August) 1875, 516–521.
———. *Miṣr li-l-Miṣriyyīn.* 4 Vols. 1884; repr., Cairo: al-Hayʾa al-Miṣriyya al-ʿĀmma li-l-Kitāb, 1998.

Al-Nasafī, Abū al-Barakāt ʿAbd Allāh b. Aḥmad b. Maḥmūd. *Kitāb Kanz al-Daqāʾiq.* [Cairo:] Maṭbaʿat Muḥammad Unsī, 1283 [1866–1867].

Nasīra, Hānī. *Wizārat al-Thaqāfa.* Cairo: Center for Political and Strategical Studies, 2003.

Nawfal, Niʾmat Allāh Nawfal al-Ṭarābulusī. *Kashf al-Lithām ʿan Muḥayyā al-Ḥukūma wa-l-Aḥkām fī Iqlīmay Miṣr wa-Barr al-Shām.* Tripoli: Jurūs Burs, 1990.

Neubauer, Eckhard. "Arabic Writings on Music: Eighth to Nineteenth Centuries." *The Garland Encyclopaedia of World Music.* 10 Vols., 6:363–86. London: Routledge, 2002.

Newman, Daniel L. "Life of al-Ṭahṭāwī." In Rifaʿa Rafiʿ al-Tahtawi, *An Imam in Paris—Account of a Stay in France by an Egyptian Cleric (1826–1831)*, 31–71. London: Saqi Books, 2011.

Ninet, John. *Au pays des khedives—plaquettes égyptiennes.* Genèva: Imprimérie Schira, 1890.

———. *Lettres d'Égypte—1879–1882.* Edited by Anouar Luca. Paris: Éditions du Centre National de la recherché scientifique, 1979.

Noorani, Yaseen. *Culture and Hegemony in the Colonial Middle East.* New York: Palgrave Macmillan, 2010.

———. "Estrangement and Selfhood in the Classical Concept of *Waṭan.*" *Journal of Arabic Literature* 47 (2016): 1–27.

Omar, Hussein. "'And I Saw No Reason to Chronicle My Life': Tensions of Nationalist Modernity in the Memoirs of Fathallah Pasha Barakat.". In *The Long 1890s in Egypt—Colonial Quiescence, Subterranean Resistance.* Edited by Marilyn Booth and Anthony Gorman, 287–314. Edinburgh: Edinburgh University Press, 2014.

Ormos, István. *Max Herz Pasha, 1856–1919: His Life and Career.* 2 Vols. Cairo: Institut français d'archéologie orientale, 2009.

Orlowska, Izabela. "The Legitimizing Project: The Coronation Rite and the Written Word." *Aethiopica* 16 (2013): 74–101.

Osterhammel, Jürgen. *The Transformation of the World—A Global History of the Nineteenth Century.* Princeton, NJ: Princeton University Press, 2014).

Owen, Roger. *Lord Cromer—Victorian Imperialist, Edwardian Proconsul.* Oxford: Oxford University Press, 2004.

Owen, Roger. *The Middle East in the World Economy 1800–1914.* 1981; London: I.B. Tauris, 2009.

Pallini, Cristina. "Italian Architects and Modern Egypt." In *Studies in Architecture, History and Culture—Papers by the 2003–2004 AKPIA@MIT Visiting Fellows*, 39–50. Cambridge, MA: The Aga Khan Program for Islamic Architecture at the Massachusetts Institute of Technology, 2004.

Pamuk, Şevket. "Interaction between the Monetary Regimes of Istanbul, Cairo, and Tunis, 1700–1875." In *Money, Land and Trade: An Economic History of the Muslim Mediterranean.* Edited by Nelly Hanna, 177–205. London: I.B. Tauris, 2002.

Papageorgiou, Ioanna. "Adelaide Ristori's Tour of the East Mediterranean (1864–1865) and the Discourse on the Formation of Modern Greek Theatre." *Theatre Research International* 33, no. 2 (2008): 161–175.

Papasian, Ed. *L'Égypte économique et financière—études financières, 1924–1925.* Cairo: Imp. Misr, 1926.
Parolin, Gianluca P. *Citizenship in the Arab World—Kin, Religion, and Nation State.* Amsterdam: Amsterdam University Press, 2009.
Peirce, Leslie P. *The Imperial Harem—Women and Sovereignty in the Ottoman Empire.* New York: Oxford University Press, 1993.
Peri, Oded. "Ottoman Symbolism in British Occupied Egypt, 1882–1909," *Middle Eastern Studies* 41, No. 1 (2005): 103–120.
Perrières, Des Carle. *Un Parisien au Caire.* Cairo: Librairie Nouvelle, 1873.
Peters, Rudolph. "Muḥammad al-ʿAbbāsī al-Mahdī (d. 1897), Grand Mufti of Egypt, and his al-Fatāwā al-Mahdiyya." *Islamic Law and Society* 1, 1 (1994): 66–82.
Philipp, Thomas. *The Syrians in Egypt, 1725–1975.* Stuttgart: Franz Steiner Verlag Wiesbaden GMBH, 1985.
Pichot, A. Pierre. *Les Invités du Khédive dans l'haute Égypte et à l'isthme de Suez.* Paris: La Revue Britannique, 1870.
Politis, Athanase G. *L'Hellénisme et l'Égypte moderne.* 2 Vols. Paris: F. Alcan, 1929.
Pougin, Arthur. *Le théâtre à l'Exposition universelle de 1889: notes et descriptions, histoire et souvenirs.* Paris: Librarie Fischbacher, 1890.
Prod'homme, J.-G., and Theodore Baker, "Unpublished letters from Verdi to Camille Du Locle (1866–1876)." *The Musical Quarterly* 17, no. 1 (1921): 73–103.
Al-Qabbānī, Sulaymān Ḥasan. *Bughyat al-mumaththilīn.* Alexandria: Jurjī Gharzūzī, [after 1902].
Qūrtanbīr. *Kitāb al-Dars al-Mukhtaṣar al-Mufīd fī ʿIlm al-Jughrāfiyya al-Jadīd.* Cairo: Maṭbaʿat Wādī al-Nīl, 1286 [1869].
Al-Rāfiʿī, ʿAbd al-Raḥmān. *ʿAṣr Ismāʿīl.* 2 Vols. Cairo: Maktabat al-Nahḍa al-Miṣriyya, 1948.
———. *Muṣṭafā Kāmil—Bāʿith al-Ḥaraka al-Waṭaniyya.* 1939; Cairo: Maktabat al-Nahḍa al-Miṣriyya, 1962.
———. *al-Thawra al-ʿUrābiyya wa-l-Iḥtilāl al-Injilīzī.* Cairo: Maktabat al-Nahḍa al-Miṣriyya, 1949.
Ramadan, Dina. "The Aesthetics of the Modern: Art, Education, and Taste in Egypt 1903–1952." Ph.D. diss., Columbia University, 2013.
Rāshid, Muḥammad. *Al-Maḥāsin al-Bahiyya fī Ḥadīqat al-Azbakiyya.* Cairo: al-Maṭbaʿa al-Khayriyya, 1291 [1874].
Re, Lucia. "Alexandria Revisited—Colonialism and the Egyptian Works of Enrico Pea and Giuseppe Ungaretti." In *A Place in the Sun—Africa in Italian Colonial Culture from Post-Unification to the Present.* Edited by Patrizia Palumbo, 163–196. Berkeley, CA: University of California Press, 2003.
Reid, Donald Malcom. "The ʿUrabi Revolution and the British Conquest." In *The Cambridge History of Egypt.* Vol. 2, *Modern Egypt from 1517 to the End of the Twentieth century.* Edited by M. W. Daly, 217–238. Cambridge: Cambridge University Press, 1998.
———. *Whose Pharaohs? Archaeology, Museums, and Egyptian National Identity from Napoleon to World War I.* Cairo: The American University of Cairo Press, 2002.
Reimer, Michael J. "Egyptian Views of Ottoman Rule: Five Historians and Their Works, 1820–1920." *Comparative Studies of South Asia, Africa and the Middle East* 31, no. 1 (2011): 149–163.

Rév, István. *Retroactive Justice: Prehistory of Post-Communism*. Stanford, CA: Stanford University Press, 2005.
Ricoeur, Paul. "Narrative Time." *Critical Inquiry* 7, no. 1 (1980): 169–190.
Riḍā, Rashīd, ed. *Ta'rīkh al-Ustādh al-Imām Muḥammad ʿAbduh*. Vols. 1 and 2. Cairo: Maṭbaʿat al-Manār, 1324 [1906–07].
Riedler, Florian. *Opposition and Legitimacy in the Ottoman Empire: Conspiracies and Political Cultures*. Abingdon: Routledge, 2010.
Rivlin, Helen Anne B. "The Railway Question in the Ottoman-Egyptian Crisis of 1850–1852." *Middle East Journal* 15, no. 4 (1961): 365–388.
Rizq, Qastandī. *al-Mūsīqā al-Sharqiyya wa-l-Ghinā' al-ʿArabī wa-Nuṣrat al-Khidīwī Ismāʿīl li-l-Funūn al-Jamīla wa-Ḥayāt ʿAbduh al-Ḥamūlī*. 4 Vols. Cairo: al-Maṭbaʿa al-ʿAṣriyya, 1936–1943.
Rizq, Yūnān Labīb. *Al-ʿAyb fī Dhāt Afandīnā—Dirāsa Tārīkhiyya Muwaththaqa min 1866 ḥattā al-Yawm*. Cairo: Dār al-Shurūq, 2008.
———. *Ta'rīkh al-Wizārāt al-Miṣriyya*. [Cairo]: Markaz al-Dirāsāt al-Siyāsiyya wa-l-Istrātījiyya bi-l-Ahrām, Waḥdat al-Wathā'iq wa-l-Buḥūth al-Tārīkhiyya, 1975.
Robinson, Paul. "Is Aida an Orientalist Opera?" *Cambridge Opera Journal* 5, no. 2 (1993): 133–140.
Rogan, Eugene. "Sectarianism and Social Conflict in Damascus: The 1860 Events Reconsidered." *Arabica* 51 (2004): 493–511.
Ronall, Joachim O. "Julius Blum Pasha (1843–1919)—an Austro-Hungarian Banker in Egypt." In *Österreich und Ägypten, Beiträge zur Geschichte der Beziehungen vom 18. Jahrhundert bis 1918*. Schriften des österreichischen Kulturinstitutes Kairo, Vol. 4, 79–108. Cairo: Österreichisches Kulturinstitut, 1993.
Rosenzweig, Roy, and Elizabeth Blackmar. *The Park and the People: A History of Central Park*. Ithaca, N.Y.: Cornell University Press, 1992.
Rosselli, John. *The Opera Industry in Italy from Cimarosa to Verdi: the Role of the Impresario*. Cambridge: Cambridge University Press, 1984.
Roussillon, Alain. "Réforme sociale et production des classes moyennes—Muhammad 'Umar et 'l'arriération des Egyptiens.'" In his *Entre réforme sociale et mouvement national*, 37–87. Cairo: Centre d'études et de documentation économiques, juridiques et sociales, 1995.
Russell, Mona L. *Creating the New Egyptian Woman: Consumerism, Education, and National Idenitity, 1863–1922*. New York: Palgrave, 2004.
Ryzova, Lucie. *The Age of the Efendiyya: Passages to Modernity in National-Colonial Egypt*. Oxford: Oxford University Press, 2014.
Sabry, Mohammed. *La genèse de l'esprit national égyptien*. Paris: [Libraire Picart], 1924.
Sacré, Amédée, and Outrebon, Louis. *L'Égypte et Ismaïl Pacha*. Paris: J. Hetzel, 1865.
Saʿd, Muḥammad Afandī. *Tuḥfat Ahl al-Fukāha fī al-Manādima wa-l-Nuzāha*. Cairo: al-Maṭbaʿa al-ʿĀmira, 1307 [1889–1890].
Sadgrove, Philip C. "Early Arabic Musical Theatre and Its European and Ottoman Influences." In *Branches of the Goodly Tree: Studies in Honor of George Kanazi*. Edited by Ali Hussein, 147–174. Wiesbaden: Harrassowitz Verlag, 2013.
———. *The Egyptian Theatre in the Nineteenth Century, 1799–1882*. 1996; repr., Cairo: AUC Press, 2007.

———. "Leyla—The First Egyptian Tragedy." *Osmanlı Araştırmaları* 7–8 (1988): 161–176.

———. "The Syrian Arab Theatre after Marun Naqqash (the 1850s and the 1860s)." *Archív Orientální* 55 (1987): 271–283.

———. "The Development of the Arabic Periodical Press and Its Role in the Literary Life of Egypt 1798–1882." Ph.D. diss., University of Edinburgh, 1983.

Al-Ṣafadī, Ṣalāḥ al-Dīn Khalīl b. Aybak. *Aʿyān al-ʿAṣr wa-Aʿwān al-Naṣr*. Vol. 4. Damascus: Dār al-Fikr, 1998.

———. *al-Wāfī bi-l-Wafayāt*. Vol. 9. Beirut: Dār Iḥyāʾ al-Turāth al-ʿArabī, 2000.

Al-Ṣaghānī. *Mawḍūʿāt al-Ṣaghānī*. Cairo: Dār Nāfiʿ li-l-Ṭibāʿa wa-l-Nashr, 1980.

Said, Edward W. *Culture and Imperialism*. New York: Vintage Books, 1993.

Sajdi, Dana. *The Barber of Damascus—Nouveau Literacy in the Eighteenth-Century Ottoman Levant*. Stanford, CA: Stanford University Press, 2013.

[Sakmānī]. *Riḥlat Sakmānī*, ed. Binyāmīn Ḥaddād. Baghdad: s. n., 2003.

Ṣāliḥ, Sulaymān. *Al-Shaykh ʿAlī Yūsuf wa-Jarīdat al-Muʾayyad*. 2 Vols. Cairo: al-Hayʾa al-Miṣriyya al-ʿĀmma li-l-Kitāb, 1990.

Sālim, Laṭīfa Muḥammad. *Fārūq wa-Suqūṭ al-Malakiyya fī Miṣr*. Cairo: Maktabat Madbūlī, 1989.

———. *Al-Quwa al-Ijtimāʿiyya fī al-Thawra al-ʿUrābiyya*. Cairo: al-Hayʾa al-Miṣriyya al-ʿĀmma li-l-Kitāb, 1981.

Sāmī, Amīn Pasha. *Taqwīm al-Nīl*. 3 Vols. 1936; repr., Cairo: Dār al-Kutub wa-l-Wathāʾiq al-Qawmiyya, 2003–2004.

Sammarco, Angelo. *Histoire de L'Égypte Moderne depuis Mohammed Ali jusqu'à l'occupation britannique (1801–1882) d'aprés les documents originaux égyptiens et étrangers*. Vol. 3: *Le Règne du Khédive Ismaïl de 1863 à 1875*. Cairo: Société Royale de Géographie d'Égypte, 1937.

Al-Sayyid, Afaf Lutfi. *Egypt and Cromer*. New York: Frederick A. Praeger, 1968.

Al-Sayyid-Marsot, Afaf Lutfi. *Egypt in the Reign of Muhammad Ali*. Cambridge: Cambridge University Press, 1984.

———. *A History of Egypt—From the Arab Conquest to the Present*. 2nd ed. Cambridge: Cambridge University Press, 2007.

Scharfe, Patrick. "Muslim Scholars and the Public Sphere in Mehmed Ali Pasha's Egypt, 1841–1841." Ph.D. diss., Ohio State University, 2015.

Schölch, Alexander. *Egypt for the Egyptians: The Socio-political Crisis in Egypt, 1878–1882*. London: Ithaca for The Middle East Centre, St. Antony's College, Oxford, 1981.

Schüller, Tonia. *Muṣṭafā Kāmil (1874–1908)—Politiker, Journalist und Redner, im Dienste Ägyptens*. Berlin: EB-Verlag, 2011.

Schwartz, Kathryn. "Meaningful Mediums: A Material and Intellectual History of Manuscript and Print Production in Nineteenth-Century Ottoman Cairo." Ph.D. diss., Harvard University, 2015.

Shafīq, Aḥmad. *Mudhakkirātī fī Niṣf Qarn*. 4 Vols. 1934; Cairo: al-Hayʾa al-Miṣriyya al-ʿĀmma li-l-Kitāb, 1994–1999.

Shārūbīm, Mīkhāʾīl. *Al-Kāfī fī Taʾrīkh Miṣr al-Qadīm wa-l-Ḥadīth*. 4 Parts in 4 Vols. Cairo: Maktabat Madbūlī, 2004.

———. *Al-Kāfī fī Taʾrīkh Miṣr al-Qadīm wa-l-Ḥadīth*. Part 5 in 2 Vols. Cairo: Maṭbaʿat Dār al-Kutub, 1998.

Sedgwick, Mark. *Muhammad Abduh*. Oxford: Oneworld, 2010.
Selim, Samah. *The Novel and the Rural Imaginery in Egypt, 1880–1985*. New York: Routledge Curzon, 2004.
Senior, Nassau William. *Conversations and Journals in Egypt and Malta*. 2 Vols. London: Sampson Law et al, 1882.
Sessa, Andrea. *Il melodramma italiano: 1861–1900*. Florence: Olschki, 2003.
Shaykhū, Luwīs. *Taʾrīkh al-Ādāb al-ʿArabiyya, 1800–1925*. 3 parts in 1 vol. Beirut: Dār al-Mashriq, 1991.
Shaw, Stanford J., and Ezel Kural Shaw. *History of the Ottoman Empire and Modern Turkey*, 2 Vols. Cambridge: Cambridge University Press, 1977.
Shiloah, Anna. *Music in the World of Islam*. Hants: Scolar Press, 1995.
Al-Shirwānī, Aḥmad b. Muḥammad. *Ḥadīqat al-Afrāḥ li-Izāḥāt al-Aṭrāḥ*. 1814; Būlāq: Dār al-Ṭibāʿa al-ʿĀmira, 1866.
[Ṣidqī, Ismāʿīl]. *Mudhakkirāt bi-Qalam Ismāʿīl Ṣidqī Bāshā*. [Cairo]: Dār al-Hilāl, 1950.
Silvera, Alain. "The First Egyptian Student Mission to France under Muhammad Ali." In *Modern Egypt*. Edited by Elie Kedourie and Sylvia G. Haim, 1–22. London: Frank Class and Co., 1980.
Şiviloğlu, Murat. "The Emergence of Public Opinion in the Ottoman Empire, 1826–1876." D.Phil. diss., University of Cambridge, 2014.
Smith, Anthony D. "Biblical Beliefs in the Shaping of Modern Nations." *Nations and Nationalism* 21, 3 (2015): 403–422.
———. *Chosen Peoples—Sacred Sources of National Identity*. Oxford: Oxford University Press, 2003.
———. *The Cultural Foundations of Nations—Hierarchy, Covenant, and Republic*. Malden: Blackwell, 2008.
Smith, Eli. "A Treatise on Arab Music, Chiefly from a Work by Mikhāil Meshākah, of Damascus." *Journal of the American Oriental Society* 1, no. 3 (1847): 171–217.
Stephan, Heinrich von. *Das heutige Ägypten*. Leipzig: Brockhaus, 1872.
Stephanov, Darin. "Minorities, Majorities, and the Monarch—Nationalizing Effects of the Late Ottoman Royal Public Ceremonies." Ph.D. diss., University of Memphis, 2012.
Steppat, Fritz. "Nationalismus und Islam bei Muṣṭafā Kāmil: Ein Beitrag zur Ideengeschichte der ägyptischen Nationalbewegung." *Die Welt des Islams*, New Ser., 4, 4 (1956): 241–341.
Strauss, Johann. "Who Read What in the Ottoman Empire (19th–20th centuries)?" *Middle Eastern Literatures* 6, no. 1 (2003): 39–76.
Tagher, Jacques. "La mission de Sarim Bey—Délégué de la Sublime Porte en Égypte (1837)." *Cahiers d'histoire égyptienne*. 2nd series; n. 4 (1949/1950), 381–408.
———. "Pietro Avoscani, artiste-décorateur et homme d'affaires." *Cahiers d'histoire égyptienne* no. 4 (1949): 306–314.
———. "Portrait psychologique de Nubar Pacha." *Cahiers d'histoire égyptienne*. first series, n. 5–6 (1949): 353–372.
———. "Psychologie du règne de Mohammad Ali." *Cahiers d'histoire égyptienne, numero special à l'occasion du centenaire de la mort de Mohammad Ali (1849–1949)*. 2nd series, no. 1 (1949): 1–17;
Tagher, Jacques, ed. *Mémoirs de A-B. Clot Bey*. Cairo: Impr. de l'Institut français d'archéologie orientale, 1949.

Tagher, Jeanette. "Les débuts du théâtre modern en Égypte." *Cahiers d'Histoire Égyptienne* 1/ 2 (1948): 192–207.
Taglioni, Charles. *Deux mois en Égypte—Journal d'un invité du Khédive*. Paris: Amyot, 1870.
[Al-Ṭahṭāwī, Rifāʿa Rāfiʿ] Cheykh Réfaha [!]. *La lyre brisée—Dythurambe de M. Agoub—Naẓm al-ʿUqūd fī Kasr al-ʿŪd*. Paris: Librairie Oriental, 1827.
[Al-Ṭahṭāwī], Rifāʿa Bey Rāfiʿ. *al-Dīwān al-Nafīs fī Īwān Bārīs aw Takhlīṣ al-Ibrīz fī Talkhīṣ Bārīz*. Beirut: Al-Muʾassasa al-ʿArabiyya li-l-Dirāsāt wa-l-Nashr, 2002. Also a *hijrī* 1265 [1849] edition.
———. *Al-Qawl al-Sadīd fī al-Ijtihād wa-l-Tajdīd*. Cairo: Maṭbaʿat Wādī al-Nīl, 1287 [1870–71].
———. *Manāhij al-Albāb al-Miṣriyya fī Mabāhij al-Ādāb al-ʿAṣriyya*. Cairo: n.a., 1286 [1869–70].
Al-Tahtawi, Rifaʿa Rafiʿ. *An Imam in Paris—Account of a Stay in France by an Egyptian Cleric (1826–1831)*. Translated by Daniel L. Newman. London: Saqi Books, 2011.
Ṭarrāzī, Fīlīb dī (Philip de Tarrazi). *Tāʾrīkh al-Ṣiḥāfa al-ʿArabiyya*. 2 Vols. Beirut: al-Maṭbaʿa al-Adabiyya, 1913, 1933.
Tauber, Eliezer. *The Emergence of Arab Movements*. London: Routledge, 1993.
Teillais, Chevalier de la. *La voyage de S. A. le Vice-Roi d'Égypte et la presse européenne*. Paris: Kugelmann, 1870.
Ther, Philipp. *In der Mitte der Gesellschaft—Operntheater in Zentraleuropa, 1815–1914*. Vienna: Oldenburg, 2006.
Tignor, Robert. *Modernization and British Colonial Rule in Egypt, 1882–1914*. Princeton, NJ: Princeton University Press, 1966.
Toledano, Ehud. *State and Society in Mid-Nineteenth-Century Egypt*. Cambridge: Cambridge University Press, 1990.
———. "The Emergence of Ottoman-Local Elites (1700-1900): A Framework for Research." In *Middle Eastern Politics and Ideas: A History from Within*. Edited by Ilan Pappé and Moshe Ma'oz, 145–162. London: Tauris, 1997.
———."Forgetting Egypt's Ottoman Past." In *Cultural Horizons: A Festschrift in Honor of Talat S. Halman*. Edited by Jayne L. Warner, 150–167. Vol. I. Syracuse, NY: Syracuse University Press, 2001.
Tollefson, Harold. *Policing Islam—The British Occupation of Egypt and the Anglo-Egyptian Struggle over Control of the Police, 1882–1914*. Westport, CT: Greenwood Press, 1999.
Tugay, Emine Fuat. *Three Centuries—Family Chronicles of Turkey and Egypt*. London: Oxford University Press, 1963.
Uçarol, Dr. Rifat. *Gazi Ahmet Muhtar Paşa—Bir Osmanlı Paşası ve dönemi*. [Istanbul]: Milliyet Yayınları, 1976.
Ulacacci, Niccola. *Pietro Avoscani—cenni biografici*. Leghorn: s.n., 1871.
ʿUmar, Muḥammad. *Kitāb Ḥāḍir al-Miṣriyyīn aw Sirr Taʾakhkhuri-him*. Cairo: Maṭbaʿat al-Muqtaṭaf, 1902.
Unsī, Muḥammad. *Al-Juzʾ al-Thānī min Talṭīf al-Uslūb wa-Takhṭīf al-ʿArabiyya ʿalā al-Qulūb aw al-Mutaʿallam li-Ḥājat al-Taʿlīm wa-l-Taʿallum fī al-Naḥw*. Cairo: Maṭbaʿat Wādī al-Nīl, 1291 [1875–76].

———. *Uslūb Jadīd wa-Ikhtirāʿ Mufīd li-Tashīl Taʿlīm Fann al-Kitāba al-ʿArabiyya*. Cairo: Maṭbaʿat Wādī al-Nīl, 1292 [1876–77].

[ʿUrābī, Aḥmad]. *The Defense Statement of Ahmad ʿUrabi the Egyptian—From the Blunt Manuscript at the School of Oriental and African Studies, London*. Edited and translated by Trevor Le Gassick. Cairo: The American University in Cairo Press, 1982.

Uzunçarşılı, İsmail Hakki, and Enver Ziya Karal. *Osmanlı Tarihi*. 8 Vols. Ankara: Türk Tarih Kurumu Basimevi, 1982–1983.

Vassalli, Luigi. *D'una rappresentazione di Sirene sopra un sarcofago egizio dell'epoca del Lagidi*. [Cairo]: [Imprimerie franco-arabe Onsy fréres], [1865].

Vaujany, H. de. *Le Caire et ses environs*. Paris: B. Plon et Cie, 1883.

Vetch, R. H. *Life, Letter, and Diaries of Lieut.-General Sir Gerald Graham*. Edinburgh: William Blackwood and Sons, 1901.

Volait, Mercedes. *Architectes et architectures de l'Égypte moderne 1830–1950—Genèse et essor d'une expertise locale*. Paris: Maisonneuve et Larose, 2005.

[Voltaire]. *Al-Rawḍ al-Azhar fī Tārīkh Buṭrus al-Akbar* [History of Peter the Great]. 1850; Cairo: Dār al-Kutub, 2013.

Wādī, Ṭāhā. *Dīwān Rifāʿa al-Ṭahṭāwī*. Cairo: Dār al-Maʿārif, 1984.

Walker, Dennis. "Egypt's Arabism: Mustafa Kamil's 1893 Play (Fath al-Andalus) On the Muslim Conquest of Spain." *Islamic Studies* 33, no. 1 (1994): 49–76.

Al-Wardī, ʿAlī. *Lamaḥāt Ijtimāʿiyya min Tārīkh al-ʿIrāq al-Ḥadīth*. 6 Vols. Baghdad: Maktabat al-Irshād, 1969–1979.

Warner, Nicholas. *An Egyptian Panorama—Reports from the 19th Century British Press*. Cairo: Zeituna, 1994.

[Wāṣif, Maḥmūd]. *Riwāyat Harūn* [!] *al-Rashīd maʿ Qūt al-Qulūb wa Khalīfat al-Ṣayyād wa yalī-hā Riwāyat al-Bakhīl wa-l-Shayṭān*. Cairo: Maṭbaʿat al-Taʾlīf, undated.

Wāṣif, Maḥmūd. *Riwāyat Hārūn al-Rashīd maʿ Qūt al-Qulūb wa Khalīfat al-Ṣayyād*. Cairo: Al-Maṭbaʿa al-ʿUmūmiyya, 1318 [1900–1901].

Watenpaugh, Keith David. *Being Modern in the Middle East: Revolution, Nationalism, Colonialism, and the Arab Middle Class*. Princeton, NJ: Princeton University Press, 2006.

Waugh, Earle H. *The Munshidīn of Egypt—Their World and Their Song*. Columbia, SC: University of South Carolina Press, 1989.

Weaver, William. *Verdi—A Documentary Study*. [London]: Thames and Hudson, 1977.

Wendell, Charles. *The Evolution of the Egyptian National Image: From Its Origins to Ahmad Lutfi al-Sayyid*. Berkeley, CA: University of California Press, 1972.

Wishnitzer, Avner. *Reading Clocks, Alla Turca: Time and Society in the Late Ottoman Empire*. Chicago, IL: Chicago University Press, 2015.

Yalman, Nur. "The Ottomans and the West: Some Thoughts on Mutual Perceptions and Good Government." *History and Anthropology* 26, 3 (2015): 345–361.

Yousef, Hoda A. "Reassessing Egypt's Dual System of Education under Ismaʿil: Growing ʿIlm and Shifting Ground in Egypt's First Educational Journal, Rawdat Al-Madaris, 1870–77." *International Journal of Middle East Studies* 40, 1 (2008): 109–130.

Yūsuf, ʿAlī. *Ayyām al-Janāb al-Khidīwī al-Muʿaẓẓam ʿAbbās al-Thānī fī Dār al-Saʿāda*. Cairo: Maṭbaʿat al-Ādāb, 1311 [1893].

———. *Muntakhabāt al-Muʾayyad—al-Sana al-Ūlā, 1890*. Cairo: Maṭbaʿat al-Muʾayyad, 1323 [1905–1906].

Zachs, Fruma. "Cultural and Conceptual Contributions of Beiruti Merchants to the Nahda." *Journal of the Economic and Social History of the Orient* 55 (2012): 153–182.

———. *The Making of a Syrian Identity—Intellectuals and Merchants in Nineteenth Century Beirut*. Leiden: Brill, 2005.

Zádori, János. *Éjszakafrikai útivázlatok I. Egyiptom*. Budapest: Szent-István Társulat, 1874.

[Zaghlūl, Saʿd]. *Mudhakkirāt Saʿd Zaghlūl*. Vol. 1. Cairo: al-Hayʾa al-Miṣriyya al-ʿĀmma li-l-Kitāb, 1987.

Zakī, Aḥmad, Bāshā. *Al-Safar ilā al-Muʾtamar*. Cairo: al-Dār al-Miṣriyya al-Lubnāniyya, 2003.

Zananiri, Gaston. *Le Khédive Ismail et l'Égypte*. Alexandria: Molco and Comp., 1923.

Zand, ʿAzīz. *Al-Qawl al-Ḥaqīq fī Rithāʾ wa-Tārīkh al-Khidīwī al-Maghfūr la-hu Muḥammad Bāshā Tawfīq*. Cairo: Maṭbaʿat al-Maḥrūsa, 1892.

Zaydān, Jurjī. *Kitāb Tārīkh Miṣr al-Ḥadīth*. Cairo: Maṭbaʿat al-Muqtaṭaf, 1889.

———. *Taʾrīkh Ādāb al-Lugha al-ʿArabiyya*. 4 Parts in 2 Vols. Beirut: Manshūrāt Maktabat al-Ḥayāt, 1967.

Al-Zayyāt, Amīn Sayyid Aḥmad, and Muḥammad ʿAṭiyya al-Kutubī. *Bulbul al-Suʿūd al-Zāhir fī al-Salāmāt al-Khidīwiyya wa-l-Alḥān al-Gharāmiyya*. n.a [1910?].

Ziya [Paşa]. *Endülüs Tarihi*. 1859; Istanbul: Qarabat ve Qaspad Maṭbaʿa, 1304 [1886–87].

Index

Abāẓa, ʿUthmān and Sulaymān, 70, 176
Abbas Hilmi, 36–38, 40–41, 44–45, 54, 56, 58, 62, 102, 272
Abbas Hilmi II, 15, 76, 201, 211, 213–14, 228–35, 248–49, 258, 268, 277, 287–99, 306
al-ʿAbbāsī al-Mahdī, Muḥammad, 259
ʿAbd al-ʿĀl Bey, 177
ʿAbd al-Fattāḥ al-Miṣrī, Muḥammad, 157, 160–61, 301
ʿAbduh, Ibrāhīm, 132
ʿAbduh, Muḥammad, 7, 78, 175, 178, 190, 206, 235, 260, 292
Abdülaziz (sultan), 19, 50, 53, 57–58, 60–63, 65, 80, 83, 92, 115, 174
Abdülhalim, 54–56, 57n41, 58, 61, 67, 81–82, 93, 154, 165, 173–74, 178, 205
Abdülhamid II (sultan), 79, 174, 178, 196–97, 205–6, 224–25, 287, 289, 297
Abdülmecid (sultan), 29, 33–34, 36, 45, 55, 59, 61–62, 112, 181
Abkāriyūs, Iskandar, 24–25, 89, 209
Abū al-ʿAdl, Amad, 226
Abū Naẓẓāra, 154, 263
Abū al-Suʿūd, ʿAbd Allāh, 41–44, 69, 125–26, 133, 141–50, 154, 161–69, 206, 225, 304
Abyaḍ, George, 251
al-Ādāb, 213
al-Aḥdab, Ibrāhīm, 166
Administration of Khedivial Theaters, 106–10
al-Afghānī, Jamāl al-Dīn, 162, 164, 172–79, 181, 205, 214, 304
Agent X, 256
Agent Z, 156, 256
Aḥmad Bey, 47–48
Ahmed Rifaat, 54–57, 58n51, 62
al-Ahrām, 170, 174–79, 189–91, 207–8, 218–20, 226–31, 236, 273, 286–87, 296
ʿĀʾida (Naqqāsh), 168–69, 220, 225–29, 287
Aida (Verdi), 14, 84, 108, 110–19, 141, 148, 152, 157, 160, 168–69, 275, 291
ʿAlam al-Dīn (ʿAli Mubārak), 152, 184
Al-Azmeh, Aziz, 7, 305
alcohol, 260–62
Al-Dars al-Tāmm (Abū al-Suʿūd), 148–49
Alexandre dans les Indes, 155
Algiers, 4
Ali Celal Pasha, 150
ʿAlī Muḥammad, 293
Ali Pasha, 22, 63, 274
ʿAli Yūsuf, 213
Allegory of the Joining of the Two Seas, 113
Almaẓ, 68, 78–79
Ālūsī, Ḥāmid Efendi, 63
al-ʿĀmilī, Bahāʾ al-Din, 76n162
Amina, 206
al-Amīra al-Iskandarāniyya (play), 161
Andalusia, 12, 77, 167, 298–302
Anderson, Benedict, 9, 13, 126
Andromaque (Racine), 169
Andrūmāk, 223
ʿAntara al-ʿAbsī, 216
ʿAntar b. Shaddād, 191–93
Antonius, George, 26–27, 306
Anṭūn, Faraḥ, 277–78
Anṭūn, Nuʿmān, 212
"Arab Acting" (*al-Muqtaṭaf*), 218
The Arab Awakening (Antonius), 26–27
Arabic: cultural Arabism and, 6–7, 118–19; Egyptian army and, 184–86; *fuṣḥā*, 15, 126–30, 132, 142, 152, 156, 160,

Arabic (*continued*)
162–63, 169–71, 218, 224, 276–78; garden culture in, 87–89; Ibrahim and, 23–28; Islam and, 73–77, 181–82; journalism and, 43–44, 131–47; Mehmed Ali and, 38–40; operas in, 125–26, 188–93, 203–4; patriotism and, 7–8, 10–13, 69–71, 128–30, 132–45, 214–28, 288–95, 305–8; theater spaces in, 13–14, 158–60, 251, 263–67. *See also* language; patriotism
Arabic Thought in the Liberal Age (Hourani), 303–4
Arab Patriotic Troupe, 216–30. *See also* Ḥijāzī, Salāma; Qardāḥī, Sulaymān
Artin Bey, 260
Arzat Lubnān (Naqqāsh), 155, 166
Āṣāf, Yūsuf, 208
ʿĀṣim, Ismāʿīl, 253
al-ʿAṣr al-Jadīd, 172
al-ʿAṭṭār, Ḥasan, 39–40, 43
aural patriotism, 13–14, 30–31, 44–48, 77–81, 85–89, 236–37, 297
Les Aventures de Télémaque (Fénelon), 220
Avoscani, Pietro, 94, 257
Ayalon, Ami, 133
aʿyān, 34–35, 51, 60, 68–69, 71–72, 163, 186, 270–71, 280
al-Azbakiyya, 86–89, 96–97, 106, 157, 159, 234, 239, 244–47, 255–60, 276–82
ʿazīz (title), 64–67
ʿAzzām, ʿAbd al-Raḥmān, 271
al-ʿAzzāzī, Khalīl, 69

Badr, Dasūqī, 227n135
Baghdad, 12, 27, 143
al-Bakhīl, 32, 156, 167n23, 169
Bakhkhāsh, Naʿūm, 24
Bakhtin, Mikhail, 12, 219
al-Bakrī, ʿAlī, 93
al-Bakrī, Muḥammad Tawfīq, 265, 268, 292
al-Bannā, Muḥammad Muḥammad, 259
Banucci, Antoine, 256
Barak, On, 93–94, 132, 144, 286
Il Barbiere di Siviglia (Rossini), 155
Baring, Evelyn, 205, 241, 268, 280, 282–83, 290
Barkey, Karen, 28
Baroche, Albert, 248
Barois, Julien, 243
al-Bārūdī, Maḥmūd Sāmī, 69, 152, 186, 210, 245
Bashīr Shihāb II, 23–25
Basiret, 130
Bāz, Rustum, 24
Beckman, Joseph, 216n52
Beirut, 8, 21, 27, 33, 45, 75, 85, 165–67, 196–97
La belle Hélène (Offenbach), 141n59, 169
Bellour, Victor, 247–48
Benjamin, Walter, 9
Benlian, Séropé, 253
Bereson, Ruth, 89, 112–13
Berger, Stefan, 8
Béroule, Elise, 108, 244
Berque, Jacques, 165, 210
body, 13, 28–30, 111–15, 162–63, 219–20, 306
Bourdieu, Pierre, 269–70
Boves, Santerres des, 232
Boyle, George, 282–83
Bravay, François, 103
The Brilliant Charms of al-Azbakiyya Garden (Rāshid), 88
Britain: Egypt's occupation by, 5–6, 164, 179–86, 193–97, 203–14, 236–37, 255–56, 258–59, 261, 264, 271, 281–91, 295–98; gardens and, 87; news and, 93; Ottoman interventions of, 27, 36, 173–75, 205–14; Tevfik and, 15, 205–10
Brubaker, Rogers, 73
Būlāq press, 43–44, 88, 133n46, 141n59
al-Burhān, 191
Burke, Peter, 111
al-Bū Saʿīdī, Ḥammūd, 88–89
Busch, Hans, 100n33
al-Bustānī, Saʿd Allāh, 220–223
al-Bustānī, Buṭrus, 75–76, 166–67
al-Bustānī, Salīm, 167–68, 178
Butovsky, Avriel, 182
Buṭrus Ghālī, Buṭrus, 266, 272

Capitulations, 260–61
Casati, Adele, 111
Castelli Press, 131

Catagay, Ali Rifaat, 80
Cattaoui, Moses, 251
censorship, 4, 254–59, 263–67
Ceride-i Havadis, 31, 62, 130
Cevdet Pasha, 29, 55
Charfeddine, Moncef, 234n138
charity, 180, 182–83, 193–96, 206, 218–19, 227, 271–73, 276, 280
The Chinese Incident (Isḥāq), 169
Choueriri, Youssef M., 6
Christians, 22–26, 30, 45, 49, 60, 165–66, 169–76, 204–5, 209–10, 260, 307
circuses, 55, 96, 106, 158, 257, 279
citizenship (Ottoman), 28, 30
Clancy-Smith, Julia, 154
Clemente, Pasquale, 246–50
Cole, Juan, 74, 125n2, 132, 165, 172, 175, 177, 255
A Collection of Beautiful Praise for the Just Prince Ismail, 69
Comédie, 90, *91*, 93, 106, 114, 157, 166, 181, 184–85, 194–95, 215–16, 239, 245, 255
Comité des Théâtres du Khedive, 238–59, 267
compensations, 67–73, 89–97
The Complete Course in Universal History (Abū al-Suʿūd), 148–49
Congress of Berlin, 172
The Conquest of Andalusia (*Fatḥ al-Andalus*, Kāmil), 288, 298–302
constitutionalism, 164–65, 172–79, 186, 302
Cook, Michael, 116
Copts, 22, 45, 129, 184, 306–7
The Count of Monte Cristo (Dumas), 141
Crabbs, Jack, 73–74
Cretan War, 37n95, 66
crime, 255–59
Crimean War, 21, 28, 30–34, 37–38, 44–48
Cromer, Lord. *See* Baring, Evelyn
cultural Arabism, 6–7, 225–28
cultural capital, 269–70, 273–74
Cuno, Kenneth, 46–47, 150, 206

al-Ḍarratayn (play), 161
Dār al-ʿUlūm, 127–28, 147–48
Davud Pasha (governor of Baghdad), 27
Dawisha, Adeed, 10
Dawn, Ernest C., 11, 305
de Blignières, Ernest-Gabriel, 240–41
de Lesseps, Ferdinand, 56, 102
democracy, 147–52
Derby, 62
Désiré, Ermé, 113
Di-Capua, Yoav, 210
Dinshaway incident, 264, 266
Dīwān al-Madāris, 129
d'Ormeville, Carlo, 108
Draneht, Paul, 84, 93–119, 153–60, 168–72, 181, 239, 246–48, 257–58, 274, 279
Dreyfus Affair, 299–300
Druze, 24–26
Duhhan, Dimitri, 177
Dupont, Octave, 248
Durrī (al-Ḥakīm), Muḥammad, 211
Dykstra, Durrell, 127

Eddine, Muhammad Emad, 82n215
Edhem, Ibrahim, 59
Edhem Pasha (play), 265
education, 15, 28–29, 39–40, 82, 127–30, 166, 173; language and, 276–78, 288–89; patriotism and, 182–83, 189, 194–95, 240, 270–71; state ministries of, 255
Egypt: Arabic in, 7, 67–73, 131–47, 152–63, 225–28; British occupation of, 5–6, 15, 100, 164, 170, 179–86, 193–97, 203–14, 236–37, 255–56, 258–59, 261, 264, 271, 281–82, 289–91, 295–98; economy of, 64–65, 239–40, 251–53, 273–76, 282–85, 304; education in, 15, 28–29, 39–40, 82, 127–30, 141–42, 166, 240, 255, 270–71, 276–78; elites of, 1, 15, 21–22, 27, 34–37, 67, 71–73, 80–81, 96–97, 102–4, 117–18, 129–30, 163–65, 172, 182–83, 186, 188–89, 209, 269–82, 291–92; European languages and, 35, 38, 40–41, 83, 86–87, 90–92, 100–103, 105–15, 118–19, 145, 167, 223–28, 231–32, 245, 248–50, 265–66, 273, 283, 307–8; historiography of, 5–7; immigration to, 165–72, 175–77, 180; Khedivate structure in, 1, 3–5, 8, 14,

Egypt (*continued*)
21, 34–37, 61–67; legal structures of, 4, 35–37, 127–28, 172–79, 186, 236–37, 254–57, 259–67, 302; Mehmed Ali's ethnicity and, 21–22, 27; military of, 22, 34–35, 44–48, 54, 58, 60, 67–68, 80–81, 184–86, 289–91; modernity and, 12–14, 87–88, 111–15, 142, 151, 248–51, 283–85; nationalism and, 6, 15; societies within, 81–83, 154, 175–77; sovereignty imagination of, 86–87, 89–97, 111–15, 130–31, 148–49, 162–63, 186, 210–13, 217, 278–82, 305–6; urbanism in, 84–89
Egypt for the Egyptians (Naqqāsh), 207
L'Égypte, 63, 179
Egyptian Brotherly Union, 227
Egyptian Theatrical Company, 250–51
Eisenstadt, Howard, 31
Emine (Ismail's daughter), 150
enterprises, 132–47
entrance fees, 273–76
Erol, Merih, 14
Ethiopia, 4–5, 49, 68, 116
Europe: Egypt's reception of, 83, 86–87, 105–15, 118–19, 145, 164–65, 189, 223–28, 231–32, 245, 265–66, 273, 307–8; modernity and, 87–88, 111–15, 119, 151, 248–51, 295; Ottoman relations with, 65–67, 170–75, 184–86
EzzelArab, AbdelAziz, 165

Fāḍil, Rifʿat and Maḥmūd, 142n61
Fahmī, ʿAbd al-ʿAzīz, 275
Fahmī, ʿAlī, 70, 146–47, 151, 186, 196–97
Fahmī, Maḥmūd, 192–93, 195–96, 210, 245
Fahmi, Mustafa (prime minister), 181, 290
Fahmy, Khaled, 6, 23, 27
Fahmy, Ziad, 255, 264, 266
Fakhrī, Ḥusayn, 246
al-Fār, Aḥmad, 234
Faraḥ, Iskandar, 252–53
al-Faraj Baʿd al-Ḍīq, 191, 216
Farīd, Muḥammad, 212–14, 291, 299
Fāris al-Shidyāq, Aḥmad, 62, 208
Farrugia, Louis, 158–59
Fatma Ismail, 114n172
La Favorite (Donizetti), 155, 291
Fawwāz, Zaynab, 269
Fayzi Pasha, 275
Fazıl, Mustafa, 47, 54–55, 57–58, 58n51, 59, 63–64, 66–67, 81, 173, 292
Figari, Antonio, 81, 101
Fikrī, ʿAbd Allāh, 71, 129–30, 133, 147, 150, 176, 186, 196–97, 206, 294
Fikrī, Amīn, 280
Filippi, Filippo, 118
fires, 244–45
firmans, 34, 37–38, 50, 58, 63–64, 66–68, 290
flesh, 12, 219–20. *See also* body
Fodor, Sandor, 116
France: Christianity and, 60; Egyptian intellectuals and, 40–41, 54, 86–87, 90–92, 100–103; gardens and, 87; Mehmed Ali's admiration for, 47–48; modernity and, 151; Ottoman war with, 21–22, 25–26; philosophy from, 74; Revolution of, 28; Tunisia and, 179; uprisings in, 150. *See also specific people*
Franz, Julius (Franz Bey), 90,94, 96–97
Freemasons, 81–83, 154, 175–77, 205
Fuad Pasha, 65, 279
Fursān al-ʿArab, 191–92
fuṣḥā Arabic. *See* Arabic

Galata Courier, 62
Galib, Osman, 287
The Garden of Pleasures for the Elimination of Sad Things, 88
gardens, 87–89. *See also* al-Azbakiyya
Garnier, Charles, 89, 94
Gasper, Michael, 271
Gay-Lussac, Jules-Ferdinand, 241
gentle revolution, 15, 151
Ghālī, Muḥammad, 176
Gharzūzī, Ḥabīb, 170, 220, 226n127
Goldziher, Ignác, 127
Granara, William, 167
Granato, Alfonso, 250
Grand, Pierre, 107, 239–42
Greek Catholics' Charitable Society, 272
Gülhane Edict, 28–29, 32

Habsburg Empire, 57, 87, 112, 117
Ḥaddād, Sulaymān, 216, 226, 234, 251
al-Ḥaddād, Sulaymān, 187
Ḥadīqat al-Akhbār, 130, 166
Ḥāfiẓ Pasha, Ismāᶜīl, 258
al-Ḥakīm, Tawfīq, 235, 274
Halim, Said, 292
Halis, Yusuf, 31, 45
Ḥamawī, Salīm, 170
al-Ḥamūlī, ᶜAbduh, 77–80, 186–87, 215, 228–31, 238, 272, 274–75, 280
Hamzah, Dyala, 39
ḥanafites, 127–28
Hānūlā, 226
Ḥaqīqat al-Akhbār, 176
harems, 53–54, 59–61, 115–16, 150–51, 256, 279, 287
al-Ḥarīrī, Kāmil, 187
Hārūn al-Rashīd (Naqqāsh), 33, 171, 179–86, 191, 219–25, 269, 277, 287
Hasan (Ismail's son), 150, 209
Ḥasanayn Ḥamza, 72, 82
Hatem, Mervat, 211
Haussmann,Georges-Eugène, 87
Hébert, Alphonse, 108
Hekekyan, Joseph, 101
hidiv-i Misir, 66
Ḥifẓ al-Widād, 219, 287
Hijaz, 24, 29, 68, 76, 116
al-Ḥijāz, 185
Ḥijāzī, Salāma, 165, 186–92, 203–4, 214–19, 225–35, 251, 273, 286, 304, 306
al-Ḥijāzī, Shihāb al-Dīn, 77
al-Hilbāwī, Ibrāhīm, 175, 179, 182, 209–10, 213
hippodrome, 86, 96, 106–7
historicization, 3, 304–5
history (genre), 21, 43–44, 147–52, 160–62, 207
History of Andalusia (Viardot), 298
History of Peter the Great (Voltaire), 43
honor, 232, 278–82, 290
horizontal patriotism, 153–54
Hoşyar, 50, 53–54, 58–62, 80–81, 83, 182, 206, 209, 281
Hourani, Albert, 41, 73–74, 178, 303–4
Les Huguenots (opera), 141
Hugo, Victor, 90
Huizinga, Johan, 2
Hunter, F. Robert, 72
al-Ḥuqūq, 223, 229
Hürriyet, 76
Hüsrev Pasha, 22, 27
Hurşid Pasha, 56
al-Ḥusaynī, Muḥammad, 212
Hüseyin Kamil (Ismail's son), 56, 150, 209, 279
al-Ḥuṣrī, Sāṭiᶜ, 6

Ibrahim, 22–29, 36, 49, 53–54, 102, 114, 209
Ibrāhīm, Sālim, 108
al-Ibshīhī, Shihāb al-Dīn, 144
al-ᶜIdwī, Ḥasan, 185
İhsanoğlu, Ekmeleddin, 48
Ilhami, 58n51
Ilyās, Edward, 168
imagined communities, 9, 69, 111–15, 219–20, 236–37, 269–78, 291–95, 303–8
impresarios, 13–14, 167, 193–96, 214–37, 245, 247–48, 250–57, 272–76, 304
Imprimerie Nationale Égyptienne, 130
India, 204
Isḥāq, Adīb, 169–72, 174–75, 180, 209
Islam: Egypt's imperial place and, 14; European understandings of, 60; gender and, 2; just rule principles and, 1, 25–26; Koran and, 141, 186–87; language politics and, 126–28, 132; laws and, 254–57, 259–67; Ottoman Empire and, 8–9, 177; patriotism and, 5–10, 40–41, 73–77, 146–47, 271–73, 289–91, 298–99, 304–5, 307–8; print technologies and, 130–31; territoriality and, 75–77
Islamic Charitable Society, 272, 276
Ismail, 37n95, 47, 66–67; Abdülaziz and, 19; Arabic representations of, 84, 118–19, 126–30, 142, 150–52, 181–82; as audience member, 156–57, 159, 168, 257, 279; death and, 81–83; deposition of, 164–65, 177–78, 241; Draneht Bey and, 104–6; European culture and, 84–85, 88–89, 92, 105–15, 119; images of, *52–53*; journalism and, 133;

Ismail (*continued*)
Ottoman-ness and, 14, 51–61, 66–67, 80–83; patriotism and, 67–73, 146–47
Ismāʿīl, Muḥammad, 108
Ismail junior (Mehmed Ali junior's son), 61
Ismāʿīl, Sayyid ʿAlī, 254–55, 264–65
Italy, 32–33, 85–86, 111–17
al-Ittiḥād al-Miṣrī, 191
al-ʿIyyādī, Muḥammad, 235–36
ʿIzzat, 226

al-Jabartī, ʿAbd al-Raḥman, 39
Jamʿiyyat al-Maʿārif, 174
Jamʿiyyat al-Ṣalība al-Adabiyya, 293
Jankowski, James, 5–6
al-Janna, 166
Jarīdat Arkān Ḥarb al-Jaysh al-Miṣrī, 141–42
al-Jawāhirjī (Sanua), 156
al-Jawāʾib, 62, 66, 96, 130, 144, 156, 208
al-Jawq al-ʿArabī, 216–28
Jews and Jewishness, 49, 227, 242–43
al-Jinān, 76, 166–70
journalism: British occupation and, 204–5, 208–9; censorship and, 4, 263–67; khedivial support for, 130–31; language politics of, 131–47; patriotism and, 39–40, 213–14, 218; political uses of, 62–63, 66, 95–96; public sphere and, 2, 132–45
Journal Officiel, 232
al-Jundī, Amīn, 25
Jūrnāl-i Khidīwī, 66
Jūrnāl ʿUmūmī li-Kāfat al-Iʿlānāt, 131

Kāmil, ʿAlī, Fahmī, 289, 293
Kāmil, Muṣṭafā, 15, 76, 266, 268–69, 277, 280–81, 288–98, 304, 306–7; photos of, *296*
Karateke, Hakan, 29
al-Kawākibī, ʿAbd al-Raḥmān, 7
al-Kawkab al-Miṣrī, 191
Keddie, Nikki R., 175
Kedourie, Elie, 303–4
Kemal, Namik, 76
Kern, Karen, 30
Khalidi, Rashid, 6–7
Khalil Agha, 59
Khalīl Yeğen Pasha, 82
Khallāṭ, Anīs, 176
Khayri, Ahmed, 210
Khayyāṭ, Yūsuf, 180–89, 194–95, 215–16, 218–19, 230, 251–53, 272–73, 277
khedivate: British relations with, 93, 204–14; class politics and, 34–35, 67–68, 102–4, 117–18, 129–30, 164–65, 182–83, 186, 269–85, 291–92; constitutionalism and, 177–78; democracy and, 147–52; immigration and, 165–72; intellectuals' relation to, 11–14, 34–35, 41–44, 46–48, 129–30, 172–79, 181–82, 288–95; language politics and, 126–47, 150–63, 214–28, 288–95; Mehmed Ali and, 21–22, 34, 49; Opera House of, 13–14, 89–97, *95*, 97–106, 111–19, 125–26, 157, 166, 181, 190–91, 203–4, 214, 227, 232, 238, 244–51, 255–59, 268, 274–76, 282–88, 290–91; Ottomanness of, 61–67, 117, 282–88, 303–8; primogeniture and, 50, 61–63, 68, 81–82; public spaces and, 105–11, 132–45, 147–63, 169–72, 182–84, 194–95, 236–50, 255–57, 259–63, 295–98; structure of, 3–5, 71–73; theater spaces and, 84, 153–62, 216–18, 238–59
Khalīfa, the Fisherman (Wāṣif), 223–24
Khuri-Makdisi, Ilham, 14, 254–55, 262
Kiamil Pasha, 36–37, 47
Koran, the, 141, 151, 186–87
Kudri Bey, 209
Kudsi-Zadeh, Albert, 172
al-Kūmī, Aḥhmad, 108, 250, 274

Lablache, Nicole, 107n140, 256
Landau, Jacob, 172
language: education and, 276–78; European contacts and, 35, 167; journalism and, 131–47; modernity and, 12–13; patriotism and, 24–25, 38–40, 49, 125–26, 152–63, 184–96, 225–28, 251, 276–78; translation and, 10, 152–63, 227, 269, 286
al-Laqānī, Ibrāhīm, 205
Larose, Léopold, 107, 246–47, 252
law: constitutionalism and, 164–65, 236–37, 302; Mehmed Ali's Egypt and, 35; Ottoman codes of, 4, 28, 30, 71–73;

public spaces and, 259–63; theaters and, 238, 254–59
Law on Theaters (1911), 266–67
Laylā (ʿAbd al-Fattāḥ al-Miṣrī), 157, 160
Laylā (singer), 230
al-Laythī, Aḥmad, 219, 294
al-Laythī, ʿAlī, 69–70, 88, 150
Leafgren, Luke, 167
Lebanon, 6, 306
Levant Herald, 62, 130
Lewis, Bernard, 10, 28–29, 46, 75
Lincoln, Abraham, 255
al-Liwāʾ, 76, 298
Louis XIV, 111–12

al-Madanī, Ibrāhīm Sīrāj, 185
Māḍī, Aḥmad, 213
al-Madrasa (journal), 294–96
al-Madrasa al-Waṭaniyya, 166
Mahd-i ʿUlya, 59
Mahmud II, 26, 29, 54
al-Maḥrūsa, 172, 191–92
Majdī, Ṣāliḥ, 45–46, 57, 69, 129, 146, 150
Majlis al-Aḥkām, 56
Majlis Shūrā al-Nuwwāb, 71–73, 82–83, 142, 177–78
Manasse, Seraphin, 90–93, 107, 114, 119, 215–16, 252
Mansour, Achille, 117
Mansur Pasha, 79, 150, 154
Maqātil Miṣr—Aḥmad Bāshā ʿUrābī (play), 235–37
Mariette, Auguste, 116–18, 148
Marin, Louis, 112
Maronite Charitable Society, 227, 229–30, 287
Maronites, 24–26
Marquis de Tard, 81
marriage, 34–35, 62, 78–79, 114, 150–52, 161, 213–14, 286
Marseillaise, 42–43, 46, 125–26
Marxism, 5n12
Maskūnās, Dīmitrī, 213
Masters, Bruce, 26
Matarci, Nukhla, 80
al-Māyis, Farḥat, 258
Mayy (Naqqāsh), 167, 187
Maẓlūm, Aḥmad, 246
McCoan, James Carlile, 58n52
Meclis-i Ahkam, 55
Le médicin malgré lui (Molière), 153
Mehmed Ali, 103; Arabic image of, 38–44; Christians under, 25–26; conquests of, 4–5; death of, 36; Draneht Bey and, 101–2, 104–5; hanafism of, 127–28; Ibrahim's Syrian campaign and, 23–29; Egypt and, 4, 14, 19, 21–22, 34, 82–83, 85; memory of, 210–13; modernity and, 89; Ottoman belonging of, 35–36; primogeniture and, 50, 61–63, 68; revival of, 291–92; scholarship on, 26–28, 48–49; territory of, 40–41; title of, 64–65
Mehmed Ali (Abbas Hilmi II's brother), 279
Mehmed Arif Pasha, 82
Mehmed Şukri, 79
Mehmed Ali, Jr., 47, 53–55
Melekper, 58
memory, 132, 147–52, 181–82, 304–5
Michelet, Jules, 89–90
middle class, 270–71, 278–82
Mikāwī, Muḥammad, 209n38
Miller, Alexei, 8
Ministry of Public Works, 239–40, 252
Miṣbāh al-Sharq, 270
Mishāqa, Mīkhāʾīl, 24, 26
Miṣr, 172, 177
al-Miṣrī, Ḥasan, 234
modernity, 43–44; democracy and, 147–52; European cultural forms and, 13–14, 119, 250–51, 283–85, 295; journalism and, 142; language and, 12–13; progress and, 87–88
Moldavia, 64
Moncrieff, Scott, 244
morality, 11–15, 41, 55–56, 105, 123, 129, 156–63, 185, 235, 255–67, 276–82, 298–301
Moreh, Shmuel, 161
Morocco, 150, 306
Mourès, Antoine, 131, 133, 220
Mubārak, ʿAlī, 40–45, 71, 76, 127–28, 146–53, 159–61, 174, 184, 212, 240–46, 291–95

al-Mufīd, 191
Muḥammad, Wafā, 277
Muḥammad ʿAlī, 73–74
Muḥarram, Khalīl, 187
Muhtar, Ahmed, 204, 217, 227, 282–84, 286–88, 297
Muḥyī al-Dīn (comedian), 218–19
Mūlyīr Miṣr (play), 160n148
al-Munbih al-Tijārī al-Miṣrī, 131, 144
Munīb, Muḥammad, 207
munshidīn, 186–87
al-Muntakhab, 191
al-Muqaṭṭam, 236, 295–96, 300
al-Muqtaṭaf, 218
al-Murūʾa wa-l-Wafā (play), 226
Mūsa, ʿAbd al-Karīm, 280
Mūsa, Salāma, 298
music. *See* aural patriotism; patriotism; songs
Muslim Charitable Society, 272
Mutaʿaṣṣiba Shanʿāʾ (play), 265
Muṭrān, Khalīl Bey, 78n180
al-Muwayliḥī, ʿAbd al-Salām, 176
al-Muwayliḥī, Ibrāhīm, 69, 131, 133n46, 155, 225, 255
al-Muwayliḥī, Muḥammad, 281
al-Muʾayyad, 213–14, 298

(al-)Nadīm, ʿAbd Allāh, 151, 182–85, 190–95, 235–36, 270, 272, 277, 289–90, 294–95
Nahman, Mattatias, 91
al-Najāḥ, 166, 191
Najī, Muḥammad, 234
al-Najjārī, Muṣṭafā Salāma, 47, 69, 116, 149
Najm, Muḥammad Yūsuf, 273
Napoleon, 43, 47
Napoleon III, 49, 62, 84
Naqqāsh, Mārūn and Niqūlā, 32–33, 45, 155, 166–67, 171, 180–81, 223, 277
Naqqāsh, Salīm Khalīl, 167–68, 171, 174, 179–81, 187, 189, 192–93, 207, 215, 227
Nāṣir al-Dīn Shah, 59, 115
nationalism, 2–3, 5–7, 9–11, 26–27, 40–41, 73–77, 164–65, 301–2, 305–8. *See also* patriotism
National Program, 177–78
nation-ness, 9–10, 30–31, 142, 147–48, 196–97, 269, 271–73, 291–95, 307–8
Naum Theatre, 92
Nawfal, Nawfal, 23–24
Nazli (princess), 292
Naẓmī, Aḥmad, 146
A Necklace of Pearls (Abū al-Suʿūd), 42
New and Old Egypt (Anṭūn), 277
New Ottoman ideology, 173
The New Tevfikian Survey (ʿAli Mubārak), 212
The New York Times, 95–96, 201, 268
Le Nil, 157
Ninet, John, 102n111
Noorani, Yaseen, 10
Nubar, Boghos, 243
Nubar Nubaryan, 64–66, 81, 103, 114, 174, 227, 240, 252
al-Nūr al Tawfīkī, 213
Nuzhat al-Afkār, 131, 155

Ömer Lufti Pasha, 170
opera: *Aida*'s performance and, 111–19; Arabic language and, 125–26, 141–42, 188–93, 218–28, 269; fires and, 244; global interest in, 91–92, 248–50; Khedivial Opera House and, 13–14, 85, 157, 166, 181, 190–93, 203–4, 214, 227, 232, 237–39, 246–51, 255–59, 274–76, 282–88, 290–91; Ottoman receptions of, 55; patriotism and, 89–97, 186–96, 286–88; privatization and, 250–51
Organic Law for the Assembly of Deputies, 186
Orientalists, 46, 127, 153, 231–32, 265–66, 307–8
Ornato, 261
Ornstein, John Maurice Isidor, 242–44
Orthodox Coptic Charitable Society, 272
Ottoman Empire: Britain and, 5–6, 27, 36, 197, 203–5, 210–13, 282–88; class politics of, 1, 34–37; Egypt's political place within, 3–5, 8–9, 14, 21–23, 36–37, 44–50, 60–67, 71–73, 90–92, 117, 162–65, 174–77, 185, 197, 210–13, 282–88, 292–98, 303–8; European culture and,

27, 65–67, 77–79, 130–31, 164–65, 170, 172–75, 182, 184–86; Islam and, 1, 9–10, 177; Ismail and, 14, 51–58, 80–83; language politics and, 7–9, 38–40; legal codes of, 4, 28, 30, 71–73, 172–79, 186, 260, 263–67; migrations within, 165–72, 180, 204–5; networks of, 1, 7–9, 175–77; patriotism and, 5–9, 28–37, 42, 176–77, 236–37

paintings, 51–54
Palmer, Elwin, 243
Papakyriacou, Marios, 100n33
Papon, Antoine August, 81
Paris World Exhibition, 86, 231
The Paths of Egyptian Hearts (al-Ṭahṭāwī), 73–75
Patriotic Party, 177–78
Patriotic Society for Aid, 180
patriotism: aesthetic representations of, 11–15, 21, 24–25, 30, 42–48, 51–54, 57, 63, 66, 68–71, 75–79, 83, 111–19, 150–52, 187, 189–91, 210–11, 219–25, 286–88, 295–98; affect and, 32–34, 38–40; aural-, 13, 30–31, 44–48, 77–81, 85–89, 297; class politics and, 67, 69, 71–73, 80–81, 117–18, 269–78; commercialism and, 228–35; as compensation, 67–73, 89–97; definitions of, 1, 5–11; education and, 15, 28–29, 39–40, 82–83, 166, 173, 182–83, 189, 194–95, 270–71, 276–78, 288–89; European homelands and, 1–3, 28–30, 32, 41–44; horizontal, 153–54; imperial contexts and, 7–11, 28–40, 42, 236–37, 303–8; journalism and, 39–40, 95–96, 130–31, 147–52, 174–75, 208–9, 213–14, 218; language and, 6–13, 24–25, 40–44, 49, 125–26, 131–47, 152–63, 169–70, 184–86, 225–28, 276–78, 307–8; Mehmed Ali and, 210–13; methodologies and, 11–14; nationalism and, 2–3, 7, 9–10; performances and, 2, 32, 67–73, 84, 89–105, 111–15, 125–26, 152–65, 171–72, 179–96, 214–28, 236–37, 268–69; religion and, 5–6, 9–10, 25–26, 40–41, 73–77, 146–47, 271–73, 289–91, 298–99, 304–5, 307–8; revolution and, 164–65; territoriality and, 5–6, 10–11, 38–48, 68–69, 75–77, 162–63, 302; vertical, 126; war and, 21, 23–28, 30–34, 44–48, 174–75, 180–81
Pavlidis, Pavlos. *See* Draneht, Paul
Peirce, Leslie, 59
Penal Code of 1883, 261–62
pensions, 244
Persian (language), 8, 66
Pertevniyal, 59, 61–62, 83
Le Petit Duc (opera), 291
petitions, 11–12, 182–84, 193, 203–4
Pīkmāliyūn, 223
plays: actors in, 169–72, 180–86, 189–91, 214–28; audiences of, 13–14, 117–18; charity and, 180, 218–19, 273–74; class politics and, 276–82; European culture and, 32–34; impresarios and, 167, 193–96, 225–29, 232–35, 237, 245, 247–48, 250–57, 272–76; language politics and, 152–63, 167, 190–91, 203–4, 251, 269; law and, 238–50, 254–59, 263–67; loyalism and, 179–86; modernity and, 11–13, 32; official sanctioning of, 244–57; patriotism and, 21, 32, 48, 125–26, 160–65, 179–86, 194–96, 236–37, 289–91; privatization of, 250–51; public spaces and, 2, 94–111; theatrical associations and, 273; translations of, 154–55, 168–69, 171–72, 227
poetry, 11, 21, 24–25, 47, 57, 63, 66, 68–71, 75–79, 89, 93, 148, 150–52, 206, 209–11
Politeama, 226
political Arabism, 7
Port Said, 192
The Present of Egyptians (ʿUmar), 270
primogeniture, 50, 61–63, 68, 81–82
print technology, 43–44, 82, 88, 126–27, 130–31, 133, 141–42, 191, 263–67
Private Domains, 94, 95n75, 108–11, 257, 275
proverbs, 21

al-Qabbānī, Abū Khalīl, 215, 218–19, 233, 235, 238, 251, 253, 265, 277

al-Qāhira, 213, 218
Qardāḥī, Christine, 189, 192, 226, 233
Qardāḥī, Sulaymān, 165, 188–204, 214–37, 245, 251–53, 262, 277, 286–87, 304–6
al-Qāsimī, Muḥammad Saʿīd, 31
Qaṭṭāwī, Moses, 251
al-Qawwās (play), 156
Quinze jours de siège (play), 257

Rifaat, Samir, 100n33
al-Rāfiʿī, Abd al-Raḥmān, 5, 56n28, 63, 289
Rāghib, Aḥmad Efendi, 108
al-Rajabī, Khalīl Aḥmad, 39
Ramaḍān, al-Sayyid Salīm, 166
Rancy, Théodore, 91
ranks, 64–67, 116
Rāshid, Muḥammad, 88
Rawḍat al-Madāris al Miṣriyya, 131–32, 141–42, 145–47, 170, 172
Re, Lucia, 116
revolutions, 164–65, 172–79, 186–87, 189–91, 205–12, 235–37, 259–60, 266, 298
Reyer, Ernest, 118
Riḍā, Rashīd, 7, 260, 265–66
Rigoletto (Verdi), 84
Ring Theatre, 244
Ristori, Adelaide, 85
Riyaz, Mustafa, 81, 174–75, 178–79, 184, 204, 213–14, 241, 290–94
Robinson, Paul, 116
Roman Catholic Charitable Society, 272
Romania, 48–49, 64
Romano, Mūrād, 216
Rushdī, ʿAbd al-Raḥmān, 246, 252–53
Russia, 15, 173, 260
Russian-Ottoman wars, 172, 175–76, 180–81, 286
Ryzova, Lucie, 271, 275, 278

Ṣabrī, Ismāʿīl, 281
Sacred Harmonic Society, 115
Sadgrove, Philip, 33, 102n111, 145, 161, 168
Said, Edward, 116
Said Pasha, 44–48, 50, 56–57, 59, 62, 68–69, 85, 102–4, 130, 192, 293
Sajdi, Dana, 31
Sakīna, 68
Salim, Latif, 213
Sālim, Laṭīfa Muḥammad, 165
al-Salīṭ al-Ḥasūd (Naqqāsh), 171
Santi Boni, 215–17, 226–27, 246, 252–53
Sanua, James, 126, 153–54, 156–63, 168–72, 175–76, 180, 193, 256, 263, 277, 304
Ṣayd al-Ḥamām, 264
al-Sayyid, Aḥmad Luṭfī, 301
Schiller, Friedrich, 90
Schölch, Alexander, 165
Scotta, Giovanni, 108n153
Second Constitutional Period (Ottoman Empire), 6
Şehname-yi Osmani, 31
Selim, Samah, 183, 271
Selim I, 19
Semiramis (opera), 125, 158
Settle, Henry, 243
Shafīq, Aḥmad, 279
Shāhīn Pasha, 176–77
Shāhīn Shāhīn, 244
Shakūr, Yūsuf, 275
Shalfūn, Buṭrus, 171
sharīʿa, 30, 127–28, 149, 259–63
Shārūbīm, Mīkhāʾīl, 268, 290, 297
Shaw, Stanford and Ezel, 37
Ṣiddīq, Ismāʿīl, 53, 68, 70–72, 78–79, 88, 126–27, 130, 157, 164, 176
Ṣidqī, Ismāʿīl, 275–76, 296
Simond, Fred W., 250
Sirrī, Ismāʿīl, 246
Société Théatrale et Artistique du Caire, 251
Society of Benevolent Intentions, 272
Society of Refined Education, 273
solidarity, 2, 10, 14, 21, 32, 74, 175, 179–86, 197, 237, 269–70, 295–98
songs, 21, 30–34, 42–48, 77–81, 85–89, 171–72, 181–82, 215, 225–28, 236–37, 297
Soschino, 215–17, 246, 252–53
Soulet, Jacques, 108
Stagni, Luigi, 250
Stephanov, Darin, 30
strikes, 192

Suarès, Raphael, 251
Sudan, 4–5, 57n42, 68, 116, 192, 205
Suez Canal, 44–45, 56, 60, 84, 86, 90, 92, 96, 102, 113, 257
Sulaymān, Ḥusayn, 258
Şura-i Askeri, 55
surveillance, 256–63
Syria (as Syrian provinces), 6, 22–29, 45, 68, 116, 165–72, 208, 234, 260, 273, 306
Syrian Orthodox Society, 272

Tahir Pasha, Ahmed, 90
al-Ṭahṭāwī, Rifāʿa Rāfiʿ, 40–42, 44–48, 66, 69, 71, 73–76, 125–26, 129, 147–50, 220
al-Tankīt wa-l-Tabkīt, 185
Tanzimat, 36–37, 48, 55
Taqlā, Bishāra, 272
Taqlā, Salīm, 208
Tartuffe (play), 152
Tasting the Branch in Its Root through the Love of the Homeland (Fahmī), 151
Tauber, Eliezer, 10
Tawfīq Charitable Society, 272
Taymūriyya, ʿĀʾisha, 210–11
al-Ṭāʾif, 191
temporality, 9–10, 12, 286
territory, 302, 305; patriotism and, 5–6, 162–63
Tevfik Pasha: Arabic representations of, 187; as audience member, 184–85, 217–18, 227–28, 253, 280–81, 287; Britain's relation to, 15, 178, 203–10; death of, 268, 289; elites and, 164–65, 241; patriotism and, 182, 217, 224–25, 236–37; primogeniture and, 61, 64n95, 81–82; revolutions and, 192–97, 201, 206–12, 235–37, 259–60
Tevhide Hanim, 62, 79, 114, 150
Tharwat, ʿAbd al-Khāliq, 275
theater. *See* khedivate; opera; plays
Le Théâtre International, 231
Théâtre Ismail, 162
Théâtre Ismail, 97
Théâtre National, 159
Thénard, Louis-Jacques, 101
al-Tijāra, 172, 179
Tilīmāk, 191, 216, 220, 223
Toledano, Ehud, 6–8, 34, 36–37, 37n95, 38, 54, 62
"To Serve Kings Is to Praise Kings" (Nadīm), 151–52
Ṭrād, Asʿad, 213
translations. *See* language
Les trois Horaces et les trois Curiaces (Corneille), 167
Tunis, 4, 8, 47–49, 174, 179
Turkish (language), 7–9, 80–81, 130, 154–55
Tusun (son of Said Pasha), 47, 58, 61

Ulman, Victor, 248
ʿUmar, Muḥammad, 270–71
unisonality, 13, 44–48, 77–81, 85–89, 218–19
Unsī, Muḥammad, 125–26, 133, 141, 144, 150–63, 169, 171–72, 180, 220, 304
ʿUrābī, Aḥmad, 151, 164–65, 184–97, 204–12, 217, 227, 235–37, 259–60, 290
urbanism, 13, 84–89, 255–57
al-Ustādh, 294
ʿUthmān Jalāl, Muḥammad, 47, 69–70, 145, 152–53, 155n118, 234, 280

Verdi, Giuseppe, 14, 78, 84, 111–12, 116–19
Verger, Amédée, 91
vertical patriotism, 126
Viardot, Louis, 298
Vivian, Hussey Crespigny, 242
Voltaire, 43

Wade, Seymour, 231–32
Wādī al-Nīl (journal and printing press), 96, 126, 131–45, *143*, 146, 148–50, 155, 158
Wahbī, Tadros,147
Walker, Dennis, 299n144
Wallachia, 48–49, 64
Wāmiq Pasha, 33–34
al-Waqāʾiʿ al-Miṣriyya, 39, 63, 69, 96, 131, 179
al-Wardī, ʿAlī, 27
Wāṣif, Maḥmūd, 223–24, 269, 277, 301

waṭaniyya (concept), 6, 10–11. *See* patriotism
al-Waṭan wa-Ṭāliʿ al-Tawfīq (Nadīm), 182–84, 191, 208, 236, 272
Watenpaugh, Keith, 305
Wendell, Charles, 73–74
Wishnitzer, Avner, 9
Wolff, Henry Drummond, 282–83, 287
women, 2, 50, 53–54, 58–63, 115–16, 182–83, 189

Xristofidis, Pavlos. *See* Draneht, Paul

Yalman, Nur, 61
al-Yāsirjī, Aḥmad, 187
Yaʿsūb al-Ṭibb, 131n32
al-Yāzijī, Nāṣīf, 25, 166
Young Ottomans, 63, 76, 234
Yousef, Hoda, 146
Yūsuf (play), 265
Yūsuf, Buṭrus, 108

Zachs, Fruma, 34
Zaghlūl, Saʿd, 205, 213, 270, 275
Zaghlūl, Aḥmad Fatḥī, 270
Zakī, Aḥmad, 290
Zaki, Mehmed, 246
al-Ẓalūm (play), 171, 273
al-Zamān, 191, 213
Zanūbiyā, 216
Zaydān, Jurjī, 167, 208, 220
Zayn, Zayn, 213
Zeki, Mehmed, 204
Zervudachi, Despina, 100n33
zevat, 34–35, 37–38, 44–45, 53–54, 58, 60, 71, 80–81, 129–30, 172, 186, 209, 270
Zeynep (daughter of Mehmed Ali), 36–37, 54–56
Zifāf ʿAntar (play), 191
Zizinia Theater, 85, 94, 180, 182, 184, 235, 241–42, 260, 262, 272, 280–81
Zurayb Bey, 279

GPSR Authorized Representative: Easy Access System Europe - Mustamäe tee 50, 10621 Tallinn, Estonia, gpsr.requests@easproject.com

www.ingramcontent.com/pod-product-compliance
Lightning Source LLC
Chambersburg PA
CBHW030431300426
44112CB00009B/951
* 9 7 8 0 6 9 1 2 0 9 0 1 2 *